TOKENS OF MEANING

CSLI Lecture Notes Number 224

TOKENS OF MEANING

Papers in Honor of Lauri Karttunen

Inroduction by
Martin Kay

edited by

Cleo Condoravdi
&
Tracy Holloway King

CSLI PUBLICATIONS
Stanford, California

Center for the Study of Language and Information
Leland Stanford Junior University
Printed in the United States
23 22 21 20 19 1 2 3 4 5

Library of Congress Cataloging-in-Publication Data

Names: Condoravdi, Cleo A., 1962- editor. | King, Tracy Holloway, 1966- editor. | Karttunen, Lauri, honoree.

Title: Tokens of meaning : papers in honor of Lauri Karttunen / edited by Cleo Condoravdi and Tracy Holloway King.

Description: Stanford : CSLI Publications, [2019] | Series: CSLI Lecture Notes ; 224 | Includes bibliographical references and index.

Identifiers: LCCN 2018056051 |
ISBN 9781684000487 (pbk. : alk. paper) |
ISBN 1684000483 (pbk. : alk. paper)

Subjects: LCSH: Linguistics. | Philology. | Karttunen, Lauri.

Classification: LCC P26.K373 T65 2019 | DDC 410–dc23

LC record available at `https://lccn.loc.gov/2018056051`

CIP

∞ The acid-free paper used in this book meets the minimum requirements of the American National Standard for Information Sciences—Permanence of Paper for Printed Library Materials, ANSI Z39.48-1984.

CSLI Publications is located on the campus of Stanford University.

Visit our web site at
`http://cslipublications.stanford.edu/`
for comments on this and other titles, as well as for changes and corrections by the author and publisher.

Contents

Acknowledgements

Cleo Condoravdi and Tracy Holloway King

Lauri touched our lives both intellectually and personally. We are better linguists and better people for having had the privilege of working with him at Xerox PARC and beyond. This volume, whose range of contributions reflects the wide scope of Lauri's work, is but a small token of our appreciation.

The volume could not have come to fruition without help from many people. First, we thank the authors for the thoughtfulness of their contributions and for their patience while we completed the volume.

Each contribution was reviewed and then revised. We wish to thank the reviewers, many of whom took time to review while working on their own contributions: Arto Anttila, Ken Beesley, Danny Bobrow, Robin Cooper, Dick Crouch, Tim Fernando, Martin Forst, Itamar Francez, Larry Horn, Mans Hulden, Ron Kaplan, Paul Kay, Tracy Holloway King, Andras Kornai, Sven Lauer, Stanley Peters, Adam Przepiórkowski, Livio Robaldo, Ida Toivonen, Annie Zaenen.

We gratefully acknowledge David Beaver who provided the perfect opportunity for us to present Lauri with an initial version of the volume at the 2016 Semantics and Linguistic Theory (SALT26) conference, where Lauri was the invited speaker.

Emma Pease provided us with guru-level Latex advice, which was sorely needed as we merged together papers from such a diverse set of authors. All remaining issues are our own. Finally, and as always, we are in debt to Dikran Karagueuzian for his tireless support of CSLI Publications and his flexibility in spanning the on-line and on-paper publication worlds.

Tokens of Meaning: Papers in Honor of Lauri Karttunen.
Cleo Condoravdi and Tracy Holloway King (eds.).

Introduction

Martin Kay

This will become a much valued book, not only because it will introduce linguists in generations to come to some new and important ideas in today's linguistics but because of the warmth of basic human understanding that one feels just behind Karttunen's theory, logic, and programs. If there is any other linguist whose writings share some of these properties, I think it would be Charles Fillmore. Fillmore found unexpected jewels in the simple sentence *May we come in?* as Karttunen did with *Wong Kwan will be lucky to break even.*

I first met Lauri Karttunen, or Lauri as I will call him from now on, in 1966 when UCLA was host to that year's Linguistics Institute in which I taught a course on parsing which Lauri attended. He wrote a term paper on the computational treatment of Finnish morphology, a topic to which he was destined to return. I like to think that the course played a role in stimulating Lauri's interest in computational linguistics. The following year, he came to the Rand Corporation in Santa Monica, California, as a member of a fellowship program that had recently been established by David Hays, who was the principal investigator of the machine translation project of which I was a member. The Rand Corporation was the first of the so-called "Federally funded research and development centers (FFRDCs)" started in 1947 to conduct coordinated programs of research to strengthen the position of the United States during the cold war. A major component of the program consisted in assessing Soviet strength in key fields of science and technology.

The launch of Sputnik on October 4, 1957 had caused considerable

Tokens of Meaning: Papers in Honor of Lauri Karttunen.
Cleo Condoravdi and Tracy Holloway King (eds.).

alarm in Washington, giving great urgency to intelligence programs concerning Soviet science and technology. A problem for the Americans was that Russian secrecy was exacerbated by the tendency of the Russians to write those documents that we could get hold of in Russian. This, in turn, gave urgency to work on machine translation and the United States government made funding available for research in this domain in the United States and abroad. I had been a member of a group working on such a project at Cambridge University when I was given the chance to go to the Rand Corporation in California in 1961.

Such little understanding as I had of computing at this stage came entirely from my experiences at Rand since, at Cambridge, my activities were restricted to entirely linguistic problems. Lauri sometimes credited me with introducing him to this or that computational technique but I am now sure that most of the useful information on computing flowed in the opposite direction. We did indeed come to work on some of the same problems in computational linguistics, notably the application of finite-state transducers to problems in morphology, and I did introduce him to Algol, a programming language that was first published in 1960 for the communication of algorithms among humans. It was not thought that it would ever be possible to actually use it on computers. It made use of characters that had no representation on punched cards and it had no mechanisms for input and output. But it did allow for recursion, which was an exciting novelty for many people, including Lauri.

Just a year after coming to Rand, Lauri gave a paper at the second International Conference on Computational Linguistics which was held in Sweden, where these conferences were given the nickname by which they are now generally known, namely "Coling". He considered some of the things that would be required of a computer that could be said to interpret natural language in any serious way. He concluded that the most challenging of these would concern the tracking of referents through a discourse. These issues quickly became the dominant concern for Lauri so that he spent less and less time on the computer. His dissertation was on "Problems of Reference in Syntax" which he submitted just after leaving Rand.

Lauri joined the Faculty of the Linguistics Department at the University of Texas at Austin where two of the people who had been particularly influential in developing his interest in semantics, namely Emmon Bach and Stanley Peters, were working. Here his interest turned towards implicative verbs and so-called "factives", which continued to be a center of interest for him. In 1973, he welcomed the opportunity to spend a year at MIT as a replacement for David Perlmutter while he was on sabbatical leave. This gave him the opportunity to interact directly with several of the most influential linguists of the day including, of course, Noam Chomsky. While there were differing views of semantics among these people, Lauri saw them essentially as variations on a basically syntactic theme.

The contrast between that syntactic and more fundamentally semantic views of meaning were highlighted for Lauri by the observation that some noun phrases depend for their proper interpretation on whether the purported referent of a preceding noun phrase is presumed to exist. In his paper *Word Play*, which he delivered when he received the Lifetime Achievement Award from the Association for Computational Linguistics in 2006, he observes that the object in the sentence *The director is looking for an innocent blond* is presumed to exist when the following sentence is *She is from Bean Blossom*, but not if it is *She must be 17 years old.*

A class of examples to which Lauri has devoted a considerable amount of attention is exemplified in the pair *John managed to get a sabbatical. It starts in September* and *John failed to get a sabbatical. *It starts in September.* The first of these entails that John did indeed get a sabbatical, the second that he did not. This proved to be an extremely rich vein running through semantics, and one that still claims considerable energy from many linguists and philosophers today, including Lauri.

Adjacent to the Stanford University campus is the Center for Advanced Study in Behavioral Sciences, a place that exists largely to provide workers in those fields with a location in which to spend sabbatical leaves. Lauri came there for this purpose in 1981 and it was natural that we should see a good deal of one another during the year because it was just down the road from the Xerox Palo Alto Research Center where Ron Kaplan and I were working at the time. I was engaged in extending the notion of unification which is built into the Prolog programming language to the realm of recursive attribute-value lists so that it would be able to play a central role in syntactic processing. This led to the development of a formalism that I called "Functional Unification Grammar" and my writing numerous programs in a language called *Lisp* which was used by many computational linguists and researchers in artificial intelligence at the time. Lauri caught the bug from me and began to write his own programs in this language. He soon started passing it on to others, such as Robin Cooper.

Lauri retained his keen interest in semantics and discourse referents to which he was due to return before long. In 1984, he joined the Artificial Intelligence Center at SRI, still only a short drive to the Xerox Palo Alto Research Center where I worked, and a modest walk to where

I lived. Stuart Shieber, one of several computational linguists at SRI had designed a syntactic formalism called PATR II which shared some of the ideas in my Functional Unification Grammar and Lauri implemented it on a computer called the Dandelion, designed and built at Xerox, and using Lisp at its very core.

In the mid 1960's, I had spent a couple of years at Berkeley on another machine translation project under the direction, this time, of Sydney Lamb. They were able to advance the cause of machine translation about as far as the other two projects in this domain that I had worked on, which is to say, not at all. However, another member of the project at that time was C. Douglas Johnson who some time later made a surprising observation about the computational power of the kind of rules that Chomsky and Halle had introduced in their very influential book "The Sound Pattern of English". Johnson was able to show that their power is considerably less than their form suggests at first glance. Essentially, they are equivalent to finite-state transducers. This in turn meant that one might hope to use them at the core of computer programs that could both generate and analyze the phonology of English and, presumably, other languages.

This work was done long after I had left Berkeley and I knew nothing of it. However, Ron Kaplan and I had become intrigued by the idea that it might be possible to create a reversible implementation of Chomsky and Halle's formalism and, in due course, were able to duplicate Johnson's result and create such a system. In 1981, we introduced these ideas to Lauri as well as to his compatriot Kimmo Koskenniemi, who was visiting from Finland. Based on these ideas, Koskenniemi constructed a system that he called "Two-level morphology" which could model both generation and analysis in morphology. Koskenniemi's results were embodied in a long and complex program in a language called "Pascal" which Lauri translated into Lisp. There was a considerable number of subsequent implementations, notably one in the C language called "PC-KIMMO" that was distributed free of charge by the Summer Institute of Linguistics. Koskenniemi's paper in this volume presents a way of conceptualizing morphology, based on his original two-level idea that makes the job of writing a morphological grammar simpler for the linguist by focusing on individual morphemes rather than widely applicable rules.

The work that Kaplan and I had done on reversible systems turned out to be applicable, with some adjustments, to Koskenniemi's formalism and this led to an efficient and practicable reversible system for morphology embodied in a program in C which was the basis of a book on morphological processing by Karttunen and Beesley. Beesley much appreciated the computational power and elegance of finite-state systems and created the Kleene programming language that he developed in his pursuit of this line of work.

Lauri's work on semantics and morphology can be approached as disjoint enterprises by linguists mainly interested in just one of these aspects of language. However, they are not separate in his mind, as Aarne Ranta makes clear in his contribution to this collection. Many have seen the principal job of the linguist to account for the supposed ability of the native speakers of a language to sort utterances into those that do, and those that do not belong to the language. Chomsky has made much of the small amount of data that children apparently need on which to base this ability. Lauri, in contrast, sees grammar as much more like a transducer between thoughts and utterances. He does not see a sharp line dividing utterances that belong to the language from those that do not. Neither do ordinary people who disagree with one another about what is in their language, and with themselves at different times and in different situations. This holistic view may account for the warmth of basic human understanding behind Karttunen's theory, logic, and programs and hence his impact not just on linguistics but on the broad linguistic community.

Major Works by Lauri Karttunen

Beesley, Kenneth and Lauri Karttunen. 2000. Finite-state non-concatenative morphotactics. In *38th Annual Meeting of the Association for Computational Linguistics*. Association for Computational Linguistics.

Beesley, Kenneth and Lauri Karttunen. 2003. *Finite State Morphology*, vol. 3 of *CSLI Studies in Computational Linguistics*. CSLI Publications.

Bobrow, Daniel, Robert Cheslow, Cleo Condoravdi, Lauri Karttunen, Tracy Holloway King, Rowan Nairn, Valeria de Paiva, Charlotte Price, and Annie Zaenen. 2007a. PARC's Bridge question answering system. In *Proceedings of the GEAF (Grammar Engineering Across Frameworks) Workshop*, pages 46—66. CSLI Publications.

Bobrow, Daniel, Cleo Condoravdi, Richard Crouch, Valeria de Paiva, Ronald Kaplan, Lauri Karttunen, Tracy Holloway King, and Annie Zaenen. 2005. A basic logic for textual inference. In *Proceedings of the AAAI Workshop on Inference for Textual Question Answering*, pages 47—51.

Bobrow, Daniel, Cleo Condoravdi, Lauri Karttunen, and Annie Zaenen. 2009. Learning by reading: Normalizing complex linguistic structures onto a knowledge representation. In *Learning by Reading and Learning to Read, Papers from the 2009 AAAI Spring Symposium, Technical Report SS-09-07*, pages 3–6. AAAI.

Bobrow, Daniel, Richard Crouch, Tracy Holloway King, Cleo Condoravdi, Lauri Karttunen, Rowan Nairn, Valeria de Paiva, and Annie Zaenen. 2007b. Precision-focused textual inference. In S. Sekine, K. Inui, I. Dagan, B. Dolan, D. Giampiccolo, and B. Magnini, eds., *Proceedings of the ACL-PASCAL@ACL 2007 Workshop on Textual Entailment and Paraphrasing*, pages 16–21. Association for Computational Linguistics.

de Paiva, Valeria, Danny Bobrow, Cleo Condoravdi, Richard Crouch, Lauri Karttunen, Tracy Holloway King, Rowan Nairn, and Annie Zaenen. 2007. Textual inference logic: Take two. In P. Bouquet, J. Euzenat, C. Ghidini, D. L. McGuinness, L. Serafini, P. Shvaiko, and H. Wache, eds., *Proceedings of the International Workshop on Contexts and Ontologies: Representation and Reasoning (C&O:RR)*, vol. 298 of *CEUR Workshop Proceedings*, pages 27—36.

Eisner, Jason, Lauri Karttunen, and Alain Theriault. 2001. Proceedings of the 5th workshop of the ACL special interest group in computational phonology (SIGPHON). *CoRR* cs.CL/0102022.

Geiger, Atticus, Ignacio Cases, Lauri Karttunen, and Christopher Potts. 2018. Stress-testing neural models of natural language inference with multiply-quantified sentences. *CoRR* abs/1810.13033.

Guingne, Franck, Florent Nicart, Jean-Marc Champarnaud, Lauri Karttunen, Tamás Gaál, and André Kempe. 2003. Virtual operations on virtual networks: The priority union. *International Journal of Foundations of Computer Science* 14(6):1055–1071.

Hakulinen, Auli and Lauri Karttunen. 1973. Missing persons: On generic sentences in Finnish. In *Chicago Linguistics Society 9*, pages 157–171.

Karttunen, Lauri. 1967. The identity of noun phrases. Technical report, the RAND Corporation.

Karttunen, Lauri. 1968. What do referential indices refer to? Technical report, the RAND Corporation.

Karttunen, Lauri. 1969a. Discourse referents. In *Third International Conference on Computational Linguistics, COLING*, pages 1–38.

Karttunen, Lauri. 1969b. *Problems of Reference in Syntax*. Ph.D. thesis, Department of Linguistics, Indiana University, Bloomington.

Karttunen, Lauri. 1969c. Pronouns and variables. In *Fifth Regional Meeting of the Chicago Linguistics Society*, pages 108–115.

Karttunen, Lauri. 1970. On the semantics of complement sentences. In *Chicago Linguistic Society 6*, pages 328–340.

Karttunen, Lauri. 1971a. Counterfactual conditionals. *Linguistic Inquiry* 2(4):566–569.

Karttunen, Lauri. 1971b. Definite descriptions with crossing coreference: a study of the Bach-Peters paradox. *Foundations of Language* pages 157–182.

Karttunen, Lauri. 1971c. Implicative verbs. *Language* 47(2):340–358.

Karttunen, Lauri. 1971d. *The logic of English predicate complement constructions*. Indiana University Linguistics Club.

Karttunen, Lauri. 1971e. Subjunctive conditionals and polarity reversals. *Research on Language and Social Interaction* 4(2):279–298.

Karttunen, Lauri. 1972. *Possible* and *must*. *Syntax and Semantics* 1:1–20.

Karttunen, Lauri. 1973. Presuppositions of compound sentences. *Linguistic Inquiry* 4:169–193.

Karttunen, Lauri. 1974a. Presupposition and linguistic context. *Theoretical Linguistics* 1:181–194.

Karttunen, Lauri. 1974b. Until. In *Tenth Regional Meeting of the Chicago Linguistic Society*, pages 284–297.

Karttunen, Lauri. 1975. On the syntax of the word *paljon* in Finnish. In *Congressus Tertius Internationalis Fenno-Ugristarum*.

Karttunen, Lauri. 1976. Discourse referents. In J. McCawley, ed., *Syntax and Semantics 7: Notes from the Linguistic Underground*, pages 363—385. Academic Press.

Karttunen, Lauri. 1977a. Syntax and semantics of questions. *Linguistics and Philosophy* 1:1–44.

Karttunen, Lauri. 1977b. To doubt whether. In *The CLS Book of Squibs*, pages 58–59.

Karttunen, Lauri. 1977c. Whichever antecedent. In *The CLS Book of Squibs*.

Karttunen, Lauri. 1983. KIMMO: A general morphological processor. In *Texas Linguistic Forum*, pages 163—186.

Karttunen, Lauri. 1984. Features and values. In *10th International Conference on Computational Linguistics and 22nd Annual Meeting of the Association for Computational Linguistics, Proceedings of COLING '84*, pages 28–33.

Karttunen, Lauri. 1986. D-PATR: A development environment for unification-based grammars. In *Proceedings of the 11th International Conference on Computational Linguistics, COLING '86*, pages 74–80.

Karttunen, Lauri. 1989a. Radical lexicalism. In *Alternative Conceptions of Phrase Structure*, pages 43–65. University of Chicago Press.

Karttunen, Lauri. 1989b. Translating from English to logic in Tarski's world. *Journal of Information Science and Engineering* 5(4):323–348.

Karttunen, Lauri. 1990. Binary encoding format for finite-state networks. Tech report SSL-90-17 [P90-00019], Xerox, System Sciences Laboratory, Palo Alto Research Center.

Karttunen, Lauri. 1993. Finite-state constraints. In *The Last Phonological Rule*, pages 173–194.

Karttunen, Lauri. 1994. Constructing lexical transducers. In *15th International Conference on Computational Linguistics, COLING*, pages 406–411.

Karttunen, Lauri. 1995. The replace operator. In H. Uszkoreit, ed., *33rd Annual Meeting of the Association for Computational Linguistics*, pages 16–23. Morgan Kaufmann Publishers/ACL.

Karttunen, Lauri. 1996a. Directed replace operator. In *Finite-state language processing*, pages 117–147.

Karttunen, Lauri. 1996b. Directed replacement. In A. K. Joshi and M. Palmer, eds., *34th Annual Meeting of the Association for Computational Linguistics*, pages 108–115. Morgan Kaufmann Publishers/ACL.

Karttunen, Lauri. 1998. The proper treatment of optimality in computational phonology: Plenary talk. In *Proceedings of the International Workshop on Finite State Methods in Natural Language Processing*, FSMNLP '09, pages 1–12. Stroudsburg, PA, USA: Association for Computational Linguistics. ISBN 975-7679-34-8.

Karttunen, Lauri. 2000. Applications of finite-state transducers in natural language processing. In S. Yu and A. Paun, eds., *Implementation and Application of Automata, 5th International Conference, CIAA 2000*, vol. 2088 of *Lecture Notes in Computer Science*, pages 34–46. Springer.

Karttunen, Lauri. 2003. Computing with realizational morphology. In A. F. Gelbukh, ed., *Computational Linguistics and Intelligent Text Processing, 4th International Conference, CICLing 2003*, vol. 2588 of *Lecture Notes in Computer Science*, pages 203–214. Springer.

Karttunen, Lauri. 2005. Finnish optimality-theoretic prosody. In A. Yli-Jyrä, L. Karttunen, and J. Karhumäki, eds., *Finite-State Methods and Natural Language Processing, 5th International Workshop, FSMNLP 2005*, vol. 4002 of *Lecture Notes in Computer Science*, pages 9–10. Springer.

Karttunen, Lauri. 2006a. A finite-state approximation of Optimality Theory: The case of Finnish prosody. In T. Salakoski, F. Ginter, S. Pyysalo, and T. Pahikkala, eds., *Advances in Natural Language Processing, 5th International Conference on NLP, FinTAL 2006*, vol. 4139 of *Lecture Notes in Computer Science*, pages 4–15. Springer.

Karttunen, Lauri. 2006b. The insufficiency of paper-and-pencil linguistics: the case of Finnish prosody. In M. Butt, M. Dalrymple, and T. H. King, eds., *Intelligent Linguistic Architectures: Variations on themes by Ronald M Kaplan*, pages 287–300. CSLI Publications.

Karttunen, Lauri. 2006c. Numbers and Finnish numerals. *SKY Journal of Linguistics* 19:407—421.

Karttunen, Lauri. 2007. Word play. *Computational Linguistics* 33(4):443–467.

Karttunen, Lauri. 2011. Beyond morphology: Pattern matching with FST. In C. Mahlow and M. Piotrowski, eds., *Systems and Frameworks for Computational Morphology - Second International Workshop, SFCM*, vol. 100 of *Communications in Computer and Information Science*, pages 1–13. Springer.

Karttunen, Lauri. 2012. Simple and phrasal implicatives. In E. Agirre, J. Bos, and M. T. Diab, eds., *Proceedings of the First Joint Conference on Lexical and Computational Semantics, *SEM 2012*, pages 124–131. Association for Computational Linguistics.

Karttunen, Lauri. 2013. You will be lucky to break even. In T. H. King and V. de Paiva, eds., *From Quirky Case to Representing Space: Papers in Honor of Annie Zaenen*, pages 167–180. CSLI Publications.

Karttunen, Lauri. 2015. From natural logic to natural reasoning. In A. F. Gelbukh, ed., *Computational Linguistics and Intelligent Text Processing – 16th International Conference, CICLing 2015*, vol. 9041 of *Lecture Notes in Computer Science*, pages 295–309. Springer.

Karttunen, Lauri and Kenneth Beesley. 1992. Two-level rule compiler. Tech Report ISTL-92-2, Xerox Palo Alto Research Center.

Karttunen, Lauri and Kenneth Beesley. 2005. Twenty-five years of finite-state morphology. In *Inquiries into Words, Constraints and Contexts. Festschrift for Kimmo Koskenniemi on his 60th Birthday*, pages 71–83.

Karttunen, Lauri, Jean-Pierre Chanod, Gregory Grefenstette, and Anne Schille. 1996. Regular expressions for language engineering. *Natural Language Engineering* 2(4):305–328.

Karttunen, Lauri, Ronald Kaplan, and Annie Zaenen. 1992. Two-level morphology with composition. In *14th International Conference on Computational Linguistics, COLING*, pages 141–148.

Karttunen, Lauri and Frances Karttunen. 1976. The clitic *-kin/-kaan* in Finnish. In *Texas Linguistic Forum 5*, pages 89–118.

Karttunen, Lauri and Frances Karttunen. 1977. Even questions. In *NELS 7: Proceedings of the Seventh Annual Meeting of the North Eastern XXX*.

Karttunen, Lauri and Martin Kay. 1985. Structure sharing with binary trees. In *23rd Annual Meeting of the Association for Computational Linguistics*, pages 133–136.

Karttunen, Lauri, Kimmo Koskenniemi, and Ronald Kaplan. 1987. A compiler for two-level phonological rules. In M. Dalrymple, R. Kaplan, L. Karttunen, K. Koskenniemi, S. Shaio, and M. Wescoat, eds., *Tools for Morphological Analysis*, pages 1–61. vol. 87-108 of CSLI Reports.

Karttunen, Lauri, Kimmo Koskenniemi, and Gertjan van Noord. 2003. Finite state methods in natural language processing. *Natural Language Engineering* 9(1):1–3.

Karttunen, Lauri and Kemal Oflazer. 2000. Introduction to the special issue on finite state methods in NLP. *Computational Linguistics* 26(1):1–2.

Karttunen, Lauri and Stanley Peters. 1976. What indirect questions conventionally implicate. In *Papers from the Twelfth Regional Meeting of the Chicago Linguistics Society*, pages 351—368.

Karttunen, Lauri and Stanley Peters. 1979. Conventional implicature. *Syntax and Semantics* 11:1–56. Presupposition.

Karttunen, Lauri and Stanley Peters. 1980. Interrogative quantifiers. In *Time, Tense, and Quantifiers*, pages 181–205.

Karttunen, Lauri and Annie Zaenen. 2005. Veridicity. In G. Katz, J. Pustejovsky, and F. Schilder, eds., *Annotating, Extracting and Reasoning about Time and Events, 10.-15. April 2005*, vol. 05151 of *Dagstuhl Seminar Proceedings*. Internationales Begegnungs- und Forschungszentrum für Informatik (IBFI).

Kay, Martin and Lauri Karttunen. 1984. Parsing a free word order language. In *Natural Language Parsing*. The Cambridge ACL series.

Kempe, André and Lauri Karttunen. 1996. Parallel replacement in finite state calculus. In *16th International Conference on Computational Linguistics, Proceedings of the Conference, COLING 1996*, pages 622–627.

Kwon, Hyuk-Chul and Lauri Karttunen. 1994. Incremental construction of a lexical transducer for Korean. In *15th International Conference on Computational Linguistics, COLING*, pages 1262–1266.

Nairn, Rowan, Cleo Condoravdi, and Lauri Karttunen. 2006. Computing relative polarity for textual inference. In *Inference in Computational Semantics*, pages 67–76.

Nerbonne, John, Lauri Karttunen, Elena Paskaleva, Gábor Prószéky, and Tiit Roosmaa. 1997. Reading more into foreign languages. In *5th Applied Natural Language Processing Conference, ANLP 1997*, pages 135–138. Association for Computational Linguistics.

Yampol, Todd and Lauri Karttunen. 1990. An efficient implementation of PATR for categorial unification grammar. In *13th International Conference on Computational Linguistics, COLING*, pages 419–424.

Zaenen, Annie and Lauri Karttunen. 1984. Morphological non-distinctiveness and coordination. In *Proceedings of the First Eastern States Conference on Linguistics*, pages 309–320.

Zaenen, Annie and Lauri Karttunen. 2013. Veridicity annotation in the lexicon? a look at factive adjectives. In *Proceedings of the 9th Joint ISO - ACL SIGSEM Workshop on Interoperable Semantic Annotation*, pages 51—58. Association for Computational Linguistics.

Zaenen, Annie, Lauri Karttunen, and Richard Crouch. 2005. Local textual inference: Can it be defined or circumscribed? In B. Dolan and I. Dagan, eds., *Proceedings of the ACL Workshop on Empirical Modeling of Semantic Equivalence and Entailment*, pages 31–36. Association for Computational Linguistics.

Part I

Semantics

1

Indefinites and Anaphora: Pivotal Problems in the History of Semantics and Pragmatics

Barbara H. Partee

1.1 Introduction

As linguists, philosophers, and logicians worked in the 1960s on developments that fed into the creation of formal semantics and pragmatics, there were some important difficulties that were hard to recognize at first. Donkey sentences, for instance, could not be understood to be a problem until formalized compositional semantic treatments had been developed for more straightforward sentences containing quantifiers and anaphora. Anaphora was a little easier to see as a problem, because it was clear that natural language pronouns did not always correspond to the logician's variables, even if Montague treated them as if they did. But it took considerable time to stop thinking of "pronominalization" as a syntactic process and focus on the interpretation of pronouns and not just their syntactic distribution. And indefinite noun phrases took even longer to emerge as a central problem for analysis, but once they did, they played a pivotal role in the development and then in the "naturalization" of formal semantics into linguistics, in motivating the introduction of theoretical innovations designed to capture some of the ways in which natural languages are importantly different from the invented logical languages whose analysis provided the early models for the formal semantics of natural language.

This paper is part of a larger project on the history of formal seman-

Tokens of Meaning: Papers in Honor of Lauri Karttunen.
Cleo Condoravdi and Tracy Holloway King (eds.).

tics. I have already written about the "starring role" of quantifiers in the history of formal semantics (Partee, 2013b). In this paper I look more closely at indefinites, which had been regarded by most logicians and logically-minded linguists as corresponding to existential quantifiers, an assumption that was gradually challenged in the 1960s and 1970s, and then radically rejected with the advent of Heim's File Change Semantics (Heim, 1982, Heim, 1983) and Kamp's Discourse Representation Theory (Kamp, 1981). My goals are to recount some interesting parts of the history of formal semantics and to simultaneously fulfill a Festschrift function in highlighting some of the contributions of Lauri Karttunen to that history.

Lauri Karttunen's work in the years leading up to his dissertation (Karttunen, 1969b) played an important role in the recognition and the development of solutions to a whole family of problems connected with indefinites. Irene Heim cites as the two main influences on her work and on her proposal to equate meaning not with truth conditions but with "context change potential" (i) Stalnaker's work on the updating of the common ground (Stalnaker, 1978) and (ii) Karttunen's work on discourse referents. Karttunen had earlier shown the inadequacy of a proposal by Partee (Partee, 1970) to distinguish specific from non-specific indefinites by means of a binary feature opposition inspired by Donnellan's (Donnellan, 1966) distinction between referential and attributive definites; as Partee reported in a footnote, Karttunen showed that in sentences with multiple layers of embedding, a binary distinction would not suffice, and scope mechanisms would be required.[1]

[1] I received a 7-page letter from Karttunen dated May 18, 1970, after the paper had been submitted to the special issue of *Synthèse* collecting papers from a 1969 conference of linguists and philosophers organized by Donald Davidson and Gil Harman. Karttunen's letter was not only full of good arguments and suggestions, but is also a beautiful example of his diplomacy. The letter begins, "Dear Barbara, Here are some comments to your paper, which I enjoyed and mostly agreed with. The criticisms below may not be in any way crucial, but I hope they are not totally irrelevant either." What follows was such a thorough and convincing demonstration of the inadequacy of my proposal for dealing with the 'referential'/'non-referential' distinction among indefinites by means of a binary feature rather than by means of a scope distinction that I considered the possibility of simply withdrawing the paper from the publication it had been submitted to. But I wasn't convinced that Karttunen's own proposals could stand, since treating the ambiguity in one-clause sentences as a scope ambiguity depended on the Generative Semantics idea of including a higher 'performative' clause on top of every simple declarative sentence; and also there were parts of the paper that Karttunen hadn't disagreed with that I thought made it still worth publishing. So in proofs in a footnote I described Karttunen's most convincing argument, agreed that my main proposal had been shown to be wrong, but not agreeing with his own proposal, concluding that at that point I knew of no satisfactory analysis. Lauri and I continued to enjoy discussing these

In the paper I review some central threads in how treatments of anaphora, indefinites, and quantification were developed from the 1960's into the 1980's, and discuss their importance for major controversies in the architecture of the grammar, especially in the relations among syntax, semantics, and pragmatics, including the rise of "dynamic semantics" and debates over its nature. A bonus topic connected with the relation of semantics to pragmatics is Karttunen's groundbreaking work on the semantics of questions, noteworthy in part for the methodological innovation of studying embedded interrogatives rather than matrix ones in order to separate the semantics of interrogative clauses from the pragmatics of asking a question.

I begin in Section 1.2 with a glimpse into a "pre-semantic" period in linguistics in the 1960's, when generative syntax was well underway but formal semantics had not come onto the scene and a number of problems later seen to involve semantics were coming to light as problems for various syntactic analyses. Then in Section 1.3 I describe some early concerns with semantics within linguistics, largely but not only within Generative Semantics, and focusing especially on Karttunen's early work leading up to his 1969 dissertation (Karttunen, 1969b) and the works he built on. In his work in that period one can see a connected path from concerns about what the phrase "identical NPs" should mean to concerns about referential indices, definiteness and specificity, and to concerns about anaphora and to the idea of discourse referents and various aspects of pragmatics.

In Section 1.4 I focus on Heim's approach to indefinites, definites, and anaphora in (Heim, 1982), work which grew out of ideas of Stalnaker about context change potential and of Karttunen about discourse referents and their lifespans. The period between Karttunen's work and Heim's was marked by the rise of formal semantics and its growing adoption in linguistics. I largely skip over that chapter of history here (see (Partee, 2011, Partee, 2013b)), making just a few pertinent observations about the rise of Generalized Quantifier theory as a result of Montague's work and the work of linguists as in (Barwise and Cooper, 1981), concentrating on the challenge to the uniform treatment of NP interpretations as generalized quantifiers that came from Heim's work.

Section 1.5 sketches parts of the beginnings of formal pragmatics and issues of the relationship of pragmatics to semantics and syntax, showing how much work on implicature and presupposition can be traced to Karttunen's concerns to pin down the contexts in which an an-

problems that interested both of us so much, and I had an early lesson in how one can deliver devastating critiques in a friendly and constructive way.

tecedent is available to be linked to an anaphoric expression. Here I briefly discuss Karttunen's groundbreaking work on the semantics of interrogatives, separate work in a different domain but I believe with similar motivation. And finally, in Section 1.6, I say a bit more about Lauri Karttunen's influences on others.

1.2 The "Pre-semantic" Period: Late 1950's into Mid-1960's

In early work on transformational grammar, the typical research problem involved identifying a family of sentence constructions that were intuitively "related", like active and passive sentences, declaratives and interrogatives, and multi-clause constructions that were intuitively related to simple "kernel" sentences (Chomsky, 1957, 1965).

In the earliest treatment of anaphora in generative grammar, Lees and Klima analyzed sentences with pronouns and reflexives as derived from sentences with full NPs (Lees and Klima, 1963), with transformations substituting a pronoun or reflexive for an identical NP. Lees and Klima focused on the differences in distribution between pronouns and reflexives, arguing with many interesting examples for the claim that the antecedent to a reflexive pronoun in English is always in the same clause, and the antecedent to a pronoun is always within a higher clause. Their work was the earliest precursor to Chomsky's Binding Theory, and some of their examples remain classic. There are many interesting and relevant constructions discussed in their work.

(1) The men threw a smokescreen around themselves. ([12], p.18)

(2) The men found a smokescreen around them. ([13], p.18)

(3) I told John to protect himself. ([14a], p.18)

(4) I told John to protect me. ([14b], p.18)

(5) *I told John to protect myself. ([14c], p.18)

Lees and Klima show evidence of awareness of some problems with the "pronominalization transformation". They follow a suggestion credited to Lila Gleitman and assume that the pronominalization and reflexive transformations are obligatory for first and second person and optional for third person: this reflects the idea that two first-person expressions in a single sentence are bound to be coreferential while two third-person expressions are not. (And they and Gleitman seem to have assumed that second-person expressions are like first-person ones, an oversimplification.)

But in their work, and even with the later addition of "referential indices" on noun phrases to indicate coreference in (Chomsky, 1965), almost all the examples used proper names. Thus the history of generative grammar had to repeat the history of the Stoics (4th – 3rd centuries BCE), as noted by (Egli, 2000): while the "pronominalization transformation" preserves meaning in (7), with a proper name as antecedent, it does not in (6), which has a very different meaning from the same sentence with somebody/a man in place of he.

(6) If somebody/a man is in Athens, it is not the case that he is in Rhodes.

(7) If Socrates is in Athens, it is not the case that he is in Rhodes.

These problems gradually entered the consciousness of linguists in the late 1960's and early 1970's. A snapshot of some of the semantic problems that were causing worries to syntacticians in the late 1960's can be found in (Stockwell et al., 1973), a compendium and synthesis of work on transformational grammar up to about 1968, basically completed in 1970 but with a few revisions made between 1970 and 1972. When that project began in 1966, a conscious decision was made to deal only with syntax, and that policy was maintained, even though the "linguistic wars" were heating up during that time.[2] In our treatment of pronominalization, we included an optional transformation of "definitization" (following an idea of S.-Y. Kuroda) to apply to the second of two identical indefinite NPs, the idea being that the decision of whether two treat two formally identical indefinites as coreferential should be reflected at that step. We treated *one(s)*-anaphora with a transformation replacing an identical noun or common noun phrase by *one(s)*, independent of referentiality. Personal pronouns themselves were analyzed as in (Postal, 1966), with *he*, *she*, etc. amounting to a surface realization of *the one(s)*.

Pronominalization was one of the first areas where problems arose that were later seen to be important semantic challenges to prevailing assumptions about syntax, if syntax was to provide the input to a systematic mapping to semantics. There were others that also involved transformations that involved some notion of identity between two NPs; many of these came to light only in the late 1960s, and some will be discussed in Section 1.3.

Common to all of the proposals that date before the Generative Semantics proposals of the late 60s is retention of the basic assumption that complex sentences are derived from (the structures underlying[3])

[2]For me, this policy caused some tension towards the end of the project, as I became increasingly interested in semantics and began to learn about Montague's work; this is described in (Partee, 2004).

[3]For brevity I speak of transformations applying to sentences; that should always

simple (kernel) sentences. In (Chomsky, 1957) transformations could apply to a single sentence, or could combine two sentences into a more complex one. In (Chomsky, 1965) all the parts underlying a complex sentence were combined in a single deep structure, but still (with very few exceptions, like a "COMP" node in a matrix sentence to provide a place for embedding of a complement clause — already in (Chomsky, 1957)) with the deep structure of each embedded clause corresponding to a complete "kernel" sentence that could in principle stand on its own. Before Generative Semantics on the one hand and Montague Grammar on the other, there were no variable-like NPs like the later "PRO" or "pro" in generative grammar, but only 'real' NPs. This widespread practice led to many problems for many transformations that depended on something like "identity" holding between two NPs.

One can get a sense of how difficult some of these problems looked from the point of view of syntax in the 1960's from the chapter on relative clauses in (Stockwell et al., 1973). The chapter discusses several different proposals for deriving relative clauses that had been and were being debated, differing in part with respect to where in the structure of the NP a restrictive relative clause originated — inside the determiner, attached to the whole NP (what is now the DP), or attached at a lower node (then NOM, now NP), and concomitantly differing on what sort of identity relation was supposed to hold between the matrix NP, or some part of it, and the corresponding NP in the relative clause. Partly semantic arguments had even led to proposals to derive some relative clauses from conjoined clauses and some (mainly with generics or universally quantified sentences) from *if*-clauses. The chapter discusses arguments for and against each of the proposals and finds serious problems for each of them (finally adopting a version of one that seemed least bad); our concerns were officially entirely syntactic, but the line between syntactic and semantic arguments was clearly not sharp, and the difficulty of trying to work out the syntax without considering semantics — and without any explicit semantics to consider — was becoming ever more evident.

Problems with the "Equi-NP Deletion" rules such as in the derivation of infinitival complements were coming to prominence as well, mostly a bit later, as discussed in (Partee, 2011). The relative order of discovery of problems related to NP identity — with anaphora first, then relative clauses, then "Equi" rules — may reflect the fact that one could and did work on the "Equi" rules using only examples with proper names for quite a long time, but that couldn't be done at all

be interpreted to mean applying to the syntactic structures of sentences.

with restrictive relative clauses, since proper names (when anarthrous) don't co-occur with restrictive relative clauses, and anaphora seems to have always been studied with a wide range of sorts of antecedents.

Indefinite NPs in the "pre-semantic" period were thought of as including only NPs with *a, an, some*, and the reduced form represented as *sm*, and their counterparts in other languages (and possibly a null indefinite article on bare plurals and bare mass terms). They figured in the *there*-transformation, which applied only when the pivot NP was indefinite, and the indefinites *someone* and *something* also served as the source of the interrogative *WH*-words *who* and *what* (Klima, 1964), leading to debates about how *what* and *which* should be distinguished — as differing in definiteness or rather as both indefinite but differing with respect to a feature "specific".

More generally, (Stockwell et al., 1973) describe a range of problems that arise from the attempt to keep their transformational syntax "conservative", problems that are spread across the chapters on Determiners, Pronominalization, Relativization, and Negation. The picture that emerges is one of syntacticians being led into semantic concerns whether they wanted to be or not (some of those who embraced semantic concerns were the pioneers of Generative Semantics), and being quite uncertain about how to deal with them.[4]

1.3 Early Concerns with Semantics in Linguistics: Late 1960's – Mid 1970's

The earliest efforts within linguistics to address the kinds of semantic problems connected with coreference and anaphora, and with definite and indefinite NPs, came from the early Generative Semanticists — Ross, Lakoff, McCawley, some of Emmon Bach's work, and others. One of the others was Lauri Karttunen. He was first attracted to transformational syntax, then recognized the potential of Generative Semantics and contributed to it, and then somewhat later became convinced that the semantics of Generative Semantics was "too syntactic", and that further advances would require exploiting the tools of model theory. But that third step will come in Section 1.4, after formal semantics has appeared on the stage. Lauri Karttunen had come to Indiana University in 1964 just after "the LSA's Linguistic Summer School that marked the beginning of Chomskyan revolution." (Karttunen, 2012, p.3) He was taken with transformational grammar and wrote a paper

[4]Postal's legendary "linguistic anarchy notes", of which (Postal, 1967) is specifically about coreferentiality, concerned problems that were *prima facie* within the domain of generative grammar, but whose solution by normal syntactic rules seemed impossible.

on existential sentences in Finnish, and planned to do his dissertation on that topic. He moved in 1967 to the Rand Corporation in Santa Monica on a research scholarship to write his dissertation and to work on computational linguistics under Martin Kay, with whom he had had a course on parsing at the 1966 Linguistic Institute at UCLA, and who "was running an exciting weekly colloquium series." (Karttunen, 2006, p.445) There he started thinking "about the similarities and differences between pronouns and logical variables" (Karttunen, 2006, p.445), and found himself writing Rand technical reports on problems of identity between NPs (Karttunen, 1967, 1968) and eventually changing his dissertation topic to pronouns and variables (Karttunen, 1969a, 1969b). In his 1967 paper, Karttunen was concerned with some difficult cases of "NP identity" that show up in the context of VP ellipsis, some from (1967b, Ross, 1967c), some Karttunen's own, some from Chomsky's lectures in the 1966 Linguistic Institute. Karttunen pointed out that some kinds of "sloppy identity" (Ross's term) in VP anaphora examples violate traditional notions of identity even with coreferentiality added. Here are three examples from (Karttunen, 1967), (4a, 5a, 6a) in the original:

(8) John scratched his arm and so did Mary. (Ross, 1967b)

(9) I saw a lion and so did you.

(10) The barber shaved himself before I could. (Chomsky, 1966 Ling. Inst. lectures)

Karttunen notes that as Ross (1967b) observed, the then-standard transformational derivation of VP-ellipsis together with the requirement that transformations preserve meaning, argued for in (Katz and Postal, 1964) and adopted in (Chomsky, 1965), would have the consequence that the ambiguous phrase *so did Mary* in (8) should be derivable from either (11) or (12), but only on certain interpretations of the two conjoined clauses.

(11) Mary scratched her arm.

(12) Mary scratched his arm.

In the case of (11), VP ellipsis should be allowed only if the possessive pronouns *his* and *her* are both interpreted reflexively; and in this case two different arms are involved. No coindexing of elements that appear in the syntax could capture that; and 'formal identity' is also violated because of the *his-her* mismatch.[5] In the case of (12), VP ellipsis should

[5]This formal non-identity of *his arm* and *her arm*, the purported underlying forms, was what gave rise to the term *sloppy identity* for what was later understood

be allowed only if the referent of *his* is the same in both conjuncts, and it does not matter whether that referent is John or not, which at the time seemed to mean that it does not matter whether the interpretation of the first clause involves a reflexive interpretation of the possessive pronoun or not.

The problems with (9) and (10) are not identical to the problems with (8), as Karttunen shows, and yet, he argues, they arise from similar deficiencies in the idea of analyzing identity of NPs in terms of formal identity plus identity of referential indices. The ambiguity of (9) concerns whether we saw the same lion or we each simply saw a lion; if the case of the same lion is treated as involving co-indexing two occurrences of *a lion*, how should the other case, which could be paraphrased with *and you saw one too*, be analyzed? And the ambiguity of (10) is still different, but similarly problematical.

Karttunen's conclusions from these and other problems raised in his 1967 paper have a positive and a negative side. The positive side is his recognition and elucidation of the problems; the negative side is that he could not see how to solve them. "The deletions — if there are any — presuppose some kind of semantic equivalence between the two clauses in question, and it just happens that this equivalence can be achieved in all of them in more than one way. All three are ambiguous, but not quite the same way. Unfortunately it also appears that this intuitive notion of semantic equivalence, which seems to play a role here, is not related to the three traditional conditions[6] in any simple fashion. ... Needless to say, presently we are unable to suggest any definition for such a notion." (Karttunen, 1967, pp.5-6)

He goes on to discuss two proposals, tentatively adopting a version of the second one, based on arguments in (McCawley, 1967):

(13) In the deep structure, some NP's are marked as referential by assigning an index to them. For each set of NP's with identical indices, only the topmost NP is expanded to a subtree in which lexical items are inserted. The rest of the coreferential NP's are unexpanded terminal symbols. The semantic component of the grammar determines the meaning of the expanded NP by processing the subtree it dominates, and the resulting set of semantic features is assigned to all NP's with that particular referential index. ([15] in Karttunen, 1967, p.13)

As he notes, such a proposal is incompatible with the notion of deep

---

to be strict semantic identity on a "bound variable" interpretation.

[6]The "three traditional conditions" are (i) identical constituent structure, (ii) morpheme-for-morpheme identity, and (iii) coreferentiality. (p.3)

structure in (Chomsky, 1965), since here there has to be some semantic interpretation before syntactic rules can operate. And selectional restrictions, proposed by Chomsky to be satisfied at deep structure, cannot be evaluated if some NP nodes have only a referential index and no lexical content.

After inconclusively discussing more puzzles, he ends by saying, "The question to be faced is this: what do referential indices refer to?" … "In retrospect it seems that the underlying motivation for postulating a transformation such as IDENTICAL NP DELETION in early transformational studies was to capture the notion of anaphoric reference without actually talking about semantics. The failure of this policy seems pretty clear now." (pp.20-21)

And that final question became the title of his 1968 paper (Karttunen, 1968), which in turn was revised into his classic paper "Discourse referents" (Karttunen, 1976), presented at CoLing 1969, but published only in 1976. In both papers, he starts by laying out a bundle of problems of five types that involve the idea of reference:

(14) (i) definite vs. indefinite NPs
(ii) generic vs. non-generic NPs
(iii) specific vs. non-specific NPs
(iv) anaphoric vs. deictic NPs and pronouns
(v) restrictive vs. appositive relative clauses and modifiers

Works on these problems that he cites in 1968 include (Annear, 1968, Bach, 1968, Baker, 1966, Gross, 1967, Jackendoff, 1968, Postal, 1966, Ross, 1967a, Ross, 1967c, Smith, 1964), a 1966 manuscript version of (Langacker, 1969), and a 1967 manuscript version of (McCawley, 1970); that list gives a good picture of the work on those problems at that time,[7] the majority of it with a generative semantics orientation or influence. Karttunen was corresponding with McCawley about pronouns at the time, and he came to a seminar of mine at UCLA, and we had discussions — he reports that I convinced him that the semantics in the generative semantics approaches was still a kind of syntax, and that

[7]Maurice Gross's paper was presented at the 1967 Congress on Logic, Methodology, and Philosophy of Science in Amsterdam, the same venue where Yehoshua Bar-Hillel had organized a symposium on "The Role of Formal Logic in the Evaluation of Argumentation in Natural Languages", whose participants included Bar-Hillel, Frits Staal, Richard Montague, Jerrold Katz, John Lyons, Jaakko Hintikka, Max Black, Eric Stenius, Michael Dummett, among others; the symposium contributions and comments were edited by Staal and published in *Foundations of Language* (Staal, 1969). I write about this symposium in the context of the development of Montague's attitudes toward the project of formalizing natural language in (Partee, 2013). But this took place before Montague's work was known to linguists.

he should learn some 'real semantics' (i.e. Montague) — something he did later on his own.[8]

In the 1968 paper, Karttunen argues that to solve this family of problems, it will be essential to look at discourse, and not just single sentences; this was an idea that went against the long-standing tenet of generative grammar that any genuinely grammatical phenomena would show up within a single sentence — perhaps a long one — and that therefore one could restrict one's attention to single sentences in working on syntax and other components of grammar. This paper also had the important example (15); Karttunen cites (Baker, 1966) as the source. Karttunen used the example to show that the discourse referent introduced by an indefinite in an opaque context has a lifespan that lasts within that opaque context. The example was repeated in (Partee, 1970), which is where Montague learned of it; he formulated rules for handling it in his "PTQ" paper (Montague, 1973), by adding a VP conjunction rule and rules to quantify a term phrase into VPs as well as into sentences; see Section 1.4.

(15) John wants to catch a fish and eat it.

During that period, around 1968-69, there was already awareness among both linguists and philosophers of the ambiguities involving indefinite NPs in classic opaque contexts as in (16), brought to prominence in the work of Quine, especially (Quine, 1960).

(16) John wants to marry a Norwegian.

Fillmore (1967) proposed analyzing it as a distinction between a [+/− specific] indefinite article, whereas Generative Semanticists like McCawley ((McCawley, 1970) was circulating in 1967) and most philosophers proposed to represent it as a scope ambiguity with an existential quantifier above or below the attitude verb *want*. I was working on the same family of problems, and having just read (Donnellan, 1966), I had the idea of trying to apply his distinction between referential and attributive definite NPs to indefinite NPs, couching the specificity distinction in similar terms. The result was (Partee, 1970) (talks and drafts circulated earlier). Similarly to Donnellan, I drew parallels between interpretations of indefinites in sentences in discourses and interpretations of indefinites in embedded clauses. I came up with a number of interesting problems that hadn't been discussed before, and I identified problems in many possible accounts, including Fillmore's specificity-based account. But I cannot say that I came up with solutions; Lauri Karttunen pointed out to me that all my examples

[8]Interview by the author with Lauri Karttunen, January 13, 2011.

of indefinites in embedded contexts had just one layer of embedding, and that when there are more layers of embedding, a single binary specificity feature cannot capture the multiplying ambiguities, but a scope account can. Rereading my paper now is like looking at the world through a fog — the puzzles were indeed difficult ones, and we didn't have many tools beyond first-order logic. (I began to sit in on Montague's classes in Fall 1968, but hadn't learned enough to make any use of his work then.) I wasn't content with the scope accounts because they didn't account for distinct interpretations of indefinites in matrix sentences — the same kind of motivation that much later led Ivan Sag and Janet Fodor to argue that one needed a specificity distinction in addition to a scope distinction (Fodor and Sag, 1982). But my own argumentation was fuzzy. When I received the letter from Karttunen that pointed out that my basic analysis was wrong, I agreed with it but didn't want to just withdraw the paper; I published it with a footnote about Karttunen's crucial critique, with the hope that the discussion of problems and critiques of all extant proposals for dealing with them would make it useful, which I think was the right decision.

Karttunen's "Discourse Referents" paper (Karttunen, 1976), the one most cited in later work on dynamic semantics and the Kamp-Heim theories of NPs and anaphora, was presented at CoLing in 1969; it is very similar to (Karttunen, 1968), but with some important innovations. In fact, this paper helps to show the relationship and natural progression among the topics that Karttunen worked on in the period 1967 – 1983, his "semantic period". Initial concerns about anaphora and rules involving "identical NPs" led to questions about "referential indices", and then to the "bundle of problems" (14)(i)-(v) above, including definite and indefinite NPs and anaphora, and working on those led to the idea that you have to examine discourse, not just sentences — there he came up with the idea of Discourse Referents. And considering their lifespans led naturally to concern with opaque contexts and other multi-clausal constructions: when an indefinite occurs in the complement of a factive verb or an unnegated implicative verb, its lifespan continues outside the embedded context. These phenomena are discussed in the "Discourse Referents" paper and in Karttunen's dissertation (Karttunen, 1969b), and mark the beginning of the fruitful line of work continued in (Karttunen, 1971, Karttunen, 1973).

So one can summarize the path of Karttunen's work from anaphora and "the identity of noun phrases" to implicative verbs and the "plugs, holes, and filters" of (Karttunen, 1973) as directed by the idea that discourse anaphora crucially involves the introduction of discourse referents whose lifespan depends on the semantic properties of the context in which they are introduced, and that crucially involves properties of the matrix verb, and the effect on it of negation and other operators.

The same paper emphasized the need to be concerned with discourse by also studying discourses that begin with a supposition of some kind and then elaborate on a hypothetical situation in which that supposition holds; the lifespan of a discourse referent introduced in connection with an indefinite in the supposition lasts as long as the discourse continues in the same hypothetical scenario. Karttunen notes the variety of such constructions, including multi-sentence texts beginning with a "Suppose ..." sentence and multiclause sentences like *if-then* constructions. And he notes that the supposition introduced in an *if*-clause may extend to following sentences, as in (18).

(17) Suppose Mary has a car. She takes me to work in it. I can drive the car too.

(18) If Mary has a car, she will take me to work in it. I can drive the car too.

(19) I wish Mary had a car. She would take me to work in it. I could drive the car too.

And it is in that paper that he notes additional scope ambiguities involving sentences with opaque verbs and multiple quantifiers, adding further evidence that a "+/− Specific" feature is not enough, and lending support to the kind of scope framework advocated in (Bach, 1968, McCawley, 1970).

Many insights concerning indefinites, anaphora, and quantifier scope in different kinds of embedding constructions were gained in this period of the late 1960s and beginning of the 1970s, led by the generative semanticists. There were not always solid theoretical foundations; Karttunen's important notion of "discourse referent" was not formalized, and there was not yet any systematic semantics connected with the proposed semantic representations. But much of the work of this period laid the foundations for later specifically linguistic contributions to formal semantics, as well as to later work on "Logical Form" in the Chomskyan tradition.

1.4 The Development of Heim's Dynamic Approach to Indefinites and Anaphora

In my papers on the history of formal semantics, such as (Partee, 2011, Partee, 2013b), I often lump together Kamp's work on Discourse Representation theory (Kamp, 1981) and Heim's File Change Semantics (Heim, 1982). In this paper I focus on Heim's work, since she explicitly cites Karttunen's work on discourse referents as one of the two principal antecedent works that she builds on, the other being Stalnaker's development of Grice's notion of "common ground" in his work on pragmatic presuppositions (Stalnaker, 1974) and on the dynamic updating of the common ground in assertion (Stalnaker, 1978).

The period between Karttunen's work at the end of the 1960's and Heim's work at the beginning of the 1980's was a period of rapid change in semantics. The period began with the Linguistic Wars (Harris, 1993) in full swing and Montague just beginning his work on natural language, yet unknown to linguists, and ended with "Montague Grammar" having broadened into "formal semantics" and formal semantics already close to the dominance in the field that it solidified by the end of the 1980's. I have described the history of that period elsewhere (Partee, 1996, Partee, 2011, Partee, 2013b); here I just briefly recapitulate some of the developments that were central to the path from Karttunen's work to Heim's.

Montague's work introduced linguists to type theory, and his higher-order typed intensional logic offered new approaches to a number of linguistic phenomena for which first-order logic was seen to be inadequate. Generalized quantifiers, whose roots can be found in Frege and which were further developed by Mostowski and Lindström (see Peters and Westerståhl, 2006) were introduced into natural language semantics by Lewis and Montague in (Lewis, 1970, Montague, 1970c, 1973) and shown to offer considerable new insight into the linguistic properties of quantifiers and noun phrases in general by the linguist-logician team of Robin Cooper and Jon Barwise (Barwise and Cooper, 1981). Montague had shown how all noun phrases, including proper names, definites, and indefinites, as well as what were more commonly thought of as quantifier phrases, could be treated as generalized quantifiers, denoting sets of properties (having the type <<e,t>,t> in extensional fragments). Barwise and Cooper showed that under that assumption, a number of linguistically significant properties of noun phrases such as the weak-strong contrast and the licensing of negative polarity items inside either or both of the two arguments of a determiner could be given an insightful formal account. They also identified some universal properties of determiners, particularly conservativity. And they went so far as to propose that the analysis of NPs (today's DPs) as generalized quantifiers is a linguistic universal.

Barwise and Cooper's work was very powerful and led to fruitful cross-linguistic work on the semantics of determiners, quantifiers, and NP's across languages. Their formal definitions provided good tools for explicating the distinctions among pairs of closely related determiners or quantifiers in a number of languages, such as the weak and strong indefinites *enkele* and *sommige* in Dutch (de Hoop, 1995). The claim that all languages have NP's that are interpreted as generalized quantifiers was not challenged until the late 1980's in an NSF project of Bach, Kratzer, and Partee, after Heim's and Kamp's work had overturned the idea that all NP's in languages like English are interpreted as generalized quantifiers. Eventually several languages were found that lacked generalized quantifiers altogether, reported in the papers (Faltz, 1995, Jelinek, 1995, Vieira, 1995) in the volume (Bach et al., 1995) that resulted from that project.

Montague's last paper, the influential "PTQ" (Montague, 1973), offered solutions to a number of puzzles relating to quantified NPs in English, including the example discussed in Section 1.3 above, *John wants to catch a fish and eat it.* One of Montague's research strategies was to try to analyze English compositionally with as little deviation from "visible" syntactic structure as possible, so he treated the infinitival complement in that sentence as a VP, not a transformed sentence, and he treated VP conjunction as base-generated (like conjunction of sentences and of NPs). He treated indefinites as existential generalized quantifiers, and he analyzed only bound variable readings of pronouns. His "Quantifying In" rules were similar in fundamental ways to the "Quantifier Lowering" rule of Generative Semantics and the later "Quantifier Raising" rule of (May, 1977), differing in the architecture of the grammar and in the semantic explicitness of their interpretation (Partee, 1997). Like his conjunction rules, his quantifying in rules operated on several different categories: sentences, VPs, and common noun phrases. So the VP *catch a fish and eat it* was analyzed as having the NP *a fish* quantified into the VP *catch* him_1 *and eat* him_1; the whole VP is then the complement of *wants to*, an opaque context.

Generalized quantifier theory, along with the rest of Montague's analyses and their extensions and adaptations by linguists, had led to solutions of many problematic aspects of anaphora, scope, and binding, but not all. In the first decade of formal semantics (which I mark as 1968-1977, starting with Montague's first paper dealing with natural language (Montague, 1968)), linguists like me were enchanted with Montague's and Lewis's demonstration that English syntax is not crazy, if all NPs can in fact be treated uniformly and categorematically as generalized quantifiers. Russell had thought it was crazy for a language to put *every man* in the same syntactic category as *Jones*. Montague and Lewis, and also independently Parsons (Parsons, 1972), showed that if you employ a higher-order logic, they can be treated uniformly. And although that seemed counterintuitive for proper names, it did not seem to cause any problems, so Montague's strategy of "generalizing to the hardest case" so as to assign to each syntactic category a single semantic type, was accepted as reasonable. And Barwise and Cooper's work added to the attraction.

Indefinites and definites were treated as generalized quantifier variants of familiar Russellian analyses as quantifiers. Puzzles arising from that analysis were observed only later.

As for anaphora, there had been progress but much was still not known. In syntax, even the distinction between bound variable anaphora and 'coreferential' anaphora was not widely appreciated before the late 1970s. Reinhart's dissertation was completed in 1976, her book published in 1983 (Reinhart, 1976, Reinhart, 1983). Among semanticists, bound variable and 'coreferential' types were distinguished, but not much more. Montague treated only bound variable anaphora explicitly; variables left free were generally assumed to function like demonstratives or 'pragmatic anaphora', getting their value from the context. There were well-known puzzles like Geach's donkey anaphora (20),(21) (Geach, 1962), Karttunen's paycheck anaphora (22) (Karttunen, 1969a), and Bach & Peters's puzzle (23) (Bach, 1970).

(20) Every man who owns a donkey beats it.

(21) If a man owns a donkey, he beats it.

(22) The man who gave his paycheck to his wife was wiser than the man who gave it to his mistress.

(23) The man who shows he deserves it will get the prize he desires.

But although these puzzles were known, formal semantic treatments of anaphora had not progressed much beyond bound variable anaphora as in Montague, and some sort of 'co-referential anaphora', vaguely pragmatic. Not until (Bach and Partee, 1980) did reflexives even get added to Montague Grammar, along with some initial discussion of the possibility of "function-argument" command as a relevant factor in constraining antecedent-anaphor relations.

Heim's dissertation topic started from a workshop I organized at the University of Massachusetts in 1978 on the topic of "Indefinite Reference", a topic I had realized was a problem but had no solution for. Heim quotes an excerpt from my circular describing the workshop in the preface to her dissertation:

> The standard view among logicians is that indefinite noun phrases like 'a tall man' are not referring expressions, but quantifier phrases, like 'every man', 'no man', and 'most men'. Yet in many respects, indefinite noun phrases seem to function in ordinary language much

> like definite noun phrases or proper names, particularly with respect to the use of pronouns in discourse. This may be simply a matter of sorting out semantics from pragmatics, but there is not to our knowledge any currently available theory that simultaneously characterizes the logical or truth-functional properties of indefinite noun phrases and accounts for their 'discourse-reference properties ...' (Heim, 1982, p.iv)

Seeing than none of the workshop participants had a solution, and the workshop didn't produce one, Heim took on the challenge of finding an adequate account of definite and indefinite noun phrases, both their similarities and their differences, including an account of how they interact with anaphora.

Right after the workshop, she wrote a manuscript "Toward a unified semantics of definite and indefinite noun phrases," treating both as variables. But she became disaffected with that, because she couldn't account for the differences between definites and indefinites. But then in the summer of 1980 she saw how the differences could come from different presuppositions of definites and indefinites. The dissertation then took about 2 years. The questions raised in the workshop concerned indefinites and their puzzling nature, and had not included anything about definites. It was Heim's idea to work on the two classes of expressions together, to try to capture not only their differences, but also how they are similar to each other and different from real quantificational NPs. Just as Lauri Karttunen had made progress by working on a family of connected problems together, Heim also carved out for herself a family of five problems:

(1) Discourse anaphora.

(24) a. John/the man/a man walked in. He looked tired.
b. #Every man/no man/more than one man walked in. He looked tired.

(2) Different "discourse" behavior of logically equivalent sentences. (This argues against a purely pragmatic account of the differences in (24)a-b.)

(25) a. One of the ten marbles is missing from the bag. It's probably under the sofa.
b. Nine of the ten marbles are in the bag. ??It's probably under the sofa. (Examples in Heim's 1982 dissertation, credited to Partee.[9])

[9]The versions given here are in (Partee, 1989, p.363, fn.13). The earliest occurrence, in a slightly different version, is example (21a-b) in (Heim, 1982, p.21).

(3) An indefinite introduces a "discourse referent" with limited lifespan.

(26) a. John wants to catch a fish and eat it. (Karttunen's (15), discussed in Section 1.3)
b. Maybe he would share it with me. (Modal subordination, like Karttunen's (19) in Section 1.3. See also (Roberts, 1987, 1990).)
c. #It's probably under the boat now.

(4) The two connected problems of "donkey sentences"

(27) a. Every man who owns a donkey beats it.
b. If a man owns a donkey, he always beats it.

Problem 1: How to explain that *it* can be anaphoric to *a donkey* in these sentences?
Problem 2: How to explain that *a donkey* seems like a *universally* quantified NP in these sentences? (And in (27)b), so does *a man*.)

(5) The quantificational variability of indefinites.

(28) An equation like this *always/often/sometimes/never* has more than one solution.

That sentence has paraphrases with '*all/many/some/no* equations like this'.

Heim's dissertation, a classic, offers solutions to these problems through several important innovations. (Kamp's solutions are in most respects similar.) One important thing she did is to treat indefinites and definites both as "variables" of type e with no independent quantificational force of their own. The difference between indefinites and definites consists in two things:

(i) for an indefinite, pick a new variable, for a definite pick an old one. (This is the core of the "anaphoric theory of definites").

(ii) the NP content of an indefinite enters into asserted content; the NP content of a definite is presupposed.

An indefinite "introduces a new file card/a new discourse referent". A definite is to be identified with an old file card/an existing discourse referent.

Heim's 1982 file change semantics and Kamp's 1981 Discourse Representation Theory are *dynamic* theories: basic semantic values for expressions are not their truth-conditions or their contribution to truth conditions, but rather their "context change potential". Truth conditions are still given by the semantics, but indirectly: the truth of a file consists in the embeddability of the file ('partial model') in a model.

Heim and Kamp came up with their theoretical innovations in response to this family of problems virtually simultaneously and independently.

Both Heim and Kamp had accounts of the "lifespan" of a discourse referent, with crucial differences between simple sentences or sequences thereof vs. quantified sentences. Both Heim and Kamp built on Stalnaker's theory of how assertions update the "common ground". Their semantics is dynamic in that the interpretation of sentences not only depends on the context, it also affects the context.

Heim's legacy includes the opening up of issues about context change, bringing Stalnaker's perspective into linguistic discussion. These issues are foundational and substantive at the same time. She also did a great deal to bring formal semantics and Chomskyan syntax together, leading to an explosion of work on the syntax-semantics interface and much-improved communication. She and her work also led to formal semantics being more within linguistic theory, reflected in the new conference SALT, which began in 1991, and the new journal *Natural Language Semantics*, of which she and Angelika Kratzer are the founding and continuing editors, begun in 1992.

The substantive legacy of her work lies in new approaches to presupposition, the dynamics of domain restriction, parallels between anaphora and presupposition (extended further in (van der Sandt, 1989), and in the strong arguments her work provided against Montague's strategy of assigning the same semantic type to all the members of a given syntactic category. Montague had unified NP semantics; Heim (and Kamp) "de-unified" it. That was the inspiration for my work on type-shifting (Partee, 1986); I wanted to find a way to be able to say that Heim and Montague were both correct, and found it in the possibility of saying that all NPs *can* be interpreted as generalized quantifiers, but some start out in simpler types and get that type only by coercion.

There has been much more work on indefinites and on anaphora since then; here my aim is to show how Karttunen's work fed into Heim's theory and how the idea that indefinites introduce a discourse referent had a major impact on the development of formal semantics, and on the beginnings of formal pragmatics, which I turn to in Section 1.5.

1.5 Some of the Beginnings of Formal Pragmatics

This section is very brief. Here I note the connection between Heim's File Change Theory and pragmatics, and also remark briefly on how Karttunen's work on the semantics of interrogatives helps to elucidate the division of labor between semantics and pragmatics.

1.5.1 Formal Pragmatics and its Relation to Semantics

Stalnaker's work on assertion and on pragmatic presupposition emphasized the fundamental pragmatic fact that a language user is always interpreting a bit of language with respect to some context, and that the process of interpreting a bit of language generally results in some updating to the context. Once that idea penetrated linguistics, which Heim's theory helped it do, the line between semantics and pragmatics became less sharp.

In some ways the distinction between semantics and pragmatics had never been very clear. The term "pragmatics" and its classic definition are due to Charles Morris (Morris, 1938). Within *semiotics*, the general science of signs (which applies to both natural languages, artificial languages, and possibly other 'sign systems'), Morris distinguished three branches: *syntax*, the study of "the formal relation of signs to one another", *semantics*, the study of "the relations signs to the objects to which the signs are applicable" (their designata), and *pragmatics*, the study of "the relations of signs to interpreters" (Morris 1938, p.6).

On this view, syntax concerns properties of expressions, such as well-formedness; semantics concerns relations between expressions and what they are "about", such as reference and truth-conditions; pragmatics concerns relations among expressions, meanings, and uses in context, such as *implicature, irony, politeness.*

But all natural languages contain some expressions that have no interpretation independent of context; even before Heim suggested that that was true of indefinite and definite NPs, there were *indexicals*, words like *I, here, now* which pick out their referent by properties of the context of the speech act in which they are used, and typically pick out different referents in different contexts. Such expressions cannot be given any semantic interpretation independent of uses in context. And in fact in the papers of Montague's that have the word "pragmatics" in their titles (Montague, 1968, Montague, 1970a), that is the only aspect of pragmatics they are concerned with: the treatment of tenses, first person pronouns, and a few other such context-dependent elements.

But for a long time, probably until Heim's work, I had held on to the idea that semantics and pragmatics were still separable, and that one could compute the semantic interpretation of a sentence autonomously from pragmatics, and then "send it" to the pragmatics to fill in the values of context-dependent variables. So a sentence like *I saw you yesterday* would be semantically interpreted as having three context-dependent variables in it, one for "I", one for "you", and one for "now", in terms of which *yesterday* can be evaluated (the day before the day that includes "now"). But the semanticists in Germany in the 1970s (especially Arnim von Stechow, and Angelika Kratzer (Kratzer, 1978, von Stechow, 1981)) had already figured out that context-dependence is more complex than that, and that there is dynamic interaction between "ordinary" semantic interpretation and the interpretation of context-dependent elements.

And with Heim's work, and work by others that soon followed it, this dynamic aspect became explicit, and the scope of "formal pragmatics" became broader, encompassing not only explicitly context-dependent elements like pronouns, demonstratives, indexicals, tenses, and expressions like *left, right, in front of, local, friend,* but also presuppositions, domain restriction, and other elements that turned out to be sensitive to the same sort of structure-dependent "lifespan" phenomena as the discourse referents associated with indefinite NPs. These phenomena are so central to semantics that the term "pragmatics" is not always applied to them; on the other hand, the term "formal pragmatics" (within linguistics) normally refers to just such things (Potts, 2009). (And in recent times, Chierchia has argued (Chierchia, 2004) that even the computation of scalar implicatures, which had been assumed to involve pragmatic principles operating at the level of the whole speech act, is in fact part of compositional interpretation, thereby opening up a lively debate about syntax, semantics, pragmatics, and the architecture of grammar.)

So the line that we traced from Karttunen's concern with identity of NPs to his recognition of the need to look at discourse and his introduction of the idea of discourse referents with limited lifespans was not only a central precursor to Heim's dynamic semantics but more broadly to formal pragmatics and the recognition of the interconnectedness of semantics and pragmatics. And as we noted in the previous section, studying the lifespans of discourse referents also led to his important work on implicative verbs, presuppositions, and related phenomena that are crucial for both pragmatics and semantics.

1.5.2 A Note on Karttunen's Work on the Semantics of Interrogatives

Lauri Karttunen's paper on interrogatives (Karttunen, 1977) was the first paper in the first issue of the journal *Linguistics and Philosophy,* the successor to *Foundations of Language,* which had been founded in 1965 by Frits Staal and colleagues to promote greater interdisciplinary collaboration in theoretical work on natural language. Before Karttunen's work, virtually all attempts to analyze the interpretation of questions had taken matrix questions as their subject matter. As a result, there had been considerable difficulty in separating out the pragmatics of the speech act of asking a question from the semantic content of the question expression. Generative semanticists had often included a higher clause structure with content something like "I ask you to tell me ...". Karttunen's brilliant methodological move was to take embedded questions as his primary object of study, and to look for a kind of meaning for them that could provide the content that would be needed for semantic composition with all sorts of embedding contexts, such as (29)-(32).

(29) John asked Mary who was coming to the party.

(30) Mary knows who is coming to the party.

(31) Whether Bill will go to the party depends on who else is going.

(32) It's not important who is coming to the party.

The attention to the full range of embedding constructions, including the interesting case of *depend on* and similar verbs, had the salutary effect of getting rid of the attention to asking and answering that is hard to avoid when focusing on direct questions. The relation between questions and their answers still plays a part in Karttunen's semantics for interrogative clauses: a question denotes the set of propositions expressed by its true answers. But the notion of 'answer' does not occur anywhere in the actual semantic composition rules; that is just a user-friendly description of the denotation.

Karttunen's work on questions was not done in a vacuum, of course, and he gives full credit to the related earlier work of Hamblin (Hamblin, 1958, 1973) and work by Belnap, Åqvist, Keenan and Hull, Hintikka, Lewis, and others. But his work became the foundation for most work on questions that followed, with interesting long-running debates on such issues as whether one can quantify into matrix questions, and about the relation between "long answers" and "short answers" (also to matrix questions), and more. And the important step he made of strictly separating the notion of the interrogative clause from the speech act of questioning paved the way to the later important work of Groenendijk and Stokhof on "the semantics of questions and the pragmatics of answers" (Groenendijk and Stokhof, 1984).

1.6 Closing Notes on Karttunen's Influence on Students, Colleagues, and the Field

Of course Lauri Karttunen's influence on the development of formal semantics and pragmatics extends well beyond what I have discussed in the first five sections of this paper, which are mainly devoted to issues in the interpretations of indefinite and other NPs, identity of NPs, and anaphora. I haven't said anything about his important work connected to presuppositions and implicatures and his pioneering classification of the different sorts of embedding verbs they interact with. That work is reflected in many of his papers from the 1970s, including the 1979 joint paper with Stanley Peters (Karttunen and Peters, 1979) arguing that many so-called presuppositions should really be analyzed as conventional implicatures. As Karttunen says, "I still think we were kind of right, but we were not successful. The only person who really picked it up, that way of doing things, was Chris Potts, and his dissertation is sort of in that spirit, trying to do sort of simultaneous parallel computation of truth-conditional meaning and implicatures."[10] Potts's published revision of that 2003 dissertation (Potts, 2005) gives credit to that work of Karttunen and Peters at many points, starting in the introduction. "That paper, called simply 'Conventional implicature', contains formal breakthroughs without which the present book would not exist." (Potts 2005, p. 2).

Karttunen did his Ph.D. work at the University of Indiana, with his 1969 dissertation directed by Fred Householder (with 'benign neglect', allowing Lauri the freedom to change his topic from syntax to semantics while working on the dissertation), and with Robert Wall as his most important mentor. The autobiographical essays (Karttunen, 2006, 2012) tell the story of how he got there as a Finnish instructor incidentally enrolled in the Linguistics Ph.D. program and was rescued by Bob Wall after two years from a sort of indentured servitude in Uralic and Altaic Studies teaching Finnish nine hours a week. Wall, who had taught him in a computational linguistics course, took him on as an assistant in the Research Computing Center and taught him his first programming languages and some formal language theory. Wall also helped him get a scholarship position at the RAND Corporation in Santa Monica in 1967, during his dissertation-writing time, and may have been instrumental in getting him a post-doctoral position at the University of Texas in 1968 (before the dissertation was actually completed), where Wall had moved and joined Emmon Bach and Stanley Peters.[11] Karttunen completed the dissertation in 1969 and was then

[10]Interview by the author with Lauri Karttunen, January 13, 2011.

[11]Karttunen reports in (Karttunen, 2006) that "I found the two [Bach and Peters] very intimidating in their suits and crew cuts. They looked like Haldeman and Ehrlichman, a pair of Nixon's aides." But he was happy to have a chance to talk with them at a San Diego conference about Bach-Peters sentences and to find out that they didn't have a solution to them; he proposed one in his dissertation. And

hired as an Assistant Professor at Texas.

When Karttunen joined the faculty at the University of Texas, David Dowty was nearing completion of his generative semantics dissertation on tense and aspect (Dowty, 1972), with Robert Wall as chairman and Emmon Bach as co-chairman of his dissertation committee. That was clearly a transition point — within a few years, Dowty, Bach, and Wall had all converted to Montague grammar, Bach had moved to the University of Massachusetts, and a new generation of graduate students had come to Texas, including three who found there — and contributed greatly to — an exciting atmosphere of discovery with the new approach to semantics that was being explored and developed at Texas.

Before I talk about the exciting atmosphere that Karttunen helped to create at Texas, let me mention the year he spent at MIT, 1972-73, as a visiting replacement for David Perlmutter for a year. Karttunen recounts "It was really because of Syntactic Structures that I ever came to linguistics, and so, like six years later, I was finally at MIT. But, somehow, the lure of syntax had faded."[12] Karttunen taught a math for linguists course in the fall, starting with Wall's textbook (Wall, 1972) and continuing with readings in Montague grammar, which he was just learning himself.[13] In the spring he taught "a seminar on my own topics: discourse referents, implicative verbs, and presuppositions. I had one star student in the seminar by the name of Mark Liberman, who wrote a Master's Thesis poking holes in my emerging ideas about presuppositions."[14] [15]

Mark Liberman recalls of that year,

> I took a couple of courses from Lauri, and the experience had a big influence on me.
>
> One was a course on the structure of Finnish, and another was a course on formal semantics/pragmatics, focusing especially on presupposition, implicature and so on.
>
> I enjoyed the content very much, but Lauri's lack of sectarian rancor was especially refreshing. I had been away from academia for several years, and found the atmosphere in Building 20 in 1972-73 very trou-

---

he was glad to have them as colleagues at Texas.

[12] Interview by the author with Lauri Karttunen, January 13, 2011.

[13] (Karttunen, 2006).

[14] (Karttunen, 2006).

[15] It was unusual to do an M.A. en route to the Ph.D. at MIT. Lauri explained to me why Mark did: "Well, he never had an undergraduate degree, he was booted out from Harvard for having carried the Dean out. And then immediately after that incident, he was drafted, and went to Vietnam. So Morris Halle kind of rescued him, got him to the MIT linguistics department. But then because he didn't have an undergraduate degree, somehow it was convenient for him to get an M.A." (Interview January 13, 2011)

bling. The general feeling was similar to the mood in C.J. Sansom's Matthew Shardlake series of historical novels about a lawyer in Tudor England. While there was no actual torture and burning of heretics in 1970s MIT linguistics, the atmosphere in other respects was reminiscent of the religious wars of the 16th century, and especially of the doctrinal maneuvering at the court of Henry VIII. So it was refreshing to see an example of someone pursuing interesting ideas in a rigorous way without ideological baggage."[16]

Karttunen was back at the University of Texas in the Fall of 1973, just in time for the arrival of the first of three graduate students who formed the core of the new generation of semantics students. [17]

Per-Kristian Halvorsen came to the University of Texas in Fall 1973, having learned from a professor in Oslo who had spent a year at UT that that was a great place for semantics because of the presence of Karttunen and Peters (and until 1972 Bach), and having been invited by a UT professor who was a Scandinavianist and who needed someone to teach Norwegian. Initially he was just to be a visitor for a year, but then he got a University Fellowship and stayed for his Ph.D. He was interested in semantics from the start.

Jim McCloskey arrived a semester later, in January 1974. His background was in Celtic studies and linguistics, "basically phonology, medieval literature, middle Irish, old Irish, that sort of thing. And I thought I was coming to Austin to do a PhD in historical phonology, and my BA thesis was a historical phonology of Old Irish". He was supported on a grant that historical linguist Winfred Lehmann had at the time, and initially saw that as his clear path to the PhD.

William Ladusaw came to Texas in Fall 1974 after getting a B.A. in Linguistics from the University of Kentucky, the second graduate in their new Linguistics major. He had had a lot of phonology, a fair amount of programming and some computational linguistics, a little logic and philosophy of language, and knew he wanted to take courses with Bob Wall.

The three had quite different backgrounds but report similar experiences after they got there. Halvorsen reports that the environment was very supportive for theoretical linguistics, and extremely lively. Even several not doing semantics themselves, like Carlota Smith at that time, and Bob King, who was Dean, were very supportive of it. And all three commented on the exciting stream of visitors who came

[16]Email to the author, December 31, 2015.

[17]What comes next is based on interviews by the author with Per-Kristian Halvorsen (January 14, 2011), James McCloskey (January 11, 2011), and William Ladusaw (January 11, 2011).

through, thanks in part to a series of grants, including David Lewis, Max Cresswell, Bas van Fraassen, Rich Thomason, and on a fairly regular basis Hans Kamp. Ladusaw recalled that in 1974-75 Bob Wall taught them modal logic using (Hughes and Cresswell, 1968) and Montague Grammar using (Thomason, 1974). Halvorsen observed that much of the teaching about Montague's work and its formal foundations was by Stanley Peters, while Karttunen was more of a practicing semanticist, slightly less formal and concerned with semantics and pragmatics. And Robin Cooper joined the department for a year, 1975-76, as a visiting replacement for Bob Wall. McCloskey noted that the NSF grants that Karttunen and Peters seemed to get fairly regularly were also an important source of support for the graduate students.

McCloskey, who arrived just a semester after Halvorsen and a semester before Ladusaw, and who felt very acutely his lack of preparation in mathematics, nevertheless reports that in his second semester, "I began to sense this stuff happening in the background, because there was Stanley Peters there at the time, and Karttunen, and then, because they had various kinds of NSF funding around their project on conventional implicatures, there was a series of guests coming through — Hans Kamp was there regularly, there were David Lewis, and Max Cresswell coming through. And at the same time, you know, Bill [Ladusaw] arrived, and I think he knew what he wanted to do before he arrived. And Per Kristian Halvorsen — Kris Halvorsen — was there. And it just seemed like the most exciting thing imaginable, you know?"[18]

Although he found it difficult, he was motivated to work to try to understand what truth-conditional compositional semantics was all about.

"I remember one turning point for me, around the time when Lauri was working on "even", and on similar particles with Fran[ces Karttunen] in Finnish, discourse particles I suppose we would call them now, I suppose. And I read their paper on "even", and ... here suddenly for the first time, you could do a kind of semantics that wasn't just writing things in small caps, you know, it was doing actual detailed nitty-gritty analysis, and making predictions and understanding really subtle facts suddenly for the first time, as far as I could tell ... That was exciting. That was tremendously exciting."[19]

McCloskey adds, "And Robin [Cooper]'s presence ... in Austin for my final year was also really important. Because he was working on the revision of his thesis, and these different ways of viewing quantification, he was developing Cooper storage and all of that. And it involved

[18] Interview by the author with James McCloskey, January 11, 2011.
[19] Interview by the author with James McCloskey, January 11, 2011.

many meetings among me and Bill and Robin and Stanley and Lauri, talking about quantification and Cooper storage, and how you might understand islands in those terms, and that was very exciting too."

Ladusaw and Halvorsen recall the collaborative atmosphere in which they developed the set of notes that turned into their valuable joint published exegesis (Halvorsen and Ladusaw, 1979) of Montague's "Universal grammar" (Montague, 1970c). By the time Robin Cooper was there in 1975-76, Montague's collected works (Montague, 1974) had become available, and Cooper taught "English as a formal language" (Montague, 1970b) in his seminar, and then a reading group formed with Ladusaw and Halvorsen as its core with the aim of working through "Universal grammar". Halvorsen notes, "That [paper] presented a challenge of understanding, and ... I think the atmosphere there was really nice and collaborative. It's not that often that you see graduate students working on a paper together, [but] Bill and I started to go through it, kind of line-by-line, trying to figure it out, and asking for help from Stanley and Lauri when we needed to, and other people."[20] Ladusaw adds, "Kris and I, we talked to Robin, ... we devoted a lot of work, and it was kind of fun, just trying to understand not just what he [Montague] was saying, but 'why on earth would you say this?' 'Why would you want this contrasting set of definitions?' I mean, just because you can define it, who cares? So we did a lot of work, and we felt like we understood the paper, and [*Linguistics and Philosophy*] was just starting up, and Bob [Wall] was the editor, and Kris and I wrote this up mostly for other graduate students, you know, having done all this work we just wrote it up... And it was never meant to be a journal article particularly, but at that point it gave us a first writing project."[21]

As Per-Kristian Halvorsen was recalling the excitement of the years when he was a graduate student there, he commented, "Yes, and what puzzles me now is — were there really just Lauri and Stanley pushing it [semantics] as faculty members? If so, they generated an enormous amount of activity. ... And I never reflected on how much activity they generated. It was truly stunning."

Stanley Peters reports that it was Karttunen who showed him how rich a field semantics could be. After listing the many papers on semantics that Karttunen had written by the time he came to Texas, Peters goes on, "So he came into ... my field of view already quite interested in meaning. And I was just a complete ignoramus, you know. I thought meaning was something so fuzzy and squishy!"[22] Peters had been learn-

[20]Interview by the author with Per-Kristian Halvorsen, January 14, 2011.
[21]Interview by the author with Bill Ladusaw, January 11, 2011.
[22]Interview by the author with Stanley Peters, January 12, 2011.

ing something about logic and was looking for problems to apply it to. He recalls that they began collaborating in the spring of 1973, between his two stints at the Center for Advanced Study at Princeton (Fall 1972, and from Fall 1973 through Spring 1975), when Karttunen was working on presuppositions and implicatures, and Peters took an interest in alternative ways of formalizing their logic. From the Fall of 1975, with both of them back at Texas, their interaction was well established, and often included Bob Wall, Robin Cooper in 1975-76, and the graduate students, and later Carlota Smith as well.

So now we know that Karttunen got Peters excited about semantics, meaning that he gets an especially big share of the credit for the wonderful environment that fostered so much important work in the early years of formal semantics at the University of Texas, as well as for all the inspiration his research has given to semanticists ever since.

References

Annear, Sandra. 1968. Relative clauses and conjunctions. In *Working Papers in Linguistics*, pages 80–109. The Ohio State University.

Bach, Emmon. 1968. Nouns and noun phrases. In E. Bach and R. T. Harms, eds., *Universals in Linguistic Theory*, pages 90–122. Holt, Rinehart.

Bach, Emmon. 1970. Problominalization. *Linguistic Inquiry* 1:121–122.

Bach, Emmon, Eloise Jelinek, Angelika Kratzer, and Barbara H. Partee, eds. 1995. *Quantification in Natural Languages. Volumes I and II*. Kluwer. Studies in Linguistics and Philosophy No. 54.

Bach, Emmon and Barbara H. Partee. 1980. Anaphora and semantic structure. In J. Kreiman and A. E. Ojeda, eds., *Papers from the Parasession on Pronouns and Anaphora*, pages 1–28. Chicago Linguistic Society.

Baker, Carl Leroy. 1966. Definiteness and indefiniteness in English. University of Illinois: M.A.

Barwise, Jon and Robin Cooper. 1981. Generalized quantifiers and natural language. *Linguistics and Philosophy* 4:159–219.

Chierchia, Gennaro. 2004. Scalar implicatures, polarity phenomena, and the syntax/pragmatics interface. In A. Belletti, ed., *Structures and Beyond: The Cartography of Syntactic Structures, Vol. 3*. Oxford University Press.

Chomsky, Noam. 1957. *Syntactic Structures*. Mouton.

Chomsky, Noam. 1965. *Aspects of the Theory of Syntax*. MIT Press.

de Hoop, Helen. 1995. On the characterization of the weak-strong distinction. In E. Bach, E. Jelinek, A. Kratzer, and B. H. Partee, eds., *Quantification in Natural Languages*, pages 421–450. Kluwer.

Donnellan, Keith. 1966. Reference and definite descriptions. *Philosophical Review* 75:281–304.

Dowty, David. 1972. *Studies in the Logic of Verb Aspect and Time Reference in English*. Ph.D. thesis, University of Texas at Austin.

Egli, Urs. 2000. Anaphora from Athens to Amsterdam. In K. von Heusinger and U. Egli, eds., *Reference and Anaphoric Relations*, pages 17–29. Kluwer.

Faltz, Leonard M. 1995. Towards a typology of natural logic. In E. Bach, E. Jelinek, A. Kratzer, and B. H. Partee, eds., *Quantification in Natural Languages*, pages 271–319. Kluwer.

Fillmore, C.J. 1967. On the syntax of preverbs. *Glossa* 1:91–125.

Fodor, Janet D. and Ivan A Sag. 1982. Referential and quantificational indefinites. *Linguistics and Philosophy* 5:355–398.

Geach, Peter T. 1962. *Reference and Generality*. Cornell University Press.

Groenendijk, Jeroen and Martin Stokhof. 1984. *Studies on the Semantics of Questions and the Pragmatics of Answers*. Ph.D. thesis, Department of Philosophy, University of Amsterdam.

Gross, Maurice. 1967. On grammatical reference. In *3rd International Congress for Logic, Methodology, and Philosophy of Science, Amsterdam*. Unpublished.

Halvorsen, P.-K. and W.A Ladusaw. 1979. Montague's "universal grammar". an introduction for the linguist. *Linguistics and Philosophy* 3:185–223.

Hamblin, C. L. 1958. Questions. *The Australasian Journal of Philosophy* 36:159–168.

Hamblin, C. L. 1973. Questions in Montague English. *Foundations of Language* 10:41–53.

Harris, Randy Allen. 1993. *The Linguistics Wars*. Oxford University Press.

Heim, Irene. 1982. *The Semantics of Definite and Indefinite Noun Phrases*. Ph.D. thesis, University of Massachusetts. published 1989, Garland.

Heim, Irene. 1983. File change semantics and the familiarity theory of definiteness. In *Meaning, Use and the Interpretation of Language*, pages 164–190. Walter de Gruyter. Reprinted in Portner and Partee, eds., 2002, 223–248.

Hughes, George and Max Cresswell. 1968. *An Introduction to Modal Logic*. Methuen.

Jackendoff, Ray S. 1968. An interpretive theory of pronouns and reflexives. Unpublished paper, M.I.T.

Jelinek, Eloise. 1995. Quantification in Straits Salish. In E. Bach, E. Jelinek, A. Kratzer, and B. H. Partee, eds., *Quantification in Natural Languages*, pages 487–540. Kluwer.

Kamp, Hans. 1981. A theory of truth and semantic representation. In J. Groenendijk, T. Janssen, and M. Stokhof, eds., *Formal Methods in the Study of Language: Mathematical Centre Tracts 135*, pages 277–322. Mathematical Centre.

Karttunen, Lauri. 1967. *The identity of noun phrases*. The RAND Corporation.

Karttunen, Lauri. 1968. *What do Referential Indices Refer to?*. The RAND Corporation.

Karttunen, Lauri. 1969a. Pronouns and variables. In *CLS*, vol. 5, pages 108–116. Chicago Linguistic Society, University of Chicago.

Karttunen, Lauri. 1969b. *Problems of Reference in Syntax*. Ph.D. thesis, Department of Linguistics, Indiana University, Bloomington, Indiana.

Karttunen, Lauri. 1971. Implicative verbs. *Language* 47:340–358.

Karttunen, Lauri. 1973. Presuppositions of compound sentences. *Linguistic Inquiry* 4:168–193.

Karttunen, Lauri. 1976. Discourse referents. In J. McCawley, ed., *Syntax and Semantics 7: Notes from the Linguistic Underground*, pages 363–385. Academic Press.

Karttunen, Lauri. 1977. Syntax and semantics of questions. *Linguistics and Philosophy* 1:3–44.

Karttunen, Lauri. 2006. Word play. *Computational Linguistics* 33:443–467.

Karttunen, Lauri. 2012. A prelude to Word Play. Unpublished manuscript.

Karttunen, Lauri and Stanley Peters. 1979. Conventional implicature. In C.-K. Oh and D. Dinneen, eds., *Syntax and Semantics, Vol. 11: Presupposition*, pages 1–56. Academic Press.

Katz, Jerrold J. and Paul M Postal. 1964. *An Integrated Theory of Linguistic Descriptions*. MIT Press.

Klima, Edward S. 1964. Relatedness between grammatical systems. *Language* 40:1–20.

Kratzer, Angelika. 1978. *Semantik der Rede: Kontexttheorie, Modalwörter, Konditionalsätze: Monographien Linguistik und Kommunikationswissenschaft 38*. Scriptor.

Langacker, Ronald. 1969. Pronominalization and the chain of command. In D. Reibel and S. Schane, eds., *Modern Studies in English: Readings in Transformational Grammar*, pages 160–200. Prentice Hall.

Lees, Robert B. and Edward S Klima. 1963. Rules for English pronominalization. *Language* 39:17–28.

Lewis, David. 1970. General semantics. *Synthèse* 22:18–67.

May, Robert. 1977. *The grammar of quantification*. Ph.D. thesis, MIT.

McCawley, James. 1967. How to find semantic universals in the event that there are any. Unpublished manuscript, Chicago.

McCawley, James. 1970. Where do noun phrases come from? In R. A. Jacobs and P. S. Rosenbaum, eds., *Readings in English Transformational Grammar*, pages 166–183. Ginn.

Montague, Richard. 1968. Pragmatics. In R. Klibanski, ed., *Contemporary Philosophy*, pages 102–121. La Nuova Italia Editrice.

Montague, Richard. 1970a. Pragmatics and intensional logic. *Synthèse* 22:68–94.

Montague, Richard. 1970b. English as a formal language. In B. Visentini et al., ed., *Linguaggi nella Società e nella Tecnica*, pages 189–224. Edizioni di Comunità.

Montague, Richard. 1970c. Universal grammar. *Theoria* 36:373–398.

Montague, Richard. 1973. The proper treatment of quantification in ordinary English. In K.J.J. Hintikka, J.M.E. Moravcsik, and P. Suppes, eds., *Approaches to Natural Language*, pages 221–242. Reidel.

Montague, Richard. 1974. *Formal Philosophy. Selected Papers of Richard Montague.* Yale University Press. Edited and with an introduction by Richmond H. Thomason.

Morris, Charles. 1938. Foundations of the theory of signs. In O. Neurath, R. Carnap, and C. Morris, eds., *International Encyclopedia of Unified Science*, pages 77–138. University of Chicago Press.

Parsons, Terence. 1972. An outline of a semantics of English. Unpublished manuscript, University of Massachusetts, Amherst.

Partee, Barbara H. 1970. Opacity, coreference, and pronouns. *Synthèse* 21:359–385.

Partee, Barbara H. 1986. Noun phrase interpretation and type-shifting principles. In J. Groenendijk, D. de Jongh, and M. Stokhof, eds., *Studies in Discourse Representation Theory and the Theory of Generalized Quantifiers*, pages 115–143. Foris.

Partee, Barbara H. 1989. Binding implicit variables in quantified contexts. In C. Wiltshire, B. Music, and R. Graczyk, eds., *CLS 25 Papers from the Twenty Fifth Meeting of the Chicago Linguistic Society*, pages 342–365. Chicago Linguistic Society.

Partee, Barbara H. 1996. The development of formal semantics in linguistic theory. In S. Lappin, ed., *The Handbook of Contemporary Semantic Theory*, pages 11–38. Blackwell.

Partee, Barbara H. 2004. Reflections of a formal semanticist. In *Compositionality in Formal Semantics: Selected Papers by Barbara H. Partee*, pages 1–25. Blackwell Publishing.

Partee, Barbara H. 2011. Formal semantics: Origins, issues, early impact. In B. Partee, M. Glanzberg, and J. Skilters, eds., *Formal Semantics and Pragmatics. Discourse, Context, and Models. The Baltic Yearbook of Cognition, Logic, and Communication. Vol. 6 (2010)*, pages 1–52. New Prairie Press.

Partee, Barbara H. 2013a. Montague's "linguistic" work: Motivations, trajectory, attitudes. In E. Chemla, V. Homer, and G. Winterstein, eds., *Proceedings of Sinn und Bedeutung*, vol. 17, pages 427–453. ENS.

Partee, Barbara H. 2013b. The starring role of quantifiers in the history of formal semantics. In V. Punčochář and P. Švarný, eds., *The Logica Yearbook 2012*, pages 113–136. College Publications.

Partee, Barbara H. with Herman L.W. Hendriks. 1997. Montague grammar. In J. van Benthem and A. ter Meulen, eds., *Handbook of Logic and Language*, pages 5–91. Elsevier/MIT Press.

Peters, Stanley and Dag Westerståhl. 2006. *Quantifiers in Language and Logic.* Oxford University Press.

Postal, Paul. 1966. On so-called 'pronouns' in English. In F. Dinneen, ed., *Georgetown University Monograph Series on Languages and Linguistics*, vol. 19, pages 177–206. Georgetown University Press.

Postal, Paul. 1967. Linguistic anarchy notes: Series a: Horrors of identity: No. 2, coreferentiality and physical objects. Unpublished manusscript, IBM, Yorktowne Heights.

Potts, Christopher. 2005. *The Logic of Conventional Implicatures*. Oxford University Press. Oxford Studies in Theoretical Linguistics.

Potts, Christopher. 2009. Formal pragmatics. In L. Cummings, ed., *The Routledge Encyclopedia of Pragmatics*, pages 167–170. Routledge.

Quine, W.V. 1960. *Word and Object*. MIT Press.

Reinhart, Tanya. 1976. *The Syntactic Domain of Anaphora*. Ph.D. thesis, MIT.

Reinhart, Tanya. 1983. *Anaphora and semantic interpretation*. Croom Helm.

Roberts, Craige. 1987. *Modal Subordination, Anaphora, and Distributivity*. Ph.D. thesis, University of Massachusetts at Amherst.

Roberts, Craige. 1990. *Modal Subordination, Anaphora and Distributivity*. Garland.

Ross, John Robert. 1967a. On the cyclic nature of English pronominalization. In *To Honor Roman Jakobson: Essays on the Occasion of his Seventieth Birthday, Vol. III*, pages 1669–1682. Mouton & Co.

Ross, John Robert. 1967b. A note on 'command'. Unpublished manuscript, MIT, Cambridge, MA.

Ross, John Robert. 1967c. *Constraints on Variables in Syntax*. Ph.D. thesis, MIT.

Smith, Carlota. 1964. Determiners and relative clauses. *Language* 40:37–52.

Staal, J.F. 1969. Formal logic and natural languages: a symposium. *Foundations of Language* 5:256–284.

Stalnaker, Robert. 1974. Pragmatic presuppositions. In M. Munitz and P. Unger, eds., *Semantics and Philosophy*, pages 197–213. New York University Press.

Stalnaker, Robert. 1978. Assertion. In P. Cole, ed., *Pragmatics*, pages 315–332. Academic Press.

Stockwell, Robert P., Paul Schachter, and Barbara H Partee. 1973. *The Major Syntactic Structures of English*. Holt, Rinehart and Winston.

Thomason, Richmond H. 1974. Introduction. In R.H. Thomason, ed., *Formal Philosophy. Selected Papers of Richard Montague*, pages 1–69. Yale University Press.

van der Sandt, Rob. 1989. Presupposition and discourse structure. In R. Bartsch, J. van Benthem, and P. van Emde Boas, eds., *Semantics and Contextual Expression*, pages 267–294. Foris.

Vieira, Marcia Damaso. 1995. The expression of quantificational notions in Asurini do Trocará: Evidence against the universality of determiner quantification. In E. Bach, E. Jelinek, A. Kratzer, and B. H. Partee, eds., *Quantification in Natural Languages*, pages 701–720. Kluwer.

von Stechow, Arnim. 1981. Presupposition and context. In U. Mönnich, ed., *Aspects of Philosophical Logic: Some Logical Forays into Central Notions of Linguistics and Philosophy*, pages 157–224. Reidel.

Wall, Robert E. 1972. *Introduction to Mathematical Linguistics*. Prentice-Hall.

2

From Missing Persons to Speech Act Participants

AULI HAKULINEN AND LEA LAITINEN

2.1 Introduction

In 1973, Lauri Karttunen and Auli Hakulinen discussed one kind of generic sentence in Finnish, where one of the major nominal constituents seemed to be missing and the finite verb of the sentence was in the third person singular form. In English, instead, the corresponding slot has to be filled with a non-specific pronoun such as *one*, *you*, or *anyone*. A generic sentence with an empty slot is exclusively about a human referent, as in (1a)-(1b).

(1) a. Tämän ohjeen ___ voi helposti ymmärtää
this-ACC instruction-ACC ___ can-3SG easily understand-INF
väärin.[1]
wrong
'This instruction *one* can easily misinterpret.'

b. Puheestani voi ___ kuulla, että olen
speech-ELA-1PX can-3SG ___ hear-INF that be-1SG
ulkomaalainen.
foreign
'From my speech *you* can hear that I am a foreigner.'

In addition to the subject position, the empty slot can appear in object and adverbial positions, when the sentence initial position is

[1]The first three examples are taken from the original Hakulinen & Karttunen paper, which did not use any glossing symbols.

Tokens of Meaning: Papers in Honor of Lauri Karttunen.
Cleo Condoravdi and Tracy Holloway King (eds.).

filled with an adverbial of place or (non-specific) time.

(2) a. Suomessa --- [OBJ] viedään aina saunaan.
Finland-INE --- take-PASS always sauna-ILL
'In Finland, one is always taken to sauna.'

b. Joskus --- [ADVL] tuntuu siltä että millään ei
sometimes --- feel-3SG it-ABL that anything-ADE NEG
ole väliä.
be-3SG difference-PAR
'Sometimes one feels that nothing matters.'

In the paper, the authors described the syntactic and semantic constraints for the kinds of structure where the slot can be left empty. They observed, for example, that the missing person construction is always allowed in a sentence where the finite verb is a modal auxiliary, as in (1), and equally, in an *if-then* compound sentence (3):

(3) Jos --- aikoo laihtua, --- lopettaa syömisen.
if --- intend-3SG slim-INF stop-3SG eating-ACC
*--- aikoo laihtua.
--- intend-3SG slim-INF
'If you want to lose weight, you give up eating. cf. One wants to lose weight'

In the missing person paper, the authors claimed to have 'just presented some facts'. Nevertheless, it inspired subsequent research that gradually spread into re-analyzing the pronominal system used for human and other animate referents. While they were concentrating on the literal meaning of the generic sentences, Hakulinen and Karttunen mentioned in passing that these expressions are often used to implicate sentences about specific persons. This, they thought, would fall in what they called 'the domain of a theory of conversation', and not be a matter of the semantics of Finnish 'in the narrow sense'. In the current paper, it is our aim to briefly report on the further development of linguistic thinking around the grammar of the third person more generally: how it gets a non-specific person reference (Section 2). We will also take up a pragmatic and/or conversation analytic aspect of the zero or 'missing person' phenomenon hinted at in their paper (Section 3). We will then look into the difference between two kinds of zero, generic and anaphoric. We are treating the anaphoric zero as not only a grammatical or textual device but also as an interactional resource, a means for conveying a stance towards its referent as a participant in the speech situation (Section 4). What this discussion amounts to will lie in the intersection of grammar, semantics and pragmatics.

As one kind of anaphoric pronoun, we will next take up the logophoric pronouns *hän* 's/he' and *he* 'they' as used in reported speech in the spoken vernacular (Section 5). We will show how the logophoric devices are put to affective use: to convey empathy or disapproval, depending on the context. In that section, our argument is slightly elaborated through looking at the further developments of the use of logophoricity in contemporary fiction. In the last section (Section 6), we are going to broaden the category of the personal pronouns by showing very briefly how the demonstrative *tämä* 'this' is used as a speech act pronoun, which has consequences for the system of personal pronouns.[2]

2.2 From Missing Person to Part of the Personal System

According to Hakulinen & Karttunen, sentences that are generic in their basic ('literal') meaning, are frequently used to implicate a specific person as well. In 1975, Hakulinen looked at the zero construction in spoken language from a pragmatic point of view. Her examples included sentences with an empty slot and a particle *sitä*.[3] When the speaker is reporting his/her own experience, with a sentence that has the zero subject, it is typically interpreted as specific; it is the particle that licenses zero constructions which would otherwise be considered as ungrammatical (3′).

(3′) Nyt *sitä* ___ aikoo laihtua.
Now PRT ___ intend-3SG lose.weight
'Now (one) intends to lose weight.'

Hakulinen suggested that the employment of the particle *sitä* has two functions. First, it permits the sentence to be grammatical even though it does not fulfill the conditions set for a generic sentence with the missing subject. Secondly, in a sentence which would be grammatical even without the particle, *sitä* conveys a subjective attitude or stance of the speaker to a situation or an event (4).

(4) Oma-ssa naveta-ssa sitä ___ sai lanto-o luu-a.
own-INE cowshed-INE PRT ___ get-SG3-PST dung-PAR shovel-INF
'In one's own cowshed one got to shovel cow dung'

In (5), the speaker is praising a method of learning; the stance could

[2]The term 'speech act pronoun' is widely used to refer to the first and second person pronouns — those of the principal speakers, i.e., 'speaker' and 'recipient' ('addressee') in a dyadic speech situation.

[3]*Sitä* is a particle that has become grammaticalized from the partitive case form of the third person pronoun *se* 'it'. As a particle, it no longer has the referring potential.

not be mediated with the zero construction without the particle.

(5) Siitä sitä ___ oppii nykysuomea!
it-ELA PRT ___ learn-SG3 current Finnish!
'From it you learn current Finnish!'

A dozen years later, Hakulinen (1987) took up again the 'missing persons', which had, in the meanwhile, been relabeled as 'zeroes' by Vilkuna (1980; also 1992). Hakulinen came up with the following suggestion for the division of labor between the uses of the two non-specific verb forms, i.e., the missing person and the so called passive form, and their relationship to the specific persons. The specific 1st-3rd person references in singular and plural are expressed either with a suffix in the finite verb, or with a pronoun and a verbal suffix agreeing with it. The two non-specific persons are expressed only with suffixes in the finite verb: either the third person or the passive.

FIGURE 1

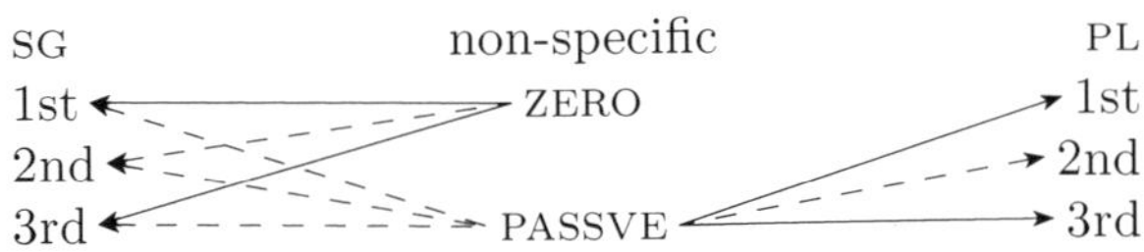

In figure 1, the dotted line signifies contextualized, implicated meaning, and the solid line is to be interpreted as the decontextualized, 'literal' meaning. Hakulinen claimed that the use of the non-specific zero constructions, which she called 'strategy of avoidance', do belong to the grammar of person, and are thereby deeply ingrained in the structure of Finnish.

The grammatical difference between the two non-pronominal choices is that the passive is plural and the third person is singular. This is reflected in the respective predicate complements.

(6) a. Sitä olla-an niin rakastu-ne-i-ta.
PRT be-PASS so lovestruck-PL-PAR.
'You (we/they) are so much in love.'

b. Sitä ___ on niin rakastu-nut.
PRT ___ be-SG3 so lovestruck-PTCP-SG-NOM
'One (me/you) is so terribly much in love!'

2.3 From Avoiding to Sharing

The term 'avoidance' in referring to the use of the zero person construction can easily be —- and it often was — misunderstood as a local strategy in any actual speech situations, reflecting the shy, withdrawn characteristic of Finns. In this section, we'll present two pieces of empirical evidence that do not support the alleged 'strategy of avoidance'. Lea Laitinen (1995, 2006) began to examine whether in actual daily conversation, the strategy of avoidance is in fact put to practice. What she found instead, was that with the zero person construction, an 'empty slot of experience' is opened up for the participants in interaction, so that an experience conveyed with the zero construction could be recognized and identified with by anyone receiving the story or telling.

Accordingly, the reference of the zero subject is multiple and distributional. Laitinen illustrated this interpretation with an extract from a piece of spontaneous conversation between three old persons, who were talking about how to pass the time (7). Otto and Kaisa are a married couple; Henry only figures as an understanding recipient of the tellings with his choice of the affiliating particle *nii* (cf. Sorjonen 2001a).

<table>
<tr><td>(7) 01 Otto:</td><td>⟶</td><td>mut että ei ___ oikeastaav voi sano-o että
but that NEG-3SG ___ in.fact can say-INF that
'But (you) can't really say that</td></tr>
<tr><td>02</td><td>⟶</td><td>täs pitkä-ks on ___ toi aika, mitenkään
here long-TRA be-3SG ___ that time in.anyway
käy-nny.
go-PTCP
it has felt (for one) particularly long in any way.'</td></tr>
<tr><td>03 Henri:</td><td></td><td>nii:i.
PRT</td></tr>
<tr><td>04 Otto:</td><td></td><td>nii.
PRT</td></tr>
<tr><td>05 Kaisa:</td><td>⟶</td><td>e:i, silloin kun ___ alkaa pitkästyttä-än
no: then when ___ begin-3SG make.tired-INF
niin ___ käy-p maate
then ___ go-3SG lying
'No, when (you) begin to get bored, then (you) go lie down,</td></tr>
<tr><td>06</td><td>⟶</td><td>[___ vetää muutama-n tunni-n une-t
___ take-3SG some-GEN hour-GEN sleep-PL
ja taas
and again
['Take a nap for a couple of hours, and again.'</td></tr>
</table>

07 Otto: ⟶ [jotain aina ___ voi-p tehäk-kin tälläse-s,
something always ___ can-3SG do-INF-CLI such-INE
[('you) can always do something
08 tälläse-s oma, näin möki-s,
such-INE own PRT cottage-INE
in this kind of cottage of your own
09 kerrostalo-i-s se on erikseen, siäl e-t voi
block-PL-INE it is different there NEG-2SG can
naputta-a
tap-INF
It's different in an apartment house, in fact,
there you can't even tap
10 ⟶ mitään oikiastaan mut täällä, tääl ___ voi-p
anything in.fact but here, here ___ can-3SG
jotain,
something
but here, here (you) can do something,
11 täs olis aina ___ vaikka kuinka piru-sti
here be-COND ___ how ever devilly
hommaa mu,
job-PAR but
there's always hell of a lot of work here (for one)
but
12 ei-hän sit nyt kerrallah mitäh tehä
NEG-CLI PRT now one.time-ALL anything do-PASS
nothing cannot be done all at once.'

In lines 1–2, Otto uses a genuinely generic construction for an experience recognizable by any elderly person. In the next turns, Kaisa is telling about her solutions to passing time ('lie down', line 5; 'taking naps', line 6) and almost simultaneously Otto brings up his possibilities for 'knocking and tapping' in a house of one's own (lines 7-11). In describing their experiences, they repeatedly use the zero constructions, each thereby explicating the claim made in lines 1-2. The last line (12) of the conversation shows that also passive can be used to construct a generic statement but one that is shared by all people collectively.[4]

As another piece of evidence for the different tasks that the passive and zero accomplish in interaction, we will present Sorjonen's (2001b) example from a doctor–patient consultation. At line 6, the doctor uses

[4]Compare this difference between the Finnish passive and zero constructions with the description of the Finnish universal quantifiers: the collective *kaikki* 'all' and the distributive *jokainen* 'every'. (Cf. VISK §740; 750; 752).

the Finnish passive, which according to Sorjonen (2001b: 92) is a doctors' means for suggesting joint activity. The passage occurs in the middle of a negotiation about coping with high blood pressure. The patient first reports on his peaceful weekend (lines 8-9) with the 1st person singular verb form. Not having received a response to this turn from the doctor, he moves on to using the zero construction (lines 11, 13). These are offered for sharing the experience or affiliating with it.

(8) (Sorjonen 2001a: 134-135)

06 D		Että mut pyri-tää ny sellasee (1.0)
		PRT but attempt-PASS now such-ILL
		mahollisimma
		most.possible-GEN
		'So but (.) (we)'ll aim at like (1.0) the best
07		parhaasee kokona[istuloksee.]
		best-ILL overall.result-ILL
		possible overall result.'
08 P:		[Kyllä nyt-ki ___ iha rauhalline
		PRT now-CLI ___ quite peaceful
		['(I) had now too quite a peaceful
09		viikonloppu ette-n tehny mitää.
		weekend that.NEG-1SG do-PTCP nothing
		weekend so that I didn't do anything.'
10		(0.5)
11 P:	⟶	Mut ei se vaikuta silti ___ .
		but NEG it have.effect still ___
		'But still it (= the medicine) doesn't have an effect (on me).'
12		(0.8)
13 P	⟶	Mut se on ainoa että ne (.)
		but it be-3SG only that those
		rahahuolet paina-vat ___ vähän
		money.worry-PL press-3PL ___ a.little
		'But the only thing is that the (.) financial worries burden (me) a little.
14		(.)
15 D		Nii::.
		PRT

Even if the patient is clearly talking about his personal experience, he can be heard to invite the doctor to 'recognize the state of affairs described, and to treat the patient's account as legitimate' (Sorjonen 2001a: 136). At line 15, after a micropause, the doctor finally responds with *nii* that carries two peaks. With this response particle, typically used for claiming affiliation[5], the doctor claims to recognize the type of experience the patient is talking about.

In sum, rather than viewing the zero person use as a strategy to avoid referring to or mentioning the co-participant, it can be seen as serving an almost opposite strategy —- that of inviting the recipient(s) to share an experience or to affiliate with it.

2.4 Anaphora — The Specific Zero

There is another third person zero used in Finnish, one with a specific interpretation, i.e., the anaphoric zero. This 'zero' is much more frequently found in languages than the generic one; it is used in English as well. The anaphoric zero is interpreted through an explicit form of reference preceding (sometimes following) it in the text or discourse. In our article (Hakulinen & Laitinen 2008), we explored the syntactic and semantic conditions of the use of anaphoric zero in written and spoken Finnish, and we found that the two zeroes are seldom confused. A good example is given below (9). As mentioned by Hakulinen & Karttunen, an *if-then* compound sentence always allows the use of an open zero construction; an example of this is (9a). In (9b), taken from a newspaper, there is a specific reference form used in the *if*-clause. However, in both cases the empty slot in the main clause is interpreted as anaphoric, i.e., co-referential with the form used in the *if*-clause.

(9) a. Jos ___ lähte-e EU-asia-n vuoksi, niin ___ saa
if ___ leave-3SG EU-thing-GEN because.of then ___ may-3SG
lähte-ä.
leave-INF.
'If (anyone) quits because of the EU, then (he) may quit.'

b. Jos Esko Aho lähte-e EU-asia-n vuoksi, niin ___
if Esko Aho leave-3SG EU-thing-GEN because.of, then ___
saa lähte-ä.
may-3SG leave-INF.
'If Esko Aho quits because of the EU, then let (him) quit.'

The use of the distinction between the two zeroes is crystallized in extract (10), taken from a conversation. The topic deals with one of the men (Topi) in a group ending up somewhere else than where he was supposed to be. Urho is telling about Topi's getting lost, referring at

[5]The term *affiliation* (also the verb *affiliate*), used by Sorjonen, is widely used in Ethnomethodological Conversation Analysis, meaning 'I feel the same way'; 'I would do a similar thing'. There is a rough correspondence to the everyday word *empathy*.

first to him with a demonstrative pronoun *tää* 'this (one)', and then, in his second clause, with an anaphoric zero: '(he) was to go'. In his turn, Topi gives an account for his misconduct by deploying the open zero construction made specific with the particle *sitä*: 'one (me) can get mixed up (when drunk)'.

(10) Urho: Ja tää ajo Ruskeasuo-lle ___
and this drive-PST-3SG NAME-ALL ___
piti Kerava-lle lähte-e.
have.to-PST-3SG NAME-ALL leave
'And this one drove to Ruskeasuo, (he) was to go to Kerava.'

Topi: Joo. (.) ei kyl sitä ___ sekko-o.
PRT NEG sure PRT ___ get.mixed.up-3SG
'Yes. (.) no, sure, (one) will get mixed up.'

In (11), a midwife (N) and a pregnant woman (M) are talking about the baby in the mother's womb. After the first mention in line 1 (*se vauva* 'the baby'), the baby is referred to by means of an anaphoric zero throughout the exchange: It can be deployed across speaker change, as the topic is salient in the situation.

(11) 1 N: No tuota mites se vauva liikkuu.
'Well uhm, how's the baby moving.'
2 M: Kyllä se liikkuu. 'It sure is moving.'
3 N: Iha hyvä. 'Right, good.'
4 M: ___ Potkii. '___ Is kicking.'
5 N: ___ Potkii vauhdilla. '___ Is kicking at full speed.'
6 M: .jooh 'Yeah'
7 Mut hirveesti niinkun ___ tunkee täältä tällee niinku –
'But terribly kind of (she is) pushing from here like this like –'

As lines 4 and 5 in example (11) illustrate, an anaphoric zero can occur in sentences beginning with or consisting only of a finite verb — in contrast to the generic zero, which requires an initial adverbial constituent or an *if-then* construction (cf. example 2 above). Answers present another case of verb initial sentences that typically involve anaphora: In Finnish, default answers to polar questions are built by repeating the finite verb of the question, as in (12) (cf. Hakulinen 2001; Hakulinen & Sorjonen 2009).

(12) Kaarina: Ol-i-ks se Joni-ki tänää tuolla vai.
be-PST-3SG-Q DEM Joni-CLI today there or
'Was Joni as well there today wasn't he.'
Reija: ___ Ol-i.
___ be-PST-3SG
'Yes.'

The majority (90%) of the examples in the database of anaphoric zeroes used in Hakulinen & Laitinen 2008 were verb initial sentences. This feature — anaphoric zero — is shared by compound sentences used in written texts and verb initial turns in spoken interaction, and it is also found in literary texts. The following batch of examples serve to illustrate the rather flexible grammatical conditions for the use of the anaphoric zero across clause boundaries: Typically, it occurs in coordinated and subordinated sentences, where the antecedent is a subject (13a) or some other initial +human NP (13b). But in addition, the anaphoric zero may take the position of an object in a passive sentence (13c). Unlike the anaphoric pronoun in Finnish, the zero 'anaphora' may also be used in subordinated clauses cataphorically, i.e., anticipating the full referential NP in the main clause (13d).

(13) a. Penttilä pit-i käsikirjoitukse-sta ja ___ halus-i
NAME like-PST-3SG manuscript-ELA and ___ want-PST-3SG
rahoitta-a se-n, mutta ___ piti si-tä liian
finance-INF it-ACC but ___ consider-PST-3SG it-PAR too
kalliina.
expensive-ESS
'Penttilä liked the manuscript and ___ wanted to finance it but ___ thought it was too expensive'

b. Ei-kä kene-stä tahansa voi tulla
NEG-CLI any.one-ELA ever can become-INF
kansainvälise-n luoka-n tähte-ä, vaikka ___
international-GEN class-GEN star-PAR even.if ___
harjoittelisi
practice-COND-3SG
'Not just anyone can become an international star even if (she'd) practice.'

c. Elli juaksi pualivälistä [kokousta] pois mut ___
NAME ran half-way [meeting] away but ___
ehdittii valita puheenjohtajaks.
have.time-PASS choose-INF chair-TRA
'Elli ran out in the middle of the meeting but they had time to elect (her) to be the chair.'

d. Kun ___ oli saanut nuoremman lapsen
when ___ be-3SG-PST young-COMP-ACC child-ACC
nukahtamaan vaunuihin, hän lähti viemään
fall.asleep-ILL pram-ILL she leave-3SG-PST take-ILL
vanhempaa puistoon.
old-COMP-PAR park-ILL
'When (she) had got the younger child to fall asleep in the pram she left to take the older one to the park.'

In the spoken vernacular, and in fiction which deploys speech and thought representation, the anaphoric zero often serves an additional task: It conveys the speaker's stance towards someone's behavior in the narrative. Example (14) is taken from a novel; the extract represents the thoughts of a young woman who is aggravated by the hypocritical behavior of her fiancé. Her stance is conveyed with the zero subject in the present tense.

(14) Olisit nyt vuokrannut peräkamarin tätä tarkoitusta varten, välähti Inkerin mielessä. ___ **Sanoo**, että minä muka olen sovinnainen ja itse ___ **istuu** äitinsä hameenhelmojen alla eikä ___ **uskalla** sormeaan liikauttaa ennen kuin äiti on mennyt ulos. Sitten kyllä ___ **ryntää** heti kimppuun.
(Marja-Liisa Vartio: *Tunteet*)
'You should have rented a back room for this purpose, thought Inkeri. **(He) says** I am supposedly conventional while*(he)* himself **sits** underneath his mum's hems and ___ **does not dare** lift a finger until mum has left. Then sure enough **(he) turns on** (me) right away.'[6]

The corresponding clauses in the English translation (14), with the explicit pronouns, are grammatically correct. However, the sentences are heard as forming a straightforward report, whereas the Finnish original with the use of the anaphoric zero all through is what conveys the understanding of the bitterness in the girl's train of thought.

In the next extract, in both languages the negative stance is at first explicitly mentioned by lexical means in the beginning of the quote (I got so mad). But the implicit means of bringing about the stance, conveyed grammatically in Finnish by the present tense and the zero anaphora, gets lost in translation.

(15) Pari päivää myöhemmin Emma kävi Koskelassa ja kertoi Hellbergin lähteneen samana iltana. Tapahtumasta hän ei ollut juuri mitään puhunut ja oli muutenkin ollut vaitelias ja synkkä. Akseli

[6]Our thanks to Kersti Juva for the English translation.

oli jonkin verran kiusaantunut ja ___pyyteli anteeksi, kun ___ oli sillä tavalla huutanut "ihmisten huoneissa", mutta ___sanoi ikään kuin selitykseksi: – Minun pisti kumminkin niin vihakseni, kun ___ rupee veteleen kaikenlaista ja ___ puhuu niin kuin hänellä olis asiassa jonkinlaiset tuomarinvaltuudet.
(Väinö Linna: *Täällä Pohjantähden alla* 1959)
A couple of days later Emma came to Koskela and said that Hellberg had left her house the same evening. She said very little about the episode and was sad and quiet as well. Akseli was somewhat troubled and asked her pardon for having shouted like that "in a decent person's house," saying by way of explanation: "I **got so mad** when**(he) started dragging** in everything and **talking** as if he had the right to judge." (Translated by Richard Impola, 2001)

The anaphoric zero can equally well express a positive stance (e.g., wonder, delight) of the narrator, as can be seen in extract (16) from a newspaper feature. Here, the reported speech is in the past perfect tense, which marks the reporting as indirect; the anaphoric zero is interpreted as referring to the speaker of the narrated speech situation.

(16) Kuitunen jutteli kisan jälkeen Pragelatoon saapuneen presidentti Tarja Halosen kanssa.
'Kuitunen talked after the competition with president T.H., who had returned to Pragelato.'
"___ Ol-i huuta-nut ääne-nsä käheä-ksi", Kuitunen
___ be-PST shout-PTCP voice-3PX hoarse-TRA NAME
kerto-i.
tell-3SG-PST
'"(She) had shouted until her voice got hoarse", told Kuitunen.'

The skiing champion (Kuitunen) told the reporter about her meeting with the President of Finland (Tarja Halonen) after the end of the competition. The president's enthusiastic words at the time of the victory are explicitly reported lexically (she had shouted till she got hoarse), whereas the enthusiasm of the narrator Kuitunen is implicitly conveyed through the anaphoric zero (___ *had shouted*).

In Section 4, we have sketched the rules of use for the anaphoric zero in ordinary prose and in everyday interaction. In addition, we have shown the ways in which it can be further exploited to convey stance in indirect discourse. Next, we will turn to another kind of anaphora, the logophoric pronouns and the logophoric use of the zero in spoken Finnish.

2.5 Logophora — The Reported Speaker's Pronoun

We are now moving on to describe the relationship of the third person pronouns to authentic speech situations with their participants. Figure 2 encompasses the vernacular system of the Finnish personal pronouns, where there is a choice between the third person pronouns *hän* and *se*, resp. *he* and *ne*. In the standard language, *hän* and *he* as personal pronouns are exclusively +human, and *se* and *ne* are demonstrative pronouns, used to refer to animals and inanimate objects. In the vernacular, however, *hän* and *he* are used as logophoric pronouns. That is, they refer in reported speech or thought to a person (human or animal) who is speaking about herself or whose behavior can be interpreted as meaningful (17). Elsewhere in a narrative, *se* and *ne* refer also to human referents.

FIGURE 2 Vernacular System for Finnish Personal Pronouns

	SG		PL
1.	minä	5.	me
2.	sinä	6.	te
3-4.	hän, se 's/he'	7.-8.	he, ne 'they'

It has been claimed that logophoricity is a unique areal characteristic of African languages, not found elsewhere (Hyman & Comrie 1981). Recently, it has been shown that third person logophoric pronouns are found, in addition, in some Northern European languages like in the Finnish vernacular and fiction, Meänkieli[7] and Saami languages (Laitinen 2005) as well as in some Latvian dialects (Nau 2006). As in African languages, even the logophoric pronouns of the Northern European languages are especially used in indirect speech. The first Finnish linguist to notice and to describe the logophoric pronouns *hän* 's/he' pl. *he* 'they' in dialects was E. N. Setälä (1883, 85). This happened almost a hundred years before Hagège (1974) coined the term 'logophoric':

(17) Se$_i$ sano että kyllä hän$_i$ tiätä-ä mitä se$_k$ tekee
s/he say-3SG.PST that PRT LOG know-3SG what s/he do-3SG
'Se$_i$ said that hän$_i$ surely knows what se$_k$ is doing.'

Setälä's example shows that *hän* is used in reported speech, as co-referential with the subject (*se*) of the reporting clause.[8] In the ensuing decades, the syntactic studies of other Finnish dialects confirmed

[7] Tornedal Finnish spoken in Northern Sweden.

[8] Under the dominance of 'verba sentiendi et dicendi', according to Setälä (1883), the word *hän* is used in the same way as Latin *sui sibi, se*.

Setälä's description. Example (18) from an old Finnish dialect shows that the logophoric pronouns can also be used in thought representation. In addition, the reporting clause can have a verb of perception, as in (19) from a Karelian dialect. In the vernacular, the logophoric pronouns can refer to animals as well as to humans (20).

(18) Se$_i$ aattel': Nyt hän$_i$ ottaa kalan.
'Se thought: Now hän takes the fish.'

(19) Velj$_i$ kun kuulj, että se tie-s hänen$_i$
brother when hear-PST-3SG that she know-PST-3SG LOG-GEN
ajatuksesa, pyörty.
thought-3PX faint-3SG-PST
'When the brother heard that she knew his thoughts, (he) fainted.'

(20) Kyl lehmä$_i$ tietä-ä mis se o hän$_i$-e
PRT cow know-3SG where it be-SG3 LOG-GEN
tillaa-se naveta-s.
space-PX3 cowshed-INE
'The cow sure knows where her place is in the cowshed.'

The logophoric use is also alive in the practice of thought representation in contemporary literature, which deviates from the pronominal use of standard Finnish. In extract (21), taken from a poem, an old woman speaker reminisces about her dog. When interpreting the motives of the animal, she uses the logophoric pronoun *hän*.[9]

(21) kyllähän minä anteeks annoin, koiralle,
eihän hän voinut tietää,
___ oli opetettu varkaita ajamaan ja käymään kiinni.
'I definitely forgave the dog
he could not know,
(he) had been taught to chase thieves and attack (them).'
(Maila Pylkkönen: Monologit)

Another fact to be noted in this example is that also the anaphoric zero can be used logophorically to convey the inner thoughts of a sentient being.

Similarly, in a speech situation, conversationalists may interpret the intentions of a non-speaking participant, for example a child, by using the logophoric *hän* (Seppänen 1998: 202-203). Extracts (22-23) are from a Christmas time family gathering. In reporting about their grandchild

[9]Peltola (in prep.) analyses the use of modal, zero and passive constructions in talking about animal referents Finnish in a different genre, i.e., contemporary radio programs dealing with nature.

baking, Maija refers to her with the pronoun *se* (22), describing the behavior of the child, whereas Matti, in his turn, first uses the logophoric zero, and then the logophoric pronoun *hän*, aligning with the child's point of view. When uttering the pronoun *hän*, Matti turns his gaze to the child.

(22) Maija: Jari-lle tuli pelkk-i-ä viiru-j-a vaan
Jari-ALL come-PST mere-PL-PAR streak-PL-PAR only
'Jari got only streaks
[kun se_i leipo Jari-lle niin
when she bake.PST Jari-ALL so
when she was baking for Jari'

Matti: [$---_i$ meinas sivut unohtu-u kun $hän_i$
--- be.about-PST-3SG edge-PL forget-INF when LOG
teki kuvio-i-ta vaan
make-3SG-PST pattern-PL-PAR only
'(she) almost forgot the edges when she kept producing patterns'

According to Seppänen (1998; 2005), gaze is used in connection with third person pronouns to regulate interaction and modify the participation framework. On the basis of her findings, it has become obvious that, in spoken interaction, there is no sharp line between certain 3rd person pronouns and the 1st and 2nd person, i.e., speech act pronouns.[10]

In another episode (23), Maija interprets the child's behavior: With only a main clause, she communicates the child's wishes to the other adults.

(23) Maija: hän halua-a tä-tä (.) mi-tä Jari-lla-kin
LOG want-3SG this-PAR hat-PAR Jari-ALL-CLI
on
be-3SG
'She wants to have what Jari is having.'

In the old tradition of vernacular storytelling, *hän* was typically used for referring to the main character even when there was no reporting clause, both in speech and thought representation. In literary fiction, the distinction between the logophoric *hän* and 'anti-logophoric' *se* is put to different kinds of use. Saukkonen (1967) discussed the phenomenon in free indirect speech representation in Veijo Meri's fiction.

[10]What Seppänen found was that e.g., *tämä* 'this', even if traditionally categorized as a demonstrative, is in fact used as a speech act pronoun. This was in fact the case in example (10) above. The sentence that includes *tä(m)ä*, when combined with a gaze, is addressed to the referent who is chosen as the next speaker.

According to him, the protagonist uses the pronoun *se* about the person he is thinking about or looking at, and the pronoun *hän* of the protagonist himself. Taking up from there, Hakulinen (1988) analyzed the ways of referring to female minor characters in the first person narrator in Meri's novels and short stories. Throughout, the narrator is a man. A prototypical logophoric *hän*, used in reported clauses, only occurs in sentence 6, whereas all the other instances of *hän* are conveying stance.

(24) 1. Ajattelin, että minun täytyi välttämättä mennä **tytön** luokse ja pyytää **siltä** anteeksi törttömäistä käytöstäni ja kertoa, mitä kauniita ajatuksia minussa oli viimeksi herännyt. [...] 2. **Tyttö** makasi sängyssä vatsallaan ja nytkähteli. 3. **Hän** itki äänettömästi. 4. Sehän riipaisi ___. 5. Istuin sängyn laidalle ja kerroin mistä olin äidin kanssa puhunut. 6. **Tyttö** sanoi, että **hän** oli kuullut. 7. Ikkunat olivat auki ja **hänen** ikkunansa ja olohuoneen ikkuna olivat kohdakkain. 8. Kerroin kaiken. 9. **Hän** pani kädet kaulaani ja suutelimme. (Veijo Meri, Yhden yön tarinat)

1. I thought that I needed to go to **the girl** and ask for **her** forgiveness of my blundering behavior and tell (her) what beautiful thoughts had recently woken up within me. [...] 2. **The girl** was lying in bed on her belly and shaking. 3. **She** cried noiselessly. 4. That was harrowing. 5. I sat down on the bed and told (**her**) what I had been talking about with mother. 6. **The girl** said **she** had heard. 7. The windows were open and **her** window and the living room window were opposite each other. 8. I told (**her**) everything. 9. **She** put (**her**) hands around my neck and we kissed. (Veijo Meri, The stories of one night)

The main purpose of example (24) is to show how the narrator uses the logophoric pronoun in main clauses throughout, conveying his stance towards the girl. Here, the choice between *se* and *tyttö* (cf. *siltä* in sentence 1; *tyttö* in sentences 1, 2, 6) respectively *hän* (sentences 3, 7 and 9) depends on the changeable stance of the male protagonist towards the girl he is observing. The pronoun *hän* is used when she has become attractive to him, that is, a potential participant in a future interaction.

In Section 5, we have surveyed some recent results on a typologically rare but in the Finnish vernacular persistent phenomenon, the logophoric status of the third person pronoun *hän* (pl. *he*) and the logophoric use of the anaphoric zero. Although logophoricity was never acknowledged as belonging to the system of third person pronouns in standard Finnish, it has been kept alive both in everyday speech and in fiction.[11]

2.6 Discussion

More than 40 years ago, the late Silva Kiuru, a university lecturer, bumped into Auli Hakulinen in the corridor of the department of Finnish, University of Helsinki. She presented Auli with the following minimal pair, and wanted to know what the following distinction would amount to:[12]

(25) a. Mikko sanoi, ettei ___ pääse ovesta.
NAME say-PST-3SG that.NEG ___ get-3SG door-ELA
'Mikko said that (he) can't get through the door.'

b. Mikko sanoi, ettei ___ ovesta pääse.
NAME say-PST-3SG that.NEG ___ door-ELA get-3SG
'Mikko said that one can't get through the door.'

Later, this was the minimal pair that Auli told Lauri in the corridor of the department of linguistics at MIT in January 1973. In some weeks' time, this encounter resulted in the paper 'Missing persons', presented in that year's regional meeting of the CLS. The paper charted the main syntactic and semantic conditions for the open zero constructions that were already partly evident in Silva's original examples.

As we have seen, the paper by Hakulinen & Karttunen inspired a range of later studies in Finland. One of the aims of the present paper was to survey the recent history: We have followed the subsequent line of thinking about the phenomenon, resulting in placing the open zero construction within the overall system of the personal forms.

With respect to the anaphoric zero in (25a), which Hakulinen and Karttunen left untouched, the subsequent research took up, besides the grammatical and semantic features, also a non-referential aspect of its use in a speech situation, i.e., the stance of the speaker to persons that are being talked about. The analysis of logophoricity, i.e., the use of the pronoun *hän*, and the logophoric use of the anaphoric zero, showed how the vernacular, and the fiction that is based on it, form a richer system than what is available in the written standard.

In discussing the grammar and semantics of the third person in Finnish, we touched on the typological characteristics of Finnish. As our discussion has hopefully shown, there was a path from each of the

[11] Today, young speakers use both the anaphoric zero and logophoric pronouns to express their ironical stance towards a person whose words they are quoting (cf. Hakulinen & Laitinen 2008, 175, example 25).

[12] See also Kiuru 1977:73.

cases discussed to the primordial use of language, i.e., interaction. This happened without the physical presence of Lauri in Finland. But the research was inspired by the Missing Persons paper, so thank you Lauri for the forty years' journey!

Glossing and Transcription Symbols

ADVL	Adverbial
ALL	Allative
CLI	Clitic
COMP	Comparative
COND	Conditional
DEM	Demonstrative
ELA	Elative
ESS	Essive
GEN	Genitive
ILL	Illative
INE	Inessive
INF	Infinitive
LOG	Logophoric pronoun
NEG	Negative
NOM	Nominative
OBJ	Object
PAR	Partitive
PASS	Passive
PL	Plural
PRT	Particle
PST	Past tense
PTCP	Participle
PX	Possessive suffix
Q	Question clitic
SG	Singular
TRA	Translative
.joo	Ingressive speech
nii:i	Extra lengthening of a vowel
(.)	Micro pause
(0.5)	Length of pause in tenths of seconds
[xxx [yyy	Starting point of overlapping speech

References

Hagège, C. 1974. Les pronoms logophoriques. *Bulletin de la Société de Linguistique de Paris* 69:287–310.

Hakulinen, Auli. 1975. Finnish 'sitä' — an instance of the interplay between syntax and pragmatics. In E. Hovdhaugen, ed., *Papers from the Second Scandinavian Conference of Linguistics*, pages 147–163. Department of Linguistics, University of Oslo.

Hakulinen, Auli. 1987. Avoiding personal reference in Finnish. In J. Verschueren and M. Pertucelli-Papi, eds., *The Pragmatic perspective. Selected Papers from the 1985 International Pragmatics Conference*, pages 141–153. Pragmatics and Beyond, Companion Series 5.

Hakulinen, Auli. 1988. Miten nainen liikkuu Veijo Meren romaaneissa. [How the woman moves in Veijo Meri's novels]. In L. Laitinen, ed., *Isosuinen nainen. Tutkielma naisesta ja kielestä*, pages 56–70. Yliopistopaino.

Hakulinen, Auli. 2001. Minimal and non-minimal answers to yes-no questions. *Pragmatics* 11(1):1—15.

Hakulinen, Auli and Lauri Karttunen. 1973. Missing persons: on generic sentences in Finnish. In C. W. Corum, T. S. Start, and A. Weiser, eds., *Papers from the ninth regional meeting of the Chicago Linguistic Society*, pages 157–171. Chicago Linguistic Society.

Hakulinen, Auli and Lea Laitinen. 2008. Anaforinen nolla: kielioppia ja affekteja. [Anaphoric zero: grammar and affect]. *Virittäjä* 112:162–185.

Hakulinen, Auli and Marja-Leena Sorjonen. 2009. Designing utterances for action: Ways of repeating the verb as a response to an assessment. In M. Haakana, M. Laakso, and J. Lindström, eds., *Comparative Conversation Analysis*, pages 124–151. Finnish Literature Society.

Hakulinen, A., M. Vilkuna, V. Koivisto, T. Heinonen, and I. Alho. 2008. Iso suomen kielioppi. [A comprehensive grammar of Finnish]. http://scripta.kotus.fi/visk/etusivu.php VISK.

Hyman, Larry and Bernard Comrie. 1981. Logophoric reference in Gocana. *Journal of African Languages and Linguistics* 3:19–37.

Kiuru, Silva. 1977. *Suomen kielen kieltohakuiset verbit.* Finnish Literature Society.

Laitinen, Lea. 1995. Nollapersoona [Zero person]. *Virittäjä* pages 337–358.

Laitinen, Lea. 2002. From logophoric pronoun to discourse particle: A case study of Finnish and Saami. In I. Wischer and G. Diewald, eds., *New Reflections on Grammaticalization*, pages 327–344. John Benjamins.

Laitinen, Lea. 2005. Hän, the third speech act pronoun in Finnish. In R. Laury, ed., *Minimal reference. The use of pronouns in Finnish and Estonian discourse*, pages 75—-106. Finnish Literature Society. Studia Fennica Linguistica.

Laitinen, Lea. 2006. Zero person in Finnish: A grammatical resource for construing human reference. In L. Campbell and M.-L. Helasvuo, eds., *Grammar from the Human Perspective*, pages 209—231. John Benjamins.

Nau, Nicole. 2006. Out of Africa: Logophoric pronouns and reported discourse in Finnish and High Latvian dialects. *Acta Linguistica Lithuanica LV* pages 55—87.

Peltola, Rea. 2016. Identifying with the non-human: Modal, zero and passive constructions with animal reference in Finnish. Unpublished manuscript, under review.

Saukkonen, Pauli. 1967. Persoonapronominien hän : se, he : ne distinktiivi oppositio. [The distinctive opposition of the personal pronouns hän : se, he : ne]. *Virittäjä* 71:286–892.

Seppänen, Eeva-Leena. 2005. Pronouns, gaze and reference. In R. Laury, ed., *Minimal reference. The use of pronouns in Finnish and Estonian discourse*, pages 75—106. Finnish Literature Society. Studia Fennica Linguistica.

Setälä, E. N. 1883. *Lauseopillinen tutkimus Koillis-Satakunnan Kansankielestä*. Finnish Literature Society. Suomi II.

Sorjonen, Marja-Leena. 2001a. *Responding in Conversation. A study of response particles in Finnish*. John Benjamins. Pragmatics and Beyond New Series 70.

Sorjonen, Marja-Leena. 2001b. Lääkärin ohjeet. [Doctor's orders]. In M.-L. Sorjonen, A. Peräkylä, and K. Eskola, eds., *Keskustelu lääkärin vastaanotolla*, pages 89–111. Vastapaino, Tampere.

Vilkuna, Maria. 1980. Referenssi ja spesies suomenkielisten tekstien tulkinnassa. Unpublished Licentiate thesis, Department of Finnish, University of Helsinki.

Vilkuna, Maria. 1992. *Referenssi ja määräisyys suomenkielisten tekstien tulkinnassa*. Finnish Literature Society. Suomi 163.

3

Accept New Substitutes: An Analysis of Reanalysis*

LAURENCE R. HORN

3.1 A Brief Trip down Memory Lane

For forty years, while seeking to plumb the depths of the intersection of pragmatics and logical semantics, I have drawn liberally on the inspiration of those who helped light the way including Paul Grice, of course, and—qua *éminence grise*—Lauri Karttunen. At a time when my fellow linguistics graduate students and I were wielding Rosenbaum's MIT dissertation as a practical guide for doing transformational grammar, we did a double-take when its title—*The grammar of English predicate complement constructions*—was slyly transformed by Lauri for his *The logic of English predicate complement constructions*, which circulated

*This work was supported in part by NSF grant BCS-1423872: The Microsyntax of Pronouns in North American English; thanks to Jim Wood and Raffaella Zanuttini, co-PIs on the grant and my two peerless collaborators on all things diversity, and to Matt Tyler, who joined Jim in carrying out Survey 7, the results of which are excerpted here. I am indebted to an anonymous reader for comments, to contributors to the American Dialect Society e-mail list for data and feedback, to Cleo Condoravdi and Tracy Holloway King for their patience, and especially to Arnold Zwicky, who inspired my study of *substitute* and offered helpful guidance along the way. Paul Kay, Michael Israel, and Scott Schwenter contributed a number of intriguing examples and valuable discussion on reverse *let alone* and *if not*. Earlier versions of this work were presented in 2015 at a meeting of the Yale Grammatical Diversity group and at the University of Geneva winter school in Macolin, Switzerland. I thank the audiences at those presentations for judgments and discussion while absolving everyone involved for any errors.

Tokens of Meaning: Papers in Honor of Lauri Karttunen.
Cleo Condoravdi and Tracy Holloway King (eds.).

(as was then almost de rigueur for influential papers in the field) as a purple mimeo samizdat.

Melding the rigorous semantics of a formal philosopher with the curiosity and *Sprachgefühl* of an empirical linguist, Lauri detailed in this study[1] the intricate web of inferences associated with factive and one- and two-way implicative predicates in the presence and absence of negation. The implicative categories, encompassing and differentiating *manage*, *fail*, and *be able*, had never been noticed before much less systematically distinguished from each other and from factives. This work, like Lauri's early treatments of discourse referents, epistemic modality, subjunctive conditionals, semi-factives, presupposition projection—and of course his seminal papers on questions and (with the collaboration of Stanley Peters) on conventional implicature in the later 1970s—served as prolegomena for fruitful work over the subsequent decades by scholars investigating compositional and lexical semantics and their interaction with pragmatic theory.

While Lauri's focus later turned to the domain of computational semantics, crowned by his Lifetime Achievement Award from the ACL, he has returned more recently, with his Stanford colleagues, to the questions animating the 1970 paper on semantic predicate types, with a new domain of inquiry on the variant readings possible for *be lucky to* and related constructions. While the version in Karttunen 2013 utilizes data from the internet, Karttunen 2014 makes crucial use of surveys conducted on Amazon Mechanical Turk (cf. Gibson et al. 2011 for an introduction to this crowd-sourcing platform and its use in linguistic research).

As it happens, my colleagues and I on the Yale Grammatical Diversity Project (https://ygdp.yale.edu/) have been employing Mechanical Turk to investigate a range of phenomena, in particular the distribution of personal and presentative datives (Wood et al. 2015). On the present occasion, I will be reporting on a mini-study in experimental semantics, utilizing MTurk to investigate possible changes in progress affecting the use and understanding of a set of constructions in flux, beginning with a reanalysis in the argument structure of *substitute* and related predicates of exchange.

3.2 Substitutes Old and New

Toward the end of 2015, a flurry of studies were released that found the consumption of red meats and, to a higher degree, processed meats to

[1] Karttunen 1970 was later distributed by the Indiana University Linguistics Club, and a shorter version of the paper was published as Karttunen 1971.

be linked to the development of cancer. News reports on television, in magazines, and on the internet displayed the results of these studies in a variety of eye-catching charts, such as the one in Figure 1, posted by Casey Dunlop for Cancer Research UK on 26 October 2015 and appearing at the web site of that group (http://tinyurl.com/qbpyng3). Note in particular the recommendation in the middle ("SWAP IT") figure, where readers are urged to "substitute ham for chicken or tuna".

FIGURE 1

For speakers who share my reading of (1),

(1) Substitute ham for chicken or tuna.

Cancer Research UK is urging readers to push away their accustomed platter of chicken or of tuna in favor of two tasty (if carcinogenic) slices of ham. Clearly, something has gone wrong.

I shall adapt Arnold Zwicky's terminology for the three distinct constructions at issue (Zwicky 2007, 2011, 2012) in this discussion:[2]

(2) Zwicky (2012) on argument structure shifts

TRADITIONAL *substitute*:	substitute NEW for OLD
TRANSITIONAL *substitute*:	substitute OLD with/by NEW [≈ replace]
REVERSED *substitute*:	substitute OLD for NEW

For traditionalists, the substitution of X (*ham*) for Y (*chicken or tuna*) can only be understood as a replacement of chicken or tuna with ham; for Casey Dunlop and other innovative *substitut*-ers, such a substitution yields (or at least can yield) a less carcinogenic and more kosher dénouement. There are also speakers in the transitional group, who can substitute ham **with**, but not (necessarily) **for**, chicken or tuna on the plausible reading; *substitute* for such speakers is an alternant of *replace*.

In connection with some of the examples to come, it should be noted that passive and unaccusative structures allow the same innovative interpretation as (1):

(3) a. Ham was substituted by chicken in this recipe.
b. Ham substitutes for chicken in this recipe.

If dictionaries can be trusted, it is still the case that most speakers (especially in the U.S.) are in the traditionalist camp. For such speakers, displaying a catalogue of instances that must (given the context and/or assumed common ground) be read with innovative uses of *substitute* can serve as a useful introduction to the reanalyzed structures.

(4) **Reversed** and **transitional** *substitute* in the wild

a. *Veganize Your Easter Brunch Menu.* Use hearty blue corn meal (we like Bob's Red Mill) with a few standard ingredients like whole wheat pastry flour, salt, and baking powder. The butter and milk are easily substituted with vegan ingredients...
—Care2 Causes, 3.28.2013 (http://tinyurl.com/n3qrxmn)

b. Fox News reports that workers at the Ground Zero site have been getting drunk on their lunch hour, "taking lunchtime at the local pub, substituting food for shots and suds!"
—from posting by Jonathan Lighter on ADS-L, 8.14.2011

c. reference to "Walt substituting Lydia's stevia for ricin"
—Paskin (2013) on Breaking Bad finale

[2] I adapt rather than adopt Zwicky's terminology by rechristening his INNOVATIVE category as TRANSITIONAL, since both non-traditional categories are innovative.

d. We're often told to substitute saturated animal fats for healthier vegetable oils.
— Care2 Causes, 11.17.2013 (http://tinyurl.com/lkwfnps)

e. Traditional moussaka is done with eggplant. What we've done is substitute eggplant for potato.
—Iron Chef America potato recipe show, via Victor Steinbok on ADS-L 11.8.2011

Compare (4e) with the constructed example in (4′), with traditional NEW for OLD *substitute*:

(4′) Traditional latkes contain potatoes. What we've done is substitute zucchini for potato.

Both traditional and innovative *substitute* can be intended when one argument is suppressed or implicit: if I tell you I substitute butter in baking, you may not know (if you haven't had me fill out a dialect questionnaire first) whether I'm planning to use butter (rather than margarine, perhaps) or whether I'm replacing butter (with vegetable shortening). And, although some may find it hard to believe, the latter reading is compatible with a sole *for*-marked argument. In the "FRESH SALADS" section of the lunch menu of Bread and Chocolate (Hamden, CT), ladies and gentlemen who lunch can opt to "substitute for baby arugula"—paying $.75 to transmogrify something unspecified into arugula.

(5) **Add** $1.75
Grilled chicken, scoop of chicken salad
or scoop of tuna salad
Substitute for Baby Arugula or Baby Spinach $.75
(http://www.breadchocolate.net/)

Even if we don't join the prescriptivists who view reversed (if not transitional) *substitute* as a sign of the apocalypse, the obvious question is *Why?* I address this question in §3.3.

3.3 First Things First: Dueling Motivations

Ignoring for now the transitional construction with the prepositions by and with, we have two possible mappings for *substitute X for Y*, repeated here from (2):

(6) a. TRADITIONAL *substitute*: substitute NEW for OLD
b. REVERSED *substitute*: substitute OLD for NEW

As it happens, each of these mappings has a powerful pragmatic (or rhetorical) strategy underlying it:

(7) a. MORE SALIENT precedes LESS SALIENT
    b. OLD precedes NEW

The first systematic catalog of the principles determining linguistic precedence or priority is due to Aristotle (*Categories*, Chapter 12, 14a26-b23; cf. also *Metaphysics* Δ11), for whom A can be prior (πρότερον) to B in a number of ways, including the two spelled out in (7):

(8) (i) WITH RESPECT TO TEMPORAL ORDER (when A precedes or is older than B)
   (ii) WITH RESPECT TO [ASYMMETRIC] IMPLICATION OF EXISTENCE (when A is implied/presupposed by B but not vice versa, e.g. 1 is prior to 2)
   (iii) WITH RESPECT TO INHERENT ORDER IMPOSED BY A GIVEN SCIENCE (elements are prior to their representation; speech segments are prior to syllables)
   (iv) "WHAT IS BETTER AND MORE VALUED IS THOUGHT TO BE PRIOR BY NATURE"
   (v) WITH RESPECT TO CAUSATION (if A causes B, A is naturally prior to B, e.g. the existence of a person is prior to the true statement that there is a person)

As emphasized by the rhetorician Quintilian (*Institutio Oratoria* 9.4.23-27), the fourth of Aristotle's rules—illustrated by the fact that "we say *men and women, day and night, rising and setting*, but not the reverse"—is a general principle of natural order (*naturalis ordo*) but a violable one. Given a default assumption that priority goes to "what is better and more valued" in conjoined (or disjoined) nominals of the kind mentioned by Quintilian (and in rather more detail by Cooper & Ross 1975, Fenk-Oczlon 1989, and Benor & Levy 2006), the hearer will recover an implicature that the speaker takes the first element to outrank the second in positivity, importance, or salience, if indeed that implicature hasn't already been conventionalized or frozen. Classic examples include *high or low, good or bad, he or she, husband and wife, gin and tonic*, and *meat and potatoes*.[3] Note that the "more salient

[3]A full account of such cases must allow for culture-specific subregularities in terms of what counts as more valued or salient in both frozen and non-frozen constituent conjunctions. For example, while male-referring terms generally precede female-referring ones (*he or she, man and woman, Mr. and Mrs., Romeo and Juliet*), female precedes male in the context of weddings, which affect the woman's status more than the man's (*bride and groom*), in kinship terms, where the woman's role is more central (*mom and dad/pop, ma and pa*), and in politeness contexts (*ladies and gentlemen*).

precedes less salient" implicature may be intended—and recovered—in cases not involving evaluative contrasts, such as the suggestion of relative importance of the two instruments in (9):

(9) Mozart wrote sonatas for piano and violin, while Beethoven wrote sonatas for violin and piano.

We can see traditional *substitute* as in (6a) as a reflex of principle (7a) priority for the more salient object—in this case the goal or replacement item rather than the source or replaced item. But that's not the end of the story.

In our own era, more or less, Strawson (1952: 80) points to the ordinary language asymmetry of English conjunctions:

> '*p* . *q*' is logically equivalent to '*q* . *p*'; but 'They got married and had a child' or 'He set to work and found a job' are by no means logically equivalent to 'They had a child and got married' or 'He found a job and set to work.'

Comments Urmson (1959: 9) along the same lines:

> In formal logic, the connectives "and" and "or" are always given a minimum meaning. . .such that any complex formed by the use of them alone is a truth-function of its constituents. In ordinary discourse the connectives often have a richer meaning; thus 'he took off his clothes and went to bed' implies temporal succession and has a different meaning from 'he went to bed and took off his trousers.'

For Grice (1981: 186), however, any temporal or causal asymmetry associated with conjoined or juxtaposed event-reporting clauses does not result from the meaning of *and*[4] but arises pragmatically from an implicature based on the "Be orderly" submaxim of Manner, thus yielding the differential interpretation of (10a,b).

(10) a. He took his trousers off and went to bed.
b. He went to bed and took his trousers off.

(See Cohen 1971, Wilson 1975, Carston 1993, 2002, Gómez Txurruka 2003, King & Stanley 2005, and Lepore & Stone 2015 for critiques of the Gricean account and for alternative analyses of conjunctive asymmetry.)

In fact, the treatment of event-denoting clausal conjunctions as iconically linked to the temporal order of those events through general but defeasible pragmatic principles antedates Grice's Be orderly submaxim by a matter of millennia. In his treatise *On the Composition of Words*,

[4]One argument adduced for this by Grice and others is the fact that asyndetic conjunctions of events, e.g. Caesar's *Veni, vidi, vici*, exhibit the same temporal asymmetry in the absence of *and*.

Dionysius of Halicarnassus (born 60 BCE) empirically investigates the "natural" word order principle (cf. Aristotle's 8i) above), a principle stipulating that events are to be reported in the order in which they occurred: what is prior in time should also be prior in word order (Dionysius 1910: 100-103; de Jonge 2008: 299) as in "The bow groaned and the string twanged loud and the arrow leapt away" (*Iliad* 4.125). But as Dionysius observes, this can't be a valid rule of logic as it's regularly violated for rhetorical effect, even by Homer himself.

A century later, the correlation between temporal and discourse priority constitutes one of the central principles of natural order in Quintilian's *Institutio Oratoria* (IX.iv.23-27). At the same, this cannot be a matter of convention: "Another piece of gross superstition is the idea that as things come first in time, so should they come first in speech." However natural the OLD PRECEDES NEW order appears in particular cases, the satisfaction of such principles depends on the requirements of clear communication and desired communicative effects, as Dionysius and Quintilian recognize.

Moving forward a couple of millennia, a sequence of integers is usually reported from smaller to larger—one or two things to say, two or three things I know about her, five and ten cents store. So if I hear on the radio that there's a major slowdown on the Merritt between Exits 48 and 42, I can infer that the bottleneck is affecting the southbound traffic (since the exit numbers decrease in that direction), not the northbound lanes. A visual illustration of the tension between our two ordering principles, MORE SALIENT precedes LESS SALIENT and OLD precedes NEW, is provided by the history of the "big board" at New Haven's Union Station giving departure and arrival information about trains. Until late 2014, the board appeared as seen in (11a). Note in particular the two Acela Express trains coming into Union Station from opposite directions, No. 2159 scheduled to arrive from Boston at 11:18 and then depart for Washington and No. 2154 scheduled to arrive from Washington at 11:30 and then depart for Boston. Unfortunately a number of Washington-bound and Boston-bound passengers not familiar with the board and reading quickly would likely end up on the wrong platform. This was due to the misreading of the information on which the train's destination in the fourth (**"To"**) column **preceded** its source in the fifth (**"From"**) column; we tend to expect "From" to precede "To" as an instance of (7b).

(11) a. Original board columns:

Time | Number | Train | To | From | Status | Track

The current configuration of the board is shown below; it will be noticed that there are now six columns, not seven: the source information has been entirely suppressed.

(11) b. New board columns:

Time | Train | Number | To | Status | Track

While passengers may miss the clacking updates of the old mechanical board, the new electronic one makes it less likely that they will head to the wrong platform. While the ordering of the columns in (11a) was presumably prompted by the high salience of the **"To"** indicator about the goal of the trajectory rather than the **"From"** indicator about its source, this was evidently not enough to withstand the power of OLD precedes NEW.

3.4 Disambiguating One's *substitutes*—or Not

In the Union Station scenario, (7b) ultimately wins out over (7a), prompting the demise of the treacherous fifth column in the (11a) board, despite the higher salience of where your train is going vs. where it's coming from. The case of *substitute X for Y* may appear different because of the role of the preposition introducing the second internal argument. The sense of *for* involved here is 'in place of' (OED s.v. *for*, 5). But the force of this consideration should not be overestimated, as seen from the reanalysis in the sole-argument attestation in (5), where the explicit *for*-marked material is offered in place of the implicit one.

To be sure, as is often the case in which apparently pernicious ambiguities arise from meaning shifts, the context will often disambiguate, preventing communication breakdown. In the case of *substitute*, the presence of definite and/or indefinite articles will often indicate which of the items in the reported or envisaged exchange is understood to be "old" and which "new", thus (virtually) resolving the potential ambiguity. Thus, a customer asking the server (12a) will be understood as using old-fashioned substitute, i.e. NEW for OLD, with *the soup* as the menu item to be replaced. In (12b), on the other, the salad is presumably the menu item to be replaced—or substituted, utilizing reverse (OLD for NEW) or transitional (OLD with NEW) *substitute*.

(12) a. Can I substitute (a) salad for the soup?
b. Can I substitute the salad for/with soup?

Similarly, even if we don't know the contents of a traditional Reuben, we can infer from the earlier exposition in the menu entry at Lefty's, an eatery at the United terminal at Denver airport, that it is fresh turkey rather than corned beef that adventurous diners are invited to try on their (pseudo-)Reubens (datum *gratia* Joel Berson, p.c. 3.22.2015).

(13) Reuben Sandwich. Shaved corned beef, Swiss cheese, sauerkraut, 1000 Island Dressing, rye bread. Make it a turkey reuben and substitute the corned beef for fresh turkey. $10.95.

Plausibility in context can also reinforce the information structure-based inference. A particularly vivid demonstration of the role of context is provided by the pig in Dan Piraro's classic Bizarro cartoon (Oct. 27, 2005) who addresses the waiter with the remark in (14).[5]

(14) The special sounds good, but can I substitute the pork chop for a fried chunk of your left buttock?

[5]See https://www.facebook.com/Page.Vegetarian/posts/497374840340941 for the actual cartoon and http://www.cafepress.com/bizarroanimals/952050 for an assortment of T-shirt spinoffs.

On the assumption that our dapper porker is far too civilized for cannibalism, only the reversed (OLD for NEW) reading is available. But here too it's the distribution of the determiners that is really decisive. The indefinite *pork chop* counterpart in (14′) conjures up a cannibal pig and a bistro with a decidedly odd selection of specials.

(14′) #The special sounds good, but can I substitute a pork chop for your left buttock?

With proper names and mass nouns, however, there's no article to help and the potential ambiguity in *substitute*—and its family members *sub* and *exchange*—is resolvable (if at all) only by discourse context and common ground.[6] There is a plethora of such problematic cites in sportive, pharmaceutical, and culinary contexts, as in (15). (Following my usual practice, I use γ to indicate examples obtained by Googling.)

(15) The 49ers substituted Kaepernick for Smith.
γYou cannot substitute Tylenol for Aspirin.
Walt substituted stevia for ricin. (cf. (4c))
γI substituted Granny Smith for Fuji apples.

With no morphosyntactic or intonational clues, not only do we find a surfeit of examples allowing either interpretation, but a given text may necessitate the disparate readings within the same passage. Thus consider the case of food and sex, which for some readers may evoke an old joke, as reproduced inter alia by Smith (2008: 13):

(16) Q: How do you know when you're using food as a substitute for sex?
A: You can't even get into your own pants.

This version assumes the traditional reading for *substitute*, as the punch line makes clear. But the advice in (17a), dispensed by Beenthere3times on the CafeMom site to a woman "banned from sex" after experiencing contractions at 30 weeks uses the innovative transitional *substitute*.[7] And the joke from (16) itself reappears in (17b), punch line and all, with reverse *substitute*:

[6]It should be noted that intonation (in particular the association of focus with new information and the anaphoric destressing of old information) often facilitates the interpretation of substitute clauses in spoken language in the absence of determiners: substitute TYLENOL for Aspirin vs. substitute Tylenol for ASPIRIN. Since our data comes largely from written sources, I will ignore the disambiguating role of stress.

[7]Of course, in principle the substitution could proceed in the opposite direction, as when the "Sex diet" popularized by Kim Kardashian and Cameron Diaz (https://en.wikipedia.org/wiki/Sex_diet) proposes substituting sex for food. But that's not the recommendation made by Beenthere3times.

(17) a. γYou want that baby in there as long a[s] possible. Substitute sex with food. lol! and maybe cool showers. (http://tinyurl.com/prou8ng)

b. γI've substituted sex for food. Now I can't even get into my own pants. (https://tinyurl.com/yb9y5e7w)

Now consider the following posting on the Ok-Pharmacy Health Blog —"IN HEALTH WE TRUST"—posted at http://www.ok-pharmacy.com/blog/are-we-eating-our-sexual-desire/:

(18) **Are we eating our sexual desire**? (Ok-Pharmacy Health Blog, 21 Mar. 2014)

There is indisputable relation between the food we consume and our sexuality. And today millions of Americans have lost their way on sexual satisfaction in a box of chocolate. Lots of people have found food as a substitute for sex.
Eating is after all accessible and gives an immediate rush of pleasure. When eating compulsively we are put in a kind of trance and unedge our real desires. So, why do we substitute sex for food?
Sex is the essential body need. Love is the main soul need. And it is the lack of them both that people compensate with food. At some time of our life it happens that a person doesn't have any sexual desire at all. Household chores, work, lack of sleep – there is no place for sex. And we start to 'chase down' our dissatisfaction with chocolates, sweets, etc. But it doesn't really work. Maybe just for a moment. And we are running off for something else, maybe spicy and hot this time[...]

The same "compensation" is described as finding food as a substitute for sex at the end of one paragraph and substituting sex for food at the end of the following paragraph.

This apparent free variation in argument structure occurs even in contexts like that in (19), an example from Beth Levin cited in Zwicky

2012, where *for* introduces the sole internal argument, whether as replaced item or replacement. The room service menu at the DoubleTree Suites in Austin offers the options in (19a) with reversed *substitute* (and an elided goal), but the same menu goes on to employ the traditional *substitute* in (19b):

(19) a. Fettucine Chipotle 12.00
Fettucine noodles in our rich and creamy chipotle sauce with grilled chicken breast.
Substitute for Shrimp 2.00

b. Signature sandwiches & burgers
All sandwiches come with a choice of regular or sweet potato fries, chips, or fresh fruit.
Substitute soup or salad for side 2.00

In both cases, the (old) source item (grilled chicken breast in (19a); side $\in$ {fries, chips, fruit} in (19b)) has been evoked in the context, so the respective goal item (shrimp; soup/salad) can only be the (new) replacement.

Definite anaphora can serve as an even clearer disambiguator for the intended direction of substitution. Leiby's pseudo-paleovore below is desperately seeking for a replacement for orecchiete, as the definite anaphor would indicate even without the additional evidence from the context and the *swap out*:

(20) I really like the sound of the orecchiette and broccoli rabe, but I'm currently on the Paleo diet...Pretty sure early man didn't have handmade orecchiette, so I shouldn't either. **Can I substitute that for something else**? Do you have any ancient grains in the kitchen? Or perhaps you could just swap out the pasta for a pile of sticks you found in the woods? (Leiby 2016)

As seen in the paleovore's plea to *swap out* the pasta, the use of disambiguating particles—especially *in* and *out*—helps secure the intended direction of substitution. A team's coach may elect to *sub(stitute) in* or *swap in Robinson for Jones* or, equivalently, to *sub(stitute)/swap/ change out Jones for Robinson.* In either case, it's Jones who takes a seat on the bench and Robinson who enters the game. Compare:

(21) a. For a more delicately flavored soup, sub in water for the vegetable stock. http://www.popsugar.com/food/Julia-Child-Potato-Leek-Soup-Recipe-24339863

b. γWhy is Mike Huckabee here [in the Republican debate]? Sub him out for the dude sitting behind [ABC reporter] Jake Tapper.

c. γI swapped in croissants for white sandwich bread and buddy it was good.

d. I'd have to ask my father to swap out his beloved Vauxhall Chevette for my Peugeot. (Courtney Maum (2014), *I Am Having So Much Fun Here Without You*, p. 108)

3.5 The Innovative *substitutes*: Evidence across Time — and across the Pond

I follow Denison (2009) and Zwicky (2012) in reconstructing the change in argument structure of substitute as involving not a simple shift from the traditional construction (substitute NEW for OLD) to the reversed construction (substitute OLD for NEW) but instead one proceeding through the transitional way-station (substitute OLD {with/by} NEW), arising in turn through the influence of the corresponding construction in which *replace* governs the prepositions *with* and *by*. The second step is the restoration of the preposition *for*. This two-stage shift is depicted in Figure 2 (= Denison 2009, Figure 1, with color added).[8]

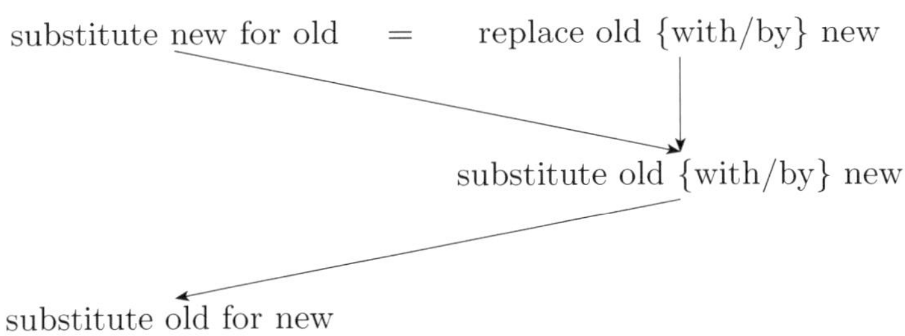

FIGURE 2

When did the reversed structure originate? Denison (2009: §3.2) takes this to be a recent development, one overlooked by lexicographers, by contrast with the transitional structure:

> The reversed pattern *V old for new* is not mentioned in the OED at all ... I take it that reversed *substitute* is a reasonably new phenomenon ... [I]t is doubtful that the reversed pattern is more than a couple of decades old at most.

Along the same lines, Denison notes the long-running prescriptive edicts against substitute OLD [with NEW], i.e. *substitute* = replace, while sub-

[8] I am grateful to Cambridge University Press for permission to reprint this figure from Denison 2009.

stitute OLD for NEW hasn't even come to the attention of usage guides in the U.K.

Whatever the merits of this observation, Denison overstates the lexicographic case somewhat. Here's the OED entry in question and a relevant cite:

(22) OED s.v. **substitute, v.**
3. b. With *with* (also *by*, later *for*). To fill the place of (a person or thing) with a replacement; = replace v. 2b.
1978 *Pop. Mech.* (*advt.*) Corvette winner may substitute automobile for $14,000 cash.

There are six cites for transitional *substitute with/by* ranging from 1839 to 2008, as against the sole (Corvette prize) cite for reversed *substitute for*, the latter taken to be a development of the former. Adds a usage note accompanying this entry: "Use in this sense has been sometimes criticized, but is now generally regarded as part of normal standard English."

A similar note adorns the better documented passive *be substituted by* (≈*be replaced by*) subentry at 3a, illustrated inter alia by the cites below:

(22′) OED s.v. **substitute, v.**
3. a. To take the place of; to become a replacement for; to supplant; = replace v. 3. **(a) In** *pass.*, **with** *by.*
1755 J. Smith *Printer's Gram.* ii. 30 Double Pica...[was] substituted by a new letter.
1863 *Life in South* II. 198 Good brandy being substituted by vile whiskey.
1900 *Arch. Surg.* 11 275 The medicine was continued a few days longer, and then substituted by the iodide of potassium.
2003 D. Brown *Da Vinci Code* (2004) lxxii. 404 In Atbash, the first letter was substituted by the last letter, the second letter by the next to last letter, and so on.

Thus, innovative substitute has a long paper trail, but chiefly in the transitional *with* or *by* form rather than as full reversed substitute OLD for NEW. But as a noun or "adjective" (i.e. modifier in a nominal compound), *substitute* appears, from the evidence in the relevant OED entries, to function only in the sense of 'replacement' or ersatz; a substitute is someone 'endowed with the authority to act on a superior's behalf' or something put forward as 'a replacement, or an alternative', never the person or thing replaced. Similarly, a substitute teacher, minister, or quarterback is always the replacement or subbed-in proxy, NEW for [implicit] OLD, not the original to be subbed out. How then did the innovative *substitute* arise, in particular in the reversed interpretation, and why has this interpretation become particularly robust in U.K. English?

Denison (2009: §3.4.2) points to the influence of football (i.e. soccer) contexts as the primary non-academic venue in which the new *substitute* is likely to occur in the U.K. Free substitution is a relatively new practice due to rule changes in British soccer, and, he notes, "The player substituted is always the **old** NP object (i.e. already on the pitch), never the **new** (on the bench)."

American sports usage is less conducive to the reanalysis of the argument structure for *substitute*, especially since this game action is typically reported in other ways. The direct object of two-place (simple transitive) *substitute* is more likely to be **new** (= "the substitute") than **old** in U.S. English. The coach typically substitutes the backup quarterback for the (injured or ineffective) starter, NEW for OLD.

If the transitional construction in which *substitute* governs *with* or *by* as its preposition rather than *for*—*substitute* OLD *with/by* NEW—is essentially an alternant of *replace*, do we ever find *replace* taking *for* rather than *with* or *by*? And if so, which interpretation does it get? While (still) rather rare, such constructions are indeed attested, and as far as I can tell are only intended and interpreted as *replace* OLD *for* NEW, exactly as with the more standard prepositions governed by *replace*:

(23) a. γIf your supporting equipment isn't allowing you to operate efficiently, it's time to **replace it for newer, more efficient, equipment**.
http://www.foodmanufacturing.com/article/2016/01/5-reasons-replace-supporting-equipment

b. γIf your toilet uses more than 1.6 gallons per flush, you can **replace it for a high-efficiency toilet** (1.28 gallons or less) and receive a $100 rebate.
http://www.recordnet.com/article/20150812/NEWS/150819892

c. He's having trouble with the whole God thing so I told him to just **replace "God" for "Jessa"** and, like, see if it helps and now I'm, like, the only thing standing between him and a crack pipe.
—Jessa on "Girls", S4E3, "Female Author" (aired January 25, 2015)

Most native English speakers rule out the possibility of *replace X for Y* entirely, including the waggish "migo" responding with tongue in cheek (and coercing a rather different sense of *for*) on a usage forum query at http://tinyurl.com/j229uwn:

(23′) *Query from shivanand:*
What's the difference between the two sentences? i.e. what is in use, an apple or an orange, in the below two sentences?
(1) Replace apple with orange.
(2) Replace apple for orange.
Response from migo:
(1) You have an apple, you take it away and put an orange in its stead.
(2) You're replacing the apple because orange wants you to.

Unlike *substitute*, where traditional NEW for OLD is under pragmatic pressure from innovative OLD for/with/by NEW, the established argument structure of *replace* already satisfies OLD precedes NEW. The object of simple transitive *replace* (*replace the teacher/minister/quarterback*) has always been unambiguously OLD, so even replacing standard *with/by* with *for* as the preposition introducing the second internal argument fails to affect the possible readings.

3.6 Other Reversals

In viewing the shift from substitute NEW for OLD to substitute OLD for NEW as an innovative reversal, and if we follow Denison, Zwicky, and implicitly the OED, viewing substitute OLD with/by NEW as a transitional stage on this path, two questions arise: Are there other constructions that have been undergone reversals? What tools can we use to systematically investigate such shifts, whether in argument structure as with *substitute* or in other constructions?

In response to the former query, consider the interpretations available for scalar correlatives like *not A let alone B, not A much less B, not A never mind B*, and *A if not B*. In canonical *let alone*, as analyzed by Fillmore, Kay & O'Connor (1988), a speaker in uttering a sentence of the form *Not X A Y let alone X B Y* presents *B* as a stronger scalar alternative to *A*. The sense is thus 'Not (even) *A*, and *a fortiori* not *B*'. The OED entry for this use of *let alone* (s.v. *let*, v.1, 18e) treats it as a specialized colloquial imperative or absolute participle, glossed as 'not to mention'. Standard examples, based on Fillmore et al. (1988), include those in (24).

(24) a. He didn't make colonel let alone general.
b. You could never get Fred to eat shrimp at McDonald's let alone squid.
c. You could never get Fred to eat shrimp, let alone Louise squid.

While (24a) is based on a lexically imposed scale—or, more accurately, rank order (see Lehrer 1974, Hirschberg 1985, and Horn 2009 on the distinction)—the construal of *let alone* in (24b,c) invokes a non-lexical but natural assumption that squid would be a more surprising or noteworthy item for Fred to eat than shrimp. (These are analogous assumptions to the ones induced by *even*; see e.g. Karttunen & Peters 1979, Kay 1990.) The attested examples in (25) further demonstrate the pragmatic nature of the relevant scales or rank orders for *let alone*, and related scalar correlatives.

(25) a. γIn all the years of their marriage, he had never *combed* Martha's hair, never mind *washed* it.

b. γYou never have any fun. When did you last get drunk, let alone laid?

c. However, there is something rather disturbing about the thought of having your pet stuck with needles, let alone seeing smoke rise from it as well.
(BNC, via Michael Israel: note the covertly negative DE licenser)

d. Before she moved to California, she had never eaten an artichoke, let alone read Neruda.
(Marly Swick (1999), *Evening News*)

The restriction described and illustrated above for the canonical construction fails to hold for many contemporary speakers, however;[9] rather than signaling 'Not (even) *A*, and *a fortiori* not *B*', the easily attested reversed let alone suggests 'Not *A*, or at least (*a debiliori?*) not *B*'. Crucially, such speakers can assign a concessive *Not A let alone B* with a concessive reading not recognized in the OED *let alone* entry.

(26) a. "These were women who were doing radio way before we had the idea let alone were born." —Interviewee on NPR describing an "all-girl radio station" in Memphis in the 1950s and 1960s. [e-mail from Paul Kay, 7/28/01]

b. "Without Clinton Portis, I don't think this team can go deep in the playoffs, let alone get in." —Sean Salisbury on ESPN, 12/15/03

[9]While a strong majority of cites for *let alone* occur in a negative context, not all speakers in present-day English restrict it to being a negative polarity item. Nor, indeed, did their predecessors. Most of the OED cites occur in the scope of NPI triggers (e.g. *It is hard to get a gardener who can prune a gooseberry-bush, let alone raise a cucumber* — 1892), but there's also this one from 1853: *It...declares that honesty, let alone that it is the right thing, is also...the wisest.* I restrict my attention in the current study to well-behaved NPI *let alone* in both traditional and reversed variants.

c. "Nobody from Victoria, let alone British Columbia, had ever made it to the NBA before." —radio interview with student-athlete from Victoria B.C. re Steve Nash, 5/19/05

d. I hope he had some idea of what use it is to know the difference between a sonorant consonant and an obstruent. But since he was commuting twice a week, just for that class, I couldn't expect him to digest let alone swallow everything. —from an e-mail message sent to Barbara Abbott, Jan. 2007

Strength correlates with unilateral entailment; in each instance of *(not) A let alone B* in (26) the *B* argument is weaker, not stronger, than the *A* argument: no team can go deep in the playoffs without getting in; if you're from Victoria you're necessarily from B.C.; to digest something requires swallowing it but not versa.

Similar reversals can be readily attested with *much less* and *never mind*, but we turn here to a related construction. The *A if not B* construction is available in two flavors (Horn 1972: §3.1.2) but in both—the concessive construction in (27a) and the suspensive construction in (27b), distinguished by prosody and NPI licensing—*B* is stronger than (unilaterally entails) *A*:

(27) a. Dolores is pretty if not exactly beautiful. [Horn 1972: (1.85b)]

b. Dolores is pretty if not downright beautiful. [Horn 1972: (1.85a)]

Similarly, it is easy to find fillers for the frame *X is one of the F-est if not the F-est [Y(s)]*, where being the F-est is a proper subcase of being one of the F-est:

(28) a. γThai paintball teams are considered to be one of the strongest, if not the strongest in Asia.

b. γQ-tips are one of the only, if not the only, major consumer products whose main purpose is precisely the one the manufacturer explicitly warns against.

c. γHe's obviously one of the best, if not the best, in the league.

But now note that the reverse order is possible (or required?) for some; reversed *if not* is paraphrasable not by 'or even' (or by 'but maybe not quite' as in (27a)-type concessives) but rather by 'or at least':

(29) a. He's the best, if not one of the best, middle linebackers in the league. —ESPN Sports radio talk show host Bob Golic on Bears' Brian Urlacher, 11/27/01

b. It's probably the best, if not one of the two or three best, offensive lines in the league. —Phil Simms, in radio interview re Kansas City Chiefs' offensive line, 11/10/02

c. Just three weeks ago we were talking about these two teams being the best in the league, if not the NFC. —Sean Salisbury on slumping Giants and Bears, ESPN SportsCenter, 11/26/06

d. This class did spark an interest in me and so I might major if not minor in linguistics. —from a student's teaching evaluation form

As with reversed *substitute* and *let alone*, one question is which speakers accept the reversed *if not*; another is which speakers prefer it. What sort of empirical study could begin to answer these questions?

3.7 Reversals and Mechanical Turk

As noted in §3.1, the Yale Grammatical Diversity Project has been conducting surveys on Amazon Mechanical Turk to help delineate the nature, amount, and type of variation exhibited by a range of grammatical constructions in U.S. English. Our methodology and experimental design is described in Wood et al. 2015. For some of the phenomena in question (see pages at https://ygdp.yale.edu/phenomena), our studies generally support standard descriptions by dialectologists as to the regional and/or ethnic variation exhibited by the distribution of such constructions as positive *anymore*, declarative negative inversion, *so don't I, needs washed*, or *I'm done my homework*. Our results have also uncovered shifts in acceptability not previously remarked on in the literature, as will be noted below. In some cases, e.g. that of "drama" or "Gen-X" *so*, variation is associated with age and possibly gender. In still other cases, such as copy-raising or verbal *rather*, we can attest individual variation that fails to correlate with any regional or social parameters.

Two particularly interesting cases are those of personal datives as in (30a) and what we call Southern dative presentatives as in (30b) (cf. Wood et al. 2015 for elaboration).

(30) a. You$_i$ need you$_i$ a new printer.

b. Here's you a new printer.

Personal datives are subject-coreferential non-argument pronouns, locally bound but non-reflexive, which contribute conventional implicatures constraining felicity without affecting truth conditions (Horn 2008, Hutchinson & Armstrong 2014). While the standard descriptions of this construction (e.g. Christian 1991, Webelhuth & Dannenberg

2006) associate personal datives with Southern and Appalachian speakers, our MTurk surveys indicate that this restriction has been weakening (Zanuttini et al. in prep). While personal datives are still more acceptable in the South among speakers older than 40, younger speakers accept them more widely across all geographical regions.[10] This generational difference can be seen even when we break respondents down into the 31–40 vs. 18–30 age groups, confirming that the construction is gradually spreading from its original geographical base.

Further, while the earlier literature stipulates that personal datives require an indefinite-marked direct object—even when the indefinite doesn't connote true partitivity (*I love me some him; He needs him some Jesus*)—this constraint is weakening among the youngest speakers in our survey (those in the 18–30 age group), many of whom accept personal datives with deictic definite objects as in (31a) and a small subset of whom even accept them with bare objects as in (31b).

(31) a. He needs him that big truck over there.
b. He wants him chocolate

The question to which we now turn is whether a similar age-based shift can be attested for the reversed interpretations of *substitute* and of the scalar correlatives discussed in §3.6. In our Survey 7, distributed and compiled by Jim Wood and Matt Tyler during the summer of 2015, we find empirical support for the spread of the reversed substitute among younger speakers, representing an apparent change in progress. The relevant pilot items on our survey are identified by survey item number along with the responses we received in Table 1.

Based on these responses, we can tentatively conclude that the reversed argument structure (substitute OLD for NEW) is most available for the speakers in the youngest group in our survey and least available for those in the oldest group, pointing to a change in progress, although additional research will be needed to confirm this.[11] None of our data

[10] In contrast to these findings on personal datives, our studies—reported in Wood et al. 2015— suggest that the distribution of the presentative dative construction illustrated in (30b) is essentially that which is standardly posited for personal datives; age appears not to be a factor in acceptability. Thus, no apparent change in progress can be detected for the presentative datives, perhaps in part because that construction lacks the social indexing that personal datives have taken on.

[11] It should be emphasized that despite the encouraging results obtained in the preliminary survey, the lack of statistical significance for most of the age-based distinctions at issue here—the one significant difference ($< .01$) being that of the oatmeal vs. pecans case—reinforces that further research, ideally utilizing a wider and more dispositive range of survey questions, will be necessary before any firm conclusions can be drawn. Thanks to an anonymous referee for stressing the need to demonstrate statistical significance and not just suggestive tendencies.

My teacher often tells John to substitute reality television for educational programming.
Q: *What does the teacher want John to watch?*

PI_1131	18-30 (%)	31-40 (%)	41-50 (%)	51+ (%)
Ed. programming	67 (54%)	42 (45%)	16 (44%)	9 (30%)
Reality TV	57 (46%)	51 (55%)	20 (56%)	21 (70%)

You can substitute pecans for oatmeal in the recipe.
Q: *Does this mean you can use oatmeal instead of pecans or pecans instead of oatmeal?*

PI_1132	18-30 (%)	31-40 (%)	41-50 (%)	51+ (%)
Oatmeal	21 (17%)	4 (4%)	2 (6%)	1 (3%)
Pecans	86 (69%)	78 (84%)	34 (94%)	28 (93%)
Either	17 (14%)	11 (12%)	0 (0%)	1 (3%)

Q: *If a menu says that* you can substitute salad for soup for $2, *which of these is true?*

PI_1133	18-30 (%)	31-40 (%)	41-50 (%)	51+ (%)
Soup costs $2 extra	39 (31%)	23 (25%)	8 (22%)	3 (10%)
Salad costs $2 extra	62 (50%)	59 (63%)	24 (67%)	20 (67%)
Unclear—either possible	23 (19%)	11 (12%)	4 (11%)	7 (23%)

TABLE 1

indicate regional or social factors other than age as relevant. It will also be seen that for many speakers, both the traditional (substitute NEW for OLD) and reversed (substitute OLD for NEW) readings are potentially available. I return below to this finding.

We also gathered data in Survey 7 on responses to scalar correlatives of the kind described in §3.6 above, presented in contexts intended to coerce reversed readings:

(32) **(not) A let alone B**:
I've never been to Paris, let alone France.
Vegetarians don't eat red meat, let alone chicken.
She's never been married, let alone had a serious boyfriend.

(33) **A if not B**:
I might major, if not minor, in chemistry.
He's the best, if not one of the best, in the whole league.

Here, our results showed no clear pattern in these cases; essentially all the respondents across age groups (and with no discernable geographic pattern) found the reversed readings available. It is not clear to us at this point whether a subtler investigation might reveal age-grading of the kind we anticipated (and found in the case of *substitute*, as Table 1 indicates) or if the shift has already progressed far enough that plausibility in context alone and not form determines the accessible readings for scalar correlatives.[12]

The difficulty of catching semantic shifts in the act is further illustrated by another construction we tested that does not involve reversed readings: the rise of metaphysical may. For many speakers of a certain age, the modality illustrated in (34) can only be epistemic.

(34) **metaphysical** *may*:
Without your help, I may not have succeeded.
If she hadn't fixed his printer, he may not have gotten the paper in on time. Fortunately, he did.
Better security may have prevented yesterday's terrorist attack.

The resultant 'for all I know' readings are anomalous in a context like those above, in which the proposition in question is known or asserted to be false.[13] For all speakers, replacing *may* with *might* or *could* renders the plausible metaphysical—and thus counterfactual—readings accessible in such contexts. As with the *let alone* and *if not* sentences, however, our respondents largely accepted all the sentences in (34).

3.8 Motivating Reversals: Some Concluding Thoughts

As we saw in (20), particles can distinguish sub/swap in NEW for OLD from sub/swap out OLD for NEW. But without disambiguating particles, *swap*, unlike *sub(stitute)*, allows only the OLD for NEW understanding. We also have trade in X for Y, where (like sub/swap out but unlike sub/swap in) the item traded is OLD (the source), not NEW (the goal), despite the preposition, as in this New York Times review by Pete Wells for Superiority Burger:

---

[12]Another confound in (33) reported by some of our colleagues is the possibility of reading these not as scalar reversals of something along the lines of *I might major—or if not, then minor—in chemistry.*

[13]cf. Karttunen 1972 for a lucid discussion of the distinction between the epistemic ('possible that') and metaphysical ('possible for') readings and the incompatibility of the former but not the latter with knowledge of falsity.

(35) [A] meatless analogue of the Philadelphia cheesesteak interests me keenly. Shaved steak had been traded in for strips of yuba, the immortal Cheez Whiz for a smooth, subtly flavorful species of cashew cheese.
http://www.nytimes.com/2015/09/02/dining/restaurant-review-superiority-burger-in-the-east-village.html

Unsurprisingly, *trade away* has the same interpretation, but more significantly so does *trade X for Y* without particles—here too only the OLD for NEW interpretation is possible.

We can illustrate this by plugging in some of the most one-sided trades in the late 20th century history of baseball, those in which a promising young player (the Mets' Nolan Ryan, the Cubs' Lou Brock) who would become a member of the Hall of Fame was obtained in exchange for an aging veteran (the Angels' Jim Fregosi, the Cardinals' Ernie Broglio) toward the end of a mediocre career. Consider these four sequences plugged into a Google search:

(36) a. "traded Jim Fregosi for Nolan Ryan"
b. "traded Nolan Ryan for Jim Fregosi"
c. "traded Ernie Broglio for Lou Brock"
d. "traded Lou Brock for Ernie Broglio"

In each of the Google hits obtained—more of them showing up for the disastrous moves (36b,d) than for the good ones (36a,c)—the missing subject refers to the team or general manager who traded **away** the direct object referent and in exchange received the *for*-object referent. Thus (36a) is invoked to laud the skill or luck of the Angels for acquiring Ryan, (36b) to bemoan the ineptitude or bad karma of the Mets in giving up on Ryan, (36c) for the good luck of the Cards, and (36d) for the typical Cub-like stupidity in giving the future superstar Brock away for a washed-up pitcher like Broglio. Sample hits are in (36'):

(36′) a. γThe Mets were also involved in what was undoubtedly the best ever trade in Angels franchise history. The Angels **traded Jim Fregosi for Nolan Ryan**. So perhaps it is a good omen that the Angels are making this trade with the Mets.

b. γThis is Bob Scheffing, the man who **traded Nolan Ryan for Jim Fregosi**. Insert colorful expletives here. [photo caption, studiousmetsimus blog site, re Mets' G.M.]

c. γHe **traded Ernie Broglio for Lou Brock**. it's the quintessential great trade... [obit for Bob Howsam, Cards G.M.]

d. γMajor League baseball: 50 years ago today, the Cubs **traded Lou Brock for Ernie Broglio**. It is considered one of the worst deals in baseball.

Note too that when these predicates of exchange appear in a simple transitive structure with the other argument unspecified, the direct object of *trade* or *swap* is always the source (OLD), not the goal (NEW). And when there **are** two arguments, definiteness doesn't matter (as it does with *substitute*): even with an indefinite definite object and a definite object of *for* only the OLD for NEW interpretation is accessible, as in this swap from the James Wesley Rawles 2009 survivalist manifesto, *Patriots: A Novel of Survival in the Coming Collapse*:

(37) In all, I swapped two hundred rounds of nine-millimeter hollow points, eleven dollars in junk silver, some hand tools, and a Fluke volt-ohm meter for the gas.
https://books.google.com/books?isbn=156975229X

We might plausibly regard the existence of these predicates of exchange with an invariant trade/swap OLD for NEW interpretation as a factor in the reanalysis of substitute NEW for OLD into substitute NEW for OLD, given that a trade or swap is a common means to effect that substitution.

We conclude with a return to the new *substitute*, buttressed by the preliminary data from our Survey 7. We not only found find empirical grounding for positing an age-based factor in the distribution of substitute OLD for NEW readings, but also a substantial group of respondents who acknowledged their acceptance of both traditional and reversed interpretations. In that light, consider the lyrics to the most celebrated musical setting our construction has enjoyed, as written by Pete Townshend and performed by The Who with Roger Daltrey on lead, released as a single in 1966 (*gratia* Matt Tyler for the reminder):

(38) **"Substitute"** (Townshend 1966)
You think we look pretty good together
You think my shoes are made of leather
But I'm a substitute for another guy
I look pretty tall but my heels are high
The simple things you see are all complicated
I look pretty young but I'm just back-dated, yeah
Substitute your lies for fact
I see right through your plastic mac
I look all white but my dad was black
My fine looking suits are really made out of sack
[...]
Substitute me for him

Substitute my coke for gin
Substitute you for my Mum
At least I'll get my washing done

While the highlighted verse may strike us as providing a significant antedate of the 1978 OED cite for substitute OLD for NEW, Denison (2009: 153) provides this footnote:

> Several colleagues have wondered whether the song 'Substitute' by The Who (released 1966) might contain some early examples of the reversal. I wrote to ask Pete Townshend, its writer, whether the line
> (i) Substitute you for my Mum
> meant 'replace you with my Mum' or 'replace my Mum with you'. The answer sent on his behalf (1 Dec. 2004) reads: 'Pete says it is the latter (viz: "YOU" are the substitute)'. In other words the song exhibits standard usage, not reversed.

But reading of the line in (i) in particular as betokening traditional substitute NEW for OLD seems quite implausible in the context. Notwithstanding the claim of Townshend's spokesperson 43 years post-recording, I side with Denison's wondering colleagues[14]: the whole point of the song is that the narrator is trying to make the best of his girlfriend's dumping him—at least he'll get his washing done, now that he's back with his mum.

Or is there another possibility? According to one analyst, the difficulty (perhaps even for the songwriter) in telling the old from the new goes deeper than it seems:

> Grammar breaks down as well. Consider the lyrics: "Substitute: me for him./ Substitute my coke for gin./(I'll) substitute you for my mum;/At least I'll get my washing done." **The consequence of incorrectly using "for" instead of "with" is to remove from the idea of substitution any contrast between authentic and ersatz. Instead, one term is as good as the other.** He (my rival) could be a substitute for me (in her affections)...or I could be her substitute for him (in our public appearances). Who knows? They are sliding signifiers. We have no idea whether the subject's taste in drinks runs to either Coca-Cola or gin, no clue as to which is the choice and which is the replacement.
> (Tyndall 2011: 33, emphasis added)

[14] And with Uberman in the interpretation if not the prescriptive attitude in a post on the sputnikmusic forum (http://www.sputnikmusic.com/forums/archive/index.php/t-338809.html) lambasting The Who for their misuse of English in the final couplet of (38): "I would assume he means his mom would do the laundry and the girl wouldn't, so shouldn't it really be: Substitute my mom for you/at least I'll get my washing done. Aside from not rhyming, of course."

We need not follow Tyndall in his prescriptive verdict on the reanalysis, much less pursue him along his every convoluted Freudian byway—

> Daltrey's unflinching rendition comports with Freud's distinction between the masochist and the self-punisher. The attitude of the masochist is truly passive, reacting to the extraneous person who has taken on the subject's role. Self-punishment represents the reflexive middle voice. Temporarily, the subject relents and resorts to such neurotic self-pity in the form of self-deprecating humor. For the moment, he returns to the maternal home with a triplet that is rounded out with comedy. Ultimately, Townshend rejects sentimentality, ending the song with a final reprise that returns to the noninfantilized real world of deceit and betrayal, sackcloth and ashes. But for that brief moment, when love is too complicated and adult life too challenging, at least my fashionable clothes will be laundered properly, as they were when I was a child. Thus the first line of that binary triplet, "substitute me for him," could as likely refer to the subject's replacement of his father in an Oedipal triangle as to any reference to the literal teenage triangle of the ostensible song. No wonder they call themselves The Who.
> (Tyndall 2011: 33)

—to appreciate his psychoanalytic riff on the inherent underspecification of *substitute X for Y* we have already witnessed. In addition to the "either" or "unclear" responses in Table 1 for those accepting both traditional and reversed readings of *substitute X for Y*, we have the evidence from the blog in (18) (substitute food for sex/substitute sex for food) and the menu in (19) (substitute X for side/substitute [X] for shrimp) where identical or parallel forms must be assigned opposite argument structures. Perhaps it is not only Townshend's substitutes that swing both ways.

For at least some speakers, as we have seen, "one term [i.e. one reading] is as good as another." In both the *substitute* cases (especially those requiring different readings within a single passage) and the *let alone/if not* cases, the form does not suffice to determine a meaning. Instead, the very existence of a replacement scenario (for the *substitute* case) or of a scale (for the scalar correlative cases) motivates the use of the construction in question, with the expectation that the hearer will be able to figure out in a given context the more plausible, and hence more likely intended, interpretation. In some cases, whether by design or by oversight, that expectation may be thwarted.

I conclude with the concession that we still have a long way to go in pinning down the trajectory of the new *substitute* and in providing a full account of the factors that affect the accessibility of substitute OLD for NEW readings (and the survival of substitute OLD for NEW readings) among younger and older speakers of English across different contexts of use. The patterning of other reversals—the innovative uses of *(not) A* let alone *B or A if not B*—is even harder to catalogue, much less predict. More and better surveys will be needed, and we will be lucky to get useful results. But I wholeheartedly endorse Lauri's vademecum (Karttunen 2014: slide 47): "Do experiments even if the data turns out to be more complex than your current theory can accommodate."

References

Aristotle. 1963. *Categories and De Interpretatione*. Clarendon Press. editor and translator J. L. Ackrill.

Benor, Sarah Bunin and Roger Levy. 2006. The chicken or the egg? a probabilistic analysis of English binomials. *Language* 82:233–78.

Carston, Robyn. 1993. Conjunction, explanation, and relevance. *Lingua* 90:27–48.

Carston, Robyn. 2002. *Thoughts and Utterances: The Pragmatics of Explicit Communication*. Blackwell.

Christian, Donna. 1991. The personal dative in Appalachian English. In P. Trudgill and J. K. Chambers, eds., *Dialects of English*, pages 11–19. Longman.

Cohen, L. Jonathan. 1971. Some remarks on Grice's views about the logical particles of natural language. In Y. Bar-Hillel, ed., *Pragmatics of Natural Language*, pages 50–68. Reidel.

Cooper, William and John Robert Ross. 1975. World order. In *Papers from the Parasession on Functionalism*, pages 63–111. Chicago Linguistic Society.

de Jonge, Casper. 2008. *Between Grammar and Rhetoric: Dionysius of Halicarnassus on Language, Linguistics and Literature*. Brill.

Denison, David. 2009. Argument structure. In G. Rohdenburg and J. Schlüter, eds., *One Language, Two Grammars? Differences Between British and American English*, pages 149–165. Cambridge University Press.

Dionysius of Halicarnassus. n.a. *On Literary Composition*. Macmillan & Co. W. Rhys Roberts, ed. & trans. 1910.

Fenk-Oczlon, Gertrud. 1989. Word frequency and word order in freezes. *Linguistics* 27:517–556.

Fillmore, Charles, Paul Kay, and Mary Catherine O'Connor. 1988. Regularity and idiomaticity in grammatical constructions: The case of *let alone*. *Language* 64:501–538.

Gibson, Edward, Steve Piantadosi, and Kristina Fedorenko. 2011. Using Mechanical Turk to obtain and analyze English acceptability judgments. *Language and Linguistic Compass* 5:509–524.

Grice, H. P. 1981. Presupposition and conversational implicatures. In P. Cole, ed., *Radical Pragmatics*, pages 183–198. Academic Press.

Hirschberg, Julia. 1985. *A Theory of Scalar Implicature*. Ph.D. thesis, University of Pennsylvania.

Horn, Laurence. 1972. *On the Semantic Properties of Logical Operators in English*. Ph.D. thesis, UCLA.

Horn, Laurence. 2008. 'I love me some him': The landscape of non-argument datives. In O. Bonami and P. C. Hofherr, eds., *Empirical Issues in Syntax and Semantics 7*, pages 169–192. Downloadable at http://www.cssp.cnrs.fr/eiss7.

Horn, Laurence. 2009. WJ-40: Implicature, truth, and meaning. *International Review of Pragmatics* 1:3–34.

Hutchinson, Corinne and Grant Armstrong. 2014. The syntax and semantics of personal datives in Appalachian English. In R. Zanuttini and L. Horn, eds., *Micro-Syntactic Variation in North American English*, pages 178–214. Oxford University Press.

Karttunen, Lauri. 1970. The logic of English predicate complement constructions. Distributed by Indiana Univeristy Linguistics Club 1971; posted at http://web.stanford.edu/˜laurik/.

Karttunen, Lauri. 1971. Implicative verbs. *Language* 47:340–358.

Karttunen, Lauri. 1972. Possible and must. In J. Kimball, ed., *Syntax and Semantics 1*, pages 1–20. Academic Press.

Karttunen, Lauri. 2013. You will be lucky to break even. In T. H. King and V. de Pavia, eds., *From Quirky Case to Representing Space: Papers in Honor of Annie Zaenen*, pages 167–180. CSLI Publications.

Karttunen, Lauri. 2014. Three ways of not being lucky. Presentation at SALT 24, NYU. Slides available at http://web.stanford.edu/˜laurik/.

Karttunen, Lauri and Stanley Peters. 1979. Conventional implicature. In C. Oh and D. Dinneen, eds., *Syntax and Semantics 11: Presupposition*, pages 1–56. Academic Press.

Kay, Paul. 1990. Even. *Linguistics and Philosophy* 13:59—-111.

King, Jeffrey and Jason Stanley. 2005. Semantics, pragmatics, and the role of semantic content. In Z. Szabó, ed., *Semantics Versus Pragmatics*, pages 111–164. Oxford University Press.

Lehrer, Adrienne. 1974. *Semantic Fields and Lexical Structure*. North-Holland.

Leiby, Alison. 2016. A few questions about the specials. *New York Times* March 23, 2016. http://www.nytimes.com/2016/03/27/opinion/sunday/a-few-questions-about-the-specials.html.

Lepore, Ernie and Matthew Stone. 2015. *Imagination and Convention*. Oxford University Press.

Paskin, Willa. 2013. Did 'Team Walt' win? *Slate* Sept. 30, 2013. http://tinyurl.com/ollv32z.

Quintilianus, Marcus Fabius. 1920. *Institutio Oratoria*. Harvard University Press. H.E. Butler, trans., Loeb Classical Library.

Rosenbaum, Peter. 1967. *The grammar of English predicate complement constructions*. Ph.D. thesis, MIT.

Smith, Karen. 2008. *The Girls-Only Dirty Joke Book*. Ulysses Press.

Strawson, P. F. 1952. *Introduction to Logical Theory*. Methuen.

Townshend, Peter. 1966. Substitute. http://www.lyricsfreak.com/print.php?id=224321.

Txurruka, Isable Gómez. 1983. The natural language conjunction 'and'. *Linguistics and Philosophy* 26:255–85.

Tyndall, Andrew. 2011. Substitute and its vicissitudes. DIVISION/Quarterly Psychoanalytic Forum 1.2: 31-33. http://www.apadivisions.org/division-39/publications/review/2011/07/substitute.aspx.

Urmson, J. O. 1959. *Philosophical Analysis: Its Development between the Two Wars*. Clarendon Press.

Webelhuth, Gert and Clare Dannenberg. 2006. Southern American personal datives: The theoretical significance of syntactic variation. *American Speech* 81:31–55.

Wilson, Deirdre. 1975. *Presupposition and Non-Truth-Conditional Semantics*. Academic Press.

Wood, Jim, Laurence Horn, Raffaella Zanuttini, and Luke Lindemann. 2015. The southern dative presentative meets mechanical turk. *American Speech* 90:291–320.

Wright, Saundra, Jennifer Hay, and Tessa Bent. 2005. Ladies first? phonology, frequency, and the naming conspiracy. *Linguistics* 43:531–561.

Zanuttini, Raffaella, Jim Wood, and Laurence Horn. In prep. Data, datives, and dialect syntax in American English. Unpublished manuscript.

Zwicky, Arnold. 2007. Another reversal. Language Log entry, Dec. 24, 2007. http://itre.cis.upenn.edu/˜myl/languagelog/archives/005255.html.

Zwicky, Arnold. 2011. More egotism. Blog entry, August 24, 2011. http://arnoldzwicky.org/2011/08/24/more-egotism/.

Zwicky, Arnold. 2012. Two remarks on reversals. Blog entry, April 28, 2012. http://arnoldzwicky.org/2012/04/28/two-remarks-on-reversals/.

4

A Few Words To Do With Multiword Expressions*

PAUL KAY AND LAURA A. MICHAELIS

4.1 Introduction

This chapter is centrally concerned with the idiom or multiword expression consisting of the words *to*, *do*, and *with*, usually in that order,[1] but not necessarily contiguous and not always in that order (3).

(1) a. Inside the flat a fruity voice was reading out a list of figures which had something to do with the production of pig iron.

b. It may have had to do with money ...

(2) a. Anorexia is not just about losing weight it has to usually do with wanting control in your life.

*We are grateful for the privilege of contributing to a volume honoring Lauri Karttunen. Given that our contribution is about the form and meaning of an idiom, we find it a welcome coincidence that after a brilliant career that began in semantics and pragmatics, and then moved into computational linguistics, Lauri has recently returned to linguistic meaning, dissecting with his accustomed mastery a highly idiomatic class of raising adjectives with protean implicative properties, e.g., *You will be lucky to break even* (Karttunen 2013). We would also like to express our gratitude for the very helpful comments of Stefan Müller and an anonymous referee.

[1]All positive numbered examples in this chapter were attested on the web in January or February 2016, except as otherwise noted. In this chapter we use the terms 'idiom' and 'multiword expression' (MWE) interchangeably. We do not intend to imply thereby that we consider the terms indistinguishable in meaning, only that the linguistic expressions with which we are concerned here are aptly characterized by either term.

Tokens of Meaning: Papers in Honor of Lauri Karttunen.
Cleo Condoravdi and Tracy Holloway King (eds.).

b. As I see it, the decolonization movement in Indian country has to do mostly with countering "white" power with "Indian" power.
c. Walter said it had something complicated to do with quantum physics.
d. In both conceptions, boredom has to do fundamentally with an experience of time and problems of meaning.
e. What does that have to do with me?
f. What has that to do with me?

(3) a. Elinor needed little observation to perceive that her reserve was a mere calmness of manner with which sense had nothing to do.
b. We implemented a recurrent-descent parser, a scanner (with which I had little to do) and a runtime Basic environment.
c. ... and my limbs moved with a positiveness and precision with which I seemed to have nothing at all to do ...

The variation in linear order observed in (3) suggests one of the main points of the chapter —- that those MWEs with fixed word order (e.g., *under the weather* (ill), *in the pink* (healthy), etc.) are not representative: many, perhaps the majority, of MWEs are syntactically flexible, and so are best analyzed as bags of lexical items whose inherent, often idiosyncratically constrained, properties determine — in concert with the canonical lexical and phrasal constructions of the grammar — the meanings and syntactic distributions of the idioms (Nunberg, Sag & Wasow 1994, O'Grady 1998, Sag et al. 2002, Ramisch 2015, Karttunen 2013, Kay, Sag & Flickinger submitted). What holds this idiom, and many other idioms, together is not any sort of phrasal template, but the syntactic and semantic potentials of its constituent lexical items. We will see that the lexical pieces of this idiom display significant syntactic freedom while nonetheless obeying fairly strict and rather idiosyncratic syntactic limitations. Our argument will be that this particular syntax and the corresponding compositional semantics is accurately predicted by a perspicuous representation of the constituent lexical items against the background of the familiar, 'core', phrasal syntax of English. This approach is in the tradition of Nunberg, Sag, & Wasow (1994).

A second general point this idiom illustrates is that MWEs usually contain fewer words than are indicated for them in dictionaries and comparably authoritative sources. The only words that all tokens of the *to do with* idiom (hereafter TDW) contain are *to*, *do*, and *with*. Some versions of TDW listed in several online sources are given in (4). Some examples lacking either *have* or *be* and exhibiting non-quantifier determiners in the NP slot occupied by *something* in (4)a,b are given in (5). Moreover, as we will see below, the syntactic and semantic roles of *something* in (4)a,b and *The issue* in (5)a are distinct.

(4) a. be/have something to do with sth [Cambridge Advanced Learner's Dictionary]
  b. be/have something to do with something [Macmillan Dictionary]
  c. have to do with [Thesaurus.com]
  d. have to do with [Collins English Dictionary]
  e. have to do with [American Heritage Dictionary of the Idioms, Second Edition]

(5) a. The issue to do with liquidity is affecting this economy too much.
  b. They asked a question to do with diversity.
  c. I am attempting to recontact Brian about a question to do with my GE Profile microwave.
  d. I had a question to do with the authenticity of painting...
  e. It's an issue to do with dietary deficiency...

In (5)a, the TDW NP occurs as subject, in (5)b as object, and in (5)c object of a preposition. In none of the examples of (5) is the TDW phrase governed by *have* or *be*, nor does the nominal preceding *to do with* contain a degree-denoting expression such as *something*, *nothing*, or *a lot*. As we will see in the next section, TDW occurs in several different syntactic environments. We show below that Sign-Based Construction Grammar (SBCG, Sag 2012, Kay & Sag 2012, Michaelis 2012, Kay, Sag, & Flickinger submitted) yields a perspicuous analysis of the TDW idiom in terms of a small number of dedicated lexical items and, notably, no phrasal constructions.

Section 2 of this chapter lays out the essential data of TDW. Section 3 deals briefly with the version in which *be* replaces *have*. Section 4 provides a brief and general introduction to SBCG. Further detail of SBCG mechanics is introduced in the formal analysis of Section 6. An informal analysis of the TDW idiom is given in Section 5 and the SBCG version in Section 6. Section 7 concludes.

4.2 The Data

We are concerned with the TDW idiom having the sense of 'having connection with/being associated with in some way'. We are thus not concerned with examples like (6), on its least context-dependent interpretation.

(6) I'm looking for something to do with the kids today and you've given me some great tips!

There are three relevant cases, or sets of cases, to be considered.

Case 1. The most commonly noticed case of TDW consists of a VP headed by a verb *have* followed by a degree-quantifying or measure expression (*something*, *nothing*, *a great deal*, *totally*, *somewhat*, etc.) followed by a TDW infinitival verb phrase, as in (7).

(7) a. OK, so the kiss had something to do with the lace and the gauze and the tassels.
b. It has nothing to do with paying tithes. It has nothing to do with perfect Church attendance.
c. It may not have a great deal to do with trades union autonomy, but trades union autonomy may have a great deal to do with guiding the destinies of society, ...
d. This has nothing to do with Eric Burdon, but somewhat to do with Iceage.

Case 2. In the second, and also frequently noticed, case, TDW again appears as an infinitival VP complement to an intransitive verb *have* (or *be*, as discussed briefly in the next section), but not preceded by a measure phrase, as illustrated in (8).

(8) a. One of the biggest climate problems has to do with what most people eat.
b. This may have to do with factors of asymmetric neurologic development, such as being right or left-handed.
c. Slavery in ancient Rome and Greece didn't have to do with your race, like it did in America.

Case 3. The third case is less frequently recognized. In this case the TDW phrase is an infinitival relative clause, modifying the head of an NP that can subserve any of the normal functions of an NP. In (9) the NP containing the TDW infinitival relative clause functions, respectively, as subject in (9)a, object in (9)b, prepositional object in (9)c, and predicate in (9)d. In Case 3, the phrase immediately preceding *to* is necessarily nominal and it is not semantically restricted to degree quantification —- see, e.g. (9)a,b — unlike the corresponding element in Case 1. Significantly there is no requirement that the TDW phrase be governed by *have* or *be*, as well as no restriction to degree quantification.

(9) a. ... an issue to do with development of a railway station has been raging...

b. Well you've asked several questions to do with the refugee crisis.

c. Many times when I am outside I will be thinking about something to do with my work or a friend ...

d. ... he knew exactly what the issue was. It is a hardware problem and nothing to do with software.[2]

4.3 The *be* Version

For Cases 1 and 2 there exist variants in which a form of *be* occurs instead of the corresponding form of *have*.[3]

(10) a. Cowardice is nothing to do with it — suicide takes considerable courage.

b. This new work is a lot to do with memory, childhood and innocence.

c. It could also be to do with the location of rooms...

d. The questions that were asked on 14 December last year were to do with looking into the assessment ...

e. What is that to do with us?

This usage appears to be a relatively recent, primarily British, innovation. It remains a minority usage in the British National Corpus and is quite rare in contemporary American usage as registered in available corpora. The BNC yields 181 (34%) raw hits for combined *is/was/were/be to do with* and 352 (66%) raw hits for combined *has/had/have to do with*. The corresponding figures in the much larger Corpus of Contemporary American English are 44 (.6%) raw hits for combined *is/was/were/be to do with* and 7,350 (99.4%) raw hits for

---

[2]We note, but do not attempt to analyze further, a special use of idiomatic *do* that refers to a social association, as illustrated by (i).

(i) But they all rejected the proposal; and said, they would have nothing to do with me any more, neither on board, nor on shore...

In this use, TDW must be the complement of *have*, both the subject and complement of *with* must denote animate entities and the degree argument must be present (??*He was unwilling to have to do with me*). In addition, the social-association interpretation appears possible only in desiderative contexts, where idiomatic *have* is the complement of a verb like *want*: ??*He does not have anything to do with me*). Idiomatic *do* in this use appears to be a negative polarity item, requiring the presence of *not* or a negative degree argument: ??*He wants to have something to do with me.* Idiomatic *do* on its social association sense appears incompatible with extraction, although extraction contexts are generally viewed as non-veridical (negative polarity) contexts: ??*What would she have to do with you?*

[3]As noted in Case 3, no particular verb governs the TDW NP.

combined *has/had/have to do with.*[4] With respect to times of attestation, the OED lists examples of the *have* version from Middle English, while the earliest citation for the *be* version is 1902. We conclude that once we have specified a special lexeme *have*, required to complete the analysis of Cases 1 and 2, to extend the analysis to the *be* usage requires no more than positing a corresponding *be* lexeme.

4.4 Sign-Based Construction Grammar

SBCG is based on a multiple-inheritance hierarchy of typed feature structures.[5] Readers acquainted with HPSG or with the kind of Berkeley Construction Grammar presented in, for example, Kay and Fillmore (1999), should find the tools and notations introduced in this paper familiar. This section does not go into details of notation. Those are explained, as necessary, as the SBCG analysis of TDW is presented in section 6.

The most important type of feature structure (FS) in SBCG is the *sign*, with subtypes *word*, *lexeme* and *phrase* (Sag 2012: 71). A *construct* is a local tree of signs. *Combinatorial constructions* define classes of constructs. *Lexical class constructions* can be thought of as filling in particular features of *listemes*, to license *lexemes*. A listeme is a minimal lexical entry that has not undergone derivational or inflectional elaboration (Sag 2012: 71, Di Sciullo & Williams 1987).

Each sign has a FORM feature, whose value is a morphological representation of the expression, notated here in standard English orthography. The other features of the sign are PHON(ology), ARG-ST (argument structure; for lexical signs only), SYN(tax), SEM(antics), and CONTEXT.[6] The value of SYN is a feature structure that specifies the features CAT(egory), VAL(ence), and MRKG (marking). CAT values are FSs assigned to various word-class types (*noun*, *verb*, etc.), and specify values for the features appropriate to that type, including Lexical Identity (LID), whose value is a list of frames.[7] The MARKING value of a lexical sign (only) is normally identified with the LID value.[8] LID

[4]These figures are not corrected for meaning and doubtless exaggerate the advantage of *have* over *be* in both corpora because of the possession sense of *have* in, e.g., (6). We find no reason to suppose, however, that the strength of this artifact would be different in the two corpora.

[5]This section is based on Kay, Sag, & Flickinger (submitted). See Sag (2012) for a comprehensive introduction to SBCG.

[6]The PHONOLOGY feature is not relevant to the material of the present chapter and will not be included in our diagrams.

[7]Typically this will be a singleton list. See Sag (2012) for greater detail.

[8]Departures from the norm will be discussed. For readers familiar with HPSG, we note that the LID feature subsumes the function of the PFORM feature and ac-

values are percolated from heads, making the identity of the lexical head available at every phrasal level; MRKG values are percolated from functors (i.e. specifiers or modifiers). Thus in an NP or N′ the identity of both the head (via the LID value) and the modifier or specifier (via MRKG value) are visible to potential governing predicators.[9]

The value of the ARG-ST feature is a list of the *signs* that are the arguments — syntactic and semantic — of a predicating lexeme. Members of the ARG-ST list reappear in the list value of the VAL feature, except when extracted or given null realization. The ARG-ST feature is limited to lexical signs; unlike the VAL feature it does not appear in phrasal signs. This limitation constitutes one aspect of the highly local nature of SBCG. The external argument is the argument that gets 'raised', 'controlled', etc. When a lexeme has an external argument, it is the first element on the ARG-ST list. There is a syntactic CAT feature, XARG, whose value is the external argument.[10] The XARG feature in effect allows a predicator that selects a given type of phrasal sign to 'see' the first argument of the verb within that phrase. As well as figuring in control and raising, the XARG feature is used to represent coreference constraints in more 'marked' constructions like copy raising, as discussed by Sag (2012: 142ff). A second property of the SBCG architecture that enforces locality is that only constructs, but not signs, have a DAUGHTERS (DTRS) feature. Since the members of the list constituting the value of the ARG-ST feature are *signs* and since a *sign* does not have a DTRS feature, it is possible for a predicator to specify properties only of its daughters, not of its 'granddaughters'. Long-distance dependencies are encoded as a sequence of local dependencies, via the GAP (aka SLASH) feature, in the tradition of GPSG and HPSG.

Like the ARG-ST feature, the VAL feature takes as its value a list of signs, corresponding to the elements that an expression can combine with:[11] the syntactico-semantic arguments of the predicator in order of increasing obliqueness, or decreasing accessibility (subject, direct object,...). Expressions including NPs, PPs, APs, and clauses have the

complishes the analogous function for lexical heads of all categories.

[9]The MARKING feature is relevant to the analysis of idioms like *bark up the wrong tree*, in which not only must *up* be able to recognize that its complement NP is headed by *tree*, but critically that *tree* is modified by an AP headed by *wrong*. Since, analysis of the TDW idiom does not involve the MARKING feature, that feature is not systematically included in the diagrams of this chapter.

[10]For convenience, we sometimes refer, somewhat loosely, to the value of the XARG feature as 'the XARG'.

[11]We say *can* combine, rather than *must* combine, because in SBCG, as in HPSG generally, raised and controlled arguments appear on the valence list (or equivalent) even though not realized locally.

empty list as their VAL value: they are 'saturated', in the sense that they already contain all of the predicator's arguments. As mentioned, the elements of the VAL list of a lexeme or word are the same signs as those appearing on the ARG-ST list, minus those that are extracted (encoded on the GAP list) or subject to null instantiation, definite or indefinite.

The value of SEM includes specifications for the features INDEX and FRAMES. We assume an indefinitely large number of referential indices *1*, *2*, ... The FRAMES feature takes a list of elementary predications[12] as its value. We adopt a frame-based conception of semantics (Fillmore 1982, 1985, Fillmore and Baker 2010). We assume further that frames form a multiple-inheritance hierarchy in which there is a first-cut bifurcation of the universe of frames into canonical frames (*c-frames*) and idiomatic-frames (*i-frames*). We assume, for example, that the idiomatic *do* of TDW means something like 'have some relation with' or 'be connected somehow with', and that its PP[*with*] complement is of the case-marking (semantically non-contributing) variety. Hence the listeme for the *do* of TDW is assigned [SEM [FRAMES *<i(diomatic)-do[rel(ation)]-fr(ame)>*]], the material in *[brackets]* expressing a rough gloss or other indication of the meaning or function of the idiomatic word. Except in the case of semantically empty lexemes like the *to* and *with* of TDW, the LID value of a lexeme is identified with its FRAMES value.

Semantically null expressions, such as the idiomatic *to* of TDW, receive the specification [SEM [INDEX *none*, FRAMES < >]]. In the case of such semantically empty lexemes, the LID value is a *non-empty* list containing a semantically null frame, which serves to identify the lexical head when it is projected to higher levels of the phrase. Accordingly, despite the fact that *to* has an empty FRAMES value, we assign it a non-empty LID value: [SYN [CAT [LID *<i-to[TDW]-fr>*]]]. In this manner, the *have* of TDW can identify a VP headed by TDW *to*; the *to* of TDW will be able to identify a VP headed by TDW *do* because of the latter's specification [SYN [CAT[LID *<i-do[rel]-fr>*]]]; and TDW *do* will be able to subcategorize for a PP headed by case-marking *with* because the latter will carry the specification SYN [CAT [LID *<with[null]-frame>*]].[13]

[12] In the present study these lists are all singleton (See Sag 2012). Roughly, SBCG frames are equivalent to the RELS of Minimal Recursion Semantics (MRS), in Copestake et al. (2005). We adopt here a simplified form of MRS, making no use of either the LTOP feature or the mechanisms for keeping track of relative scoping relations. We make limited use of the LABEL feature, which is explained where first employed.

[13] We treat infinitive *to* as a highly defective auxiliary verb in the phrase structure grammar tradition (Gazdar, Pullum & Sag 1982, see also Pullum 1981).

The basic mechanism for preventing idiom words — like *beans* in *spill the beans* or *do* in TDW — from appearing in contexts where they are not lexically governed by the appropriate idiom predicator involves the feature VAL. Canonical (non-idiomatic) predicators are lexically specified as requiring all members of their VAL list to be non-idiomatic, that is, [LID <*c-frame*>]. By contrast, an idiomatic predicator such as idiomatic *spill* requires a direct object that is idiomatic, i.e. one whose LID value (and hence that of its lexical head) contains a particular *i-frame*, to wit: *i-beans[secret]-fr*. Similarly, the VAL value of the infinitive-taking verb *to* of TDW specifies a VP complement whose LID value is <*i-do[rel]-frame*>.

We will have occasion below to talk about the verb *have* that plays a role in the TDW idiom. We will discover that this verb, like the TDW infinitive *to*, is a subject-raising verb that contributes nothing to the semantics. Although this *have* is idiomatic in the sense that it plays a role in a MWE, the LID of an idiom-governing verb like TDW *have* does not contain an *i-frame* because a phrase headed by such a predicator can be a complement of an ordinary predicator. This circumstance is exemplified by the *spill* of the *spill the beans* in (11)a and by the *have* of TDW in (11)b and (11)c.[14]

(11) a. We both began to spill the beans about our relationships...
b. Some historians believe it has something to do with handicrafts that the first Strigolniki were engaged in ...
c. Others believe it has to do with how you got your financing or who distributed your film.

In (11)b and (11)c the complement of *believe* is a clause headed by TDW *have*, illustrating the fact that the highest predicator in an MWE has to bear a *c-frame* LID.

4.5 The Analysis

In this section we provide an informal description of our analysis of TDW. In the next we show how this analysis is expressed more formally in SBCG.

4.5.1 Case 1

We repeat in (12) an example of Case 1 of the TD idiom, given above as (7)a.

[14]The *to* of TDW does have an *i-frame* LID because it must be recognizable to TDW *have*. It is not the case, however, that any infinitive-marking verb *to* that can take a VP idiom complement has a special form restricted to that complement.

(12) OK, so the kiss had something to do with the lace and the gauze and the tassels.

As mentioned, in Case 1, when an element intervenes between TDW *have* and TDW *to*, it must denote a degree-measuring expression, such as *something*, *a little*, *little*, *plenty*, *a great deal*, *somewhat*, etc. In a sentence like (13)a, in which the NP intervening between *have* and *to* is not a degree-quantifier, *it*-cleft (version (13)b) and *wh*-cleft (version (13)c) are possible. However, in a sentence genuinely illustrating Case 1, in which the intervening element is a degree-quantifying expression, neither *it*-cleft nor *wh*-cleft are possible, for reasons we discuss below. These facts establish that the *have* of (13)a,b,c are the ordinary 'possessive' *have*, not the special *have* of TDW. Example (13)d exemplifies Case 1, and the (13)e (*it*-cleft) and (13)f (*wh*-cleft) examples show that in Case 1 the string corresponding to *something to do with your computer* is not a constituent.

(13) a. if any of you guys has a problem to do with his computers [please keep in touch and we can solve [i]t].
b. If it's a problem to do with his computer that any of you guys have... (invented)
c. If what any of you guys have is a problem to do with his computer... (invented)
d. If your problem has something to do with your computer we can solve it. (invented)
e. *If it's something to do with your computer that your problem has we can solve it. (invented)
f. *If what your problem has is something to do with your computer we can solve it. (invented)

It follows from the fact that Case 1 examples require the intervening element to be a degree-quantifier that cases in which a non-degree quantifier intervenes, like (13)a-c, are instances of the familiar 'possessive' *have.* The intervening degree-measuring expression found in Case 1 examples, like those expressions that intervene between the control verb *promise* and its infinitival complement in (14)a and (14)b, do not form an NP constituent with the following infinitival VP.

(14) a. I have promised Lord Henry to go with him.
b. She was much affected, and promised immediately to set about the great work of seeking the salvation of her soul.

Similarly, the object of possessive *have* can be topicalized (15)a, but not the superficially similar [*something to do with* NP] string in a Case 1 sentence like (15)b, as shown in (15)c.

(15) a. A problem with a computer Einstein would never have. (invented)
b. Einstein's problem would never have something/anything to do with a computer. (invented)
c. *Something/Anything to do with a computer Einstein's problem would never have.

In our proposed analyses of Case 1 sentences, *have* is a subject raising verb with a non-subject argument directly following the verb that fails to have all the properties of a direct object. In this regard *have* functions like *promised* in (14).

Turning now to the semantics of Case 1, in a sentence like (16), the modern Nahuatl language is asserted to have an association with the language of the Aztecs and 'only a little' is asserted to express the strength of that association. The latter effect is achieved, as we will see below, by 'only a little' binding a degree variable in the *i-do[rel]-frame* that idiomatic *do* introduces into the semantics of the sentence.

(16) Today, the modern Nahuatl language has only a little to do with the language spoken by the Aztecs.

4.6 Case 2

The relevant examples, like those in (8), the first of which is repeated as (17), contain the verb *have* and lack a degree quantifier between *have* and *to*.

(17) One of the biggest climate problems has to do with what most people eat.

These examples show that the degree-quantifier of Case 1 is an optional argument of *have* syntactically and that semantically the degree of association can simply remain unspecified. This observation comports with the fact that pairs of sentences like (18)a and (18)b appear to be indistinguishable in denotation.

(18) a. It had something to do with love.
b. It had to do with love.

As mentioned, TDW *to* subcategorizes for a VP headed by TDW *do*, which in turn subcategorizes for ordinary case-marking PP[*with*]. Since *to* is a semantically inert subject-raising verb, like TDW *have*, in (17) the denotatum of *One of the biggest climate problems* is identified with an entity that is associated (to an unspecified degree) with the denotatum of *what most people eat*.

4.6.1 Case 3

In this case the word-string [NP_1 *to do with* NP_2] is analyzed as a freestanding NP, headed by NP_1, which can subserve any of the normal functions of a referential or predicative NP, as illustrated in (9); (9)a is repeated as (19).

(19) ... an issue to do with development of a railway station has been raging ...

The string [*to do with* NP] is analyzed as an infinitival relative clause, modifying, for example, *issue* in (19).[15]

4.7 The Analysis Implemented in SBCG

The challenging problem for the analysis of TDW is to formulate the listemes for *do* (and to a lesser extent *to*, and *have*) in such a way that the TDW phrase can serve as a subject-raising verbal complement (Cases 1 and 2) and an infinitival relative clause (Case 3), and yet not license further imagined possible syntactic configurations, such as a finite clause like (20)a, a modifying gerund phrase like (20)b, a *for* ... *to* infinitival clause, as in (20)c, a TDW infinitival VP governed by a subject raising verb other than *have*, as in (20)d, and so on.

(20) a. *The problem does with fleas. 'The problem has to do with fleas'
  b. *I have a problem doing with my kitchen. 'I have a problem to do with my kitchen'
  c. *Her mother doesn't want for her to do with him anymore. 'Her mother doesn't want her to have to do with him anymore.'
  d. *This film appears to do with the war. 'This film has to do with the war.'

[15] It is tempting to assume that infinitival relative clauses attach to NP. Sag 1997 argues convincingly that *wh*-relatives attach to NP. He argues further, though, that non-finite relatives attach to N′, in order to account for the fact that bare relatives precede *wh*-relatives. However, simple infinitival relatives do not necessarily precede *wh*-relatives, as seen in (i).

(i) I need someone who I can trust to talk to.

We note that a saturated nominal word, such as *something*, might qualify as an NP in the intended sense of having an empty VALENCE list (See also Sag 2012: 80, fn. 22), although Sag (1997: 36-37 note) suggests analyzing words like *something* as *some thing*, which would support the proposal that infinitival relatives attach to N′. We will not attempt to settle that matter here, nor will we present an SBCG formulation of the construction(s) licensing infinitival relative clauses. For detailed analysis of English relative clauses in constructional HPSG, see Sag 1997.

We will argue that SBCG, as represented in Boas & Sag (2012) and Kay, Sag, & Flickinger (submitted) makes possible a perspicuous implementation of the analysis sketched in this section.

4.7.1 *with*

Case-marking *with* is not an idiomatic lexeme restricted to the TDW idiom. However, it provides a good starting point for our analysis, both because it is required in the TDW idiom and because case-marking *with* furnishes a convenient opportunity to introduce some of the notation of SBCG. The lexical entry ('listeme') for *cm-with* is given in (21).

(21)
$$\begin{bmatrix} \textit{cm-p-word} & \\ \text{FORM} & \langle \textit{with} \rangle \\ \text{ARG-ST} & \langle \textsc{y}\text{:NP}_y \rangle \\ \text{SYN} & \begin{bmatrix} \text{CAT} & \begin{bmatrix} \textit{prep} & \\ \text{XARG} & \textit{none} \\ \text{LID} & \langle \textit{with[cm]-fr} \rangle \end{bmatrix} \\ \text{VAL} & \langle \textsc{y} \rangle \end{bmatrix} \\ \text{SEM} & \begin{bmatrix} \text{INDEX} & y \\ \text{FRAMES} & \langle\rangle \end{bmatrix} \end{bmatrix}$$

The notation in italics at the top of the AVM indicates a case-marking prepositional word. The second row tells us the morphological form of this word. Lists are surrounded by <angled brackets>. ARG-ST abbreviates *argument structure.* We see that this word has a single argument, an NP whose index is *y*, and which is tagged with the feature-structure tag Y. The SYN value is represented by an AVM containing the features CAT and VAL. The CAT value is a FS of type *preposition* with external argument (XARG) indicated as *none* — consonant with the 'case-marking' function — and whose lexical identity (LID) identifies this word, and any phrase it projects, as headed by case-marking *with.* The VAL value is a singleton list containing the tag Y, identifying it with the single member of the ARG-ST list. The SEM value shows that the referential INDEX of this word, which will be projected to the INDEX of the PP it heads, is identified with that of its unique (object) argument. This fact, along with the fact that the FRAMES list is empty, completes the specification of a preposition with 'case-marking' function.[16]

[16]Situations in which the FRAMES value is the empty list constitute the only circumstance considered in this chapter in which the LID and FRAMES values are not identified, Cf. fn. 8.

We now want to consider the structure of a PP projected by case-marking *with.* The combinatorial construction that assembles a case-marking preposition, one which makes no semantic contribution and has no XARG, with its NP object is the Saturational Head-Complement Construction (Sag 2012: 152), shown in (22). The construction is called 'saturational' because there is no XARG that needs to be controlled or realized outside of the PP.

(22) Saturational Head-Complement Construction (↑ *headed-construct*)
sat-hd-comp-cxt ⇒

$$\begin{bmatrix} \text{MTR} & \begin{bmatrix}\text{SYN} & x!\left[\text{VAL} < >\right]\end{bmatrix} \\ \text{DTRS} & <z> \oplus L{:}nelist \\ \text{HD-DTR} & z{:}\begin{bmatrix} word & \\ \text{SYN} & x{:}\begin{bmatrix} \text{CAT} & \begin{bmatrix} prep & \\ \text{XARG} & none \end{bmatrix} \\ \text{VAL} & L \end{bmatrix} \end{bmatrix} \end{bmatrix}$$

The statement in (22) defines the type *saturational-head-complement-construct*, which is the class of FSs named by the type designation preceding the double-shafted arrow and constrained by the feature-structure description expressed in the AVM following the arrow. The notation (↑ *headed-construct*) indicates that the type *saturational-head-complement-construct* is a subtype of *headed-construct* (Sag 2012: 154). A *construct* is a FS that defines a local tree, a mother immediately dominating one or more daughters. In the AVM there is a mother (MTR) feature, a daughters (DTRS) feature, and a head daughter (HD-DTR) feature. By definition, the mother and each of the daughters are of type *sign*, and since the *sat-hd-comp-cxt* type is a subtype of *headed-construct*, instances of *sat-hd-comp-cxt* inherit the constraints defined (in analogous fashion) for *headed-construct.*[17] In the mother's SYN value the first thing encountered is the compound tag symbol '*x*!'. In the head daughter's SYN value we find the compound tag symbol '*x*:'. Pairs of elements so tagged (one ending in '!' and one either ending in ':' or lacking a punctuation mark) are identical except for the parts in which they are explicitly shown to differ (Sag 2012:126 note). In this case, the SYN values of the MTR and HD-DTR are identical, except that the MTR's VAL list is empty. The HD-DTR's CAT feature indicates a preposition with no XARG, a case-marking preposition. The DTRS feature is a list

[17] We do not show the details here. For more on the headed constructions and on the formal nature of the SBCG type hierarchy, see Sag (2012).

consisting of the head daughter (note the *z* tag) followed (as indicated by the symbol '⊕') by a non-empty list, which is identified (via the list tag *L*) with the VAL list of the head daughter.

The listeme for *Paris*, following Sag's (2012: 108-109) treatment of proper names, is given in (23). The construct *with Paris* — licensed by the listeme for case-marking *with* (21), the Saturated Head-Complement Construction (22), and the listeme *Paris* — is given in (24).[18]

(23)
$$\begin{bmatrix} \textit{word} & \\ \text{FORM} & <\textit{paris}> \\ \text{ARG-ST} & <> \\ \text{SYN} & \begin{bmatrix} \textit{pn} & \\ \text{CAT} & [\text{LID} <\textit{paris-fr}>] \end{bmatrix} \\ \text{SEM} & \begin{bmatrix} \text{INDEX} & y \\ \text{FRAMES} & \left\langle \begin{bmatrix} \textit{name-fr} & \\ \text{NAME} & <\textit{paris}> \\ \text{ENTITY} & y \end{bmatrix} \right\rangle \end{bmatrix} \end{bmatrix}$$

[18] FSs are enclosed in boxes. FS descriptions are enclosed in [square brackets].

(24)

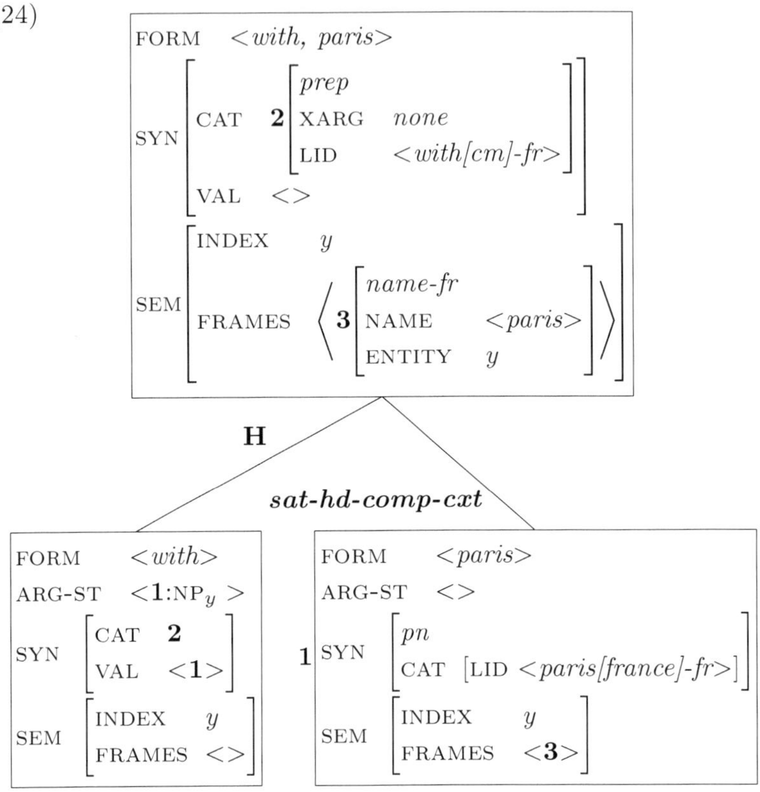

The **H** on the left descending branch indicates the head daughter ([FORM <*with*>]), whose single argument (**1**:NP$_y$) is also its unique valent (**1**). As a case-marking preposition *with*'s SEM value shows an empty FRAMES list and its INDEX (y) is identified with that of its object. The non-head daughter ([FORM <*paris*>]) has the internal structure specified in (23).[19] The mother constituent ([FORM <*with, paris*>]) inherits its SYN|CAT value (**2**) from the head daughter. According to the Saturated Head Complement Construction, its VAL value is the empty list, since the unique valent of the head daughter is realized as the non-head daughter (**1**). The mother's INDEX (y) is inherited from the head daughter. Since a mother constituent inherits the frames of all its daughters according to the Principle of Compositionality (Sag et

[19]Since we are dealing here with a sign, modeled by a FS, rather than a class of FS as in (22), the AVM is enclosed in a box instead of square brackets. Here, as elsewhere, to simplify diagrams as much as possible, features not germane to the topic at hand are not shown.

al. 2003) and since the FRAMES list of *with* is empty, the only frame in the mother's LIST is the unique frame (**3**) of the non-head daughter.

Starting with the phrase *with Paris*, shown as the top box in (24), proceeding word by word we build up the VP *do with Paris*; then the VP *to do with Paris*; then the VP *have to do with Paris*, exemplifying Case 2; and the VP *has something to do with Paris*, exemplifying Case 1. Subsequently, we address the derivation of the NP *something to do with Paris*, exemplifying Case 3, in which *to do with Paris* is not a VP but an infinitival relative clause.

4.7.2 *do*

The special word *do* is at the heart of the TDW idiom. The listeme for TDW *do* is shown in (25).

(25)
$$
\begin{bmatrix}
\textit{intrans-v-word} & \\
\text{FORM} & \langle \textit{do} \rangle \\
\text{ARG-ST} & \langle X{:}\text{NP}_x, Y{:}\text{PP}_y, [\text{LID}\ \langle \textit{with[cm]-fr}]] \rangle \\
\text{SYN} & \begin{bmatrix} \text{CAT} & \begin{bmatrix} \text{LID} & \langle Z \rangle \\ \text{XARG} & X \\ \text{VF} & \textit{base} \end{bmatrix} \\ \text{VAL} & \langle X, Y \rangle \end{bmatrix} \\
\text{SEM} & \begin{bmatrix} \text{FRAMES} & \left\langle Z{:}\begin{bmatrix} \textit{i-do[rel]-fr} & \\ \text{DEGREE} & \textit{index} \\ \text{TRAJECTOR} & x \\ \text{LANDMARK} & y \end{bmatrix} \right\rangle \end{bmatrix}
\end{bmatrix}
$$

TDW *do* is an intransitive verb word with the morphological form *do*, as shown in the top two rows of the AVM. This intransitive verb word finds a precedent in intransitive uses of *do* like *This will do* and *She is doing just fine*. Its ARG-ST list has two members, an NP with INDEX x and a PP with INDEX y, identified as the case-marking PP[*with*] by its LID value <*with[cm]-fr*>.[20] Skipping for a moment to the semantics in the bottom row, we find a single frame, *i-do[rel]-fr*, expressing the information that a TRAJECTOR x bears an unspecified scalar relation to a LANDMARK y of a DEGREE to be determined. Thus the values of the TRAJECTOR and LANDMARK semantic arguments are identified with the respective indices of the NP and PP syntactic arguments. The

[20] Paths in AVMs may be abbreviated. In (25), [SYN [CAT [LID <*with[null]-fr*>]]] is rendered [LID <*with[null]-fr*>].

CAT value shows this verb word to be of base form, which eliminates (20)a,b, repeated as (26).

(26) a. *The problem does with fleas. 'The problem has to do with fleas'

b. *I have a problem doing with my kitchen. 'I have a problem to do with my kitchen'

The XARG value is identified with the NP_x argument and the LID value is identified with the FRAMES value, as is canonical. Examples like those in (27) are ruled out by the fact that TDW *to* will be assigned the *i-frame i-to[TDW]-fr* and the only predicators that can accept as a complement a constituent with [LID <*i-to[TDW]-fr*>] are TDW *have* and *be*.

(27) a. *Her mother doesn't want for her to do with him anymore. 'Her mother doesn't want her to have to do with him anymore.' (=(20)c)

b. *I expect the film to do with the war. 'I expect the film to have to do with the war.'

The TDW VP *do with Paris* is licensed by the word *do*, the PP *with Paris*, and the Predicational Head-Complement Construction (28), which licenses VPs, along with other head-complement phrases such as canonical PPs, and certain APs, and N-bars. The Predicational Head-Complement Construction differs from the Saturational Head-Complement Construction in that it projects from heads with non-empty VAL values. The Predicational Head-Complement Construction appears in (28).

(28) **Predicational Head-Complement Construction** (↑ *headed-construct*)

$$pred\text{-}hd\text{-}comp\text{-}cxt \Rightarrow \begin{bmatrix} \text{MTR} & [\,\text{SYN } X!\,[\text{VAL } \langle Y \rangle]] \\ \text{DTRS} & \langle Z \rangle \oplus L{:}nelist \\ \text{HD-DTR} & Z{:}\begin{bmatrix} word & \\ \text{SYN} & X{:}\begin{bmatrix} \text{CAT} & [\text{XARG } Y] \\ \text{VAL} & \langle Y \rangle \oplus L \end{bmatrix} \end{bmatrix} \end{bmatrix}$$

The construction in (28) defines the type *predicational-head-complement-construct* as the class of constructs that obey the constraints depicted in the AVM to the right of the arrow. There is a mother feature MTR, a daughters feature DTRS, and a head daughter feature HD-DTR. The mother's and head daughter's syntax differ only in the facts (i) that the mother, like all phrases, lacks an ARG-ST feature and (ii) that the mother's VAL list consists only of the XARG (y). The other members of the daughter's VAL list, indicated by the list tag L, are realized as sisters to the head daughter, as displayed in the value of the DTRS feature. The DTRS list consists of the head daughter followed by its non-XARG complements.

The construct whose mother is the TDW VP *do with Paris* appears in (29).

(29)

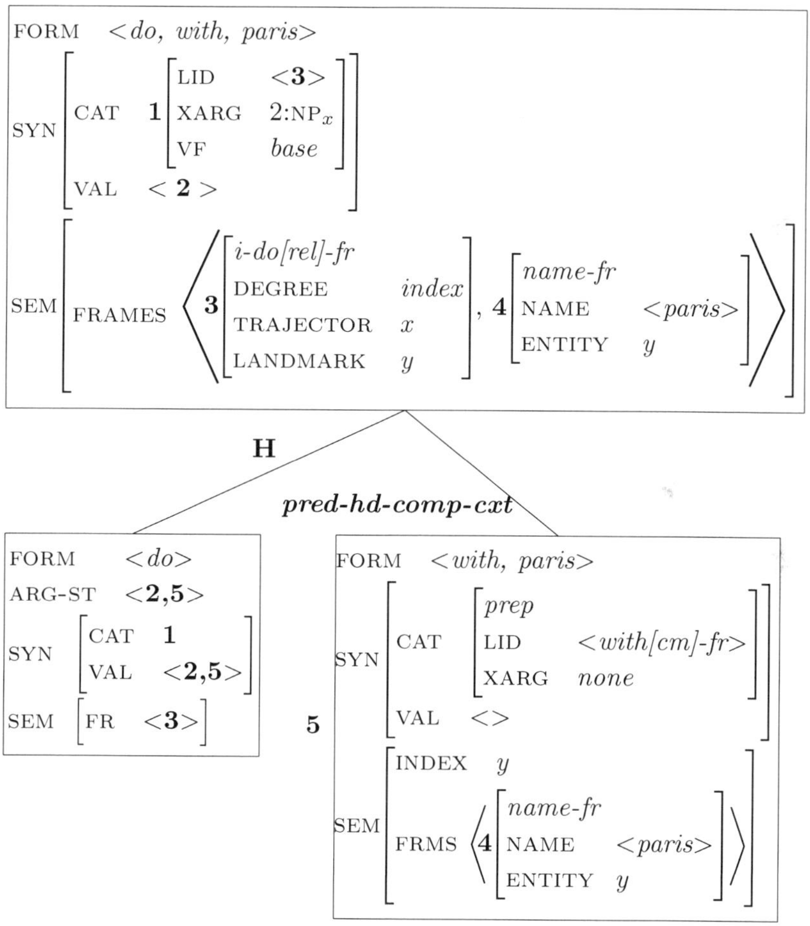

In construct (29), the mother, *do with Paris*, inherits its CAT value (**1**), from the head daughter *do*, specifying [LID <*i-do[rel]-fr*>] (**3**), [XARG

NP$_x$] (**2**), and, [VF *base*]. The two members of the mother's FRAMES list, *i-do[rel]-fr* (**3**) and *name-fr* (**4**) are inherited from the head and non-head daughters, respectively.[21] Regarding the arguments of the head daughter, the tag **2** identifies the XARG of the mother, and the tag **5** identifies the unique valent of the head daughter — consequently, also the non-head daughter.

4.7.3 *to*

TDW *to* has both a verb and a complementizer version, the former heading the VP in cases 1 and 2 and the latter heading the infinitival relative clause in case 3.[22] We consider the verb TDW *to* in this section and complementizer TDW *to* later. The TDW verb *to* shares many of the properties of the common infinitival verb *to*. It is nevertheless unique in that (1) TDW *to* requires specifically that its base-form VP complement be specified [LID <*i-do[rel]-fr*>], and (2) TDW *to* bears an idiomatic LID value, <*i-to[TDW]-fr*>, which ensures that a VP headed by TDW *to* can only serve as complement for a verb that specifies this LID in its VAL list, the unique verbs with this property being TDW *have* and *be*. In (30) we show the SELECT value as *none*, which contrasts with the complementizer version, whose SELECT value will be non-null. The listeme for the verb TDW *to* appears in (30).

(30)
$$\begin{bmatrix} \textit{sraising-verb-word} & \\ \text{FORM} & \langle \textit{to} \rangle \\ \text{ARG-ST} & \left\langle \begin{array}{l} X\text{:NP}, \\ Y\text{:VP}[\text{LID } \langle \textit{i-do[rel]-fr} \rangle] \end{array} \right\rangle \\ \text{SYN} & \begin{bmatrix} \text{CAT} & \begin{bmatrix} \text{LID} & \langle \textit{i-to[TDW]-fr} \rangle \\ \text{XARG} & X \\ \text{SELECT} & \textit{none} \\ \text{VF} & \textit{inf} \end{bmatrix} \\ \text{VAL} & \langle Y \rangle \end{bmatrix} \\ \text{SEM} & \begin{bmatrix} \text{INDEX} & \textit{none} \\ \text{FRAMES} & \langle \rangle \end{bmatrix} \end{bmatrix}$$

Since TDW *to* is shown at the top of the AVM to be of the type

[21] According to SBCG's Principle of Compositionality (Sag 2012: 146, Sag et al. 2003), in a construct the mother's FRAMES list represents the merger of the FRAMES lists of the daughters.

[22] Verbs and complementizers share many properties and are grouped together in the type hierarchy of SBCG as the two immediate subtypes of the type *verbal* (Sag 2012: 81-82).

s(ubject)raising-verb-word no further indication of the identity of the indices of the XARG and the complement VP's XARG valent are displayed in diagram (30). The ARG-ST shows an NP XARG and a VP complement with [LID <*i-do[rel]-fr*>]. The CAT value shows the VERB FORM (VF) to be *inf*, the XARG to be identified with the NP argument, and the LID to contain the idiomatic frame *i-to[TDW]-fr*, which ensures that a VP headed by TDW *to* can complement only TDW *have* (or *be*).

The VP *to do with Paris*, is licensed by TWD *to* (30), the Predicational Head-Complement Construction (28), and the VP *do with Paris* the mother of (29). The construct whose mother is the TDW VP *to do with Paris* is given in (31).

(31)

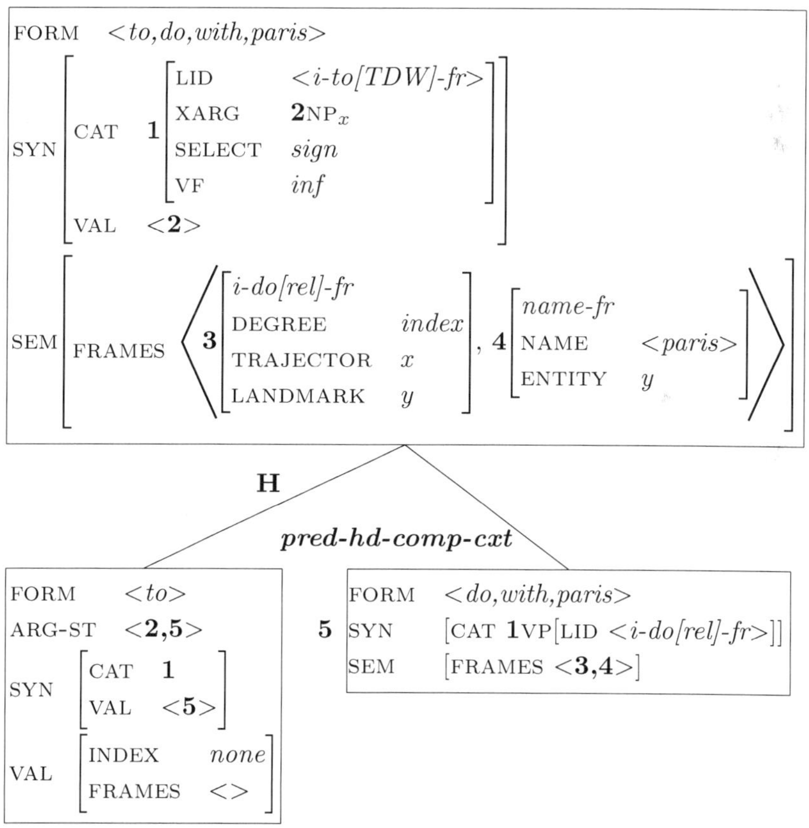

In the mother FS of (31), the phrase *to do with Paris*, the CAT value (**1**) is identified with that of the head daughter *to* — exemplifying a property of all headed phrases — and includes the specifications [VF *inf*], [XARG NP$_x$] and [LID <*i-to[TDW]-fr*>]. The mother's frames, *i-do[rel]-fr* (**3**) and *name-fr* (**4**), are inherited from the non-head daughter *do with paris* (**5**), which satisfies the unique VAL requirement of the head daughter, *to*.

4.7.4 *have*

The listeme for TDW *have* is shown in (32).

(32)
$$\begin{bmatrix} \textit{sraising-v-lxm} & \\ \text{FORM} & \langle \boldsymbol{\mathit{have}} \rangle \\ \text{ARG-ST} & \left\langle \begin{array}{l} X{:}\text{NP},\ Y{:}\text{XP}\begin{bmatrix}\text{FRAMES}\left\langle \ldots \begin{bmatrix}\textit{deg-quant-fr} & \\ \text{MEASURE} & w\end{bmatrix}\ldots\right\rangle\end{bmatrix}, \\ Z{:}\text{VP}\begin{bmatrix}\begin{bmatrix}\text{LID} & \langle \textit{i-to[TDW]-fr}\end{bmatrix} \\ \begin{bmatrix}\text{FRAMES} & \left\langle\ldots\begin{bmatrix}\textit{i-do[rel]-fr} & \\ \text{DEGREE} & w\\ \ldots & \end{bmatrix}\ldots\right\rangle\end{bmatrix}\end{bmatrix} \end{array} \right\rangle \\ \text{SYN} & \begin{bmatrix}\text{CAT} & \begin{bmatrix}\textit{verb} & \\ \text{LID} & \langle \textit{have[TDW]-fr}\rangle \\ \text{XARG} & X\end{bmatrix} \\ \text{VAL} & \langle X, Y^{ini}, Z\rangle\end{bmatrix} \\ \text{SEM} & \begin{bmatrix}\text{INDEX} & \textit{none} \\ \text{FRAMES} & \langle\rangle\end{bmatrix} \end{bmatrix}$$

TDW *have* licenses examples like those in (18) repeated as (33)a, exemplifying Case 1, and (33)b, exemplifying Case 2.

(33) a. It had something to do with love
b. It had to do with love.

Like TDW *to*, TDW *have* is a subject-raising verb. Its ARG-ST specifies, in addition to an XARG NP (X) and an infinitival VP complement (Z), an additional measure-phrase argument (Y). The Y argument contains a degree-quantifying frame whose MEASURE value w binds the value of the DEGREE argument of the *i-do[rel]-frame* of the Z argument. In the CAT value, the XARG status of the X argument is expressed and the LID value is shown to be a canonical frame, since a phrase headed by TDW *have* can be embedded under a canonical predicate, as in (34).

(34) His rationale was that this area of the spine innervated the pancreas, which was believed to have something to do with diabetes.

All three arguments appear in the VAL list. However, the second, Y, argument carries the superscript *ini*, standing for 'indefinite null instantiation'. Fillmore 1986 discusses the fact that some arguments of predicators can, when optionally omitted, be construed in a manner analogous to the existential closure of indefinites (Heim 1982, and much subsequent research; recently Ruppenhofer and Michaelis 2014).[23] The SEM value of (32) shows TDW *have* to contribute nothing to the semantics of a phrase in which it occurs — aside from the tense or aspect information it may host — despite the important syntactic role *have* often plays in the idiom.

The VP *have to do with Paris* illustrates Case 2. The head daughter of the construct shown in (35) contains a TDW *have* word based on the TDW *have* lexeme that has undergone the Indefinite Null Instantiation derivational construction and therefore lacks a valent corresponding to the Y valent in (32) and also contains an *exist-fr* (**5**) whose value w binds the DEGREE value in the *i-do-[rel]-fr* of the non-head daughter and the mother, as determined by (32).

[23]Indefinite null instantiation is implemented in SBCG by a derivational construction not shown here whose unique daughter contains a valent XP_x^{ini} and in which (i) the mother's VAL list lacks XP_x^{ini} and (ii) the mother's FRAMES list adds to the FRAMES list of the daughter an *exist-fr* whose bound variable (BV) value is x. Analogously, the Definite Null Instantiation Construction eliminates a daughter's XP_x^{dni} valent and inserts a *the-frame* in the mother's FRAMES list, binding x.

(35)

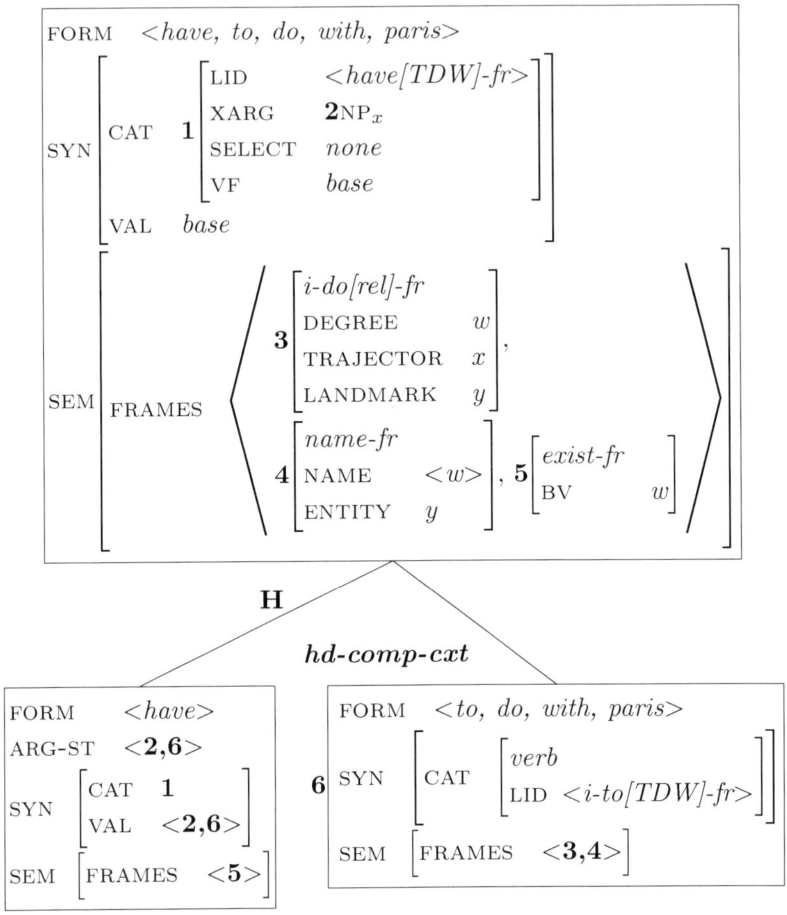

4.7.5 The TDW phrase as infinitival relative clause

We consider next an example of Case 3, *something to do with Paris*, as a freestanding NP in a sentence like (36)a. In the freestanding NP case there is no restriction to XPs expressing a measure of degree, as mentioned above and shown in (36)b.

(36) a. Every time I read something to do with Paris I end up crying.
b. I recently read an article to do with mares and foals.

We have noted that the string *something to do with Paris* has a different analysis in an expression like *The book has something to do with Paris* and an expression like *The book concerns something to do with Paris*. In the former case *something to do with Paris* is a VP in which *something* plays an adverbial role, like the word *plenty* in (37).

(37) The war had nothing to do with him. But it had plenty to do with Magdalena.

In the latter case *something to do with Paris* is a noun phrase and *to do with Paris* is an infinitival relative clause modifying the nominal (NP or N) *something*. Whereas in the former case *to* is a verb, in the latter *to* is a complementizer. Unlike the infinitive verb TDW *to*, the complementizer *to* that introduces TDW infinitival relatives is not a special, idiomatic word, restricted to TDW complements, as shown in (38).

(38)
$$\begin{bmatrix} \textit{complementizer-word} & \\ \text{FORM} & \langle \textit{to} \rangle \\ \text{ARG-ST} & \langle \text{Y:VP}[\text{VF } \textit{base}] \rangle \\ \text{SYN} & \begin{bmatrix} \text{CAT} & \begin{bmatrix} \text{LID} & \langle \textit{i-to[null]-fr} \rangle \\ \text{XARG} & \textit{none} \\ \text{SELECT} & [\text{CAT } \textit{noun}] \\ \text{VF} & \textit{inf} \end{bmatrix} \\ \text{VAL} & \langle \text{Y} \rangle \end{bmatrix} \\ \text{SEM} & \begin{bmatrix} \text{INDEX} & \textit{none} \\ \text{FRAMES} & \langle\rangle \end{bmatrix} \end{bmatrix}$$

The listeme pictured in (38) differs from that shown in (30) by indicating that it is a *complementizer-word*, specifying a single argument: a VP complement constrained only to [VF *base*] (rather than one constrained to [LID <*i-do[rel]-fr*>]), by eliminating the XARG of (30), and by specifying a non-null SELECT value.[24]

We assume that words like *something*, *everything*, *somebody*, etc. belong to a type *quantifier-noun-word*, which is a subtype of both *noun* and *quantifier*. The listeme for the word *something* is given in (39).

[24]Nouns, N-bars, and NPs are all of category *noun*. We avoid taking a position on whether infinitival relatives modify N-bars or NPs.

(39)
$$\begin{bmatrix} \textit{quant-nominal} & \\ \text{FORM} & <\textit{something}> \\ \text{ARG-ST} & <> \\ \text{SYN} & \begin{bmatrix} \text{CAT} & \begin{bmatrix} \textit{noun} & \\ \text{LID} & L \end{bmatrix} \\ \text{VAL} & <> \end{bmatrix} \\ \text{SEM} & \begin{bmatrix} \text{INDEX} & x \\ \text{FRAMES} & L{:}\left\langle \begin{bmatrix} \textit{exist-fr} & \\ \text{BV} & x \\ \text{REST} & l \end{bmatrix}, \begin{bmatrix} \textit{thing-fr} & \\ \text{LABEL} & l \\ \text{INST} & x \end{bmatrix} \right\rangle \end{bmatrix} \end{bmatrix}$$

We assume that listemes in this class contain both a *quantifier-fr*, e.g. *exist-fr*, and a RESTRICTION (REST) frame, viz. *thing-fr* or *person-fr*, although nothing here turns on that assumption.[25] Additionally we assume that at least some quantifier frames, including this one, are subtypes of *degree-quantifier-fr*. The NP *something to do with Paris*, is licensed by *something* (39), the infinitival relative clause *to do with Paris*, and the Head Functor Construction (40).[26] The derivation tree of the NP *something to do with Paris* as it appears in (36)a is shown in (41).

(40) Head-Functor Construction (↑ *headed-construct*)
hd-func-cxt⇒

$$\begin{bmatrix} \text{MTR} & [\text{SYN } X![\text{MRKG M}]] \\ \text{DTRS} & \left\langle \begin{bmatrix} \text{SYN} & \begin{bmatrix} \text{CAT} & [\text{SELECT } Y] \\ \text{MRKG} & M \end{bmatrix} \end{bmatrix}, \; Y{:}[\text{SYN } X] \right\rangle \\ \text{HD-DTR} & Y \end{bmatrix}$$

The Head-Functor Construction, based on the work of Van Eynde 2006, 2007 and Allegranza 1986, 1998, unites specifiers and modifiers as 'functors', bearing non-null values for the SELECT feature. The entire

[25] The LABEL feature of Minimal Recursion Semantics, of which we make only occasional use in this chapter, allows the representation of hierarchical relations among frames in the 'flat', list structures of MRS. In (39) the two tokens of the LABEL variable *l* show that *thing-fr* is the value of the RESTRICTION feature of *exist-fr*.

[26] We assume for simplicity of exposition that all modifier-head structures are licensed by the Head-Functor Construction.

syntax of the mother is inherited from the head daughter except for the MARKING value, which is mentioned in (40) for completeness although it plays no role in this chapter.

(41)

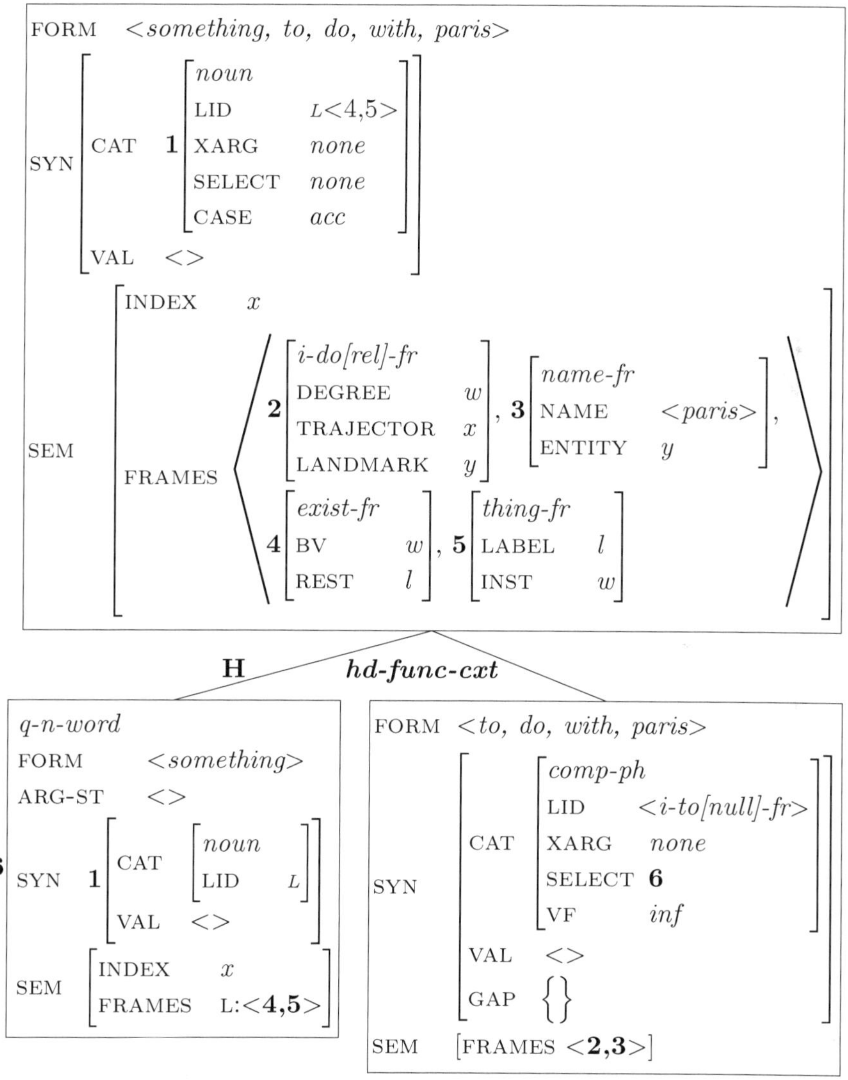

In the head-functor construct *something to do with Paris* (41), the mother is a noun phrase, i.e. of type *noun* with [VAL < >], and inherits

its CAT value from the head daughter *something.* The mother's XARG and SELECT features both have value *none.* In the mother's SEM value the INDEX x is inherited from the head daughter *something.* The *exist-fr* (**4**) and the *thing-fr* (**5**) are also inherited from the head daughter, and the remaining frames, *i-do[rel]-fr* (**2**) and *name-fr* (**3**), are inherited from the non-head (modifier) daughter *to do with Paris.* The non-head daughter's CAT feature shows it to be *verbal*, with [LID <*i-to[null]-fr*>], [XARG none], [VF *inf*], and to SELECT the head daughter *something* (**6**). The VAL list is empty.

As we have noted, the constituent bearing [FORM <*to, do, with, Paris*>] in (41) is different from the constituent with the same FORM value in (31) and (35). The former is a clause, specifically an infinitival relative clause, while the latter is a VP. In the VP of (31) and (35) the trajector argument is successively raised from the XARG of *do* to the XARG of the auxiliary verb *to.* For the infinitival relative clause of (41), we follow the main lines of the analysis of simple infinitival relative clauses of Sag (1997: 469-470). The trajector XARG of *do*, instead of raising, appears in the GAP (formerly SLASH) set of *do* and does not appear on the VAL list, where it could be the target of raising. In this case *to* is not an auxiliary verb but a complementizer. The GAP content is constructionally bound off below the CP level, so at the clausal level, where the SELECT (formerly MOD) value is coindexed with the erstwhile solitary member of the GAP set, the GAP set itself is empty.[27]

4.8 Conclusion

We have shown that the idiomatic character of TDW, like that of many other multiword expressions, is exclusively lexical: both *to* and *do* are verbal heads with idiosyncratic valence requirements. Simply put, *to* selects a VP headed by *do* and *do* selects a PP headed by *with.* The resulting combination, licensed by the Predicational Head-Complement Construction, is selectable by an idiomatic subject-raising lexeme, *have* (or *be*), which also contributes a degree argument or licenses its existential closure. Alternatively a TDW phrase can constitute an infinitival relative clause, in which case there is no restriction of the preceding phrase to a degree-quantifier. Idiomatic *do*, despite its restricted combinatorial potential, is compositionally interpreted, denoting an association between two entities, the first of which is expressed by the non-locally-

[27] As discussed in footnote 15, for Sag (1997) the SELECT (MOD) value is an N′ rather than an NP. Also the features have different names and in some cases somewhat different definitions, but are sufficiently alike for present purposes: GAP replaces SLASH, SELECT replaces MOD, [VAL < >] replaces [SUBJ <PRO>] in this context, and CAT replaces HEAD.

instantiated subject and the second of which is expressed by the object of the *with*-headed PP. SBCG has provided us with a precise framework in which to express this analysis and to predict exactly those syntactic configurations in which TDW occurs and does not occur.[28]

Idioms frequently contain fewer words than is often supposed, e.g., by the compilers of idiom dictionaries and other presumed authorities. However, not all words that are necessary parts of an idiom occur only in that idiom. An example is the requirement of canonical case-marking *with* in the TDW idiom. The reverse is the case with TDW *have*, which illustrates the fact that some words which appear only in an idiom are not required in all instances of that idiom. For most idioms, the phrase-structural configurations in which their words can appear derives exclusively from the syntactic potentials of the words themselves, which often mirror the syntactic properties of canonical words with similar meanings, subject of course to idiosyncratic limitations. The syntactic privileges of occurrence of the *beans* of *spill the beans* is a subset of the syntactic privileges of occurrence of the word *secrets*. The meanings of the phrases and sentences in which most idioms occur are composed by the same processes as compose the meanings of phrases and sentences that contain no idiom words, and most phrasal idioms, properly analyzed, contain no phrasal information.

References

Allegranza, Valerio. 1998. Determination and quantification. In *Linguistic Specifications for Typed Feature Structure Formalisms*, pages 281–314. Official Publications of the European Communities. vol. 10 of Studies in Machine Translation and Natural Language Processing.

Allegranza, Valerio. 2007. *The signs of determination: Constraint-based modelling across languages*, vol. 16. Peter Lang. SABEST: Saarbrücker Beiträge zur Sprach- und Translationswissenschaft.

[28]Using the LFG framework, Müller (2016) describes an allied lexicalist approach to the benefactive and resultative argument structures in English and German, motivating it on typological grounds. He argues that by representing these patterns as f-structures of lexical classes rather than as phrasal configurations we gain generalizations across languages with radically different constituent structures. Müller also points out that a version of the TDW idiom exists in German (p.c.), as illustrated in (i).

(i) a. Das hat nichts mit Peter zu tun.
b. This has nothing with Peter to do.
c. This has nothing to do with Peter.

The TDW idiom also occurs throughout the Romance languages, often with a verb meaning 'see', and doubtless beyond, subject in every case to the syntactic patterns of the language in question. The lexical analysis of idioms enables us to see commonalities across languages that would otherwise remain obscure.

Di Sciullo, Anna Marie and Edwin Williams. 1987. *On the Definition of Word*. MIT Press.

Eynde, Frank Van. 2006. NP-internal agreement and the structure of the noun phrase. *Journal of Linguistics* 42:139–186.

Fillmore, Charles J. 1986. Pragmatically controlled zero anaphora. In *Proceedings of the Berkeley Linguistics Society 12*, pages 95–107.

Fillmore, Charles J. and Paul Kay. 1995. Construction grammar. Unpublished ms., University of California, Berkeley.

Gazdar, Gerald, Geoffrey Pullum, and Ivan A. Sag. 1982. Auxiliaries and related phenomena in a restrictive theory of grammar. *Language* 58:591–638.

Heim, Irene. 1982. *The semantics of definite and indefinite noun Phrases*. Ph.D. thesis, University of Massachusetts, Amherst. Published in 1989 by Garland, New York.

Karttunen, Lauri. 2013. You will be lucky to break even. In T. H. King and V. dePaiva, eds., *From Quirky Case to Representing Space: Papers in Honor of Annie Zaenen*, pages 167–180. CSLI Publications.

Kay, Paul and Ivan A. Sag. 2012. Discontinuous dependencies and complex determiners. In H. Boas and I. Sag, eds., *Sign-Based Construction Grammar*, pages 211–238. CSLI Publications.

Kay, Paul, Ivan A. Sag, and Dan Flickinger. submitted. A lexical theory of phrasal idioms.

Michaelis, Laura A. 2012. Making the case for construction grammar. In H. Boas and I. Sag, eds., *Sign-Based Construction Grammar*, pages 31–69. CSLI Publications.

Müller, Stefan. 2016. Flexible phrasal constructions, constituent structure and (cross-linguistic) generalizations: A discussion of template-based phrasal LFG approaches. In D. Arnold, M. Butt, B. Crysmann, T. H. King, and S. Müller, eds., *Proceedings of the Joint 2016 Conference on Head-driven Phrase Structure Grammar and Lexical Functional Grammar*, pages 457–477. CSLI On-line Publications.

Nunberg, Geoffrey, Ivan A. Sag, and Thomas Wasow. 1994. Idioms. *Language* 70:491–538.

O'Grady, William. 1998. The syntax of idioms. *Natural Language and Linguistic Theory* 16:279–312.

Pullum, Geoffrey K. 1981. The category status of infinitival *to*. *University of Washington Working Papers in Linguistics* 6:55–72.

Ramisch, Carlos. 2015. *Multiword expressions acquisition: A generic and open framework*. Springer. Theory and Applications of Natural Language Processing series XIV.

Ruppenhofer, Josef and Laura A. Michaelis. 2014. Frames and the interpretation of omitted arguments in English. In S. K. Bourns and L. Myers, eds., *Linguistic Perspectives on Structure and Context: Studies in Honor of Knud Lambrecht*, pages 57–86. Benjamins.

Sag, Ivan A. 1997. English relative clause constructions. *Journal of linguistics* 33(2):431–483.

Sag, Ivan A. 2012. Sign-based construction grammar: An informal synopsis. In H. C. Boas and I. A. Sag, eds., *Sign-Based Construction Grammar*, pages 69–202. CSLI Publications.

Sag, Ivan A., Timothy Baldwin, Francis Bond, Ann Copestake, and Dan Flickinger. 2002. Multiword expressions: A pain in the neck for NLP. In *Lecture Notes in Computer Science 2276*, pages 1–15.

Sag, Ivan A., Thomas Wasow, and Emily M. Bender. 2003. *Syntactic Theory: A Formal Introduction*. CSLI Publications. 2nd ed.

Van Eynde, Frank. 2007. The big mess construction. In S. Müller, ed., *The Proceedings of the 14th International Conference on Head-Driven Phrase Structure Grammar*, pages 415–433. CSLI Publications.

5

Liminal *Until*[*]

CLEO CONDORAVDI AND ITAMAR FRANCEZ

5.1 Introduction

Temporal modifiers headed by *until* are known to behave differently when modifying telic and atelic predicates. As demonstrated in (1) and (2), with atelic predicates (states and activities) *until* is acceptable in both positive and negative clauses, while with telic predicates (accomplishments and achievements) it is only acceptable with negation. Based on this difference, two types of *until* have been recognized, at least descriptively (Klima 1964, Horn 1970, 1972, Heinämäki 1974, Karttunen 1974, Mittwoch 1977, Hitzeman 1991, Declerck 1995, Tovena 1996, de Swart 1996, Giannakidou 2002, Condoravdi 2008, Israel 2011, Bassa-Vanrell 2017).

(1) Durative *until*
  a. It was (not) dark until she pulled the curtains.
  b. They played until the bar closed down.

(2) Punctual *until*
  a. Mary didn't get home until noon.
  b. *Mary got home until noon.

*Thanks to Adam Przepiórkowski for comments on a previous version of the paper. Part of this work was conducted during a fellowship of Cleo Condoravdi at the Oslo Center for Advanced Study at the Norwegian Academy of Science and Letters.

Tokens of Meaning: Papers in Honor of Lauri Karttunen.
Cleo Condoravdi and Tracy Holloway King (eds.).

A prominent approach, one that Lauri Karttunen argued for in Karttunen (1974), assumes two distinct lexical items, durative *until* ($until^D$) and punctual *until* ($until^P$), with different semantic properties. Durative *until* — and on approaches that do not recognize lexical ambiguity, *until* in general — has a selectional restriction for atelic predicates, usually modeled in terms of divisive reference.[1] Proponents of the lexical ambiguity approach may differ on how they derive the contrast with telic and atelic predicates, but all agree on two points. The first point is that punctual *until* is a negative polarity item. This explains the contrast in (2), on the assumption that negation scopes over the temporal modifier. In (2a) $until^P$ appears in the scope of negation and is, therefore, licensed. (2b) is unacceptable because it contravenes some requirement on either construal of *until*. On the one hand, punctual *until* remains unlicensed in the absence of negation, and on the other, the selectional restriction of durative *until* for an atelic predicate is not satisfied. The second point is that the semantic hallmark of sentences with punctual *until* are the implications in (3) (see Condoravdi 2008 for more extensive discussion).

(3) Implicational profile of punctual *until*:
  a. **Actualization**: (2a) implies that Mary got home.
  b. **Temporal location**: (2a) implies that Mary got home at noon.

A key contrast between punctual and durative *until*, which any analysis must derive, is in their inferential profiles. While any implication of cessation that arises with durative *until* is cancellable, the actualization implication of punctual *until* is not. (4) exemplifies the contrast.

(4) a. The lake was warm until early September, and, alarmingly, it stayed warm until December.
  b. The lake didn't get warm until early August, #and, alarmingly, it didn't get warm even then.

Analyses that reduce punctual *until* to durative *until*, such as Heinämäki (1974) and Mittwoch (1977), attribute the pattern in (1) and (2) to the independently required selectional restriction of *until*. The contrast in (2) is explained by assuming that the temporal modifier scopes over negation, which produces a derived stative predicate and thus satisfies the selectional restriction of the temporal modifier.

[1] A predicate P has divisive reference relative to a given argument position iff its denotation in any model is closed under the subpart relation relative to that argument position. For predicates over temporal intervals, divisive reference is the subinterval property.

In avoiding lexical ambiguity, such approaches are ostensibly more parsimonious, but they face the challenge of deriving the actualization implication in (2a), and hence of explaining the contrast in inferential behavior seen in (4). The fact that the actualization implication of punctual *until* is conventional whereas the cessation implication of durative *until* is pragmatic constitutes a strong argument in favor of positing ambiguity.

This contribution presents new data that complicate the empirical picture, casting doubt on the view that punctual *until* is polarity sensitive, and revealing that its implicational behavior is significantly more complicated than has been realized in the literature. We maintain the hypothesis that *until* is lexically ambiguous between (i) a durative adverbial that can give rise to cancellable implicatures of cessation and (ii) a frame adverbial that cannot occur with simple, non-quantified sentences headed by telic predicates and that gives rise to non-cancellable inferences. We show that this frame adverbial is not polarity sensitive, and that the non-cancellable inference it gives rise to is more general than the actualization inference found with telic predicates under negation. We demonstrate that existing analyses do not derive the non-cancellable inferences observed in the relevant cases, but argue that Karttunen's basic insight, namely that these inferences are contextual entailments arising from the interaction between what sentences with the frame adverbial *until* presuppose and what they assert, is correct. Specifically, we propose, following Condoravdi (2008), that the non-durative, frame adverbial *until* describes the temporal location of a presupposed transition within a contextually familiar interval. We, therefore, name this adverbial *liminal until.* We provide an informal but precise characterization of the transition, and point out the challenges of formalizing our characterization within a compositional framework. Punctual *until* turns out to be a special case of liminal *until.*

5.2 Punctual and Durative *until*

Karttunen (1974) introduces his analysis of punctual *until* this way:

> The basic idea is this: there are different ways of drawing inferences from utterances. Some of the inferences we feel entitled to are based on knowing the logical form of the sentence that was spoken, some of them are presuppositional inferences based on the knowledge of the kind of situation in which we would be entitled to say such a thing, and finally there are inferences that arise from the interplay of these two kinds. I propose that the inference from [(2a) to (3b)] is of this third type and that the inference from [(2a) to Mary didn't get home before noon] is a matter of logical form. (p. 292–293)

He proposes that the truth-conditional temporal meaning of punctual *until* is the same as that of *before*. Punctual *until* has, in addition, presuppositional content that is responsible for the actualization inference, and ultimately for the inference of temporal location, which makes *until time t* appear synonymous with *at time t*. Specifically, sentences of the form 'A Until^P T' presuppose (A AT T) $\vee$ (A BEFORE T) and assert A BEFORE T. With negation, the assertion is NOT (A BEFORE T), which taken together with the presupposition, entails A AT T.

Condoravdi (2008) follows the main idea of Karttunen's analysis but recasts both the presuppositional and the truth-conditional content of *until*^{P}. She proposes an analysis in which a modifier [*until*^{P} α], where α denotes time t, presupposes a transition within a contextually salient interval I, between a maximal initial subinterval, I_{NEG}, in which the modified by *until*^{P} α is not instantiated and a minimal final subinterval, I_{POS}, in which it is, and uncertainty about when the transition occurred. α is associated with a set of alternatives, Alt_α, including α itself. The alternatives denote disjoint subintervals of I, which are epistemic alternatives for when the phase transition from I_{NEG} to I_{POS} might have occurred.[2] For example, the modifier *until noon* in (2a) presupposes that a contextually familiar interval I is divisible into a maximal interval I_{NEG} within which she didn't arrive, and a minimal interval I_{POS} in which she did. Since the time of the transition is not settled, in different possibilities I_{NEG} extends up to, and I_{POS} starts at, different times that are elements of Alt_{noon}. The assertive contribution of punctual *until* is that the modified eventuality description, in this case `she arrive`, is instantiated in the interval $[lb(I), t)$ which stretches from the left boundary of I up to, but not including, t (forming a convex interval with t). In (2a), where negation has to scope over *until*, the assertion is that it is not the case that `she arrive` is instantiated within $[lb(I), t)$ The non-cancellable inference, that she arrived at noon or later, arises, as in Karttunen's analysis, as an entailment of the assertion given the presupposition. Since it is presupposed that she arrived within an interval stretching from $lb(I)$ to one of the times in Alt_{noon}, and given the assertion that she did not arrive within $[lb(I), \texttt{noon})$ it follows that, if the sentence is true, she arrived at noon or later.[3]

Condoravdi's (2008) analysis of durative *until* is that, like punctual *until*, [*until*^{D} α], where α denotes time t, delivers an interval that stretches from the left boundary of a contextual interval I up to t. Durative *until* requires an atelic predicate and it asserts that this pred-

[2] This is a (generalized) reconstruction of Karttunen's disjunctive presupposition.

[3] The inference that she arrived at noon and not later is argued to be a pragmatic scalar inference, see Condoravdi (2008) for discussion.

icate is true of the interval $[lb(I), t)$. This means that both punctual and durative *until* expand the time that is given by their complement backwards but differ in the kind of modifier they produce. Punctual *until* forms a frame modifier, while durative *until* forms modifier. Durative *until* can scope over and under negation, yielding the throughout-not and the not-throughout readings, respectively. For durative *until* any further implications about the predicate not holding of a bigger interval, one that extends past the time specified by its complement, arise pragmatically, hence the contrast in (4).

The assumption that durative and punctual *until* are two different lexical items is not uncontroversial, but there are good arguments for making it in addition to the contrast in (4) (see Condoravdi (2008) for elaboration of, and extensive arguments against, the alternatives). One familiar argument is that various languages draw a lexical distinction between punctual and durative *until*. A more indirect argument is that analyses like Karttunen's and Condoravdi's, in which punctual *until*, but not its durative counterpart, is associated with a presupposition of change within a temporal interval, naturally relate this item to a family of polarity sensitive, scalar items that serve as its counterparts in other languages, such as German *erst* (Löbner (1989), see Condoravdi (2008) for discussion). We point out here another argument, namely that, in English, punctual and durative *until* can be distinguished by their interaction with the scalar particles *only* and *even*. While durative *until*, which is not inherently scalar, can be modified by both particles, as in (5a) and (6a), punctual *until*, which is inherently scalar, cannot be modified by either.

(5) a. She stayed only until noon.
    b. She didn't arrive (#only) until noon.

(6) a. She stayed even until after they closed for the night.
    b. She didn't arrive (#even) until after they closed for the night.

On the type of analysis of punctual *until* described above, this contrast is natural and anticipated. Since durative *until* only contributes information about the duration of an event, it can naturally be contrasted with potential longer durations (in the case of *only*) or shorter ones (in the case of *even*). Punctual *until*, on the other hand, contributes information about which of a set of alternative times is the earliest time at which a presupposed transition occurs. The kind of scalar information that *even* and *only* would supply is already lexically encoded by punctual *until*. Since there cannot be more than one earliest time in a set of times (one time cannot be more or less earliest than another), there is no way to build more scalarity on top of the lexically encoded one for *only* and *even* to operate on.

An issue raised by Condoravdi (2008) but left unresolved is why (2a) does not have a reading without the actualization implication. Such a reading should be available on a construal with durative *until* scoping over negation. One potential line of explanation is that $until^D$ selects for predicates with a property other than divisive reference, which would differentiate between negated atelic and negated telic predicates. Another potential line of explanation exploits the truth-conditional equivalence of $until^D$ and $until^P$ in this configuration and attributes the unavailability of $until^D$ to the principle of Maximize Presupposition (Heim 1991), construed in such a way so that competition is between logical forms.

5.3 *Until* without Negation

This section presents a host of cases in which an *until*-phrase modifies a predicate in the absence of negation, giving rise to non-cancelable inferences similar to — though, not identical to — those found with punctual *until*, but not found with durative *until*.

The attested example in (7a) and that in (7b) involve a telic verb with an indefinite plural subject with a cardinality specification. The sentential predicate is arguably also telic, as seen by the contrasts in (8). This implies that the *until* seen here is not a durative *until*, which, like *for*, would be incompatible with such a clausal predicate.

(7) a. Hundreds died until the epidemic ran its course.[4]
b. Dozens of solicitors came by my house until I put up the 'no soliciting' sign.

(8) a. Hundreds died in just a few minutes.
b. # Hundreds died for a few hours.
c. Dozens of solicitors came by my house in a short time.
d. # Dozens of solicitors came by my house for a long time.

(7a) and (7b) imply that there was a steady stream of deaths or visits of solicitors to my house before the time specified by the temporal clause. In addition, (7a) gives rise to the inference that after the epidemic ran its course, the rate of epidemic-induced deaths decreased. Similarly, (7b) gives rise to the inference that once the 'no soliciting' sign was put up, visits from solicitors stopped or at least decreased. In both cases, the inference is not cancellable. Admittedly, in the case

[4] Sheldon H. Harris, Factories of Death: Japanese biological warfare and the American coverup, London: Routledge, 1994, p. 97

of (7a) there is strong pragmatic pressure for this inference. But the same kind of inference can be observed when the content of the temporal clause is independent from that of the main clause, as in (9), where government intervention could have been ineffectual, in which case the rate of deaths would have continued unchanged, or it could have increased the number of deaths just as well as decreased them.

(9) Hundreds died until the government intervened.

The examples in (10) involve the upward entailing determiner *many* on a cardinal reading. The inference in (10a) is that once the conference started, the number of people I managed to talk to dropped, in (10b) that once the course requirements were made public registration dropped.

(10) a. I managed to talk to many people until the conference started.
b. Many students registered for the class until I posted the course requirements.

In (11) the subject NP features the quantifier *more and more*, which expresses, roughly, that the cardinality of the intersection of its restrictor and scope sets increases over time. The non-cancellable inference here is that the increase in registration ended once the course requirements were posted.

(11) More and more people registered for the class until I posted the course requirements.

The same kind of inference of change can be observed when the main clause features a downward entailing expression, except in the opposite direction. In (12), the subject NP contains the downward entailing determiner *few*. The inference in (12a) is that once Hungary opened the border, the number of people who managed to leave increased. In (12b), it is that once the course was advertised the number of registrations increased. The type of inference seen with (12a) and (12b) shows up even in (12c) and (12d), where it is pragmatically less plausible. (12d) suggests, for example, that discouraging the students from taking the class had the opposite effect.

(12) a. Few people managed to leave until Hungary opened its border.
b. Few students registered for the class until I advertised the course.
c. Few people managed to leave until Hungary closed its border.
d. Few students registered for the class until I started discouraging them from taking it.

The non-cancellability of the inferences with these instances of *until* can be observed by considering the contrast between *until* and other frame adverbials with similar meanings. The same inferences that arise with *until* arise with *before*, but with *before* they are clearly cancellable, as shown by (13) and (14).

(13) a. I managed to contact many people before the conference started, and many more later.
b. #I managed to contact many people until the conference started, and many more later.

(14) a. Few people managed to leave before Hungary closed its border and no one afterwards.
b. #Few people managed to leave until Hungary closed its border and no one afterwards.

(15) shows a similar contrast between *until* clauses in the relevant (non-negated) context and the temporal modifier *over the course of the summer*.

(15) a. #Many people registered until early registration was over, and many more afterward.
b. Many people registered over the course of the summer, and many more afterwards.

5.4 Liminal *until*

The descriptive generalization emerging from the previous section is that liminal *until* is, like punctual *until*, a non-durative frame adverbial which, unlike its durative counterpart, gives rise to uncancellable inferences. Liminal *until*, however, differs from punctual *until* in two respects. First, it is not polarity sensitive. Second, the inference it gives rise to is not always **actualization**, but a more general inference of transition. For example, (12a) above does not give rise to the inference that few people managed to leave Hungary overall. Rather, liminal *until* can be said to give rise to an inference of a transition, a change in polarity, within the contextual interval, with respect to the matrix sentence radical. Something that was the case up to the time specified by the *until* phrase is no longer the case afterwards, or else something that was not the case becomes the case. This section discusses the implications of these findings for the analysis of *until*.

The emergent description of liminal *until* raises two interrelated problems. The first is how to characterize and derive the general transition inference it gives rise to, relating it to that of punctual *until*, which, ideally, would come out to be a special case. The second is explicating the particular transitions that are inferred in the cases that do not feature negation. This latter problem is especially acute in the cases featuring upward monotone quantifiers, in which the inferred transition seems to be the opposite of actualization of a property of eventualities expressed by the matrix sentence radical. For example, if it was true that dozens of solicitors came by my place until just before I put up a 'no soliciting' sign, then it remains equally true within any larger interval ending at any later point that dozens of solicitors came by my house, even if solicitors stopped coming after the sign went up.

Extending existing analyses devised only for the case of punctual *until* to the more general liminal *until* is, therefore, not straightforward. Analyses that rely crucially on the presence of negation are clearly non-starters, since none of the cases discussed above feature negation. Analyses that only recognize a durative *until* face the same problem here as they do in the case of negation. Even when the matrix clauses feature atelic predicates, positing that the predicate in examples like (12a), repeated here as (16), is in the scope of durative *until* provides no way of explaining the key property such examples share with sentences featuring punctual *until*, namely that the inference it gives rise to, that the number of people who managed to leave Hungary *after* the border opened increased, is indefeasible.[5]

(16) Few people managed to leave until Hungary opened its border.

Karttunen's (1974) analysis discussed above also cannot be easily extended to cover liminal *until*, since the presupposition and assertion he proposes will not yield the desired inference. Applying Karttunen's analysis, one would say that this sentence presupposes that few people managed to leave Hungary either before or when it opened its border. The assertion would be that few people managed to leave before Hungary opened its borders. This assertion, however, does not in any way lead to any indefeasible inference about how many, if any, people managed to leave after the border was opened. generated.

Applying Condoravdi's (2008) analysis to (16) would yield the presupposition that there is a transition within a contextually supplied interval I, containing the time of Hungary opening its border. The transition is with respect to the property expressed by the clausal predicate

[5]Given the atelicity of the clausal predicate in (16), the question arises what excludes a construal with durative *until* in this case. This is the same kind of question as the one raised at the end of section 5.2, namely why (2a) does not have a reading without the actualization implication. Whatever explanation is the proper one for the original case would also apply to liminal *until*.

and based on the truth-conditional content the time of the transition is implied to be no earlier than the opening of the border. The presupposed transition is further specified to be from a maximal initial subinterval I_{NEG} of I not satisfying the property corresponding to the matrix clause, to a minimal final subinterval I_{POS} satisfying it. This presupposition, however, is contradicted by the asserted content. Assuming that the property of intervals expressed by the matrix sentence is the property of containing few events of people leaving Hungary, the presupposed transition ends up being from an interval in which there are many events of leaving (that is, not few), to one in which there are few. However, according to the asserted content, the first phase of the interval, the subinterval of I that ends just before the opening of the border, is an interval in which few departures occurred.

We contend that what is needed to allow Condoravdi's analysis to capture liminal *until* is a generalization of the nature of the presupposition. Liminal *until* presupposes that the interval extending from a contextual left boundary to the time mentioned in the temporal clause contrasts with all of its relevant superintervals with respect to the instantiation of a property associated with the matrix clause. Relaxing the requirement that $I_{\text{NEG}} \prec I_{\text{POS}}$, allowing instead the two phases to occur in either order, the assertive content of (16) would determine that the interval stretching from $lb(I)$ to a time just before Hungary opens its borders, $[lb(I), t_{open})$, is an improper subinterval of I_{POS} ($[lb(I), t_{open}) \subseteq I_{\text{POS}}$) and scalar reasoning determines that $[lb(I), t_{open})$ is identical to I_{POS}. If the interval $[lb(I), t_{open})$ is the maximal interval within which only few people managed to leave, then this implies that more people left within the interval $[t_{open}, rb(I)]$,[6] that is after Hungary opened its border. The analysis can capitalize on the fact that the truth of a sentence with a downward monotone quantifier is not persistent over superintervals.

Intuitively speaking, (16) border marked a change in the number of people leaving and presupposes that, within the contextually relevant interval starting at some left boundary l_B, there is a change in the number of events of leaving Hungary, and that this change happens within an interval ending in one of the alternative times to the time t_{open} at which Hungary opens its borders (including t_{open} itself). The assertion is that the number of events of leaving Hungary within the interval ending just before t_{open} is low. Given the presupposition, this leads to the inference that within some interval beginning in l_B and ending at the time t_{open} at which Hungary opened its borders, or perhaps later,

[6] $rb(I)$ is the right boundary of I.

the number of events of leaving Hungary is not low, and hence that it has increased, which is the desired inference.

Under these assumptions, punctual *until* is indeed just a special case of liminal *until*, the special case that arises when the interval extending from a contextual left boundary to the time mentioned in the temporal clause is asserted to not instantiate the property of intervals expressed by the matrix clause. With a telic predicate and no quantifiers, as in the classic cases considered in the literature and exemplified by (2), the temporal ordering between I_{NEG} and I_{POS} has to be $I_{\text{NEG}} \prec I_{\text{POS}}$. On the ordering $I_{\text{POS}} \prec I_{\text{NEG}}$, the asserted and the presuppositional content of the sentence would be in conflict, just like we saw above for (16) in the case where $I_{\text{NEG}} \prec I_{\text{POS}}$. On this view then, the apparent polarity sensitivity of punctual *until* is due to the fact that only under negation are its asserted and presuppositional contents compatible. Whether a language has liminal or only punctual *until* depends on how specific the presuppositional content of its *until* is. If the presupposition requires that $I_{\text{NEG}} \prec I_{\text{POS}}$, then the language has only punctual *until*. If the presupposition is more general, requiring only that a transition occur, thus allowing for either temporal ordering, the language has the more general liminal *until*.[7]

The cases that remain problematic are the ones involving upward entailing cardinals, such as (7b), repeated in (17).

(17) Dozens of solicitors came by my house until I put up the 'no soliciting' sign.

Specifically, what needs to be explicated is what property of intervals features in the presupposed contrast in these cases and how it is to be extracted from the matrix clause. Taking this property to simply be instantiation of the property of eventualities encoded by the matrix sentence radical would yield the wrong results. The reason is that the analysis proposed would then generate the inference that, within an interval ending at the time when I put up the sign or later, it is false that dozens of solicitor came by my house. This, however, will be false in any context in which (17) is true, since by the time the sign was put up, the dozens of visits have already occurred, and this remains true throughout any longer interval.

What seems to be required here is a way to extract from the matrix sentence, `dozens of solicitors come by my house`, a property that can be said to hold within an interval ending just before the sign was put up, but not persisting through longer intervals. Intuitively formulated,

---

[7]It may well be that what we observe in English is a change in progress, where *until*'s presuppositional content has been generalized.

the required property of intervals is the property of containing regular visits by solicitors at a certain rate, a rate that, over a period of the same length as the interval stretching from l_B to the time at which the sign was put up, yields dozens of visits. Presumably, this is the same kind of property of intervals as features in assertions in the progressive, such as (18).

(18) Dozens of people are visiting the museum these days (but it might not last).

Given such a property, the analysis would yield the desired results. For (17), for example, the inference would be that the interval stretching from l_B up to but not including the time at which the sign was put up contrasts with all of its alternative superintervals in showing such a rate of visits. Putting up the sign generates a drop in the rate, making it the case that for all intervals that extend beyond the time at which the sign was put up, the overall rate of visits is one that does not generate dozens of visits for an interval of the same length as the period from l_B up to the hanging of the sign.

We leave the puzzle of how to extract such a property in a general way that works for all cases, and within a compositional framework, as a present to Lauri and a prospect for future work.

References

Bassa-Vanrell, Maria del Mar. 2017. *Scope, Scalarity, and Polarity in Aspectual Marking: The case of English 'until' and Spanish 'hasta'*. Ph.D. thesis, University of Texas at Austin.

Condoravdi, Cleo. 2008. Punctual *Until* as a scalar NPI. In S. Inkelas and K. Hanson, eds., *The Nature of the Word: Essays in honor of Paul Kiparsky*, pages 631–655. Cambridge, Mass: MIT Press.

de Swart, Henriëtte. 1996. Meaning and use of *not ... until*. *Journal of Semantics* 13(3):221–263.

Declerck, Renaat. 1995. The problem of *not ... until*. *Linguistics* 33(1):51–98.

Giannakidou, Anastasia. 2002. UNTIL, Aspect, and Negation: A Novel Argument for Two Untils. *Semantics and Linguistic Theory (SALT)* 12:84–103.

Heim, Irene. 1991. Artikel und Definitheit [Articles and definiteness]. In A. von Stechow and D. Wunderlich, eds., *Semantik: Ein internationales Handbuch der zeitgenössischen Forschung*, pages 487—-535. Berlin: de Gruyter.

Heinämäki, Orvokki. 1974. *Semantics of English Temporal Connectives*. Ph.D. thesis, University of Texas at Austin.

Hitzeman, Janet. 1991. Aspect and adverbials. *Semantics and Linguistic Theory (SALT)* 1:107–126.

Horn, Lawrence. 1970. Ain't it hard (anymore). In *Papers from the 6th regional meeting of the Chicago Linguistic Society (CLS 6)*, pages 318–327.

Horn, Laurence. 1972. *On the Semantic Properties of Logical Operators in English*. Ph.D. thesis, University of California, Los Angeles.

Israel, Michael. 2011. *The Grammar of Polarity: Pragmatics, Sensitivity, and the Logic of Scales*. Cambridge: Cambridge University Press.

Karttunen, Lauri. 1974. Until. In *Papers from the 10th regional meeting of the Chicago Linguistic Society (CLS 10)*, pages 283–297.

Klima, Edward S. 1964. Negation in English. In J. A. Fodor and J. J. Katz, eds., *The Structure of Language: Readings in the Philosophy of Language*, pages 246–323. Englewood Cliffs, N.J.: Prentice-Hall.

Löbner, Sebastian. 1989. German *Schon - Erst - Noch*: An integrated analysis. *Linguistics and Philosophy* 12(2):167–212.

Mittwoch, Anita. 1977. Negative sentences with *until*. In *Papers from the 13th regional meeting of the Chicago Linguistic Society (CLS 13)*, pages 410–417.

Tovena, Lucia. 1996. *Studies on Polarity Sensitivity*. Ph.D. thesis, University of Edinburgh.

6

Talking about (Quasi-)Higher-Order Uncertainty

DANIEL LASSITER

6.1 Introduction

Theories of the lexical semantics of modal language live in the shadow of modal logic. Being a junior partner in this relationship has many advantages for us linguists: we get to make use of technical results that come from modal logic, and we benefit from the linguistic insights of smart philosophers, many of whom might not bother with natural language if they didn't think that modal expressions hold some philosophical interest. Still, the technical apparatus of modal logic was developed by people whose main academic interest was definitely not the lexical semantics of one corner of the vocabulary of a single Germanic dialect. For those of us who do (for whatever reason) care deeply about the vocabulary of English for its own sake, we should of course be cautious about borrowing *in toto* theories that were designed to elucidate philosophical issues—issues whose import does not depend on the quirks of any natural language. For each such case, it is important to examine the borrowed theory carefully in order to ensure that its empirical predictions make sense of the grammatical and inferential properties of the item in question.

Lauri Karttunen was perhaps the first linguist to make this point clearly and forcefully, in his "Possible and Must" (Karttunen, 1972). He did so by exploring an extension of Hintikka (1962)'s influential logic of knowledge and belief to English expressions of epistemic modality—*possible, may, perhaps, must,* and *have to* among others—and showing

Tokens of Meaning: Papers in Honor of Lauri Karttunen.
Cleo Condoravdi and Tracy Holloway King (eds.).

that the empirical predictions of the extended theory failed to match up with the intuitive interpretations of the English expressions in various ways. Lauri was careful to emphasize that these findings only impugned the application of standard systems of modal logic to the lexical semantics of epistemic modals in English: "I will argue that the principles on which our use of *possible* and *must* in ordinary language appears to be based are different from any of the well known standard systems that have been studied by logicians" (p.3). The same systems could still be relevant to the lexical semantics of other items, and to the elucidation of philosophical issues that are independent of the semantics of English: "[T]his is an interesting fact about ordinary language, but it should not be misconstrued as evidence against other modal systems" (ibid.).

Lauri's insights in "Possible and Must" have generated a significant literature, especially around his novel observation that the intuitive interpretation of *must* is weaker than that of the necessity operator in standard modal logics of knowledge. A few of the papers in this still-growing collection are Groenendijk and Stokhof 1975, Kratzer 1991, von Fintel and Gillies 2010, Lassiter 2016, Mandelkern 2016, Goodhue 2018. Thanks to "Possible and Must", there is now a consensus among linguists that *must* differs in some important ways from the $\Box$ operator of modal logic S5—though there is still no consensus about exactly what the difference is. S5 is the most obvious way to interpret linguists' usual gloss of *must, might, perhaps, possible* etc. as $\forall$- or $\exists$-quantifiers over a "set of epistemically possible worlds" which contains the actual world. Under certain common (though not uncontroversial) assumptions, these quantifiers correspond to the $\Box$ or $\Diamond$ of a normal modal logic where accessibility is an equivalence relation (reflexive, transitive, and symmetric).

In this paper I want to talk about another property of epistemic modals in English that apparently differentiates them from the S5 modal operators: the fact that they can be nested in a non-trivial way. A key property of S5 is that iterated modals reduce to the innermost. For example,

$$\Box\Box\phi \Leftrightarrow \Box\phi$$
$$\Box\Diamond\phi \Leftrightarrow \Diamond\phi$$
$$\Box\Diamond\Box\phi \Leftrightarrow \Box\phi,$$

and so on. In S5, piling modal operators on top of an already modalized formula has no semantic effect. This is due to the fact that accessibility in S5 is an equivalence relation. The worlds accessible from w are exactly the same as the worlds accessible from any world accessible from

w. If all of the worlds you can access in one step from w verify ϕ, then all of the worlds you can access in two steps will also verify ϕ. So, $\Box\phi$ holds at w if and only if $\Box\Box\phi$ does.

However, as Moss (2015, 2018) discusses in detail, this property does not seem to characterize English accurately. In examples like those in (1), there are two epistemic expressions, one of which takes scope immediately above the other. Yet both appear to make a separate contribution to the meaning of the sentence, in violation of the S5 principle that the epistemic expression that takes wider scope should be semantically vacuous.

(1) a. This book is an odyssey, a journey up through the mists of time from the remote past. It ... explores what must perhaps be the most fundamental of all questions — who we are. (Dunbar, 2004, p. 7)

b. Alice is a likely hire, and Bob might be a likely hire. (Moss, 2015)

c. "At this point, it's probably unlikely that we'll trade Doc," Ricciardi said Tuesday. (*San Jose Mercury News*, 7/21/2009)

This paper is an interim report on a project with two main components. Taking a probabilistic perspective on epistemic modality, I attempt to connect the interpretation of nested epistemics with theories of uncertainty that have been developed in philosophy and psychology, but without a focus on natural language. I then report on a study that explores the distribution of examples following the pattern in (1) in a large corpus of *New York Times* articles. I suggest that the examples of nested epistemics found in this corpus vary in the kind of uncertainty involved: in most of them, one or both of the modals is not epistemic (talking about information) but rather objective ('worldly', 'stochastic': talking about chance as a genuine feature of an indeterministic world). If this is right, then many or most naturalistic examples that follow the pattern in (1) do not technically constitute counter-examples to the S5 reduction property, because one or both of the modal operators is not being interpreted epistemically. While there are a few examples where true higher-order uncertainty may be implicated, I will suggest that the lower modal in these examples may be interpreted by 'objectivizing' the relevant probability measure, treating it as a contingent feature of the world rather than as a contextually fixed parameter of evaluation.

If the tentative generalizations floated here about the interpretation of nested epistemics hold up, then we have a situation that is interestingly different from the cases that Lauri discussed in his groundbreaking 1972 paper. There, Lauri showed that certain intuitions derived from the study of epistemic logic were misleading and should be discarded when doing modal semantics for English. Here, we have a case where what appears to be a straightforward counter-example to the S5 reduction property—cases where such modals are nested but both make a semantic contribution—may not constitute a counter-example after all. Instead, it points to an interesting ambiguity in the kind of uncertainty that "epistemic" expressions trade in.

6.2 A Compositional Puzzle

When dealing with examples like (1), these are some key questions that we need to resolve:

A) What do these sentences mean?

B) How can we define a compositional interpretation procedure for the meanings in (A)?

C) How do the meanings of uncertainty expressions relate to what we know about the psychological representation of uncertainty?

Compositionality is a crucial principle that should guide our investigation. That is, it is desirable to have a single theory of the meaning potential that *probably* contributes in examples (2a) and (2b)—not just methodologically, but also psychologically because such an analysis helps to explain the productive use and interpretation of modal language.

(2) a. The time is now near at hand, which must probably determine whether Americans are to be free men or slaves ... (G. Washington)[1]

b. This time will probably determine whether Americans are to be free men or slaves.

I will assume that unembedded *probable, probably*, and *likely* are interpreted as indicating that the proposition that it embeds has high probability (Yalcin, 2005, 2007, 2010, Swanson, 2006, 2015, Lassiter, 2010, 2015, 2017). Roughly:

(3) probably $\phi \Leftrightarrow P(\phi) > .5$

A probabilistic interpretation is also appropriate for complex expressions built from *probable* and *likely* such as *improbable, very likely, probability*, and *more likely than not*: see Lassiter 2015, 2017 for compositional details.

[1] Example borrowed from Moss (2015). The quote is from a speech delivered on August 26, 1776, before the Battle of Long Island.

In addition, I will assume—rather more controversially—that certain other epistemic expressions including *possible, might, must* and *certain* are also interpreted directly in terms of probabilities. *Possible* and *might* mean roughly probability greater than 0, and *certain* and *must* mean probability 1 or something close to it. For a detailed analysis of these expressions and their relationship to *probable* and *likely* see Lassiter 2015, 2016, 2017. If you do not like the latter set of assumptions, feel free to think of it as a simplification for expository purposes, holding place for a more elaborate theory which captures the probabilistic entailments of these expressions in a more complicated way.

The question, then, is how to embed the interpretation of *probably* etc. in a way that correctly predicts the interpretation of Washington's utterance in (2a). In principle, there is a straightforward way to make this happen: we can treat probabilities as being dependent on both the context and the world of evaluation. For example, we might suppose that example (1c) has roughly the truth-conditions sketched in (7).

(4) *It's unlikely that we'll trade Doc* is true in context c, relative to world w, iff $P_{c,w}$, the probability measure associated with the beliefs of the speaker in c, assigns a value less than .5 to the proposition that "we" will trade Doc.

This kind of meaning would embed smoothly:

(5) *It's probably unlikely that we'll trade Doc* is true in context c', relative to world w', iff $P_{c',w'}$ assigns a value greater than .5 to the proposition generated by abstracting over the world variable in the interpretation of (7).

More compactly:

$$[\![1c]\!]^{c',w'} = 1 \text{ iff } P_{c',w'}(\{w \mid P_{c',w}(\textbf{we trade Doc}) < .5\}) > .5$$

On this approach, the probability measure associated with *unlikely* is world-dependent. So, we can abstract over the world variable and associate *unlikely to trade Doc* with an ordinary proposition: the set of worlds where the probabilistic beliefs of (e.g.) the speaker assign low credence to a trade.[2]

There are several reasons to be skeptical of this interpretation of (1c). Most importantly, it does not quite capture the right meaning.

[2]Of course, we might want to relax the assumption that the probability measure is uniquely associated with the speaker, reverting to, say, some kind of group belief. There are decent arguments for thinking of epistemic modals in this way, but it does not help here: the speaker of (1c) is equally unlikely to resolve his uncertainty about whether a trade is unlikely by polling the opinions of others around him, except inasmuch as they are informative about relevant worldly matters.

According to (5), *It's probably unlikely that we'll trade Doc* expresses the speaker's uncertainty about his own beliefs. In the context of the example—reporting a sports manager's deliberations about staffing—this is not what the speaker of (1c) seems to intend. If it were, the right way to resolve his uncertainty about Doc's prospects on the team would be soul-searching: to try to get clear about his own beliefs so that he could be sure whether he thought trading Doc was truly unlikely. However, the example does not convey the kind of epistemic self-doubt that interpretation (5) implies. The manager is more likely to resolve his uncertainty by keeping tabs on Doc's performance and other such worldly matters. In other words, example (1c) does not seem to express a failure of introspection, but rather uncertainty about how future events will unfold and so influence an eventual decision. This is the first hint of an idea that I will explore in more detail below: the interpretation of nested modal *unlikely* is not about anyone's credence, but about certain features of the world that are considered indeterminate and chancy.

Concerns about how to capture agreement and disagreement provide a second reason to question whether probabilistic expressions really make reference to anything like a context-and-world-dependent measure $P_{c,w}$. (See, for example, Knobe and Yalcin 2014 and references therein.) If two people argue about whether it is likely to rain, it does not seem right to suppose either that they are arguing about what one of them believes, or that they are talking about their own beliefs and thus really not disagreeing. This is an old puzzle that has generated a significant literature, and I do not want to add to it here—except to point out that many thinkers have suggested that disagreement phenomena problematize the assumption that the world and context of evaluation jointly determine an information state relevant to evaluation. If they do not, then we may not be justified in assuming that epistemic sentences are always determinately true or false in a given context. In other words, the content of epistemic sentences may not always be associated with a classical proposition. The resolution of this contentious debate will bear heavily on the question of whether the simple-minded account of embedded epistemics sketched above is tenable.

Yalcin (2007) provides a now-famous argument against associating matrix epistemic expressions with a world-bound interpretation (along with several further arguments that I will not review here). If the interpretation described above were right, there should be a proposition associated with sentences like (6):

(6) It rained yesterday but it's unlikely that it rained yesterday.

Yalcin dubs these "epistemic contradictions". They contrast with merely Moore's-paradoxical sentences (e.g., *It rained yesterday but I don't believe that it did*) in that the latter embed sensibly in contexts where epistemic contradictions remain odd.

(7) a. ✓ Suppose that it rained yesterday but I don't believe that it did.

b. # Suppose that it rained yesterday but it's unlikely that it did.

(7a) makes perfect sense: we are asked to consider a situation where I fail to believe something true. In contrast, (7b) remains bizarre. The world-bound interpretation of epistemic expressions sketched above predicts a reasonable meaning for it, though: we are asked to suppose that we are in a world w which has the characteristics that (a) it rained, and (b) the speaker (group, etc.) assigns low credence to the proposition that it rained. So, (7b) should have a sensible interpretation akin to "Suppose that it rained yesterday but I (we, etc.) doubt that it did".

Yalcin (2007)'s solution relies on a different parameterization of the semantic evaluation function, where epistemic modals are associated with an information state that is not determined by the world of evaluation. For present purposes, we can treat this as a probability measure that is directly supplied as a parameter of evaluation. In effect, Yalcin replaces the schema (8) that we assumed above with (9).

(8) $[\![\phi \text{ is likely}]\!]^{c,w} = 1 \text{ iff } P_{c,w}([\![\phi]\!]^{c,w}) > .5$

(9) $[\![\phi \text{ is likely}]\!]^{c,w,P} = 1 \text{ iff } P([\![\phi]\!]^{c,w,P}) > .5$

Since worlds and probability measures are independent parameters of evaluation, they can now be shifted independently by embedding operators. Yalcin's explanation for the oddity of (7b) makes crucial use of this fact. The embedding verb *suppose* not only operates on the world parameter, but also on the probability measure. In effect[3]:

(10) $[\![x \text{ supposes } \phi]\!]^{c,w,P} = 1 \text{ iff } \forall w' \in S(x,w)\text{: } [\![\phi]\!]^{c,w',P(\cdot|S(x,w))}$,

where $S(x,w)$ is the set of worlds compatible with what x is supposing at world w, and $P(\cdot \mid S(x,w))$ is the probability-measure parameter restricted to the set of worlds compatible with what x is supposing at w. Crucially, we do *not* interpret the embedded occurrence of ϕ relative to a probability measure associated with the universally-quantified world

[3]This presentation is somewhat modified and simplified from Yalcin's official system, but it should be enough to make the crucial point that epistemic contradictions can be used to motivate a non-world-bound interpretation of subjective probability expressions.

variable (like so: $\forall w' \in S(x, w) : [\![\phi]\!]^{c,w',P_{c,w}}$). Instead the P-parameter is modified so as to reflect the global changes in information required by supposing that it's raining.

The payoff of these modifications is that it predicts the contrast in (7) between embedded Moore's-paradoxical sentences and epistemic contradictions. To fulfill the order in (7a), you have to make sure that (11) is satisfied:

(11) $\forall w' \in S(\textbf{you}, w)$: $[\![\text{rain yesterday}]\!]^{c,w',P'}$ and $[\![\text{I don't believe (rain yesterday)}]\!]^{c,w',P'}$,

where $P' = P(\cdot \mid S(\textbf{you}, w))$. This is readily satisfiable. On the other hand, (7b) requires you to suppose something impossible:

(12) $\forall w' \in S(\textbf{you}, w) : [\![\text{rain yesterday}]\!]^{c,w',P'}$ and $[\![\text{(rain yesterday) is unlikely}]\!]^{c,w',P'}$
$= \forall w' \in S(\textbf{you}, w) : [\![\text{rain yesterday}]\!]^{c,w',P'}$ and $P'([\![\text{rain yesterday}]\!]^{c,w',P'}) < .5$

Recall that P' is P conditioned on the set of worlds compatible with what is being supposed. So, to fulfill the condition in (12) one would have to find a set of supposition-worlds with the property that it rained in each, but the probability of rain conditional on these same supposition-worlds is low. It is not possible to fulfill this command because the probability of rain, conditional on a set of worlds in which it is raining, can only be 1. This accounts for the oddity of (7b), in contrast to the unremarkable (7a).

The key property of Yalcin's system that makes this solution possible is the presence of independently shiftable parameters providing a world of evaluation and a relevant informational background (probability measure). Now, this account has been challenged on both empirical and theoretical grounds: see Dorr and Hawthorne 2013, Moss 2015, Stojnić 2017, Ninan 2018, Mandelkern 2018. Rather than considering whether there is some way out, I would like to consider what Yalcin's conclusion implies for the analysis of nested epistemics like *probably unlikely*. Here it is:

(13) $[\![\text{probably (unlikely } \phi)]\!]^{c,w,P} = 1$ iff $\text{P}(\{w' \mid [\![\text{unlikely } \phi]\!]^{c,w',P}\}) > .5$
$= 1$ iff $P(\{w' \mid P(\{w'' \mid [\![\phi]\!]^{c,w'',P}\}) < .5\}) > .5$

Note that nothing in the interpretation of ϕ depends on the variable w' that is extracted over in the interpretation of the outer modal *probably*. As a result the set of worlds w' that verify the condition $P(\{w'' \mid [\![\phi]\!]^{c,w'',P}\}) < .5$ is either all of them (if this condition holds) or none of them (if it fails). If the condition holds and all worlds have this property, the outer condition has probability 1 and the sentence is true. If it fails and no worlds have this property, the outer condition has probability 0 and the sentence is false. In effect, *It's probably unlikely that we'll trade Doc* is true if and only if *It's unlikely that we'll trade Doc* is.

In general, the prediction of Yalcin's domain semantics is that the interpretation of nested probability operators should be controlled by the meaning of the innermost operator. This is very close to the S5 reduction property discussed above.[4] As we observed above, this prediction does not seem to be correct for nested epistemics: both modals make separate contributions to the meaning of *It's probably unlikely that we'll trade Doc.*

Accepting Yalcin's analysis puts us in a bind, then: getting the right interpretation of epistemics embedded under attitude verbs like *suppose* seems to require a semantics that makes the wrong prediction when epistemics are embedded under other epistemics. Moss (2015, 2018) responds to this tension by proposing a radically revised semantic theory built around sets of probability measures, with deep revisions to the type-theoretic properties of the system, the interpretations of connectives, and a number of other adjustments. While Moss' system is attractive in many ways and has significant philosophical motivation, I want to explore whether it is possible to account for the interpretation of nested epistemics in a way that is compatible with Yalcin's explanation of epistemic contradictions, without major revisions to other aspects of the semantic theory.

In what follows I will explore the idea that we can deal with nested epistemics by importing a distinction among several different kinds of probability. These distinctions have considerable independent philosophical, psychological, and linguistic motivation. Independence of the probability measure from the world of evaluation makes sense for one prominent kind of probability, subjective credence. However, epistemic language can also make reference to mind-independent features of the

[4]Indeed, Yalcin's system has an intimate connection to S5: "informational consequence" as he defines it is equivalent to necessary consequence in S5, i.e., classical consequence when a $\Box$ is prefixed to every sentence. See Schulz 2010 for a detailed discussion of this point.

There is an extra wrinkle when we expand the account to include probability operators. If the outer modal is a downward-monotone probability operator that excludes probability 1—such as *unlikely* or *less than 30% probability*—it maps a true inner condition to false because it has probability 1, and a false inner condition to true because it has probability 0. In effect, downward monotone nesting probability operators function as negation. Sentences where the outermost operator is non-monotone—like *exactly 50% chance* or *between 80 and 90% likely*—are predicted to be trivially false since they exclude both probability 0 and probability 1, which are the only values available in a vacuous abstraction.

world—facts about propensity and about the distribution of properties in a class—that are conceptually determined by objective features of the world of evaluation. On the account that I will pursue, epistemics that are nested under other epistemics generally take on one of these worldly interpretations. This gives us a surprisingly simple theoretical account of these initially vexing constructions: nested epistemics are generally associated with ordinary propositions and embed just like non-modal sentences. In addition, it allows us to maintain Yalcin's account of epistemic contradictions while also leaving room for non-trivializing interpretations of nested epistemics.

To begin, I will discuss how the distinction between various kinds of probability has been made in philosophy and psychology, and then use this discussion to inform the classification of some examples drawn from a large corpus of news text.

6.3 Two Kinds of Probability

Philosophers of probability have distinguished between subjective and objective probability (e.g., Hacking 1975, Lewis 1980, Gillies 2000). Subjective probability, also known as "credence" or "degree of belief", is a property of individuals' psychological states. Pure subjective uncertainty might involve questions about unique events that have a determinate answer, but for which we lack certain key information. For example, I have no idea whether Plato was taller than Aristotle, but I do know that there is a determinate answer to this question. My uncertainty is of the purely subjective type.

Objective probability, also known as "chance" or "propensity", is a non-psychological property of the world. A truly stochastic event—say, the time that it takes for a certain radioactive particle to decay—is intrinsically chancy, independent of what anyone believes about it, or indeed whether any agents exist. Along similar lines, the particle might be said to have a certain propensity to decay within a given period of time. While the extension of this kind of reasoning to non-quantum events is metaphysically controversial, it is natural to think of certain kinds of macroscopic events as non-deterministic and intrinsically random as well. A flip of a fair coin has a 0.5 chance of coming up heads, independent of what anyone thinks about it; this is a fact about the world. If I draw a ball at random from a well-mixed urn with 3 red and 7 green balls in it, there is a 0.3 chance of getting a red ball. The roll of a die, a deal of a card from a well-shuffled pack, and the result of a future sporting event whose outcome depends on many chance factors might all be thought to have a similar character. Naturally, we can also have mixed uncertainty: for instance, I might be uncertain about whether a given coin was fair, so that I am subjectively uncertain about the value of a certain objective chance (Lewis, 1980).

One way to gain an intuitive feel for the distinction is to imagine yourself being in possession of all immediately causally relevant information about an event. For example, suppose that you were in immediate possession of all relevant information about the factors influencing an event's outcome. The only thing that you do not have direct observational evidence of is the actual outcome. Would you still have any uncertainty about the outcome? If not, you are dealing with a case of purely subjective probability. Otherwise, the situation includes at least some degree of inherent stochasticity, i.e., objective chance. Of course, the problem with this heuristic is that it relies on the intuitive notion of "immediately causally relevant" information. If the event in question involves a coin flip or weather conditions, a layperson and a physicist might resolve this expression in radically different ways. But, for most of us, it is natural to suppose that there would be a certain amount of inherent stochasticity in coin flips, draws from an urn, the outcomes of sporting events, atmospheric events, and the like.

This latter point brings out one of the reasons why the extent of objective chance is controversial in philosophy: does it exist beyond the quantum level? I want to sidestep such metaphysical questions by taking a psychological perspective on meaning, like much work in semantics and reasoning that investigates the implicit metaphysical assumptions of human language and cognition without addressing questions of the ultimate accuracy of these assumptions (cf. Bach 1986). We are not worried here about whether coin flips really involve objective chance, but whether people typically believe that it does, and whether such a belief influences the way that they communicate about uncertainty. So, it makes sense to turn to the psychological literature for clues about whether and to what extent people are sensitive to such a distinction in reasoning, decision-making, and communication.

Psychologists have distinguished two kinds of uncertainty that mirror the philosophical discussion. "Singular external" (Kahneman and Tversky, 1982) or "aleatory" (Ülkümen et al., 2015) uncertainty involves events that are considered to be intrinsically random and essentially unpredictable. This type of uncertainty is intuitively the same as objective chance, as long as we are willing to extend the latter concept well beyond the quantum level. These authors argue that our knowledge of external uncertainties is generally due to reasoning about specific cases, e.g., about the physical characteristics of a certain coin, or about the likely trajectory of an arrow fired from a bow pointed in a particular direction, under specific atmospheric conditions. Corresponding to subjective probability is what psychologists have called "internal" (Kahneman and Tversky, 1982) or "epistemic" (Ülkümen et al., 2015) uncertainty.[5] This is the kind of uncertainty that we have about in-principle knowable features of the world, such as the length of the Nile, or Plato and Aristotle's relative heights.

In any case, given the proliferation of terminology in this domain, it will be useful to declare the labels that I will use at this point.

- **O**bjective probability, a world-bound property of events involving inherent randomness
  - abbreviation: "**O**-probability" or just "**O**"
  - cf.: chance, propensity, singular external uncertainty, aleatory uncertainty, stochasticity, randomness, indeterminism
- **S**ubjective probability, relating to an agent's information about an in-principle knowable event
  - abbreviation: "**S**-probability" or just "**S**"
  - cf.: credence, degree of belief, internal uncertainty, epistemic uncertainty, (lack of) information

(The best labels would perhaps be "chance" and "credence", which are widely used in the philosophical literature on probability, but these will be less useful as abbreviations later on since they begin with the same letter.)

There is considerable evidence for the linguistic and psychological reality of this distinction. On the psychological side, we have, for example, decision-making experiments which suggest that the distinction influences choice behavior. People prefer to place bets on events whose objective chance is known, rather than on those which involve pure subjective uncertainty or a mixture of subjective uncertainty and objective chance. For instance, Ellsberg (1961) famously observed that people generally prefer to bet on a binary event whose objective probability is known to be 50% rather than an event about which they have no information about objective probabilities, so that it could be anywhere in the $[0, 1]$ range—even if they are indifferent between the two possible outcomes in both cases.

While this example involves a mixture of subjective and objective uncertainty, it is possible to separate the two cleanly by considering how people's betting behavior is affected by whether the chancy event has already occurred. Brun and Teigen (1990) show that, when given

[5] The label "epistemic" is unfortunate, since it is really subjective beliefs that are relevant, regardless of whether the beliefs in question constitute knowledge.

the choice between placing a bet on an event with known chances before or after it has occurred, people prefer to bet in advance. This is surprising: we would expect a strict Bayesian to be indifferent, since the subjective probability of winning the bet remains the same if there is no prospect of gaining information about the outcome once it has occurred. This result suggests that there is a preference for betting under pure O-uncertainty rather than pure S-uncertainty, and so, *a fortiori*, that people make this distinction psychologically. Relatedly, Rothbart and Snyder (1970) found that experimental participants had greater confidence in their predictions about the roll of a die if the die had not yet been rolled. Their participants were also willing to bet more money on the outcome of the roll before it had happened.

The latter findings are consonant with Kahneman and Tversky (1982)'s claim that people believe in a sharp asymmetry between past and future: past events are in-principle knowable, but future events—unless they are impossible or inevitable—involve external uncertainty. Coming from a different perspective, Lewis (1980) likewise makes a past/future asymmetry central to his theory of the relationship between subjective probability and objective chance. Note that the temporal dimension is also important in resolving what is "in-principle knowable". As a rule, past events are in-principle knowable, and uncertainty about them is of the purely subjective type. Future events may or may not be chancy: for instance, there is an objective chance of rain tomorrow, but no chance that $3 + 3$ will fail to equal 6 tomorrow. However, many interesting future events are chancy, and involve a mixture of subjective and objective uncertainty.

Turning to linguistic traces of the subjective/objective distinction, Ülkümen et al. (2015) addressed this question with a corpus study of uncertainty expressions in *New York Times* articles published in 2008-2009. They extracted all instances of a predetermined list of phrases from these articles, including "sure", "confident", "certain", "chance", "likely", "likelihood", and "probability", and asked annotators to rate them on a number of dimensions including perspective, control over the event's outcome, source of uncertainty, and locus of uncertainty (internal or external). A key finding was that uncertainty expressions vary in whether they are typically used to discuss subjective or objective probabilities. The most interesting result was that there was a clear preference for *likely, chance, likelihood*, and *probability* when the locus of uncertainty was external (objective), and for *sure, confident, certain* when the locus of uncertainty was internal (subjective). While the result was far from categorical, it was highly reliable.

This aspect of Ülkümen et al. (2015)'s study reveals two interesting facts. First, the subjective/objective distinction is immediately relevant for communicating about uncertainty, and not just indirectly via its effects on reasoning and decision-making. Second, the association between particular items and particular types of uncertainty is not categorical. While it is not clear how it should be explained semantically, it would be a mistake to hard-code this association into the semantics of the various expressions. For example, while Ülkümen et al. (2015) found that *likely* is much more frequently used to talk about objective chances, it is easy to find examples where the only sensible reading involves pure subjective uncertainty.

(14) a. An accident report into a light aircraft's crash landing at East Midlands Airport earlier this year has revealed the most likely cause was an incorrectly fitted screw in the landing gear. (web)

b. [T]he residential-scale reservoirs ... were likely used around 900 B.C. It's likely that the systems were lined with a thick, clay "plaster" that allowed the areas to hold the water instead of seeping away. (web)

Presumably the cause of the plane crash under discussion is a fixed fact about the world: investigators simply have subjective uncertainty about what this cause was, and an incorrectly fitted screw is the best hypothesis. Similarly, viewed from the present day, the way that certain reservoirs were constructed and used thousands of years ago is clearly not a matter of objective chance. Subjective uncertainty is all we can muster.

Contrariwise, it may also be that *certain* can express pure objective chance in examples such as "It is certain that everyone will eventually die". (But not, of course, in the frame "x is certain that ...".) However, it is more difficult to show that this is strictly objective since someone who is in a position to assert the ubiquity of death will presumably also be in a state of maximal subjective confidence about the truth of the same proposition.

6.4 The Distributional Interpretation

A third kind of probability that seems to be linguistically relevant is what I will call "distributional" probability, involving information about frequencies or proportions in a reference class. (Abbreviation: **D**-probability.) This corresponds to what Kahneman and Tversky (1982) call "Distributional external" uncertainty, and is related to some versions of the frequentist interpretation of probability. D-probability is the kind that is relevant when we imagine ourselves constructing an ad hoc group of real-world individuals or events, and considering the distribution of properties within this group. It can be operationalized as the proportion of individuals in the group that satisfies a certain predicate, analogous to the proportional reading of the quantifiers *few* and *many* (Partee, 1988). Equivalently, D-probability can be thought of as the chance that a randomly sampled member of the group would satisfy the predicate. The following web examples illustrate.

(15) a. The eight anti-seizure medications in the study came in 37 colors and four shapes. Overall, a change in color saw about a 20 percent additional likelihood that a prescription would lapse.

b. At the University of Nebraska College of Law [in 2006] ... [t]he probability that a Hispanic resident with the credentials of the average black admittee would be admitted was 43 percent.

In these and many other examples of D-readings, there is an indefinite or a bare plural within the scope of a probability expression. The indefinite is apparently not interpreted as an existential quantifier. For example, neither scopal order in (16) captures the interpretation of (15a), on either an objective or a subjective interpretation of the probability measure *prob*. Letting b be the implied baseline from which "additional" deviation is being measured in this example:

(16) a. $\exists x[\mathbf{prescription}(x) \wedge \mathit{prob}(\mathbf{lapse}(x)) = b + 0.20]$

b. $\mathit{prob}(\exists x[\mathbf{prescription}(x) \wedge \mathbf{lapse}(x)]) = b + 0.20$

The first reading in (16) deals with uncertainties involving some particular prescription; the second is about the probability that *any* prescription would lapse. Neither corresponds to the natural interpretation of (15a). Rather, this example is about the probability that a randomly selected member of a certain real-world class (those prescriptions, among those on which the study gathered data, for which the color of the pills had changed) had a certain property (not being renewed by the patient). Similarly, the claim being made in (15b) is that, among the class of Hispanic applicants who had the overall credentials of an average black admittee, 43% were admitted. This is obviously different from the claim that, for some Hispanic applicant x with certain credentials, the probability that x would be admitted was or is 43% (subjectively or objectively). It is also different from a claim about the probability that a Hispanic applicant (any Hispanic applicant) with these credentials would be admitted. The chance that there would be *at least one* such applicant admitted was presumably much higher prospectively, and retrospectively it is either 1 or 0. (This holds both objectively, and subjectively given that all relevant admissions data were available.)

D-readings are not restricted to sentences with indefinites, or to *likely*, *probable*, and their derivatives. For example, (17) is an example with generic *you* and the noun *chance*.

(17) In fact, in 2000, which was one of the last years that I was mayor, it was 191 for crime in the country. For example, in Boston, there was a 59 percent greater chance you'd be the victim of a crime than in New York City. (Rudy Giuliani, Republican Presidential Primary debate, September 5, 2012)

(18) contains two instances, one with a bare plural and *chance*, and one with a gerundive phrase and *likelihood*.

(18) There was a 67 percent greater chance that black patients would not receive treatment compared with white patients; and being single, divorced, separated, or widowed as compared with being married or having a domestic partner also increased the likelihood of not getting definitive treatment.

It would be interesting to develop a compositional interpretation for distributional readings of probability expressions—building, perhaps, on theories that treat indefinites as denoting free variables or choice functions, and on theories of genericity and their interaction with indefinites, plurals, etc. It might even turn out that apparent *D*-readings could be reduced to a generic interpretation of *S*- or *O*-readings. Since indefinites and bare plurals play an important role in the theory of genericity, this might help to explain the frequent occurrence of indefinites with an apparent free-variable interpretation in examples of *D*-readings.[6] However, I do not have a clear sense of how such a reduction would work in the details.

Absent some theoretical reduction along the lines just mentioned, examples like (15) appear to motivate a third type of uncertainty in the interpretation of English probability expressions, corresponding to frequentist probability, and which has not been studied previously from a linguistic perspective. *D*-probability is, like *O*-probability, a non-psychological feature of the world—as real as rain, sleet, or snow once the relevant class of individuals has been specified. Since objective facts about the world are sufficient to determine the proportion of individuals in a certain class that satisfy a certain property, it is natural to expect the interpretation of distributional probability expressions to be indexed to the world of evaluation.

[6]Many thanks to a helpful reviewer for pressing me to consider this possibility.

6.5 An Informal Corpus Study of Nested Epistemics

Our main goal here is to understand the interpretation of examples involving nested epistemics, where one epistemic expression occurs in the immediate scope of another. I pointed out that a compositional interpretation of these examples would be very simple if we had a way to "objectivize" probabilities, tying them to the world of evaluation rather than some parameter of evaluation or other non-world-bound feature of interpretation. Now we have two such ways—objective probability and distributional probability—and some evidence that at least some "epistemic" expressions are genuinely ambiguous in whether they express subjective, objective, or distributional probability.

If we wish to explain embedded occurrences of epistemics in the most conservative possible way—with epistemic modals taking a propositional argument—this would suggest the following strong hypothesis: *Embedded epistemics always have a world-bound interpretation.* That is, we should find examples of modals indicating O-, D-, and S-uncertainty in matrix position, but those embedded under another epistemic expression should always have an O- or D-interpretation.

As a result, we do not expect singly embedded examples to show the full 3x3 typology of ambiguities that is in principle available. The $X > S$ reading (for any $X \in \{S, O, D\}$) is ruled out if the relevant subjective probability measure is provided by a parameter of evaluation that is independent of the world of evaluation, as we are assuming. This assumption is borrowed from previous work, especially Yalcin 2007, and could of course be discarded by relaxing this assumption or by giving a more complex theory of embeddings (as in Moss 2015, 2018).

On the other hand, we might find that S-readings are not totally unembeddable: $S > S$ readings might occur when an agent is genuinely uncertain about her own beliefs, due to psychological limitations (e.g., time pressure rendering it difficult to reason through a problem, so that one's own implicit beliefs have not yet emerged). This is in fact what I expect to find: when embedded S-readings occur, they should be in rare cases where it is pragmatically sensible for someone to express (un)certainty about her own subjective (un)certainty.

In this section I will evaluate these hypotheses in a rough-and-ready way against examples of nested epistemics. Except where noted explicitly, the examples are drawn from the NYT-Eng section of the Gigaword corpus, comprising 1.4 million words of *New York Times* newswire. The NYT examples were selected by retrieving all sentences in which two or more of the following items occurred within the same clause (as delimited by the punctuation marks [!,;.?]).

probable, probably, improbable, likely, certain, sure, definitely, possible, possibly, impossible, must, might, may, maybe, perhaps.

To keep the study to a manageable size I did not include many relevant items such as *confident, clear, clearly, dubious, think, believe, know, doubt, chance, likelihood, probability, possibility, confidence.*

This search technique returned a large number of hits, most of them irrelevant: for example, examples of *must* with a deontic interpretation, *certain* in expressions such as *a certain individual*, and examples in which the two modals were not in a scopal relation (e.g. *It is very probable or even certain that ...*). However, within this collection I was able to find a substantial number of examples which do appear to be genuine nested epistemics.

I selected for discussion here examples that had a relatively clear intended meaning, and which were relevant to a theoretically interesting point. All interpretations are my own. A controlled evaluation using trained, hypothesis-naïve annotators would of course be preferable, but this will have to wait for future work.

6.5.1 Subjective Uncertainty about Casually Relevant Chance Factors ($S > O$)

It is relatively easy to find examples in which an author expresses subjective uncertainty about chance factors. For example, (19) appears to have this character.

(19) Nuclear war is as likely, and perhaps more likely, in our time than at any point during the Cold War because superpower constraints are much weaker ... (perhaps > more likely)

The message is that complex, interacting geopolitical forces have conspired such that the objective probability of nuclear war is (definitely) at least as high as at any point during the Cold War—and that the information available to the author renders it possible that this objective probability is even higher. So, *perhaps more likely* has a $S > O$ reading.

Here is another, somewhat more complex example.

(20) Despite starting 29th in today's Samsung/Radio Shack 500, Gordon had a spring in his step on Saturday at Texas Motor Speedway after posting the fourth-fastest lap during the final practice session. "We're probably the dark horse for sure," Gordon said. "Our cars have been really, really fast lately. ... Maybe Sunday will be our day."

I believe that the intended scopal order here is *for sure* > *probably.*

Assuming this, Gordon's message seems to be that he is subjectively certain that objective features of the world (his team's abilities, other teams' performances) will be arranged so that his team probably performs above expectations on Sunday.

(21) To build a large database of people who are interested in participating as links in the chain, Watts' team has set up a Web site ... Participants will receive e-mail messages asking them to help locate a target person by forwarding e-mail to a personal contact who might be likely to know the target.

As I understand this example, Watts' team is asking participants to identify people who might (given their information about the individuals in question) be likely (given objective facts about that individual, such as their location and activities) to know the target.

The following is a relatively clear case, where subjective *definitely* embeds the epistemic expression *much more likely*. The latter is explicitly justified in terms of current conditions in the global economy—a radically indeterminate macrostructure if there ever was one.

(22) "You can be guaranteed of rocketing commodity prices if and when the global economy starts working together," said Bond. "We've definitely got conditions now where commodity price squeezes are much more likely than they were in the past."

(23) has a similar character:

(23) The new federal law makes most legal immigrants ineligible for Supplemental Security Income ... All those people might be likely applicants for Home Relief.

If I understand correctly, the intended interpretation of (23) is that, for each newly ineligible immigrant x, it is subjectively possible that x would be likely (in light of objective facts about the individual and the application process) to apply for Home Relief. (As an aside, (23) is a counter-example to von Fintel and Iatridou (2003)'s "epistemic containment" constraint, which forbids quantifiers from taking scope directly above an epistemic modal. See Swanson 2010 for additional counter-examples.)

6.5.2 Subjective Uncertainty about Distributional Probabilities ($S > D$)

The only good candidate of a potential $S > D$ example that I have located is (24):

(24) We do have an enemy, and it is definitely possible that what you consider a "word from God" could in fact be demonic and be "a

word from satan." (web)

An $S > O$ reading of this example is not very plausible, since it is presumably a determinate present fact whether a given communication is from God or from Satan (or indeed from neither). If so, only $S > S$ and $S > D$ would make sense here. My interpretation of this example goes as follows: the author is expressing maximal confidence in the claim that Satan has the ability to deceive people into thinking that his words come from God. In other words, the author is confident that—among the class of communications that his audience consider to be "words from God"—a non-zero proportion of these are in fact "words from Satan". If so, the quantity that he is maximally confident of is a distributional probability.

6.5.3 $D > S$?

I have found no corpus examples that clearly indicate a $D > S$ interpretation. Here is an invented example that has been suggested to me:

(25) He is a Republican; so, it's unlikely that he is probably a pacifist.

To the extent that the example makes sense, it suggests distributional reasoning: if you sample an individual at random from the class of Republicans, it is unlikely that the individual sampled will be one who is probably a pacifist. We might imagine, after sampling an individual, being forced to infer from observables whether the individual is a pacifist. In any case, if example (25) is intelligible it may provide another argument that subjective readings of probability expressions can be embedded under other epistemic operators.

6.5.4 Multiple layers of objective uncertainty ($O > O$)

Most of the examples that follow could also be interpreted as $S > O$. The best $O > O$ candidates seem to involve well-informed speculation about the future, which (as we noted above) people seem to treat as open and in-principle unknowable.

(26) NBA Commissioner Adam Silver said Wednesday night that it's "probably unlikely" for Orlando to host the 2017 NBA All-Star Game because the city hosted the exhibition just several years ago, in 2012. ... Silver answered that Orlando's chances are slim "only because the game was here in 2012 and there are some other teams that haven't had an All-Star Game in a long time ... But having said that, this was a great experience down here in 2012, and I'm sure we won't be waiting to go to 29 other teams before we come back here." (*Orlando Sentinel*, 2/25/15)

Here Silver expresses uncertainty about the future value of a set of variables—other teams' levels of interest—which are known to be causally relevant to Orlando's chances of getting the Game. (This choice is ultimately under Silver's control.) It's hard to be sure that the "probably" here is of the objective sort, but if it is, this is an $O > O$ example.

(27) Tom McGowan, the town planner, suggested that if critical sites needed protection that could not be provided in any other way, "a very focused proposal might be likely to receive favor." He cited such vulnerable open areas as Routes 118 and 254, both entry roads into the village center.

We might think to treat (27) as $D > S$, but I think that this would be incorrect: McGowan is not discussing the prospects of a proposal randomly selected from a known class, but rather noting that, if a focused proposal is written, it *might* (depending on its characteristics) be *likely* (depending on the planning commission's internal deliberations) to receive favor. If so, this can be read as an $O > O$ example.

6.5.5 Genuine Higher-order Uncertainty ($S > S$)

Many theorists have wished to ban true higher-order uncertainty, of the $S > S$ variety, for philosophical or computational reasons. It's true that allowing higher-order uncertainty makes the semantics more complicated, and that it conflicts with certain theoretical positions about the nature of belief or introspection. Still, it may be a real thing. Here are some examples that could be analyzed as $S > S$ readings.

(28) "I believe in a 'yes' victory, but I'm definitely not certain," said Prime Minister Goran Persson ...

I do not see any real alternative but to understand this example as an expression of Persson's higher-order certainty about the non-maximal value of his own subjective degree of belief. Here is another similar example:

(29) This book is an odyssey, a journey up through the mists of time from the remote past. It explores what must perhaps be the most fundamental of all questions - who we are. (Dunbar 2004, p. 7)

As I understand it, the author is not at all sure about what the most fundamental of all questions is—but he is virtually certain that it *might* be "who we are". So, this looks like another $S > S$ reading.

Once we have opened this can of worms, further candidates start to appear.

(30) Mr. Nolan must certainly be rubbing his conspiratorial hands with glee as he hears that the arrival of Primark has meant that other stores are now looking to make a new home in Truro. (web)

This example would typically be interpreted as modal concord. This is not an unreasonable analysis, but note that examples (28) and (29) cannot be treated in this way since the modals are not matched in strength. Perhaps some constructions that could plausibly be used to express concord can also yield to a nested analysis. I am tempted to read (30) as expressing higher-order confidence, either about the author's own certainty or about the appropriate degree of certainty for conversational partners to adopt in light of the evidence available.

I do not know whether any of these examples will hold up in the end: perhaps they can all be explained away in some other fashion. But it may also be that authors sometimes wish to express (un)certainty about their own beliefs, about how their beliefs will stabilize upon reflection, or about what the appropriate degree of belief is for people with access to a given body of information.

6.6 Distributional Considerations

There appear to be significant gaps in the distribution of nested modals in the Gigaword-NYT corpus. For example, none of the following occur in the same clause in the corpus.

- *definitely ... may/(im)probable*
- *impossible ... definitely/maybe*
- *perhaps ... definitely*
- *possibly ... improbable/probable*
- *improbable ... probably/certain/definitely/may/must/perhaps/possibly/sure*

In a corpus as large as this one, where many combinations are attested by numerous examples, these gaps are striking. Some of them may be explicable in terms of Ülkümen et al. (2015)'s observations about preferred interpretations of modals: as I mentioned above, they point out that *certain, sure, confident*, and expressions derived from them tend to deal with subjective uncertainty, while *likely, likelihood, chance, probability* and their derivatives prefer an external (objective or perhaps distributional) interpretation. If such preferences do exist, then we might be able to explain certain gaps by pointing to the semantic ill-formedness, or pragmatic infelicity, of the preferred readings of certain combinations.

6.7 Embedding Epistemics Simple-mindedly

One of the goals of this paper is to consider the prospects of a simple-minded analysis of nested epistemics: probability expressions of all stripes embed propositions (sets of possible worlds), and anything that can serve as their direct argument must pick out a set of possible worlds. If we start with Yalcin (2007)'s hypothesis that subjective probabilities come into the composition via a parameter that is independent of the world of evaluation, we expect that subjective probability expressions should not embed non-trivially, but objective and distributional probability expressions—being world-bound—should.

The examples tentatively analyzed as $S > S$ in section (6.5.5) do not yet refute this position, but they do problematize it somewhat. If we wish to hold onto a simple theory of embeddings, we may have to "objectivize" subjective probabilities in some cases, treating them as features of the world about which we can be uncertain. There does not seem to be any technical barrier to doing so, though there might be philosophical reasons to try to find a way around it. Alternatively, we could frame a more complicated theory of embeddings, as Moss (2015, 2018) does. While this theory does many things well, it is definitely much more complex and radical in its semantic and philosophical implications than the simple-minded approach suggested here.

This bring us back to the vacuity issue from section 1. Do multiple epistemics reduce to the innermost in English, as they do in S5 and (in a slightly more complicated way) on Yalcin (2007)'s account? On face, the answer is a clear "no": the nested examples that we have analyzed have complex, subtle interpretations that definitely are not equivalent to the same sentences with the outermost modal deleted. However, the English data do not decide this question if there is a subtle ambiguity in the interpretation of the modal expressions, as I argued that there is in many cases. A convincing test of the empirical claim would have to involve $S > S$, $O > O$, or $D > D$ interpretations. $D > D$ readings do not seem to occur among the examples that I have found. (I am unsure what they would even mean.) Various examples did occur that could plausibly be analyzed as $S > S$ or $O > O$, but these could probably be re-interpreted in some other way by a dedicated proponent of the S5 reduction property.

This conclusion is somewhat unsatisfying, since we do not know for sure yet whether reduction holds. Reduction does have two nice features that might make it worth pursuing, though. First, it may allow us to maintain Yalcin (2007)'s account of epistemic contradictions in light of problem cases involving nested epistemics noted by Moss (2015,

2018). Second, it means that we will have to continue doing what Lauri taught us many years ago: continue to take inspiration from logic and philosophy, but evaluate every idea inspired from these sources carefully against empirical data. The only major methodological development to report is that taking a probabilistic perspective on modal semantics allows to draw additional inspiration from the rich tradition of philosophical and psychological work on belief, reasoning and choice that is tied in to probabilistic modeling and statistics.

References

Bach, Emmon. 1986. The algebra of events. *Linguistics and Philosophy* 9(1):5–16.

Brun, Wibecke and Karl Halvor Teigen. 1990. Prediction and postdiction preferences in guessing. *Journal of Behavioral Decision Making* 3(1):17–28.

Dorr, Cian and John Hawthorne. 2013. Embedding epistemic modals. *Mind* 122(488):867–913.

Dunbar, Robin. 2004. *The Human Story*. Faber & Faber.

Ellsberg, Daniel. 1961. Risk, ambiguity, and the Savage axioms. *The quarterly journal of economics* pages 643–669.

Gillies, Donald. 2000. *Philosophical theories of probability*. Psychology Press.

Goodhue, Daniel. 2018. *Must p* is felicitous only if *p* is not known. To appear in *Semantics & Pragmatics*.

Groenendijk, Jeroen and Martin Stokhof. 1975. Modality and conversational information. *Theoretical linguistics* 2(1-3):61–112.

Hacking, Ian. 1975. *The emergence of probability: A philosophical study of early ideas about probability, induction and statistical inference*. Cambridge University Press.

Hintikka, Jaako. 1962. *Knowledge and Belief: An Introduction to the Logic of the Two Notions*. Cornell University Press.

Kahneman, Daniel and Amos Tversky. 1982. Variants of uncertainty. *Cognition* 11(2):143–157.

Karttunen, Lauri. 1972. Possible and must. In J. Kimball, ed., *Syntax and semantics*, vol. 1. Seminar Press.

Knobe, Joshua and Seth Yalcin. 2014. Epistemic modals and context: Experimental data. *Semantics and Pragmatics* 7:1–21.

Kratzer, Angelika. 1991. Modality. In A. von Stechow and D. Wunderlich, eds., *Semantik: Ein internationales Handbuch der zeitgenössischen Forschung*, pages 639–650. Walter de Gruyter.

Lassiter, Daniel. 2010. Gradable epistemic modals, probability, and scale structure. In N. Li and D. Lutz, eds., *Semantics & Linguistic Theory (SALT) 20*, pages 197–215. CLC Publications.

Lassiter, Daniel. 2015. Epistemic comparison, models of uncertainty, and the disjunction puzzle. *Journal of Semantics* 32(4):649–684.

Lassiter, Daniel. 2016. *Must*, knowledge, and (in)directness. *Natural Language Semantics* .

Lassiter, Daniel. 2017. *Graded Modality*. Oxford University Press.

Lewis, D. 1980. A subjectivist's guide to objective chance. In R. Jeffrey, ed., *Studies in inductive logic and probability*, pages 263–293. University of California Press.

Mandelkern, Matthew. 2016. A solution to Karttunen's problem. To appear in *Proceedings of Sinn und Bedeutung 2016*.

Mandelkern, Matthew. 2018. Bounded modality. To appear in *The Philosophical Review* .

Moss, Sarah. 2015. On the semantics and pragmatics of epistemic vocabulary. *Semantics and Pragmatics* 8:1–81.

Moss, Sarah. 2018. Probabilistic knowledge .

Ninan, Dilip. 2018. Relational semantics and domain semantics for epistemic modals. *Journal of Philosophical Logic* 47(1):1–16.

Partee, Barbara. 1988. Many quantifiers. In *Proceedings of ESCOL*, vol. 5, pages 383–402.

Rothbart, Myron and Mark Snyder. 1970. Confidence in the prediction and postdiction of an uncertain outcome. *Canadian Journal of Behavioural Science/Revue canadienne des sciences du comportement* 2(1):38.

Schulz, Moritz. 2010. Epistemic modals and informational consequence. *Synthese* 174(3):385–395.

Stojnić, Una. 2017. One's modus ponens: Modality, coherence and logic. *Philosophy and Phenomenological Research* 95(1):167–214.

Swanson, Eric. 2006. Interactions With Context. Ph.D. thesis, MIT.

Swanson, Eric. 2010. On scope relations between quantifiers and epistemic modals. *Journal of Semantics* .

Swanson, Eric. 2015. The application of constraint semantics to the language of subjective uncertainty. *Journal of Philosophical Logic* pages 1–26.

Ülkümen, Gülden, Craig R Fox, and Bertram F Malle. 2015. Two dimensions of subjective uncertainty: Clues from natural language. To appear in *Journal of Experimental Psychology: General*.

von Fintel, Kai and Anthony Gillies. 2010. Must... stay... strong! *Natural Language Semantics* 18(4):351–383.

von Fintel, Kai and Sabine Iatridou. 2003. Epistemic containment. *Linguistic Inquiry* 34(2):173–198.

Yalcin, Seth. 2005. A puzzle about epistemic modals. *MIT Working Papers in Linguistics* 51:231–272.

Yalcin, Seth. 2007. Epistemic modals. *Mind* 116(464):983–1026.

Yalcin, Seth. 2010. Probability operators. *Philosophy Compass* 5(11):916–937.

7

Surprise for Lauri Karttunen*

Floris Roelofsen

7.1 Introduction

This paper is written in honor of Lauri Karttunen's seminal contributions to formal semantics, in particular his work on discourse referents (Karttunen, 1969), presuppositions (Karttunen, 1973, 1974) and questions (Karttunen, 1977). The present paper is connected to all these lines of work, suggesting that a long-standing issue concerning question embedding verbs like *surprise*, raised in Karttunen (1977), can be resolved by assuming that such verbs involve a presupposition that is sensitive to the discourse referents introduced by their complement.

The first issue that Karttunen (1977) considers in his article on embedded questions is whether all such questions should be taken to belong to the same syntactic category. In particular, he raises the issue whether *wh*-questions should be treated as belonging to the same syntactic category as *whether*-questions. Karttunen (p. 5) writes:

> "These two types of questions have virtually the same syntactic distribution. Nearly all verbs which take *wh*-questions as complements

*This paper further develops a proposal initially made in joint work with Michele Herbstritt and Maria Aloni (Roelofsen, Herbstritt, and Aloni, 2016). I am grateful to Ivano Ciardelli, Alexandre Cremers, Donka Farkas, Jeroen Groenendijk, Anna Szabolcsi, Nadine Theiler, Wataru Uegaki, Thom van Gessel, and an anonymous reviewer for discussion and feedback on earlier versions of the paper, and to audiences in Utrecht and Göttingen, especially Jakub Dotlacil, Sven Lauer, Rick Nouwen, Hedde Zeijlstra, and Sarah Zobel for helpful questions and comments on presentations of the paper. Finally, financial support from the Netherlands Organization for Scientific Research (NWO) and the European Research Council (ERC, grant agreement number 680220) is gratefully acknowledged.

Tokens of Meaning: Papers in Honor of Lauri Karttunen.
Cleo Condoravdi and Tracy Holloway King (eds.).

also take *whether*-questions. A verb which doesn't allow embedded *wh*-questions in general doesn't complement with *whether*-questions either. This is illustrated in (1) and (2).

(1) a. John knows what they serve for breakfast.
    b. John knows whether they serve breakfast.

(2) a. *John assumes what they serve for breakfast.
    b. *John assumes whether they serve breakfast.

There are two classes of exceptions to this generalization, both of which seem marginal to me. So-called 'emotive factives', such as *amaze*, *surprise*, and *bother* take *wh*-questions but do not allow *whether*-questions. Dubitative verbs, such as *doubt*, *question*, and *be dubious*, have the opposite characteristic. This is shown in (3) and (4).

(3) a. It is amazing what they serve for breakfast.
    b. *It is amazing whether they serve breakfast.

(4) a. *I doubt what they serve for breakfast.
    b. I doubt whether they serve breakfast.

The ungrammaticality of (3b) and the grammaticality of (4b) pose problems for me and require some special treatment. Nevertheless, it seems correct to assume, in the light of the great majority of cases of overlapping distribution, that *wh*-questions and *whether*-questions should be assigned to the same syntactic category."

In much subsequent work on questions, Karttunen's conclusion has been taken to heart. However, if *wh*-questions and *whether*-questions are indeed taken to be of the same syntactic category, a semantic or pragmatic explanation is needed for the contrasts in (3) and (4). Our focus will be on the first type of contrast, i.e., on emotive factive verbs like *amaze*, *surprise*, *bother*, *disappoint*, *please*, etcetera, which can take *wh*-questions as their complement but not *whether*-questions. We refer to this phenomenon as the **whether* puzzle.[1]

Several accounts of the puzzle have been suggested; some semantic in nature (d'Avis, 2002, Abels, 2004, Nicolae, 2013, Romero, 2015), others pragmatic (Guerzoni, 2007, Sæbø, 2007). Each of these proposals, however, still has certain shortcomings.[2] In particular, as already

[1] A semantic explanation of the second type of contrast, involving verbs like *doubt*, has been suggested in Pruitt and Roelofsen (2011), Farkas and Roelofsen (2012), Biezma and Rawlins (2012). However, as soon as we look beyond English such a semantic explanation becomes highly problematic, since the cross-linguistic behavior of verbs like *doubt* is far from stable. For instance, Italian *dubitare* only licenses *that*-complements, no *whether*- or *wh*-complements. See also footnote 12.

[2] Only a very brief discussion of these previous proposals is included here. For more extensive discussion see Roelofsen, Herbstritt, and Aloni (2016).

noted by Egré (2008), one of the assumptions that is crucial for the pragmatic approaches, namely the assumption that emotive factives involve so-called *speaker factivity* (Guerzoni and Sharvit, 2007), faces systematic counterexamples. Furthermore, as pointed out in Roelofsen et al. (2016), these approaches do not account for examples that are somewhat more complex than the ones above, e.g., ones like (5) where the subject is quantificational rather than referential.

(5) *Every guest was amazed whether he got breakfast.

The semantic approach initiated by d'Avis (2002) and further developed by Abels (2004), on the other hand, accounts for the fact that emotive factives do not take plain polar *whether*-questions as their complement, but it does not account for the fact that such verbs do not take *alternative questions* as their complement either, as illustrated in (6).

(6) *It is amazing whether they serve eggs for breakfast, or cereals.

Finally, the semantic accounts of Nicolae (2013) and Romero (2015) predict that emotive factives are not only incompatible with *whether*-complements, but also with *wh*-complements receiving a strongly exhaustive interpretation. This prediction is controversial: while Heim (1994) and Guerzoni and Sharvit (2007), among others, have indeed claimed that *wh*-complements under emotive factives cannot receive a strongly exhaustive interpretation, more recently Klinedinst and Rothschild (2011) and Theiler (2014) have argued that they *can*, and experimental results of Cremers and Chemla (2016) seem to confirm this. These results are unexpected on Nicolae's and Romero's explanations of the **whether* puzzle.[3] An additional problem for Romero's account is that it only applies to alternative questions. As noted by Romero herself, it remains to be seen whether it can be extended to polar questions.

We offer an account of the puzzle that explains the unacceptability of both polar and alternative questions, including cases with quantificational subjects, which does not need to assume speaker factivity, and which does not rely on any mechanism that prohibits strongly exhaustive *wh*-complements under emotive factives.

Interestingly, while mainly concerned with question embedding, the account is tightly connected to two other areas where Karttunen's work has been highly influential as well. Namely, the key idea is that emotive factive verbs involve a *presupposition* (Karttunen, 1973, 1974) that is sensitive to the *discourse referents* (Karttunen, 1969) introduced by

[3]See Romero (2016) for some ideas on how Cremers and Chemla's results might be reconcilable with her proposal.

their complements. While it is generally accepted that the discourse referents introduced by matrix questions are important to understand their role in discourse, in particular their potential to license discourse anaphora, we argue here that this dynamic aspect of meaning is also crucial for understanding embedded questions and the verbs that take such questions as their complement.

7.2 Proposal

In order to get a handle on the puzzle, we first need to understand what the crucial difference is between *wh*-questions and *whether*-questions, and second, what the relevant difference is between emotive factives and other question embedding verbs. We will consider these two issues in turn.

7.2.1 The Difference between *wh*-questions and *whether*-questions

A first important observation is that it is impossible to account for the given contrast between *wh*-questions and *whether*-questions just in terms of their answerhood/resolution conditions. To see this, consider the following examples (see Romero, 2015, for a different example making the same fundamental point).

(7) *Context: Ann and Chris have placed an order online. They are kept up to date about the status of the order, which is first 'in progress' and then at some point turns into 'sent'. Ann looks at her email and then tells Chris:*

a. It is surprising what the status of the order is.

b. *It is surprising whether the order is still in progress.

The two embedded questions in these examples have exactly the same resolution conditions: if a certain piece of information resolves one of them, then it resolves the other as well. And yet, the *wh*-question in (7a) is licensed while the *whether*-questions in (7b) is not. So to account for the **whether* puzzle, we have to look beyond resolution conditions. What is it, then, that distinguishes *whether*-questions from *wh*-questions?

Our answer is based on a contrast that is parallel to the one in (7), though this time it involves two *matrix* questions, rather than embedded ones, and the contrast between them concerns their ability to license *yes/no* responses.

(8) *Context: Ann and Chris have placed an order online. They are kept up to date about the status of the order, which is first 'in progress' and then at some point turns into 'sent'. Ann hasn't*

looked at her email for a while so she asks Chris about the status of the order.

a. Ann: Is the order still in progress?
Chris: Yes, it is. / No, it isn't.

b. Ann: What is the status of the order?
Chris: *Yes, it is. / *No, it isn't.

The two questions in (8), just like their embedded counterparts in (7), have exactly the same resolution conditions. Thus, in order to explain the difference that exists between them when it comes to licensing *yes/no* responses, we again have to look beyond resolution conditions. In this case, however, it is quite clear in which direction we should look. Namely, it is natural to think of *yes* and *no* as anaphoric expressions, and we know that such expressions are only interpretable in the presence of suitable antecedents. Plausibly, then, what explains the contrast between the polar question in (8a) and the *wh*-question in (8b) is that the former introduces a discourse referent that can serve as an antecedent for *yes* and *no*, while the latter doesn't. This is indeed what is assumed in recent accounts of *yes/no* responses (e.g., Krifka, 2013, Roelofsen and Farkas, 2015).

The hypothesis that we will pursue is that the difference between polar questions and *wh*-questions that is responsible for the contrast in (8)is also responsible for the contrast in (7). We assume that this difference, in general terms, concerns the semantic objects that the two types of questions bring into **salience**—or, in the terminology of Roelofsen and Farkas (2015), the semantic objects that they **highlight**. It is natural to assume that such highlighted objects become available as discourse referents, serving as potential antecedents for subsequent anaphoric expressions. This makes it possible to account for the contrast in (8). On the other hand, we will show that it also leads to an account of the **whether* puzzle, under the assumption that emotive factive verbs like *surprise* are sensitive to the semantic objects highlighted by their complement.

To make this more concrete, let us consider the sentences in (9) and see which semantic objects they may plausibly be taken to highlight.

(9) a. They serve breakfast.
b. Do they serve breakfast?
c. Do they serve eggs for breakfast, or cereals?
d. What do they serve for breakfast?

First, following Krifka (2013) and Roelofsen and Farkas (2015), we assume that both the declarative in (9a) and the polar question in (9b) highlight the proposition 'that they serve breakfast'. Indeed, it appears that this proposition can be anaphorically referred to by *yes* and *no*:

(10) They serve breakfast. / Do they serve breakfast?
  a. Yes. $\leadsto$ they serve breakfast
  b. No. $\leadsto$ they don't serve breakfast

Similarly, we assume that the alternative question in (9c) highlights two propositions: 'that they serve eggs for breakfast' and 'that they serve cereals for breakfast'. These propositions cannot be referred to by *yes* and *no*, presumably because these expressions require a *unique* most salient antecedent, just like anaphoric pronouns (Krifka, 2013, Roelofsen and Farkas, 2015); however, the two highlighted propositions *can* be referred to by means of anaphoric expressions that have slightly more descriptive content, like *the former* and *the latter*.

(11) Do they serve eggs for breakfast, or cereals?
  a. The former. $\leadsto$ eggs
  b. The latter. $\leadsto$ cereals

Finally, we assume that the *wh*-question in (9d) does not highlight a proposition, but rather a *property*, i.e., a function from entities to propositions (cf., Groenendijk and Stokhof, 1984, Krifka, 2001, Aloni et al., 2007, Roelofsen and Farkas, 2015). More specifically, we assume that the property highlighted by (9d) is the function that maps every entity x to the set of worlds where x is served for breakfast:[4]

(12) $\lambda x.\lambda w.\textsf{they-serve-for-breakfast}(x)(w)$

Groenendijk and Stokhof (1984) assume that this property is anaphorically accessed in the interpretation of short answers to the given question, as in (13)[a], and even in the interpretation of full sentential answers, to compute their exhaustive interpretation, as in (13)[b].[5]

[4]Groenendijk and Stokhof (1984) call this the *abstract* of the question.

[5] It should be noted that Groenendijk and Stokhof's account of short answers and exhaustivity are not uncontroversial. On the one hand, some authors have argued that short answers actually involve *ellipsis*, and their interpretation involves reconstructing the syntactic structure of the elided material rather than purely anaphoric access to the semantic property made available by the question (see, e.g., Merchant, 2005 for such a proposal, and Jacobson, 2012 for a critique of it). On the other hand, some authors have argued that the exhaustive interpretation of answers to questions comes about through pragmatic reasoning, rather than a semantic process that involves anaphoric access to the property made salient by the question (see, e.g., Westera, 2017). Be this as it may, it remains plausible to assume that *wh*-questions bring a certain property into salience which could in principle serve as the antecedent for subsequent anaphora, and which could play other roles in the interpretation process as well.

(13) What do they serve for breakfast?

a. Eggs and cereals. $\rightsquigarrow$ they only serve eggs and cereals

b. They serve eggs and cereals. $\rightsquigarrow$ they only serve eggs and cereals

To generalize over the various cases considered, it is useful to view propositions as 0-place properties. All sentence types considered, then, highlight one or more n-place properties, where $n \geq 0$ is the number of *wh*-elements in the sentence. The declarative in (9a) and the polar question in (9b) both highlight a single 0-place property, i.e., a proposition, the alternative question in (9c) highlights two 0-place properties, i.e., two propositions, and the *wh*-question in (9d) highlights a 1-place property.

Now let us turn to the *embedded* variants of (9a)-(9d), given in (14a)-(14d):

(14) a. *Peter knows* that they serve breakfast.

b. *Peter knows* whether they serve breakfast.

c. *Peter knows* whether they serve eggs for breakfast, or cereals.

d. *Peter knows* what they serve for breakfast.

Of course, the simplest assumption is that these embedded clauses highlight exactly the same properties/propositions as the corresponding matrix clauses. For declaratives, *wh*-questions, and alternative questions, this assumptions indeed seems uncontroversial. In the case of polar questions, however, it has been argued by Starr (2014, p.6) that there is in fact a difference in highlighting between matrix and embedded cases. Namely, Starr argues that, while a matrix polar question like (9b) only highlights the proposition 'that they serve breakfast', an embedded polar question headed by *whether* also highlights the proposition 'that they don't serve breakfast'. He further argues that this is specific for embedded polar questions headed by *whether*; ones that are headed by *if* instead highlight only one proposition, just like the corresponding matrix question. The argument rests on the empirical claim that the choice between *if* and *whether* influences the anaphoric availability of the positive answer. To substantiate this claim, Starr offers the following minimal pair (the judgments given here are his):

(15) a. I wonder if Bob will dance. Then Leland will dance.

b. I wonder whether Bob will dance. ??Then Leland will dance.

This contrast, however, does not seem to be very clear-cut. There are certainly many cases in which anaphoric reference to the positive answer to a *whether*-question embedded under *wonder* is fine, as illustrated in (16)-(17):

(16) I wonder whether you are still interested to go see the show, because then I'll have to make a reservation.

(17) There is an incomplete backup and I wonder whether that's the problem. If so, is it ok to delete it? [from the web]

It seems fair to conclude that more empirical work is needed to determine what exactly is highlighted by *whether*-complements. It is clear, however, that there are only two natural options: either they highlight one proposition, just like the corresponding matrix question and, presumably, the corresponding *if*-complement, or they highlight two propositions, the one highlighted by the corresponding matrix question as well as its set-theoretic complement. We will not try to settle here which of these assumptions is right. Rather, we will show that on either assumption, the **whether* puzzle can be accounted for. For now, note that on either assumption there is a contrast between polar and alternative questions on the one hand and *wh*-questions on the other; the former highlight 0-place properties, i.e., propositions, while the latter highlight n-place properties, with $n \geq 1$.

So we have found a semantic distinction between *whether*-questions and *wh*-questions, one that is motivated by considerations involving anaphora, independently from the empirical phenomenon that we aim to account for here. What about the other ingredient of the puzzle, emotive factive verbs? What distinguishes them from other verbs, and how does this distinguishing feature interact with the difference in highlighting between *whether*-questions and *wh*-questions?

7.2.2 The Difference between Emotive Factives and Other verbs

An Empirical Contrast

We start with an empirical observation due to d'Avis (2002): when *surprise* takes a *wh*-question as its complement, it triggers a strong existential presupposition. For instance, (18) below implies that something is served for breakfast, and this implication is preserved under negation.

(18) It is surprising what they serve for breakfast.

$\rightsquigarrow$ they serve something for breakfast

(19) It is not surprising what they serve for breakfast.

$\rightsquigarrow$ they serve something for breakfast

This presupposition seems to be characteristic for emotive factives in general. For instance, (20) also implies that something is served for breakfast, and this implication is again preserved under negation.

(20) It is disappointing/pleasing what they serve for breakfast.
$\leadsto$ they serve something for breakfast

(21) It is not disappointing/pleasing what they serve for breakfast.
$\leadsto$ they serve something for breakfast

Note that it is odd to cancel the existential implication with *if anything*.

(22) It is surprising what they serve for breakfast, *if anything.

(23) It is disappointing/pleasing what they serve for breakfast, *if anything.

This contrasts with other verbs:

(24) The hotel manager knows/will tell you what they serve for breakfast, if anything.

Intensional, Extensional, and Instance-related Verbs

Which general feature of emotive factives could be behind the existential presupposition observed by d'Avis? We propose the following. Intuitively, emotive factives, when taking a wh-question as their complement, express a certain emotion/attitude (surprise, disappointment, happiness, et cetera) about one or multiple **true instances** of the property highlighted by the wh-question. For instance, to be surprised at who passed the exam is to be surprised about one or more people who did in fact pass the exam that they did. So, in order to be surprised at who passed, there has to be someone who passed.

Other verbs behave differently. First consider other factive verbs like *know*, *remember*, and *discover*. These express knowledge, memory, and discovery, respectively, of the **true extension** of the property highlighted by the wh-question, not necessarily of any true instances of this property—in case the true extension of the property is empty, there are no such instances. For example, to discover who passed the exam is to discover of the set of people who did in fact pass that they are the ones who did. If nobody passed the exam, this set of people is empty. However, one can still discover who passed the exam in this case, because, unlike in the case of *surprise* and other emotive factives, such a discovery does not have to involve any true instances of the property highlighted by the question, it just concerns the true extension of this property.

Leaving the realm of factive verbs and turning to non-factives like *be certain*, *agree*, and *wonder*, we again find a shift in subject matter. Namely, these verbs are not about the *true* extension of the property highlighted by the wh-question, i.e., its extension in the actual world, but rather about the **intension** of this property, or equivalently, its various extensions across different possible worlds. Thus, these verbs certainly do not express an attitude pertaining specifically to one or multiple true instances of the property highlighted by their complement, and as a consequence they do not require the existence of such true instances. For example, one can very well wonder who passed the exam if in fact nobody did. The wondering does not have to be about some particular person who passed.

These considerations lead us to a refinement of the traditional distinction between extensional and intensional question-embedding verbs, made by Groenendijk and Stokhof (1984) and adopted in much subsequent work. This basic distinction separates verbs like *know*, *remember*, and *discover* on the one hand from ones like *be certain*, *agree*, and *wonder* on the other. Under this classification, emotive factives fall into the class of extensional verbs, together with *know*, *remember*, and *discover*. What we have seen, however, is that within this general class a further natural distinction can be made. On the one hand, verbs like *know*, *remember*, and *discover* express attitudes about the true extension of the property highlighted by their *wh*-complement, while emotive factives like *surprise* and *disappoint* actually express attitudes about something more specific, namely one or more true instances of this property. To mark this distinction, we will only refer to the former as proper extensional verbs, and to the latter as **instance-related** verbs. Our hypothesis is that all verbs which have been earmarked in the literature as 'emotive factives' are instance-related verbs, and that it is this property which explains their incompatibility with *whether*-questions. Let us see why.

Instance-related Verbs Presuppose the Existence of True Instances

Since instance-related verbs express attitudes about true instances of the property highlighted by their wh-complement, it is natural to assume that they presuppose the existence of such true instances. To make this more precise, let us say that an n-place property P has a true instance in a world w just in case there is a tuple t of n individuals such that $P(t)$ is true in w. Note that if P is a 0-place property, i.e., a proposition, then it has a true instance in w just in case it is itself true in w.

The existential presupposition of instance-related verbs can then be formulated as follows.

(25) **Existential presupposition of instance-related verbs**

Instance-Related verbs presuppose that every property highlighted by their complement has a true instance in the world of evaluation.

To illustrate this, consider again the example in (18). The *wh*-complement in this sentence highlights a 1-place property:

(26) $\lambda x.\lambda w.\mathsf{they\text{-}serve\text{-}for\text{-}breakfast}(x)(w)$

The presupposition triggered by *surprise*, then, is that this property has a true instance in the world of evaluation, i.e., that something is served for breakfast. This is exactly the existential requirement observed by d'Avis (2002).

Now consider what the presupposition in (25) amounts to when *surprise* takes a declarative complement, as in (27):

(27) It is surprising that they serve breakfast.

In this case, the complement highlights a 0-place property, i.e., a proposition, namely the proposition 'that they serve breakfast':

(28) $\lambda w.\mathsf{they\text{-}serve\text{-}breakfast}(w)$

The presupposition triggered by *surprise*, then, is that this proposition is true—a standard *factivity* presupposition. So, when applied to a *wh*-complement the presupposition postulated in (25) yields the existential requirement observed by d'Avis, and when applied to a declarative complement it yields standard factivity.

Notice that the existential presupposition in (25 requires that *every* property that is highlighted by the complement clause (rather than, say, *at least one* of these properties) should have a true instance in the world of evaluation. To justify this, we have to consider a somewhat more complex case.

(29) It is surprising what they serve for breakfast and what they serve for lunch.

$\leadsto$ Presupposition: they serve something for breakfast and something for lunch

Assuming that the conjunctive complement in (29)highlights two 1-place properties, each contributed by one of the *wh*-clauses, the observed presupposition is predicted by (25). It is crucial in this case that *every* property highlighted by the complement is required to have a true instance, rather than just one of these properties.

One might be tempted to raise an objection against this argument by pointing out that (29)may actually be seen as an elided version of (30) below, where conjunction does not apply to the interrogative complement clauses but rather to the declarative root clauses (the part that must be elided in order to obtain (29)is displayed in gray).

(30) It is surprising what they serve for breakfast and *it is surprising* what they serve for lunch.

Under this analysis, it is possible (given certain assumptions about presupposition projection) to derive the conjunctive presupposition of (29) even if the existential presupposition associated with instance-related verbs just requires that at least one of the properties (rather than every property) highlighted by the complement clause have a true instance.

This does not invalidate our argument, however, for two reasons. First, while (29) *could* indeed be seen as an elided version of (30), it could also be analyzed as involving conjunction directly at the level of the interrogative complement clauses. Thus, if we adopted a weaker formulation of the existential presupposition in (25), it would still be predicted that (29) *has a reading* under which it only presupposes that something is served for either breakfast or lunch—a prediction that should be avoided.

Moreover, it is easy to construct a variant of (29) which is immune to the objection considered here. A case in point is (31).

(31) It is only surprising what they serve for breakfast and what they serve for lunch. (...It is not surprising what they serve for dinner)
$\rightsquigarrow$ Presupposition: they serve something for breakfast and something for lunch

The conjunctive presupposition is still present, and clearly this sentence cannot be analyzed as an elliptical version of (32) below, where conjunction again applies to the declarative root clauses instead of the interrogative complement clauses.[6]

(32) It is only surprising what they serve for breakfast and *it is only surprising* what they serve for lunch.

Another potential objection, brought up an anonymous reviewer, concerns cases like (33), where the two interrogative complements are *disjoined* rather than conjoined.

[6]We refer to the appendix of Roelofsen et al. (2016) for some further discussion of this issue, including supporting evidence from Hungarian, which, according to Szabolcsi (1997, 2015), overtly marks whether the two interrogative clauses in cases like (29) are directly conjoined or first composed with the verb before conjunction applies.

(33) It is surprising what they serve for breakfast or what they serve for lunch; I forget which meal they are open for.

The reviewer suggests that the existential presupposition as formulated in (25) wrongly predicts that (33)should be anomalous, because the sentence would inconsistently presuppose that something is served for breakfast and something is served for lunch, while also implying that only one of those meals is available.

Upon closer inspection, however, this prediction does not arise. After all, as we saw for the conjunctive case in (29) above, (33)may be analyzed as an elided version of (34) below, where the disjunction does not apply directly to the interrogative complement clauses but rather to the declarative root clauses.

(34) It is surprising what they serve for breakfast or *it is surprising* what they serve for lunch; I forget which meal they are open for.

Under this analysis no contradiction arises. Thus, (33) is not predicted to be anomalous.

We conclude that there are good reasons to formulate the existential presupposition of instance-related verbs as we did in (25). With this in place, we now specify concrete, semi-formal lexical entries for some emotive factives.

Lexical Entries for some Emotive Factives

Below we provide semi-formal entries for *surprise*, *bother*, and *please*. We consider three different verbs in order to show that they can all be taken to follow the same pattern. We assume that this extends to other emotive factives as well; in particular, we take it that all emotive factives have the same presuppositional component (conditions 1 and 2 below). After having spelled out the entries for *surprise*, *bother*, and *please*, we will zoom in on the case of *surprise* and discuss some specific features of its entry in more detail.

(35) $[\![\phi \textit{ surprises } x]\!]^w$ is defined iff conditions 1-2 below hold, and true iff 1-3 hold:

1. Every property P highlighted by ϕ has at least one **true instance** in w;
2. One or more of these true instances, $P(t_1), \ldots, P(t_m)$, where $m \geq 1$, are such that x **believes** $P(t_1) \wedge \ldots \wedge P(t_m)$ in w;
3. $P(t_1) \wedge \ldots \wedge P(t_m)$ is incompatible with x's **prior expectations** in w.

(36) $[\![\phi \textit{ bothers } x]\!]^w$ is defined iff conditions 1-2 below hold, and true

iff 1-3 hold:

1. Every property P highlighted by ϕ has at least one **true instance** in w;
2. One or more of these true instances, $P(t_1), \ldots, P(t_m)$, where $m \geq 1$, are such that x **believes** $P(t_1) \wedge \ldots \wedge P(t_m)$ in w;
3. $P(t_1) \wedge \ldots \wedge P(t_m)$ is incompatible with x's **preferences** in w.

(37) $[\![\phi \textit{ pleases } x]\!]^w$ is defined iff conditions 1-2 below hold, and true iff 1-3 hold:

1. Every property P highlighted by ϕ has at least one **true instance** in w;
2. One or more of these true instances, $P(t_1), \ldots, P(t_m)$, where $m \geq 1$, are such that x **believes** $P(t_1) \wedge \ldots \wedge P(t_m)$ in w;
3. $P(t_1) \wedge \ldots \wedge P(t_m)$ satisfies x's **preferences** in w.

To illustrate the predictions that arise from the entry for *surprise* when it takes a *wh*-complement, consider the following example:

(38) It surprises Peter who came to the party.

First of all, it is predicted that this sentence presupposes that at least one person came to the party. Second, the sentence is predicted to presuppose that for one or more people who came, Peter believes that they came. And finally, if $t_1, \ldots, t_m$ are the people of which Peter correctly believes that they came, the sentence is predicted to assert that the fact that $t_1, \ldots, t_m$ came is incompatible with Peter's prior expectations.

For instance, if Mary, Bill, and Susan came, Peter only believes of Mary that she came, and he had not expected Mary to come, the sentence is predicted to be true. If Mary, Bill, and Susan came, Peter believes of Mary and Bill that they came, and he had not expected that they would both come (e.g., because they are known to hate and avoid each other), the sentence is also predicted to be true. On the other hand, if Peter knows that Mary and Bill came but Susan didn't, while he had expected Susan to come as well, the sentence is not predicted to be true.

As mentioned at the outset, there is disagreement in the literature concerning the exact range of possible interpretations of *wh*-questions under *surprise*. While George (2011, 2013) proposes that *surprise* only allows for non-exhaustive ('mention-some') readings of *wh*-complements, Heim (1994) and Guerzoni and Sharvit (2007) suggest that it only allows for weakly exhaustive readings, and Klinedinst and Rothschild (2011) and Theiler (2014) argue that strongly exhaustive readings are also possible. Experimental results of Cremers and Chemla (2016) confirm the availability of strongly exhaustive readings. At a more fine-grained level, Spector and Egré (2015) argue that the epistemic presuppositional component of the verb (our condition 2) should involve strong exhaustivity, though not the assertive component (our condition 3). Finally, Theiler (2014) distinguishes between a *literal* and a *deductive* reading of the verb, and argues that strong exhaustivity arises only on the deductive reading.

We do not want to and do not need to take a stance in this debate. The predictions of our entry as formulated above are in line with George (2011, 2013), but the entry could easily be adapted in order to generate exhaustive readings, and the distinction between literal and deductive readings could be incorporated as well. As far as we can see, this would not affect our account of the **whether* puzzle.

Now let us consider the predictions that arise from the entry in (35) when *surprise* takes a declarative complement. Consider the following example:

(39) It surprises Peter that Mary came to the party.

In this case the complement highlights a 0-place property, i.e., a proposition, namely the proposition that Mary came to the party. The sentence is predicted, first of all, to presuppose that this proposition is true. This captures the fact that *surprise* is a factive verb. Second, the sentence is predicted to presuppose that Peter believes that Mary came to the party. And finally, it is predicted to assert that the fact that Mary came is incompatible with Peter's prior expectations. These predictions appear to be right.

Two general features of our entry for *surprise* are worth emphasizing. First, as we have just exemplified, the entry applies in a uniform way to declarative and interrogative complements. This contrasts with the most common approach to responsive verbs, which is to view their declarative-embedding variant as basic, and then to *reduce* their interrogative-embedding variant to their declarative-embedding variant (see, e.g., Karttunen, 1977, Lahiri, 2002, Spector and Egré, 2015). Although we cannot substantiate our choice for a uniform approach in any detail here, we would like to note that this choice is not arbitrary; we believe that the uniform approach has significant advantages over the reductive one (see Theiler et al. 2018).

Second, note that our entry for *surprise* does not make direct reference to the truth conditions or resolution conditions of the complement ϕ; rather, it only makes reference to the properties/propositions that are highlighted by ϕ. While this keeps the entry neat and simple, it is not essential for our account of the **whether* puzzle. What *is* essential is that the presupposition requiring the existence of at least one true instance (condition 1) is formulated in terms of highlighting. The other two conditions could in principle be formulated in terms of truth/resolution conditions rather than highlighted properties/propositions.

Related to this, one may wonder whether the truth/resolution conditions of a sentence may in general be *derived* from the properties/propositions that it highlights. In that case, our semantics would not have to compute truth and resolution conditions recursively at all. However, this is not possible. To see this, recall that a declarative sentence (e.g. *Bill is sleeping*) and the corresponding polar question (e.g., *Is Bill sleeping?*) both highlight the same proposition. Clearly, the two sentences do not have the same truth/resolution conditions. Thus, highlighting cannot in general *replace* truth/resolution conditions as the core notion of our semantics.[7]

7.2.3 Back to the *whether Puzzle

We have seen that when *surprise* takes a *wh*-complement, the presupposition that every property highlighted by the complement has to have at least one true instance amounts to the existential requirement observed by d'Avis, and when *surprise* takes a declarative complement, the presupposition amounts to standard factivity. Now, what if *surprise* takes a *whether*-complement?

Polar Questions

Let us first consider a case with a polar interrogative complement:

(40) *It surprises Peter whether Mary came to the party.

Recall that we considered two possible hypothesis as to what is highlighted by polar interrogative complements. One possibility is that *whether Mary came to the party* only highlights the proposition 'that Mary came to the party', just like the corresponding matrix polar question. The other possibility, argued for by Starr (2014), is that, in addition, it also highlights the proposition 'that Mary didn't come to the

[7] If we leave declarative sentences and truth conditions out of the picture, focusing solely on questions, then highlighting *could* be taken as the basic notion of our semantics, with resolution conditions as a derived notion. Such an approach is explicitly taken in Aloni et al. (2007) and in a sense already implicit in Groenendijk and Stokhof (1984). As noted above, what we call the property highlighted by a question is referred to in this earlier work as the *abstract* of the question.

party'.

We will consider both possible hypotheses in turn, starting with the second because it yields the most straightforward account of the **whether* puzzle. Recall that *surprise* presupposes that every property/proposition highlighted by its complement has a true instance in the world of evaluation. This means that, if the complement in (40)highlights both the proposition 'that Mary came to the party' and the proposition 'that Mary didn't come to the party', then (40) as a whole presupposes that both of these propositions are true in the world of evaluation, something that is impossible. So the sentence has a contradictory presupposition, and the same holds for any other sentence in which *surprise* takes a polar *whether*-complement. This systematic contradictoriness can be taken to account for its perceived ungrammaticality.[8]

Now consider the other possible hypothesis as to what is highlighted by polar interrogative complements.[9] Under this hypothesis, (40) is predicted to presuppose that Mary came to the party and that Peter knows this, and to assert that Mary's presence is incompatible with Peter's prior expectations. Note that this is precisely the same as what our account predicts for (39), which differs from (40) only in that it involves a declarative complement rather than a *whether*-complement. This equivalence does not rely on any specific feature of the example under consideration; it occurs systematically, whenever an emotive factive verb takes a polar interrogative complement. We propose that this systematic equivalence, together with the fact that declarative complements are plausibly less complex than polar interrogative complements in terms of processing,[10] and therefore more likely to ensure communicative success, explains why emotive factive verbs do not license polar interrogative complements. That is, in the spirit of neo-Gricean pragmatics (e.g., Horn, 1984) and bidirectional optimality theory (e.g., Blutner, 2000), we take this to be a case where one construction is **blocked** with regard to a certain interpretation because that same interpretation can be expressed by another construction in a better way, i.e., one

[8]See Gajewski (2002) for a general discussion of explaining perceived ungrammaticality in terms of systematic contradictoriness or triviality.

[9]Even if Starr (2014) is right that this hypothesis is not suitable for *whether*-complements, what follows would still be needed to account for the fact that polar *if*-complements are just as bad under emotive factives as polar *whether*-complements.

[10]We assume, as is quite widely done, that computing the semantic value of a polar interrogative complement involves the same operations that are needed to compute the proposition expressed by the corresponding declarative complement, plus an additional operation (roughly, 'adding the complement proposition'). For a more in-depth discussion of this issue, see Farkas and Roelofsen (2017).

that reduces processing effort and thereby increases the likelihood of communicative success.

Such blocking effects have been found in many other empirical domains as well. An example discussed by both Horn (1984, p.24) and Blutner (2000, p.194) is that of 'disjoint reference effects', illustrated in (41):

(41) John washed him. $\rightsquigarrow$ him $\neq$ John

The pronoun *him* cannot be taken to refer to John in this configuration, because that would yield an interpretation that could be expressed by (42) as well:

(42) John washed himself.

Assuming that the range of possible antecedents of reflexive pronouns like *himself* is heavily constrained by the grammar, using such a reflexive pronoun instead of a non-reflexive one is much more likely to ensure communicative success. Hence, the availability of (42) blocks coreference in (41).[11]

Interestingly, there is one particular phenomenon that has been explained in terms of blocking which is very closely related to the phenomenon we are trying to explain here. Namely, as noted by Adger and Quer (2001), there is a peculiar contrast between *whether*- and *if*-complements in certain contexts. For instance, while the *whether*-complements in (43a) and (44a) are perfectly acceptable, the corresponding *if*-complements in (43b) and (44b) are not.

(43) a. The bartender told me whether I was drunk.
 b. *The bartender told me if I was drunk.

(44) a. Jones admitted whether he was drunk.
 b. *Jones admitted if he was drunk.

Eckardt (2007) proposes an account of this contrast in terms of blocking. Given her lexical semantics for verbs like *tell* and *admit* and her treatment of *whether*- and *if*-complements, sentences like (43b) and (44b), in contrast with ones like (43a) and (44a), are systematically equivalent with ones where the *if*-complement is replaced by the corresponding *that*-complement. Given this equivalence, Eckardt reasons precisely as we did above: *if*-complements are blocked in these constructions because they are arguably more complex than *that*-clauses

[11] This example of blocking is only briefly discussed in Horn (1984) and Blutner (2000). See Levinson (2000), Kiparsky (2002), Beaver (2004), and Mattausch (2004), among others, for full-fledged theories of pronominal anaphora where blocking plays an important role.

in terms of processing, and therefore non-optimal. To the extent that this account is correct, it provides independent support for the idea that the selectional restrictions of clause-embedding verbs are partially determined by blocking effects, in particular ones resulting from the competition between *if*/*whether*-complements and *that*-complements.

It should be emphasized that the account we are proposing, as well as theories of other phenomena in terms of blocking, are compatible with the possibility that certain blocking effects are fully grammaticalized (see, e.g., Levinson, 2000, Blutner and Strigin, 2011). That is, it may well be that the competition between polar interrogative complements and declarative complements under emotive factives does not play a role anymore in actual processing, but has been the driving force behind a diachronic development which has led to the ungrammaticality of the non-optimal construction.

Finally, before turning to the case of alternative questions, let us note that our account is reminiscent of the pragmatic approaches of Guerzoni (2007) and Sæbø (2007), briefly mentioned in the introduction, in that they also allude to competition between declarative and polar interrogative complements. There are, however, two crucial differences. First, on our account the competition is not with one out of two declarative complements (*that Mary came* or *that Mary didn't come*), depending on which one is true in the world of evaluation, but rather always with the same declarative complement, which is simply obtained by replacing *whether* with *that*. As a consequence, we do not need to include speaker factivity as an additional assumption, something we identified as a weakness of the pragmatic approach.

Second, our semantics predicts that replacing a polar interrogative complement by the corresponding declarative complement does not yield a stronger interpretation, but rather the *same* interpretation. This renders a polar interrogative complement systematically dispreferred w.r.t. the corresponding declarative complement, whose semantic computation involves less effort and is therefore more likely to be interpreted as intended. Thus, while our account also has a pragmatic component, it is not *quantity* based ("the speaker should have been more informative"), but rather *manner* based ("the speaker could have expressed the same meaning in a way that would have been easier to process and would thus have been more likely to lead to successful communication").[12]

[12]It would be problematic for the present account if there were verbs which, when combined with a *whether*-complement, would systematically yield exactly the same

Alternative Questions

Now let us consider a case where the complement of *surprise* is an alternative question.

(45) *It surprises Bill whether Susan is drinking coffee or tea.

Here, the complement highlights two 0-place properties, i.e., two propositions, namely 'that Susan is drinking coffee' and 'that Susan is drinking tea'. The verb presupposes that both of these properties have a true instance in the world of evaluation. Since the properties are 0-place, this again just means that they have to be true. So the verb contributes the presupposition that Susan is drinking both coffee and tea.

From here we can proceed in either one of two ways. A first option is to adopt the commonplace assumption that alternative questions by themselves, i.e., independently of the embedding verb, imply that *exactly one* of the listed alternatives holds (see, e.g., Karttunen and Peters, 1976, Roelofsen and van Gool, 2010, Biezma and Rawlins, 2012). In our example, this implication says that Susan is drinking either coffee or tea, but *not both.* This is incompatible with the presupposition generated by the verb. Thus, the sentence as a whole comes out contradictory, and this explains its oddness.

If we do not want to rely on any specific assumption about the implications of alternative questions, there is also another way to account for the oddness of (45). This explanation starts with the observation that (45)comes out equivalent to (46), with a conjunctive declarative

interpretation as when combined with the corresponding declarative complement, and yet would not be perceived as ungrammatical with a *whether*-complement. At first sight, *doubt* appears to be such a verb. For instance, *I doubt whether Eric will come* and *I doubt that Eric will come* are both grammatical and seem to mean roughly the same. Upon closer inspection, however, there might be subtle differences in meaning between *doubt whether* and *doubt that* constructions. According to the American Heritage dictionary (www.ahdictionary.comwww.ahdictionary.com):

> "The choice of what conjunction to use following *doubt* and *doubtful* is a perennial usage problem. [...] When the expectation for the outcome is negative, *that* tends to be used. Some 86 percent of the Usage Panel prefer *that* in the sentence *I doubt [that/whether/if] it will rain tomorrow* (where the expectation is that it probably won't rain), with *whether* getting the preference of only 6 percent and *if* getting 7 percent. Note that, in certain kinds of sentences, the choice of conjunction can carry subtle differences in implication. *That* is the best choice when the truth of the clause following *doubt* is assumed, as in negative sentences and questions. Thus *I never doubted for a minute that I would be rescued* implies "I was certain that I would be rescued." By the same token, *Do you doubt that you will be paid?* may be understood as a rhetorical question meaning "Surely you believe that you will be paid," whereas *Do you doubt whether you will be paid?* expresses a genuine request for information (and might be followed by *Because if you do, you should make the client post a bond*)."

complement:

(46) It surprises Bill that Susan is drinking coffee and tea.

Given this equivalence, we could argue, just as in the case of polar questions, that alternative questions are ruled out under verbs like *surprise* through competition with declarative complements, which are preferable because they are less complex and therefore also more likely to lead to successful communication.

Thus, the two possible explanations for the infelicity of alternative questions under emotive factives are parallel to the two possible explanations we gave for the infelicity of polar questions under such verbs. The first possible explanation is that the relevant constructions, under certain (independently motivated) auxiliary assumptions, involve contradictory presuppositions. The second possible explanation, which does not require any auxiliary assumptions, is that they are blocked through competition with declarative complements.

A Quantificational Case

Now let us consider a case with a quantificational subject, which we mentioned in the introduction as a problem for the pragmatic approaches of Guerzoni (2007) and Sæbø (2007).

(47) *Every guest was surprised whether he got breakfast.

Our explanation for the oddness of this sentence is essentially the same as that for (40). Namely, due to the existential presupposition of *surprise*, we predict that (47)is semantically equivalent with (48), which involves a declarative complement rather than a polar interrogative complement.

(48) Every guest was surprised that he got breakfast.

This equivalence, together with the lower complexity of the declarative complement, accounts for the infelicity of (47) through blocking. Thus, quantified cases do not require any additional stipulations.

Concealed Questions

There is one additional prediction that is worth mentioning before concluding. Consider the following contrast, pointed out by Martin Stokhof:

(49) a. *Whether they serve breakfast is surprising.
b. The answer to the question whether they serve breakfast is surprising.

This example shows that, whereas *surprise* does not license a plain polar question as its complement, it does license a so-called 'concealed question' concerning the answer to that polar question. This contrast is expected on our view, under the assumption that concealed questions involve a type-shifting operation that turns the determiner phrase (here, *the answer to the question whether they serve breakfast*) into a *wh*-question concerning the identity of the referent of that phrase (*What is the answer to the question whether they serve breakfast*), an assumption that has been argued for in some detail in Aloni and Roelofsen (2011).[13] Concealed questions are, under this assumption, expected to pattern with *wh*-questions rather than with *whether*-questions, and thus correctly predicted to be licensed under emotive factives.

7.3 Summary and Outlook

We have posited that emotive factive verbs like *surprise*, *bother*, and *please* are, unlike other factive verbs like *know*, *remember*, and *discover*, not just about the true extension of their complement clause, but rather about something more specific, namely, about one or more **true instances** of the properties that are *highlighted* by their complement. As a natural consequence, these verbs presuppose that every property highlighted by their complement has at least one true instance in the world of evaluation.

When the complement is declarative, this presupposition amounts to a standard factivity presupposition. In the case of a *wh*-complement, it amounts to the requirement that there be at least one individual that has the property highlighted by the question, in line with empirical observations by d'Avis (2002). And finally, in the case of *whether*-complements, the proposed analysis predicts oddness, either due to contradictory presuppositions or to systematic equivalence with the corresponding declarative complements.

Central to our account is the notion of highlighting, which was initially motivated by observations concerning *yes*/*no* responses and other kinds of propositional anaphora. If highlighting is indeed an important aspect of the semantics of questions, one would expect it to be relevant for other question-related phenomena as well, beyond anaphora and the interaction with question-embedding verbs. It seems that there are indeed many such phenomena. We will give one brief illustration here, having nothing to do with anaphora or question embedding but rather with the felicity conditions of questions in discourse.[14]

---

[13] Several other approaches to concealed questions exist as well (see, e.g., Nathan, 2006, Schwager, 2007, Romero, 2010, Frana, 2013). We refer to Aloni and Roelofsen (2011) for comparison.

[14] Beyond the phenomena discussed here, highlighting has also played a role in

Consider the following contrast:

(50) A: Is Peter coming for dinner tonight?
B: Is he in town this week?

(51) A: Is Peter coming for dinner tonight?
B: #Is he out of town this week?

This contrast is striking because the response questions in (50) and (51) are equivalent in terms of resolution conditions. Both questions elicit a choice between two alternatives: 'in town' and 'out of town'. But they differ in which alternative they highlight: the first highlights the 'in town' alternative, the second highlights the 'out of town' alternative. Apparently this matters.

The contrast is perhaps even more marked if we insert the particle *even* (see Iatridou and Tatevosov, 2015, for discussion of this use of *even* in polar questions):

(52) A: Is Peter coming for dinner tonight?
B: Is he even in town this week?

(53) A: Is Peter coming for dinner tonight?
B: #Is he even out of town this week?

Notice that from A's question, B can infer that *if* Peter is out of town, then A would not be able to confirm this—otherwise she would not have asked whether he is coming for dinner. So, if A can answer B's response question, the answer must be that Peter is in town. Let us say that the 'out of town' alternative in B's question is *doomed.*

These examples suggest the following preliminary generalization:

(54) *Preliminary generalization: Don't highlight doomed alternatives!* If a speaker asks a question Q and one of the alternatives in $[\![Q]\!]$ is doomed, i.e., it can be inferred in the context of utterance that the addressee will not be able to confirm it, then the speaker should not highlight this alternative.

However, the following response questions are fine:

(55) A: Is Peter coming for dinner tonight?
B: Isn't he out of town this week?

(56) A: Is Peter coming for dinner tonight?
B: He is out of town this week, isn't he?

recent work on conditionals (Onea and Steinbach, 2012, Starr, 2014), modified numerals (Coppock and Brochhagen, 2013), and discourse particles (Csipak and Zobel, 2014, Rojas-Esponda, 2014).

Assuming that these response questions highlight the 'out of town' alternative (which can be justified by considering what *yes* and *no* mean in response to these questions), these are counterexamples to our preliminary generalization.

Interestingly, a rising declarative highlighting the 'out of town' alternative is again infelicitous:

(57) A: Is Peter coming for dinner tonight?
B: #He is out of town this week?

In Farkas and Roelofsen (2017) it is argued based on other contrasts between rising declaratives and tag questions that, while both signal that the speaker has access to some evidence for the highlighted alternative, rising declaratives indicate that the speaker's credence in this alternative is at most low (possibly even zero), while tag questions signal that the speaker's credence in the highlighted alternative is moderate to high.

It is often assumed that high negation questions also signal that the speaker is epistemically biased towards the highlighted alternative. It seems reasonable to assume that the speaker's credence in the highlighted alternative must be moderate to high in this case as well, just like in the case of tag questions. This, then, leads to the following revised generalization:

(58) *Refined generalization: Only highlight doomed alternatives if probable!*
If a speaker asks a question Q and one of the alternatives in $[\![Q]\!]$ is doomed, then she should only highlight this alternative if she believes that it is true with moderate to high confidence, and in this case the form of the question should signal that she has such a belief.

This generalization may have to be further refined, and of course one would ultimately like to derive it from more basic principles. This is left for future work. For now, we conclude that the notion of highlighting seems to be useful not only in capturing phenomena to do with anaphora and question embedding, but also in characterizing the felicity conditions of questions in discourse.

Taking a step back, one could ask what all these phenomena have in common. The answer is that they all bring out certain contrasts between different types of questions that are indistinguishable in terms of resolution conditions. These contrasts may concern two 'opposing' polar questions (e.g., *Is he in town?* versus *Is he out of town?*), a polar question and a *wh*-question (e.g., *Is the order still in progress?* versus

What is the status of the order?), or any other combination. Whenever we find such contrasts, we could ask whether they might be due to the fact that the different types of questions bring different properties or propositions into salience. If so, highlighting will most likely be useful in accounting for the observed contrasts.

References

Abels, Klaus. 2004. Why surprise-predicates do not embed polar interrogatives. *Linguistische Arbeitsberichte* 81:203–222.

Adger, David and Josep Quer. 2001. The syntax and semantics of unselected embedded questions. *Language* pages 107–133.

Aloni, Maria, David Beaver, Brady Clark, and Robert van Rooij. 2007. The dynamics of topics and focus. In M. Aloni, A. Butler, and P. Dekker, eds., *Questions in Dynamic Semantics*. Elsevier.

Aloni, Maria and Floris Roelofsen. 2011. Interpreting concealed questions. *Linguistics and Philosophy* 34(5):443–478.

Beaver, David. 2004. The optimization of discourse anaphora. *Linguistics and Philosophy* 27(1):3–56.

Biezma, Maria and Kyle Rawlins. 2012. Responding to alternative and polar questions. *Linguistics and Philosophy* 35(5):361–406.

Blutner, Reinhard. 2000. Some aspects of optimality in natural language interpretation. *Journal of Semantics* 17(3):189.

Blutner, Reinhard and Anatoli Strigin. 2011. Bidirectional grammar and bidirectional optimization. In *Bidirectional optimality theory*, pages 221–248. John Benjamins.

Coppock, Elizabeth and Thomas Brochhagen. 2013. Diagnosing truth, interactive sincerity, and depictive sincerity. In *Proceedings of SALT 2013*, pages 358–375.

Cremers, Alexandre and Emmanuel Chemla. 2016. A psycholinguistic study of the exhaustive readings of embedded questions. *Journal of Semantics* 33(1):49–85.

Csipak, Eva and Sarah Zobel. 2014. A condition on the distribution of discourse particles across types of questions. In *Proceedings of NELS 44*, pages 83–94.

d'Avis, Franz-Josef. 2002. On the interpretation of *wh*-clauses in exclamative environments. *Theoretical linguistics* 28(1):5–31.

Eckardt, Regine. 2007. The syntax and pragmatics of embedded yes/no questions. In K. Schwabe and S. Winkler, eds., *On Information Structure, Meaning and Form*, pages 447–467. Amsterdam: John Benjamins.

Egré, Paul. 2008. Question-embedding and factivity. *Grazer Philosophische Studien* 77:85–125. Special issue on Knowledge and Questions edited by F. Lihoreau.

Farkas, Donka F. and Floris Roelofsen. 2012. Polar initiatives and polarity particle responses in an inquisitive discourse model. Presented at the Amsterdam Colloquium, December 2011, and at the Newcastle Workshop on the Syntax of Answers to Polar Questions, June 2012.

Farkas, Donka F. and Floris Roelofsen. 2017. Division of labor in the interpretation of declaratives and interrogatives. *Journal of Semantics* 34(2):237–289.

Frana, Ilaria. 2013. Quantified concealed questions. *Natural Language Semantics* 21(2):179–218.

Gajewski, Jon. 2002. L-analyticity and natural language. Manuscript, MIT.

George, Benjamin Ross. 2011. *Question embedding and the semantics of answers*. Ph.D. thesis, University of California, Los Angeles.

George, Ben Ross. 2013. Which judgments show weak exhaustivity? (and which don't?). *Natural language semantics* 21(4):401–427.

Groenendijk, Jeroen and Martin Stokhof. 1984. *Studies on the Semantics of Questions and the Pragmatics of Answers*. Ph.D. thesis, University of Amsterdam.

Guerzoni, Elena. 2007. Weak exhaustivity and *whether*: a pragmatic approach. In T. Friedman and M. Gibson, eds., *Proceedings of Semantics and Linguistic Theory (SALT 17)*, pages 112–129.

Guerzoni, Elena and Yael Sharvit. 2007. A question of strength: on NPIs in interrogative clauses. *Linguistics and Philosophy* 30(3):361–391.

Heim, Irene. 1994. Interrogative semantics and Karttunen's semantics for *know*. In R. Buchalla and A. Mittwoch, eds., *The Proceedings of the Ninth Annual Conference and the Worshop on Discourse of the Israel Association for Theoretical Linguistics*. Jerusalem: Academon.

Horn, Laurence R. 1984. Towards a new taxonomy of pragmatic inference: Q-based and R-based implicatures. In D. Schiffrin, ed., *Meaning, Form, and Use in Context*, pages 11–42. Georgetown University Press.

Iatridou, Sabine and Sergei Tatevosov. 2015. Our even. To appear in Linguistics and Philosophy.

Jacobson, Pauline. 2012. The myth of silent linguistic material. Presented at the Second East Asian School on Logic, Language, and Computation, Chongqing, China.

Karttunen, Lauri. 1969. Discourse referents. In *Proceedings of the Conference on Computational linguistics*, pages 1–38. Association for Computational Linguistics.

Karttunen, Lauri. 1973. Presuppositions of compound sentences. *Linguistic inquiry* 4(2):169–193.

Karttunen, Lauri. 1974. Presupposition and linguistic context. *Theoretical linguistics* 1(1-3):181–194.

Karttunen, Lauri. 1977. Syntax and semantics of questions. *Linguistics and Philosophy* 1:3–44.

Karttunen, Lauri and Stanley Peters. 1976. What indirect questions conventionally implicate. In *CLS 12: Papers from the Twelfth Regional Meeting*, pages 351–368. Chicago Linguistic Society.

Kiparsky, Paul. 2002. Disjoint reference and the typology of pronouns. In I. Kaufmann and B. Stiebels, eds., *More than Words*. Berlin: Academie Verlag.

Klinedinst, Nathan and Daniel Rothschild. 2011. Exhaustivity in questions with non-factives. *Semantics and Pragmatics* 4(2):1–23.

Krifka, Manfred. 2001. For a structured meaning account of questions and answers. *Audiatur Vox Sapientia. A Festschrift for Arnim von Stechow* pages 287–319.

Krifka, Manfred. 2013. *Ja, nein, doch* als sententiale anaphern. Manuscript, ZAS Berlin.

Lahiri, Utpal. 2002. *Questions and answers in embedded contexts*. Oxford University Press.

Levinson, Stephen. 2000. *Presumptive Meanings*. MIT press.

Mattausch, Jason. 2004. Optimality theoretic pragmatics and binding phenomena. In *Optimality theory and pragmatics*, pages 63–90. Springer.

Merchant, Jason. 2005. Fragments and ellipsis. *Linguistics and Philosophy* 27(6):661–738.

Nathan, Lance. 2006. *On the Interpretation of Concealed Questions*. Ph.D. thesis, MIT.

Nicolae, Andreea Cristina. 2013. *Any questions? Polarity as a window into the structure of questions*. Ph.D. thesis, Harvard.

Onea, Edgar and Markus Steinbach. 2012. Where question, conditionals and topics converge. In M. Aloni, V. Kimmelman, F. Roelofsen, G. Weidmann-Sassoon, K. Schulz, and M. Westera, eds., *Logic, Language, and Meaning. Selected papers from the 18th Amsterdam Colloquium*, pages 42–51. Berlin Heidelberg: Springer.

Pruitt, Kathryn and Floris Roelofsen. 2011. Disjunctive questions: prosody, syntax, and semantics. Presented at a seminar at the Georg August Universität Göttingen. Available via www.illc.uva.nl/inquisitivesemantics.

Roelofsen, Floris and Donka F. Farkas. 2015. Polarity particle responses as a window onto the interpretation of questions and assertions. *Language* 91(2):359–414.

Roelofsen, Floris, Michele Herbstritt, and Maria Aloni. 2016. The **whether* puzzle. To appear in *Questions in Discourse*, edited by Klaus von Heusinger, Edgar Onea, and Malte Zimmermann.

Roelofsen, Floris and Sam van Gool. 2010. Disjunctive questions, intonation, and highlighting. In M. Aloni, H. Bastiaanse, T. de Jager, and K. Schulz, eds., *Logic, Language, and Meaning: Selected Papers from the Seventeenth Amsterdam Colloquium*, pages 384–394. Berlin: Springer.

Rojas-Esponda, Tania. 2014. A QUD account of German *doch*. In U. Etxeberria, A. Fălăuş, A. Irurtzun, and B. Leferman, eds., *Proceedings of Sinn und Bedeutung 18*, pages 359–376.

Romero, Maribel. 2010. Concealed questions with quantifiers. In M. Aloni, H. Bastiaanse, T. de Jager, and K. Schulz, eds., *Logic, Language, and Meaning, selected and revised papers from the Amsterdam Colloquium*, pages 21–31. Springer.

Romero, Maribel. 2015. Surprise-predicates, strong exhaustivity and alternative questions. In *Semantics and Linguistic Theory*, vol. 25, pages 225–245.

Romero, Maribel. 2016. Strong exhaustivity, alternative questions and monotonicity: Some thoughts on Cremers and Chemla (2016). Handout presented at the XPrag workshop *Disjunction Days: Theoretical and experimental perspectives on the semantics and pragmatics of disjunction*, June 2016.

Sæbø, Kjell Johan. 2007. A whether forecast. In B. ten Cate and H. Zeevat, eds., *Logic, Language, and Computation*, pages 189–199. Springer.

Schwager, Magdalena. 2007. Keeping prices low: an answer to a concealed question. In A. Gronn, ed., *Proceedings of Sinn und Bedeutung XII*.

Spector, Benjamin and Paul Egré. 2015. A uniform semantics for embedded interrogatives: An answer, not necessarily the answer. *Synthese* 192(6):1729–1784.

Starr, William B. 2014. What 'if'? *Philosophical Imprint* 14(10):1–27.

Szabolcsi, Anna. 1997. Quantifiers in pair-list readings. In A. Szabolcsi, ed., *Ways of Scope Taking*, pages 311–347. Springer.

Szabolcsi, Anna. 2015. Can questions be directly disjoined? Presented at the Chicago Linguistics Society conference (CLS 51).

Theiler, Nadine. 2014. *A multitude of answers: Embedded questions in typed inquisitive semantics*. University of Amsterdam, MSc thesis.

Theiler, Nadine, Floris Roelofsen, and Maria Aloni. 2018. A uniform semantics for declarative and interrogative complements. *Journal of Semantics* 35(3):409–466.

Westera, Matthijs. 2017. *Exhaustivity and intonation: a unified theory*. Ph.D. thesis, Institute for Logic, Language and Computation, University of Amsterdam.

8

How not to Project the Satisfaction Theory of Projection (on Karttunen) *Or: Who has a Proviso Problem?*[*]

ITAMAR FRANCEZ

8.1 Introduction

The *satisfaction-based conception of presupposition*, originating in early work by Stalnaker and Karttunen, is arguably the dominant conception of presupposition in linguistic semantics. According to this conception, presuppositions are conditions imposed by linguistic expressions on contexts, such that if the conditions are not satisfied by a context, the expressions cannot, in that context, be assigned an interpretation. In the simplest cases, where a sentence presupposes a proposition, the expression can be interpreted only in contexts that entail this proposition (for Karttunen) or in which that proposition is accepted as common ground (for Stalnaker).[1]

[*]I thank Cleo Condoravdi, Sven Lauer, Julian Grove and Greg Kobele for discussion and criticism of the issues discussed here. I thank María Biezma and Maribel Romero for the opportunity to present initial thoughts and solicit feedback at their *Conditionals at the crossroads* workshop at the University of Konstanz. I have also benefited from feedback from Yasu Sudo, Matt Mandelkern, Raj Singh, Jacopo Romoli, and Paul Elbourne, who read earlier versions out of which this paper grew.

[1]Though both Stalnaker and Karttunen conceive of presuppositions as preconditions on contexts, they do not have exactly the same view of presupposition. For

Tokens of Meaning: Papers in Honor of Lauri Karttunen.
Cleo Condoravdi and Tracy Holloway King (eds.).

This conception of presupposition has the attractive feature that it very naturally captures cases in which the presupposition of an expression is not propositional, as is the case with familiarity presuppositions (Heim 1982 and much subsequent work). It also allows us to model one of the key insights of Karttunen (1974), discussed below and often overlooked, that even in cases in which an expression is intuited to carry a propositional presupposition, it is not always possible to say what that presupposition is independently of context. This is the case, for example, with additive *too*, discussed by Heim (1990, 1992), and used by Stalnaker (2002) to illustrate his version of the same point, namely that in some cases, a speaker clearly presupposes a proposition in uttering a sentence, yet there is no proposition that must be accepted as common ground in all contexts in which the sentence is acceptable.

In an influential paper, Geurts (1996) coins the term *satisfaction theory* to name a set of dynamic semantic analyses of presupposition projection. Geurts' main argument is that the satisfaction theory suffers a detrimental, insurmountable problem, which he calls "the proviso problem". The problem is that the satisfaction theory's predictions about the projection behavior of conditionals[2] do not match their actual projection behavior:

> "In particular, the satisfaction theory often predicts presuppositions of the form $\phi \rightarrow \psi$, where the intuitively perceived presupposition is simply ψ." (p. 260)[3]

According to Geurts (p. 259), "the ideas underlying the satisfaction theory go back to Stalnaker (1973, 1974) and Karttunen (1974). They were shaped into an explicit theory by Heim (1983)". Indeed, the general conception in the subsequent literature is that satisfaction theory, as shaped by Heim, is advocated by Karttunen in Karttunen (1974). Thus, Van Rooij (2007) discusses "the satisfaction theory of presupposition, as motivated by Karttunen (1974) and Stalnaker (1974) and implemented by Heim (1983) and others", and Singh (2007) directly cites "Karttunen 1974, Stalnaker 1974, Heim 1983, Beaver 2001, von Fintel (2006)[4], among others" as instances of "satisfaction theories".

Furthermore, Geurts' paper implies that the satisfaction theory suf-

---

Stalnaker, presupposition is a pragmatic notion, an interlocutor attitude, whereas for Karttunen, it is a semantic one, having to do with semantic context change (though Karttunen describes it as pragmatic in Karttunen 1974). This difference is not discussed here.

[2]Also disjunctions, but I will be exclusively concerned with conditionals here.

[3]Here and throughout, $\rightarrow$ corresponds to material implication unless noted otherwise.

[4]von Fintel (2006) is an earlier, manuscript version of von Fintel (2008).

fers the proviso problem *because* it is based on a problematic conception of presupposition. This is already implied by the very term "satisfaction theory". The implication is strengthened, on the one hand, by presenting the satisfaction theory as an explicit implementation of Stalnaker and Karttunen's ideas,[5] and on the other hand, by contrasting the satisfaction theory with one that does not employ the satisfaction-based conception of presupposition and does not suffer the proviso problem.

This paper does not aim to make a contribution to the theory of projection[6] or towards solving the proviso problem. My aim is, rather, to clarify and contextualize, largely through exegesis, the relation between the ideas about presupposition and projection expressed in Karttunen (1974), the dynamic theory of projection Geurts calls 'satisfaction theory', the satisfaction-based conception of presupposition, and the proviso problem. In particular, I make the following two points:

(i) Contrary to the impression one might get from the literature, the "satisfaction theory" as defined and criticized by Geurts, namely the theory of projection for conditionals developed in Heim (1983), does not implement the ideas presented in Karttunen (1974).

In fact, I argue that Karttunen's entire project can be taken to be antithetical to the construction of a theory that predicts context invariant presuppositions for conditionals (and complex expressions more generally).

(ii) Contrary to an implication of Geurts' paper, the reason satisfaction theory suffers the proviso problem is not that it assumes a satisfaction-based conception of presupposition.

Rather, satisfaction theory suffers the proviso problem because it identifies the presuppositions of an expression, specifically those of conditionals, with the minimal definedness conditions determined by a standard dynamic semantics. A proponent of the satisfaction-based conception of presupposition,[7] such as Karttunen is in no way committed to such an identification. On the contrary, the ideas put forth in Karttunen (1974) explicitly call for maintaining the satisfaction-based conception of pre-

[5]Though, as noted above, Karttunen and Stalnaker's ideas differ significantly. In particular, Stalnaker, unlike Karttunen, is not adopting a dynamic approach to semantics at all. The idea they *do* share is that presuppositions should be conceived of as conditions that need to be satisfied for successful interpretation.

[6]Projection is not a property of presupposition alone, but of a variety of inferences. Recently, Simons et al. (2010) have argued that projection is a general property of all implications that are not *at issue*, i.e. do not serve to resolve an open issue of privileged relevance in the context of discourse.

[7]Here I am echoing comments already made in Beaver (2001) and van Rooij (2007).

supposition, while rejecting the idea that it is possible, or desirable, to predict what a conditional presupposes from the presuppositions of its constituent sentences, precisely because of Karttunen's insight mentioned above, namely that what a conditional presupposes depends on context.

8.2 Satisfaction and Projection

Influenced by Stalnaker's pragmatic analysis of presupposition, Karttunen articulated an influential way of modeling the satisfaction-based conception of presupposition, i.e. the (arguably Fregean) idea that a presupposition is a precondition for the interpretability of a sentence. Specifically, he proposed to model presuppositions as conditions imposed by expressions on contexts, bodies of information on which utterances of such expressions operate. Within a dynamic conception of interpretation, sentence meanings are viewed as operations on contexts, and a presupposition is a condition that a context must satisfy in order for a sentence meaning to operate on it. In the simplest case, contexts are sets of worlds and presuppositions are stated in terms of propositions. To say that a sentence S presupposes p is to say that in order for S to carry out its conventionally determined operation on a context c, c must entail p. A context c entails a proposition p iff $c \subseteq p$. The conditions imposed by expressions on contexts, however, need not be propositions. In Heim's (1982) influential familiarity theory of definiteness, a definite description imposes the requirement that the context contain a particular discourse referent.

Much literature on presupposition, however, has been concerned with a problem that arises on any conception of what presuppositions are, namely the problem of presupposition projection, the relation between the presuppositions of simple expressions and those of complex expressions that contain them. The satisfaction-based conception of presupposition, obviously, does not in itself provide an account of projection. It is no more a full fledged grammatical account of presupposition than the conception of meaning as contribution to truth conditions is a full fledged grammatical account of denotational semantics.

8.3 Karttunen's Insight

Karttunen (1974) proposed to link the satisfaction-based conception of presupposition to the projection problem in an interesting and surprising way. A crucial empirical observation of Karttunen's, exemplified in (1) (example 3 in Karttunen 1974), is that what at least some compound sentences presuppose is not fixed, but depends on the properties of the context in which they are uttered.

(1) a. If Dean told the truth, Nixon is guilty too.
b. If Haldeman is guilty, Nixon is guilty too.
c. If Miss Woods destroyed the missing tapes, Nixon is guilty too.

(1a) presupposes the guilt of someone other than Nixon. (1b) does not. (1c) does in a context in which destroying tapes is not considered a crime, but does not in a context in which it is. In light of these examples, Karttunen suggests (already in Karttunen 1973) the descriptive generalization in (2) about the presuppositions of conditionals.

(2) **Karttunen's generalization**:
The presuppositions of *if* A, B (with respect to a context X) consist of:
a. all the presuppositions of A (with respect to X) and
b. all the presuppositions of B (with respect to $X \cup A$) except those that are entailed by $X \cup A$ and are not entailed by X alone.

This generalization correctly describes the facts. That what a conditional presupposes depends on context is captured by clause (2b), which states that which presuppositions of the consequent B are presupposed by the conditional depends on what is entailed by $X \cup A$, and this, of course, depends on what X is like. In Karttunen's example, adding the information that Miss Woods destroyed the tapes will lead to the contextual entailment that she is guilty in a context which entails that destroying tapes is a crime, but not in a context that does not entail this. There is, however, also something clearly wrong with the way (2b) is stated, since whether an expression conventionally imposes a condition on contexts or not must be determinable independently of whether any given context satisfies that condition or not. For example, the sentence *God stopped hiding* presupposes that God was hiding, regardless of whether any given context satisfies the presupposition or not. The clause in (2b), however, states that whether or not a conditional *if* A *then* B imposes the conditions conventionally associated with B on a context depends on whether the context satisfies them or not.

What Karttunen sets out to demonstrate is that the satisfaction-based conception of presupposition makes it possible to state when a context satisfies the presuppositions of a conditional without committing to what those presuppositions are. In other words, it makes it possible to account for the empirical generalizations without stating a theory of projection, without making the theoretical commitment that the presupposition of a complex expression are predictable solely from those of its constituent parts, and, crucially, without making the empirically problematic assumption that one can state what an expression presupposes independently of context. The statement he offers is in (3), which forms the basis for his more general statement of when a context satisfies the presuppositions of a complex expression.

(3) Context X satisfies-the-presuppositions-of *If* A *then* B just in case (i) X satisfies-the-presuppositions-of A, and (ii) $X \cup A$ satisfies-the-presuppositions-of B.

(3) shifts the theoretical burden from predicting what a complex expression presupposes to predicting what it takes for a context to satisfy a complex expression's presuppositions.

This shift is of great consequence. Its importance lies not only in the fact that it allows Karttunen to better express the descriptive generalization in (2), but also because it enables an account of the context dependence of presupposition, of those cases in which it is not possible to point to a general condition that an expression imposes on all contexts, but it is possible to say, in a general way, what it takes for a context to satisfy whatever condition that is. An example is the case, mentioned earlier, of expressions with anaphoric presuppositions, such as additive *too* and definite descriptions. A particularly revealing example of the explanatory potential of distinguishing presuppositions from the different ways in which contexts can satisfy them is Condoravdi and Gawron's (1996) analysis of definite implicit arguments, where different ways of satisfying a familiarity presupposition account for distinct interpretations. Having explicated Karttunen's observation and theoretical move, I turn to what Geurts calls the satisfaction theory of presupposition and the proviso problem.

8.4 Satisfaction Theory and the Proviso Problem

The target of Geurts' paper, what he calls "the satisfaction theory", is a particular theory of presupposition projection developed within dynamic semantics, which assumes a particular definition of presupposition, a definition that, in turn, utilizes a satisfaction-based conception of presupposition. The theory, first articulated formally in Heim (1983), is very familiar and I do not reproduce it here in detail. Informally put, the idea behind it is that sentence meanings are operations on contexts, and stating the presuppositions of a simple expression is stating the conditions under which the conventional meaning of the sentence, the operation on contexts it conventionally performs, is defined. For example, the linguistic intuition that an expression S presupposes a proposition p is captured by making the operation that S conventionally performs on contexts defined only for contexts that entail p. Heim's theory of projection is simply that the presupposition of any complex expression are that expression's minimal definedness conditions as determined by the minimal definedness conditions of its parts and the dynamic semantics of the operators or connectives that put the parts together. As Geurts points out, this is a highly attractive theory, since it makes the projection properties of any expression a direct side effect of its dynamic semantics.

Unfortunately, argues Geurts, the predictions this theory makes do not match the empirical facts. He points out that, according to Heim's theory, the presupposition of an expression is defined as in (4) (where $c[\phi]$ is the context resulting from the operation ϕ performs on c). The equivalent definition found in Heim (1983) is given in (5).

(4) ϕ presupposes χ iff for all c, $c[\phi]$ is not defined unless c satisfies χ.

(5) S presupposes p iff all contexts that admit S entail p.

Geurts then observes that, given the definition in (4) and the standard assumptions about semantics and definedness for conditionals in (6), conditionals are predicted to have conditional presuppositions. A conditional $\phi \rightarrow \psi_r$ (where ψ_r means ψ presupposes r) is predicted to be defined in a context c whenever ψ_r is defined in $c[\phi]$, which is whenever c entails $\phi \rightarrow r$.

(6) $c[\phi \rightarrow \psi]$ is defined iff $c[\phi]$ is defined and $c[\phi][\psi]$ is defined.

As an example, consider (7).

(7) If it's raining, then it's stopped snowing.

As a matter of descriptive fact (where what is being described are native speaker intuitions), (7) presupposes that it was snowing. But if (4) is the definition of presupposition, then, given (6), (7) is wrongly predicted to presuppose that if it is raining, then it was snowing. This is because, according to (6), (7) is defined in all and only those contexts c such that c[*it's raining*] satisfies the presupposition of *it stopped snowing*, and this is the case exactly when c entails *if it's raining, it was snowing*. This is the proviso problem, and much work has been dedicated to reacting to it (Heim 1983, Beaver 1999, van Rooij 2007, Singh 2007, Schlenker 2011, Lassiter 2012, Lauer 2015 among others).

As discussed above, the general conception in the literature is that the satisfaction theory is a formal explication of the ideas of Stalnaker and Karttunen. The theory clearly employs their satisfaction-based conception of presupposition, the view that presuppositions are conditions on contexts. This, together with Geurts' discussion, also mentioned above, of van der Sandt's (1989) DRT based "binding" theory, which is *not* rooted in the satisfaction-based conception of presupposition and does not suffer the proviso problem, invites the inference that the proviso problem arises for satisfaction theory because of the conception of presupposition it employs. For example, Geurts ends his paper with the following statement: "The binding theory views a presupposition as an agile creature that sets itself off to either find its antecedent or become accommodated. The satisfaction theory, on the other hand, pictures presuppositions as lethargic beings that keep hanging around in the neighborhood, content to get local satisfaction. The main purpose of this paper was to show that presuppositions are more demanding than that."

8.5 How not to Project the Satisfaction Theory of Projection (on Karttunen)

Neither the diagnosis of the proviso problem as rooted in the satisfaction-based conception of presupposition[8] nor the claim that satisfaction theory embodies Karttunen's ideas are warranted. First, as the discussion in section (8.3) should make very clear, Karttunen, working within a satisfaction conception of presupposition, goes to great pains to *not* predict conditional presuppositions for conditionals. On the contrary, the entire point of his move, as elaborated above, is to be able to deal with his descriptive generalization (2), that conditionals presuppose different things in different contexts, and therefore to avoid making context independent predictions about what they presuppose, predicting instead what the set of contexts that can satisfy their presuppositions is. So, not only is the satisfaction theory not an implementation of Karttunen's ideas, its premises are practically antithetical to his.

Second, the proviso problem arises for the satisfaction theory not because it is rooted in a satisfaction-based conception of presupposition, but because it employs the definition of presupposition in (4) and (5). These definitions of presupposition obliterate Karttunen's distinction between the presuppositions of an expression and what it takes for a context to satisfy them.

On Karttunen's theory of contextual satisfaction, a context c satisfies

[8] A diagnosis which Geurts himself changes elsewhere (p. 292), where he attributes the proviso problem not to the conception of presupposition on which the satisfaction theory is based, but rather to what the theory says about projection: "presuppositional requirements are inevitably weakened because of the way they are transmitted to the global context."

the presuppositions of conditional $\phi \rightarrow \psi_r$ in exactly the following kinds of context:

(i) c entails r

(ii) c does not entail r, but $c[\phi]$ does.

For any context c of the type in (i) or (ii), it is also true that $c[\phi]$ entails r, and therefore any such context is of the type in (iii) (contexts of type (i) are trivially of type (iii)).

(iii) c entails $\phi \rightarrow r$

(iii) is therefore the minimal condition for a context to satisfy the presuppositions of a conditional.

The definition of presupposition in (4), and hence what Geurts calls the satisfaction theory, identifies the presupposition of a conditional with this minimal condition, and hence makes the prediction that conditionals with presuppositional consequents have conditional presuppositions. As already pointed out above, however, the satisfaction-based conception of presupposition in no way requires us to make this identification.[9] In fact, Geurts himself provides a different characterization of presupposition, the one in (8), immediately before proposing (4).

(8) If ϕ presupposes χ, then $c[\phi]$ isn't defined unless c satisfies χ.

(8) says that if an expression ϕ presupposes something, then $c[\phi]$ is not defined unless c satisfies the condition that is the presupposition of ϕ.[10] The reverse is part of the definition of presupposition espoused by the satisfaction theory, but it is not part of the satisfaction-based conception of presupposition. It might very well be that $c[\phi]$ is not defined unless c satisfies some condition, but that the condition that is the presupposition of ϕ is a stronger one.[11] Given a standard dynamic semantics in which basic presuppositions induce (but are not identified with) definedness conditions, a conditional $\phi \rightarrow \psi_r$ is clearly not defined in a context c unless c satisfies $\phi \rightarrow r$. The conclusion that this is what the conditional presupposes, however, is not merited by the assumption that presuppositions are admissibility conditions. The actual presuppositions of a conditional (like those of additive *too*) are

---

[9] van Rooij (2007) points to Beaver (2001) as an example of a theory couched in this conception of presupposition that does not make the identification.

[10] Recall that presuppositions need not be propositions.

[11] Turning the *if* in (8) into an *iff* is clearly wrong if the goal of defining presupposition formally is to capture the notion of presupposition employed in linguistic theory, namely the backgrounded inferences associated with linguistic expressions by virtue of grammatical convention. It would entail that every sentence presupposes any number of tautologies, an intuition that native speakers never have, essentially emptying the term presupposition of empirical content.

themselves context dependent, and one can state when they are satisfied **without** making any context independent predictions about what they are. So, the source of the proviso problem is not the satisfaction-based conception of presupposition, but the definition of presupposition employed in the analyses of projection that Geurts calls the satisfaction theory.

If the presuppositions of a conditional can be satisfied both by contexts of type (i) and contexts of type (ii) above, one obviously would like to know: when does a conditional require a context to be of type (i), and when does it require the weaker type (ii)? This is the problem raised by Karttunen's theory of presuppositions as conditions on contexts, but it is not the projection problem. It is the problem of accounting for the role of context in determining what an expression presupposes. Van Rooij's (2007) idea is that a conditional requires its input context c to be of type (i) when the information contained in the antecedent ϕ is not enough to ensure that $c[\phi]$ entails r no matter what c looks like. In other words, when ϕ and r are conditionally independent of each other. For example, in (7) above, the presupposition of the consequent is that it was snowing. Adding the information that it is raining to a context c is not generally enough to secure the inference that it was snowing. If c, for example, contained worlds in which it was snowing as well as ones in which it was not, there is no assurance that the subset of c in which it is raining does not also contain both kinds of worlds, in which case c will not be a context of type (ii). In this case, therefore, the context is required by the conditional to be of the type in (i), and so the conditional is correctly predicted to presuppose that it is snowing.[12] This explanation is not only compatible with, but is couched within, a satisfaction theory of presupposition. A related idea that brings in pragmatic considerations of plausibility can be found in Beaver (1999, 2001).

8.6 Conclusion

Geurts (1996) demonstrates that what he calls the satisfaction theory of presupposition makes systematically wrong predictions about the presuppositional behavior of conditionals, a problem which he calls the

[12] In cases such as (i), the presupposition of the consequent is the antecedent itself. In this case, the information contained in the antecedent is necessarily enough to ensure entailment of the consequent regardless of what the original context is like. Consequently, our intuition is that no condition is imposed, and hence that nothing is presupposed:

(i) If Sara has a brother, her brother likes latkes.

proviso problem. The satisfaction theory is claimed by Geurts and others to implement the ideas of Stalnaker and Karttunen, and Geurts' discussion implies (inadvertently, see fn. 8) that the source of the problem is the satisfaction-based conception of presupposition. This note shows that the ideas put forth in Karttunen (1974) about the presuppositions of conditionals are very different from the ideas about projection embodied in the satisfaction theory, and that the satisfaction theory suffers the proviso problem not because it assumes that presuppositions are conditions on contexts but rather because it identifies presupposition with minimal definedness conditions. This is a fortunate result, because it means we do not have to throw away a perfectly satisfactory baby just because we might not yet able to explain exactly where we got the water for the bath.

References

Beaver, David. 1999. Presupposition accommodation: A plea for common sense. In L. S. Moss, J. Ginzburg, and M. de Rijke, eds., *Logic, language, and computation, Volume 2*, pages 21–44. Stanford: CSLI Publications.

Beaver, David. 2001. *Presupposition and assertion in dynamic semantics*. Stanford, CA: CSLI publications.

Condoravdi, Cleo and Jean Mark Gawron. 1996. The context-dependency of implicit arguments. In M. Kanazawa, C. Piñón, and H. deSwart, eds., *Quantifiers, Deduction and Context*, pages 1–32. Stanford, CA: CSLI Publications.

von Fintel, Kai. 2008. What is presupposition accommodation, again? *Philosophical perspectives* 22(1):137–170.

Geurts, Bart. 1996. Local satisfaction guaranteed: A presupposition theory and its problems. *Linguistics and Philosophy* 19(3):259–294.

Heim, Irene. 1982. *The semantics of definite and indefinite noun phrases*. Ph.D. thesis, University of Massachusetts Amherst.

Heim, Irene. 1983. On the projection problem for presuppositions. In *Proceedings of the WCCFL 2*, pages 114–126.

Heim, Irene. 1990. Presupposition projection. In R. van der Sandt, ed., *Reader for the Nijmegen Workshop on Presupposition, Lexical Meaning, and Discourse Processes, University of Nijmegen*.

Heim, Irene. 1992. Presupposition projection and the semantics of attitude verbs. *Journal of semantics* 9(3):183–221.

Karttunen, Lauri. 1973. Presuppositions of compound sentences. *Linguistic Inquiry* 4(2):169–193.

Karttunen, Lauri. 1974. Presupposition and linguistic context. *Theoretical Linguistics* 1:81–194.

Lassiter, Daniel. 2012. Presuppositions, provisos, and probability. *Semantics and Pragmatics* 5(2):1–37.

Lauer, Sven. 2015. Biscuits and provisos: providing unconditional information by conditional means. In E. Csipak and H. Zijelstra, eds., *Sinn und Bedeutung 19*, pages 357–374.

Schlenker, Philippe. 2011. The proviso problem: a note. *Natural Language Semantics* 19(4):395–422.

Simons, Mandy, Judith Tonhauser, David Beaver, and Craige Roberts. 2010. What projects and why. In *Semantics and linguistic theory*, vol. 20, pages 309–327.

Singh, Raj. 2007. Formal alternatives as a solution to the proviso problem. In *Proceedings of Semantics and Linguistic Theory*, vol. 17, pages 264–281.

Stalnaker, Robert. 1973. Presuppositions. *Journal of philosophical logic* 2(4):447–457.

Stalnaker, Robert. 1974. Pragmatic presuppositions. In M. Munitz and P. Unger, eds., *Semantics and Philosophy*, pages 197–213. New York University Press.

Stalnaker, Robert. 2002. Common ground. *Linguistics and philosophy* 25(5):701–721.

van der Sandt, Rob A. 1989. Presupposition and discourse structure. In R. Bartsch, J. van Benthem, and P. van Emde Boas, eds., *Semantics and Contextual Expression*, pages 267–294. Dordrecht: Foris.

van Rooij, Robert. 2007. Strengthening conditional presuppositions. *Journal of Semantics* 24(3):289–304.

Part II

Meaning and Reasoning

9

Natural Language Inference Using an Ontology

Marisa Ferrara Boston, Richard Crouch, Erdem Özcan, and Peter Stubley

The initial version of this paper was written some years back (c. 2014), and has lain around gathering at least two strata of dust. The background to it is buried deeper, and was at best only partially published in connection with the PARC 'Bridge' system (Bobrow et al., 2007). Publication is largely a Markov process, where, with a few exceptions, the overhead of remembering how you got to your present state is profitless. Lauri's work provides one of the exceptions to this Markov principle, and we hope he will forgive us for using him as a pretext for brushing this work off as new. Following the advice of the late Danny Bobrow, we are further exploiting this pretext to extend the original unpublished paper to provide a fuller introduction to this approach to natural language inference, the lack of which has caused complaints from Lauri and others. The initial paper evaluated a rather inconclusive effort to fold information extracted from the Cyc ontology (Lenat and Guha, 1990) into a natural-logic style inference system. We have preserved the original evaluation section, but extended the background description beyond what would normally be found in conference proceedings.

The work was done when the authors were at Nuance Communications. Since then all but the last (alphabetically listed) author have moved elsewhere. But we are grateful to have been in an environment where work on statistical NLP, natural language semantics, and ontological reasoning co-occurred, and sometimes co-existed. Straddling

Tokens of Meaning: Papers in Honor of Lauri Karttunen.
Cleo Condoravdi and Tracy Holloway King (eds.).

these three stools without falling between them is, we feel, a necessary balancing act—even if the circus trick has yet to be pulled off with elegance. Lauri's supporting foundations for our attempt at this should be evident to anyone familiar with his work on factives and implicatives (Nairn et al., 2006), since it furnishes a basis for accounting for the impact of semantic context and intensionality on inference. And inference is, after all, the cornerstone of semantics; one of the fields that Lauri has done so much to guide.

9.1 Introduction

This paper describes some old and previously unpublished work on a natural language inference engine (NLIE) used within a question answering system. The goal of the system was to use a search engine to retrieve passages from a document base in response to a question. A combination of textual and formal inference re-ranks and if necessary recombines the passages to provide answers to the question.

The work described provides three extensions to earlier work connected with the PARC 'Bridge' system (Bobrow et al., 2007). First, it reformulates its Abstract Knowledge Representation (AKR), and reasoning with it, in graphical terms. This is more than just a notational convenience to make the treatment more accessible to computer scientists: explicit graph dominance simplifies the account of inference. Second, the natural-logic style inference engine associated with the graphical AKR is embedded within a broader variety of statistical features. Third, world knowledge from both the Cognition semantic lexicon (Dahlgren, 1988) and the Cyc ontology (Lenat and Guha, 1990) is incorporated in an effort to move beyond merely taxonomic, subclass/super-class reasoning. The evaluation section of this paper looks at the impact of introducing this extra world and lexical knowledge.

9.2 Motivation

Our focus is on a question answering system that finds answers from natural language text corpora and other sources. Consider the question-answer pair in Example 1.

(1) **Q:** What's that movie where Tom Cruise is a pilot?
A: Top Gun
Relevant passage: Lieutenant Pete "Maverick" Mitchell (Tom Cruise) flies an F-14A Tomcat off USS Enterprise.

One possible way to answer this question is to populate a formal knowledge base through information extraction from a source like IMDB, map the question to the same ontology, and use logical inference to find the answer. This presupposes that all the necessary information from the corpus can be extracted and canonicalized into the ontology ahead of time. While this is a feasible approach for predictable relationships (e.g. casts/directors of films, release dates), it is less plausible for more open-ended content like plot descriptions. To deal with such cases, the aim is to use formalized knowledge bases where possible, but to supplement this with passage retrieval over text, and natural language inference to compare retrieved passages to questions. Thus, given the knowledge that "Top Gun" is a movie starring Tom Cruise, the passage (1) retrieved from the movie's plot summary ought to be sufficient to complete the answer.

But in order to make this inference it is necessary to know that an F-14 is an airplane, and that pilots fly airplanes. Simple lexical overlap, even allowing for synonyms and hypernyms, is insufficient to adequately connect the question to the passage.

One solution is the Cognition semantic lexicon (Dahlgren, 1988). This proprietary lexicon is the largest hand-curated resource available for the English language to our knowledge, and contains information on over 500,000 lexical items. Each lexical item has word sense disambiguation information, syntactic and semantic categories, definitions, taxonomic links, and naive semantic relations. These relations include the crucial world knowledge link we need between pilots and their occupation of flying airplanes. This, along with some other inference through ontological hierarchies on airplanes, allows us to answer this question. In addition, this lexicon improves our accuracy on an internal textual entailment test set and the recent SemEval textual entailment task (Marelli et al., 2014).

The naive semantics in the Cognition lexicon is deliberately geared towards archetypal semantic relations: the kind of information that any competent speaker of the language would associate with words. The boundaries of this archetypal, linguistic world knowledge are somewhat vague, and even if they were clear there would inevitably be gaps in coverage in the lexicon. Following the recommendations of our ontologist colleagues, we therefore experimented with further extending Cognition's linguistic world knowledge by extracting additional information from the Cyc ontology.

9.3 System overview

Figure 1 depicts our question answering system, which consists of a pipeline of components.

The first is a question analysis component that parses the question

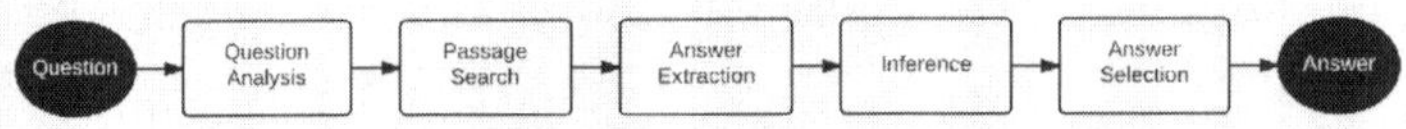

FIGURE 1 The architecture of our question-answering system

and produces a semantic representation. This representation helps form search queries over text sources, which the search component uses to pull passages that are related to the question and extract candidate answers. Both search and answer extraction are tuned for high recall at the expense of precision: the inference engine is used to select and combine high precision passages to furnish answers.

The language analysis component uses the ClearNLP parser (Choi, 2012), which produces dependency parses of the inputs. These structures are then fed into a semantic rewrite component (Crouch, 2005). This makes use of the lexical databases and world knowledge from Cognition and Cyc to build a graphical semantic representation of the inputs. Language analysis is applied both to questions, and to the contents of the document collection.

Passage retrieval (Crouch et al., 2016) uses a pair of Lucene indexes. The first is a conventional document index supplemented to contain synonym codes. The second is a passage index. Each sentence in each document is indexed along with additional information obtained from the document structure (e.g. document title, hierarchy of section titles leading to the passage, row and column headings if the passage occurs in a table). Passage retrieval first selects relevant documents, and then uses the passage index to find appropriate passages within the selected documents. This approach to passage retrieval returns better formed passages than conventional passage search on Watson's 'title oriented documents', (Ferrucci, 2012), and without the need to alter document content. As a convenience, semantic graphs for passages are stored as payloads in the passage index.

The NLIE (fig. 2) uses textual entailment to determine whether the extracted passages support the answer (Harabagiu and Hickl, 2006, Ferrucci, 2012). It is a statistical system that combines various string, linguistic, and logical features to determine whether the passage entails or contradicts the answer, and is built much in the style of other statistical systems (Roth and Sammons, 2008, Zanzotto et al., 2006, Hickl et al., 2008). These features can be classified as term matching (e.g. string, lemma, part of speech, Brown clusters (Liang, 2005)), path matching (e.g. lemma and skip bigrams based on surface and dependency structures), and semantic features (e.g. semantic relation and dependency

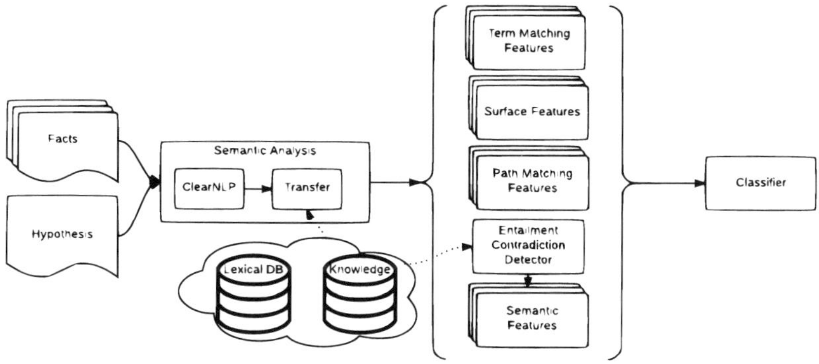

FIGURE 2 Architecture of NLIE

path matches, predicate-argument matches based on Brown clusters). All the features are fed into a Weka logistic regression classifier (Hall et al., 2009) that outputs the predicted entailment class. Our system is trained on a combination of established training sets, including SemEval 2014 (Marelli et al., 2014) and RTE 1-3 (Dagan et al., 2006, Bar-Haim et al., 2006, Giampiccolo et al., 2007).

The most significant of the NLIE features is an inference algorithm based on natural logic (MacCartney and Manning, 2007, Angeli and Manning, 2014), which modifies the PARC entailment-contradiction detector (ECD) (Crouch and King, 2007). This operates on graphical semantic representations of questions and passages, as described below.

9.4 Semantic Graphs

The graphs used as semantic representations are a graphical reformulation of the Abstract Knowledge Representation (AKR) used in the PARC Bridge system (de Paiva et al., 2007, Bobrow et al., 2007). AKR splits out a number of different levels of representation, principal amongst which are a conceptual and a contextual level. The conceptual level gives the basic predicate-argument structure, but excludes Boolean and intensional aspects of meaning; these are represented at the contextual level. This means, for example, that the conceptual representation of a sentence and its negation are the same; the difference only registers at the contextual level. In the same vein, intensional predicates introducing hypothetical or anti-veridical contexts (e.g. *believe, wish, prevent*) look structurally no different from regular extensional predicates (e.g. *see, touch*) at the conceptual level. For example, "Negotiations prevented a strike" and "Negotiations caused a strike" have parallel conceptual structures: *prevent(negotiation, strike)* and *cause(negotiation, strike)*. The existence or otherwise of the strike is only expressed at the contextual level.

As pointed out in Condoravdi et al. (2001), this conceptual/contextual split is only coherent if the terms in the conceptual structure are seen as referring to concepts and sub-concepts, rather than to individuals and collections of individuals. The conceptual representation *prevent(negotiation, strike)* needs to be read as talking about some sub-concept of prevention that is dually restricted by some sub-concept of negotiation and some sub-concept of strike. Whether there are any instances of these sub-concepts is expressed at the contextual level. The word "prevent" induces a non-factual context for its object. The contextual structure indicates that in the true, top level context there is an instance of the prevention and negotiation concepts, but no instance of the strike context.

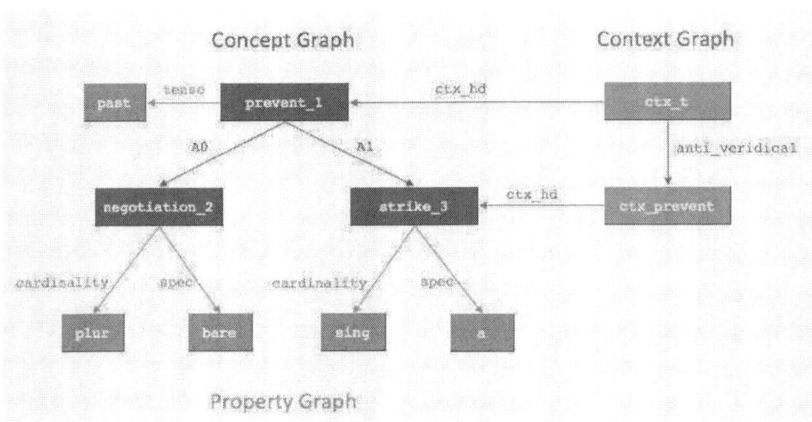

FIGURE 3 Concept, Context & Property graphs for "Negotiations prevented a strike"

The graph in Figure 3 shows three concept nodes and two context nodes. Each concept node represents some sub-concept of its lexical concept; thus `prevent_1` represents some sub-concept of the concept `prevent`. Each context node is linked to a concept node via a context head relation. The context graph asserts that the head concept for each context is instantiated in that context. Thus it asserts that there is an instance of the sub-class `prevent_1` involving negotiations and strikes in the top level context, and that there is an instance of the (prevented) `strike_3` in the lower context. The anti-veridical relation linking the two contexts implies that `strike_3` is uninstantiated in the

9.5 Entailment and Contradiction Detection

Entailment and Contradiction Detection (Crouch and King, 2007) implements a version of what has come to be known as "Natural Logic" (MacCartney and Manning, 2007). This performs inference by determining specificity relations between words, phrases, and sentences. For example, *dog* is more specific than *mammal*; *x saw a dog* is consequently more specific than *x saw a mammal*; and so *John saw a dog* is more specific than *John saw a mammal*. This means that an instance of John seeing a dog counts as an instance of John seeing a mammal.

Entailment and contradiction relations arise from the combination of specificity and instantiation relations:

- An instance of a more specific concept also counts as an instance of any concept that is more general. So instantiation of a specific concept entails instantiation of a more general concept. Consequently, to claim that a specific concept has an instance while a more general lacks one would be a contradiction.
- If a general concept lacks any instance, then any concept more specific also lacks an instance. So uninstantiation of a general concept entails the uninstantiation of any more specific concept. Consequently, to claim that a general concept lacks any instances while a more specific one has an instance would be a contradiction.

Logical relations of entailment and contradiction thus emerge from the interactions between the concept and context graphs. Taken on its own, the concept graph can only deal with relations like semantic specificity or similarity.

In normal positive / upward monotone contexts, it follows that the specific entail the general. In terms of question answering: an answer is a more specific instance of a question—*Did John see a mammal? Yes, John saw a dog.* But in negative / downward monotone / anti-veridical contexts the (negated) general entails the specific: *John did not see a mammal* entails that *John did not see a dog.*

In brief, ECD first determines specificity relations between pairs of individual concept nodes, one from the premise graph and one from the conclusion graph. These initial specificity judgments are then updated in light of the further concept restrictions placed on the nodes within their own graph. The context graph is then used to determine which concepts are instantiated or uninstantiated within which contexts. Instantiation and specificity are finally combined to determine entailment relations.

world assignment.

9.5.1 Initial Term Matching

The first operation is to identify potential matches between concept nodes in the conclusion (i.e. question) and premise (i.e. answer graphs). Ideally, this is just a matter of correctly mapping words to senses and/or concepts located in a taxonomic hierarchy, and using the hierarchy to determine the specificity relation (sub-class, super-class, equal, disjoint, possibly overlapping / unconnected). Three modifications of this a required to deal with different cases.

First, the mapping from words to concepts may be incomplete. In such cases, one can fall back to surface form or stem matches between words in the premise and conclusion to infer a relation of equality. At somewhat greater risk, one could treat a sufficiently high cosine similarity between semantic word vectors (Mikolov et al., 2013) as an indication of equality (inducing hypernym and antonym relations from word vectors is currently something of a black art).

Second, it may not be possible to do complete lexical disambiguation on a word. In this case, multiple concepts and lexical expansion graphs are introduced, one for each sense. These are marked as being mutually exclusive to prevent matching cross-talk between different senses of the same word.

Third, the premise and conclusion graphs may have been extended to include additional concepts induced by lexical or domain knowledge (e.g. "pilot" will induce further relations between flying and planes). Over-eager matching between induced terms can harm accuracy. To limit this, we do not allow matches against induced terms in the premise graph. In other words, for question answering, lexical and domain extension is only performed on the question, and not on the candidate answer passages. Expanding on one side only is safe provided that lexical and domain knowledge is complete in the following sense: if the word "pilot" induces a relation between flying and planes, then "fly" should induce a relation between planes and pilots, and "plane" should induce a relation between flying and pilots.

Co-reference links (e.g. for pronouns) also need to be factored into the initial term matching. This is done by closing the set of term matches under co-reference links.

The result of initial term matching is a further graphical structure containing the premise and conclusion graphs, plus a match sub-graph. The match sub-graph contains edges linking matched premise and conclusion nodes and recording the initial specificity relation of the match.

9.5.2 Updating Match Specificity

Having made initial term matches between individual lexical items, it remains to be seen how the specificity of these matches is affected by the restriction structures in the premise and conclusion graphs. For example, while *dog* is a sub-class of *mammal*, it is not a sub-class of *white mammal* (not all dogs are white). Specificity updates are recorded on the match edges, along with the justifications for those updates.

The update proceeds in three phases. The first works bottom up in the matches in the premise and conclusion graphs to take account of concept restrictions. Relative clauses are dealt with in a second phase. The final phase accounts for the effects of property restrictions: typically cardinality and determiner constraints.

Concept Restrictions

Each match is updated in turn to account for concept restrictions in the premise and conclusion graphs. Consider a match between a conclusion term C and a premise term P, [C, P]. Investigation of the restriction structures may show that C and/or P are restricted to more specific concepts than was accounted for in the initial match. If so, the initial match specificity is updated as follows:

- C is more specific than initially assumed:
  equals, sub-class ⇒ sub-class
  super-class, unconnected ⇒ unconnected
  disjoint ⇒ disjoint
- if P is more specific than intially assumed:
  equal, super-class ⇒ super-class
  sub-class, unconnected ⇒ unconnected
  disjoint ⇒ disjoint

To determine updates to the match specificity of [C,P], we proceed as follows

- If neither C nor P have any concepts restricting them, keep the initial match specificity .
- If C has additional restrictions but P does not, then C is more specific than was accounted for in the initial match, and the match specificity should be updated accordingly.
- Likewise, if P has additional restrictions but C does not, update the match specificity according to P becoming more specific.
- If C and P both have restrictions, then all the match specificities on the restriction nodes must first be updated.

  Then, for each restriction, Cr, on the conclusion term, C:

- If Cr has a match with some premise term Pm, find out whether the node P dominates Pm (i.e. Pm is a direct or indirect restriction on P).
- If Pm is not a restriction on P, then Cr counts as a restriction on C that is not matched by any corresponding restriction in the premise graph. This makes C more specific, so update the match accordingly.
- If Pm is a restriction on P, then find the updated specificity of the [Cr,Pm] match.
  If Cr is more specific than Pm, update the [C,P] match as C has become more specific.
  If Pm is more specific than Cr, update the [C,P] match as P has become more specific.
  If the [Cr,Pm] match is equality, the [C,P] match remains unchanged.
  If the [Cr,Pm] match is unconnected, the [C,P] becomes unconnected.
  If the [Cr,Pm] match is disjoint, then [C,P] remains disjoint if it was to begin with, otherwise it becomes unconnected
- Sometimes there will be more than one possible match for a Cr term restricting C. In this case, we have to make copies of the [C,P] match, and separately explore the match updates according to the various [Cr, Pm] matches.

After dealing with each Cr restriction, if there are any restrictions on P that were not matched with a Cr, this means that P is more specific than initially assumed. Update the match specificity accordingly.

Scoring Restriction Paths

For a match [C,P], we only looks at direct restrictions, Cr, on C. If Cr matches some premise term Pm, then two possibilities exist for the connection between P and Pm. Either there is a directed path from P to Pm (i.e. Pm is a direct or indirect modifier of P). Or there is an undirected path from P to Pm (i.e. there might be some distant relation between P and Pm). These undirected paths will not necessarily capture a coherent connection between P and Pm, still less one that parallels the connection between C and Cr. But one can optionally update the [C,P] match as though the path were a directed one, to give a looser way of updating specificities.

If indirect and undirected matches are permitted, match edges [C,P] are supplemented by a set of pairs of restriction paths. For each Cr and matching Pm, the edge records the ⟨C,role,Cr⟩ and

$\langle$P,role$_1$,P1,...,role$_n$,Pm$\rangle$ paths. These path pairings may or may not be plausible candidates for semantically equivalent paths. Given enough training data, the plausibility of a given path pairing could be estimated. In the absence of sufficient data we heuristically compute a plausibility dependent on (a) the length of the paths, and (b) whether either path cross from one sense of a word to another.

Relative Clauses

Relative clauses like *the dog that barked* are odd in that the noun *dog* is restricted by the head of the relative clause, *barked*, but the noun is at the same time an argument/restriction of the relative clause. That is, the concept graph is not guaranteed to be acyclic. To break these cycles, relative clause restrictions are excluded from the initial round of updating matches via concept restriction.

For a match [C,P], suppose that in the C has a relative clause restriction, Cr. If there is a matching restriction Pr on P, we can update the [C,P] according to the specificity of the [Cr,Pr] match. This is true whether Pr is a regular concept restriction of a relative clause restriction. Otherwise, if the relative clause restriction is unmatched, then C becomes more specific than initially assumed, and the [C,P] match is updated accordingly.

After all the conclusion relative clauses have been dealt with, we look to see if there any remaining unmatched premise relative clauses, Pr. If Pr matches a conclusion term that has C as a descendant, then update [C,P] with the specificity of this match. Otherwise there is an unmatched premise restriction, and so [C,P] is updated to account for the fact that P was more specific than originally assumed.

Determiners

Once the effects of relative clauses have been taken into account, we need to deal with the effect of determiner and cardinality restrictions in the property graph. Some determiners can flip the specificity of a match.

(2) John fed a black dog $\Rightarrow$ John fed a dog.
John fed a dog $\not\Rightarrow$ John fed a black dog.

(3) John fed every black dog $\not\Rightarrow$ John fed every dog.
John fed every dog $\Rightarrow$ John fed every black dog.

Determiners can have different monotonicity properties on their restrictions and bodies. Positive or upward monotonicity (+) means that entailment is preserved when concepts become more general. Negative or downward monotonicity (–) means that entailment is preserved when concepts become more specific. Monotonicity is undefined when one

Monotonicity Restr	Body	**Determiners**	**Examples**
+	+	some, at least N	some old men are keen gardeners $\Rightarrow$ some men are gardeners some men are gardeners $\not\Rightarrow$ some old men are keen gardeners
–	+	all, every	all men are keen gardeners $\Rightarrow$ all old men are keen gardeners all old men are keen gardeners $\not\Rightarrow$ all men are keen gardeners
–	–	no, at most N	no men are gardeners $\Rightarrow$ no old men are keen gardeners no old men are keen gardeners $\not\Rightarrow$ no men are gardeners
u	u	exactly N	exactly 3 old men are keen gardeners $\not\Rightarrow$ exactly 3 old men are gardeners $\not\Rightarrow$ exactly 3 men are gardeners
u	+	most, many	most men are keen gardeners $\Rightarrow$ most men are gardeners most old men are gardeners $\not\Rightarrow$ most men are gardeners
u	–	few:	few men are gardeners $\Rightarrow$ few men are keen gardeners few men are keen gardeners $\not\Rightarrow$ few men are gardeners

TABLE 1 Monotonicity properties of selected determiners

cannot predict persistence of an entailment just by looking at specificity of concepts. Some of the common determiners are classified in table 1.

It turns out that all determiners that are downward monotone in their second (body) argument ("no", "few", "at most N") can be treated as a negated version of a determiner that is upward monotone in the second argument (no = not some, few = not many, at most N = not at least N). The effects of this are captured by including a negation in the semantic graphs containing these determiners. Monotonicity entailments in the first (restriction) argument are dealt with through a determiner table that captures such facts as *all* $\langle$*subclass*$\rangle$ $\models$ *some* $\langle$*superclass*$\rangle$, e.g. *all dirty water* $\models$ *some water*. This table is used to update the specificity on matches for terms with the corresponding determiners in the property graph.

9.5.3 Determining Entailment Relations

Once all the term matches have been fully updated according to the structure of the premise and conclusion graphs, the entailment relation between the two graphs can be determined. It is at this point that context structure becomes important.

First, we look for any contradictions. A contradiction requires one term in a positive context being matched with a term in a negative context. Specifically, the two terms must be the context heads of their respective contexts. If the conclusion term is positive and more or equally specific than the negative premise term (e.g. a (young) man :: no man), then a contradiction occurs. If it more general (a man :: no young man), then no determination can be made. Likewise, if the conclusion term is in a negative context and the positive premise term is equally or more specific, then a contradiction occurs.

If there are no contradictions, then a search is made for entailments. This looks for the highest level, non-vacuous conclusion term(s). If it occurs in a positive context, then it needs to match a text term in a positive context that is as or more specific. If it is in a negative context, it must match a negative text term that is as or more general.

If an entailment is not found, the relation is neutral. In the case of neutrality, there one can consider lower confidence guesses at contradiction or entailment on the basis of the specificity of the initial term matches rather than the updated values.

9.6 Incorporating Additional Knowledge

9.6.1 Adding Cognition lexical information

The initial term-matching layer is where the lexical and world knowledge bases are used in order to enhance the mappings between surface words that are present in the fact and hypothesis text. That is, the semantic representations produced by the ClearNLP parser and rewrite semantics are augmented by lexical data obtained from lexicons and world knowledge bases, including mappings from words to concepts, to thesaural groups/synonym classes, and to naive semantics.

As mentioned above, the main role of the Cognition lexicon in our system is to increase term matching for the ECD component. This not only serves to improve the accuracy of ECD itself, but also helps with other semantic features we derive from ECD (such as the number of term matches it finds). It is in fact these ECD-derived features which provide the most benefit to our system.

Example 4 provides an abbreviated example of the Cognition lexical entry for "pilot". We provide the definition and a few of the naive semantic relations, and do not list the morphosyntactic features or taxonomic links. Each naive semantic relation is made of a triple including the semantic relation, the arguments, and its behavior (**i**nherent or **t**ypical). The crucial relation for our working example is highlighted below. Here, the **typical function** of a pilot is to **fly** an **aircraft**. The numeric marker on **fly** helps with word sense disambiguation (in this case, it is the second sense of "fly").

(4) **`pilot`**
```
Definition: n, v: (be or act as) someone who guides
(usually a ship or plane).
Naive semantics: [behavior,confident,t],[age,adult,t],
[requirement,training,i],[tools,airplane,t],
[function,fly2(A,noun,B)&aircraft(B),t],
[function,operate(_,noun,A)&vehicle(A),t],
[domain,war,i],[what_enables,train4(bef,someone,subj),t],
[goal,reach(aft,subj,A)&destination(A),t],
[constituency,guide(_,subj,obj),t],
[goal,reach(justaf,obj,pobj),t]
```

At this time, we are only using the arguments of the relations in the ECD term matching component. We relax term matches such that if one hypothesis contains the term "pilot" and the other "fly" and "aircraft", ECD finds a match. Notice, however, that this still does not allow us to get the working example as F-14 does not map to "aircraft". ECD makes use of Cognition's ontological representations of concept generalizations which allow for this mapping, but we do not detail this process here.

9.6.2 Adding Cyc naive semantic relations

As can be seen the lexical entry example presented in Section 9.6.1, the lexicon holds precise naive semantic relations that can aid in term matching. But, these relations are not extensive for all words in the lexicon. Further, an NLIE that makes crucial use of these relations will encounter difficulties when moved to another task, such as one in the medical domain. We therefore created Cognition-style naive semantic relations from the ResearchCyc knowledge base to determine how well we can automatically generate these relations from an extensive ontology.

Another advantage of interfacing with Cyc through the Cognition lexicon is that it provides a way to map from natural language to Cyc.

Rather than executing queries to Cyc for world knowledge using the terms in the text and the hypothesis directly, we interface through the word-sense disambiguated Cognition lexicon, which can aid in the mapping.

We began by augmenting the Cognition lexicon with more naive semantic relations for frequent words since these will be most able to help with our current internal test set. We chose approximately 80,000 of the highest-frequency Cognition words that appear in Wikipedia (in this case, these are all words that appear more than five times).

The first step is creating a mapping between Cognition and Cyc. Our initial strategy is fairly simplistic: we take the lexical item and search Cyc's natural language denotations. A sample query is provided in Example 5.

(5) (termPhrases ?DENOT CharacterString "pilot")

The query then returns a Cyc concept (or several), like "Aviator". These mappings are often ambiguous and contain non-atomic terms, but at the early stage of the process we decided to leave these in. Because we get very few mappings (only 16% of the Cognition lexical items in the Wikipedia frequency list could be mapped to Cyc), we do not restrict or disambiguate at this time.

Once we have mappings, we find relations between the mapped words. This restriction is required due to the nature of the Cognition lexicon: we need to be sure that both arguments of the relation are in the lexicon if this is going to be of any use for term matching. We fire off a query that searches for everything that a concept like Aviator has a relation to, as in Example 6.

(6) (relationAllExists ?REL AVIATOR ?CONCEPT2)

This returns a set of related concepts. We restrict some of the relations because they are not often useful, but otherwise, if we can map the second concept into Cognition, we keep the relation. Example 7 shows a sample relation for pilot. This link is not very informative, and the method does not return the crucial link between pilots and airplanes. This requires a more sophisticated query, and we are currently making progress on integrating these kinds of queries into this automatic method, as discussed in Section 9.7.

(7) `[anatomicalParts, eyebrow, i]`

9.7 Evaluation

We use a series of ablation studies to determine the efficacy of Cognition and Cyc in our system. Our results are reported on an internal test

Ablation name	Description	Internal Test	SemEval 2014
Base	Without the ECD feature	.437	.723
ECD	With ECD and its derived features	.598	.780
CogLex	ECD + Cognition, no naive semantics	.608	**.821**
CogWorld	ECD + full Cognition	.629	.814
Cyc	ECD + full Cognition + Cyc relations	**.632***	.814*

TABLE 2 Ablation accuracy results for each test set. The * indicates results that do not demonstrate a statistically significant increase (McNemar, 1947).

set consisting of 717 text-hypothesis pairs, many of which are pulled from test sets like FraCaS (Cooper et al., 1996), RTE, and SemEval (Marelli et al., 2014). The ablations follow a standard set-up where we incrementally increase the amount of information available to the NLIE while holding everything else equal in the system.

We also ran our system against the SemEval 2014 textual entailment challenge. In this case, we changed our training set to take into account only the SemEval2014 training data, and then ran against the full test set[3]. Table 2 provides a description of each experiment and our results for both sets.

The most significant jump in results for both our internal set and for SemEval comes from the addition of ECD. This component provides a sophisticated set of inference rules that allow us to move beyond surface matching. Although ECD is sensitive to lexical information on its own, it is the addition of Cognition's large, hand-curated representations that allows NLIE to return the best results. Our best result for SemEval places us in the top five for the competition (although we did not officially participate).

One interesting result from this work is that world knowledge is not helpful on all sets. The world knowledge is what allows us to determine the inference between pilots and flying airplanes in Example 1, and is therefore a necessity for the kind of inference we need in question answering. In our internal test set the addition of this information improves accuracy, but it does not improve accuracy for SemEval. If

[3]No training was applied to restriction path scores in ECD, which is an area still to be investigated. Training was only used to adjudicate between various inference features, of which ECD was just one.

we consider the SemEval 2014 data, though, many of these pairs were built to explicitly test semantic inference. World knowledge, while not entirely removed, is not as important as it is for sets like those from RTE.

Another issue is that we have not found Cyc to increase accuracy significantly. We believe the approach we are using is still too simplistic to be helpful because of a number of limitations: we are looking at frequent words, we get few mappings, we do not disambiguate concepts, we do not use the Cyc ontological hierarchy, and we are searching for all relations. We are currently working towards more sophisticated automatic generation techniques that work around these limitations.

Regardless, we find that our natural logic-style feature augmented by the Cognition lexicon provides the best accuracy for our system, and allows us to perform within the top five of reported SemEval 2014 results.

9.8 Conclusion

The main purpose of this paper was to present a long overdue description of an approach to entailment and contradiction detection. The first version of this system was created in 2006/2007, but not really described beyond a patent disclosure. The system described here has been somewhat modified to act on semantic graphs rather than abstract knowledge representations, but is otherwise true in spirit to the original. We believe that our semantic graphs provide a solid foundation for combining textual inference with more formal taxonomic and logical inference, while also being able to deal with inferences involving intensional and modal contexts.

The importance of both natural language and common sense inference to the textual entailment task is well-known (Dagan et al., 2006, LoBue and Yates, 2011), yet acquiring both and extending them to new domains remains difficult. The types of questions we would like to answer in our system require sophisticated components that can aid with both types of inference when there is little lexical overlap. In our case, this requirement is met by (a) including additional lexical and domain knowledge as an extra sub-graph in the graphical representation of sentence meaning, and (b) applying a contextually aware version of natural logic to compute inferences.

Incorporating lexically oriented information from Cognition seems to have more of an impact than incorporating world knowledge from Cyc. We cannot be completely sure about this, since an ablation without Cognition but with Cyc was not performed, and we are no longer in a position to perform this experiment. But one of the major difficulties with using Cyc is the somewhat patchy connection between the ontology and language. Though there are links from Cyc concepts and relations to English words and synsets, around 90% of Cyc lacks explicit connection to language, and constitutes an ontological form of dark matter. One can speculate as to why links to natural language are treated as an afterthought. One speculation is that language is seen as inherently messy and unstructured, and at best constitutes a noisy channel for talking about the formal and precise concepts to be found in a real world ontology. We find this view of language to be misguided. Language can be mapped onto highly structured graphical objects, and provides a remarkably precise and flexible way of describing the world. Where it differs from standard ontologies is in the degree of canonicalization it offers. Language can describe the same fact in many ways, and moreover one (ambiguous) statement can be used to describe several different facts. Ontologies aim at something much closer to a one-to-one mapping between statements and facts. But this should not be taken as grounds for dismissing language as unstructured.

References

Angeli, Gabor and D. Christopher Manning. 2014. Naturalli: Natural logic inference for common sense reasoning. In *Proceedings of the 2014 Conference on Empirical Methods in Natural Language Processing (EMNLP)*, pages 534–545. Association for Computational Linguistics.

Banarescu, Laura, Claire Bonial, Shu Cai, Madalina Georgescu, Kira Griffitt, Ulf Hermjakob, Kevin Knight, Philipp Koehn, Martha Palmer, and Nathan Schneider. 2015. Abstract meaning representation (AMR) 1.2.2 specification. `github.com/amrisi/amr-guidelines/blob/master/amr.md`.

Bar-Haim, R., Ido Dagan, Bill Dolan, L. Ferro, Danil Giampiccolo, Bernardo Magnini, and I. Szpektor. 2006. The second PASCAL recognizing textual entailment challenge. In *Proceedings of the second PASCAL Challenges Workshop on Recognizing Textual Entailment*.

Bentivogli, Luisa, Ido Dagan, Hoa Trang Dang, Danilo Giampiccolo, and Bernardo Magnini. 2009. The fifth pascal recognizing textual entailment challenge. In *Proceedings of Text Analysis Conference (TACÂ'09*.

Bhagat, Rahul and Eduard H. Hovy. 2013. What is a paraphrase? *Computational Linguistics* 39(3):463–472.

Bobrow, Daniel G., Cleo Condoravdi, Richard Crouch, Valeria de Paiva, Lauri Karttunen, Tracy Holloway King, Rowan Nairn, Lottie Price, and Annie Zaenen. 2007. Precision-focused textual inference. In *Proceedings of the ACL-PASCAL Workshop on Textual Entailment and Paraphrasing*, RTE '07, pages 16–21. Stroudsburg, PA, USA: Association for Computational Linguistics.

Bos, John. 2016. Expressive power of abstract meaning representations. *Computational Linguistics* 42(3):527–535.

Choi, Jinho D. 2012. *Optimization of Natural Language Processing Components for Robustness and Scalability*. Ph.D. thesis, University of Colorado at Boulder, Boulder, CO, USA. AAI3549172.

Condoravdi, Cleo, Richard Crouch, Martin van den Berg, John O. Everett, Valeria de Paiva, Reinhard Stolle, and Daniel G. Bobrow. 2001. Preventing existence. In *Formal Ontology in Information Systems: Proc. FOIS-2001*, pages 162—-173.

Cooper, Robin, Dick Crouch, Jan Van Eijck, Chris Fox, Johan Van Genabith, Jan Jaspars, Hans Kamp, David Milward, Manfred Pinkal, Massimo Poesio, and Steve Pulman. 1996. *Using the framework*. The FraCaS Consortium, technical report lre 62-051 d-16 edn.

Copestake, Ann, Dan Flickinger, Ivan Sag, and Carl Pollard. 2005. Minimal recursion semantics: An introduction. *Journal of research on language and computation* 3(2–3):281–332.

Crouch, Dick. 2005. Packed rewriting for mapping semantics to KR. In *In Proceedings Sixth International Workshop on Computational Semantics*.

Crouch, Richard, Lauri Karttunen, and Annie Zaenen. 2006. Circumscribing is not excluding: A response to Manning. http://web.stanford.edu/ laurik/publications/reply-to-manning.pdf.

Crouch, Richard S., Marisa F. Boston, A. Erdem Ozcan, and Peter R. Stubley. 2016. Text indexing and passage retrieval. US Patent App. 14/485,176.

Crouch, Richard S and Tracy Holloway King. 2007. Systems and methods for detecting entailment and contradiction. US Patent 7,313,515.

Dagan, Ido, Oren Glickman, and Bernardo Magnini. 2006. The PASCAL Recognising Textual Entailment challenge. In *Proceedings of the First International Conference on Machine Learning Challenges: Evaluating Predictive Uncertainty Visual Object Classification, and Recognizing Textual Entailment*, MLCW'05, pages 177–190. Berlin, Heidelberg: Springer-Verlag. ISBN 3-540-33427-0, 978-3-540-33427-9.

Dahlgren, Kathleen. 1988. *Native Semantics for Natural Language Understanding*. Norwell, Massachusetts: Kluwer Academic Press.

de Paiva, Valeria, Daniel G. Bobrow, Cleo Condoravdi, Richard Crouch, Lauri Karttunen, Tracy Holloway King, Rowan Nairn, and Annie Zaenen. 2007. Textual inference logic: Take two. In *Contexts and Ontologies Representation and Reasoning*, pages 27–36.

Ferrucci, D. A. 2012. Introduction to "This is Watson". *IBM J. Res. Dev.* 56(3):235–249.

Giampiccolo, Danilo, Bernardo Magnini, Ido Dagan, and Bill Dolan. 2007. The third PASCAL recognizing textual entailment challenge. In *Proceedings of the ACL-PASCAL Workshop on Textual Entailment and Paraphrasing*, RTE '07, pages 1–9. Stroudsburg, PA, USA: Association for Computational Linguistics.

Hall, Mark, Eibe Frank, Geoffrey Holmes, Bernhard Pfahringer, Peter Reutemann, and Ian H. Witten. 2009. The weka data mining software: An update. *SIGKDD Explor. Newsl.* 11(1):10–18.

Harabagiu, A and Andrew Hickl. 2006. Methods for using textual entailment in open-domain question answering. In *In Proceedings of ACL 2006*, pages 905–912.

Hickl, Andrew, Jeremy Bensley, John Williams, Kirk Roberts, Bryan Rink, and Ying Shi. 2008. Recognizing textual entailment with LCC's groundhog system. In *In Proc. of the Second PASCAL Challenges Workshop*.

Kamp, Hans and Uwe Reyle. 1993. *From Discourse to Logic; An Introduction to Modeltheoretic Semantics of Natural Language, Formal Logic and DRT*. Kluwer.

Lenat, Douglas and Ramanathan V. Guha. 1990. *Building Large Knowledge-Based Systems: Representation and Inference in the Cyc Project*. Addison-Wesley.

Liang, Percy. 2005. Semi-supervised learning for natural language. Master's thesis, MIT.

LoBue, Peter and Alexander Yates. 2011. Types of common-sense knowledge needed for recognizing textual entailment. In *Proceedings of the 49th Annual Meeting of the Association for Computational Linguistics: Human Language Technologies: Short Papers - Volume 2*, HLT '11, pages 329–334. Stroudsburg, PA, USA: Association for Computational Linguistics. ISBN 978-1-932432-88-6.

MacCartney, Bill and Christopher D. Manning. 2007. Natural logic for textual inference. In *Workshop on Textual Entailment and Paraphrasing at ACL 2007*.

Magka, Despoina, Boris Motik, and Ian Horrocks. 2012. Modelling structured domains using description graphs and logic programming. In *Proc. of the 9th Extended Semantic Web Conference (ESWC 2012)*, pages 330—-344.

Manning, Christopher D. 2006. Local textual inference: it's hard to circumscribe, but you know it when you see it–and nlp needs it. http://nlp.stanford.edu/ manning/papers/LocalTextualInference.pdf.

Marelli, Marco, Luisa Bentivogli, Marco Baroni, Raffaella Bernardi, Stefano Menini, and Roberto Zamparelli. 2014. Semeval-2014 task 1: Evaluation of compositional distributional semantic models on full sentences through semantic relatedness and textual entailment. In *Proceedings of the 8th International Workshop on Semantic Evaluation (SemEval 2014)*, pages 1–8. Dublin, Ireland: Association for Computational Linguistics and Dublin City University.

McNemar, Quinn. 1947. Note on the sampling error of the difference between correlated proportions or percentages. *Psychometrika* 12(2):153–157.

Mikolov, Tomas, Kai Chen, Greg Corrado, and Jeffrey Dean. 2013. Efficient estimation of word representations in vector space. *CoRR* abs/1301.3781.

Nairn, Rowan, Cleo Condoravdi, and Lauri Karttunen. 2006. Computing relative polarity for textual inference. *Inference in Computational Semantics (ICoS-5)* pages 67–76.

Quine, W.V.O. 1960. *Word and Object*. MIT Press.

Robaldo, Livio. 2010. Independent set readings and generalized quantifiers. *Journal of Philosophical Logic* 39(1):23–58.

Roth, Dan and Mark Sammons. 2008. A unified representation and inference paradigm for natural language processing. Tech. Rep. UIUCDCS-R-2008-2969, UIUC Computer Science Department.

Zaenen, Annie, Lauri Karttunen, and Richard Crouch. 2005. Local textual inference: Can it be defined or circumscribed? In *Proceedings of the ACL Workshop on Empirical Modeling of Semantic Equivalence and Entailment*, EMSEE '05, pages 31–36. Stroudsburg, PA, USA: Association for Computational Linguistics.

Zanzotto, F. M., A. Moschitti, M. Pennacchiotti, and M. T. Pazienza. 2006. Learning textual entailment from examples. In *In Proc. of the 2nd PASCAL Challenges Workshop on Recognising Textual Entailment*, pages 50–55.

10

From Language to Reasoning: Going from Y to X in Many Dimensions*

ANNIE ZAENEN, DANNY BOBROW, CLEO CONDORAVDI, LUCAS CHAMPOLLION, AND LIZ COPPOCK

10.1 Introduction

The ultimate goal of Natural Language Processing (NLP) is automatic Natural Language Understanding (NLU). Natural language understanding is not a matter of language alone but also relies on world knowledge and on reasoning. In the computational world, this knowledge is typically not available as a model of the world itself but as a deductive system, such as a theorem prover, with, in general, rather incomplete background axioms about the world. On the linguistic side, NLP systems may provide a semantic interpretation that exploits the compositional devices of formal semantics but leaves most content words unanalyzed.

Lexical resources are supposed to help fill the gap by decomposing the meaning of lexical items into a representation that can interact with (and enrich) the axioms of the theorem prover. However, these

*Thanks to Lauri Karttunen and to the audiences of the workshop on Spatial Relations at Stanford (March 2009), the Texas Linguistic Forum (November 2009), SemFest 2010, and the Linguistics departments at the University of Gothenburg and the University of Edinburgh for discussion of this work. Thanks also to Tracy Holloway King for useful comments on a previous version of the paper. Sadly, Danny Bobrow could not read the final version of this paper. We dedicate the paper to his memory.

Tokens of Meaning: Papers in Honor of Lauri Karttunen.
Cleo Condoravdi and Tracy Holloway King (eds.).

resources reflect the concerns of lexical semantics as practiced in linguistics and often the analysis of lexical items is subordinate to a theory of the mapping between 'conceptual structure' and syntax. As a result, the analysis of lexical items is mainly motivated by syntactic regularities and the semantic characteristics of lexical items are mainly studied to find invariants in the mapping between lexical classes and syntax. A prime example is Levin (1993). This work has led to many valuable insights but it does not study lexical classes from the point of view needed for the integration of lexical information into a reasoning system. Typically, lexical resources do not make distinctions between uses where an implicit parameter varies. (1a) is treated the same way as (1b), so there is no indication that (1a) involves a change of psychological state and (1b) a change of location.

(1) a. Mary went from hope to despair.
    b. Mary went from California to Texas.

This is justified in the linguistic context in which the resource was developed, but it is not sufficient in a computational context where the aim is to ascertain whether a statement allows for a specific inference, such as whether Mary has ever been in California or in Texas.

What needs to be added to well-established linguistic and computational linguistic endeavors is a type of lexical semantic analysis that is both explicit and attuned to the inferential potential of lexical items. We describe here a very small part of such an enterprise: the development of adequate representations for *from-to* phrases with nominal arguments referring to entities in the physical domain and their combination with predicates that denote gradual change either of location or along a scale. Our discussion is aimed at making explicit which linguistic distinctions need to be made and what kind of world knowledge is needed to ensure the right interpretation.

From-to phrases are a good subject for a case study because they are at the intersection of lexical and compositional semantics and have been discussed extensively within the conceptual approach. Especially relevant within this tradition are the approaches of Jackendoff and Fillmore. Specifically, we rely on semantic treatments found in Jackendoff (1996), Gawron (2005), Gawron (2009), Zwarts (2005), and Fong (1997). More generally, we are indebted to the insight of Fillmore and his collaborators that it is not possible to study lexical semantics without paying attention to the conceptualization of reality that underlies it (see, for instance, Fillmore and Atkins (1992)). In the computational domain, our work overlaps in some respects with, and complements in others, recent work by Pustejovsky and his students (see, for instance,

Pustejovsky and Moszkowicz (2011)).

The paper is organized as follows. In section 10.2 we exemplify the problem we want to examine. In section 10.3 we sketch the overall architecture of the NLU system we have in mind. In section 10.4 we sketch how to represent the required information in such a system and discuss how our representations are built up. Then, in section 10.5, we examine whether this type of analysis can be implemented on a large scale given the current state of computational linguistics and the lexical resources it requires.

10.2 The Variety of Interpretations of *from-to* Phrases

This study focuses on a subset of *from-to* phrases with verbal predicates. *From-to* phrases are, *par excellence*, the expressions of *paths*. We take *paths* to be one dimensional objects consisting of points in space, time or on some abstract scale, ordered by a precedence relation and a part-of relation. We assume that paths are convex, that is, that they have no gaps, but allow for overlap. The use of *from-to* phrases presupposes paths with a starting point and an end point.

Suppose our system is given input sentences such as the following:

(2) a. Eric went from Palo Alto to Menlo Park.
b. The road went from Palo Alto to Menlo Park.
c. The meeting went from 3 p.m. to 5 p.m.
d. The temperature went from 20 degrees to 30 degrees.
e. The room went from 20 to 30 degrees.

We would like the system to be able to draw related but different inferences from examples (2a) – (2e). From (2a) it should infer that Eric was in Palo Alto before being in Menlo Park, while for (2b) it should infer that one part of the road is in Palo Alto and another part is in Menlo Park.[1] Sentence (2c) should be understood as being about an event that began at 3 p.m. and ended at 5 p.m. The desired entailments for the two last sentences are less clear: the most immediate interpretation for example (2d) is that the temperature was 20 degrees at some time and 30 degrees at a later time. This temporal dimension can be made explicit, as in example (3).

(3) The temperature went from 20 degrees to 30 degrees from 11 a.m. to 11:30 a.m.

However, it is easy to create a context in which the change is over space instead of being over time:

[1] Note that the sentence does not entail that the road starts in Palo Alto and ends in Menlo Park.

(4) The temperature went from 20 to 30 degrees from the front to the back of the room.[2]

Examples (2d), (3), and (4) imply change in the value of the function *temperature*. Example (2e) illustrates an additional problem: instead of having the function name in the subject position, we can also have an argument of the function, in this case, the room.[3] The two *from-to* phrases in (3) and (4) clearly play two different roles: one indicates the range of the variation of the function values, and the other the time or space over which this change in range occurs, hence additional arguments of the function. We will call the first type *range*-denoting and the second type *extent*-denoting.

These examples show that sentences that have substantially the same syntax and even use the same main verb can exhibit very different relations between their parts. The first question we want to address is how to explicate these differences, and the second question is how to get from the words used in these sentences to the information needed about the entities talked about to ensure the right interpretation in each case.

The verb *go* is not the only one that exhibits the behavior that we are interested in, although it is certainly the most flexible one. The difference in interpretation between (2a) and (2b) can also be found with manner-of-motion verbs, such as *zigzag* or *run*.

(5) a. Eric zigzagged from one end of the room to the other.
  b. The path zigzags from one end of the village to the other.
  c. Eric ran from Palo Alto to Menlo Park.
  d. The show ran from mid-September to the end of December.

It is also useful to compare the interpretation of motion predicates with that of degree achievements.[4] Like motion predicates, degree achievement predicates can have stative uses, as in (6).

(6) a. The road widens from Palo Alto to Menlo Park.

---

[2]While (3) and (4) have the indicated interpretations, the implied change need not be in one direction:

(i) This summer, the temperature went from 20 degrees to 30 degrees.

(i) seems only to entail that the temperature varied from 20 to 30 degrees, not that 20 degrees was the temperature at a starting point or 30 degrees the temperature at an end point. We come back to this case in section 10.4.4.

[3]Another pair like this, in a domain that we will not discuss further, is

(i) The price went from 100 to 200 dollars.
(ii) The ticket went from 100 to 200 dollars.

[4]See Dowty (1979) and Abusch (1985). Examples of degree achievements include *widen*, *age*, and *cool*.

b. The road widens from 12 to 24 feet.

Although both (6a) and (6b) could be about the same situation, involving change in the spatial domain, the two *from-to* phrases describe two different aspects of the situation: the distance over which the change in width manifests itself, as in (6a), and the amount of the width, a spatial scale, as in (6b). As with cases where a function is named by an argument or is implied, here again, where a function is part of the meaning of the verb, it is useful to distinguish between an *extent* restricting phrase, seen in (6a), and a *range* restricting one, seen in (6b).

In what follows, we will mainly discuss intransitive sentences that are syntactically very close to the ones given above, but the analysis should extend to the set of related transitive verbs, like *widen* in (7).[5]

(7) a. They widened the road from Menlo Park to Palo Alto.
b. They widened the road from 12 to 24 feet.

To make our treatment explicit, in the next section we describe the representational framework that we are assuming and the notation that we are using.

10.3 NLU Architecture

We assume a system that automatically analyzes input sentences and canonicalizes linguistic expressions into an explicit disambiguated representation of relations that can interface with standard axioms as used by reasoners. We call these canonicalized logical forms abstract knowledge representations (AKR).

Typically such systems are composed of a pipeline of several modules. In the system in which we implemented our analysis, we relied on a syntactic parser, the XLE parser, a domain independent, ambiguity enabled dependency parser, based on a broad coverage, hand-coded, LFG-based grammar of English that analyzes the input text syntactically into functional and constituent structures (Maxwell and Kaplan, 1991). Functional structures (f-structures) are dependency structures that encode all semantically relevant morphosyntactic features, such as tense or definiteness, and localize arguments in control and long-distance dependency constructions.

These syntactic dependency structures are then further translated into linguistic semantic representations, introducing terms for tokens of content words, flattening embedded structures to clausal form, and

[5]There are subtle differences in interpretation between the transitive and the intransitive versions that we will not address here. For instance, the transitive versions are less easily interpreted as stative.

assigning scope to sentential modifiers such as negation, modals, and sentence-level adverbs like *allegedly* or *predictably* (Crouch and King, 2006). Flattening replaces embedded expressions with complex internal structure, such as clausal complements, with atomic first order terms, so-called contexts. The information about the level of embedding of an expression is preserved by associating its content with the corresponding context.

Such linguistic semantic representations are normalized to the more uniform abstract knowledge representations (AKR), described in more detail below (see also Bobrow et al. (2007)). A central feature of AKR is the use of concepts and subconcepts instead of instances (see Condoravdi et al. (2001) for motivation). The normalization component can be implemented as a set of recursive, resource sensitive rewrite rules (Crouch, 2005). The exact form of the steps of prior analysis is, however, not relevant to the analysis proposed, which we assume to be compatible with other syntactic and semantic parsers.

We envision the AKR language as similar in form to a Description Logic in which objects, relationships and eventualities are reified (see Bobrow et al. (2005)). The reification has two properties that are useful for any semantic manipulation and reasoning system. The first property is the use of a neo-Davidsonian notation. Verbal relation arguments are linked by role-name to a single value, reducing relations of variable arity to a series of binary relations and allowing new roles to be added as needed. The second property is that, thanks to reification, expressions do not have to be nested, as they are linked through their names. This significantly simplifies the manipulations that can be done in the rewrite system.

As said above, an adequate AKR needs a representation of contexts (see Condoravdi et al. (2001) and Nairn et al. (2006)), but this structure will not play a role in what follows, since none of our examples involves clausal embedding or scope-taking elements. We will not discuss it further and will limit our attention to a conceptual structure specifying the types of events and objects referred to in a sentence. Predicates and their arguments or modifiers are related via role relations, including thematic roles and temporal or spatial relations. The inventory of roles extends the set of semantic or thematic roles often assumed in linguistic analyses so as to also represent modifiers and to specify cardinality restrictions and quantifier information.

In principle, each content word is mapped to its corresponding concept in an ontology. This type of mapping is, however, currently not available on a sufficiently large scale. We use WordNet (Fellbaum, 1998) as a surrogate for the taxonomic part of an ontology, because it is the largest available resource for mapping English words into an (approximate) abstraction hierarchy through WordNet's hypernyms. Where omissions or extra entries become a problem, we patch WordNet. Apart from being spotty and idiosyncratic, WordNet is a poor substitute for the kind of ontology needed for NLU because it does not have the full structure of an ontology. For instance, it does not specify the attributes or restrictions of classes in a systematic way.

In addition to the conceptual structure, a temporal structure represents qualitative relations between time intervals and events mentioned in the text (Bobrow et al., 2007). Tense, aspect, and temporal modifiers all contribute to temporal interpretation by locating the event described by a clause relative to a temporal perspective and possibly other times determined by temporal modifiers. The temporal perspective is, by default, the time of utterance, designated with Now.

To make this more concrete, (8) is the AKR representation of a simple sentence.

(8) *The boy ate an apple before noon.*
subconcept(boy:3,[boy-1])
subconcept(eat:4,[eat-1])
subconcept(noon:5,[noon-1])
subconcept(apple:6,[apple-1])
role(theme,eat:4,apple:6)
role(agent,eat:4,boy:3)
role(when,eat:4,Interval(before,Now))
role(when,eat:4,Interval(before,noon:5))

The representation involves four subconcepts. The mapping to their corresponding concepts in the ontology, in this case WordNet as a stand-in, is indicated in square brackets. The roles that link the arguments to the verb (*eat*) are theme for *the apple* and agent for *the boy*. The 'when' role clauses indicate that the event takes places before the speaking time (Now) and before noon.

10.4 AKR Representation of *from-to* Phrases

In section 10.2 we gave an informal overview of the various interpretations that are possible for *from-to* phrases in the physical domain, occurring with verbs indicating gradual change, be it spatial or scalar, and in stative expressions. In this section we develop a representation to capture these interpretations within the framework sketched in the previous section.

The approach that we take to these phenomena is most directly inspired by Jackendoff (1996), Gawron (2005), and Gawron (2009)[6] but our aim is different from that of these authors. On the one hand, we do not intend to elucidate all the aspects of the meaning of path expressions. As said above, we limit ourselves to expressions that describe paths in the physical world and even for those we are only interested in starting and end points, ignoring, for instance, manner of motion. On the other hand, we aim to integrate the analysis in an NLU system.

As proposed in Jackendoff (1996), the basic concept we need to represent sentences such as those in section 10.2, is that of *path*. We will represent this in our notation as a concept restricted by two roles, the *initial* role and the *final* role. This leads to the (incomplete) representational schema in (9).

(9) subconcept(path:n,[ ])
role(initial,path:n,*term1*)
role(final,path:n,*term2*)

The first question we need to address is the ontological status of a path. Even when we focus solely on sentences such as (2a), it is clear that this cannot be the most prevalent physical sense in WordNet, specified as "any artifact consisting of a road or path affording passage from one place to another", since Eric might well have gone through the fields or the bushes, where there is no such path. The WordNet sense that comes the closest is "a line or route along which something travels or moves", which has as its hypernyms 'line' (a spatial location defined by a real or imaginary unidimensional extent) and 'location' (a point or extent in space). However, these are still linked to a spatial dimension, whereas the uses in (2c) and (2d) show that the notion of path that is embodied in *from-to* expressions does not necessarily have such a spatial dimension. A WordNet notion that comes closer to covering the relevant notion of path is that of sense 2 of 'interval' (a set containing all points between two given endpoints). If we choose to have paths be of the type 'interval', however, it is clear that we have to categorize them further depending on the domain of their denotations (e.g., space or time). We will represent this information through a choice of dimensions. The initial and final points of a path are related in some way to the point/interval/region named by the complements of *from* and *to*. We use *-at-* to represent the relation of inclusion.[7] The chosen

[6]More distantly related sources of inspiration are Talmy (2006) and Verkuyl (1999).

[7]The relation of inclusion is the default one when *from* and *to* take NP rather than PP complements. Compare *from Palo Alto to Menlo Park* and *from near Palo Alto to beyond Menlo Park*.

dimension will determine the domain of the subpart relation, which can be temporal, spatial, or scalar. Adding this information to the representation we have the more complete schema for *path* in (10).

(10) subconcept(path:n,[interval-2])
role(dimension,path:n,[location, time, scale, ...])
role(initial,path:n,*domain-subpart*(-at-,region:n))
role(final,path:n,*domain-subpart*(-at-,region:m))

This representation schema specifies a path whose initial point is "located at/within" region:n and whose final point is "located at/within" region:m. We assign path terms the second synset in WordNet for the word 'interval', as this seems to be the most adequate.[8] This approach allows us to maintain unidimensional paths like those in Jackendoff (1996), in contradistinction to proposals such as those by Verkuyl (1999) that see paths as spatio-temporal. The importance of this will become clear in the analysis developed below. On a multi-dimensional notion of path, it would be difficult to unify the different ways *from-to* expressions function.

In our approach, the path term is related to the term corresponding to the verbal predicate. The *from-to* phrases are used to specify restrictions on the path term and do not translate into thematic roles, such as SOURCE or GOAL, to relate a verbal predicate and a complement NP. Our representation embodies the view that source and goal are not independent notions: even when only one of them is specified explicitly in a sentence, the other one and a path between them is assumed to exist.

Before returning to the examples above that involve predicates that often indicate a change of state, we look at *from-to* phrases functioning as extent restricting. They are conceptually the simplest, but as we will see, they can be of different dimensions and can co-occur in the same predication.

10.4.1 Uncorrelated Readings: Extent Restricting *from-to* Phrases

States and non-punctual events occupy space and time and these can be specified by spatial and temporal path phrases. Examples of such *extent* restricting uses of *from-to* phrases are given in (11).

(11) a. The bridge was unusable from Yerba Buena Island to Oakland.

[8] The chosen WordNet synset may not be completely adequate. As we said earlier, the WordNet synsets are used as a stand-in ontology for the system but for the desired understanding to be possible it will need to be replaced with more adequate resources. We touch on this issue in sections 10.4.6 and 10.5.

b. The bridge was unusable from Sunday to Friday.

c. We worked from Sunday to Friday.

There is an interesting contrast between (11a) and (11b): while (11a) implies that only a part of the bridge was unusable, (11b) implies that the totality of the bridge was unusable (during the specified time). In (11a) the implication seems to be due to the fact that the *from-to* modifier functions as if it targeted the subject argument rather than the predicate. *From-to* phrases function as extent restrictions mainly with state-denoting predicates but, as example (11c) indicates, they also occur with activity verbs. In that case, the modifier is normally temporal.[9]

In all these cases, the *from-to* phrase simply delimits the time or space over which the activity takes place or the state holds. The most straightforward example of this use is (11a). We will develop a representation for this example in steps.

(12) AKR **representation of a locational extent path**
subconcept(path:23,[interval-2])
role(dimension,path:23,location)
role(initial,path:23,location(-at-,Yerba Buena Island:4))
role(final,path:23,location(-at-,Oakland:6))

This piece of representation specifies that there is a path with an initial point located within Yerba Buena Island and a final one located within Oakland. For this path the dimension is locational and the domain-subparts are locations.

We combine this with the usual elements of the AKR representation corresponding to the predicate and the subject, which yields (13).[10]

[9]When a locational *from-to* phrase occurs with an activity verb, we obtain the extent reading only if the verb is in the progressive, as the following contrast shows:

(i) The people were working from Paris to Lyon.

(ii) The people worked from Paris to Lyon.

(i) has a reading where people are working over a region including the path specified by the *from-to* phrase, with the people distributed over that region. However, (ii) only has a reading that implies movement: the sentence implies that people were moving from Paris to Lyon while working, for example, on a plane or a train. It appears then that the extent reading arises only with temporally homogeneous predicates, like lexically stative predicates and predicates in the progressive. The movement reading imposed by the simple past tense seems to be a type of coercion. We have no explanation of why the coercion goes in the direction it does, that is, why it does not create a progressive reading for the past tense.

[10]We use here a shortcut in the representation of *be unusable* using the non-existent synset be-unusable-2, as the treatment of the copula *be* is outside the scope of the paper and WordNet does not have a synset for *unusable*.

(13) AKR **for sentence with locative extent** ***from-to*** **phrase**
(first approximation)
subconcept(bridge:10,[bridge-2])
subconcept(be-unusable:1,[be-unusable-2])
subconcept(Oakland:6,[town-1])
subconcept(Yerba Buena Island:4,[town-1])
subconcept(path:23,[interval-2])
role(dimension, path:23,location)
role(theme,be-unusable:1,bridge:10)
role(initial,path:23,location(-at-,Yerba Buena Island:4))
role(final,path:23,location(-at-,Oakland:6))

This representation is incomplete in that it introduces a path that is not linked to anything else in the sentence. This is easily remedied with the introduction of a role that links the path to the main predicate of the sentence, thus adding (14) to (13).

(14) role(position,be-unusuable:1,path:23)

We encode the locational extent with a *position* role for the path term. As we will see later, we assign a different role to the path term with movement predicates and yet a different one with scalar predicates.

Note that (11a) is synonymous with 'The bridge was unusable between Yerba Buena Island and Oakland'. This is somewhat unexpected on the assumption that paths are directed intervals. As we have seen *from-to* phrases can modify both predicates that express directed change and predicates that are state-denoting, as in this case. When there is no directed change denoted and there is no inherent directionality in the domain of the *from-to* modifier, the directional value of the *from-to* phrase is neutralized: it has nothing to apply to. We will call the readings where *from A to B* implies *from B to A* symmetrical. In our representation, the fact that (11a) has a symmetrical reading is encoded by the choice of the *position* role. With temporal *from-to* phrases we get a directed interpretation, because time is conceived as directed and the direction of the path can be interpreted.

To complete the representation of (11a) there is one detail that needs to be improved upon: the sentence implies that the unusable path is a subpart of the bridge, but nothing so far relates the path term to the bridge term. To make this explicit we introduce the new role spatially-Subsumes, ending up with the representation in (15).[11]

[11]It might come as a surprise that the locational path is linked to the main predicate and not to the THEME given that we said above that the *from-to* modifier functioned as if it targeted the subject. Note, however, that the sentence does not

(15) AKR **for sentence with locative extent *from-to* phrase** (final)
(*The bridge was unusable from Yerba Buena Island to Oakland.*)
subconcept(bridge:10,[bridge-2])
subconcept(be-unusable:1,[be-unusable-2])
subconcept(Oakland:6,[town-1])
subconcept(Yerba Buena Island:4,[town-1])
subconcept(path:23,[interval-2])
role(dimension, path:23,location)
role(theme,be-unusable:1,bridge:10)
role(initial,path:23,location(-at-,Yerba Buena Island:4))
role(final,path:23,location(-at-,Oakland:6))
role(position,be-unusuable:1,path:23)
role(spatiallySubsumes,bridge:10,path:23)
role(when,be-unusable:1,interval(before,Now)

As example (11b) shows, there are also temporal extents. The representation for those is parallel to the ones we have developed above, as is illustrated in (16).

(16) AKR **for sentence with a temporal extent *from-to* phrases**
(*The bridge was unusable from 3 p.m. to 5 p.m.*)
subconcept(bridge:10,[bridge-2])
subconcept(be-unusable:1,[be-unusable-2])
subconcept(Oakland:6,[town-1])
subconcept(Yerba Buena Island:4,[town-1])
subconcept(from-to-timespan:11,[time-period-1])
role(initial,from-to-timespan:11,timepoint(-at-,3 p.m.))
role(final,from-to-timespan:11,timepoint(-at-,5 p.m.))
role(temporallySubsumes,time(be-unusuable:1),
from-to-timespan:11)
role(when,be-unusable:1,interval(before,Now)

Temporal paths correspond to time-periods in our ontology and hence get the more specific synset time-period-1, while the term corresponding to them is designated as *from-to-timespan*. We link the temporal path to the time of being unusable with a *temporallySubsumes* role. The link to the time of the event corresponding to the clausal predicate is a general characteristic of temporal modifiers. The role *temporallySubsumes* correctly captures that the sentence specifies that the bridge was unusable between Monday and Friday without precluding that it could have been unusable for a longer period. In this case, the sentence has

mean the same thing as 'The bridge from A to B was unusable.' Here, in fact, the bridge as a whole is implied to be unusable and the *from-to* phrase serves to pick out the bridge talked about.

a directional interpretation because time is always considered to have a direction, whereas this is not the case for space.

When a predicate is modified by two extent restricting *from-to* phrases, as in (17), the eventuality is delimited in two ways, over time and in space.

(17) The bridge was unusable from Yerba Buena Island to Oakland from Monday to Friday.

The meaning of (17) can be represented in a straightforward way with the machinery that we have introduced up to now, by combining the individual contributions of the two modifiers, as shown in (18).

(18) AKR **for sentence with both temporal and locational extent *from-to* phrases:**
(*The bridge was unusable from Oakland to Yerba Buena Island from Monday to Friday.*)
subconcept(bridge:10,[bridge-2])
subconcept(be-unusable:1,[be-unusable-2])
subconcept(Oakland:6,[town-1])
subconcept(Yerba Buena Island:4,[town-1])
subconcept(path:23,[interval-2])
subconcept(from-to-timespan:11,[time-period-1])
role(dimension, path:23,location)
role(position,be-unusuable:1,path:23)
role(initial,path:23,location(-at-,Yerba Buena Island:4))
role(final,path:23,location(-at-,Oakland:6))
role(spatiallySubsumes,bridge:10,path:23)
role(temporallySubsumes,time(be-unusuable:1),
from-to-timespan:11)
role(initial,from-to-timespan:11,timepoint(-at-,Monday))
role(final,from-to-timespan:11,timepoint(-at-,Friday))
role(when,be-unusable:1,interval(before,Now)

The two modifiers are independent of each other. The path corresponding to one is associated by the position role with the main predicate of the sentence and the path corresponding to the other restricts the time during which the predicate holds. We call this the **uncorrelated** reading. It contrasts with correlated readings, discussed in the next subsection.

To sum up, in this subsection we have illustrated uses of *from-to* phrases that function as *extent* restrictors on the eventualities that are denoted by the predicates that they modify. In extent readings, directional interpretations are imposed by the predicate or the path dimension itself: temporal *from-to* phrases are intrinsically directed but locational ones are not. A moment's reflection will convince the reader that, although they have *go* as the main predicate, examples (2b) and (2c) in section 10.2 are of the *extent* type.

10.4.2 Correlated Readings: Change-denoting *from-to* Phrases:[12]

In this subsection, we turn first to the meaning of examples (6a) and (6b) in section 10.2 and compare them with those discussed in the previous subsection. After that we return to example (2a).

In examples (6a) and (6b), we again have two different paths and, as a first approximation, we could represent them in a similar way to what we did before. This would be unsatisfactory, however, since such a representation would tell us nothing about how the widening of the road occurs (remember that the *position* role links the path to the main predicate but does not imply a directional reading). The meaning of sentence (6a) clearly implies that the road is wider in Menlo Park than in Palo Alto. The meaning of sentence (6b) gives the width of the road at the beginning and at the end of the widening eventuality.

To understand the difference in nature between these two *from-to* phrases, it is easier to look at an example where the change in width, as well as the extent over which this change occurs, are expressed explicitly, as in (19).

(19) The road widens from 12 to 24 feet from Palo Alto to Menlo Park.

Here we have two paths but the relation between them is different from that found in the previous subsection. *From 12 to 24 feet* gives the range of the widening, whereas *from Palo Alto to Menlo Park* gives us a restriction on the extent over which this widening takes place. The denotation of the two paths is also of a different nature: the first one indicates a scale, whereas the second is the familiar type of a path between two locations.

We need to extend our representations to capture these differences. First we will introduce a new path role, the *scale* role. Scalar paths are not located in space or time. For instance, it makes no sense to assert that 12 feet is located in California, or north of Palo Alto. Different scales measure different things and in this case the verb indicates clearly what is measured, namely, the width. This is the *dimension* of this scalar path. The dimension of the other path is the already introduced *location*.

The second *from-to* phrase gives us the direction in which the widen-

[12] *Change* is understood here as not being limited to the temporal dimension but also including differences over a spatial domain.

ing occurs: we can conclude from this sentence that the road is 12 feet wide in Palo Alto and 24 feet wide in Menlo Park (but the sentence does not specify where exactly the change occurs, or whether it is done abruptly or gradually). To represent these entailments we need more than the association of two paths with the *widen* predicate. The two paths need to be functionally related to each other, as is, to our knowledge, first discussed in Jackendoff (1996) and further developed in Gawron (2005) and Gawron (2009). We call these readings **correlated**. We use the *path-map* predicate to express a width function that has the second path as its domain and the first as its range. More generally, the higher-order predicate, **path-map(F,D,R)**, relates a function F and two partially ordered sets D and R. The path-map relation expresses that the image of D under F is equal to R.[13] For example, the representation in (20) expresses that the road's width is a function that takes its arguments from the extent of one path (path:7) and maps them to points on the width path (path:4). Combined with the already familiar notation about paths, these additions give us the representation in (20) for sentence (19).

(20) *The road widens from 12 to 24 feet from Palo Alto to Menlo Park.*
subconcept(widen:13,[widen-1])
subconcept(Palo Alto:8,[town-1])
subconcept(Menlo Park:9,[town-1])
subconcept(road:1,[road-2])
subconcept(path:4,[interval-2])
subconcept(path:7,[interval-2])
role(theme,widen:13,road:1)
role(scale,widen:13,path:4)
role(dimension,path:4,width)
role(initial,path:4,width(-at-,12 feet))
role(final,path:4,width(-at-,24 feet))
role(position,widen:13,path:7)
role(dimension,path:7,location)
role(initial,path:7,location(-at-,Palo Alto:8)
role(final,path:7,location(-at-, Menlo Park:9)
role(spatiallySubsumes,road:1,path:7)

[13]Depending on what F, D and R are, this mapping may also be order preserving, i.e., for all elements x, y in D, if x precedes y, then F(x) precedes F(y), but this cannot be assumed in all cases. In general, the only thing we know about the function is that there is a functional correspondence between the initial and the final values of the two paths.

role(when, widen:13,interval(includes,Now)
path-map(function(width,road:1),path:7,path:4)

The domain of the function does not have to be a location. In (21), for instance, the domain is temporal. The representation for this type of sentence is straightforward.

(21) The crack widened from 2 to 4 cm from 3 p.m. to 4 p.m.

Widen is an example of a degree achievement.[14] When there is only one path expressed with this type of verb, as in examples (6a) and (6b), the existence of the other type of path is understood. When only the range path is given, the understood domain path can be either temporal or locational. The preferred interpretation will depend on the aspect of the verb. The stative aspect in example (6b) leads to a locational interpretation. For the sentences in (7), a salient interpretation is that the road is widened over its whole extent over a non-expressed period of time. In (22) we give the representation for the stative case. Note that the term path:7 corresponds to an inferred, not explicitly mentioned, path that is the part of the road exhibiting the specified widening.

(22) *The road widens from 12 to 24 feet.*
subconcept([widen:13,[widen-1])
subconcept(road:1,[road-2])
subconcept(path:7,[interval-2])
subconcept(path:4,[interval-2])
role(theme,widen:13,road:1)
role(scale,widen:13,path:4)
role(dimension,path:4,width)
role(dimension,path:7,location)
role(initial,path:4,width(-at-,12 feet))
role(final,path:4,width(-at-,24 feet))
role(position,widen:13,path:7)
role(spatiallySubsumes,road:1,path:7)
role(when,widen:13,interval(includes,Now))
path-map(function(width,road:1),path:7,path:4)

Change-denoting paths do not occur only with degree achievement verbs. In example (3) we can see something similar. In this case we again have two paths and a similar relation to the one in the previous example: one path gives the range of the change of temperature and

[14] In English, most degree achievements are derived from gradable adjectives, such as *wide* or *cool*. When this is the case, the meaning of degree achievements is systematically related to the meaning of the underlying adjective (see Hay et al. (1999) and Deo et al. (2013)).

the other one restricts the period over which this change took place. Along predictable lines, the sentence will get the representation in (23).

(23) *The temperature went from 20 to 30 degrees from 11am to 11:30am.*
subconcept(go:5,[go-1])
subconcept(temperature:1,[temperature-2])
subconcept(path:4,[interval-2])
subconcept(path:7,[interval-2])
subconcept(from-to-timespan:11,[time-period-1])
role(theme,go:5,temperature:1)
role(scale,go:5,path:4)
role(dimension,path:4,temperature)
role(initial,path:4,temperature(-at-,20 degrees))
role(final,path:4,temperature(-at-,30 degrees))
role(initial,from-to-timespan:11,timepoint(-at-,11 a.m.))
role(final,from-to-timespan:11,timepoint(-at-,11:30 p.m.))
role(temporallySubsumes,time(go:5),from-to-timespan:11)
role(when,go:5,Interval(before,Now))
path-map(function(temperature,?),from-to-timespan:11,path:4,)

Here the relation between the main predicate and the range-denoting path is again that of *scale* but the *dimension* is *temperature*. The path-map maps from time (domain) to temperature (range). The function has one unexpressed argument (represented above by '?'): the sentence specifies when the temperature change occurred but it does not specify where. By contrast, in example (2e) this argument is expressed but we need to infer from the rest of the sentence that the first argument of function is temperature. We leave it to the reader to construct the representation for this example.

We now come to (2a), which is the kind of example that illustrates the prototypical use of a *from-to* phrase. As our paraphrase in section 10.2 indicates, there is a hidden temporal dimension as well as the explicit spatial one. Apart from the inference that Eric was in Palo Alto and in Menlo Park (and on a connected path that links both locations), we also infer that he was in Palo Alto *before* he was in Menlo Park.[15] Moreover, in this case the starting point of the locational path (in Palo Alto) is mapped on the starting point of the temporal interval that constitutes his going and similarly for the end point. To make this explicit we include a path-map relation in our representation, ending up with (24).

(24) *Eric went from Palo Alto to Menlo Park.*

[15]It may well be that this follows from the way the physical world in organized but the NLU system must be able to reason about this world knowledge.

subconcept(Eric:1,[male-2])
subconcept(Palo Alto:2,[location-1])
subconcept(Menlo Park:3,[location-1])
subconcept(go:4,[go-1])
subconcept(path:5,[interval-2])
role(theme,go:4,Eric:1)
role(mpath,go:4,path:5)
role(dimension,path:5,location)
role(initial,path:5,location(-at-,Palo Alto:2)
role(final,path:5,location(-at-,Menlo Park:3)
role(when,go:4,interval(before,Now))
path-map(function(location,Eric:1),time(go:4),path-5)

The role that links the path to the main predicate in this case is *mpath* (movement path). This choice of role reflects that movement verbs compose with *from-to* phrases in a way that is different from that of stative verbs. Here the location of Eric is a function that maps the time of the going event to the spatial path. In the proposed representation, the temporal dimension is the domain and the spatial path is the range of the function.

10.4.3 A Note on the Syntax of *from-to* Phrases

So far, we have paid no attention to the syntactic role of the *from-to* phrases, which is clearly not always the same. For the examples in subsection 10.4.1, the *from-to* phrases are not subcategorized for by the verb but they are compatible with it. We assume that this compatibility is ensured by the lexical specification of the verb. In such cases the *from-to* phrase forms one unit, as seen in (25)

(25) a. *From Sunday the bridge was unusable to Friday.
b. From Sunday to Friday the bridge was unusable.
c. *To Oakland the bridge was unusable from Yerba Buena Island.
d. From Yerba Buena Island to Oakland the bridge was unusable.
e. *To Friday we worked incessantly from Sunday.
f. From Sunday to Friday we worked incessantly.

This situation is different from the one we find with the verb *go*. In that case the *from* and the *to* phrases are clearly subcategorized for and obligatory. Syntactically, we have two arguments, as indicated by the examples in (26). For degree achievements and manner-of-motion verbs, the *from* and the *to* phrases behave as two syntactic units, suggesting that they are also syntactically subcategorized for.

(26) a. *From Yerba Buena Island to Oakland the road went.

b. From Yerba Buena Island the road went to Oakland.
c. *From 20 to 30 degrees the temperature went.
d. From 20 degrees the temperature went to 30.
e. *From 12 to 24 feet the road widened.
f. From 12 feet the road widened to 24.

Thus, apart from their different semantic functions and denotations, *from-to* phrases also seem to exhibit syntactic variations that do not correlate in a simple way with their semantic differences.

10.4.4 The Components of the Representations

In the previous subsections we discussed different types of *from-to* phrases. We now summarize the distinctions that we have made. First, we have divided *from-to* phrases according to the **domain of their denotations**. We distinguish temporal, locational and scalar *from-to* phrases. We encode this as their *dimension*. For locational and scalar paths we explicitly give a dimension. For the temporal paths we have distinct notational devices that make it unnecessary to express the dimension explicitly. All the locational paths have the same dimension, *location*, whereas for the scalars we have several dimensions, depending on the meaning of the verbs. These dimensions impose ontological conditions on the initial and final points of the path. The temporal paths require their initial and final points to be time points or periods and the spatial ones locations, whereas for the scalars, each scale imposes its own, e.g., *widen* requires a width and hence an expressions that can be the value of that. We have only discussed *width* and *temperature*, but there are many more (e.g., *length*, *height*, *weight*, *speed*, etc.).

We have studied *from-to* phrases with two different types of denotations: **extent** in time or space and **range** on a scale. We have shown that such phrases, depending on the predicate that they combine with, can have two different modification relations to their predicate. We thus distinguish between **uncorrelated** and **correlated** modification. When there is only one explicit or implicit path, it is obviously an uncorrelated one. When there are two,[16] they are uncorrelated when their initial and final points are not aligned. The paths represent independent restrictions in two different dimensions, as discussed in subsection 10.4.1. Correlated modification implies a functional relation between

[16]It is possible to construct sentences with three *from-to* phrases:

(i)From 2001 to 2002, the road widened from 2 lanes to 4 lanes from Palo Alto to Menlo Park.

It is more difficult to figure out what they mean. For the authorss of this paper, only two of the phrases can have a correlated reading, the third one is an uncorrelated one (here the preposed temporal phrase).

the two paths. One path, a temporal or a spatial one in the examples given, is the domain of the function and the other, a spatial or a scalar one in the examples above, is the range of the function. This correlated modification leads to a change reading (where change can be over time or over space). A complicating factor is that one of the paths can be implicit.

This analysis has led us to propose different **roles** to represent the composition of the denotation of the *from-to* phrases. The roles depend on the denotation of the predicate that they modify. Locational extent phrases compose via a *position* role, range restricting scalar phrases compose with a *scale* role, and locational range restricting phrases compose via an *mpath* role. The temporal extent restricting paths have a role that links the time span to the time of the event denoted by the predicate.

This gives us the following categorization of the examples in section 10.2.[17]

Correlated (time to location)	(2a)
Correlated (time/location to scale)	(2d), (2e)
Correlated (time to scale)	(3), (7)
Correlated (location to scale)	(4), (6a), (6b)
Uncorrelated	(2b), (2c)

Another aspect we touched on briefly is whether the combination of the verbal predicate and the *from-to* phrase indicates a direction, whether we have a symmetrical reading or not. Our assumption is that, when the verbal predicate does not express directed change/movement and the domain of the modifier is not inherently ordered, the reading will be symmetrical because there is no direction for the *from-to* phrase to specify. Note that this requires that sentences like (2b) be assumed to not imply movement. A fictive movement analysis would predict a non-symmetrical reading.

Temporal *from-to* paths are always *extent* restricting. This raises the question whether the possible function-domain pairings are further constrained. As we have already seen, spatial paths can have both

[17]We classify our predicates differently from Gawron, who has a notion of dynamic predicate that conflates two, to our mind, unrelated classes: dynamic predicates defined in the traditional sense (e.g., Comrie (1976)) as predicates that require continuous input of energy, and change-denoting predicates. For example, 'The bell rang' is a dynamic predicate in the traditional sense, but it does not denote a change. 'The road widened from 3m to 5m' is a dynamic predicate in Gawron's sense, but it does not describe an eventuality that requires continuous input of energy.

functions but the scalar paths we have seen up to now are all *range* restricting. Is this always the case though?

There are cases of scalar *from-to* phrases where an interpretation that assumes a functional correspondence mapping becomes rather strained. Consider (27).

(27) The temperature ranged from 20 degrees to 30 degrees.

Here the verb itself expresses that we are talking about a range but if a temporal or spatial extent path is expressed, as in (28), we do not get a correlated reading.

(28) From the beginning to the end of the summer, the temperature ranged from 20 degrees to 30 degrees.

We conclude that there are scalar paths that have an uncorrelated reading. In fact, *go* too might allow such readings: (29) does not seem to imply that the temperature was 20 degrees at the beginning of the summer and 30 degrees at the end (see footnote 2). It simply says that the temperature remained in the 20-to-30 degree range.

(29) This summer, the temperature went from 20 degrees to 30 degrees.

For some speakers it also seems possible to get the uncorrelated reading for (30).

(30) From the beginning to the end of the summer, the temperature went from 20 degrees to 30 degrees.

The ability to imagine fluctuations depends very much on the situation described. In the case of (31), one is not very likely to get an interpretation where the road fluctuates between these two states of affairs.

(31) This summer, the road (width) went from 12 to 24 feet.

It is clear that the initial situation has to be one with a road of width of 12 feet and the final one has to be one with a road of width of 24 feet. Here we seem to have a clear case of a functional link between the expressed scalar path and a non-expressed temporal path. For some predicates, there seem to be clear restrictions on the type of readings we can get, for instance, *widen* and *rise* seem always to have correlated readings and *be unusable* and the like are always uncorrelated, but other predicates are rather malleable.[18]

---

[18]Our representation for a scalar with an uncorrelated reading with a verb like *range* is as follows:

The temperature ranged from 20 to 30 degrees.
subconcept(range:5,[range-1])

10.4.5 Inferences

The representations we have presented are designed so as to enable a set of basic inferences to be drawn from *from-to* sentences. One such inference is about the relation of the THEME to the initial and final points of the *from-to* path(s), including whether the THEME is in a different location at the end of the described event than at the beginning. Below we characterize these inferences and sketch how the linguistic expressions involved in each case determine which inferences will arise.

A crucial step for the appropriate inferences to be drawn is determining whether the paths are correlated or uncorrelated. Uncorrelated paths do not imply change in the way we have defined it. Correlated paths imply change, be it over time or over space. The THEME role in these sentences can be either an individual-denoting expression (*the bridge, Eric*) or a function-denoting one (*the temperature*).

When we have one path or two uncorrelated paths, the inferences with respect to the THEME depend on whether the THEME is a function-denoting NP or not. When it is not a function, we can conclude that a **subpart** of the THEME is in a particular state at the starting point and another subpart is in a different state at the final point of the path. What these states themselves are depends on the arguments of the *from* and the *to* phrase. They will either be locations, time points, or points on a scale. This should be clear for examples such as (2b) and (2c),[19] as well as for (32a). It might be less clear for (32b).

(32) a. The clouds extended from the Golden Gate to the Bay Bridge.
b. The room ranged from 30 to 50 degrees.

In (32b) there is an understood function (the temperature) but it is still true that part of the room was at 30 degrees and another part was at 50 degrees. This is clearly so for the locational interpretation but it is also true for the temporal one on the assumption that over time the

---

subconcept(temperature:1,[temperature-2])
subconcept(path:4,[interval-1])
role(theme,go:5,temperature:1)
role(scale,range:5,path:4)
role(dimension, path:4,temperature)
role(initial,path:4,temperature(-at-,20 degrees))
role(final,path:4,temperature(-at-,30 degrees))
role(when,range:5,Interval(before,Now))

Here there is no correlation because *range* implies that the temperature stays within the boundaries of the scalar path, and hence there is no directed change.

[19] We assume that an event-denoting expression, such as *meeting*, constitutes a time period and that time-period has as its subparts the beginning (5 p.m.) and the end point (7 p.m.).

room corresponds to different time slices of the spatio-temporal entity denoted by *the room*. When the THEME denotes a function, as in (27), it is clearly the boundary values of the function that are indicated by the initial and the final points of the path.

With correlated paths where neither of them, be it implicit or explicit, is temporal, there is directed change but no movement. In these non-movement cases, what we can conclude about the THEME depends again on whether the THEME denotes a function or not. When the THEME is not a function, we conclude that a subpart of the THEME is in a particular state at the initial point of the path and that another subpart is in a particular state at the end. When the THEME is a function, the boundary values of that function are the initial and final points of the path.

When we have a correlated path with a temporal dimension, we can have movement. In that case the THEME as a whole is in a different position at the end of the event from its position at the beginning, as in (2a). But this is not the only possibility. Consider (33), where the state of the room on a temperature scale is lower at the end of the period than at the beginning.

(33) The room cooled from 5 to 7 p.m.

In this case, there is directed change along the temporal dimension but there is no movement in the ordinary sense. A way to construe this interpretation is, similarly to that of (32b), that a temporal slice of the room is in the initial state and another in the final state, with the other temporal slices in between.

The following informally stated rule schemas use properties of the AKR representation of *from-to* sentences to determine whether the paths are correlated or uncorrelated. This information can then be used to draw the kinds of inferences discussed above. The rules are sensitive to the presence of particular specifications in the representation (indicated by the prefix +), as well as to the absence of others (indicated by the prefix −).

if [+ role(temporallySubsumes, time(predicate:z), from-to-timespan:x),
  − path-map(function(dimension), from-to-timespan:x, path:y)]
→ uncorrelated temporal path

if [+ role(spatiallySubsumes, entity:z, path:x),
  − path-map(function(dimension), path:x, path:y)]
→ uncorrelated spatial path

if [+ role(scale, predicate:x, path:y),
  – path-map(function(dimension), path:x, path:y)]
→ uncorrelated scalar path

if [+ role(scale, predicate:x, path:y),
  + role(temporallySubsumes, time(predicate:x), from-to-timespan:z),
  + path-map(function(dimension), from-to-timespan:z, path y)]
→ correlated temporal and scalar paths
  (function changing over time)

if [+ role(scale, predicate:v, path:y),
  + role(spatiallySubsumes, entity:z, path:x),
  + path-map(function(dimension), path:x, path:y)]
→ correlated spatial and scalar paths
  (function changing over space)

if [+ role(mpath, predicate:x, path:y),
  + path-map(function(location), time(predicate:x),path:y)]
→ correlated temporal and spatial paths
  (movement)

Looking at the set of inferential patterns discussed in this subsection, we see that to confine the discussion of the inferential properties of change-of-state and so-called movement verbs to the case in which movement is expressed ignores many of their uses and would lead to the inability to draw basic inferences which are at the core of what is communicated with the use of such predications.

10.4.6 Lexical and Ontological Resources

In our system, roles and dimensions are introduced by rules that are assumed to take the output of the syntactic parse of the sentence as input. The exact form of these rules need not concern us here. Still, an important question for NLP is where the information comes from that allows us to determine which role connects a path with the verb and what dimension it has. As the examples in section 10.2 show, the verb is not necessarily the place to look: the examples in (2) all use the verb *go* but they involve a variety of dimensions and roles for their paths. Further examples of *go* with other scalars can be easily found. For instance, on the model of (4), we can have (34).

(34) a. The crack went from 2 to 4 cm from the back to the front of the room.
  b. The crack went from 2 to 4 cm from 3 p.m. to 4 p.m.

What all these cases show is that the information can come from various elements in the sentence or the broader textual context. Moreover, in some cases information about, say, the dimension can come from the arguments of *from* and *to*, whereas in other cases this information can come from the verb. *Widen*, for instance, imposes the dimension of width, but in examples like (34a) the information about the dimension has to come from the arguments of *from* and *to* and the subject. In example (34b), the first *from-to* phrase gives us the information that the path is on a scale pertaining to spatial dimensions but it does not tell us whether it is length, width, depth, or height. In example (34a), the second *from-to* phrase, the extent path, gives us the length dimension of the crack, whereas the width interpretation is natural for the first *from-to* phrase.

Similar problems arise with respect to the determination of the roles. Example (2a) and (2b) seem to have straightforward interpretations: the path role is m(ovement)path in (2a) and position in (2b). At first blush, this is the kind of information that can be straightforwardly lexically encoded: people move and roads do not, so we could give our lexical entries a feature, for instance '±moveable'. Further reflection shows that this will not do. Take (35).

(35) a. The train went from one end of the station to the other.
b. The train went from Paris to Istanbul.

In this case two interpretations are available: in (35a) the likely (although not necessary) interpretation is that the length of the train is such that it covers that of the whole station; in (35b) the obvious interpretation is the movement one. These examples show that in certain cases, general ontological classifications will not be enough to disambiguate such sentences: the ends of the station and Paris and Instanbul are all locations. Whatever ontological classification is given to train, it will presumably not change from a moving to a stationary one. The interpretation depends on specific world knowledge about the typical length of trains, the distance between Paris and Instanbul and the distance between two ends of a station. It is the characteristics of the entities that the lexical items refer to that determine what can be said, not the items themselves. In the right circumstances any object can cover an extent, as seen in (36).

(36) We asked the boys to lie down head to toe and they went from the front door to the back door, covering the whole length of the school.

Some more or less stable relations between syntax and semantics can help us determine which analysis to give. For instance, the starting and end points of paths with the roles *position* or *mpath* are referential. As such, they tend to be expressed by proper names or by a noun phrase with a determiner. There are, however, exceptions:

(37) a. He ran from where I put to ball to where the field ends.
b. His tattoo goes from head to toe.
c. The path meanders from mountain to mountain.

Manner of motion verbs are surprisingly uninformative: many of them can have a moving object, or a stationary object, or a function, such as *the temperature*, as their subject. The combinations in (38) are all possible.

(38) Liz/the road/the temperature went/crawled/moved/meandered from X to Y.

With verbs of inherent directed motion, the verb contributes a polarity for the direction but very little else, as example (39) illustrates.

(39) Liz/the road/the temperature descended/climbed/ascended/fell/ tumbled from X to Y.

Again, whatever information there is about the type of path or the dimension has to come from the THEME or from the *from-to* arguments. *From-to* arguments can give the necessary information about the dimension (locations, money, time, degrees) but when they are scalar or temporal, the measurement units will often be omitted and we will have to rely on the THEME to indicate the dimension.

Degree achievements tend to be more specific, as they indicate the dimension (e.g., width, temperature). One complication is that the subject can denote the function whose values change (e.g., *the temperature*) or an argument of the function (e.g., *the room*). We can expect lexicons to contain many of the function names but it is not clear that they will be of great help with the arguments. Some interpretation preferences correlate with syntactic variation: as we already observed, the differences between transitive and intransitive versions seem to correlate with a preference for, respectively, the spatial and the temporal interpretation.

These considerations show that, at the limit, the possible linguistic interpretations of these expressions need to be constrained by world knowledge. On a linguistic level, it shows that the verbal predicates often contribute surprisingly little to the interpretation. It is only through the combination with their arguments that we can select or constrain their meaning. This means that we need a better typing of these arguments. For instance, our ontology should not only know that meetings are social affairs, the WordNet hypernym, but also that they are time periods that go, stretch, run, etc. in the temporal dimension, whereas cracks have spatial dimensions. The information about these arguments needs to be encoded in such a way that mutual constraints can be expressed. For instance, if the *from-to* arguments refer to a temperature scale, the THEME needs to be interpreted as referring to the temperature function and if it happens to be *the room*, the interpretation needs to be coerced into the temperature function applied to the room.

10.5 Research Directions

Even if ontologies have their limits, as illustrated by examples like (35), we do need ontologies to give us the right characteristics of the entities underlying our lexical items. We also need adequate mappings from lexical items to ontological categories. Work in this direction is done, for instance, in the framework of the Generative Lexicon (Pustejovsky and Moszkowicz, 2011), but by and large such ontologies and mappings are currently not available.

Natural language processing applications, however, have taught us that even if humans can do surprising things and language can express surprising thoughts, most of the time, the kind of reality described by language is rather predictable. Consequently, the functionality of these ontologies can up to a certain point be mimicked by probabilistic feature assignments to lexical items. We can assume that, with a high probability, *Eric* will be the THEME of a predication with an *mpath*-role related path, whereas *the road* will be the THEME of a predication with a *position*-role related path. In other cases, however, we need overall lexical co-occurrence statistics in order to assign the right representations. A small study we ran (Zaenen et al., 2010) produced surprising findings (like paintings turning out to be among the most mobile entities in this construction) and thus revealed the challenges of this work. Work on distributional semantics could be of great help here, but it is not clear whether it will be easy to make the right distinctions. This would require the development of appropriate training data, which is labor intensive.

Lexical knowledge resources are constructed with concerns that can be at odds with what is needed for the kind of NLU considerations presented in this paper. For instance, FrameNet talks about fictive movement as possible with some predicates but does not discuss the difference in inferences between fictive and real movement. It also treats change of position on a scale as totally different from either fictive or real movement and, at the same time, leaves many distinctions unexplored. VerbNet, based on Levin (1993), puts *go* in several verb classes, but there are just two for physical movement: class 47.7 (*meander*-type verbs) and class 51.1 (verbs of inherent directed motion). The first class corresponds to the use exemplified in (2b), the second one corresponds to example (2a). In both cases we only get the information that the subject is a *theme*.[20] *Rise* has the same role assignment in one of its meanings. *Widen* has a patient role and is in the same class as *break*. It is clear that these semantic role assignments do not do justice to the fine-grained relations between the various elements of the sentences that are necessary for an NLU system. The semantic frames in VerbNet sometimes give further information but only for very specific meanings. If there is anything that the analysis we have given above demonstrates, it is that to account for the inferential properties of lexical items we need an approach to the lexicon that goes beyond, and in certain cases against, the one found in linguistic lexical semantics. Specifically, in the case at hand, it is not possible to separate verbal semantics from the contribution of the prepositional arguments and the theme argument.[21]

10.5.1 Reasoning about Time and Space

Our analysis presupposes the existence of reasoners that can take the explicit representations that we propose and reason on the basis of them. In our representations we do not say anything about what degrees and centimeters, or locations and times are. We assume that reasoning systems will have the right axioms about these types of entities. In fact, very little of this exists. Whereas there are implementations of temporal reasoners, mainly based on the work of Allen (1983), computational spatial reasoning is in its infancy and the spatio-temporal reasoning that is necessary in several of the cases that we have discussed is nearly non-existent. Some first steps are proposed in recent work by Pustejovsky and Moszkowicz (2011), building on earlier work in Kurata and Egenhofer (2007) and Galton (2000). More generally, fine-grained analyses such as the one given above, can be exploited only if they interface with domain specific knowledge representations that can act as constraints on the linguistically possible interpretations. In the joint SRI-PARC project Quadri: Intelligent Question Answering in the HIV Domain, we have collaborated with some of the developers of SNARK

[20] There is no explicit information given about the combination with *from-to* complements. This is more an omission than a question of principle; it would be straightforward to add the information that the *from*-phrase indicates a *source* and the *to*-phrase a *destination*, as is the case with other verb classes. See Zaenen et al. (2008) for discussion of the inconsistencies of VerbNet with respect to directionals.

[21] Current revisions to VerbNet (Hwang et al., 2014, Palmer et al., 2017) and recent work in the Generative Lexicon (Pustejovsky et al., 2016) are making steps in the desired direction.

(Stickel et al., 2000) to develop such a complete, end-to-end system from a surface form to the desired entailments in the medical domain (Waldinger et al., 2011, Richardson et al., 2011).

10.6 Conclusion

In this paper we discussed how to represent sentences with *from-to* modifiers in a way that allows the correct inferences to be made. We showed that there are different meanings depending on whether change is implied or not. We also showed that verbs of motion contribute actually very little to the meaning representation and that the meanings and the referents of the arguments are extremely important in determining the right reading. In addition to word knowledge, world knowledge is essential to arrive at the right inferences.

References

Abusch, Dorit. 1985. *On verbs and time*. Ph.D. thesis, University of Massachusetts Amherst.

Allen, James F. 1983. Maintaining Knowledge about Temporal Intervals. *Communications of the ACM* 26:832–843.

Bobrow, Daniel, Robert Cheslow, Cleo Condoravdi, Lauri Karttunen, Tracy, Rowan Nairn, Valeria de Paiva, Lotti Price, and Annie Zaenen. 2007. PARC's Bridge question answering system. In *Proceedings of the GEAF (Grammar Engineering Across Frameworks) Workshop*, pages 46–66. Stanford, CA.: CSLI Publications.

Bobrow, Daniel, Cleo Condoravdi, Richard Crouch, Valeria de Paiva, Ronald Kaplan, Lauri Karttunen, Tracy King, and Annie Zaenen. 2005. A basic logic for textual inference. In *Proceedings of the AAAI Workshop on Inference for Textual Question Answering*, pages 47–51. Pittsburgh, PA: American Association for Artificial Intelligence.

Comrie, Bernard. 1976. *Aspect: An Introduction to the Study of Verbal Aspect and Related Problems*. Cambridge: Cambridge University Press.

Condoravdi, Cleo, Richard Crouch, John Everett, Valeria de Paiva, Richard Stolle, Daniel Bobrow, and Martin van den Berg. 2001. Preventing existence. In C. Welty and B. Smith, eds., *Formal Ontology in Information Systems*, pages 162–173. New York: Association for Computing Machinery Press.

Crouch, Richard. 2005. Packed rewriting for mapping semantics to KR. In *Proceedings of the Sixth International Workshop on Computational Semantics*.

Crouch, Richard and Tracy King. 2006. Semantics via f-structure rewriting. In *Lexical Functional Grammar Conference 2006*. Konstanz, Germany.

Deo, Ashwini, Itamar Francez, and Andrew Koontz-Garboden. 2013. From change to value difference in degree achievements. *Semantics and Linguistic Theory* 23:97–115.

Dowty, David. 1979. *Word Meaning and Montague Grammar: The Semantics of Verbs and Times in Generative Semantics and in Montague's PTQ*. Dordrecht, Holland: D. Reidel Publishing Company.

Fellbaum, Christiane, ed. 1998. *WordNet: An Electronic Lexical Database*. Cambridge, MA: MIT Press.

Fillmore, Charles and B. T. Sue Atkins. 1992. Towards a Frame-based Lexicon: The Semantics of RISK and its Neighbors. In A. Lehrer, E. F. Kittay, and R. Lehrer, eds., *Frames, Fields and Contrasts: New Essays in Semantic and Lexical Organization*, pages 75–102. Hillsdale, NJ: Lawrence Erlbaum Associates.

Fong, Vivienne. 1997. *The Order of Things: What Directional Locatives Denote*. Ph.D. thesis, Stanford University.

Galton, Antony. 2000. *Qualitative spatial change*. Oxford: Oxford University Press.

Gawron, Jean Mark. 2005. Generalized Paths. *Semantics and Linguistic Theory* 15:327–344.

Gawron, Jean Mark. 2009. The Lexical Semantics of Extent Verbs. Manuscript, San Diego State University.

Hay, Jennifer, Chirstopher Kennedy, and Beth Levin. 1999. Scale structure underlies telicity in degree achievements. *Semantics and Linguistic Theory* 9:127–144.

Hwang, Jena D., Annie Zaenen, and Martha Palmer. 2014. Criteria for identifying and annotating caused motion constructions in corpus data. In *Proceedings of the Ninth International Conference on Language Resources and Evaluation (LREC'14)*, pages 1297–1304. Reykjavik, Iceland.

Jackendoff, Ray. 1996. The Proper Treatment of Measuring Out, Telicity, and Perhaps Even Quantification in English. *Natural Language and Linguistic Theory* 14:305–354.

Kurata, Yohei and Max Egenhofer. 2007. The 9+ intersection for topological relations between a directed line segment and a region. In *Proceedings of the Workshop on Behaviour Monitoring and Interpretation*, pages 62–76.

Levin, Beth. 1993. *English Verb Classes and Alternations: A Preliminary Investigation*. Chicago, IL.: University of Chicago Press.

Maxwell, John T. and Ronald M. Kaplan. 1991. A method for disjunctive constraint satisfaction. In M. Tomita, ed., *Current Issues in Parsing Technology*, vol. 126 of *The Springer International Series in Engineering and Computer Science (Natural Language Processing and Machine Translation)*, pages 173–190. Boston, MA: Springer.

Nairn, Rowan, Cleo Condoravdi, and Lauri Karttunen. 2006. Computing relative polarity for textual inference. In *Inference in Computational Semantics (ICoS) 5*, pages 67–76.

Palmer, Martha, Claire Bonial, and Jena D. Hwang. 2017. VerbNet: Capturing English verb behavior, meaning and usage. In S. Chipman, ed., *The Oxford Handbook of Cognitive Science*. Oxford: Oxford University Press.

Pustejovsky, James and Jessica L. Moszkowicz. 2011. The qualitative spatial dynamics of motion in language. *Spatial Cognition & Computation* 11:15–44.

Pustejovsky, James, Martha Palmer, Annie Zaenen, and Susan Brown. 2016. Integrating VerbNet and GL predicative structures. In *Interoperability for Semantic Annotation (ISA-12)*. Portoroz, Slovenia.

Richardson, Kyle, Daniel Bobrow, Cleo Condoravdi, Richard Waldinger, and Amar Das. 2011. English access to structured data. In *Fifth International Conference on Semantic Computing (ICSC 2011)*, pages 13–20. IEEE Computer Society.

Stickel, Mark E., Richard J. Waldinger, and Vinay K. Chaudhri. 2000. *A Guide to SNARK (2000)*.

Talmy, Leonard. 2006. The fundamental system of spatial schemas in language. In B. Hampe, ed., *From perception to meaning: Image schemas in cognitive linguistics*, vol. 29 of *Cognitive Linguistics Research (CLR)*, pages 199–234. Berlin: Mouton de Gruyter.

Verkuyl, Henk. 1999. *Aspectual Issues. Studies on Time and Quantity*. Stanford, CA: CSLI Publications.

Waldinger, Richard, Daniel Bobrow, Cleo Condoravdi, Amar Das, and Kyle Richardson. 2011. Accessing structured health information through English queries and automated deduction. In *AAAI Spring Symposium: Artificial Intelligence and Health Communication*, pages 70–73. Association for the Advancement of Artificial Intelligence.

Zaenen, Annie, Daniel Bobrow, and Cleo Condoravdi. 2008. The encoding of lexical implications in VerbNet predicates of change of locations. In *Proceedings of the Sixth International Conference on Language Resources and Evaluation (LREC'08)*, pages 387–390. Marrakech, Morocco.

Zaenen, Annie, Cleo Condoravdi, Daniel Bobrow, and Raffael Hoffmann. 2010. Supporting rule-based representations with corpus-derived lexical information. In *First International Workshop on Formalisms and Methodology for Learning by Reading (FAM-LbR '10), NAACL HLT*, pages 114–121. Stroudsburg, PA: Association for Computational Linguistics.

Zwarts, Joost. 2005. Prepositional Aspect and the Algebra of Paths. *Linguistics and Philosophy* 28:739–779.

11

Integrating Implicative Commitments

Valeria de Paiva and Gerard de Melo

11.1 Introduction

Natural language processing systems, even when given proper syntactic and semantic interpretations, still lack the common sense inference capabilities required for genuinely understanding a sentence. Recently, there have been several studies developing a semantic classification of verbs and their sentential complements, aiming at determining which inferences people draw from them. Such constructions may give rise to implied commitments that the author normally cannot disavow without being incoherent or without contradicting herself, as described for instance in the work of Lauri Karttunen. In this paper, we model such knowledge at the semantic level by attempting to associate such inferences with specific word senses, drawing on WordNet and VerbNet. This allows us to investigate to what extent the inferences apply to semantically equivalent words within and across languages.

Understanding what a text means requires more than just decoding its syntactic and semantic structure. Rather, it typically involves drawing additional inferences beyond the information that it immediately conveys. Even when supplied with proper syntactic and semantic interpretations of a sentence, current natural language processing systems still lack the common sense inference capabilities required to interpret it in the way humans do. Given a sentence such as "John missed that Mary had left", we are inclined to infer that Mary had indeed left. In contrast, given the sentence "John pretended that Mary had left", we

Tokens of Meaning: Papers in Honor of Lauri Karttunen.
Cleo Condoravdi and Tracy Holloway King (eds.).

are inclined to suppose the opposite. Although both sentences share a common structure, involving verbs with sentential complements, there are clear differences in the types of implicative commitments the author is making. Such sentences have been studied in detail in the work of Karttunen.

We have been working on inferential properties of linguistic expressions to enable automated reasoning for natural language understanding. In particular, we are interested in linguistic expressions that can be said to 'flip' (e.g. change from true to false) or 'erase' (if X is a true proposition, 'Mary said X' can be true or false) the truth values naturally associated with some other expressions. For instance, hearing that "John prevented Mary from leaving", we are inclined to suppose that Mary has not left and that there might be reasons for this not leaving.

Textual inferences may be based on purely linguistic knowledge, assumptions about language use by collaborative rational agents, knowledge about the world, or any combination thereof, and it is important to recognize how much of this information can be codified in the lexicon.

The semantics of complement constructions is an important part of textual inference. Karttunen's seminal work on English complement constructions (Karttunen, 1971) makes the point that while it is valid and helpful to classify verbal constructions according to their syntactic characteristics, e.g., whether they take propositional complements, it is also valid and even more useful to classify them according to their semantic characteristics, such as the *factivity* or *implicativity* of complements. Karttunen's more recent work, with Condoravdi and Nairn (Nairn et al., 2006), and, independently with Zaenen (Zaenen and Karttunen, 2013), takes a more empirical route and discovers the factivity and implicativity behavior by examining corpora on the web. We follow this tradition, aiming for as broad coverage as possible. As remarked in Nairn et al. (2006) this type of semantic information is not available in, or deducible from any public lexical databases such as WordNet (Fellbaum, 1998), VerbNet (Kipper et al., 2008) or FrameNet (Baker et al., 1998), by itself. Hence, they had to compile their own tables of "implication signatures" for a large class of complement-taking constructions. To create these tables, Nairn, Condoravdi and Karttunen write

> "[we took] the verbs in order of decreasing frequency in the British National Corpus (BNC), we determined their natural implications (if any). Judgments were based on agreement by multiple annotators using resources such as Google search and the Linguist's Search Engine to sample the relevant constructions in the wild."

Of the 1,250 relevant verbs in that sample, they classified 400 in a first pass and ended up with 108 involving `that` complements (`compex-that`) and 114 with infinitive complements (`xcomp-inf`). The original lists are available from CSLI at `http://web.stanford.edu/group/csli_lnr/Lexical_Resources/`.

Our hypothesis is that implicative commitments derive from the semantics of the involved words and hence are somewhat independent of the particular choice of word among a set of synonyms, certainly grammatical theory independent, and perhaps to some degree also language independent. While there are certainly exceptions to this, our system can only get better as we provide more relevant data points to it so as to enable more accurate generalizations.

Based on this hypothesis, our previous work (de Melo and de Paiva, 2014) took the marked implicative and factive verbs from Karttunen et al., as distributed by CSLI, and made them more semantic, by considering the various meanings of these verbs and marking in the Princeton WordNet (Fellbaum, 1998) of those synsets that corresponded to the relevant senses of the verbs.

The work in this paper extends the original lexical resource into a system that is able to generalize beyond the specific markings found in the lexicon. Our system operates on Universal Dependencies (Nivre et al., 2016) and uses semantic relatedness assessments to infer information for words not in the lexicon. To make this system more complete, we have also integrated information from additional sources beyond what was in our initial resource. These include implicative commitments based on adjectives and context-creating nouns. We have also worked with annotators to obtain initial lists of markings for Brazilian Portuguese.

11.2 Related Work

Such differences have been examined in detail by recent studies that have attempted to develop a classification of verbs (and verb-noun collections) that take sentential complements (Karttunen, 2012). Similar analyses can be made with respect to other constructions, e.g. to study adjective constructions like "It is confusing that Mary has left" vs. "It is improbable that Mary has left" (Zaenen and Karttunen, 2013). Likewise, one can also study implicative commitments regarding the existence of entities. For instance, "She cancelled the meeting" generally leads us to believe that there was no meeting, while "They caused a strike" means that a strike did occur (Amaral et al., 2012).

Certain sentences give rise to implied commitments that the author normally cannot disavow without being incoherent or without contradicting herself. Previous work has developed detailed classifications of words and their implicative commitments at the lexical level (Nairn et al., 2006). In this paper, we build on this work but attempt to model such knowledge about commitments at the semantic level instead. For this, the commitments are tied to specific word senses, drawing on WordNet and VerbNet as sense inventories. We rely on automatic disambiguation methods to produce a lexicon of sense-specific implicative commitments. Among other things, this allows us to investigate to what extent such inferences also apply to semantically equivalent words within and across languages. Our findings indicate that they are for the most part preserved when transitioning from words to synonym sets, and at least most of the English classifications collected by Nairn et al. (Nairn et al., 2006) seem to transfer to other languages such as Portuguese as well.

11.3 Preliminaries

Karttunen's seminal "The Logic of English Predicate Complement Constructions" (Karttunen, 1971) makes the point that while it is valid and helpful to classify verbal constructions according to their syntactic characteristics, e.g. whether they take propositional complements, it is also valid and even more useful to classify them according to their semantic characteristics, such as the *factivity* of complements. The term *factive verb* introduced by Kiparsky and Kiparsky (Kiparsky and Kiparsky, 1970) refers to the notion that any simple assertion using one of these verbs (e.g. "John knew that Mary had left") commits the speaker to the belief that the complement sentence ("Mary had left"), just by itself, is also truc.

Karttunen observes that it is sometimes "possible to show that there is a definite connection between the semantic properties of a verb and certain syntactic characteristics", and thus goes on to investigate parts of this connection. The syntactic characteristics referred to are that these are propositional complement constructions, while the semantic characteristics are what he refers to as the "logic" in the title of his book. The latter is more general than simply factivity. In fact, 35 years later, as part of a project to extract information from text for question answering, Karttunen, together with Nairn and Condoravdi (Nairn et al., 2006) presented an algorithm for detecting author commitment to the truth or falsity of complement clauses based on their syntactic type and on the meaning of their embedding predicate. They also created a small lexicon of around 300 verbs spelling out the implicative commitments that these verbs indicate. This was the starting point of our work. We contend that such implicative commitments are best described at the semantic level, as one would hope given Karttunen's choice of the word "logic" in the title of his seminal work.

The same applies to other sources and forms of implicative commitments. For instance, in some cases, nouns can induce factivity commitments. As an example, "John took the opportunity to sing" entails that he did sing (Price et al., 2008). Similarly, adjectives, too, can be marked for factivity and implicativity, as in a recent study (Zaenen and Karttunen, 2013) that collected such annotations using Amazon Mechanical Turk (`https://www.mturk.com/`). Additionally, one can study implicative commitments relating to existential and temporal aspects (Amaral et al., 2012).

Throughout this paper, we are adopting a generalized, somewhat underspecified notion of implicativity that subsumes factivity, entailment, and presupposition, calling them "implicative commitments" for want of a better name. This notion as described by Nairn et al. (Nairn et al., 2006) seems more robust and clear-cut, as exemplified in their small lexicon. So no attempt will be made in the following to distinguish between the several components of the "implicative commitments".

However, it is clear that our lexicon would have to be just one of several ingredients in any natural language understanding systems aimed at fully assessing the *factuality* of textual content, as defined by Saurí and Pustejovsky's in Saurí and Pustejovsky (2009, 2008, 2012). We might want to know whether an event mentioned in the text has really occurred in the world. Who is the source of the information? What is the stance of the author of the text? Does the author indicate whether he or she believes the source?

This encompassing problem is also discussed by Karttunen and Zaenen in Karttunen and Zaenen (2005). They call "veridicity" what we can ascertain from the text itself about the stance of the author as far as her text is concerned. As they explain

> When somebody says or writes *The earth is flat* or *The king of France is bald* because (s)he is a liar or ill-informed, nothing in these linguistic expressions in themselves alerts us to the fact that they do not correspond to situations in the real world. But a text does give us information about the stance its author takes vis-à-vis the events or states described. When somebody says *Bill acknowledges that the earth is round*, we know something about the author's as well as Bill's beliefs in the matter.

A different perspective is taken in Saurí and Pustejovsky's FactBank corpus and factuality studies (Saurí and Pustejovsky, 2009, 2008, 2012).

The work in FactBank is an attempt to mark the implicative commitments of **both the author and some participants of the events**, in some given text. As Saurí and Pustejovsky explain

> Identifying the veracity, or factuality, of event mentions in text is fundamental for reasoning about eventualities in discourse. Inferences derived from events judged as not having happened, or as being only possible, are different from those derived from events evaluated as factual. Event factuality involves two separate levels of information. On the one hand, it deals with polarity, which distinguishes between positive and negative instantiations of events. On the other, it has to do with degrees of certainty (e.g., possible, probable), an information level generally subsumed under the category of epistemic modality.

Thus their work is not concerned with what the author's stance with respect to his/her text, but with some over-arching version of the actuality of events, as determined by the reader.

The work on FactBank has been extended by the Stanford NLP group (de Marneffe et al., 2011), who re-annotated the same sentences using workers on Amazon Mechanical Turk, given their stance that textual entailment is to be measured in terms of the understanding of text by ordinary people, not the one of logicians, philosophers, or linguists. De Marneffe, Manning, and Potts explain (de Marneffe et al., 2011)

> Natural language understanding depends heavily on assessing veridicality — whether the speaker intends to convey that events mentioned are actual, non-actual, or uncertain. However, this property is little used in relation and event extraction systems, and the work that has been done has generally assumed that it can be captured by lexical semantic properties. Here, we show that context and world knowledge play a significant role in shaping veridicality. We extend the FactBank corpus, which contains semantically driven veridicality annotations, with pragmatically informed ones. Our annotations are more complex than the lexical assumption predicts but systematic enough to be included in computational work on textual understanding. They also indicate that veridicality judgments are not always categorical, and should therefore be modeled as distributions.

Thus following Karttunen and Zaenen, we make a distinction between factuality (what has actually happened in the world) contrasting it with veridicity (what the author of the utterance conveys about what has happened in the world). While we agree that in the long run we will need distributions of veridicality judgements for sentences that require opinions and assessing the trustworthiness of sources, we believe that there is a level of assessment that can be coded up in the lexicon. It is rarely disputed that if a text says "John admitted that he was guilty" then the author of the text believes that the embedded clause "John is guilty" is true. Whether the readers of the text should or should not believe the text they are reading (the veridicality of the text) is an orthogonal question. We are only concerned with the fact that by using the predicate "admit" the authors of the sentence indicates that their stance is that John was guilty. That is, we are concerned with the veridicity of the sentence, not its veridicality, which is much harder to ascertain. In particular veridicality of sentences depends on the veridicity of authors that are not lying and that are well-informed. Deciding whether authors are not lying and whether they are well-informed (or not) is much harder than deciding what the linguistic text tells us.

While veridicality or factuality is a possible long term goal, we instead start from the less lofty goal of *veridicity*, a level of assessment that we believe can be coded up in the lexicon. As Karttunen and Zaenen put it:

> It is useful to distinguish between two ingredients that go into determining the truth value of utterance, one is the trustworthiness of the utterer and the other is the stance of the utterer vis-à-vis the truth of the content. The latter we will call the veridicity of the content [...].

The classification chosen by Nairn et al. (Nairn et al., 2006) focuses on cases in which the author's commitment to the truth of a complement clause arises solely from the larger sentence it belongs to, leaving aside other sources of information about the beliefs of the author. Note that it can be difficult to decide between *entailments*, that is, what the author is actually committed to, and the more pragmatic notion of *conversational implicatures*, that is, what a reader/hearer may feel entitled to infer. For example, "Ed did not refuse to participate" might lead the hearer to conclude that Ed participated. But the speaker could continue with "He was not even eligible" indicating the opposite.

The tags used to describe the implicative commitments of lexical items need to distinguish several types of context-specific behaviors. Some words yield an entailment in both affirmative and negated environments but there are others, "one-way implicatives", that yield entailments only in one or the other environment. Furthermore, the entailment may be either positive or negative depending on the polarity of the environment. Altogether Nairn et al. provide us with a table of "implication signatures" for a large class of complement-taking constructions. These implication signatures can be stacked together, which gives rise to their algorithmic solution for dealing with more complex phrases (Nairn et al., 2006).

11.4 Integrating Annotations

In this paper we advance the state-of-the-art in that, instead of associating implicative commitments just with lexical items, we associate them with word senses, as represented by synsets given by the lexical resource WordNet (Fellbaum, 1998). These subsequently, in Section 11.5, shall allow us to relate new words to the word senses covered in the lexicon.

Our input is a set of resources that describe implicative commitments at the lexical level (included the Nairn et al. lexicon and further resources listed later on in Section 11.6.1). Our output will contain descriptions of implicative commitments at the sense level.

Generally speaking, an input entry at the lexical level consists of a partially instantiated construction and a set of tags describing the implicative commitments of that construction in particular contexts. The construction may involve one or more lexical items to be disambiguated. For instance, often, there is simply a single verb like "to find" in a syntactic frame expecting a subject and a *that*-complement ("John found that Mary had arrived"). Instead of describing the construction for a specific lexical item like "to find", we can instead characterize it at a more abstract semantic level, allowing an instantiation with several additional words ("notice", "discover", etc.). We thus have to disambiguate the word "to find" in order to establish which senses are relevant and know which sense-specific synonyms can be assumed to give rise to the same commitments.

In some cases, the construction may also involve two lexical items that need to be disambiguated. For instance, the construction may involve both the verb "avoid" and a description of its possible arguments, described by the word "event". These will then both be mapped to WordNet synsets, and WordNet's synset hierarchy will allow us to to recognize specific instantiations, e.g. "avoiding a strike" vs. "avoiding a road bump" – In the first case, there is no strike, whereas in the second case, the road bump remains.

11.4.1 Sense Mappings and Disambiguation

Our goal is thus to map one or more input lexical items $e = (l, p, f)$ on the one side, each consisting of a lemma l, part-of-speech tag p, and syntactic frame marker f, to one or more candidate WordNet synsets s on the other side. For example, our input entry could be for the lemma "admit" with part-of-speech tag `verb`, and a marker for a syntactic frame with infinitival complement (as in "The report was admitted to be incorrect"). WordNet lists a total of 8 verb senses for the input lemma "admit". For instance, the first WordNet sense for "admit" refers to the process of allowing people to enter a building, and the second one refers to admittance into a group or a community. These do not reflect the meaning that our input entry is targeting. Our system instead needs to choose the WordNet sense for *declaring to be true or admitting the existence or reality or truth of something.*

In order to achieve such disambiguated mappings in the case of verbs, we draw on another traditional lexical resource, VerbNet (Kipper-Schuler, 2005). VerbNet is a lexicon of Levin-style verb classes (Levin, 1991) based on the syntactic frames of English verbs. Since the input lexicons often refer to specific syntactic frames, e.g. for sentential complements, the syntactic characterizations present in VerbNet can help us pick relevant senses.

For a given input entry e with lemma l, let $W(l)$ denote the set of WordNet senses and $V(l)$ denote the set of VerbNet senses for l. We first use the following similarity function to score the candidate VerbNet senses $v \in V(l)$:

$$\text{sim}(e, v) = \frac{1}{|V(l)|}\left(\epsilon + \max_{f_v \in F(v)} \text{sim}(f_v, f)\right) \tag{11.1}$$

Here, the strength of association between e and one of the verb senses $v \in V(l)$ first of all depends on the number of candidates $|V(l)|$. Additionally, we obtain the relevant VerbNet class and its syntactic frame information from VerbNet, using $F(v)$ to denote the set of syntactic frames associated with the VerbNet class of v.

We rely on a simple rule-based similarity measure between syntactic descriptors f_v from VerbNet and descriptors f from the original lexicon, which in our case are based on PARC's Bridge system (Bobrow et al., 2007). For instance, VerbNet's `NP V that S` would match the `V-SUBJ-COMPEXthat` descriptor from the Bridge system but not `V-SUBJ-OBJexpl-XCOMPinf`. While this similarity function clearly prefers VerbNet senses that have at least one matching syntactic frame, we still retain the remaining VerbNet senses as possible candidates by setting ϵ to a small constant greater than 0, because VerbNet's syntactic frame descriptions are not always complete.

We then use these VerbNet similarities to help us in scoring the candidate WordNet synsets $s \in W(l)$:

$$\text{sim}(e, s) = \begin{cases} \epsilon + \sum_{v \in V(l)} \dfrac{\max_{s_v \in V_w(v)} \text{sim}(s_v, s)}{1 + |V_w(v)|} \text{sim}(e, v) & s \in W_p \\ 0 & s \notin W_p \end{cases} \tag{11.2}$$

Here, first of all, for a given part-of-speech tag p, W_p denotes the global set of all WordNet senses for that part-of-speech tag. If we are attempting to disambiguate an entry e for which the part-of-speech tag p denotes adjectives, for instance, then only adjective synsets $s \in W_p$ receive a non-zero similarity score.

For a given VerbNet sense v, we use $V_w(v)$ to denote the set of WordNet synsets mapped to v. For this, we make use of the existing disambiguated mappings between VerbNet and WordNet provided with the former. VerbNet's verb senses tend to be more coarse-grained, as their induction was mainly guided by syntactic considerations. Thus for a given VerbNet sense v, the set $V_w(v)$ may contain multiple WordNet synsets. We compare these synsets with our current synset of interest s, simply by using the identity function as the similarity measure $\text{sim}(s_v, s)$, although there are also many existing WordNet sense similarity measures that could be plugged in here. If none of the synsets $s_v \in V_w(v)$ are similar, then the overall value of $\text{sim}(e, s)$ will turn out to be just a small $\epsilon > 0$. In contrast, if there are similar synsets, we discount using the set cardinality $|V_w(v)|$, based on the intuition that the score should be higher if there are fewer possible synset matches and thus less ambiguity.

These scoring functions thus allow us to select likely WordNet synsets for a given input entry.

11.4.2 Lexicon

Once we have disambiguated all the lexical items involved in the construction based on the disambiguation procedure described above, we can assign the implicative commitment tags associated with the original construction to our newly sense-disambiguated version of the construction. The latter refers to specific senses of lexical items, thus eliminating possible confusion about which senses are meant in the case of ambiguous words. At the same time, the latter is more general by enabling us to instantiate the construction with alternative synonymous words, rather than forcing us to select the original lexical item.

In addition to the new sense-specific implicative commitment markings, our final lexicon incorporates information from WordNet, VerbNet, and other lexical resources. For a given word, we list a number of (potentially overlapping) senses. Each sense corresponds either to a WordNet synset or to a VerbNet sense or to both, based on the mappings between the two resources provided with VerbNet.

For some of these word senses, we now have information about constructions they can be involved in and the implicative commitments that are entailed when relevant words with those senses (or hyponym senses) are used in those specific constructions. The implicative commitments are provided as properties of the constructions, marked using tags like `fact_p` (based on the ones in the original lexicons). The constructions are linked to specific word senses and thus our lexicon describes the implicative commitments that words with a corresponding word sense entail when used in the corresponding syntactic constellation.

Additionally, our lexicon also provides references to other resources. For every sense corresponding to a VerbNet entry, we list the corresponding FrameNet (Baker et al., 1998) frames, relying on the SemLink project's mappings between VerbNet and FrameNet (Bonial et al., 2013). For every sense corresponding to a WordNet entry, we also include the relevant SUMO (Niles and Pease, 2001) concepts based on the pre-existing WordNet-SUMO mappings (Niles and Pease, 2003).

We make use of the RDF standard for information interchange, but our data can be converted to any number of other formats, including simple tab-separated-value files. It is clear that this is just a first step towards a freely available open "unified" lexicon in the spirit of Crouch and King (Crouch and King, 2005). In future work, we additionally hope to add presupposition relationships between different verbs, as studied by Temper and Frank (Tremper and Frank, 2013) (e.g., given "Spain *won* the tournament", one may presuppose that Spain *played* in the tournament). Another possible extension is to mine corpora for information about downward entailment as proposed by Danescu-Niculescu-Mizil et al. (Danescu-Niculescu-Mizil et al., 2009).

11.5 Implicative Commitments for Sentences

Our current work extends the original lexical resource into a natural language understanding system that is able to generalize beyond the specific markings found in the lexicon.

11.5.1 Syntactic Analysis

Our system starts from syntactic analyses in terms of Universal Dependency annotations (`http://universaldependencies.org/`).

Our system needs to recognize what in more theoretical work we called *context markers*. Some verbs that denote context markers are not as informative as factives or implicatives. Instead of assigning a new truth value to the propositions that are nested into the contexts they introduce, they simply make these contexts opaque. Thus if I say *John opened the door*, you may conclude that I think that John opened the door, assuming that I do not usually lie. If I say *John managed to open the door* you may wonder whether there was a problem that made it difficult to open the door or not, but you can still conclude that *John opened the door.* And if I say *Mary prevented John from opening the door* you may rationally conclude that *John opened the door* is false, i.e John did not open the door. However, for a sentence like *Mary said that John opened the door*, the stance of the author remains unclear. We do not know if they believe Mary to be a well-informed and honest person and hence believe that John did open the door, or if they do not believe the stated fact, but do not want to say it directly. There are many synonyms for the verb *to say*, and these introduce a context in the representation that one could decide to consider factive, for instance, if one considers a source such as *The New York Times* as always reputable and reliable. In order to recognize syntactic context-introducing verbs that do not allow for any clear inference, e.g., for the verb *to say*, we extend the lexicon with relevant markings of such verbs. Subcategorization frame information helps in this process, but is under-realized both in Princeton WordNet and in VerbNet. Thus, we extended the lexicon by marking around a thousand instances in our Implicative Lexicon.

11.5.2 Prediction

Given an identified context-inducing word, we rely on our lexicon to infer relevant implicative commitments. For words covered by the lexicon, it is just a matter of recognizing them within the syntactic structure of the sentence. When a new word, not covered by the lexicon, is encountered, we rely on a measure of semantic similarity to find relevant points of reference in the lexicon that allow us to guess the implicative behavior of the new word.

To this end, we rely on the Open Multilingual WordNet (Bond and Foster, 2013), which combines data from a number of multilingual WordNet-like projects, including the Princeton WordNet for English (Fellbaum, 1998) and our own OpenWN-PT (Rademaker et al., 2014). For a given target word, we retrieve its list of word senses from the multilingual WordNet data. Then, we rely on the Wu-Palmer semantic relatedness measure between synsets to relate these senses to the entries in our lexicon. The output markings are a weighted sum of the markings of the nearest neighbours.

In the long run, we endeavor to build on our previous work to lay the basis of a multilingual resource and system that can help us to achieve better and more fine-grained inferential results than the ones we have for recognizing textual entailment in English nowadays. As the accuracy of most textual entailment recognition systems remains below 60% (Zanzotto and Pennacchiotti, 2010), there is much room for improvement.

11.6 Results

11.6.1 Data

For our input, we relied on the lexicons from Nairn et al. (Nairn et al., 2006) and related papers, as distributed by CSLI[1], the creation of which was largely DARPA-funded, in the context of the AQUAINT project.

A lexicon entry consists of a lemma, a syntactic category descriptor, one or more tags to describe the implicative commitment behavior, and frequently also an example sentence for the lemma in the respective syntactic frame highlighting such a possible implicative commitment.

In addition to the simple factives data and the simple implicatives data, we also included the more recent phrasal implicatives data (Karttunen, 2012), which captures implicative behaviors that depend on the specific arguments of a verb. We likewise included the CSLI data about the factivity of adjectival statements, e.g. "It is accurate that John informed the president" vs. "It is untrue that John informed the president," as well as the reduced set of markings on nouns from the appendix of Price et al. (Price et al., 2008).

Moreover, we incorporated the CSLI infinite temporal markings data, which provides information about possible temporal shifts in addition to factivity information. For instance, for a sentence like "Mary persuaded Ed to cook dinner", the cooking can happen after the persuasion, while for "Mary let Ed cook dinner" the cooking typically is simultaneous with the letting. Finally, we created a lexicon of entries about existential commitments, drawing on analyses in the Amaral et al. paper (Amaral et al., 2012), among other sources.

To disambiguate all of this data with respect to WordNet, we made use of the algorithm described in Section 11.4.1, choosing the highest-ranked synset for each lexical item in the input. In the case of ties (in particular for the nouns and adjectives, where the VerbNet-based heuristics do not apply), we chose the top WordNet synset in terms of WordNet's original frequency-based sense ranking.

Table 1 summarizes the results of this process. For each category of information, we describe the number of lexical items in the input and the relevant number of candidate senses in VerbNet and WordNet. We then list the number of annotated entries in the input and in our disambiguated output. Since for many data types, annotated entries only refer to a single lexical item, these numbers are often quite correlated. On a random sample of 20 simple implicatives, our automatic disam-

[1] `http://www.stanford.edu/group/csli_lnr/Lexical_Resources/`

TABLE 1 Implicative Commitment Data

	Lexical Items			Annotated Entries	
		VN	WN		
Data Type	Input	Cand.	Cand.	Input	Disamb.
Simple factives	108	188	486	108	108
Simple implicatives	114	223	950	114	114
Phrasal implicatives	17	67	584	14	14
Factiv. of adj. comp.	278	0	449	278	225
Factiv. of extraposed adj. comp.	695	0	1,534	695	623
Factiv. of noun comp.	112	0	304	112	108
Temporal implicatives	86	160	811	86	86
Existential commitments	74	101	428	62	62

biguation had a precision of 75.0%. This is a reasonable result given that we are using fine-grained WordNet word senses and that particularly for verbs we have to choose from a very large set of candidates, as can be seen in Table 1. We could not reliably assess the recall of our disambiguation, because for many of the rarer word senses, it is more difficult to establish whether the same implicatives hold as for the primary senses of those lexical items.

In any case, we are currently in the process of relying on human annotators to correct and extend our data, giving us a more complete set of reliable WordNet sense annotations.

11.6.2 Discussion

One of the low hanging fruits of using our sense-specific implicative markings is the extension of coverage it affords. For example the original lexical markings repository provides the marking for "to bother" but not for its WordNet synonym "to trouble", as in "It troubled Ed that Mary was about to leave". Similarly there is a marking for "to acknowledge" as in "They acknowledged that the report was correct" but not for "to concede" in the same frame.

Obviously, not all synonyms can be used in the syntactic frame specified by the annotation entry. WordNet's synonym sets are semantically motivated, and as such may include words with different syntactic behavior. Thus the extension only applies to words with compatible syntactic behavior. For example, "to hate" is marked as factive as in "Ed hated to leave the party" or "Ed hated that Mary went home". The synonymous verb "to detest" was not marked in the original lexicon, but is a possible synonym listed by our lexicon.

Another advantage of a semantic approach is that we can more accurately describe the behavior of words when this behavior depends on the semantic context. For example, if you have "wasted your chance to go to Paris", then you probably did not go, whereas if you "wasted your money to go to Paris", then you probably did go (Karttunen, 2012). Similarly, "He withdrew his hand" does not affect the existence of the hand, while "He withdrew his offer" does reflect a change regarding the existence of the offer. Our lexicon distinguishes the two cases based on the semantic type of the complement. Given a novel example, an NLP system can make use of WordNet's hypernym hierarchy or of WordNet-based semantic relatedness measures to determine which of the two cases is more likely.

Of course, our lexicon nevertheless lacks descriptions to account for certain more involved contexts. It seems difficult to account for all possible context-specific behaviors. For example, while "to cause something" generally implies that that something comes to be, there are also examples like "The decree was causing a revolution when it was revoked", from which one is likely to conclude that a revolution was ultimately avoided (Amaral et al., 2012).

11.6.3 Cross-Lingual Applicability

Our WordNet sense markings not only enable us to find new synonyms, but also allow us to look up non-English equivalents in sense-aligned non-English versions of WordNet, such as EuroWordNet (Vossen, 1998) and UWN (de Melo and Weikum, 2009).

We have additionally arranged for a human-created Portuguese translation of the Nairn et al. lexicon and examples footnoteThe authors would like to thank Henrique Oliveira for his help with the Portuguese translations. and checked that most of the inferential behavior is preserved under direct translations. Some anecdotal observations can be made about this translation. First, as expected, the translation tends to indicate more English verbs, with subtle variations of meaning, going to a single Portuguese verb, for example "abhor" and "abominate" mapping to "abominar", or "acknowledge" and "recognize" to "reconhecer", or, more telling, "amaze"/"astonish"/"surprise" going to "surpreender". All the factive verbs and their examples provided by Nairn et al. seem to work in Portuguese, very much like in English. This is despite some non-direct translations, for example sometimes a single work in English like "affect" becomes a phrasal verb in Portuguese "fazer de conta" (make believe), or "to perplex" becomes "deixar perplexo". Things are not always as clear-cut on the implicatives and their examples. More work is needed here.

11.7 Conclusion

In this paper, we modeled the common sense inference capabilities required for genuinely understanding a sentence as knowledge at the semantic level by associating such inferences with specific word senses, drawing on WordNet and VerbNet. This allowed us to determine to what extent the inferences apply to semantically equivalent words within and across languages. Our preliminary lexical resources are available from `http://lexvo.org/implicative-lexicon/`.

Much work remains to be done, both for multiple languages and for extending the kinds of inferences we can deal with. We are actively integrating additional data. Incorporating new data resources requires aligning and integrating their entries into the Implicative Lexicon. We are also drawing on the large-scale entailment and contradiction detection (ECD) corpora that have appeared in recent years (Marelli et al., 2014, Bowman et al., 2015). Other future sources include the work of Lin and Pantel (Chklovski and Pantel, 2004), of Burchardt and Frank (Burchardt and Frank, 2006) of Tremper and Frank (Tremper and Frank, 2011, 2013) and of Dagan and collaborators (Lotan et al., 2013, Stanovsky et al., 2017). We continue to expanded the Implicative Lexicon to include implicative commitments based on adjectives and context-creating nouns (Gurevich et al., 2008). The implicative commitments of adjectives and nouns are less understood than those of verbs and we hypothesize that our knowledge-based approach will help to abstract across different parts of speech.

Finally, by making our lexicon and techniques available to the research community, we hope to encourage research into and the creation of similar resources for multiple languages. Our efforts to develop the Implicative Lexicon for Brazilian Portuguese indicate that English resources can be used to bootstrap Brazilian Portuguese ones but cannot be directly ported from one language to another.

References

Amaral, Patricia, Valeria de Paiva, Cleo Condoravdi, and Annie Zaenen. 2012. Where's the meeting that was cancelled? existential implications of transitive verbs. In *Proceedings of the 3rd Workshop on Cognitive Aspects of the Lexicon*, pages 183–194. Mumbai, India: The COLING 2012 Organizing Committee.

Baker, Collin F, Charles J Fillmore, and John B Lowe. 1998. The Berkeley FrameNet project. In *Proceedings of the 17th international conference on Computational linguistics-Volume 1*, pages 86–90. Association for Computational Linguistics.

Bobrow, Daniel G., Bob Cheslow, Cleo Condoravdi, Lauri Karttunen, Tracy Holloway King, Rowan Nairn, Valeria de Paiva, Charlotte Price, and Annie Zaenen. 2007. PARC's Bridge and Question Answering system. In T. H. King and E. M. Bender, eds., *Proceedings of the GEAF07 Workshop*, pages 46–66. Stanford, CA: CSLI.

Bond, Francis and Ryan Foster. 2013. Linking and extending an open multilingual wordnet. In *ACL (1)*, pages 1352–1362.

Bonial, Claire, Kevin Stowe, and Martha Palmer. 2013. Renewing and revising SemLink. In *Proc. 2nd Workshop on Linked Data in Linguistics*. Pisa, Italy.

Bowman, Samuel R., Gabor Angeli, Christopher Potts, and Christopher D. Manning. 2015. A large annotated corpus for learning natural language inference. In *Proceedings of the 2015 Conference on Empirical Methods in Natural Language Processing (EMNLP)*. Association for Computational Linguistics.

Burchardt, Aljoscha and Anette Frank. 2006. Approaching textual entailment with lfg and framenet frames. *Proc. of the Second PASCAL RTE Challenge Workshop* .

Chklovski, Timothy and Patrick Pantel. 2004. Verbocean: Mining the web for fine-grained semantic verb relations. In *Proceedings of EMNLP, vol 4*.

Crouch, Dick and Tracy Holloway King. 2005. Unifying lexical resources. In *Proceedings of the Interdisciplinary Workshop on the Identification and Representation of Verb Features and Verb Classes*. Saarbruecken, Germany.

Danescu-Niculescu-Mizil, Cristian, Lillian Lee, and Richard Ducott. 2009. Without a "doubt"? Unsupervised discovery of downward-entailing operators. In *HLT-NAACL*, pages 137–145. The Association for Computational Linguistics. ISBN 978-1-932432-41-1.

de Marneffe, Marie-Catherine, Christopher D. Manning, and Christopher Potts. 2011. Veridicality and utterance meaning. In *Proceedings of the Fifth IEEE International Conference on Semantic Computing: Workshop on Semantic Annotation for Computational Linguistic Resources, Stanford, CA.*. IEEE Computer Society Press.

de Melo, Gerard and Valeria de Paiva. 2014. Sense-specific implicative commitments. In *Computational Linguistics and Intelligent Text Processing*, pages 391–402. Springer Berlin Heidelberg.

de Melo, Gerard and Gerhard Weikum. 2009. Towards a Universal Wordnet by learning from combined evidence. In *Proceedings of the 18th ACM Conference on Information and Knowledge Management*, CIKM '09, pages 513–522. New York, NY, USA: ACM. ISBN 978-1-60558-512-3.

Fellbaum, Christiane, ed. 1998. *WordNet: An Electronic Lexical Database*. The MIT Press. ISBN 026206197X.

Gurevich, Olga, Richard Crouch, Tracy Holloway King, and Valeria de Paiva. 2008. Deverbal nouns in knowledge representation. *Journal of Logic and Computation* 18:385–404.

Karttunen, Lauri. 1971. *The logic of English predicate complement constructions.*. Bloomington, IN: Publications of the Indiana University Linguistics Club.

Karttunen, Lauri. 2012. Simple and phrasal implicatives. In *Proceedings of the First Joint Conference on Lexical and Computational Semantics - Volume 1: Proceedings of the Main Conference and the Shared Task, and Volume 2: Proceedings of the Sixth International Workshop on Semantic Evaluation*, SemEval '12, pages 124–131. Stroudsburg, PA, USA: Association for Computational Linguistics.

Karttunen, Lauri and Annie Zaenen. 2005. Veridicity. In *Annotating, Extracting and Reasoning about Time and Events. Dagstuhl Seminar Proceedings 05151, G. Katz, J. Pustejovsky, F. Schilder (eds.), Dagstuhl*. Germany: Dagstuhl, Germany.

Kiparsky, Paul and Carol Kiparsky. 1970. Fact. In M. Bierwisch and K. E. Heidolph, eds., *Progress in Linguistics: A Collection of Papers*, pages 143–73. The Hague: Mouton.

Kipper, Karin, Anna Korhonen, Neville Ryant, and Martha Palmer. 2008. A large-scale classification of english verbs. *Language Resources and Evaluation* 42(1):21–40.

Kipper-Schuler, Karin. 2005. *VerbNet: A Broad-Coverage, Comprehensive Verb Lexicon*. Ph.D. thesis, University of Pennsylvania.

Levin, Beth. 1991. *English Verb Classes and Alternations: A Preliminary Investigation*. University of Chicago Press.

Lotan, Amnon, Asher Stern, and Ido Dagan. 2013. Truthteller: Annotating predicate truth. In *Proceedings of the 2013 Conference of the North American Chapter of the Association for Computational Linguistics: Human Language Technologies*, pages 752–757.

Marelli, Marco, Stefano Menini, Marco Baroni, Luisa Bentivogli, Raffaella Bernardi, and Roberto Zamparelli. 2014. A SICK cure for the evaluation of compositional distributional semantic models. In *Proceedings of LREC 2014*.

Nairn, Rowan, Cleo Condoravdi, and Lauri Karttunen. 2006. Computing relative polarity for textual inference. *Inference in Computational Semantics (ICoS-5)* pages 67–76.

Niles, Ian and Adam Pease. 2001. Toward a Standard Upper Ontology. In C. Welty and B. Smith, eds., *Proceedings of the 2nd International Conference on Formal Ontology in Information Systems (FOIS-2001)*.

Niles, Ian and Adam Pease. 2003. Linking lexicons and ontologies: Mapping WordNet to the Suggested Upper Merged Ontology. In *Proceedings of the IEEE International Conference on Information and Knowledge Engineering*, pages 412–416.

Nivre, Joakim, Marie-Catherine de Marneffe, Filip Ginter, Yoav Goldberg, Jan Hajic, Christopher D. Manning, Ryan McDonald, Slav Petrov, Sampo

Pyysalo, Natalia Silveira, Reut Tsarfaty, and Daniel Zeman. 2016. Universal dependencies v1: A multilingual treebank collection. In N. C. C. Chair), K. Choukri, T. Declerck, M. Grobelnik, B. Maegaard, J. Mariani, A. Moreno, J. Odijk, and S. Piperidis, eds., *International Conference on Language Resources and Evaluation (LREC 2016)*. Paris, France: European Language Resources Association (ELRA). ISBN 978-2-9517408-9-1.

Price, Charlotte, Valeria de Paiva, and Tracy Holloway King. 2008. Context inducing nouns. In *COLING 2008: Proceedings of the workshop on Knowledge and Reasoning for Answering Questions*, pages 9–16. Manchester, UK: Coling 2008 Organizing Committee.

Rademaker, Alexandre, Valeria de Paiva, Gerard de Melo, Livy Real, and Maira Gatti. 2014. Openwordnet-pt: A project report. In *Proceedings of the 7th Global WordNet Conference (GWC 2014)*.

Saurí, Roser and James Pustejovsky. 2008. From structure to interpretation: A double-layered annotation for event factuality. In *The 2nd Linguistic Annotation Workshop, LREC, Marrakech. May 26-27, 2008*. Morocco.

Saurí, Roser and James Pustejovsky. 2009. Factbank: A corpus annotated with event factuality. *Language Resources and Evaluation* 43(3):227–268.

Saurí, Roser and James Pustejovsky. 2012. Are you sure that this happened? Assessing the factuality degree of events in text. *Computational Linguistics* 38(2).

Stanovsky, Gabriel, Judith Eckle-Kohler, Yevgeniy Puzikov, Ido Dagan, and Iryna Gurevych. 2017. Integrating deep linguistic features in factuality prediction over unified datasets. In *Proceedings of the 55th Annual Meeting of the Association for Computational Linguistics (Volume 2: Short Papers)*, vol. 2, pages 352–357.

Tremper, Galina and Anette Frank. 2011. Extending fine-grained semantic relation classification to presupposition relations between verbs. *Bochumer Linguistische Arbeitsberichte* page 129.

Tremper, Galina and Anette Frank. 2013. A Discriminative Analysis of Fine-Grained Semantic Relations including Presupposition: Annotation and Classification. In S. Dipper, H. Zinsmeister, and B. Webber, eds., *Dialogue and Discourse, Special Issue on Annotating Pragmatic and Discourse Phenomena*, pages 282–322.

Vossen, Piek, ed. 1998. *EuroWordNet: A Multilingual Database with Lexical Semantic Networks*. Springer. ISBN 0792352955.

Zaenen, Annie and Lauri Karttunen. 2013. Veridicity annotation in the lexicon? a look at factive adjectives. In *Proceedings of the 9th Joint ISO - ACL SIGSEM Workshop on Interoperable Semantic Annotation*, pages 51–58. Potsdam, Germany: Association for Computational Linguistics.

Zanzotto, Fabio Massimo and Marco Pennacchiotti. 2010. Expanding textual entailment corpora from wikipedia using co-training. In *Proceedings of the 2nd Workshop on The People's Web Meets NLP: Collaboratively Constructed Semantic Resources*, pages 28–36. Beijing, China: Coling 2010 Organizing Committee.

Part III

Syntax and Beyond

12

Sentence Embedding Predicates, Factivity and Subjects*

PRANAV ANAND, JANE GRIMSHAW, AND VALENTINE HACQUARD

12.1 Sentence Embedding Predicates

In this paper, we examine the subjects that embedding predicates can take. We limit ourselves to those proposition embedding predicates that fit into the sentential complement schema in (1), excluding predicates that only take expletive subjects:

(1) subject predicate $[_{CP}$ *that* ...]

This study reveals two generalizations, which demarcate a class of predicates which express a communicative act, or "discourse move", which we refer to as "communicative predicates", following Anand and Hacquard (2014). These include the verbs analyzed in Grimshaw (2015) as formed from the universal predicate SAY.

First, communicatives (e.g., *claim*, *say*) show unexpected flexibility in the types of subjects they can take (the **subject generalization**): they allow certain inanimate subjects, like "*books*" or "*reviews*", but not others, like "*plates*", as shown in (2). In this, they differ from **doxastic** (e.g., *believe*, *know*) and **emotive** (e.g., *love*, *hate*) predicates, which take animate subjects exclusively, as shown in (3). They also differ from **inferential** predicates (e.g. *demonstrate*), which allow inanimate subjects of any kind, as shown in (4).

*We would like to thank an anonymous reviewer for insightful comments and suggestions.

Tokens of Meaning: Papers in Honor of Lauri Karttunen.
Cleo Condoravdi and Tracy Holloway King (eds.).

(2) a. The critic claims that the food is good here.
b. The (critic's) review claims that the food is good here.
c. #The (critic's) empty plate claims that the food is good here.

(3) a. The critic {believes/hates} that the food is good here.
b. #The (critic's) review {believes/hates} that the food is good here.
c. #The (critic's) empty plate {believes/hates} that the food is good here.

(4) a. The critic demonstrated that the food is good here.
b. The (critic's) review demonstrates that the food is good here.
c. The (critic's) empty plate demonstrates that the food is good here.

Second, we show that communicatives exhibit an interesting generalization: while some doxastic (e.g., *know*) and emotive (e.g., *love*) predicates are factive (i.e., they entail and presuppose the truth of the proposition expressed by their complement), we find that no communicative predicate is truly factive (the **factivity generalization**).

Our starting point for the subject constraint is Anand & Hacquard (2009), who propose that the contrast illustrated in (2) and (3) diagnoses a difference in attitude predicate argument structure, indexed by semantic category: doxastic predicates like *believe* require subjects that are sentient (i.e., animate entities capable of cognitive states). In contrast "proffering" predicates such as *claim*, which express a communicative act, can take a limited set of inanimate subjects that are "Repositories of Information" (R-of-Is), such as *book* or *review*, i.e., entities that are associated with propositional content. But what exactly counts as such a repository? While *books* and *reviews* seem to work, *notepads* do not, as shown in (5). We will argue that the difference between *reviews* and *notepads* is that the former are possible discourse agents, that is, they are entities capable of making a move in discourse, as opposed to merely being associated with information content.

(5) #The critic's notepad claims that the food is good here.

In this paper, we report on a broader and deeper examination of such subjects. We examine four types of subjects — sentient animates, agentive R-of-Is (*book*, *review*), non-agentive R-of-Is (*notepad*), and general inanimates (*glove*, *plate*) — and four semantic categories of predicates — communicatives (*claim*), doxastics (*believe*), emotives (*love*), and inferentials (*demonstrate*), based on our intuitions about their meaning. Drawing on several hundred verbs and adjectives across our four categories, we ask which of our subject types can combine with which of our semantic categories of predicates. Our main goal here is to test the robustness of the subject and factivity generalizations, and to see what apparent counterexamples can tell us about the semantic and syntactic profile of communicative predicates, and the nature of the communicative acts that they are used to report.

We find that communicatives split our subject classes in half. Sentient beings (e.g., *John*) and agentive R-of-Is (like *books*) are both felicitous subjects of these predicates, but non-agentive R-of-Is (*transcripts*) and inanimates more generally (*bloody gloves*) are not. The interpretation that we pursue here is that communicative predicates do not partition their subjects by notional sentience. That is, the contrast above between *believe* and *claim* with respect to the felicity of R-of-I subjects seems to exemplify a more robust generalization about cognitive and speech-act predicates in general. Still, we show that communicative predicates do not uniformly accept R-of-I subjects (e.g., *mumble*, *apologize*). Building on the analysis of SAY verbs in G (2015), we argue that such predicates involve meaning components that render them incompatible with R-of-I conversational agents.

Because the two generalizations distinguish communicative predicates, one further correlation emerges in the work we report here: there is a negative correlation between allowing R-of-I subjects and factivity. That is, no factive predicate allows agentive R-of-I subjects.

12.2 The Subject Generalization

12.2.1 Why Subjects?

While "alternations" exhibited by various predicates have been a central focus of research in argument structure, predicates combining with clausal complements have been less intensively studied. And where work does exist on such predicates, it has focused primarily on the syntactic or semantic types of complements, not the restrictions on their subjects. The aim is to develop theories of predicate meaning and possible subject meanings that, when coupled, would predict subject-predicate felicity. In some domains we do seem to have met something akin to this goal. Consider the theory of thematic roles, and in particular the hypothesis that some predicates can combine only with Experiencers (sentient entities that necessarily experience a cognitive state). As Experiencers must be animate, a predicate which allows only Experiencer subjects (external arguments) will combine only with animate DPs and will never combine with CPs in subject position. This predicts the paradigm in (6) for *hate*:

(6) a. #That stone hates the weather.
b. The tourist hates the weather.
c. #That it is raining hates the weather.

The predicates under discussion here may seem at first blush like *hate*, admitting only animate subjects. Minimally, they *allow* animate subjects quite naturally:

(7) a. John {believes, thinks, knows} that the earth is flat.
b. John {claims, argues} that the earth is flat.
c. John {demonstrated, implied} that the earth is flat.

However, once we turn to inanimate subjects, interesting restrictions emerge, cutting apart both the predicates in (7a-c) and the kinds of subjects they can combine with. Here, we review some of the distinctions that A&H (2009, 2014) make. First, while "doxastic" predicates like those in (7a) require a sentient subject, "proffering" predicates (what we refer to here as "communicatives"), i.e., predicates that express a communicative act, like those in (7b), can take inanimate subjects such as *book* or *review*. A&H (2009, 2014) argue that what allows proffering verbs like *claim* or *argue* to combine with such subjects is that these verbs only require agents capable of making discourse contributions. While books are not sentient, they can still be discourse participants in generic conversations. Being non-sentient, they are incapable of *thoughts*, and hence cannot combine with verbs like *believe* or *know*. This is illustrated in the examples below, adapted from A&H (2009).

(8) a. #The book {believes, knows} that the earth is flat.
b. The book {claims, reports} that the earth is flat.
c. The book {demonstrates, implies} that the earth is flat.

Second, inanimate subjects that are not repositories of information, such as *plate* or *time of death*, cannot be discourse participants. They thus can appear with neither doxastics nor communicatives. Interestingly, predicates of "inference" such as *demonstrate* allow such subjects:

(9) a. #The time of death {believes, knows} that the butler is the murderer.
b. #The time of death {claims, reports} that the butler is the murderer.
c. The time of death {demonstrates, implies} that the butler is the murderer.

The cases in (7-9) suggest a complex interplay between predicate, subject, and felicity. Doxastics are only felicitous with sentient subjects, while communicative predicates like *claim* and *report* admit sentient subjects and agentive R-of-I subjects, and inferentials allow both of these and inanimates more generally. A&H (2009) split inanimates in two: the repository of information type (like *book*) and the inanimate (like *glove*). However, what counts as a repository of information is not entirely clear — Does it simply mean that the object is associated with content in some vague way? Or is there a more substantive notion?

12.2.2 Books, Notepads, and Plates

There are two types of distinctions in the literature that we may lean on to help answer the above questions. One comes from the literature on polysemy (e.g., Pustejovsky (1995), Cruse (2000), and Asher (2010)), which extensively discusses the ability of terms like *book* to predicate either of the physical object (e.g. *having a red cover*) or the propositional content encoded in the physical object (e.g., *being an adaptation of a film*). It is possible that this chimerical quality is necessary for being a "repository" of information. If it is necessary, it may or may not be sufficient. To investigate this further, we consider two kinds of repositories: items like *book* and items like *transcript* or *audio recording*. Both of these show physical object-propositional content polysemy: books and transcripts are both artifacts with natural physical forms that also allow us to speak of the content physically encoded (e.g., they can both be *confusing*). However, books can be seen as *adaptations* or *longwinded* or *conceited* (which pertain to the agent involved in the creation of the R-of-I), while transcripts cannot. This difference, we believe, connects to differences in the purposes driving the creation of books or transcripts (i.e., part of Pustejovsky's telic quale). Transcripts and recordings are made to memorialize some bit of action, which need not even be even linguistic. Books, on the other hand, can be created to encode arguments and claims for the reader to access and interact with.

But something more needs to be said beyond the terms "memorialize" and "encode" if we are to understand this distinction. Here, we will follow A&H (2009) in suggesting that books do not merely *encode* arguments, but *make* them as communicative agents within a discourse (see G (2015) for an alternative conception of nouns like *book* as locations rather than agents). Under this view, when one reads a book, one enters into a conversation with it. In this way, *the book* is an acceptable subject of a predicate like *claim* insofar as the book can be conceived of as making commitments within a discourse (Farkas & Bruce 2010, Condoravdi & Lauer 2012). This is a matter of course for books that set up argumentative claims, like many works of non-fiction. In contrast, works of fiction do not regularly establish a set of commitments in a rational exchange of information, and hence, like *transcript*, are less acceptable subjects for proffering predicates (10a). However, they may be used by predicates of intentional presentation (10b), unlike *transcript*:[1]

(10) a. The {biography, #novel, #transcript} claimed that Einstein was autocratic.

b. The {biography, novel, #transcript} portrays Einstein as autocratic.

Of course, it is still possible to single out the commitments a particular line of text would commit someone to, both for novels and for transcripts:

(11) The last line of the {novel, transcript} claims that Einstein was autocratic.

What this discussion suggests is a three way split among non-sentient subjects. On the one hand, there are elements without the object-propositional content polysemy, including artifacts like *glove* that lack any propositional content and proposition denoting elements which have no physical aspect, like the concealed question interpretation of the phrase *the time of death.* On the other, there are repositories of information like *transcript* and *book*, which do. But as we have seen, R-of-Is themselves need to be split in two. Some, like *book*, are capable of making commitments in discourse; we will call these Agentive R-of-Is. Those that cannot, like *transcript*, we will call Non-agentive R-of-Is. In what follows, we will sample from all three of these categories.

12.2.3 Subjects and Predicates

Our goal in this work is to be as comprehensive as we can reasonably be in examining the space of predicates. For verbs, we examined a list of *that*-clause embedding verbs that one author (JG) has compiled over several years, and excluded all verbs that did not allow the frame in (1) with a non expletive subject. This yielded 436 distinct morphemes, with a larger number of verb senses (472), since some morphemes have more than one sense. Although we attempted to supplement this list with existing lexical resources (FrameNet and VerbNet) and corpus extractions, the manually-collected list turned out to be far more accurate and complete than those resources. For adjectives, there was very little in existing resources, so we chose to extract them from text. First, we extracted all instances in Annotated Gigaword (Napoles *et al.*

[1]Thanks to an anonymous reviewer for suggesting we discuss the commitments of novels.

2012) of adjectives that are found with a *that*-clause complement in the machine-generated parses. We then pruned that noisy list manually to those that fit the frame in (1) with a non expletive subject. This yielded 153 unique adjectives. We split our proposition-taking predicates into four semantic classes, based on their intuitive meaning, as described in (12). For each of these predicates, we judged whether they could take four different types of subjects, described in (13):

(12) **Types of predicates**

- **Communicatives** (which include Grimshaw's SAY predicates, A&H (2009, 2014)'s "profferings"): predicates that express communicative acts (e.g., *claim*, *report*)
- **Doxastics**: predicates that express beliefs (e.g., *believe*, *know*)
- **Emotives**: predicates that express emotions (e.g., *hate*, *love*)
- **Inferentials**: predicates that express demonstrations (e.g., *show*, *demonstrate*)

(13) **Types of subjects**

- **Sentient beings**, which can be experiencers (*John*)
- **Agentive repositories of information**: R-of-Is which can be discourse agents (*book*, *article*, *review*)
- **Non-agentive repositories of information**: R-of-Is which cannot be discourse agents (*data*, *transcript*)
- **Inanimates**: Inanimate objects that lack propositional content (*plate*, *time of death*)

As for the protocol for the investigation itself, the judgments were sufficiently subtle (involving keeping track of word sense and syntactic structure) that we decided to pursue an annotation study, leaving an experimental acceptability follow-up for another occasion. The procedure for this was the following: for each predicate, two of the authors were presented with the various subject possibilities as schematized in (14) below and had to specify whether the subject-predicate combination was valid, invalid, or unknown. We allowed ourselves to see all of the possible subjects at once. After performing this task independently, we met to discuss and adjudicate our results. Our pre-adjudication reliability was reasonably high (pairwise Cohen's kappa = .76), suggesting that this task was sufficiently well-founded for experts to perform it reliably. All of our predicates are listed and grouped by semantic class in the Appendix, along with information about whether they allow R-of-I subjects and whether they are factive.

(14) {*The book?; The transcript?; The glove?*} VERB/BE ADJ that the Earth was flat.

	Sentient	Agentive R-of-I	Non-Agentive R-of-I	Inanimate
	John	*book*	*transcript*	*bloody glove*
Communicative *claim*	√	√	#	#
Doxastic *believe*	√	#	#	#
Emotive *hate*	√	#	#	#
Inferential *imply*	√	√	√	√

TABLE 1 Predicted felicity of subject-predicate combinations.

	Sentient	Agentive R-of-I	Non-Agentive R-of-I	Inanimate
	John	*book*	*transcript*	*bloody glove*
Communicative 319	319	**199**	0	0
Doxastic 124	124	**35**	0	0
Emotive 159	159	**13**	0	0
Inferential 23	23	23	23	23
Total 625	625	270	23	23

TABLE 2 Counts of felicitous subject-predicate combinations.

Our hypothesized interactions of predicate and subject are provided in Table 1, under the assumption that the Agentive/Non-Agentive R-of-I distinction is relevant for felicity with communicative predicates. Table 2 provides a summary count of the felicitous subject-predicate combinations for the forms we considered. For the most part, the expectations in Table 1 were confirmed: where we expected infelicity, there are very few predicates that seem to combine with the relevant subject, and where we expect felicity, the majority of predicates can take the relevant subject type.

Two kinds of exceptions to our predictions (bolded in Table 2) arise. First, some doxastic and emotive predicates seem to combine successfully with Agentive R-of-I subjects (about 28% and 8% respectively). We would expect 0 instead of 35 and 13 in the doxastic and the emotive rows. Second, some communicative predicates do not combine with them (about 38%). We would expect 319, instead of 199 in the communicative row. We consider each of these in the following sections: section 2.4. discusses communicative predicates, and why some do not allow R-of-I subjects; section 2.5 discusses doxastic and emotive predicates, and why some do allow R-of-I subjects.

12.2.4 Subjects of Communicative Predicates

Quite a few communicatives are infelicitous with Agentive R-of-I subjects, as noted above. The partial list in (15) illustrates. For a more complete list, see the Appendix.

(15) Communicatives infelicitous with Agentive R-of-I subjects:
cackle, enthuse, exclaim, explode, frown, fume, gasp, gesticulate, mumble, whisper...

We propose that the behavior of these verbs is explicable in a more articulated theory of their semantic structure, based on Grimshaw's (2015) analysis of SAY verbs, the subset of communicatives which are compatible with CP complements, and combine with clausal quotations, as well as main clauses.

(16) a. "We will", the principal reported, "have the best record in the state".
b. The principal claimed, "We will have the best record in the state".

Many verbs that are often grouped together (e.g. as *verba dicendi*) are not instances of SAY and do not share these characteristics, e.g. *discuss, speak, utter.* These verbs report events of linguistic formulation, or "speech events", but do not do so *in the same way* as SAY verbs. In particular they do not report the content or illocutionary force of what was linguistically encoded, and hence do not allow a CP or quoted clause as in (16). At most they report the topic, e.g. *speak for 10 minutes, discuss the situation.*

All of our communicative predicates take clausal complements, and a majority of them are SAY verbs. However we included some predicates such as *impart* and *guarantee*, which express a communicative act, but are not SAY verbs, and do not combine with quoted clauses (34 out of 319). As far as our subject generalizations are concerned, these additional predicates behave like the SAY verbs. The Appendix lists all of the communicative predicates, whether they are SAY verbs or not, and whether or not they allow agentive R-of-I subjects.

The proposal in G (2015) is that SAY verbs, including *ask, assert, mutter,* and *bitch* and even *think (to oneself)* all realize the schema (17), which can be enriched with additional material, such as the illocutionary force of the speech act or the means by which it is executed.

(17) SAY { Agent / Linguistic Content / Goal }

They share the universal abstract core predicate SAY, which combines with clausal complements and direct quotations, because these correspond to the "Linguistic Content" component in (17). Canonically SAY verbs combine with an Agent that produces linguistic material potentially directed toward some Goal (i.e., Addressee). This core (without any additional enriching structure) is lexicalized in English by the verb *say*.

When SAY is enriched by illocutionary force it is realized as *ask*, *assert* or *report* among other possibilities. This hypothesis makes it possible to characterize complementation possibilities for these verbs in a principled fashion, see Grimshaw (in prep.). (*Force* is subsumed under "discourse role" in G (2015).) Alternatively SAY can combine with independent intransitive verbs which denote activities that can result in the production of linguistically coded information. The enriching element, "means" (to realize the verb as *mutter*) or affective "attitude" (to realize it as *bitch*), imposes its own constraints on the (now shared) subject.

(18) How SAY verbs are constructed

SAY-**plus-Force**	Question	SAY + Q	*ask*
SAY-**by-Means**	Means	SAY + mutter	*mutter*
SAY-**with-Attitude**	Attitude	SAY + bitch	*bitch*

When two components combine, the shared subject argument is subject to the restrictions governing both components. For *bitch*, for instance, the Agents of *bitch* and SAY are identified with each other. Informally, the subject of SAY-*bitch* is both a "bitcher" and a "sayer".

(19) a. *bitch* { Agent / Goal or Target }

b. SAY-*bitch* { Agent / Linguistic Material / Goal or Target }

Since agentive R-of-I subjects are possible for the verb *say* itself, the ill-formedness of *book* as the subject of *whisper* or *bitch* must be attributed to a clash between the nature of the subject and the representation of the means or attitude component. While *bitch* as an activity predicate combines with *book* as a subject, *whisper* does not. This correctly predicts that SAY-whisper will not take agentive R-of-I subjects but SAY-*bitch* will:

(20) a. #The book whispered that the Governor never had a fair trial.
b. #The book whispered about the trial.
c. The book bitched (that the Governor never had a fair trial).
d. The book bitched about the trial.

The effects in (20) reflect the difference between predicates characterizing the means of linguistic production on the one hand (*whisper*, *mutter*), and affective attitude on the other (*bitch*, *gripe*), i.e. the SAY-means versus SAY-attitude distinction. The SAY-by-means verbs describe the physical act of emitting language, and agentive R-of-I subjects are therefore incompatible with all of them.

Just as the internal structure of a SAY verb controls the subjects the verb is compatible with, it also affects compatibility with complements such as *a few words*, which describe emitted linguistic units rather than the content of the linguistic material. This is illustrated in (21), based on examples in G (2015). SAY-by-means verbs are grammatical with *a few words*, as shown in (21a). In contrast, verbs of affective attitude (21b) or force (21c) disallow such complements:

(21) a. John {whispered, muttered} a few words.
b. *John {bitched, griped, grieved, rejoiced} a few words.
c. *John {asked, reported} a few words.

This contrasts with affective attitude verbs like *bitch* and *gripe*, which cannot combine with linguistic units as their complements (21b).[2]

Recall that no communicative predicate is compatible with non-agentive R-of-I subjects (like *transcript*, *corpus*, *archive*, or *data*). We claim that this is because although these elements do denote repositories of information, they are incompatible with the SAY schema: they are not agentive in the relevant sense.

Given what we said above, this would suggest that such subjects should be infelicitous with *say*, a prediction that does not at first appear to be borne out:

(22) The {transcript, corpus, archive, data} says that Bill is the murderer.

Our proposal is that in felicitous instances, the subject is functioning not as an Agent in any respect, but rather as the grounding for a conclusion. These are instances where *say* is not a manifestation of the SAY schema, but is used as an inferential, like *show*, *demonstrate*, *tell*, and *imply*. As the argument structure of inferentials is itself a complex

[2] A few additional communicatives cannot take R-of-I subjects. They are: *add in*, *put in*, *tell*, *throw in*, *publish*, *record*, *verbalize*.

topic, we simply provide two diagnostics that this is a distinct sense of *say*. First, we note that under this reading, *say*, like the inferentials, allows a host of subjects that SAY verbs do not — inanimates, facts, events:

(23) a. {The bloody glove, (The fact) that he is sweating, Him sweating} says that Bill is the murder.
b. #{The bloody glove, (The fact) that he is sweating, Him sweating} claims that Bill is the murder.

Second, G (2015) notes that all SAY verbs allow their linguistic material to be instantiated by direct quotation; non-SAY verbs do not admit clausal quotation. Turning to *say*, we see that its compatibility with clausal quotation co-varies with the subject. Both sentient and agentive R-of-I subjects permit it, in contrast to the other subjects allowed by inferentials:

(24) a. {John, the book} says, "This is the best restaurant you'll ever go to."
b. *{The transcript, The bloody glove, (The fact) that he is sweating, Him sweating} says, "This is the best restaurant you'll ever go to."

What (23-24) suggest, then, is that the use of *say* in (22) is not an instantiation of the SAY schema.

Let us now turn to the case of SAY-plus-force verbs, such as *assert*, *ask*, and *report*. These verbs enrich the SAY schema with a specification of the role of the linguistic material in discourse, which specifies how the speech act in question integrates into the larger conversational structure. Like other SAY verbs, these all combine with quoted clauses (see Grimshaw 2013, 2014). As SAY verbs, these all will be restricted to the usual SAY subjects: sentient elements and agentive R-of-I elements. Although, in principle, one could imagine additional restrictions that would militate in favor of sentient agents exclusively, our examination of SAY-plus-force verbs revealed none that prohibit agentive R-of-I subjects. Thus, sentient subjects and agentive R-of-I subjects are divided only by SAY-by-means verbs, which come with an inference of physical production.

Human speakers are not the only possible subjects for embedding verbs which canonically report human speech acts. Subjects of these verbs are governed by general principles which require compatibility between components of verb meanings and verbal arguments. As a further illustration, we note that the very factors which distinguish among verbs which take *that*-clause complements also partition speech-related verbs that do not allow clausal complements at all. For instance, while *discuss* cannot take *that*-clauses, it shows the same subject properties as SAY-plus-force verbs and affective attitude SAY verbs: it allows sentient and agentive R-of-I subjects, and excludes the other subject types. The verb *speak* can only take sentient subjects, patterning like *whisper* in being a verb of physical linguistic unit emission. This suggests that the factors which govern subject-verb compatibility hold broadly.

12.2.5 Subjects of Doxastic and Emotive Predicates

There are a few emotive and doxastic predicates that combine with agentive R-of-I subjects, several of which have communicative senses. Only a handful of **emotive** predicates allow R-of-I subjects (13 out of 159). They are listed in (25) below:

(25) **Emotives felicitous with agentive R-of-I subjects**: *deplore, exult, adamant, despair, fear, hope, hopeful, optimistic, obsess, pessimistic, sanguine, suspicious, worry*

When an emotive predicate combines with a R-of-I subject like *book*, the resulting sentence reports a preference expressed by the book. That is, despite being classed as emotive, all of the predicates in (25) can be used to report on speech acts, and hence should be acceptable with agentive R-of-I subjects. The sentence in (26), for instance, reports that the book expresses the hope/fear that our sources of fossil fuels will be depleted by 2030:

(26) The book {hopes/fears} that our sources of fossil fuels will be depleted by 2030.

One important question we leave aside here is why among the emotives only those in (25) seem to be acceptable as reporting expressed preferences (e.g., why *fear* and not *afraid*?).[3] However, we note in passing that, interestingly, most of these predicates encode both emotive and doxastic content (they correspond to Anand & Hacquard's (2013) "emotive doxastics"). The verb *hope*, for instance, not only expresses a preference for *p*, but further requires that *p* be a doxastic possibility for its subject. However, as the Appendix shows, many other "hybrid" attitudes do not allow agentive R-of-I subjects.

The proportion of **doxastic** predicates that allow R-of-I subjects is larger (35 out 124). Many of these predicates also have a communicative sense, which we take to be responsible for allowing these R-of-I subjects.

[3] An anonymous reviewer suggests that those emotive predicates that disallow R-of-I subjects are ones with greater "mental agitation", and hence ones that require sentience. We leave a more detailed exploration of this idea to future work.

The remaining verbs fall into three subclasses: predicates of "forecast"; predicates of "assumption"; and predicates of "reasoning":

(27) **Doxastics felicitous with Agentive R-of-I subjects**
Communicative sense: *calculate, conclude, deem, determine, forecast, generalize, hold, judge, predict, rationalize*
Forecast: *anticipate, envisage, envision, forecast, foresee, predict, prognosticate, project*
Assume: *appreciate, assume, discern, make out, recognize, accept, assume, estimate, figure, presuppose, posit, postulate, suppose, surmise, trust*
Reason: *diagnose, establish, reason, reckon, verify*

We believe that the felicity of these predicates with agentive R-of-I subjects is a symptom of something larger: these are not intrinsically predicates involving a sentient "thinker". For instance, the fact that agentive R-of-Is can appear as subjects of predicates of forecast follows from the fact that discourse agents can make predictions about the future, independent of sentience. Similarly, when *book* subjects combine with predicates of reasoning, the resulting sentence describes a chain of argumentation that is made explicit in the book. Again, discourse agents are capable of delivering an argument, without necessitating sentience. Finally, the ability of *book* subjects to combine with the class of predicates of assumption show that agentive R-of-Is can not only make discourse moves (assertions), but they do so against a set of background assumptions, which can explicitly be described using these predicates of assumption. Again, assumptions do not require sentience.

12.3 Factivity and Subject Variation

12.3.1 Factivity and Communicatives

As we have seen, agentive R-of-I subjects differentiate communicative predicates from doxastics and emotives. This leads us to ask what other properties cut the pie the same way. One possible place to go hunting is factivity, since the classic factive attitude predicates are cognitive factives (*know, figure out, realize*) and emotive factives (*love, hate, be surprised*) (Kiparsky & Kiparsky 1970, Karttunen and Peters 1979). And yet, there seem to be some communicative predicates that are also understood as factive (*acknowledge, admit*).

In order to ascertain the robustness of the doxastic/emotive-factivity correlation, we investigated which of the predicates described in section 2 were factive, veridical or neither. While different authors make different assumptions about veridicality and factivity, here we understand these terms as follows: both factives (e.g., *know*) and veridicals (*be true that*) have a veracity entailment. As an illustration, both factive *know* in (28a) and veridical *be true* in (28b) entail (28c):

(28) a. John **knows** that it is raining.
b. It is **true** that it is raining.
c. It is raining.

Factives differ from veridicals in that this veracity entailment gets foregrounded with veridicals, but backgrounded ("presupposed") with factives. Evidence for this backgrounding comes from the fact that the veracity inference typically projects out of negation, questions and antecedents of conditionals. Unlike in (30), a speaker uttering any of the sentences in (29) seems to presuppose that it is raining.

(29) a. John doesn't **know** that it is raining.
b. Does John **know** that it is raining?
c. If John **knows** that it's raining, he'll take an umbrella.

(30) a. It's not **true** that it is raining.
b. Is it **true** that it is raining?
c. If it's **true** that it's raining, John will take an umbrella.

We thus subjected each of the predicates from section 2 to the family of sentences test. What we found upon close investigation of all of these predicates is that none of the putatively factive communicative predicates are actually factive. We thus have the following generalization (see A&H 2014 on communicatives, G 2015 on SAY verbs).

(31) **The factivity generalization**: No communicative predicate is factive. We only find factivity amongst the doxastics (*know*, *discover*, *learn...*), and emotives (*hate*, *love...*).

In what follows, we discuss several potential counterexamples to this generalization and show that the predicates are not factive.

12.3.2 Some Potential Counterexamples

To begin with, certain speech reports have been argued to be factive (Schlenker 2010, Egré & Spector, *to appear*):

(32) Did Mary tell her parents that she's moving to Australia?

A speaker uttering (32) seems to be presupposing that Mary is moving to Australia. Note, however, that while verbs like *tell*, *announce* or *say* can have factive *uses* as in (32), where the speaker seems to take for granted the truth of the complement clause, these verbs do not have a veracity entailment, as the lack of contradiction in (33) shows:

(33) Mary told her parents that she's moving to Australia, but she's not.

Hence, these verbs are not truly factive (and are not listed as factive in the Appendix): they lack a veracity entailment that can be backgrounded. Given our understanding of factivity as backgrounding of an entailment, (33) would come out contradictory. We argue that the apparent factivity in (32) has to do with how speakers use attitude and speech reports in context, and the flexibility in what they can foreground and background with an attitude report (see also Simons 2007, Simons *et al.* 2010; Dayal and Grimshaw 2009).

With the assertion of a speech report, the speaker can either foreground the speech report, or its content. Consider the contexts in (34) and (35). In (34), the "main point" of B's utterance seems to be about what Mary said: it is carried by the main clause of the predicate report. In (35), on the other hand, the main point of B's utterance seems to be carried by the complement clause. In this context, what matters is Mary's whereabouts, not her claims. The main clause gets a parenthetical interpretation, and seems to merely play an evidential role (see Simons 2007).

(34) A: What kind of crazy claim is Mary making these days?
B: She told her parents she's moving to Australia.

(35) A: Is Mary going to be here next month? I'd like to invite her to my party.
B: She told her parents she's moving to Australia.

Hence, with communicative predicates, the speaker can easily appear to proffer the content of the complement clause, and choose to foreground the main clause or the complement clause.

Returning to (32), the speaker seems to take for granted that Mary is moving to Australia, and to ask about whether she informed her parents of that fact. Why should this be? All else equal, we assume that Mary should be a reliable source of information about whether she's moving to Australia or not. All else equal then, we assume that the interesting question is whether she has informed her parents of that fact. But here again this assumption can easily disappear, depending on context. If we know Mary to be a compulsive liar, we might assume that the question in (32) is not so much about Mary's whereabouts, but about her claims, in which case the factivity illusion disappears.

A few communicatives (*acknowledge* and *admit*; listed as "factive" in the Appendix) seem less prone to contextual manipulation, and thus more stubbornly factive. These verbs allow *book* subjects, and are hence communicative given our analysis.

(36) a. The book acknowledges that the earth is flat.
b. Does the book acknowledge that the earth is flat?

Both (36a) and (36b) seem to presuppose that the earth is flat. However, even in this case, A&H (2014) argue that there is no veracity entailment, which means that there is no factivity. However, these verbs have other presuppositions, which can be exploited to yield an inference very close to a factive presupposition. Verbs like *acknowledge* and *admit* seem to presuppose that their subject was the last hold out for acceptance of their complement in the common ground of the reported communicative act. Once the subject acknowledges or admits *p*, *p* becomes accepted in the reported common ground. Assuming that no further relevant information leads to *p* being removed later from the common ground, we assume that *p* still holds in our common ground. However, *p* is not entailed in our world. This can be seen by creating enough distance from the reported common ground and our common ground (from A&H 2014: 75)

(37) In Ancient Greece it was widely accepted that the Earth was flat. Eratosthenes however thought that it was round. After his peers demonstrated to him that he couldn't be right, he finally {acknowledged/admitted} that the Earth was flat.

Based on this evidence, A&H (2014) propose that there is a gap in factivity: no communicative is factive. In section 3.5, we briefly explore what might underlie this gap.

12.3.3 Factivity and Subjects

Given our factivity generalization, according to which no communicative is factive, and our subject generalization, according to which only communicatives allow agentive R-of-I subjects, (putting aside the inferentials, which allow all kinds of inanimate subjects), we expect that no factive predicate will take R-of-I subjects. There are, however, counterexamples to this generalization from both the emotives and the doxastics, which we briefly discuss here.

There are two emotive factives that seem to allow R-of-I subjects, namely *exult* and *deplore*. These verbs interestingly seem to lose their factivity when they combine with a R-of-I subject, as the lack of contradiction in (38) seems to show.

(38) The book$_1$ deplores that Iraq$_2$ has weapons of mass destruction, which it$_2$ doesn't.

Several factive doxastics also allow R-of-I subjects, namely those in

(39):

(39) *appreciate, discern, make out, recognize.*

These verbs all seem to be predicates of assumption. As we argued in section 2.5, such predicates make reference to background assumptions that discourse agents (including agentive R-of-Is) can make. Perhaps what explains the apparent factivity of these predicates is the backgrounded status of such assumptions, which may give rise to an illusion of factivity, as we argued for *acknowledge*. Predicates of assumption would refer to backgrounded commitments in the reported common ground. Barring reasons to assume that our common ground differs from the reported common ground, we would expect these presuppositions to hold in our common ground as well, making these predicates appear factive. And again, with enough distance, the use of such predicate would not require that the speaker be commited to the truth of the complement in a sentence like (40):

(40) Eratosthenes' book recognized that the Earth was flat.

12.3.4 Factivity and Frame

A particularly powerful case for the allergy of communicatives to factivity comes from predicates that can appear in multiple argument structural frames. Consider the cases of *worry* and *obsess* which can (atypically uniquely) appear with its individual argument as either subject or object (trading with the proposition denoting CP):

(41)

		Factive?	Agentive R-of-I?
a.	{Mary, The book} worries that the plan will fail.	N	Y
b.	That the plan will fail worries {Mary, #the book}.	Y	N

As indicated in (41), the alternation simultaneously affects both the factivity of the predicate and whether it admits agentive R-of-I individuals. When the subject is the individual argument, agentive R-of-I elements are felicitous, and there is no veracity entailment for the proposition denoted by the CP (instead, it is taken to be epistemically possible for the subject). In contrast, when the proposition-denoting CP is the subject, a factive inference arises (and hence a speaker asserting (41b) seems to be committed to a rather definitive claim about the future) and agentive R-of-I subjects are infelicitous.

To our knowledge, *worry* and *obsess* are unique in being possible in both the syntactic frames in (41) without overt morphological modification. However, the pattern in question is more general. In general, the

	that-clause-V-DP	DP-V-*that*-clause	DP-be-A-*that*-clause	
obsess	Factive	**Non factive**	Non factive	*obsessed*
worry	Factive	**Non factive**	Non factive	*worried*
concern	Factive	*	Non factive	*concerned*
distress	Factive	*	Factive	*distressed*
upset	Factive	*	Factive	*upset*
doubt	*	**Non factive**	Non factive	*doubtful*
resent	*	Factive	Factive	*resentful*
scare	Factive	*	Non factive	*scared*
frightened	Factive	*	Non factive	*frightened*
fret	*	**Non factive**	Non factive	*fretful*
hope	*	**Non factive**	Non factive	*hopeful*
grieve	Factive	Factive	*	

TABLE 3 Predicate-frame correlations with factivity and admission of agentive R-of-I subjects. Forms in a frame that allow agentive R-of-I subjects are in **boldface**.

frame *that*-clause-V-DP is uniformly factive, and agentive R-of-I objects are systematically forbidden. DP-V-*that*-clause and DP-be-Adj-*that*-clause frames (where the adjective is derived from the relevant verb), in contrast, are more diverse: sometimes they are factive (*be surprised*) and sometimes they are not (*be obsessed*). What we find is that agentive R-of-I subjects are systematically excluded from factive sentences, regardless of whether they are formed from a passive verb or not. For instance, in the DP-V-*that*-clause frame, *obsess* and *worry* are able to take a R-of-I subject (42a). However, in the *that*-clause-V-DP, which is exclusively factive, these verbs cannot take a *book* subject (42b). Table 3 provides several instances of this pattern.

(42) a. The book {worries, obsesses} that Iraq has weapons of mass destruction.

b. # That Iraq has weapons of mass destruction {worries, obsesses} the book.

We take the existence of this pattern, regardless of which predicate is possible in any given frame, as an argument that communicative predicates are incompatible with factivity.

12.3.5 Explanations for the Factivity Gap Generalization

We have seen three kinds of distributional evidence that communicative predicates cannot be factive: first, there are very few potentially factive communicative predicates; second, the potentially factive ones do not seem to actually be so under further scrutiny; finally, factive predicates seem to lose their factivity in frames/forms where they take agentive R-of-I subjects. What then might be the source of this incompatibility?

In principle, it is possible that the combination of a communicative event and factivity is somehow conceptually inconceivable, independent of language. Absent a clear logic for conceptual combination, it is hard to know how to investigate such an idea. Nonetheless, there is some indirect evidence that inconceivability is not driving things, namely, the fact that we had to argue that *tell* and *admit* are not factive. If such interpretations were not possible, we would expect that the pragmatically enriched meanings for (32)-(35), which have a very similar profile, would also be impossible.

While we are skeptical of an explanation based on conceptual incompatibility, it may be the case that we are witnessing a linguistic constraint on lexical meaning. For example, if lexical meaning can be decomposed into formal representations in some logical system, it may be that the representations of "being a communicative event" and "being factive" are syntactically incompatible. Formalizing this in a satisfactory way requires careful consideration about what the representation for "being factive" should be, especially since most argument structural representation systems focus on encoding relational concepts (agent, goal, etc.). Thus, while we remain interested in examining this kind of approach, saying anything more requires going well beyond the scope of this paper.

In closing this speculative discussion, we would like to highlight a different possible explanation that is less often invoked in formal semantics circles: functional pressures on lexicalization. Horn (1972) observes systematic gaps in the kinds of logical operator meanings that get lexicalized in natural language. While we find words like *some*, *all*, and even *no*, there do not seem to be words *nall*, that express the meaning *not all*. Similarly, while we find words like *and*, and *or*, there do not seem to words *nand*, that express the meaning *not and*. Why should this be? Horn argues that these lexical gaps can be provided a functional explanation by considering not just the semantics of particular words, but also what (enriched) meanings can be expressed with just a few words. In particular, the meanings *not all* and *not and* can easily be conveyed via scalar implicatures: a speaker using some in a context where the stronger term all would have been appropriate seems to imply *not all* from their choice of using *some* rather than *all*. Because such meanings can easily be pragmatically derived, there is no need for a language to lexicalize such words, and hence such lexicalizations should be rare.

As we have seen in (32)-(35), the kind of enrichment we see with *not all* occurs with speech reports. That is, speech reports are pragmatically employed by a speaker in order to commit to the truth of the complement clause, especially when the complement is most relevant to the topic of conversation. A speaker can thus use a speech report to indirectly assert the complement clause (this is why Hooper 1975 calls such predicates "assertives"). As a result, pursuing an analogy with Horn's explanation for *nall*, there is no functional pressure to lexicalize a factive communicative, since such meanings are easily pragmatically communicated.

The problem for this kind of explanation is making sure it does not run amok. If all lexicalization were subject to stringent functional utility pressures having to do with relevance-based pragmatics, open class vocabularies should be very tiny indeed. Figuring out how to respond to this concern will likely come with more precisely formalizing the nature of the pragmatic calculations being invoked, a challenge we leave to further work.

12.4 Conclusions and Prospects

In this paper we have reported on a fairly systematic investigation of the subject-taking properties of several hundred *that*-clause embedding predicates in English. We have argued on the basis of this investigation that the preliminary claims of A&H (2009) are largely right: sentence embedding ("attitude") predicates split between those that select for sentient entities (experiencers) and those that select for communicative agents. These are what A&H (2009) called agentive repositories of information —- entities that can be understood as interlocutors in generic conversations. We also showed that a finer-grained understanding of the landscape of SAY-verbs can derive why not all of them are compatible with these arguments. The subjects that SAY-verbs occur with follow general principles which relate the semantic components of the verbs to their complement-taking capacities as well as their subject possibilities. In future research, we hope to extend this to other communicatives, and to further pursue the properties of communicative verbs.

We also showed that this same split in attitudes is reflected in a somewhat orthogonal-seeming dimension: which predicates are factive. We find that no communicative predicate is truly factive. Given the relatively large attitude and speech vocabulary under consideration, this gap is rather surprising, and calls for an explanation. We've briefly touched on various lines that one could pursue.

We see this investigation as a start toward a more articulate understanding of attitude meaning and, more generally, *that-clause* embedding predicates. One large hole in our understanding at present is the structure of inferential predicates. We have argued that *say* has an inferential sense, but we do not at present know what restrictions, if any, inferentials possess. The structure of inferentials also looms large in our exploration of factivity. We have argued that there are no factive communicatives, but what we have in fact shown is that several putative counterexamples do not even possess a veracity entailment. If that is the case generally, then it is not merely the case that there are no factive communicatives. Rather, we would have a stronger generalization: communicative predicates are incompatible with veracity entailments. Examining this stronger claim will require us to take a closer look at putative veridical communicatives and determine if they truly are veridical. Inferentials may be one case to examine: *John demonstrated that it's raining* seems to entail that the complement is true, an entailment that does not survive questioning or negation. But is *demonstrate* actually veridical (what happens when one adds an overt experiencer *to Mary*)? And is it truly a communicative, or something else? Answering this seemingly minor question could be central in understanding how communicative predicates may be enriched with additional meaning.

Lastly, we hope that this investigation can eventually help to shed light on the (natural language) metaphysics of discourse moves — who can make such a move, what is required for such a move, and what such moves require of the context and the participants. We have shown that the answer is far from trivial, since some, but not all, repositories of information are licit subjects of such predicates. Karttunen (1977) was instrumental in showing us that the semantics and pragmatics of questions are best disentangled by looking at embedded questions. In turn, we hope that looking at the subjects of predicates referencing speech acts can similarly help to clarify issues where the pragmatics and semantics seem at first inextricably mixed.

Appendix

DOXASTICS		
$\surd$*agentive* **R-o-I subject**	**Factive**	*appreciate, discern, make out, recognize*
	Non factive	*accept, anticipate, assume,* ***calculate, conclude, deem, determine,*** *diagnose, envisage, envision, establish, estimate, figure,* ***forecast****, foresee,* ***generalize, hold, judge,*** *presuppose, posit, postulate,* ***predict****, prognosticate, project,* ***rationalize****, reason, reckon, suppose, surmise, trust, verify*
#agentive **R-o-I subject**	**Factive**	*absorb, acknowledge, ascertain, aware, catch on, catch, comprehend, conscious, detect, discover, figure out, find out, forget, get, glimpse, grasp, hear, ignorant, intuit, know, learn, mindful, mystified, notice, observe, puzzled, realize, recall, recollect, register, remember, see, smell, surprised, take in, unaware, understand, uninformed, unsurprised, well-aware*
	Non factive	*agree, believe, bet, certain, clueless, cocksure, cognizant, conceive, confident, consider, convinced, decide, deduce, disagree, doubt, doubtful, dream, dubious, expect, fancy, fantasize, feel, find, gather, guess, hallucinate, imagine, infer, internalize, note, overhear, paranoid, perceive, positive, pray, presume, resolve, ruminate, sense, skeptical, sure, suspect, think, uncertain, unconvinced, unsure, visualize, wish, work out*

Boldface: predicate also has a communicative sense.

Some of these doxastics further fall into the following sub-classes:

Forecast predicates: *anticipate, envisage, envision,* ***forecast****, foresee,* ***predict****, prognosticate, project*

Assume predicates: *appreciate, discern, make out, recognize, accept, assume, estimate, figure, presuppose, posit, postulate, suppose, surmise, trust*

Reason predicates: *diagnose, reason, reckon, verify, establish*

EMOTIVES		
√*agentive* R-o-I subject	**Factive**	***deplore, exult***
	Non factive	*adamant, despair, fear, hope, hopeful, optimistic, obsess, pessimistic, sanguine, suspicious, worry*
#agentive R-o-I subject	**Factive**	*abashed, abhor, accept, admire, adore, aggrieved, aghast, agonize, amazed, amused, angry, anguished, annoyed, apologetic, apoplectic, appalled, appreciate, appreciative, ashamed, astonished, astounded, awed, bear, befuddled, bemused, bewildered, bitter, calm, care, celebrate, cherish, concerned, delighted, delirious, depressed, depressing, despairing, despise, detest, disappointed, disgruntled, disgusted, dislike, dismayed, displeased, dissatisfied, distraught, ecstatic, elated, embarrassed, enjoy, envious, euphoric, excited, exhilarated, exultant, face, flabbergasted, fortunate, frantic, freak out, frightened, furious, giddy, glad, gleeful, grateful, gratified, grieve, happy, hate, heartbroken, heartsick, impatient, incredulous, indignant, irate, jealous, joyful, jubilant, leery, like, livid, loathe, love, lucky, mad, mind, nervous, oblivious, outraged, overjoyed, pained, peeved, pissed, pleased, proud, regret, regretful, remorseful, rejoice, relish, resent, resentful, respect, rue, sad, satisfied, scared, self-aware, shocked, sorrowful, sorry, stand, thankful, tolerate, unabashed, unconcerned, uneasy, unfazed, ungrateful, unhappy, unimpressed, unlucky, uptight, value, wistful, worry, wrathful*
	Non factive	*afraid, anxious, apprehensive, desire, dread, fearful, fretful, keen, maniacal, overconfident, petrified, prefer, resolute, self-assured, upbeat, wary, worried*

Boldface: also has a (nonfactive) communicative sense.

Inferentials		
√*agentive* R-o-I subject	**Factive**	*betray*
	Non factive	*assure, certify, confirm, demonstrate, guarantee, highlight, hint, illustrate, implicate, imply, indicate, manifest, mean, prove, reassure, show, signal, reveal, suggest, teach, underline*
#agentive R-o-I subject	**Factive**	—
	Non factive	—

COMMUNICATIVES		
√*agentive* **R-o-I subject**	**Factive**	*acknowledge, admit*
	Non factive	*add, admonish,* ***advertize****, advise, advocate, affirm, agonize, agree, allege,* ***animadvert****, announce, answer, argue, ask, assert, assure, attest, aver, bark, bawl, beef, beg, bellow, beseech, bitch, blabber, bleat, blubber, bluster, boast, brag, bray,* ***bring in, bring up****, burble, calculate, caution,* ***certify****, charge,* ***cite****, claim, clarify, clear, command, comment, complain, concede, conclude, concur, confess, confirm, conjecture, contend, continue, [be]* ***correct****, corroborate, counter,* ***criticize****, declare, decree,* ***deem****, demand, demur,* ***deny, deplore****, detail,* ***determine****, dictate,* ***disagree****, disclose, dispute, divulge,* ***document****, elaborate, emphasize,* ***emphatic****, explain,* ***explicit****, expostulate, exult, forecast, foretell, forewarn, fret, fuss,* ***generalize****, gloat, go on, grant, gripe, grouse, grumble,* ***guarantee****, guess, gush, hazard, hint, hold, hypothesize,* ***impart, incorrect****, indicate, inform, insinuate,* ***insistent****, instruct, intimate, jest, joke, josh, judge, kvetch, lament, lay out, leak,* ***leave out****, let slip, lie, maintain, marvel,* ***mean****, mention, muse, note (down), object, observe,* ***omit****, opine,* ***overemphasize****, philosophize, plead, pledge, point out, preach, predict, proclaim, profess, promise, prophesy, propose, protest,* ***publicize****, put out, question, quip, radio in, ramble, rant, rationalize, rave, reaffirm, reassure, recommend, reemphasize, reflect, reiterate, rejoice, relate, relay, remark, remind, remonstrate, repeat, reply, report, request, respond, retort, reveal,* ***right****, say,* ***share****, signal, soliloquize, specify, speculate, spell out, state,* ***steadfast****, stipulate, stress, submit, suggest, swear, tease, telegraph, theorize, threaten,* ***tout, unveil****, urge,* ***unanimous, vehement****, venture, vow, warn, whine*

#agentive R-o-I subject	**Factive**	—
	Non factive	*add in, apologize,* ***apprise****, babble, blurt, blurt out, boom, burst out, cackle, call, call in, call out, carol, chant, cheer, chime in, chirp, chortle, chuckle, cluck, confide, coo, cry, cry out, editorialize, enthuse, exclaim, explode, fib, frown, fume, gasp, gesticulate, gesture, get in, get out, giggle, glare, grimace, grin, groan, grunt, harrumph, hiss, holler, insist, jot down, laugh, let out, moan, move, mumble, mutter, notify, order, pray, pretend, pronounce,* ***publish****, put in, rage, read, read out, recite,* ***record****, roar, rule, scoff, seethe, shout, shout out, shrug, sigh, sign, sing, smirk, snap, snarl, sneer, snicker, sniff, snort, snuffle, sob, splutter, sputter, squall, squawk, squeak, squeal, stammer, stutter, tell, testify, text, think, throw in, thunder, tisk, trill, trumpet, tweet, twitter,* ***verbalize****, wail, warble, wave, wheeze, whimper, whisper, whistle, whoop, write, yammer, yap, yell, yell out, yelp, yodel*

Boldface: communicative predicates that are not SAY verbs.

References

Anand, Pranav and Valentine Hacquard. 2009. Epistemics with attitude. In *Proceedings of SALT 18*, pages 37–54.

Anand, Pranav and Valentine Hacquard. 2013. Epistemics and attitudes. *Semantics and Pragmatics* 6.8:1–59.

Anand, Pranav and Valentine Hacquard. 2014. Factivity, belief and discourse. In L. Crnic and U. Sauerland, eds., *The Art and Craft of Semantics: A Festschrift for Irene Heim*, pages 69–90. MITWPL.

Asher, Nicholas. 2010. *Lexical semantics in context*. Cambridge.

Condoravdi, Cleo and Sven Lauer. 2012. Imperatives: Meaning and illocutionary force. In C. Piñón, ed., *Empirical issues in syntax and semantics 9*, pages 37–58.

Cruse, D. Alan. 2000. Aspects of the micro-structure of word meanings. In Y. Ravin and C. Leacock, eds., *Polysemy: Theoretical and Computational Approaches*. Oxford University Press.

Dayal, Veneeta and Jane Grimshaw. 2009. Subordination at the interface: A quasi-subordination hypothesis. Manuscript, Rutgers.

Farkas, Donka and Kim Bruce. 2010. On reacting to assertions and polar questions. *Journal of Semantics* 27(1):81–118.

Grimshaw, Jane. 2013. Quotes, subordination, and parentheticals. Manuscript, Rutgers University.

Grimshaw, Jane. 2014. Quotes, clausal complements, and parentheticals. Manuscript, Rutgers University.

Grimshaw, Jane. 2015. The light verbs say and SAY. In I. Toivonen, P. Csúri, and E. van der Zee, eds., *Structures in the Mind: Essays on Language, Music, and Cognition*, pages 79–99. MIT Press.

Grimshaw, Jane. in prep. Questions and issues in wh complementation. Manuscript, Rutgers University.

Hooper, Jane. 1975. On assertive predicates. In J. Kimball, ed., *Syntax and semantics, volume 4*, pages 91–124. Academy Press.

Horn, Lawrence R. 1972. *On the semantic properties of logical operators in English*. Ph.D. thesis, UCLA.

Karttunen, Lauri. 1977. Syntax and semantics of questions. *Linguistics and Philosophy* 1:3–44.

Karttunen, Lauri and Stanley Peters. 1979. Conventional implicature. In C.-K. Oh and D. A. Dinneen, eds., *Syntax and Semantics 11, Presupposition*, pages 1–56. Academic Press.

Kiparsky, Carol and Paul Kiparsky. 1970. Fact. In M. Bierwisch and K. Heidolph, eds., *Progress in Linguistics*, pages 143–73. Mouton.

Napoles, Courtney, Matthew Gormley, and Benjamin Van Durme. 2012. Annotated gigaword. In *Proceedings of the Joint Workshop on Automatic Knowledge Base Construction and Web-scale Knowledge Extraction*, pages 95–100.

Pustejovsky, James. 1995. *The generative lexicon*. MIT Press.

Schlenker, Philippe. 2010. Local contexts and local meanings. *Philosophical Studies* 151:115–142.

Simons, Mandy. 2007. Observations on embedding verbs, evidentiality and presupposition. *Lingua* 117:1037–1056.

Simons, Mandy, Judith Tonhauser, David Beaver, and Craige Roberts. 2010. What projects and why. In N. Li and D. Lutz, eds., *Proceedings of Semantics and Linguistic Theory*, vol. 20, pages 309–327. CLC Publications.

Spector, Benjamin and Paul Egré. to appear. A uniform semantics for embedded interrogatives: An answer, not necessarily the answer. *Synthese*.

13

Multiple Center-embedding in Spoken English*

FRED KARLSSON

13.1 Introduction

A center-embedded clause is surrounded on both sides by major constituents (excluding subordinators) of the superordinate clause, e.g. all the three relative clauses in (1):

(1) [A person [who, [when riding a cycle, [not being a motor vehicle,] on a road or other public place,] is unfit to ride through drinks or drugs,] shall be guilty of an offence.] (*British Road Traffic Act*, 1972; Hiltunen 1984: 115).

Based on extensive evidence from seven European languages, I have concluded that the maximal empirically demonstrable (but extremely rare) degree of multiple clausal center-embedding in written language is three, as in (1) (Karlsson 2007). Double clausal center-embeddings, as in (2), are somewhat more common but still utterly rare:

(2) [For an analysis of the possible modifications [of which the pathological termination of an act [which is not according to law] is susceptible] we have therefore ...] (Bentham 1945: 121)

In total 119 authentic written double center-embeddings were found in the seven languages under scrutiny. Of these twenty-two occurred in the written Brown and LOB corpora totaling two million words.

*Thanks to Laurence Horn for valuable comments on the preliminary version of this paper.

Tokens of Meaning: Papers in Honor of Lauri Karttunen.
Cleo Condoravdi and Tracy Holloway King (eds.).

This yields an estimated incidence of one double center-embedding per 90,000 words. Thus double center-embedding is a real (but rare) construction type in present-day written English. However, triple center-embeddings were not found in Brown or LOB, indicating extreme rarity.

No systematically collected data nor motivated interpretations have been published on the incidence and nature of multiple center-embedding in spoken English. This is the topic of the present paper.

In the literature I have found just one authentic instance of a multiple spoken center-embedding, the double center-embedding in (3).

(3) [It's ironic [that I'm here, [where the man [the trophy [I won] is named after] coached.]]]

The utterance (3) contains a double center-embedding under two finally-embedded clauses. Laurence Horn (2000) reported the provenience of (3) as being:

> [a]ttested from Tony De[g]rate, winner of the Vince Lombardi trophy as a college senior at the U. of Texas, upon being cut from the Green Bay Packers professional football team, which had won five championships under their legendary coach Vince Lombardi.[1]

Horn (p.c.) had transcribed the sentence on hearing Degrate utter it on the sports segment of a television news program on 8 October 1985. The sentence also occurs in precisely the form (3) in The Milwaukee Journal in October 1985.[2] Clearly (3) must be deemed both grammatical and acceptable, so at least one clear instance of spoken double center-embedding is at hand.

13.2 Material and method

The spoken-language corpora consulted are:

(i) The CHRISTINE Corpus, Release 2 (henceforth CHRISTINE), compiled and annotated by Geoffrey Sampson, Alan Morris and Anna Rahman, cf. Sampson (2000). The material was drawn from the demographic section of the spoken materials of the British National Corpus (BNC, Hoffmann & al. 2008). CHRISTINE set out to extend Sampson's (1995) SUSANNE analytic scheme to cover spoken English, and particularly spontaneous, informal spoken English. The 147 identified

[1] http://linguistlist.org/issues/11/11-269.html [accessed 13 September 13 2015].

[2] https://news.google.com/newspapers?nid=1499&dat=19851004&id=SWgaAAAAIBAJ&sjid=VyoEAAAAIBAJ&pg=7077,3829810&hl=en [accessed 22 September 2015]. Upon accessing the link on 12 September 2016 I noted that Google had discontinued it. A scanned version of the relevant passage from The Milwaukee Journal (apparently from 9 October 1985) is available via my home page as the file Degrate_1985.PDF.

speakers were drawn from all social classes and regions of the United Kingdom in the 1990s. The number of sentence-size chunks is 6125 and the number of words (excluding hesitations, repetitions etc.) around 80,500.

(ii) The International Corpus of English - Great Britain, ICE-GB (Nelson 1998). ICE-GB contains one million words of spoken and written British English collected in 1990-1993. All three parts of the spoken dialogue part of the corpus (henceforth called ICE-GB-DIAL) were analyzed in detail: (a) private direct conversations (338 speakers, 185,193 words, texts s1A1-s1A90), (b) private telephone calls (36 speakers, 20,415 words, texts S1A91-S1A100), and (c) public dialogues (altogether 446 speakers, 171,059 words, texts S1B1-S1B80), distributed over classroom lessons (42,208 words), broadcast discussions (43,921 words), broadcast interviews (22,147 words), parliamentary debates (21,060 words), legal cross-examinations (21,179 words), and business transactions (20,544 words). The total number of words now considered in ICE-GB-DIAL is 376,667.

The analysis of the materials in CHRISTINE and ICE-GB described in (i) and (ii) yielded a few relevant examples of double center-embedding. The structural patterns thus detected were checked for occurrence in:

(iii) the whole demographically sampled and regionally unrestricted spoken conversational dialogue part of the British National Corpus, BNC, containing 4,233,962 words.

(iv) The Pear Story material of Chafe (1980, ed.), some 16,000 words, was checked.

As for methodology, the annotation scheme of CHRISTINE covers all details of spoken English grammar and is specifically geared towards treating the intricacies of everyday speech. The explicit and detailed syntactic coding, including constituent labeling and bracketing of relative clauses (coded Fr), adverbial clauses (Fa), and nominal clauses (Fn), makes possible sophisticated automatic searches, including searches for multiple center-embeddings by means as simple as regular expressions (when the syntactically coded files were first enriched by some preprocessing). All the potentially relevant 1900 examples thus spotted of complex local combinations of subordinate clauses were analyzed manually.

ICE-GB, too, provides detailed syntactic labeling and bracketing which are the basis of an integrated search system (ICECUP = The ICE Corpus Utility Program), making possible the formulation of Fuzzy Tree Fragments (FTFs) by which data satisfying the search keys may be retrieved. FTFs were formulated for all combinations of two dependent clauses (category cl = clause) over the combinations of the features rel(ative with explicit relative pronoun), zrel (relative without relative pronoun), indrel (independent relative clause), sub(ordinate clause with subordinator), and zsub (subordinate clause without subordinator), yielding 25 combinations (rel+rel, rel+zrel, rel+sub etc). From ICE-GB-DIAL 3703 instances of such dependent clauses in dependent clauses were retrieved, which were manually inspected to check whether there were any multiple center-embeddings.

Even if tagged corpora like the British National Corpus are highly useful for making automatic searches, the syntactic structures possibly instantiating multiple center-embeddings are so convoluted and subtle (cf. example (3)) that most of the basic analysis must be conducted by manual inspection of 'promising' complex examples. Multiple center-embedding almost always involves one or two relative clauses, but, as (3) shows, these are frequently instantiated by omission of the relative pronouns and such zeroes are not explicitly coded in tagged corpora such as BNC. They can only be spotted by hand.

13.3 Results

CHRISTINE contains some 300 relative clauses, 750 adverbial clauses, and 840 complement (nominal, *that*-) clauses. Not a single instance was found of double center-embedding of any combination of these subordinate clause types, either as self-embedding such as relative center-embedding in relative center-embedding, or as combinations of different clause types, e.g. adverbial center-embedding in nominal center-embedding.

The most colloquial and thereby fundamental part of ICE-GB, i.e. the private direct conversations, contains two candidates for instantiating spoken double center-embedding. First consider (4) where the brackets offer one possibility of interpreting the levels of clausal embedding.

(4) [I mean like I said to quote the example again of of Debbie [who said, [when describing both a woman [she didn't like] and a man [she didn't like] the very first quality she didn't like was uhm weak] (ICE-GB s1a-037 164)

The first instance of *[she didn't like]* is here the candidate for being the lower member of a double center-embedding. If it were, the subsequent material should be the end of the *when*-clause, and its subsequent material should be the end of the main clause. But rather the *when*-clause seems to end in an anacoluthon after the second instance of *[she didn't like]*. (4) does not qualify as an unequivocal double center-embedding.

(5) [I think ideally the one [*that* [I'd like] missed out] is uhm is the fifth.] (ICE-GB s1a-026 051)

Utterance (5) contains an italicized relative Raised from a lower clause, epiphenomenally making *I'd like* center-embedded. But (5) is a double center-embedding only under the traditional hypothesis that *that* starting the relative clause is taken to be a relative pronoun and a constituent integrated in the argument frame of the finite verb, i.e. it functions as grammatical subject. Another possible interpretation is that *like* is not a verb form but an adverb-like filler, 'sorta'. If so, (5) would have only one level of center-embedding.

However, Huddleston & Pullum (2003: 1056-57) argue that it would rather be a subordinator. If this interpretation is correct, (5) does not contain a double center-embedding because it would have a subordinator starting the upper clause, not a fully integrated major constituent. So their status of is contentious. But a structure like (6), if found, surely would count as a double center-embedding, because here *which* is an integrated grammatical subject of *are crap*:

(6) [M Comedies [which [everybody thinks] are crap] I like].

The ICE-GB private conversations do in fact provide an instance very close to (6), differing by having a non-finite verb in the infinitive clause (7) and the relative object fronted from CE-2:

(7) [M and the second set [which [she didn't want] to play] I won three two] (ICE-GB s1a-083 007)

Simple net search on the word string *which everybody thinks are* turns out an example just like (7) from scripted speech, originally rendered in double quotes (8), namely in a testimony by professor Byron Spencer in a hearing in the Parliament of Canada, November 27, 2006. One more was found in the public dialogues of ICE-GB (9):

(8) [The popular view is [that increases in health care costs, [which [everybody thinks] are obviously attributable to population aging,]] will break the bank ...][3]

(9) [... and people on the basis of the voluminous reading [which [I know] you've all done] are invited to uh ask the speaker questions] (ICE-GB s1b-016 010)

So far the conclusion must be that spoken English does allow, albeit very rarely, double center-embedding when relatives are Raised over reporting verbs. Note that the clauses involved are referentially light,

[3]http://www.parl.gc.ca/Content/SEN/Committee/391/agei/rep/repintfeb07-e.htm) [accessed 23 September 2009].

i.e. short (2-4 words) and heavily populated by pronouns with known or general discourse referents, no full noun phrases: *which – she* in (7), *which – everybody* in (8), and *which – I* in (9).

Another rare subcase of spoken double center-embedding was spotted in four utterances belonging to the public conversations in ICE-GB, the last three of which were uttered by the same speaker in the British Parliament in the course of a few seconds:

(10) [... one of your fellow rabbis [who [as they say] preferred to remain anonymous] was reported as saying ...] (ICE-GB s1b-047 021)

(11) [... many of those groups uh [who are sometimes adverted to as people [who have missed out [if you like] in these developments]] uh have been increasingly brought in.] (ICE-GB s1b-058 045)

(12) [... some twenty million of the workforce [that is [as the honorable gentleman says] ninety-one percent] uh are working for employers with occupational sick-pay schemes.] (ICE-GB s1b-058 046; same speaker as in 045)

(13) [A particularly striking feature of the report [which [as I say] we commissioned in nineteen eighty-eight] is the growth in coverage in manual occupations.] (ICE-GB s1b-058 068; same speaker as in 045, 046)

The shared feature of these is that the deepest center-embedding is a comment clause, i.e. a disjunctive supplement in the sense of Quirk et al. (1989: 1112-8). Comment clauses like *as they say*, *if you like*, *that is* are not structurally integrated in the matrix clause, and they are metatextual, idiom-like and play only minor roles in advancing the discourse purpose of the speaker. Semantically they (albeit not (7)) typically hedge or express the speaker's certainty or emotional attitude. These very semantic properties are shared by examples (5)-(9). Furthermore, (10)-(13) are brief and pronoun-populated, just like the relatives Raised over reporting verbs. Deeply embedded clauses are well-known to prefer pronouns over full NPs, especially in subject position (see Karlsson (2007: 381) for references). A shared feature of all of (3-13), with the possible exception of (5), is that they don't have the characteristic nested structure of (3) in which an element in each of the higher two levels is coindexed with a gap one level more deeply embedded.

The original version of the Pear Stories comprised some twenty American speakers freely retelling the contents of a silent film, approximately 16,000 words (Chafe 1980, ed.). These texts were manually examined in search for multiple center-embeddings; none were found.

Given the authentic examples found so far, I constructed tens of generalized search keys for examining the spoken conversational dialogue part of BNC, e.g. '_{ART} _{N} _{ART} _{N} _PNP' covering sequences like *the man the trophy I* in (3) (substituting different pronouns for the NPs), and '_PNQ as _PNP say' (again with pronoun substitutions) covering sequences like *who as they say* in (10).[4] No such multiple center-embeddings were found in the conversational part of BNC.

13.4 Discussion

Detailed scrutiny of the roughly 457,000 relevant spoken words in the CHRISTINE and ICE-GB corpora revealed that double center-embedding in spoken English is extremely rare. A handful of uncontroversial examples were retrieved, all of a syntactically restricted and somewhat stereotypical nature. Extensive focused searches of the ten times larger spoken materials of BNC did not yield any additional positive evidence for the productivity of this structural option. Center-embedding of degrees greater than two do not exist in spoken English.

Reich's (1969) early hypothesis of the (practical) non-existence of authentic multiple center-embedding is thus corroborated, if understood to refer to spoken language (which Reich did not state explicitly). The few relevant authentic English instances discussed above are minor short pronoun-laden comment clauses and relatives Raised over reporting verbs, whose discourse importance and functional load are negligible. Example (3) as well involves Raising and several pronouns and zeroes.

I am aware of just one other attempt at systematically addressing the question what the status of multiple clausal center-embedding is in spoken language. Laury & Ono (2010) analyzed some 1000 clause-like units from each of Finnish and Japanese telephone and face-to-face conversations but found no instances of multiple center-embedding. The practical absence of multiple center-embedding seems to be a general phenomenon.

The finding that only one cycle of clausal center-embedding is normally to be found in conversation, the most basic and evolutionarily primary form of language, is relevant for the current discussion on syntactic recursion and its role in language phylogeny (e.g. van der Hulst 2010 (ed.), Hurford 2012). Center-embedding is the full-blown form of recursion creating structural depth whereas left recursion (initial embedding) and right recursion (final embedding) are closely related to plain iteration.

The one-cycle restriction on spoken central recursion renders dubi-

[4] ART = article, N = noun, PNQ = relative pronoun, PNP = personal pronoun.

ous the claim by Hauser, Chomsky & Fitch (2002) that unconstrained recursion would have been the all-important property constituting the essence of the 'faculty of language in the narrow sense' (FLN). Notice that Fitch (2010) seems to have retreated from this position because he does not talk about FLN any more nor does he elevate recursion to phylogenetic primacy.

References

Bentham, Jeremy. 1945. *The Limits of Jurisprudence Defined*. Columbia University Press. Ed. C. Everett.

BNC. 2008. See Hoffman et al.

Chafe, Wallace L., ed. 1980. *The Pear Stories: Cognitive, Cultural, and Linguistic Aspects of Narrative Production*. Ablex Publishing Corp.

Corpus, CHRISTINE. 2000. See Sampson (2000).

Fitch, William Tecumseh. 2010. *The Evolution of Language*. Cambridge University Press.

Hauser, Marc D., Noam Chomsky, and William Tecumseh Fitch. 2002. The faculty of language: What is it, who has it, and how did it evolve? *Science* 298:1569–1579.

Hiltunen, Risto. 1984. The type and structure of clausal embedding in legal English. *Text* 4:107–121.

Hoffmann, Sebastian, Stefan Evert, Nicholas Smith, David Lee, and Ylva Berglund Prytz. 2008. *Corpus Linguistics with BNCweb. A Practical Guide*. Peter Lang. http://www.natcorp.ox.ac.uk/ [accessed 11 November 2014].

Horn, Laurence. 2000. Disc: Newmeyer: Language form and language function. Posting on Linguist List, Vol-11-269, Tue Feb 8 2000. URL=http://listserv.linguistlist.org/pipermail/linguist/2000-February/009590.html.

Huddleston, Rodney and Geoffrey K. Pullum. 2003. *The Cambridge Grammar of the English Language*. Cambridge University Press.

Hurford, James R. 2012. *The Origins of Grammar. Language in the Light of Evolution*. Oxford University Press.

ICE-GB. 1998. See Nelson (1998).

Karlsson, Fred. 2007. Constraints on multiple center-embedding of clauses. *Journal of Linguistics* 43:365–392.

Laury, Ritva and Tsuyoshi Ono. 2010. Recursion in conversation: What speakers of Finnish and Japanese know how to do. In H. van der Hulst, ed., *Recursion and Human Language*, pages 69–91. De Gruyter Mouton.

Nelson, Gabby. 1998. *The International Corpus of English. The British Component. ICE-GB. Getting started*. Survey of English Usage, University College London. CD-ROM.

Quirk, Randolph, Sidney Greenbaum, Geoffrey Leech, and Jan Svartvik. 1989. *A Comprehensive Grammar of the English Language*. Longmans.

Reich, Peter. 1969. The finiteness of natural language. *Language* 45:831–843.

Sampson, Geoffrey. 1995. *English for the Computer. The SUSANNE Corpus and Analytic Scheme*. Clarendon Press.

Sampson, Geoffrey. 2000. CHRISTINE corpus: Documentation. http://www.grsampson.net/ChrisDoc.html [accessed 23 March 2015].

van der Hulst, Harry, ed. 2010. *Recursion and Human Language*. De Gruyter Mouton.

14

Notes on Finnish Nonfinite Clauses*

PAUL KIPARSKY

Dear Lauri: This brief description of the morphosyntax of Finnish nonfinite clauses does not meet your high standards of formalization and exhaustive data coverage, but I offer it in the hope that it will be an interim step towards one that does. I draw attention to the close match of the morphology of their participial and infinitival heads with their syntax, and to the sentential properties of propositional participial complements (*referatiivinen lauseenvastike*), which unlike other types of participial clauses have external arguments rather than nominal specifiers and verbal rather than adjectival heads. As always in Finnish syntax, structural cases play a big role in the analysis. I argue that they are decomposed into features which are defined at three levels of grammar.

14.1 Participles and Infinitives

14.1.1 The Morphological Data in Summary

Finnish nonfinite verb forms assign case to their objects like finite verbs, but unlike finite verbs they are inflected for case and have either genitive or controlled PRO subjects. Three convergent morphosyntactic criteria divide them into PARTICIPLES and INFINITIVES.[1] (1) Participles distinguish the verbal inflectional categories of voice and aspect, infinitives do not. (2) Participles head nominalized clauses that function as

*A warm thank you to Ida Toivonen for her careful review, and to the editors for their patience.

[1]See Manninen 2012 for arguments that these verb forms and the clauses that they head are nonfinite.

Tokens of Meaning: Papers in Honor of Lauri Karttunen.
Cleo Condoravdi and Tracy Holloway King (eds.).

heads of propositional complements and adjuncts, and of adjectival and adverbial modifiers (relative clauses), whereas infinitives head nominalized VPs, functioning as arguments when they bear direct cases, and as adjuncts when they bear oblique cases. (3) Participles can have overt subjects, marked with genitive case, while infinitive complements require obligatory control.

(1) Participles vs. infinitives

	1. Participles	2. Infinitives
Functional verbal categories	Voice and aspect	No voice or aspect
Syntactic function	Adjectival or nominal	Nominal
Subject	Genitive	Obligatory control (PRO)

Participles and infinitives can each be divided into two types, DIRECT and OBLIQUE, according to whether they bear structural case or oblique ("inherent") case. DIRECT PARTICIPLES function as predicates and modifiers (non-finite relative clauses), and in addition head nonfinite propositional clauses that function as direct arguments equivalent to finite *that*-clauses, gerunds, and ECM constructions. (2) shows the participle stems of *tuo-* 'bring'.

(2)

	Active	Passive
Non-Perfect	*tuo-va*	*tuo-ta-va*
Perfect	*tuo-nut*	*tuo-tu*

(3a-d) illustrate the adjectival (relativizing) function of the participles in (2). The modal construction with a genitive subject (3e,f) is restricted to the non-perfect passive participle.[2]

(3) a. **tule-va** ja **mene-vä** hallitus
come-PTC.N and go-PTC.N government.N
'the incoming and the departing government'

[2]In the glosses, PTC = Participle, INF = Infinitive, PRF = Perfect, PAS = Passive, PRS = Present, PST = Past, N = Nominative, A = Accusative, G = Genitive, INST = Instrumental, ALL = Allative, INS = Inessive, ILL = Illative, ADS = Adessive, TRNS = Translative. Unmarked categories such as Non-Perfect aspect, Active voice, and Singular number are generally not glossed. Examples here and below come from literary and colloquial internet sources, complemented for the sake of clarity of exposition with constructed sentences (mostly about bears). I am grateful to Arto Anttila and Lauri Karttunen for sharing their acceptability judgments; I take full responsibility for any errors.

b. **usko-tta-va** asian-tunti-ja
believe-PAS-PTC.N thing-know-er.N
'a/the credible expert'

c. **men-nyt** vuosi
go-PRF.PTC.N year.N
'the past year'

d. valtuusto-lle **tuo-tu** esitys
commission-ALL bring-PRF.PAS.PTC proposal.N
'a/the proposal brought to the commission'

e. Linksysi-n reiti-tt-im-i-ssä on **mado-n**
Linksys-G route-CAUS-INST-PL-INS be.3SG worm-G
men-tä-vä reikä.
go-PAS-PTC.N hole.N
'Linksys' routers have a hole that a worm can go through.'

f. **yhde-n maat-ta-va** sänky
one-G lie-PAS-PTC.N bed.N
'a/the bed for one person to lie in'

Direct participles also combine with the copula into periphrastic forms.

(4) a. on tuo-va 'is to bring'
b. on tuo-ta-va 'is to be brought'
c. on tuo-nut 'has brought'
d. on tuo-tu 'has been brought'

OBLIQUE participles, traditionally called "SECOND INFINITIVES" for historical reasons, but participial by the three criteria in (1), bear inessive case or instrumental case ("instructive" in Finnish grammatical terminology), and form temporal adjunct clauses.

(5) Oblique participle forms (adjuncts)

		Active	Passive
Non-Perfect	Inessive	*tuo-de-ssa*	*tuo-ta-e-ssa*
	Instrumental	*tuo-de-n*	—
Perfect	Partitive	*tuo-tu-a*	—

The inessive is added both to the active stem and to the passive stem. The instrumental case is restricted to the active stem, and has, in addition to its temporal use (6c), also a manner or means interpretation (6d). The perfect counterpart, also active, is supplied by the partitive of the perfect passive *-(t)tu-* participle, see (6e,f).[3] The active participles

[3]This is one of several uses of the Partitive as an inherent case rather than as a structural case.

can have a genitive subject, see (6a,c,e).[4]

(6) a. Kehu las-ta tois-ten las-ten **kuul-le-ssa**.
praise-IMP child-PRT other-PL.G child-PL.G hear-PTC-INS
'Praise a child while the other children hear.'

b. Mi-hin suoja-udu-taan **kuul-ta-e-ssa** yleinen
what-ILL cover-INCH-PAS hear-PAS-PTC-INS general.A$_{\text{N}}$
vaaramerkki?
danger-sign.A$_{\text{N}}$
'Where does one take cover on hearing the general alarm signal?'

c. Vanhemma-t saa-vat riidel-lä las-ten-kin
parent-PL.N may-3PL fight-INF child-PL.G-TOO
kuul-le-n.
hear-PTC-INST
'It's OK for parents to fight even in earshot of the children.'

d. Istu-i-mme jala-t maa-ta **koske-tta-e-n**.
sit-PST-1PL foot-PL.N ground-PRT touch-CAUS-PTC-INST
'We sat with our feet touching the ground.'

e. Ainei-sto hävi-te-tään heti se-n
material.A$_{\text{N}}$ disappear-CAUS-PAS immediately it-G
tul-tu-a tarpee-ttoma-ksi.
become-PTC-PRT need-less-TRNS
'The material is destroyed as soon as it is no longer needed.'

f. Se-n **kuul-tu-a** Minttu pyörä-ht-i ympäri.
it-A$_{\text{G}}$ hear-PTC-PRT Minttu turn-MOMENT-PST.3SG around
'When she heard that, Minttu suddenly turned around.'

INFINITIVES are aspectless and voiceless. Like participles, they are divided by their case inflection into a direct and an oblique type, which together cover approximately the territory of English infinitives and gerunds. The direct form of the infinitive in /-ta-/,[5] the traditional "FIRST INFINITIVE", makes direct propositional arguments that function as subjects and objects.

[4] In anticipation of the upcoming discussion I gloss morphosyntactic Accusative Case with a subscript showing the morphological case that expresses it. For example, the object in (6b) and (6e) bears abstract morphosyntactic Accusative Case, realized as morphological nominative case by the rules to be stated in (21) below. This will become important shortly, but until then the reader may ignore the subscripts.

[5] Marked by an abstract consonant -*C*, see (9). The -*C* is realized in phonologically regular ways, including gemination of a following consonant, which is not indicated in the orthography or in the examples given here.

(7) a. Halus-i-n **ampu-a** karhu-n.
want-PST-1SG shoot-INF bear-A$_G$
'I wanted to shoot a/the bear.'

b. **Ymmärtä-ä** o-n **anta-a** antee-ksi.
understand-INF be-3SG give-INF pardon-TRNS
'To understand is to forgive.'

With the translative singular case ending, infinitives in /-ta-/ head purpose clauses similar to *for to*-infinitives. They have an obligatory possessive suffix that identifies the person/number of its controlled null (PRO) subject.

(8) Ot-i-n aikalisä-n **tuo-da-kse-ni** kuri-a
take-PST-1SG timeout-**A**$_G$ bring-INF-TRNS-1SG discipline-PRT
peli-i-mme.
game-ILL-1PL
'I took a timeout in order to bring discipline to our game.'

"Third infinitives" in *-ma* are inflected with oblique cases and make adverbial clauses with functions determined by those cases.

(9) Oblique ("third") infinitives in *-ma*

Illative *-Vn*	*tuo-ma-an* 'to bring'
Elative *-sta*	*tuo-ma-sta* 'from bringing'
Adessive *-lla*	*tuo-ma-lla* 'by bringing'
Abessive *-tta*	*tuo-ma-tta* 'without bringing'
Instructive *-n*	*tuo-ma-n* (archaic, e.g. *pitää tuoman* 'is obliged to bring')

An ending homonymous with the "third infinitive" in *-ma*, and etymologically related to it, also functions as a relativizer. In this function, it is by our criteria really a participle (traditionally called the "agent participle"), with all the participial hallmarks: it allows passive voice and perfect aspect, heads attributive relative clauses, takes a genitive subject, and triggers possessive agreement.

(10) a. (Minä) nä-i-n Mati-n **tuo-ma-n** karhu-n.
(I) see-PST-1SG Matti-G bring-PTC-A$_G$ bear-A$_G$
'I saw the bear that Matti brought.'

b. (Sinu-n$_i$) **tuo-ma-lla-si$_i$** karhu-lla ol-i
you-G bring-PTC-ADS-2SG bear-ADS be-PST.3SG
upea talja.
fine.A$_N$ pelt.A$_N$
'The bear that you brought had a magnificent pelt.'

c. Karhu o-n minu-n$_i$ **tuo-ma-ni**$_i$.
bear.N be-3sg me-G bring-PTC-1SG
'The bear is brought by me.'

The *-ma-* participle can also be affixed with the privative suffix /-ttoma-/ (nom. *-ton*) to furnish the negation of the adjectival uses of the other participles:

(11) a. *parantu-ma-ton* (1) 'incurable', (2) 'uncured', respectively negating *parantu-va* 'healing, convalescing' and *parantu-nut* 'cured'
b. *taipu-ma-ton* (1) 'inflexible', (2) 'not bending', (3) 'unbent', respectively negating *taipu-va* 'flexible' (e.g. *taipuva lanka* 'a flexible wire'), 'bending, curved' (e.g. *taipuva liike* 'an oblique movement'), and *taipunut* 'bent' (e.g. *taipunut lanka* 'bent wire')
c. *syö-mä-tön* (1) 'not having eaten', (2) 'not eaten', (3) 'without eating' (*syömätön päivä* 'a day without eating'), the first two meanings respectively negating *syönyt* 'having eaten' and *syöty* 'eaten'

14.1.2 The Syntactic Data in Summary

In addition to the three basic properties in (1), the various infinitival and participial clauses are distinguished by a range of other syntactic properties. For our purposes the most important ones are:

(12) a. the case of the head,
b. the occurrence of possessive agreement on the head,
c. the order of adverbs with respect to the head,
d. the possibility of extraction from the clause,
e. transparency of the nonfinite clause to partitive and nominative case marking on its direct object by the superordinate clause,
f. the normal order of the nonfinite clause with respect to the superordinate clause, and
g. the possibility of independent temporal reference in the nonfinite and superordinate clauses.

These properties are determined for a given nonfinite verb form by its specific syntactic function in the matrix sentence. Descriptively, nonfinite clauses function as: (A) *direct arguments*, viz. subjects and direct objects, (B) *oblique arguments* and *VP adverbials*, primarily adverbs that express goal, manner, or means, (C) *adjunct adverbials* of time and purpose, and (D) attributive modifiers corresponding to relative clauses.

What follows is a synopsis of the basic syntactic data to be accounted for, organized according to these four functions.

(13) Functions and properties of nonfinite clauses in Finnish

(A) Direct arguments	(A1) *ampu-va, -nut, -ttu*	(A2) *ampu-a*
Type of head	Direct participle /-va, -nut, -ttu/	Direct infinitive /-taC/
Function of clause	Subject, object	Subject, object
Marking of clausal head	/-n/	—
Clausal subject	Genitive	PRO
Genitive Subject incorporation?	No	—
Extraction possible?	Marginally	Yes
Transparent to partitive rule?	Depends on scope and factivity	Yes
Transparent to nominative rule?	Yes	Yes
Order w.r.t. main clause	Follows main clause	Follows main clause
Independent temporal reference	Yes	No

(B) Oblique comps, VP adverbs	(B1) *ampu-e-n*	(B2) *ampu-ma-an, -lla, ...*
Type	Oblique participle /-te-/	Oblique infinitive /-ma-/
Function	Manner and circumstance	Goal and means
Marking of clausal head	Obl. (inst.)	Obl. (ill., ads., ...)
Clausal subject	Genitive	PRO
Genitive Subject incorporation?	Yes	—
Extraction possible?	No	No
Transparent to partitive rule?	Depends on scope and factivity	Yes
Transparent to nominative rule?	Optionally	Yes
Order w.r.t. main clause	Variable	Variable
Independent temporal reference	Yes	No

(C) Adjunct adverbials	(C1) *ampu-e-ssa*	(C2) *ampu-a-kse-ni*
Type	Oblique participle /-te-/	Direct infinitive /-ta-/
Function	Temporal clauses	Purpose clauses
Marking of clausal head	Oblique (local cases, partitive)	Oblique (translative case)
Clausal subject	Genitive	PRO
Genitive Subject incorporation?	Yes	—
Extraction possible?	No	No
Transparent to partitive rule?	Yes	Yes
Transparent to nominative rule?	Yes	—
Order w.r.t. main clause	Variable	Variable
Independent temporal reference	Yes	No

(D) Attributive modifiers	(D1) *ampu-va, -nut, -ttu, -ma*
Type	Direct ptc. /-va, -nut, -ttu, -ma/
Function	Relative clauses
Case of clausal head	Agrees with modified N
Clausal subject	Genitive
Genitive Subject agreement?	No
Extraction possible?	No
Transparent to partitive rule?	No
Transparent to nominative rule?	No
Order w.r.t. main clause	Prenominal
Independent temporal reference	Yes

"Variable" word order as per the table does not include contrastive focus fronting, which can apply to all clauses. It is of course affected by discourse information structure (functional sentence perspective).

14.2 Direct Arguments: Propositional Complements (Data Set A)

We begin with the participial and infinitival complement clauses in set A.

14.2.1 Case Assignment

The clause types in (13A) are subject and object complements with propositional force. Participial complements (13A1) function as objects of verbs such as "say", "think", "want", and as subjects of intransitive verbs such as "appear" and "become evident". The examples in (14) demonstrate the construction of participial complement clauses. The *-n* suffix of the participle is glossed for now as *-C*; I will argue later that it is a Complementizer and not a Case ending.

(14) a. Ties-i-n heidä-n tappa-nee-n / tappa-va-n karhu-n.
know-PST-1SG they-**G** kill-PRF.PTC-C / kill-PTC-C bear-$\mathbf{A_G}$
'I knew that they had killed / were (would be) killing a/the bear.'

b. E-n tien-nyt heidä-n tappa-nee-n /
Not-1SG know-PRF.PTC they-G kill-PRF.PTC-C /
tappa-va-n karhu-n / karhu-a.
kill-PTC-C bear-$\mathbf{A_G}$ / bear-**PRT**
'I didn't know that they had killed / were (would be) killing a/the bear.'

c. Ties-i-n metsä-ssä tape-tu-n karhu-n/karhu.
know-PST-1SG forest-ILL kill-PRF.PAS.PTC-C bear-$\mathbf{A}_{\mathrm{G}}$/bear.$\mathbf{A}_{\mathrm{N}}$
'I knew a bear to have been killed in the forest.'

d. Nyt tiede-tään tape-tu-n karhu/*karhu-n.
now know-PRS.PAS kill-PRF.PAS.PTC-C bear.$\mathbf{A}_N$/bear-$\mathbf{A}_G$
'It is now known that a bear has been shot.'

e. Eilen ilmen-i ammu-tu-n karhu/ *karhu-n.
yesterday turn-OUT-PST.3SG shoot-PRF.PAS.PTC-C bear.$\mathbf{A}_N$/ bear-$\mathbf{A}_G$
'It turned out yesterday that a bear was shot.'

I assume that structural cases are represented by values of the cross-classifying features [±H(ighest) R(ole)] and [±L(owest) R(ole)] (see e.g. Kiparsky 2001). At the level of argument structure, these features represent grammatical relations/functions. Abstract structural Case features are assigned to Theta-roles (lambda-abstractors) according to their depth in Semantic Form. This yields the four basic abstract grammatical relations distinguished in the typological literature.

(15) a. [+HR,+LR] Intransitive Subject (S)
b. [+HR,−LR] Transitive subject (A)
c. [−HR,+LR] Direct Object (O)
d. [−HR,−LR] Indirect object (D)

At the morphosyntactic level, the features define structural Cases. The syntax constructs the optimal match between the abstract Case array built on a Semantic Form and the morphosyntactic structural Case features of syntactic arguments. Structural Cases are most simply treated as purely differential entities, marked only with the negative values of the features:

(16) a. Nominative: [ ]
b. Ergative: [−LR]
c. Accusative: [−HR]
d. Dative: [−HR,−LR]

For example, assume that a language has a verb "show", decomposed into "cause to be able to see", and that it has Nominative, Accusative, and Dative (but not Ergative) structural Case. The Semantic Form (17a) provides three Theta-roles, which are assigned abstract Case and optimally matched with structural Case as shown in (17b):

(17) a. λzλyλx[x CAUSE [CAN [y SEE z]]]

b. λz λy λx

$$\begin{array}{ccc} \begin{bmatrix}-\mathrm{HR}\\+\mathrm{LR}\end{bmatrix} & \begin{bmatrix}-\mathrm{HR}\\-\mathrm{LR}\end{bmatrix} & \begin{bmatrix}+\mathrm{HR}\\-\mathrm{LR}\end{bmatrix} \\ | & | & | \\ \begin{bmatrix}-\mathrm{HR}\end{bmatrix} & \begin{bmatrix}-\mathrm{HR}\\-\mathrm{LR}\end{bmatrix} & \begin{bmatrix}\ \end{bmatrix} \end{array}$$

A language's repertoire of morphosyntactic structural Case is determined by its morphology and functional categories. Arguments can get morphosyntactic Case features from case morphology, from the agreement relations they enter into, and/or from the structural positions they occupy. (This is the major locus of differences between languages.)

From this perspective, diatheses ("relation-changing processes") are operations on the feature [±HR].

(18) a. Passive: demotes (existentially binds) [+HR] (valency reduction).
b. Antipassive: demotes [−HR] (all but the highest Theta-role, intransitivization).
c. Causative: adds/promotes [+HR] (valency increase).
d. Applicative: adds/promotes [−HR] a non-highest Theta-role (transitivization).

For example, Finnish passive morphology existentially binds the [+HR] role and assigns it the feature [+Human], without "promoting" the object, which remains morphosyntactically Accusative (e.g. (21c)).[6]

The abstract Nominative (subject) argument of a participial clause, as in any adnominal context, is always genitive. The unmarked morphosyntactic expression of abstract Accusative (object) arguments is Partitive Case (Vainikka & Maling 1996: 186 ff.). Partitive Case is invariably assigned to complements of nonverbal categories, such as adjectives, numerals, quantifiers, and interjections, to all negated objects, and to objects of a proper subclass of atelic verbal predicates. The marked morphosyntactic expression of abstract Accusative Case, restricted to the objects of a certain class of verbs in affirmative contexts, is morphosyntactic Accusative Case, which is morphologically expressed on nouns as genitive or nominative depending on the syntactic context, and on personal pronouns as accusative.

[6] On Finnish passives, see Manninen & Nelson 2004. In Kiparsky 2013 I propose a typology of passives from this point of view.

The above three-level distinction must be made in one way or another in order to describe the case marking of objects in Finnish, but there are several ways of doing it, some of which differ in their theoretical assumptions, others only terminologically. The grammatical function "object" is here identified as abstract Accusative Case, specified on Theta-grids as as [−HR]. This is based on the idea that grammatical relations and structural cases are defined by the same features but at different levels of grammar (Semantic Form and argument structure). Abstract Accusative Case is realized as morphosyntactic Partitive or Accusative, as mentioned in the preceding paragraph. Morphosyntactic Accusative is treated in two different ways by Finnish grammarians. Some call it accusative case, and consider genitive-marked, nominative-marked, and accusative-marked objects to be different "forms" of accusative case.[7] Others (notably Hakulinen et al. 2004) identify morphosyntactic Accusative as a distinct grammatical function "total object", and refer to its respective morphological case realizations as accusative object, genitive object, and nominative object.

Theory and terminology aside, what is important and uncontroversial here is that genitive, nominative, and accusative as object markers are not just allomorphs of a single morphological case. All are identical with existing morphological cases that have independent uses, and their distribution as object markers is governed by complex *syntactic* conditions, not by morphological context as would be expected of allomorphs (see particularly (20b) below).

(19) and (20) provide a synopsis of structural object case in Finnish.

(19) Abstract Accusative Case is realized

a. as morphosyntactic Accusative Case on the complement of an affirmative quantitatively determinate VP,

b. as morphosyntactic Partitive Case elsewhere (in any other type of VP, and on the complement of any nonverbal category).

(20) Morphosyntactic Accusative is realized

a. as morphological accusative on personal pronouns (except *se* "it", which patterns morphologically with demonstrative and interrogative pronouns),

b. otherwise as morphological genitive if the object is singular and the clause can have an overt structural subject (Anttila

[7] For example, *nominatiivin kaltainen akkusatiivi*, *nominatiivimuotoinen akkusatiivi*, *nominatiiviakkusatiivi*, or *päätteetön akkusatiivi* "nominative-like (or nominative-shaped) accusative", "nominative-accusative", "endingless accusative".

& Kim 2017, cf. Vainikka & Brattico 2014 for a different formulation),

c. otherwise as morphological nominative.

Clause types with nominative objects by (20c) include imperatives, bare infinitives ("to see Naples and to die"), passives (which in Finnish do not involve "promotion" of the object), and clauses with "quirky case" subjects.[8]

It is because of these complexities that I add to morphosyntactic Accusative in the glosses a subscript showing the morphological case by which it is expressed, as already mentioned. For example, the objects of the sentences in (21) bear abstract and morphosyntactic Accusative Case, realized in (21a) as morphological genitive case, in (21b) as morphological nominative case, and in (21c) as morphological accusative case.

(21) a. Hän ampu-i karhu-n
he.N shoot-PST.3SG bear-A_G
'He shot the/a bear.'

b. ammu karhu!
shoot-IMPER bear.A_N
'Shoot the/a bear!'

c. häne-t näh-dään
he-A_A see-PAS
'He is seen.'

To further help the reader, I capitalize the names of the abstract and morphosyntactic Cases (e.g. Accusative) and use lower case for the names of morphological cases (accusative, nominative, genitive).

As if matters are not already complicated enough, the assignment of Partitive and Accusative morphosyntactic Case by (19) as well as the condition (20b) on morphological case assignment can be evaluated both within a participial clause and within the larger clause that contains it. The object of the participial clause can take its cue *either* from the participle that governs it, *or* from the main clause. This is the source of the case variation we have seen in (14). Thus, in sentence (14b), the object can be Partitive because of the negation in the main clause, or Accusative (realized as morphological genitive case) because the participial clause is affirmative. In (14c), the morphosyntactically Accusative object is realized either (and in fact preferably) as mor-

[8] Weather verbs count as having a subject even though it is mostly missing, e.g. *eilen (taivas) satoi pysyvän lumen* 'yesterday (the sky) precipitated a permanent snow', where the Accusative *lumen* is morphologically genitive.

phological accusative because the main clause has an agreeing subject, but it can also be morphological nominative because its own clause is subjectless. In (14d) and (14e), the morphosyntactically Accusative object is morphologically nominative because neither the main verb nor the participle has an agreeing subject. For an in-depth study of these intricate data and the structural factors that condition the variation of morphological object case in nonfinite clauses see Anttila and Kim (2017), which argues for a bottom-up cyclic (stratal) model of structural case assignment.[9] An alternative also worth exploring is that the variation is due to optional RESTRUCTURING of nonfinite clauses in the sense of Wurmbrand (2014, 2015).

With respect to case assignment, then, participial complement clauses are neither fully opaque domains, nor totally transparent ones, but complexly translucent.

14.2.2 The Sentential Character of Participial Propositional Clauses

In this section I argue that participial propositional clauses are structurally analogous to finite sentences in several respects. Their genitive subjects are true external arguments, except that they are not nominative because they cannot agree with the non-finite verbal predicate. Genitive subjects of other nonfinite clauses, on the other hand, pattern more like genitive possessors of nominals. I argue that the genitive subjects of participial propositional clauses are external arguments, structurally higher than possessors of NPs, that the clauses are CPs rather than NPs, and that their participial predicate is truly verbal, not adjectival like most participles.

The first argument that the genitive subject of a participial propositional clause is an external argument and not a possessor is that it does not possessor-agree with the participle. Possessor-agreement is a hallmark of genitive possessors of nouns (22a), and also of genitive subjects of other participles, such as specifiers of oblique participles ("second infinitives") (22b), and of agent participles (22c). The genitive possessor is normally omitted, unless it is emphasized, but the possessive suffix is required regardless.

[9] The classic empirical studies of the variation are Itkonen 1976, 1981. See also Vainikka and Brattico 2014, with a different approach. In addition, the variation is sensitive to as yet unexplored semantic, stylistic and discourse factors. The distribution of the partitive in particular seems to be affected by factivity and the scope of negation (Hakulinen and Karlsson 1970:31, 1979:365). A speaker uttering (14b) who presupposes that a bear-shooting had taken place or would take place would be likely to use the Accusative; the Partitive would might register a non-committal attitude, and perhaps surprise or even skepticism.

(22) a. (minu-n$_i$) karhu-ni$_i$
(my-G) bear.N-1SG

b. (minu-n$_i$) ampu-e-ssa-ni$_i$ karhu-n
me-G shoot-INF-ILL-3SG bear-A$_G$
'as I shot the/a bear'

c. (teidä-n$_i$) ampu-ma-nne$_i$ karhu
(you.pl-G) shoot-INF-2PL bear.N
'the/a bear that you shot'

Possessor agreement does *not* apply in participial propositional clauses:

(23) a. Ties-i-t minu-n$_i$ ampu-va-n
know-PST-2SG me-G shoot-PRF.PTC-C
(*ampu-va-ni$_i$) karhu-n.
(shoot-PRF.PTC.C-1SG) bear-A$_G$
'You know that I (have) shot the/a bear.'

b. Selvis-i teidä-n$_i$ ampu-nee-n
transpire-PST-2PL you.PL-C shoot-PRF.PTC-C
(*ampu-nee-nne$_i$) karhu-n.
(shoot-PRF.PTC.C-2PL) bear-A$_G$
'It became clear that you had shot the/a bear.'

In the first and second persons, the possessive suffix can be used provided the pronoun is omitted. Following Toivonen 2000, I assume this is not agreement plus obligatory pronoun deletion but rather pronoun incorporation, or pronominal inflection. The point is that in (22) the possessive suffix is fine even if the pronoun is omitted, as it normally is, unless it is emphasized. Since possessor agreement otherwise takes place between a genitive specifier and its nominal head, the systematic lack of possessor agreement in participial propositional complements like (23) supports the claim that the genitive subject of participial complements is not a genitive specifier of a participial nominal, but a subject-like external argument.

A second argument is that the genitive subject of propositional participial clauses can be raised into the main clause, as in (24b), whereas possessive genitives cannot be so raised in Finnish. A fortiori, such raised subjects cannot possessor-agree with the participle either.

(24) a. Ilmen-i he-i-dän ol-lee-n suku-a
appear-PST.3SG they-PL-G be-PRF.PTC.-C kin-PRT
bin Ladeni-lle.
bin Laden-ALL
'It turned out that they were related to bin Laden.'

b. He ilmen-i-vät ol-lee-n suku-a bin Ladeni-lle.
they.N appear-PST.3PL be-PRF.PTC.-C kin-PRT bin Laden-ALL
'They turned out to have been related to bin Laden.'

A third argument that the genitive subject of participial complements is not a specifier of the participle comes from extraction. In Finnish, possessors cannot be extracted:

(25) a. Si-llä väite-tään saa-du-n selv-i-lle auringo-n
it-ADS claim-PAS get-PTC-C clear-PL-ALL sun-G
sijainti pilvi-en läpi.
location.A_N cloud-G.PL through
'It is claimed that the sun's location has been detected with it through the clouds.'

b. *Mi-n-kä$_i$ si-llä väite-tään saa-du-n selv-i-lle e_i
what-G-Q it-ADS claim-PAS get-PTC-C clear-PL-ALL
sijainti pilvi-en läpi?
location.A_N cloud-G.PL through
'What is the location of claimed to have been detected with it through the clouds?'

Neither can genitive specifiers of tenseless nonfinite complements such as the third infinitive (26a) and the oblique participle ("second infinitive") (26b) (by the Left Branch Condition, Ross 1967: 127).

(26) a. *Kene-n$_i$ väit-i-t e_i ampu-ma-n karhu-n
who-G claim-PST-2SG shoot-INF-A_G bear-A_G
paina-nee-n 500 kilo-a?
weigh-PRF.PTC-C 500 kg-PRT
'The bear shot by whom did you claim weighed 500 kg?'

b. *Kene-n$_i$ itk-i-t e_i ampu-e-ssa karhu-n?
who-G claim-PST-2SG shoot-INF-INS bear-A_G
'Who did you weep while he shot the/a bear?'

In contrast, subjects can be extracted from participial object complements as readily as objects can:

(27) a. Kene-n väit-i-t ampu-nee-n hän-tä?
who-G claim-PST-2SG shoot-PRF.PTC-C he-PRT
'Who did you claim shot at him?'

b. Ke-tä väit-i-t häne-n ampu-nee-n?
who-PRT claim-PST-2SG he-G shoot-PRF.PTC-C
'Who did you claim he shot at?'

As expected, there is no extraction from subject clauses:

(28) a. *Kene-n ilmen-i ampu-nee-n hän-tä?
who-G become-clear.PST.3SG shoot-PRF.PTC-C he-PRT
'Who did it become apparent had shot at him?'

b. *Ke-tä ilmen-i häne-n ampu-nee-n?
who-PRT become-clear-PST.2SG he-G shoot-PRF.PTC-C
'Who did it become apparent he had shot at?'

Fourth, the structural genitive subject of the participial propositional clause is diagnosed by the obligatory morphological genitive realization of the Accusative object in examples such as (29).

(29) Tiede-tään Mati-n näh-nee-n karhu-n (*karhu).
know-PST.PAS Matti-G see-PRT-C bear-$\mathbf{A_G}$ (bear.$\mathbf{A_N}$)
'It is known that Matti has seen a/the bear.'

If the participial propositional clause counted as structurally subjectless, the object would receive the nominative form of Accusative case by (20), since the main clause is certainly subjectless. For the object to get the genitive form of Accusative case, the genitive subject *Matin* of the participial clause (29) must be a structural subject. In contrast, (20) diagnoses "quirky" genitive subjects such as the one in (30) as nonstructural. They induce the nominative (short) form of the object's Accusative Case:

(30) Häne-n pitä-ä ampu-a karhu.
He-G must-3SG shoot-INF bear.$\mathbf{A}_N$
'He has to shoot a/the bear.'

A fifth argument that the genitive argument in participial propositional clauses is a structural subject and not a possessor is that it can be a generic null subject pro_{arb}. In Finnish pro_{arb} can be a subject (Hakulinen & Karttunen 1973) but it cannot be a possessor (Vilkuna 1989): contrast (31a) and (31b). So, the fact that participial propositional clauses can have generic pro_{arb} subjects, as in (31c), supports the claim that they have structural subjects and not possessors. Moreover, they can be subjectless under the same conditions as subjects of finite clauses. For example, gerunds can have the impersonal passive form, see (31d).

(31) a. Siellä ∅ voi tanssi-a.
there *pro* can-3SG dance-INF
'One can dance there.'

b. *On mukava katsel-la ∅ valokuv-i-a.
be-3SG nice look-at-INF *pro* photo-PL-PRT
'It's nice to look at one's photos.'
(OK only without an implied possessor:
'It's nice to to look at photos.')

c. Siellä väite-tään ∅ voi-va-n tanssi-a.
there claim-PST.PAS *pro* can-PTC-C dance-INF
'It is claimed that one can dance there.'

d. Siellä väite-ttiin voi-ta-va-n tanssi-a.
there claim-PST.PAS can-PAS-PTC-C dance-INF
'It was claimed that there is dancing there.'

Having established that propositional participial complements have a subject that bears structural case, we can build an argument that they are CPs. Structural case must be assigned, or licensed, by something. What could that assigner or licenser be? We can eliminate the possibility that the subject gets its genitive by agreement with the *-n* ending of the participle. Although the ending of the participle looks like a genitive, it is not a genitive at least synchronically. First, the participle ends in invariant *-n* even if the subject is genitive plural; the participle may not get the genitive plural ending:

(32) Huomas-i-n heidä-n ampu-nee-n/*ampu-ne-i-den
notice-PST-1SG they-**G** shoot-PRF.PTC-C/shoot-PRF.PTC-PL-**G**
karhu-n.
bear-$\mathbf{A}_{G}$
'I noticed that they had shot a/the bear.'

Secondly, the participle has the same form even if the subject is not genitive but has oblique (quirky) case (see (33)).

(33) Tiede-tään häne-llä ole-va-n (*ole-va-lla) avain.
know-PST.PAS he-**ADS** be-PRS.PTC-C (be-PRS.PTC-**ADS**) key-A_{N}
'It is known that he has a/the key.'

So the subject and the participle's *-n* are not in any kind of agreement relation.

The second source of the subject's genitive case to consider is that it comes from 'ECM' style case-marking by the matrix verb. This alternative too can be easily eliminated. The genitive case of the complement's subject cannot be assigned by the verb of the matrix clause because it is always genitive even if the matrix verb requires some different case on its object. For example, *huomat-* 'notice' assigns regular structural case to its object: genitive alternating with accusative in personal pronouns, and with nominative in subjectless sentences. But its clausal complements always have inherent genitive subjects.

(34) a. Huomas-i-t minu-n saapu-nee-n.
notice-PST-2SG I-G arrive-PRF.PTC-C
'You noticed that I had arrived.'

b. Huomas-i-t minu-t/karhu-n.
know-PST-2SG me-$\mathbf{A}_{\mathbf{A}}$/bear-$\mathbf{A}_{\mathrm{G}}$
'You knew me/a/the bear.'

And *odotta-* 'wait' assigns partitive case to its object. But its clausal complements always have inherent genitive subjects.

(35) a. Odot-i-t minu-n saapu-va-n.
wait-PST-2SG I-G arrive-PRS.PTC-C
'You expected me to arrive.'

b. Odot-i-t si-tä.
wait-PST-2SG it-**PRT**
'You expected it.'

Furthermore, intransitive verbs like *selvit-* 'become clear' never assign any case to objects. But they also have complements with genitive subjects:

(36) a. Selvis-i hänen ampu-nee-n karhu-n.
become-clear-PST-3SG he-G shoot-PRF.PTC-C bear-$\mathbf{A}_{\mathrm{G}}$
'It became clear that he had shot the bear.'

b. Se (*se-n) selvis-i.
it-**N** (it-**G**) become-clear-PST-3SG
'It became clear.'

The conclusion is that the genitive case on the subject of the participial complement cannot come from the matrix verb by some kind of 'ECM' case marking.

The remaining possibility is that the genitive case is assigned by a complementizer. The natural candidate for the complementizer is the invariant ending *-n* of the participle, which we have been glossing as -C. This appears to be the element that confers a full clausal complement status on the participle and allows it to function as an argument.

Treating propositional participial clauses as CPs has the added benefit that the complementizer can be the locus of their selectional restrictions. Unlike English gerunds, Finnish propositional participial clause never function as external arguments. That is, they can be objects of transitive verbs such as "say", "think", "want", "prove", "remember" and "hear", and subjects of presentational intransitives like "appear" and "become evident", as in (23), but they cannot be subjects of such predicates as "be obvious", "prove", "mean", or "please".

(37) *Mati-n ampu-nee-n karhu-n suututt-i Liisa-a.
Matti-G shoot-PRF.PTC-C bear-A_G anger-PST.3SG Liisa-PRT
'That Matti had shot the/a bear angered Liisa.'

This could be accounted for by assigning it the abstract Case feature [+LR], which makes it incompatible with transitive subjects (external arguments), which are valued [−LR].

If propositional participial complements are full CP clauses, they are extended verbal projections and their heads should be verbs. The verbal character of participial complements is confirmed by their rejection of compounding, see (38a,b). In Finnish verbs do not usually undergo compounding, wheras adjectives and nouns do so regularly. This criterion converges with the earlier ones in drawing the boundary between propositional participial complements and other participles, such as participial modifiers like (38c) and adjuncts (type C1 temporal clauses) like (38d).

(38) a. Saate-taan mainit-a testamenttaaja-n puoliso-n
can-PAS mention-INF testator-G spouse-G
ole-va-n läsnä.
be-PTC-C present
'It can be mentioned that the testator's spouse is present.'

b. *Saate-taan mainit-a testamenttaaja-n puoliso-n
can-PAS mention-INF testator-G spouse-G
läsnä-ole-va-n.
present-be-PTC-C
'It can be mentioned that the testator's spouse is present.'

c. Pelkkä läsnä-ole-va-n puoliso-n vakuutus ei
mere present-be-PTC-G spouse-G assurance.N not.3SG
riitä.
suffice.INF
'The mere declaration by a/the spouse who is present is not sufficient.'

d. Piere-skele-tte-kö puoliso-n läsnä-ol-le-ssa?
fart-FREQ-PL2-Q spouse-G present-be-PTC-INS
'Do you fart in the presence of your spouse?'

e. Puoliso-n läsnä-ol-o on tärkeä-ä.
spouse-G present-be-N be.3SG important-PRT
'The presence of a/the spouse is important.'

If we assume a lexicalist syntax, the complementizer is morphologically attached, and not a syntactic functional head to which the verb head-moves. This explains the lack of subject/object extraction asymmetries noted at (27), since extraction of subjects is blocked by syntactic complementizers but allowed in the absence of syntactic complementizers, e.g. *Who do you think (*that) came* (the "*that*-trace effect", Perlmutter 1971, Rizzi 1982, Lasnik and Saito 1992, Pesetsky 1982, 2015).

(39) *Kuka luule-t että tul-i?
who think-2SG that come-PST.3SG
'Who do you think came?'

Although propositional participial complements are sentential constituents (CPs), they still do not have *all* the functional structure that finite clauses have. They are incompatible with negation (in the standard language at least), as in (40a), and as far as I know in all dialects with tense/mood, such as the potential in (40b).

(40) a. *Ilmen-i ei ammu-tu-n karhu-a
turn-out-PST.3SG not.3SG shoot-PRF.PTC-C bear-PRT
'No bear turned out to have been shot.'

b. *Sano-i-t ampu-ne-tu-n karhu-n
say-PST-2SG shoot-POT-PRF.PTC-C bear-$\mathbf{A}_G$
'You said that a bear had probably been shot.'

We will assume that participial clauses are Tns/AspPs and that the *-n* is a complementizer that allows them to function as propositional arguments. So the morphology of each type of nonfinite verb faithfully mirrors the functional categories of the phrase it heads. The syntax could be built from the morphology, just as well as the other way round.

(41)

Infinitive clauses:					[VP]
Oblique participial clauses:			[Tns/AspP	[VoiceP	[VP]]]
Propositional part. clauses:		[CP	[Tns/AspP	[VoiceP	[VP]]]]
Finite clauses: [CP	[PolP	[MoodP	[Tns/AspP	[VoiceP	[VP]]]]]]

14.2.3 Propositional Infinitive Complements

Infinitival object clauses (data set A2) are simple in comparison. They are obligatory control constructions, always transparent to the case marking rules. That is, case is determined by the main clause, as shown in (42).

(42) The first infinitive, bare form, subject control (data set A2):

a. Halus-i-n ampu-a karhu-n.
want-PST-1SG shoot-INF bear-$\mathbf{A}_G$
'I wanted to shoot a/the bear.'

b. Lupas-i-n he-i-lle ampu-a karhu-n.
promise-PST-1SG them-ALL shoot-INF bear-**A**$_G$
'I promised them to shoot a/the bear.'

c. E-n halun-nut ampu-a karhu-a (*karhu-n).
not-1SG want-PRF.PTC shoot-INF bear-**PRT** (*bear-**A**$_G$)
'I didn't want to shoot / shoot at a/the bear.' (part. object)

d. Halut-tiin ampu-a karhu.
want-PST.PAS shoot-INF bear.**A**$_N$
'One/we wanted to shoot a/the bear.' (nom. object)

In (42c), the object must be partitive due to the negation in the main clause, and in (42d), the object must be partitive case due to the subjectless verb in the main clause.

The same pattern of obligatory transparency to object case assignment holds in complements with object control, also having the bare form of the first infinitive. This construction is restricted to a small group of verbs, principally *antaa* 'let, give', *suoda, sallia* 'allow', and optionally *käskeä* 'command' (Penttilä 1963: 483).

(43) The first infinitive, bare form, object control (A2):

a. Anno-i-n heidä-n ampu-a karhu-n.
let-PST-1SG them-**G** shoot-INF bear-**N**$_G$
'I let them shoot a/the bear.'

b. E-n anta-nut heidä-n ampu-a karhu-a.
not-1SG let-PRF.PTC them-**G** shoot-INF bear-**PRT**
'I didn't let them shoot a/the bear.' (downstairs partitive object)

c. Heidä-n anne-ttiin ampu-a karhu.
them-**G** let-PST.PAS shoot-INF bear.**A**$_N$
'They were allowed to shoot a/the bear.' (downstairs nominative object)

d. *E-n anta-nut ammu-ta karhu-a.
not-1SG let-PRF.PTC shoot-INF bear-**PRT**
'I didn't let a/the bear be shot.' (no passive infinitives!)

Recall that infinitives have no voice (see (1)), hence the passive (43d) is ungrammatical.

Curiously, the clausal subject following these verbs (*heidän* in (43a)) is a morphologically invariant genitive, and does not show that usual morphological accusative/genitive/nominative variation by (20). This might suggest that it is actually a downstairs subject genitive like the subject genitives of the previous section. However, its behavior with the reflexive *itse*, which requires an antecedent in the same clause, clearly shows that it is an object of the main clause. The reflexive *itse* is grammatical in (44a), just as in vanilla object control sentences like (44b):

(44) a. Anno-i-n itse-ni näh-dä karhu-n.
let-PST-1SG self-(**G**)-1SG shoot-INF bear-$\mathbf{A}_G$
'I let myself see a/the bear.'

b. Pakot-i-n itse-ni näke-mää-n karhu-n.
force-PST-1SG self-(**N**)-1SG see-INF bear-$\mathbf{A}_G$
'I forced myself to see a/the bear.'

But the clause-bounded reflexive *itse* is not allowed in (45a,b,c), where it belongs syntactically to the lower clause.

(45) a. *Sano-i-n itse-ni näh-nee-n karhu-n.
say-PST-1SG self.G-1SG see-PRF.PTC.C bear-$\mathbf{A}_G$
'I wanted myself to see a/the bear.'

b. *Halus-i-n itse-ni näh-dä karhu-n.
let-PST-1SG self.G-1SG see-INF bear-$\mathbf{A}_G$
'I wanted myself to see a/the bear.'

c. *Nuku-i-n itse-ni näh-de-ssä karhu-n.
sleep-PST.PAS self.GEN)-1SG see-PTC-INS bear-$\mathbf{A}_G$
'I slept while myself saw a/the bear.'

Historically, the invariant genitive object of (43) has been considered the remnant of a now lost dative case. However, Inaba 2015 provides weighty evidence against its native origin from a dative, and suggests that it arose in 15th-16th century translations from Swedish. Whatever its origin, it does arguably have the thematic role of an indirect object, with the clausal object complement expressing the theme role. Other constructions with invariant genitives in dative function are those in (46) (Penttilä 1963: 343-4).

(46) a. Siellä on lapse-n hyvä nukku-a.
there-ADS be-3SG child-G good-N sleep-INF
'That's a good place for a/the child to sleep.'

b. Minu-n käy hyvin.
me-G go.3SG well
'I'm doing well.'

For the sake of completeness and in order to further document the difference in case assignment and possessive agreement between participial complement clauses and other non-finite constructions, I conclude with a brief review of data sets B, C, and D.

14.3 Oblique Complements and VP Adverbials (Data Set B)

Constructions B1 and B2 in (13) comprise complements and VP adverbials with oblique participles and oblique infinitives. In type B1, the subject of participles can be an overt genitive nominal (47a). It is omitted if it is identical to the matrix subject (presumably a case of anaphoric control rather than functional control). Case usage is variable, but the trend seems to be that the Accusative object is regularly a morphological genitive if the main clause has an overt subject (47b), and otherwise either genitive (47c,e) or nominative (47d,f).

(47) Participial adverbial of manner or circumstance, instrumental of 2nd participle (B1):

a. Humalainen mies ahdistel-i nais-ta kaikk-i-en
drunk.N man.N harass-PST.3SG woman-PRT all-PL-**G**
nähd-e-n.
see-PTC-INST
'A/the drunk man harassed a/the woman with everyone seeing.'

b. Kävel-i-mme maatila-n poikki pitä-e-n piene-n
walk-PST-1PL farm-G across hold-PTC-INST little-A$_\mathrm{G}$
tauo-n.
break-A$_\mathrm{G}$
'We walked across the farm, taking a little break.'

c. Vede-ttiin rata nelisen kerta-a läpi,
pull-PST-PAS track.A$_\mathrm{N}$ about four time-PRT through,
väli-ssä aina pitä-en piene-n tauo-n.
between-INS always hold-PTC-INST little-A$_\mathrm{G}$ break-A$_\mathrm{G}$
'We traversed the track four times, taking a little break each time.'

d. Laskeudu-taan vasem[m]a-lle pitä-en pieni
descend-PRS.PAS left-ALL hold-PTC-INST little-A$_\mathrm{N}$
tauko.
break.A$_\mathrm{N}$
'One descends to the left, taking a little break.'

e. Oikea kaista jatku-u teh-de-n mutka-n.
right.N lane.N continue-3SG make-PTC-INST bend-A$_\mathrm{G}$
'The right lane continues, making a bend.'

f. Perjantai-na men-nään Frankfurti-in teh-de-n
Friday-ESS go-PRS.PAS Frankfurt-ILL make-PTC-INST

mutka Luxemburgi-n kautta.
bend.A_N Luxemburg-G via
'We leave on Friday for Frankfurt, with a detour via Luxemburg.'

Like other adverbial clauses, these can also precede the main clause. My intuition is that they are then more likely to act as a separate domain of case assignment, but I have not been able to find enough corpus data to confirm this.

The corresponding oblique infinitive constructions (B2), which express goal and means, cannot have an overt subject, and are transparent domains of case assignment. Goal complements with the illative of the oblique infinitive (B2) are controlled by the lowest direct argument ([+LR]) – that is, by the subject of intransitive matrix clauses (48) and by the object of transitive matrix clauses (49):

(48) a. Matti rupes-i ampu-ma-an karhu-n.
Matti begin-PST-3SG shoot-INF-ILL bear-**A_G**
'Matti began to shoot the/a bear.'

b. Matti ei rupea ampu-ma-an karhu-a.
Matti not-3SG begin shoot-INF-ILL bear-**PRT**
'Matti does/will not begin to shoot the/a bear.'

(49) Object control
a. Pakot-i-n häne-t ampu-ma-an karhu-n.
force-PST-1SG him/her-**A** shoot-INF-ILL bear-**A_G**
'I forced them to shoot a/the bear.'

b. E-n pakotta-nut hän-tä ampu-ma-an karhu-a.
not-1SG force-PST.PTC him/her-**PRT** shoot-INF-ILL bear-**PRT**
'I didn't force them to shoot (at) a/the bear.' (part. object)

c. *Pakot-i-n ammu-tta-ma-an karhu-n.
force-PST-1SG shoot-PAS-INF-ILL bear-**A_G**
'I forced a/the bear to be shot.' (no passive infinitives!)

d. Matti pakote-ttiin ampu-ma-an karhu.
Matti-**A_N** force-PST.PAS shoot-INF-ILL bear.**A_N**
'Matti was forced to shoot a/the bear.' (nom. object)

Means adverbials with adessive of the oblique infinitive (B2) are always controlled by the subject ([+HR]):

(50) a. Voit-i-n mitali-n ampu-ma-lla karhu-n.
win-PST-1SG medal-A_G shoot-INF-ADS bear-**A_G**
'I won the/a medal by shooting a/the bear.'

b. E-n voitta-nut mitali-a ampu-ma-lla karhu-a.
not-1SG win-PST.PTC medal-**PRT** shoot-INF-ADS bear-**PRT**
'I didn't win the/a medal by shooting (at) a/the bear.' (part. object)

c. Mitali voite-ttiin ampu-ma-lla karhu.
medal-$\mathbf{A}_N$ win-PST.PAS shoot-INF-ADS bear-$\mathbf{A}_N$
'A/the medal was won by shooting a/the bear.' (nom. object)

Negated means adverbials are expressed by the inherently negative abessive case on the infinitive, which obligatorily triggers partitive case on the clausal object.

(51) Means adverbial, abessive of the oblique infinitive (B2):

a. Voit-i-n mitali-n ampu-ma-tta karhu-a.
win-PST-1SG medal-**G** shoot-INF-ABESS bear-**PRT**
'I won the/a medal without shooting (at) a/the bear.' (part. object)

b. E-n voitta-nut mitali-a ampu-ma-tta karhu-a.
not-1SG win-PST.PTC medal-**PRT** shoot-INF-ABESS bear-**PRT**
'I didn't win the/a medal without shooting (at) a/the bear.' (part. object)

c. Mitali voite-ttiin ampu-ma-tta karhu-a.
Medal.$\mathbf{A}_N$ win-PST.PAS shoot-INF-ABESS bear-**PRT**
'A/the medal was won without shooting (at) a/the bear.' (part. object)

14.4 Adjunct Adverbials (Data Set C)

The adjunct adverbials in data set C have genitive subjects in participles and obligatory control in infinitives, just as we have seen in the other data sets. Infinitives are transparent to case assignment, as before.

(52) Infinitival adjuncts: purpose clauses (C2)

a. Näh-dä-kse-mme karhu-n mei-dä-n pitä-ä matkusta-a
see-INF-TRNS-1PL bear-$\mathbf{A}_G$ we-G must-3SG travel-INF
Lappi-in.
Lapland-ILL
'In order to see a/the bear we must travel to Lapland.'

b. E-n tul-lut näh-dä-kse-ni karhu-a.
not-1SG come-PST.PTC see-INF-TRNS-1SG bear-**PRT**
'I didn't come to see a/the bear.'

Genitive subjects of participial adjuncts differ from genitive subjects of participial complements in creating an opaque domain for case assignment. This is illustrated in (53).

(53) Participial adjuncts: temporal clauses (C1):

a. E-n odotta-nut häne-n tappa-e-ssa-an karhu-n
not-1SG wait-PRF.PTC he-G kill-PTC-INS-3P bear-$\mathbf{A}_G$
(*karhu-a).
(bear-**PRT**)
'I didn't wait while he killed the bear.'

b. Odote-ttiin häne-n tappa-e-ssa-an karhu-n (*karhu).
wait-PST.PAS he-G kill-PTC-INS-3P bear-$\mathbf{A}_G$ (bear.$\mathbf{A}_N$)
'One/we waited while he killed the bear.'

c. Itki-n tape-tta-e-ssa karhu (*karhu-n).
weep-PST.1SG kill-PAS-PTC-INS bear.$\mathbf{A}_N$ (bear-$\mathbf{A}_G$)
'I cried when a/the bear was killed.'

d. Tape-tta-e-ssa karhu (*karhu-n) o-n ol-ta-va
kill-PAS-PTC-INS bear.$\mathbf{A}_N$ (bear-$\mathbf{A}_G$) be-3SG be-PAS-PTC
varovainen.
careful.N
'When a/the bear is being killed, one must be careful.'

e. Tape-ttu-a-ni taas karhu-n, ...
kill-PRF.PTC-PRT-1SG again bear-$\mathbf{A}_G$
'after (my) having killed a bear again, ...'

Unlike the genitive subjects of CP participial complements, the genitive subjects of participial adjuncts follow the nominal pattern. The data in (54) parallel the NP data in (55). Thus we have possessive agreement in (54a) and in (55a), and so on.

(54) a. Mi-tä kissa-si_i teke-e (sinu-n_i) poissa
what-PRT cat-POSS.2SG do-2SG (you-G) away
ol-le-ssa-si_i (*or:* ...ol-le-ssa-si_i poissa)?
be-PTC-INS-POSS.2SG
'What does your cat do when you are away?'

b. Mi-tä kissa-si_i teke-e Peka-n_j poissa
what-PRT cat-POSS.2SG do-2SG Pekka-G away
ol-le-ssa(*-an_j) (...ol-le-ssa poissa?)
be-PTC-INS
'What does your cat do when Pekka is away?'

c. Mi-tä kissa-si_i teke-e ulkona ol-le-ssa-an_i
what-PRT cat-POSS.2SG do-2SG out-ESS be-PTC-INS-POSS3
(...ol-le-ssa-an_i ulko-na)?
'What does your cat do when it is outside?'

d. *Mi-tä kissa-si_i teke-e itse-$nsä_i$
what-PRT cat-POSS.2SG do-2SG self.G-POSS.3SG

ol-le-ssa(-an$_i$) ulko-na?
be-PTC-INS(-POSS3) out-ESS
'What does your cat do when it is outside?'

(55) a. Matti istu-i (sinu-n$_i$) auto-ssa-si$_i$
Matti sit-PST-3SG (you-GEN) car-INS-2SG
'Matti was sitting in your car.'

b. Matti istu-i Peka-n auto-ssa
Matti sit-PST-3SG Pekka-G car-INS
'Matti was sitting in Pekka's car.'

c. Matti$_i$ istu-i häne-n$_{*i,j}$ auto-ssa-an$_{*i,j}$
Matti sit-PST-3SG (he-GEN) car-INS-3SG
'Matti$_i$ was sitting in his$_{*i,j}$ car.'

d. Matti$_i$ istu-i auto-ssa-an$_i$
Matti sit-PST-3SG car-INS-3SG
'Matti$_i$ was sitting in his$_i$ car.'

e. *Matti$_i$ istu-i itse-nsä$_i$ auto-ssa
Matti sit-PST-3SG self-3SG car-INS
'Matti$_i$ was sitting in his$_i$ car.'

14.5 Attributive Modifiers (Data Set D)

Passives have no agent phrases in Finnish, so the passive participle *-ttu* cannot be have an agent.[10]

(56) a. Ammu-ttu karhu
shoot-PTC bear.N
'a/the shot bear'

b. *(Sinu-n) ammu-ttu(*-si) karhu
you-G shoot-PTC-2P bear.N
'a/the bear shot by you'

c. *Sinu-n ammu-ttu karhu-si
you-G shoot-PTC bear-NOM-2P
'a/the bear shot by you' (grammatical on the reading 'your shot bear')

[10]Interestingly, sentences of the form (56c) are fully grammatical as agentive passives in a number of languages that are typologically similar to Finnish, including Northern Ostyak (shown here), Armenian, Dagur (Mongolian), Uighur, and Yakut (Sakha); see Hale 2002, Nikolaeva 1999, Kornfilt 2008.

(i) (ma) xans-əm/tinij-əm me:pək-e:m
my write-PST.PTC/SELL-PSTPRT book-1SG
'the book I wrote/sold' (literally 'my written/sold book')

Instead of the ungrammatical (56b) we must use the "agent participle" in *-ma-*, which forms relative clauses with genitive subjects. Possessor agreement then applies, as expected:

(57) Sinu-n ampu-ma-si karhu
you-G shoot-INF-2P bear.N
'a/the bear shot by you'

They allow compounding as freely as participial clauses of types B and C, which suggests that they are adjectival clauses; contrast the propositional (CP) participial clause (58b).

(58) a. pois-juokse-va karhu
away-run-PTC.N bear.N
'a/the bear that is running away'

b. *Huomas-i-n karhu-n pois-juokse-va-n (OK: juoksevan pois)
notice-PST-1SG bear-G away-run-PTC.C
'I noticed that a/the bear was running away.'

Another indication that genitive subjects of *-ma* complements are specifiers of their participial heads, like that of all participial clauses except propositional (CP) participial clauses, is that extraction from them is constrained by the Left Branch Condition.

(59) *Kene-n$_i$ löyde-ttin e_i ampu-ma karhu?
who-G find-PST.PAS shoot-PTC.N bear.N
'Who was a bear shot by found?'

14.6 Conclusion

The functional syntactic structure of Finnish nonfinite clauses is a transparent reflection of the overt morphological makeup of their participial and infinitival lexical heads. This implies the viability of a lexicalist analysis in which morphology merges morphemes into words, endowing them with functional features that determine how they are merged by syntax into sentences. Taking the morphology at face value and letting it constrain the syntax obviates the need for invisible syntactic functional heads and syntactic word-building rules. Participial propositional clauses were argued to be CPs with external arguments, unlike other nonfinite clauses, whose genitive specifiers behave syntactically like possessors.

References

Anttila, Arto and Jong-Bok Kim. 2017. Locality and variation in Finnish structural case. *Natural Language and Linguistic Theory* 35:581–634.

Hakulinen, Auli and Lauri Karttunen. 1973. Missing persons: On generic sentences in Finnish. In *CLS9: Papers from the Ninth Regional Meeting*, pages 157–71. Chicago Linguistic Society.

Hale, Kenneth. 2002. On the Dagur object relative: Some comparative notes. *Journal of East Asian Linguistics* 11:109–122.

Inaba, Nobufumi. 2015. *Suomen datiivigenetiivin juuret vertailevan menetelmän valossa*. Suomalais-Ugrilainen Seura. Suomalais-ugrilaisen Seuran Toimituksia 272.

Itkonen, Terho. 1976. Syntaktisten vaikutusyhteyksien luonteesta [On the nature of syntactic interactions]. *Virittäjä* 80:52—81.

Itkonen, Terho. 1981. Katson minulla olevan oikeus. In *Näillä näkymin: Kirjoituksia nykysuomesta ja sen huollosta*, pages 86—116. Suomalaisen kirjallisuuden seura.

Kiparsky, Paul. 2001. Structural case in Finnish. *Lingua* 111:315–376.

Kiparsky, Paul. 2005. Absolutely a matter of degree: The semantics of structural case in Finnish. https://web.stanford.edu/~kiparsky/Papers/partitive.ho.pdf.

Kiparsky, Paul. 2013. Towards a null theory of the passive. *Lingua* 125:7–33.

Kornfilt, Jaklin. 2008. Subject case and Agr in two types of Turkic RCs. In *Proceedings of WAFL 4*, vol. 56, pages 145–168. MIT Working Papers in Linguistics.

Lasnik, Howard and Mamoru Saito. 1984. On the nature of proper government. *Linguistic Inquiry* 15:235–289.

Manninen, Satu and Diane Nelson. 2004. What is a passive? the case of Finnish. *Studia Linguistica* 58:212–251.

Nelson, Diane. 2012. Diagnosing finiteness in embedded nominalised clauses. *Finno-Ugric Languages and Linguistics* 1:82–88.

Nikolaeva, Irina. 1999. *Ostyak*. LINCOM.

Perlmutter, David M. 1971. *Deep and surface structure constraints in syntax*. Holt, Rinehart and Winston.

Pesetsky, David. 1982. Complementizer-trace phenomena and the nominative island condition. *The Linguistic Review* 1:297–344.

Pesetsky, David. 2015. Complementizer-trace effects. Ms., MIT http://ling.auf.net/lingbuzz/002385.

Rizzi, Luigi. 1982. Negation, wh-movement and the null subject parameter. In *Issues in Italian syntax*, pages 117–185. Foris.

Ross, John. 1967. *Constraints on variables in syntax*. Ph.D. thesis, Massachusetts Institute of Technology.

Toivonen, Ida. 2000. The morphosyntax of Finnish possessives. *Natural Language and Linguistic Theory* 18:579–609.

Vainikka, Anne and Pauli Brattico. 2014. The Finnish accusative: Long distance case assignment under agreement. *Linguistics* 52:73—124.

Vainikka, Anne and Joan Maling. 1996. Is partitive case inherent or structural? In J. Hoeksema, ed., *Partitives. Studies on the Syntax and Semantics of Partitive and Related Constructions*. Mouton de Gruyter.

Wurmbrand, Susi. 2014. Restructuring across the world. In L. Veselovská and M. Janebová, eds., *Complex Visibles Out There*, pages 275–294. Olomouc: Palacký University.

Wurmbrand, Susi. 2015. Restructuring cross-linguistically. http://ling.auf.net/lingbuzz/002514/current.pdf.

15

Formal Aspects of Underspecified Features*

RONALD M. KAPLAN

15.1 Introduction

Hierarchical feature structures were introduced as early as the 1970s as an attractive representation for certain abstract syntactic dependencies (e.g. Kaplan, 1975a,b; Kay, 1979). They became a central point of contrast between the phrase-structure representations of transformational theories of syntax and an emerging family of nonderivational linguistic theories including LFG and HPSG (Kaplan and Bresnan, 1982, Pollard and Sag, 1987). Feature structures provide a simple and uniform representation that formalizes both grammatical relations and morphosyntactic properties. They also support a formal notion of modularity in that the representation of a complete utterance satisfies a conjunction of constraints that are contributed independently by its constituent words and phrases. The constraints may even arise from separate levels of linguistic description. Among its other benefits, this arrangement allows for individual constituents to specify only partially the features of a larger syntactic unit, sharing with other constituents or with global

*I am grateful to Miriam Butt, Mary Dalrymple, Anette Frank, Tracy Holloway King, John Maxwell, Annie Zaenen, and other participants in the long-running LFG Parallel Grammar Consortium. I am also very much indebted to Lauri Karttunen, for his early forays into this arena of linguistics and computational linguistics and for enlightening discussions of these and many other issues over a very long period. An earlier version of this material was presented in 2007 at the London Workshop on Features, organized by Anna Kibort. I thank Anna and other workshop participants for their helpful comments and suggestions.

Tokens of Meaning: Papers in Honor of Lauri Karttunen.
Cleo Condoravdi and Tracy Holloway King (eds.).

declarations the burden of defining a full grammatical analysis.

In this paper we examine several varieties of partially specified features that have appeared from time to time in the linguistic literature. We classify these values roughly according to their formal characteristics as unspecified, underspecified, unmarked, default, and indeterminate. For each of these we discuss the linguistic intuition being expressed, the descriptive apparatus used to express it, and whether or how it shows up in syntactic representations. An additional consideration has to do with whether or how potential consumers (elsewhere in syntax, in semantics, or perhaps in some application scenario) assign an interpretation to the different types of partially specified features. For the most part we frame our discussion within the formal machinery of LFG, taking advantage of LFG's clear distinction between syntactic descriptions and syntactic structures. But we also point out some relations to HPSG principles and to early proposals of Karttunen (1984) and Zaenen and Karttunen (1984).

15.2 Unspecified Values

The impoverished case system of English provides a good example of values that may appear in some feature structures but may be systematically omitted from others. Most pronouns in English are restricted in their syntactic distribution by virtue of their case features:

(1) They/*them saw them/*they.

This distribution can be accounted for by lexically marking pronouns with their particular case features, as in (2), and providing phrase structure rules with annotations that assert appropriate values of those features (3):

(2) *they* $(\uparrow \text{PRED}) = \text{‘PRO’}$
$(\uparrow \text{CASE}) = \text{NOM}$

(3) $\text{S} \longrightarrow \underset{\substack{(\uparrow \text{SUBJ}) = \downarrow \\ (\downarrow \text{CASE}) = \text{NOM}}}{\text{NP}} \quad \text{VP}$

$\text{VP} \longrightarrow \text{V} \quad \underset{\substack{(\uparrow \text{OBJ}) = \downarrow \\ (\downarrow \text{CASE}) = \text{ACC}}}{\text{NP}}$

The collection of constraints for the one grammatical sequence in (1) (its f(unctional)-description in LFG parlance) will have the f-structure (4) as its only minimal model, its LFG f(unctional)-structure. This structure shows that the feature CASE is fully instantiated in both subject and object (and omits for brevity other syntactic features (NUM,

PERS, etc.) that are not relevant to the point at hand):

(4)
$$\begin{bmatrix} \text{PRED} & \text{`SEE}\langle\text{SUBJ, OBJ}\rangle\text{'} \\ \text{TENSE} & \text{PAST} \\ \text{SUBJ} & \begin{bmatrix} \text{PRED} & \text{`PRO'} \\ \text{CASE} & \text{NOM} \end{bmatrix} \\ \text{OBJ} & \begin{bmatrix} \text{PRED} & \text{`PRO'} \\ \text{CASE} & \text{ACC} \end{bmatrix} \end{bmatrix}$$

The f-descriptions for the three ungrammatical sequences are not satisfiable because the CASE values asserted by the lexical entries are inconsistent with the values defined by the rules. These constraints thus ensure the proper distribution of pronoun forms in local configurations, but otherwise the CASE values in English seem to have no grammatical relevance. They do not interact with other syntactic constituents and they have no significance for semantics or any other consumer of syntactic representations.

English common nouns differ systematically from pronouns in that they all can appear freely in either subject or object position. This could be accounted for by simply omitting any mention of the CASE feature in common noun lexical entries (5), leaving that feature completely unconstrained:

(5) *dog* N $(\uparrow \text{PRED}) = \text{`DOG'}$

Given the rules in (3), the f-description for sentence (6a) would give rise to the f-structure (6b) in which CASE values have been instantiated in both positions:

(6) a. The dog chased the cat.

b.
$$\begin{bmatrix} \text{PRED} & \text{`CHASE}\langle\text{SUBJ, OBJ}\rangle\text{'} \\ \text{TENSE} & \text{PAST} \\ \text{SUBJ} & \begin{bmatrix} \text{PRED} & \text{`DOG'} \\ \text{CASE} & \text{NOM} \end{bmatrix} \\ \text{OBJ} & \begin{bmatrix} \text{PRED} & \text{`CAT'} \\ \text{CASE} & \text{ACC} \end{bmatrix} \end{bmatrix}$$

These instantiated values have no grammatical relevance beyond their local configurations, as for pronouns, but they do not even control the local distribution of different forms. Their appearance in f-structure serves no grammatical purpose and nothing is lost by leaving them out:

(7)
$$\begin{bmatrix} \text{PRED} & \text{`CHASE}\langle\text{SUBJ, OBJ}\rangle\text{'} \\ \text{TENSE} & \text{PAST} \\ \text{SUBJ} & \begin{bmatrix}\text{PRED} & \text{`DOG'}\end{bmatrix} \\ \text{OBJ} & \begin{bmatrix}\text{PRED} & \text{`CAT'}\end{bmatrix} \end{bmatrix}$$

LFG has always had a preference for smaller syntactic descriptions (5) and less cluttered syntactic representations (7), to avoid spelling out features and values that are needed only to complete a paradigm.[1] The challenge is to provide for concise lexical entries and uncluttered f-structures when features and values have no import while still enforcing the proper distributional requirements in other situations.

The LFG formalism makes a distinction between "defining" constraints and "checking" constraints.[2] The defining constraints in an f-description specify the values that must appear in its minimal model, while checking constraints test for additional properties that must be satisfied by any minimal model so defined. A checking constraint can test whether a feature does or does not appear in an f-structure regardless of its value (positive and negative existential checks) or whether a feature does or does not have a particular value (positive or negative value checks). Existential checks are notated by expressions (possibly with the negation operator) that designate the f-structure location of the target feature. LFG value checks are traditionally notated by a subscript "c" attached to equalities and other operators.

Suppose now that we replace the CASE-defining constraints in the rules (3) with the CASE-checking constraints in (8):

(8)
$$\begin{array}{lll} \text{S} \longrightarrow & \underset{\substack{(\uparrow \text{SUBJ}) = \downarrow \\ \neg(\downarrow \text{CASE}) \vee (\downarrow \text{CASE}) =_c \text{NOM}}}{\text{NP}} & \text{VP} \\ \text{VP} \longrightarrow & \text{V} & \underset{\substack{(\uparrow \text{OBJ}) = \downarrow \\ \neg(\downarrow \text{CASE}) \vee (\downarrow \text{CASE}) =_c \text{ACC}}}{\text{NP}} \end{array}$$

[1] This preference for more succinct descriptions and more succinct f-structures should not be confused with the "Economy of Expression" principle. The latter has been proposed as a principle only for choosing among alternative constituent structures and strings that can express the meaning that a given f-structure might represent. For discussion see Dalrymple et al. (2015) and references therein.

[2] What we are labeling here as "checking" constraints are called "constraining" assertions by Kaplan and Bresnan (1982) and elsewhere in the LFG literature. We use a different terminology to avoid confusion with the less technical and more conventional notion of a constraint.

Here we see disjunctions of negative existentials with positive value checks: an f-structure is satisfactory if either it has no CASE feature ($\neg(\downarrow$ CASE$)$, as for common nouns and the pronoun *it*) or its CASE is defined in a way appropriate for its grammatical function (as in other pronouns' lexical entries). As intended, the concise f-structure (7) is an acceptable minimal model for sentence (6a)'s f-description while the more elaborated (4) is acceptable for the pronoun example. Checking for but not defining the specific values NOM and ACC rejects only pronouns that are misplaced.

The f-structure structure (7) is a valid syntactic representation with respect to LFG theory, but it might stand in violation of some of HPSG's core principles. Feature structures in HPSG must not only satisfy the constraints associated with the words and phrases in a given sentence, they must also be *well-typed* with respect to the definitions and relations declared in a separate type lattice (Pollard and Sag, 1994). In particular, an acceptable feature structure for a sentence must be *complete* in that it contains an attribute for all and only type-appropriate features. It must also be *sort-resolved*, having a most specific value for each of its attributes. Thus if CASE is specified as an appropriate noun-phrase feature in an HPSG type lattice, the minimal model (7) would have to be extended with explicit but uninformative values.

As another example of an unspecified and uninstantiated value, consider the fact that English main clauses must contained tensed verbs (9):

(9) John likes/*liking Mary.

Tensed verbs carry a TENSE feature, as in (10a), and thereby form a natural class that can be distinguished from participles (10b) (and infinitives) by the positive existential constraint $(\uparrow$ TENSE$)$ in (10c):

(10) a. *likes* V $(\uparrow \text{PRED}) = \text{'LIKE}\langle\text{SUBJ, OBJ}\rangle\text{'}$
$(\uparrow \text{TENSE}) = \text{PRES}$

b. *liking* V $(\uparrow \text{PRED}) = \text{'LIKE}\langle\text{SUBJ, OBJ}\rangle\text{'}$
$(\uparrow \text{PARTICIPLE}) = \text{PRES}$

c. $$\text{S} \longrightarrow \underset{(\uparrow \text{SUBJ}) = \downarrow}{\text{NP}} \quad \underset{\substack{\uparrow = \downarrow \\ (\uparrow \text{TENSE})}}{\text{VP}}$$

This directly expresses the tensed-S linguistic intuition without adding a feature (e.g. [TENSE NONE]) whose only purpose would be to group together the different kinds of untensed forms to simplify a different kind of syntactic check.

15.3 Underspecified and Disjunctive Values

Common nouns in English are typically inflected for singular or plural number, but there are well-known examples where the different numbers are expressed by a single form. It is an accident of English that the word *sheep* taken out of context can denote either a single animal or several. As with CASE, this fact can be expressed by leaving the number completely unmarked (11).

(11) *sheep* N ($\uparrow$ PRED) = 'SHEEP'

NUM resembles CASE in that its underspecified values may be resolved by agreement with constituents elsewhere in the sentence:

(12) a. The sheep eats grass.

b.
$$\begin{bmatrix} \text{PRED} & \text{`EAT}\langle\text{SUBJ, OBJ}\rangle\text{'} \\ \text{TENSE} & \text{PRESENT} \\ \text{SUBJ} & \begin{bmatrix}\text{PRED} & \text{`SHEEP'} \\ \text{NUM} & \text{SG}\end{bmatrix} \\ \text{OBJ} & \begin{bmatrix}\text{PRED} & \text{`GRASS'}\end{bmatrix}\end{bmatrix}$$

Here the NUM feature for *sheep* is instantiated to SG because of a defining constraint (e.g. ($\uparrow$ SUBJ NUM)= SG) provided separately by the verbal inflection.

However, there are situations where the syntactic context provides no further constraints to instantiate the NUM value. If NUM is unmarked for both *sheep* and *ate*, the f-description for sentence (13a) will have the f-structure (13b) as its only minimal model:

(13) a. The sheep ate grass.

b.
$$\begin{bmatrix} \text{PRED} & \text{`EAT}\langle\text{SUBJ, OBJ}\rangle\text{'} \\ \text{TENSE} & \text{PAST} \\ \text{SUBJ} & \begin{bmatrix}\text{PRED} & \text{`SHEEP'}\end{bmatrix} \\ \text{OBJ} & \begin{bmatrix}\text{PRED} & \text{`GRASS'}\end{bmatrix}\end{bmatrix}$$

This is the concise, LFG-preferred structure for this sentence, but it ignores the fact that NUM is a feature that typically receives an interpretation by the semantic consumer of syntactic representations. In the absence of a NUM feature, the semantic component might remain agnostic about the number of sheep. Or it might use information from another source (e.g. from an HPSG type lattice or other declaration) to interpret the absent value as an ambiguity between two (non-minimal) extensions that have either SG (as in (12b)) or PL filled in for the NUM attribute.

It would be a mistake to interpret an omitted value as either vague or ambiguous if English happened to be a language that sometimes marks an additional number, say DUAL, that is not compatible with *sheep*. In that case the lexical entry would have to include an additional constraint to impose that restriction. The allowable values could be enumerated either in an explicit disjunction (14a) or a more concise set-membership assertion (14b):[3]

(14) a. $(\uparrow \text{NUM}) = \text{SG} \vee (\uparrow \text{NUM}) = \text{PL}$

b. $(\uparrow \text{NUM}) \in \{\text{SG}, \text{PL}\}$

For both formulations the eventual value is not pinned down precisely but still the choice is not left completely open. Both give rise to two minimal models, one with SG and one with PL, if the sentence carries no other constraints.

Karttunen (1984) explored an approach to feature underspecification wherein partially restricted values can be encoded in a single structure. He considered an attribute-value matrix to be a hybrid data structure that incorporates Boolean constraint formulas (as in an LFG f-description) in addition to atomic feature values (as in an LFG f-structure model). On this view a disjunctive specification of alternative values (14) in the description logic can be replaced by a compact specification of a disjunctive value (15a).[4]

(15) a. $(\uparrow \text{NUM}) = \text{SG}{\vee}\text{PL}$

b.
$$\begin{bmatrix} \text{PRED} & \text{`EAT}\langle\text{SUBJ, OBJ}\rangle\text{'} \\ \text{TENSE} & \text{PRESENT} \\ \text{SUBJ} & \begin{bmatrix} \text{PRED} & \text{`SHEEP'} \\ \text{NUM} & \text{SG}{\vee}\text{PL} \end{bmatrix} \\ \text{OBJ} & \begin{bmatrix} \text{PRED} & \text{`GRASS'} \end{bmatrix} \end{bmatrix}$$

The disjunctive value then shows up to represent those alternatives in a single matrix (15b).

Karttunen was working within a framework that focused particularly on unification-based methods for solving conjunctions of feature-structure constraints. In that context he defined an extension to the

[3]The syntactic value restriction could also be imposed by a lexical inequality $(\uparrow \text{NUM}) \neq \text{DUAL}$, possibly leaving the feature uninstantiated. But then a semantic consumer would need some other signal to know that only DUAL had been excluded.

[4]Karttunen (1984) used a set-bracket notation to code disjunctive values. Here we use an explicit disjunction operator so as to avoid confusion with the sets that LFG allows as f-structure values, as in (14b).

conventional solution algorithms in order to implement the intuitive, logical properties of disjunctive values while still trying to maintain the incremental character of the unification solution process.[5] Karttunen (1984) and Zaenen and Karttunen (1984) noted, however, that disjunctive values cannot always be regarded, linguistically or computationally, as just an abbreviation for fully spelled out disjunctions of primitive constraints; we return to this point in Section 15.6.

Karttunen (1984) discussed another example of constrained underspecification as a further illustration of his proposal for coding Boolean constraints in feature-structure values. Rather than enumerating a collection of five fully specified combinations of number and person for the agreement of subjects with non-third-singular-present-tense verbs, he suggested the single compact attribute-value representation (16a), which corresponds to the Boolean negation in the LFG description (16b):

(16) a. $\left[\text{AGREEMENT} \quad \left[\neg \begin{bmatrix} \text{PERS} & 3 \\ \text{NUM} & \text{SG} \end{bmatrix}\right]\right]$

b. $\neg \left(\begin{array}{l} (\uparrow \text{SUBJ PERS}) = 3 \\ (\uparrow \text{SUBJ NUM}) = \text{SG} \end{array} \right)$

These both express a dependency on the instantiation of underspecified values for two different features. As for disjunctive values, Karttunen sketched how to propagate negative values through a unification constraint-solving process. In LFG, f-description negations are interpreted as Boolean satisfiability conditions on the properties of minimal models.

15.4 Conventionally Unmarked Values

As noted, there is a preference in LFG for smaller syntactic representations that are not cluttered with predictable features and values. In the examples above we observed that a consumer may interpret an accidentally absent value by choosing freely from a set of alternatives (perhaps restricted by information from other sources). Unremarkable values of certain features can also be systematically omitted from syntactic structures in a way that reduces uninformative clutter but still allows syntactic dependencies to be enforced. Checking-constraints elsewhere in the grammar can assign a specific meaning to a value that is

[5] Karttunen's proposal for unifying hybrid structures with embedded constraints was a precursor to the more general sound and complete packing method for solving arbitrary Boolean constraints later put forward by Maxwell and Kaplan (1991).

not instantiated in a minimal model. Consumers can be informed of the intended interpretation, if necessary, by explicit marking conventions.

The PERSon feature resembles English CASE in that values other than 3 are only specified for personal pronouns. Third person traditionally has been taken as the unmarked value, which suggests that it should not be defined in common-noun lexical entries and should not be instantiated in corresponding f-structures (in contrast to the representation in (16)). Yet it still must satisfy the subject agreement constraints of present-tense verbs. For non-third-singular inflections we can replace the specific-value test in (16) with the inner-most negative existential in (17a) to verify that the PERS feature does not appear in the minimal model:

(17) Not third-person singular:

a. $\neg \left(\begin{array}{c} \neg(\uparrow \text{SUBJ PERS}) \\ (\uparrow \text{SUBJ NUM}){=}\text{SG} \end{array} \right)$

b. $(\uparrow \text{SUBJ PERS}) \vee (\uparrow \text{SUBJ NUM}){=}\text{PL}$

(18) Third-person singular:

$\neg(\uparrow \text{SUBJ PERS}) \quad (\uparrow \text{SUBJ NUM}){=}\text{SG}$

This can be reduced to the simpler formulation (17b) by applying de Morgan's law, introducing a positive existential constraint, and noting that PL and SG are the only values possible for NUM (discounting the hypothetical DUAL value of our earlier discussion). A common-noun singular subject will fail this disjunctive test because PERS is uninstantiated and the number mismatches. A plural subject or a first or second person pronoun will meet this condition. In contrast, the agreement requirements of third person singular present tense verbs are expressed by the conjunction of constraints (18), the complement of (17b). Existential constraints, both positive and negative, are the key formal device for assigning a syntactic interpretation to an unmarked value.

Karttunen (1984) offered a related account of person-marking within his Boolean-value framework. He also represented third person as the unmarked, uninstantiated value, but coupled this with an encoding of first and second person in terms of more primitive features, CONVERSANT and SPEAKER. He then proposed values for the marked persons to cover the way that person features resolve in coordination constructions. Dalrymple and Kaplan (2000) considered more complex patterns of feature resolution under coordination, also decomposing atomic values into more primitive representations.

Since the person feature that supports syntactic agreement is also relevant to semantic interpretation, the semantic component must also recognize the intended meaning of an uninstantiated value. We can borrow from phonology the notion of a marking convention to provide for cross-component communication. A marking convention in phonology (e.g. (19a)) indicates how to fill out a feature matrix with unexceptional values that do not play a role in the normal course of a derivation. Using the f-description notation of LFG, an analogous syntactic convention might be provided as (19b):

(19) a. u NASAL $\Rightarrow$ −NASAL
b. $\neg(f$ PERS$)$ $\Rightarrow$ $(f$ PERS$)$=3

Given our preference for smaller, uncluttered syntactic representations, we do not regard this as an instruction for expanding the f-structure in advance of further interpretation but rather as information that a consumer can use to guide its interpretation of an uninstantiated input. Accordingly, for any f-structure unit f for which a consumer requires a specific value of PERS, an uninstantiated value is to be interpreted as if it had been instantiated as 3.

15.5 Default Values

Whereas an unmarked value simply does not appear in f-structure, a default feature value is one that does appear but only when no other syntactic constraints combine to define a different value. A default specification is useful when it is difficult or inconvenient to locate all the places in the grammar and lexicon where explicit assertions would be needed to define the intended value. Thus a default typically has the effect of reducing the complexity of grammatical descriptions but it does not serve the purpose of reducing clutter in the corresponding feature structure. A default can be regarded as a syntax-internal marking convention as opposed to a convention at the interface between separate components of grammar.

Dalrymple et al. (2004) point out that default values can be asserted in LFG f-descriptions by simple disjunctions of positive existential and value-defining constraints. Consider a language (not English) in which all nouns must be case-marked, there are explicit rules for assigning ACC, GEN etc., and NOM is the default when none of the other case-assigning rules have applied. The disjunction (20) expresses that generalization:

(20) $(\uparrow$ CASE$)$ $\vee$ $(\uparrow$ CASE$)$ = NOM

The existential is satisfied if the value is instantiated in a minimal model, either to one of the other values or perhaps redundantly to

NOM. If the value is not elsewhere asserted, then the defining constraint applies to install the default NOM. We see that these default constraints are always satisfiable, that their effect at most is only to extend a minimal model. Dalrymple et al. (2004) also propose a parameterized template as a more succinct way of encapsulating the fact that a designator takes a default value. They define the template

(21) DEFAULT(D V) $\equiv$ D $\vee$ [D = V]

so the disjunction (20) can be expressed as DEFAULT(($\uparrow$ CASE) NOM).

A default specification has a "notation scope" in that it appears in an individual rule or lexical entry with LFG metavariables $\uparrow$ and $\downarrow$ that denote the f-structure units corresponding to particular phrase structure nodes. But the "value scope", the possible sources of non-default values, can be much broader, since values can propagate through conspiracies of defining constraints associated with distant nodes. This may not always be desirable. For example, the CASE feature for a noun phrase may or may not be defined by any of its lexical or morphological components, and the f-description at the NP level (ignoring the default) may also leave the value unspecified. If the value scope extends beyond the NP, any defining constraints provided by the larger context will have priority over the default. But suppose the proper generalization is that the CASE feature is intrinsic to the lexical make up of an NP and is only to be checked by the larger context. Then the value scope must be restricted to take into account only the f-description of the NP subtree.

The f-description notation of Kaplan and Bresnan (1982) does not enable this refined degree of control. However, in the context of the XLE system for parsing and generating with LFG grammars, Crouch et al. (2008) introduced a special formal device that can be used to restrict the scope of a default to a particular phrase-structure constituent:

(22) Definition of COMPLETE:
Let c be an arbitrary existential constraint and let COMPLETE(c) appear as an annotation on the right-hand side of a phrase-structure rule expanding category X.

Then all occurrences of c in the f-description provided by the subtree under X are replaced by FALSE if the minimal model for that f-description does not include a value for c.

Assume that a constituent is defined as COMPLETE for the existential constraint implicit in a default value specification and that a value is not otherwise defined in that subtree. Then the existential constraint in the default disjunction is FALSE and the value-defining alternative must be applied. The phrase-structure rule in (23) illustrates how this would work:

(23) NP $\longrightarrow$ Det N
Complete((↑ case))
Default((↑ case) nom)

If case is left uninstantiated by other syntactic, morphological, and lexical constraints within the NP, the default nom will be asserted. The effect of complete is to reduce the value scope of the default to its notation scope.

This is a relatively lightweight approach to the problem of defaults in feature representations, relying as it does on the traditional checking and defining constraints of the LFG description language and the distinction between descriptions and models. In this way it differs from proposals that depend on operations, like priority union (Kaplan, 1987) and default unification (Lascarides et al., 1996), that recursively combine larger feature structures in defeasible ways. The description approach is more limited in its expressive power but does not require an elaborate mathematical analysis or special implementation techniques.

15.6 Indeterminate Values

Karttunen (1984) and Zaenen and Karttunen (1984) were among the first to call attention to a descriptive and technical challenge for feature-based theories of grammar, like LFG and HPSG. They pointed out that equality assertions (and corresponding unification methods) and standard Boolean operations cannot directly account for grammatical constructions where a given form appears to satisfy simultaneously two or more conflicting requirements on a feature value. Such a feature is considered to have an indeterminate value.

German determiners and nouns typically agree in number and case (24) and contexts that impose incompatible agreement constraints, such as the coordinated determiners in (25), are not acceptable:

(24) des/*der Professors (genitive singular)
the professor's

*des/der Professoren (genitive plural)
the professors'

(25) der Antrag des oder *der Professors
der Antrag *des oder der Professoren
'the petition of the professor or professors'

The word *Dozenten* is a syncretic form that expresses both numbers in the genitive case and agrees with both determiners separately (26). Surprisingly, that word can also satisfy the agreement constraints of both determiners in a single construction (27):

(26) des Dozenten (genitive singular)
the docent's

der Dozenten (genitive plural)
the docents'

(27) der Antrag des oder der Dozenten
'the petition of the docent or docents'

If both the determiner and the noun constrain the NUM value of the NP, as suggested by (24) and (25), then the normal interpretation of equality as a transitive relation would lead to the contradiction that the NP's NUM is both SG and PL and that the construction is ungrammatical. This would be the expected result whether the NUM feature of *Dozenten* is left unspecified or specified as a disjunction of values. Karttunen (1984) conjectured that a special interpretation of his disjunctive values might give a correct account of indeterminate behavior but he did not expand on that possibility.

Karttunen (1984), Zaenen and Karttunen (1984), and other researchers have examined indeterminate values as they interact with the distributive properties of coordination, but the phenomena is more widespread. Another classic example, discussed by Groos and van Reimsdijk (1979) and Ingria (1990), is the indeterminacy of CASE that shows up in the German free relative. The relative pronoun *wer* in (28a) is explicitly marked as nominative and thus satisfies the compatible CASE requirements of the matrix and relative adjectives. Sentence (28b) is ungrammatical because *wer* does not match the SUBJ CASE that *geholfen* requires. Again, the surprise is that the conflicting requirements in (28c) are simultaneously satisfiable with the CASE-indeterminate pronoun *was*.

(28) a. Wer nicht stark ist muss klug sein
who not strong is must clever be
NOM SUBJ=NOM SUBJ=NOM
'Who isn't strong must be clever'

b. *Wer nicht geholfen wird, muss klug sein
who not helped is must clever be
NOM SUBJ=DAT SUBJ=NOM
'Who isn't helped must be clever'

c. Ich habe gegessen was übrig war
I have eaten what left was
OBJ=ACC SUBJ=NOM
'I ate what was left'

Within the LFG framework Dalrymple and Kaplan (2000) proposed a set-based alternative to atomic values as an encoding for indeterminate features. Instead of leaving the CASE value for *was* unspecified or specified by a disjunction of atomic values (29a), the fact that *was* is compatible with NOM and ACC is represented by a set (29b) containing those two elements:[6]

(29) a. *was*: $(\uparrow \text{CASE}) = \text{NOM} \vee (\uparrow \text{CASE}) = \text{ACC}$
b. *was*: $(\uparrow \text{CASE}) = \{\text{NOM, ACC}\}$

The adjectives then test for CASE-compatibility by membership statements:

(30) *gegessen*: $\text{ACC} \in (\uparrow \text{OBJ CASE})$
übrig: $\text{NOM} \in (\uparrow \text{SUBJ CASE})$

Both membership statements are true of the indeterminate value (29b). In contrast, the pronoun *wer* carries the definition $(\uparrow \text{CASE})=\{\text{NOM}\}$ and so is compatible only with NOM membership constraints.

This formalization captures the core intuitions of indeterminacy by means of mathematically simple descriptions and representations that exist independently in the LFG framework. Set-values may restrict the range of elements (e.g. *was* excludes GEN and DAT) but mutually incompatible requirements are not inconsistent. Used in this way, sets behave as the narrow-scope disjunctions foreshadowed in Karttunen's (1984) sketch of disjunctive values.

Dalrymple et al. (2009), however, considered more complicated patterns of indeterminacy that cannot be handled directly by the set representations and constraints of the Dalrymple and Kaplan proposal. Their set-based solution circumvents the transitivity of equality, so that incompatible constraints are not in conflict. But Dalrymple et al. and others discuss an array of examples where some constraints on an otherwise indeterminate form do have the effect of reducing the matching possibilities for other constraints.

---

[6]Note the difference between a set-equality assertion (29b) and a set-membership assertion (14b) for the CASE value. The latter is logically equivalent to a disjunction (29a) over the set's elements and results in alternative f-structures each of which has an atomic value for CASE. An equality provides for a single f-structure with a set value that represents the lack of specificity.

For instance, the German syncretic plural form *Papageien* 'parrot' is indeterminate with respect to any of the cases. In particular it can appear with a plural dative modifier *alten* when it is the object of a dative-object verb (31a):

(31) a. Er hilft alten Papageien
he helps old parrots
OBJ=DAT DAT NOM/ACC/DAT/GEN
'He helps old parrots'

b. *Er hilft alte Papageien
he helps old parrots
OBJ=DAT NOM/ACC NOM/ACC/DAT/GEN

But the sentence becomes ungrammatical if the DAT modifier is replaced by a form that is compatible only with NOM or ACC (31b). The indeterminacy of the head noun is restricted by agreement with the modifier and the NP therefore does not meet this verbal requirement (see Dalrymple et al. (2009) for further discussion and justification of this analysis).

These examples, and many similar ones, call for a more flexible way of asserting and testing an indeterminate value. Dalrymple et al. (2009) propose to represent such a value by an expanded feature matrix that essentially encodes the characteristic function for a set of atomic values. They represent CASE as a submatrix with attributes NOM, ACC, DAT, and GEN whose possible values are + (that form may satisfy a corresponding case requirement) or − (that form may not satisfy a corresponding case requirement). An unspecified value represents an indifference as to the presence or absence of that case. This encoding allows for finer-grained control over indeterminate values by means of an incremental accumulation of partial constraints.

Returning to the German free relative (28), the fact that the indeterminate pronoun *was* cannot match DAT or GEN is indicated by negative values for those features (32). Positive values for NOM and ACC are specified as a functional uncertainty to ensure that at least some value for CASE is marked for nominal heads, even if there are no other constraints. The predicate adjectives are specified positively for the cases that they require but leave the other cases unspecified.

(32) *was*: $(\uparrow \text{CASE GEN}) = -$
$(\uparrow \text{CASE DAT}) = -$
$(\uparrow \text{CASE } \{\text{NOM}|\text{ACC}\}) = +$
gegessen: $(\uparrow \text{OBJ CASE ACC}) = +$

übrig: $(\uparrow \textsc{subj case nom}) = +$

Given these assertions, the feature matrix (33) will be the CASE encoding for the pronoun *was* as it is shared between the matrix and relative clauses.

(33)
$$\begin{bmatrix} \text{NOM} & + \\ \text{ACC} & + \\ \text{GEN} & - \\ \text{DAT} & - \end{bmatrix}$$

On this proposal a nominal modifier is specified as negative for all of the cases it disallows but left unspecified for all compatible cases. Thus, for the feature values of the adjectival lexical entries relevant to (31) we have:

(34) *alten*: $((\text{ADJ} \in \uparrow)\ \text{CASE NOM}) = -$
$((\text{ADJ} \in \uparrow)\ \text{CASE ACC}) = -$
$((\text{ADJ} \in \uparrow)\ \text{CASE GEN}) = -$

alte: $((\text{ADJ} \in \uparrow)\ \text{CASE DAT}) = -$
$((\text{ADJ} \in \uparrow)\ \text{CASE GEN}) = -$

The inside-out functional designators $(\text{ADJ} \in \uparrow)$ denote the f-structure unit corresponding to the NP that these adjectives modify, as in standard LFG treatments. For the examples in (31) the CASE of *Papageien* is unconstrained while the OBJ of *hilft* encodes a restriction just to DAT:

(35) *Papageien*: $(\uparrow \text{CASE}\ \{\text{NOM}|\text{ACC}|\text{DAT}|\text{GEN}\}) = +$

hilft: $(\uparrow \text{OBJ CASE DAT}) = +$

With these specifications the f-structure for sentence (31a) is (36):

(36)
$$\begin{bmatrix} \text{PRED} & \text{`HELFEN}\langle\text{SUBJ, OBJ}\rangle\text{'} \\ \text{TENSE} & \text{PRES} \\ \text{SUBJ} & \begin{bmatrix} \text{PRED} & \text{`PRO'} \end{bmatrix} \\ \text{OBJ} & \begin{bmatrix} \text{PRED} & \text{`PAPAGEIEN'} \\ \text{NUM} & \text{PL} \\ \text{ADJ} & \left\{ \begin{bmatrix} \text{PRED} & \text{`ALT'} \end{bmatrix} \right\} \\ \text{CASE} & \begin{bmatrix} \text{NOM} & - \\ \text{ACC} & - \\ \text{GEN} & - \\ \text{DAT} & + \end{bmatrix} \end{bmatrix} \end{bmatrix}$$

For (31b) the negative DAT value for *alte* is inconsistent with *hilft*'s positive specification.

We can interpret these feature submatrices as the characteristic functions of the indeterminate sets of the earlier Dalrymple and Kaplan (2000) proposal, taking a +-valued attribute to indicate that the corresponding set contains that designated CASE. We might even adopt a special convention of representing these submatrices in minimal models as the sets so defined, in which case the f-structure (36) would appear as the more succinct and perhaps more intuitive (37):

(37)
$$\begin{bmatrix} \text{PRED} & \text{`HELFEN}\langle\text{SUBJ, OBJ}\rangle\text{'} \\ \text{TENSE} & \text{PRES} \\ \text{SUBJ} & \begin{bmatrix} \text{PRED} & \text{`PRO'} \end{bmatrix} \\ \text{OBJ} & \begin{bmatrix} \text{PRED} & \text{`PAPAGEIEN'} \\ \text{NUM} & \text{PL} \\ \text{ADJ} & \left\{ \begin{bmatrix} \text{PRED} & \text{`ALT'} \end{bmatrix} \right\} \\ \text{CASE} & \left\{ \text{DAT} \right\} \end{bmatrix} \end{bmatrix}$$

The LFG formalism, however, makes available a more direct way of arriving at this f-structure. As an alternative to a submatrix of binary-valued attributes, the effect of narrowing the membership possibilities for an indeterminate CASE set can also be achieved by means of the f-structure subsumption operator (Zaenen and Kaplan, 2002). The subsumption relation $A \sqsubseteq B$ holds between two sets A and B of atomic values if and only if $A \subseteq B$. As a consequence, for atomic-valued sets A, B, and C, if $A \sqsubseteq B$ and $A \sqsubseteq C$, then $A \subseteq B \cap C$.

Suppose we recode the CASE specifications for indeterminate nominal heads like *was* and *Papageien* as in (38). This allows the CASE value for *was* to be {NOM, ACC}, excluding DAT and GEN as before (29b). But subsumption rather than equality allows the narrowing of *Papageien* to smaller sets in the presence of other constraints.

(38) *was*: $(\uparrow \text{CASE}) \sqsubseteq \{\text{NOM, ACC}\}$
Papageien: $(\uparrow \text{CASE}) \sqsubseteq \{\text{NOM, ACC, DAT, GEN}\}$

In particular, subsumption can impose the additional restrictions of indeterminate modifiers, as illustrated in (39a). The CASE for the NP *alten Papageien* can contain only {DAT}. This satisfies the membership requirement of *hilft* (39b), and sentence (31a) will be assigned the target f-structure (37).

(39) a. *alten*: $((\text{ADJ} \in \uparrow)\ \text{CASE}) \sqsubseteq \{\text{DAT}\}$

alte: $((\text{ADJ} \in \uparrow)\ \text{CASE}) \sqsubseteq \{\text{NOM}, \text{ACC}\}$

b. *hilft*: $\text{DAT} \in (\uparrow \text{OBJ CASE})$

In contrast, the indeterminate CASE for *alte Papageien* will reduce to {ACC} and remain incompatible with the membership assertion of *hilft*.

Dalrymple et al. (2009) also make use of featural decomposition to account for what has been called "second-order" indeterminacy. The Russian examples (40) (taken from (22) and (23) of Dalrymple et al. (2009)) show that a predicate can impose indeterminate constraints on its argument:

(40) a.

On	proždal	zvonka	naprasno.
he	waited-for	call	in.vain
	OBJ=ACC/GEN	GEN	

'He waited in vain for a (phone) call.'

b.

On	proždal	svoju	podrugu	Irinu	naprasno.
he	waited-for	self's	girlfriend	Irina	in.vain
	OBJ=ACC/GEN		ACC		

'He waited for his girlfriend Irina in vain.'

On their account the predicate *prošdal* assigns a + value to either of the ACC or GEN features as in (41a).

(41) *prošdal*: $(\uparrow \text{OBJ CASE}\ \{\text{ACC}|\text{GEN}\}) = +$

This CASE uncertainty implicitly distributes over coordination sets and thus accounts for the grammaticality of (42) (example (24) of Dalrymple et al. (2009)):

(42)

Včera	ves'	den'	on	prošdal	svoju	podrugu	Irinu	i
yesterday	all	day	he	waited-for	self's	girlfriend	Irina	and
				OBJ=ACC/GEN		ACC		

zvonka	ot	svoego	brata	Grigorija.
call	from	self's	brother	Gregory
GEN				

'Yesterday he waited all day for his girlfriend Irina and for a call from his brother Gregory.'

The same effect is achieved on the subsumption approach by a membership disjunction (43) that is explicitly declared to be a distributive property (cf. Dalrymple and Kaplan, 2000; Kaplan and Maxwell, 1988; Kaplan, 2017; Przepiórkowski and Patejuk, 2012).

(43) *prošdal*: $\text{ACC} \in (\uparrow \text{OBJ CASE}) \vee \text{GEN} \in (\uparrow \text{OBJ CASE})$

Both approaches extend to the second-order configuration wherein the indeterminate predicate requirement is applied to indeterminate arguments (example (26) of Dalrymple et al. (2009)):

(44) On ždal mat' i mal'čika.
he waited-for mother and boy
OBJ=ACC/GEN NOM/ACC ACC/GEN
'He waited for his mother and a boy.'

The common element of both approaches is that an indeterminate feature is not reduced to an atomic value in the minimal model.

15.7 Conclusion

The general architecture of feature-based grammars allows syntactic structures with particular properties to arise from the sometimes unpredictable interaction of modular and independent syntactic descriptions. A key aspect of this architecture is that values that are unspecified or underspecified in one place may be constrained in larger contexts but in some cases may even remain unresolved. We surveyed several varieties of underspecification that differ as to the linguistic intuitions they embody. We described how these differences correlate with the kinds of assertions that appear in lexical entries and syntactic rules, the values that appear in corresponding feature structures, and the information that may be needed by other grammatical components to assign appropriate interpretations. It is important to recognize that the various forms of underspecification have different consequences for grammatical analyses, but we have seen that they can all be formulated in terms of the basic formal mechanisms that feature grammars have traditionally made available.

References

Crouch, Dick, Mary Dalrymple, Ronald M. Kaplan, Tracy Holloway King, John T. Maxwell, III, and Paula S. Newman. 2008. *XLE Documentation*. Palo Alto Research Center, Palo Alto, CA.

Dalrymple, Mary and Ronald M. Kaplan. 2000. Feature indeterminacy and feature resolution. *Language* 76(4):759–798.

Dalrymple, Mary, Ronald M. Kaplan, and Tracy Holloway King. 2004. Linguistic generalizations over descriptions. In M. Butt and T. H. King, eds., *On-Line Proceedings of the LFG2004 Conference*. Stanford: CSLI Publications.

Dalrymple, Mary, Ronald M. Kaplan, and Tracy Holloway King. 2015. Economy of expression as a principle of syntax. *Journal of Language Modelling* 2(3):377–412.

Dalrymple, Mary, Ronald M. Kaplan, John T. Maxwell, III, and Annie Zaenen, eds. 1995. *Formal Issues in Lexical-Functional Grammar*. Stanford: CSLI Publications.

Dalrymple, Mary, Tracy Holloway King, and Louisa Sadler. 2009. Indeterminacy by underspecification. *Journal of Linguistics* 45:31–68.

Groos, Anneke and Henk van Reimsdijk. 1979. Matching effects in free relatives: A parameter of core grammar. In A. Belletti, L. Brandi, and L. Rizzi, eds., *Theory of Markedness in Generative Grammar: Proceedings of the 1979 GLOW Conference*, pages 171–216. GLOW, Pisa: Scuola Normale Superiore di Pisa.

Ingria, Robert J. P. 1990. The limits of unification. In *Proceedings of the 28th Annual Meeting of the ACL*, pages 194–204. Association for Computational Linguistics, Pittsburgh.

Kaplan, Ronald M. 1975a. On process models for sentence analysis. In D. Norman and D. Rumelhart, eds., *Explorations in Cognition*, pages 117–135. San Francisco, CA: W. H. Freeman & Co.

Kaplan, Ronald M. 1975b. *Transient Processing Load in Relative Clauses*. Ph.D. thesis, Harvard University.

Kaplan, Ronald M. 1987. Three seductions of computational psycholinguistics. In P. Whitelock, M. M. Wood, H. L. Somers, R. Johnson, and P. Bennett, eds., *Linguistic Theory and Computer Applications*, pages 149–188. London: Academic Press. Also published as CCL/UMIST Report No. 86.2: Alvey/ICL Workshop on Linguistic Theory and Computer Applications: Transcripts of Presentations and Discussions. Center for Computational Linguistics, University of Manchester. Reprinted in Dalrymple et al. (1995, 337–367).

Kaplan, Ronald M. 2017. Preserving grammatical functions in LFG. In V. Rosén and K. De Smedt, eds., *The very model of a modern linguist: In honor of Helge Dyvik*, pages 127–142. Bergen: Bergen language and linguistic studies.

Kaplan, Ronald M. and Joan Bresnan. 1982. Lexical-Functional Grammar: A formal system for grammatical representation. In J. Bresnan, ed., *The Mental Representation of Grammatical Relations*, pages 173–281. Cambridge, MA: MIT Press. Reprinted in Dalrymple et al. (1995, 29–130).

Kaplan, Ronald M. and John T. Maxwell, III. 1988. Constituent coordination in Lexical-Functional Grammar. In *Proceedings of the International Conference on Computational Linguistics (COLING88)*, pages 303–305. International Committee on Computational Linguistics. Reprinted in Dalrymple et al. (1995, 199–210).

Karttunen, Lauri. 1984. Features and values. In *Proceedings of the 10th International Conference on Computational Linguistics (COLING)*, pages 28–33. Stanford, CA.

Kay, Martin. 1979. Functional grammar. In *The Fifth Annual Meeting of the Berkeley Linguistics Society*, pages 142–158. Berkeley Linguistics Society, Berkeley, California.

Lascarides, Alex, Ted Briscoe, Nicholas Asher, and Anne Copestake. 1996. Order independent and persistent typed default unification. *Linguistics and Philosophy* 19(1):1–90.

Maxwell, John T., III and Ronald M. Kaplan. 1991. A method for disjunctive constraint satisfaction. In M. Tomita, ed., *Current Issues in Parsing Technology*, pages 173–190. Dordrecht: Kluwer. Reprinted in Dalrymple et al. (1995, 381–401).

Pollard, Carl and Ivan A. Sag. 1987. *Information-based Syntax and Semantics: Vol. 1: Fundamentals*. Stanford, CA: Center for the Study of Language and Information.

Pollard, Carl and Ivan A. Sag. 1994. *Head-Driven Phrase Structure Grammar*. Chicago: The University of Chicago Press.

Przepiórkowski, Adam and Agnieszka Patejuk. 2012. On case assignment and the coordination of unlikes: The limits of distributive features. In M. Butt and T. H. King, eds., *On-Line Proceedings of the LFG2012 Conference*, pages 479–489. Stanford: CSLI Publications.

Zaenen, Annie and Ronald M. Kaplan. 2002. Subsumption and equality: German partial fronting in LFG. In M. Butt and T. H. King, eds., *On-Line Proceedings of the LFG2002 Conference*. Stanford: CSLI Publications.

Zaenen, Annie and Lauri Karttunen. 1984. Morphological non-distinctiveness and coordination. In *Proceedings of the Eastern States Conference on Linguistics*, pages 309–20. Columbus, Ohio.

Part IV

Finite State Methods and Grammars

16

A History and Overview of the Kleene Programming Language*

Kenneth R. Beesley

16.1 Introduction

16.1.1 What is Kleene?

Kleene[1] is a high-level finite-state programming language in the tradition of the AT&T Lextools (Roark and Sproat, 2007),[2] OpenGrm Thrax,[3] the SFST-PL language (Schmid, 2005),[4] and especially the Xerox/PARC Finite State Toolkit (Beesley and Karttunen, 2003),[5] all of which provide higher-level programming formalisms built on top of low-level finite-state libraries. Kleene itself is built on the OpenFst li-

*Sincere thanks are due to the OpenFst team and all who made that library available. A special personal thanks goes to Mans Hulden, who graciously shared his algorithms for interpreting alternation rules and language-restriction expressions, and who went to great lengths to help me understand and re-implement them. I also acknowledge and thank my SAP Labs colleagues Paola Nieddu and Phil Sours, who contributed to the design and implementation of Kleene, and my SAP boss Michael Wiesner, who supported the open-source release. Finally, I thank Lauri Karttunen, who introduced me to finite-state linguistics and has always been an inspirational friend and mentor.

[1]Kleene is named after mathematician Stephen Cole Kleene (1909–1994), `http://en.wikipedia.org/wiki/Stephen_Cole_Kleene`, who investigated the mathematical properties of regular sets and invented the metalanguage of regular expressions.

[2]`http://www.research.att.com/~alb/lextools/`

[3]`http://openfst.cs.nyu.edu/twiki/bin/view/GRM/Thrax`

[4]`http://www.ims.uni-stuttgart.de/projekte/gramotron/SOFTWARE/SFST.html`

[5]`http://www.fsmbook.com`

Tokens of Meaning: Papers in Honor of Lauri Karttunen.
Cleo Condoravdi and Tracy Holloway King (eds.).

brary, developed by Google Labs and NYU's Courant Institute (Allauzen et al., 2007).[6]

Using Kleene, one can specify and construct finite-state machines (FSMs)—including acceptors and two-projection transducers—using regular expressions, a rich alternation-rule syntax, and right-linear phrase-structure grammars. The regular expressions are based, as far as possible and appropriate, on the syntax of Perl-like regular expressions, which are already familiar to many programmers. The language also supports variables, lists, functions, scoped blocks, `if-else` expressions, and `while` loops. Pre-edited scripts can be run from the command line, and a graphical user interface (GUI) can be used for learning, interactive experimentation, and testing.

Kleene can be used to implement spelling-checkers and spelling-correctors, phonetic models, tokenizers, morphological analyzers, part-of-speech disambiguators, shallow parsers, and many other applications for natural language processing. Future plans include text-to-speech generation and speech recognition.

16.1.2 Inspiration and Pre-History

The main inspiration behind Kleene is the Xerox/PARC Finite State Toolkit, created and maintained for over twenty-five years under the leadership of Lauri Karttunen, whom I first met at the 1988 COLING conference in Budapest, where I attended his workshop on Two Level Morphology. This early implementation of finite-state programming was ultimately based on some findings of Ronald Kaplan and Martin Kay of the Xerox Palo Alto Research Center (PARC) (Kaplan and Kay, 1981, Karttunen et al., 1987, Kaplan and Kay, 1994), and it was ingeniously formalized into a workable framework, called Two-Level Morphology, by Kimmo Koskenniemi at the University of Helsinki (Koskenniemi, 1983, 1984, Antworth, 1990).[7] Karttunen popularized Two Level Morphology first at the University of Texas at Austin, and later at SRI International and finally at Xerox/PARC, where Kaplan and Kay had built a library of finite-state algorithms in INTERLISP. In the late 1980s, Karttunen and various assistants at Xerox Research started a project to port the library, first to Common Lisp and then to C, and to build a set of higher-level programming languages on top of the library.

The result of Karttunen's work, now known as the Xerox or PARC Finite State Toolkit,[8] is still available and widely used, both in busi-

[6] `http://www.openfst.org`

[7] For a more detailed account of the early history, from the Xerox point of view, see Karttunen and Beesley (2005).

[8] The Xerox Palo Alto Research Center (Xerox PARC) was established in 1970 and

ness and research.[9] It is believed to have been used in programming courses at over seventy universities, and an informal (and no doubt incomplete) survey that I performed in 2013 found that it had been used to write morphological analyzers and related applications for over a hundred languages around the world, including of course the commercially interesting European languages, but also Basque, Irish, and Welsh; Hindi and Urdu; Persian and Armenian; Malay and Indonesian; Arabic, Hebrew, and Amharic; Chinese; dozens of Uralic, Saami, and other Nordic languages; eleven Mongolian languages; seven American Indian languages; seven Bantu languages; and even Khoekhoegowab, one of the Khoisan languages famous for their click consonants.

Going back to 1988, I was working for ALPNET and had recently been assigned to write a morphological analyzer for Arabic, a task that appeared daunting, to say the least. After attending Karttunen's workshop at COLING, I saw a glimmer of hope, reimplemented Two Level Morphology in Common Lisp (an implementation that was later ported to C by my colleague Stuart Newton), and led a small team notably including Arabist Tim Buckwalter in writing a successful analyzer (Beesley et al., 1989, Beesley, 1991). The Arabic project was saved by the discovery of Two Level Morphology, and I've been using, documenting, and promoting various implementations of finite-state programming ever since.

In 1990, with support from Karttunen, I was hired by Microlytics, a Xerox spin-off company, where I was assigned as a liaison to the linguistic researchers at PARC. There I helped Karttunen to implement and document the Twolc language/compiler (Karttunen and Beesley, 1992). When Karttunen relocated to Grenoble, France, in 1993 to join the new Xerox Research Centre Europe, he contracted with a business unit of Xerox to develop commercial finite-state morphological analyzers (and eventually tokenizers, part-of-speech disambiguators and shallow parsers) for Spanish, Portuguese, Italian, and Dutch; and Karttunen brought me to Grenoble in 1994 to lead the morphological-analyzer projects. I remained there, mostly under his leadership, for twelve years. He has always been the best possible boss, mentor, and friend.

16.1.3 Clones of the Finite State Toolkit

The Xerox/PARC Finite State Toolkit comprises the low-level **C-fsm** library, written in C, and three high-level languages built on top of it:

---

was spun off as PARC Incorporated, a wholly owned subsidiary of Xerox, in 2002.

[9] `http://www.fsmbook.com`

- **Twolc**: a language for compiling alternation rules written in the classic Koskenniemi-style two-level formalism,
- **Lexc**: a language based on right-linear phrase-structure grammar, used mainly to describe morphotactics, and
- **Xfst**: an interactive interface to the C-fsm library

The Xfst scripting language evolved over the years into a programming language for compiling regular expressions and a rich variety of alternation rules into FSMs; and it eventually became possible to compile Lexc source files directly from Xfst, rendering the separate Lexc interface largely unnecessary. The alternation rules of Xfst, called Replace Rules, were an extension of the regular-expression syntax, and by at least the year 2000 Xerox researchers and developers had enthusiastically abandoned Twolc rules in favor of the new Replace Rules, which have a different syntax and geometry of combination. By 2003, when the book *Finite State Morphology* was published (Beesley and Karttunen, 2003), documenting the Finite State Toolkit, Twolc was considered so uninteresting and obsolete that a chapter documenting it was removed from the manuscript; the book therefore documents only Lexc and Xfst.[10]

Although the Finite State Toolkit has been freely available for decades for non-commercial research and academic use, commercial use has always required a paid license, and this has prompted the development of some clones. Much to the surprise of Xerox researchers, Twolc remained and today still remains popular in Scandinavia and Finland, where the formalism originated, and it has been reimplemented as part of the Helsinki Finite-State Technology (HFST) project.[11] Parts of HFST, which also supports Xfst and Lexc syntax, and provides a number of runtime tools, are available under a variety of licenses, including the GNU Library or Lesser General Public License Version 2.0 (LGPLv2), the GNU General Public License Version 2.0 (GLPv2), and the Apache License, Version 2.0.

An excellent clone of Xfst, including its ability to compile Lexc source files, is Foma, created and maintained by Mans Hulden, who also implemented the underlying finite-state library from scratch (Hulden, 2009a,b).[12] Many grammars written originally in Lexc and Xfst compile "out of the box" using Foma, which is available under the Apache License, Version 2.0.

---

[10]The chapter on Twolc is available at `http://www.fsmbook.com`.

[11]`http://hfst.sourceforge.net`, `http://sourceforge.net/projects/hfst`

[12]`http://en.wikipedia.org/wiki/Foma_(software)`, `http://code.google.com/p/foma/`

16.1.4 Why Yet Another Language?

Given that the Finite State Toolkit is readily available, at least for non-commercial use, and that the Foma and HFST clones are available under less restrictive licenses; and considering that an online Registry of Finite-State Technology lists over sixty finite-state projects and implementations,[13] one might well ask why a new finite-state programming language like Kleene is needed. In my opinion, the Finite State Toolkit has some extremely attractive features that I have tried to emulate in Kleene:

- The Lexc and Xfst languages provide a suitably high level of abstraction from the underlying C-fsm library, allowing developers to think in terms of regular languages and regular relations instead of the states and arcs of the FSMs.
- Each FSM created by Lexc and Xfst contains a record of its own private alphabet of known symbols (the "sigma"), and special reserved arc labels can refer to and match "other" or "unknown" symbols, i.e., any symbols not in the private alphabet. This powerful feature makes it unnecessary for developers to hand-define the alphabet, facilitating development, though it does considerably complicate the implementation of the interpreters.
- Though far from perfect, the extensive documentation, mostly in the book *Finite State Morphology* and on `http://www.fsmbook.com`, has allowed developers around the world to learn the languages and use them successfully.

At the same time, there are some infelicities in the Finite State Toolkit that I believed could and should be improved upon when designing Kleene:

- Xerox (and later the spun-off PARC) have a perfect right to require payment for commercial use of the Finite State Toolkit, which was developed over many years at considerable expense, but this has been an obstacle to adoption for many projects. Both the clones (HFST and Foma) and Kleene aimed from the beginning to relax commercial licensing. Foma, Kleene, and Kleene's underlying OpenFst library are all available under the Apache License, Version 2.0, which allows commercial usage without a licensing fee or royalties.[14] The Kleene source code is also open-source, allowing users to examine, correct, augment, and even adopt the code if the project should ever be abandoned by its original maintainer(s).

[13] `https://kitwiki.csc.fi/twiki/bin/view/KitWiki/FsmReg`

[14] `http://www.apache.org/licenses/LICENSE-2.0`

- The Finite State Toolkit does not support weighted FSMs.[15] Kleene is built on the OpenFst library, which supports weighted FSMs under a variety of semirings, though Kleene currently supports only the default Tropical Semiring.
- Memories vary and grow dim, but as I recall, the Xfst language began life in early 1990 as one developer's interactive framework, originally named ifsm, for testing finite-state algorithms as they were being ported from INTERLISP to C. Central to Xfst (and its predecessors) is a stack onto which arguments are pushed and from which arguments are popped to perform an operation, much like an old Hewlett-Packard calculator. However, whereas other stack-based interfaces push arguments onto the stack and invoke operations based on the order of Reverse Polish notation, the Xfst stack is implemented backwards, which, frankly, confuses most learners.[16] Kleene eliminates the stack altogether.
- The fact that there are two separate languages, Lexc and Xfst, by itself presents problems. Each of these languages has its own syntax and semantics, and its own special characters. When using regular expressions inside Lexc, one must revert to using the Xfst regular-expression syntax. It is all too easy for developers to fall into the cracks between the two languages, which leads to many bugs. Kleene combines the capabilities of Lexc and Xfst into a single programming language.
- The languages of the Finite State Toolkit have simple terminal-based interfaces, which creates challenges for portability and the handling of Unicode characters.[17] Kleene has a GUI implemented using the

---

[15] There were, over the years, two separate attempts to add weights to the C-fsm library and thus to Lexc and Xfst, but these efforts were not sustained long enough and were ultimately unsuccessful.

[16] An ordered arithmetic operation such as the subtraction (5 - 2) is represented in Reverse Polish notation as `5 2 -`. To perform this operation on a Hewlett-Packard calculator, one follows the order of the Reverse Polish notation, first pushing 5 on the stack, then 2, and then invoking the subtraction operation. The subtraction algorithm first pops 2 off the top of the stack and uses it as the *second* argument; then it pops 5 off the top of the stack and uses it as the *first* argument. Then it effectively computes (5 - 2) and pushes the result, 3, back on top of the stack.

In contrast, in Xfst, if Fsm1 and Fsm2 encode regular languages, and you want to compute (Fsm1 - Fsm2) on the stack, you must first push Fsm2, then Fsm1, and then invoke the subtraction operation. The Xfst subtraction operation will then pop Fsm1 off the stack and use it as the *first* argument; and then it will pop Fsm2 off of the stack and use it as the *second* argument. So, when pushing arguments onto the stack for an ordered operation like (Fsm1 - Fsm2) in the Xfst interface, or in an Xfst script, instead of thinking in terms of the Reverse Polish order, `Fsm1 Fsm2 -`, one must think of the order `Fsm2 Fsm1 -`, which many find backwards.

[17] At SRI International and Stanford's Center for the Study of Language and In-

highly portable Java Swing library, using text widgets that are inherently Unicode capable. Unicode text can be entered using standard Java input methods and rendered correctly.[18]

- Although the documentation of the Finite State Toolkit is unusually rich, the 2003 book *Finite State Morphology* was traditionally paper-published by CSLI, with the copyright held by the publisher. The languages continued to evolve, especially with improvements in the handling of Unicode, and yet hopes for an updated second edition never materialized. When an ebook version was finally offered, the publisher wanted it to conform to the printed book as closely as possible, so only minor corrections were possible.[19] The Kleene User Manual, which is a constant work-in-progress, is currently 300 pages long and is freely downloadable from `http://www.kleene-lang.org`.
- Xfst began to be used by developers almost immediately after it first became available, and then it evolved over more than twenty-five years, all the time under considerable pressure to maintain backward compatibility. Predictably, the resulting Xfst programming language and regular-expression syntax are less than ideal.

Indeed, it seems that in Xfst development, syntax was never a high priority. One former C-fsm library developer has even expressed the view that no serious thought at all was ever given to syntax. The C-fsm and Xfst developers were generally happy as long as they had a

formation (CSLI) in the mid 1980s, Karttunen wrote a fancy graphical user interface for the two-level rule compiler that was written on top of PARC's original INTERLISP library, which supported sophisticated graphics on the Xerox Dandelion computers ("D-machines"). It included windows and menus and icons for each rule, and one could edit, compile and test each rule separately, and visualize the resulting automata. Karttunen and Kaplan used this interface in a morphology class that they taught at the 1987 LSA Institute at Stanford.

After moving from SRI to Xerox in 1987, and it became evident that INTERLISP had no future, Karttunen switched to Common Lisp, which did not support the graphical features that made INTERLISP so nice on the D-machines. When it soon became obvious that Common Lisp had no future either, Karttunen switched to C, and all the energy and enthusiasm for building fancy graphical user interfaces had dissipated.

[18]Java has a better-than-average commitment to handling Unicode, but it's not perfect. Suitable fonts must be installed in the user's Java framework, and proper display of some orthographies depends on the evolving capabilities of the Swing library's rendering engines. From inside or outside the GUI, Kleene can process pre-edited scripts in any standard encoding.

[19]The paperback, cloth-bound, and electronic versions of the book are available from CSLI at `http://web.stanford.edu/group/cslipublications/cslipublications/site/1575864347.shtml`.

way, no matter how awkward, to test their new algorithms.[20]

From the learner's point of view, not only must he/she juggle two different programming languages—Lexc and Xfst—but the regular-expression syntax of Xfst differs in a number of arbitrary and completely unnecessary ways from the syntax of the Perl-like regular expressions that are already familiar to many programmers.[21] Of course, there are numerous subtle differences among the implementations of regular expressions in programming languages and operating systems (Friedl, 2006), and there are major semantic differences between Perl-like "regular" expressions (which aren't really regular) and true regular expressions (as in Xfst, Foma, SFST, OpenGrm Thrax, etc.) that denote regular languages and regular relations, but the arbitrary differences in the Xfst syntax are an annoying obstacle to many learners. As far as possible and appropriate, Kleene tries to use the familiar syntax of Perl-like regular expressions. From the beginning, Kleene was designed under the guiding principle that Syntax Matters.

16.1.5 Kleene History

While at Xerox Research from 1994 to 2006, I presented several proposals to redesign the Xerox finite-state programming languages, and even tried to implement an entirely new language, called Rx or XRX, based on a new weighted finite-state library called WFST that was being developed by my colleagues André Kempe and Tamás Gaál (Kempe et al., 2003). All of these efforts were spectacularly unsuccessful.

After leaving Xerox and joining Inxight in 2006, I began to implement Kleene from scratch as a private hobby project, initially working only on syntax and arithmetic expressions until the OpenFst library became available in mid 2007. Inxight was subsequently acquired by Business Objects, and Business Objects was in turn acquired by SAP, which adopted and supported Kleene development from 2008 to 2011, after which the project was canceled.[22] On 4 May 2012, SAP released Kleene as free, open-source code under the Apache License, Version 2.0,[23] at which time it effectively reverted to being my one-man hobby project again. I'm grateful to my SAP bosses for allowing Kleene to

[20] In the academic field of finite-state computing, new algorithms are considered "scientific" and worthy of publication and presentation in papers at conferences. Reports on finite-state programming languages and projects using them, no matter how challenging and useful they might be, are often relegated to the poster session.

[21] Perl-like regular expressions are now found also in Python, Java, and many other programming languages.

[22] My SAP colleagues Paola Nieddu and Phil Sours also worked on Kleene and related runtime code during those three years.

[23] `http://www.apache.org/licenses/LICENSE-2.0.html`

TABLE 1 Kleene Regular-Expression Assignment Examples

```
$var = dog ;
$var = d o g ;          // equivalent to dog
$var = ~( a+ b* c? ) ; // language complementation
$var = \~ \+ \* \? ;  // literalized special characters using backslash
$var = "~+*?";        // literalized characters inside double quotes
$var = "dog" ;        // unnecessary literalization, equivalent to dog
$myvar = (dog | cat | horse) s? ;
$yourvar = [A-Za-z] [A-Za-z0-9]* ;   // symbol union as in Perl
$hisvar = ([A-Za-z]-[aeiouAEIOU])+ ; // subtraction of languages
$itsvar = [^a-z] ;                   // complement character union
$hervar = (bird|cow|elephant|pig) & (pig|ant|bird) ; // intersection
$ourvar = (dog):(chien) ∘ (chien):(Hund) ;            // composition
$theirvar = [a-z]+ ( a <0.91629> | b <0.1> ) ; // weights in brackets
```

escape the oblivion of the bit bucket.

The paper continues with a brief description the Kleene language, the current state of development, and plans for the future.

16.2 Implementation

The Java-language Kleene parser, implemented with JavaCC and JJTree (Copeland, 2007),[24] is Unicode-capable and portable. The GUI, the environment and the interpreter are hand-written in Java. Successfully parsed statements are reduced to abstract syntax trees (ASTs), which are interpreted by calling C++ functions in the OpenFst library via the Java Native Interface (JNI).

16.3 Kleene Syntax

16.3.1 Regular Expressions

Basic Kleene assignment statements have a regular expression on the right-hand side, as shown in table 1. As in Perl regular expressions, simple alphabetic characters are literal, and concatenation is indicated by simple juxtaposition, with no overt operator. Parentheses can be used to group expressions. The postfixed `*` (the "Kleene star"), `+` (the "Kleene plus"), and `?` denote zero-or-more, one-or-more, and optionality, respectively.[25] Again as in Perl regular expressions, square-bracketed expressions have their own internal syntax to denote character unions, including character ranges such as `[A-Z]`. The union operator is `|`. Basic regular operations missing from Perl regular expressions

[24] `https://javacc.dev.java.net`

[25] The terms "Kleene star" and "Kleene plus" are used generally in the field, recognizing Stephen Cole Kleene, the inventor of regular expressions.

TABLE 2 Basic Perl, Kleene, and Xfst Regular Expression Syntax

<table>
<tr><th></th><th>Perl</th><th>Kleene</th><th>Xfst</th></tr>
<tr><td>zero or more</td><td>a*</td><td>a*</td><td>a*</td></tr>
<tr><td>one or more</td><td>a+</td><td>a+</td><td>a+</td></tr>
<tr><td>optional</td><td>a?</td><td>a?</td><td>(a)</td></tr>
<tr><td>iteration n times</td><td>a{2}</td><td>a{2}</td><td>a^2</td></tr>
<tr><td>iteration n to m times</td><td>a{2,4}</td><td>a{2,4}</td><td>a^{2,4}</td></tr>
<tr><td>union</td><td>|</td><td>|</td><td>|</td></tr>
<tr><td>concatenation</td><td>abc</td><td>abc or a b c</td><td>a b c or {abc}</td></tr>
<tr><td>literalized special symbol</td><td>\+</td><td>\+</td><td>%+</td></tr>
<tr><td>any symbol (wildcard)</td><td>.</td><td>.</td><td>?</td></tr>
<tr><td>grouping</td><td>(...)</td><td>(...)</td><td>[...]</td></tr>
<tr><td>symbol union</td><td>[a-z]</td><td>[a-z]</td><td>"a-z"</td></tr>
<tr><td>complement symbol union</td><td>[^a-z]</td><td>[^a-z]</td><td>\"a-z"</td></tr>
<tr><td>variable</td><td></td><td>$name</td><td>name</td></tr>
<tr><td>user-defined symbol</td><td></td><td>'name'</td><td>name</td></tr>
<tr><td>intersection (language)</td><td></td><td>&</td><td>&</td></tr>
<tr><td>subtraction (language)</td><td></td><td>-</td><td>-</td></tr>
<tr><td>complement (language)</td><td></td><td>~</td><td>~</td></tr>
<tr><td>cross-product</td><td></td><td>:</td><td>:</td></tr>
<tr><td>weight</td><td></td><td><0.1></td><td></td></tr>
</table>

include cross-product (`:`), composition (∘ or `_o_`), language intersection (`&`), language subtraction (`-`), and language negation (prefixed ∼). Weights under the Tropical Semiring are indicated as floating-point literals or arbitrarily complicated arithmetic expressions inside angle brackets, e.g., `<0.1>`.

Special characters can be literalized with a preceding backslash or inside double quotes, e.g., `\*` or `"*"` denotes a literal asterisk rather than the Kleene star. To improve the human readability of expressions, whitespace characters are not significant, unless they appear inside square brackets or are explicitly literalized inside double quotes or with a preceding backslash.

In a language like Kleene where alphabetic symbols are literal, and the expression `dog` denotes three literal symbols, *d*, *o*, and *g*, concatenated together, there must be a way to distinguish variable names from simple concatenations of letter symbols. The Kleene solution is to prefix variable names that are bound to FSM values with a dollar-sign sigil, e.g., `$myvar`. Once bound to an FSM value, a variable name can be used inside subsequent regular expressions, as in the following example, which models a fragment of Esperanto verb morphology.

```
$vroot = don | dir | pens | ir ;
// Comment: "give", "say", "think", "go"
$aspect = ad ;  // habitual/repeated aspect
$vend = as | is | os | us | u | i ;
// pres, past, fut, cond, subj, inf
$verbs = $vroot $aspect? $vend ; // using defined variables
```

The final definition of `$verbs` specifies that a verb starts with an obligatory root, followed by an optional aspect morpheme, and terminated with an obligatory tense/mood verb suffix.

Similarly, names of functions that return FSMs are distinguished with the `$^` sigil. To denote less common operations, rather than inventing and proliferating new and arguably cryptic regular-expression operators, Kleene provides a set of predefined functions including

`$^reverse(`*regexp*`)`
`$^invert(`*regexp*`)`
`$^inputProj(`*regexp*`)`
`$^outputProj(`*regexp*`)`
`$^contains(`*regexp*`)`
`$^ignore(`*regexp, regexp*`)`
`$^copy(`*regexp*`)`

Users can also define their own functions, and function calls that return FSMs are regular expressions that can appear as operands inside larger regular expressions. The following trivial example defines a function that takes two FSM arguments, unions them, and returns the resulting FSM.

```
// function definition
$^myunion($a, $b) {
    return $a | $b ;
}

// function call
$myfsm = $^myunion(dog, cat) ;
```

Of course, this example is not only trivial but unnecessary because the user can simply use the union operator, `|`, directly.

For a more interesting example, consider the following script that produces an FST that performs analysis and generation of regular Spanish -ar verbs, limited here to the present indicative forms.[26]

```
// A simple Kleene script for modeling
// the conjugation of Spanish regular -ar verbs
// (limited here to the present indicative)

// First define a union of Spanish regular -ar
// infinitive forms, the traditional dictionary-
// citation form.  Later expand the union to cover
// thousands in this class.

$regSpanArInf =
  amar
| cantar
| hablar
| imaginar
| meditar
;

//  Construct the FST that maps abstract strings like
//  amar[Verb][PresInd][1P][Sg] to amo,
//  amar[Verb][PresInd][1P][Pl] to amamos, etc.
//  and vice-versa

$conjRegSpanAr =
// convert (amar):(amar) to (amar):(am),
// mapping the infinitive ending ar to the empty
// string (denoted "") on the lower side
( $regSpanArInf _o_  (.* .:"" .:"") )

// concatenate [Verb] and [PresInd] "tags"
// on the upper side, mapped to the empty string
// on the lower side
( '[Verb]' '[PresInd]' ):""

// then concatenate the conjugation tags and endings
(
    ( '[1P]' '[Sg]' ) : o
```

[26]The spanverbs.kl script, available from `www.kleene-lang.org/downloads/downloads.html`, uses similar functions to handle all verb classes in all conjugations, but not yet including clitic pronouns.

```
|    ( '[2P]' '[Sg]' ) : (as)
|    ( '[3P]' '[Sg]' ) : a
|    ( '[1P]' '[Pl]' ) : (amos)
|    ( '[2P]' '[Pl]' ) : (ais)
|    ( '[3P]' '[Pl]' ) : (an)
)
;

// Define $^analyze and $^generate functions for
// convenience in testing

$^analyze($surfaceWd) {
return $^upperside($conjRegSpanAr _o_ $surfaceWd) ;
}

$^generate($abstractStr) {
return $^lowerside($abstractStr _o_ $conjRegSpanAr) ;
}

// Some simple tests

pr $^analyze(amamos) ;
// Output: amar[Verb][PresInd][1P][Pl]

pr $^analyze(ama) ;
// Output: amar[Verb][PresInd][3P][Sg]

pr $^generate(amar '[Verb]' '[PresInd]' '[1P]' '[Sg]') ;
// Output: amo

pr $^generate(amar '[Verb]' '[PresInd]' '[1P]' '[Pl]') ;
// Output: amamos

pr $^generate(amar '[Verb]' '[PresInd]' '[3P]' '[Pl]') ;
// Output: aman

pr $^analyze(cantamos) ;
// Output: cantar[Verb][PresInd][1P][Pl]

pr $^analyze(canta) ;
// Output: cantar[Verb][PresInd][3P][Sg]
```

TABLE 3 The Simplest Kleene Alternation-Rule Templates

input-expression -> *output-expression*
input-expression -> *output-expression* / *left-context* _ *right-context*

```
pr $^generate(cantar '[Verb]' '[PresInd]' '[1P]' '[Sg]') ;
// Output: canto

pr $^generate(cantar '[Verb]' '[PresInd]' '[1P]' '[Pl]') ;
// Output: cantamos

pr $^generate(cantar '[Verb]' '[PresInd]' '[3P]' '[Pl]') ;
// Output: cantan
```

16.3.2 Alternation-Rule Syntax

Alternation rules, called rewrite rules or replace rules in other traditions, compile into finite-state transducers (FSTs) and are commonly used to model phonetic and orthographical alternations. Kleene provides a rich variety of alternation-rule types, comparable to the Replace Rules of the Finite State Toolkit (Beesley and Karttunen, 2003, pp. 130–82), but implemented using algorithms kindly supplied by Mans Hulden (2009a). The reimplementation of the basic algorithms in Java and OpenFst, starting from Hulden's Foma notation; the implementation of an interpretive framework to allow the general use of multiple contexts, two-level contexts, and parallel rules; and the design of the new alternation-rule syntax were some of the biggest challenges during Kleene development.

Simple Traditional Rules

The simplest rules have the templates shown in table 3, and are interpreted into transducers that map the input to the output in the specified context (if any). The *input-expression*, the *output-expression*, the *left-context*, and the *right-context* can be arbitrarily complicated regular expressions, with the semantic limitation that they must all denote acceptors. Where a context is indicated, either the left context or the right context can be omitted. For example,

```
a -> b
```

denotes the regular relation that maps each *a* in the input string to *b* in the related output string(s), no matter what the context might be. The rule

```
s -> z / [aeiou] _ [aeiou]
```

maps *s* to *z* if and only if it appears between vowels. Rules can have multiple contexts, separated by || as in the following example, which maps *s* to *z* when it appears between vowels or at the beginning of the input. The # is interpreted as a string boundary.

```
s -> z / [aeiou] _ [aeiou] || # _
```

Such simple right-arrow rules will apply if and only if the input expression and at least one of the contexts match the input. As in the Finite State Toolkit, Kleene FSTs are visualized as having an upper projection and a lower projection, and right-arrow rules have a kind of downward bias, usually read as mapping from upper-projection input strings to lower-projection output strings.

Syntactic variations of the arrow allow a range of semantic variations:

`->`	obligatory downward mapping
`->?`	optional downward mapping
`{max}->`	maximum left-to-right downward matching
`{min}->`	minimum left-to-right downward matching
`{max}->?`	optional maximum left-to-right downward matching
`{min}->?`	optional minimum left-to-right downward matching

Left-arrow rules, with an upward bias, are also supported.[27]

Fancy Rules

Using Hulden's algorithms, Kleene also supports rules with two-level contexts, which are not available in Xfst. Where the single underscore _ separates a left context and a right context that are to be interpreted as one-level, the Unicode DOUBLE LOW LINE ‗, U+2017, causes the contexts to be interpreted as two-level. As usual, either of the context sides can be omitted. Instead of the DOUBLE LOW LINE, which is not available in many fonts, one can use the ASCII equivalent sequence _2_. For example,

```
a -> e / s:z _2_ s:z
```

maps *a* to *e*, but only when the *a* is surrounded by *s*s on the input projection and *e* is surrounded by *z*s on the output projection. The mapping of *s* to *z* in the context would be accomplished by some other rule applied in parallel, typically using the built-in special function

[27] What are not yet supported are rules with right-to-left minimum or maximum behavior.

`$^parallel`. The FST resulting from the following parallel-compiled rules maps *asasas* to *azezas*.

```
$^parallel(a -> e / s:z _2_ s:z,
           s -> z / [aeiou] _ [aeiou])
```

As an even simpler example,

```
$^parallel(a -> b, b -> a)
```

compiles into a single FST that maps *a* to *b*, *b* to *a*, *abba* to *baab*, etc. The rules can be as complex as desired, with or without contexts, mixing different kinds of arrows, and there are currently no known restrictions on the kinds of rules that can be interpreted in parallel.[28]

Sometimes it is useful to write rules with contexts that will accept anything (the universal language .*) on the input side, but something concrete on the output side. The rule

```
a -> b / (.*):b  _2_
```

maps *a* to *b* if and only if the input *a* is preceded, on the *output* projection, by *b*. This has the effect of mapping *baaa* to *bbbb* because the rule effectively creates its own left context. Such rules can be used to model phenomena that seem to have a domino effect from left to right, including vowel harmony.

Similarly, the rule

```
a -> b / _2_  (.*):b
```

maps *a* to *b* if and only if the input *a* is followed, on the *output* projection, by *b*. This rule maps *aaab* to *bbbb*. Such rules can be used to model phenomena that seem to have a domino effect from right to left, including umlaut.

Kleene also supports rules with `where` clauses that define local variables and compile as sets of parallel rules. The following rule, which models devoicing of consonants at the end of a word,

```
$Voiced -> $Unvoiced / _ #
{where   $Voiced ∈ $@(b, d, g),
       $Unvoiced ∈ $@(p, t, k)
}
```

is equivalent to three rules compiled in parallel:

[28]The greatest limitation on compiling rules in parallel is the ability of the rule writer to comprehend all the rule interactions and potential conflicts. In particular, two-level contexts must often be specified with great care, as in the classic Two-Level Morphology rules.

```
$^parallel(b -> p / _ #,
           d -> t / _ #,
           g -> k / _ #)
```

The ∈ (U+2208, ELEMENT OF) operator can also be typed with the ASCII equivalent _E_. The `$@(`*regex*`, ...)` syntax denotes a literal list of FSMs.

Using `where` clauses, one can easily implement simple-substitution ciphers such as the classic Caesar Cipher, wherein each letter was substituted by the letter three steps later in the alphabet, e.g., A was replaced by D, B was replaced by E, C was replaced by F, etc. At the end of the alphabet, the mapping wrapped around to the beginning so that X was replaced by A, Y by B, and Z by C. The following script uses the common convention of treating the plaintext as consisting only of lowercase letters, and the ciphertext as consisting only of uppercase letters. Arbitrarily, the script is written to generate (apply downwards) from a plaintext string to the corresponding ciphertext string.

```
// Define $@plainletter and $@cipherletter
//    as lists of FSTs
$@plainletter =  $@(a,b,c,d,e,f,g,h,i,j,k,l,
     m,n,o,p,q,r,s,t,u,v,w,x,y,z) ;

$@cipherletter = $@(D,E,F,G,H,I,J,K,L,M,N,O,
     P,Q,R,S,T,U,V,W,X,Y,Z,A,B,C) ;

$ucfilter = ~$^contains([A-Z]) ;

// Define $caesar as an FST that maps from each plainletter
//    to its corresponding cipherletter, and vice versa
$caesar = $ucfilter
    _o_
    $pl -> $cl {where $pl _E_ $@plainletter,
                      $cl _E_ $@cipherletter} ;

// Define some convenient functions for testing
$^encipher($plainstring) {
    return $^lowerside($plainstring _o_ $caesar) ;
}
$^decipher($cipherstring) {
    return $^upperside($caesar _o_ $cipherstring) ;
```

```
}

pr $^encipher("attack at dawn") ;
// => DWWDFN DW GDZQ

pr $^decipher("DWWDFN DW GDZQ") ;
// => attack at dawn
```

Because of the `where` clause, the basic `$pl -> $cl` rule is expanded by the interpreter into twenty-six rules compiled in parallel. The rule is downward-oriented, like all right-arrow rules, so it maps *a* uniquely down to *D*, but when it is applied upward, it maps *D* to both *a* and *D*; the `$ucfilter`, which matches all and only strings that do not contain any uppercase letter(s), when composed "on top of" the rule ensures that a lower-side *D* maps up uniquely to *a*, allowing the `$caesar` FST to be used for both enciphering and deciphering.

In addition, Kleene supports transducer-style rules that express the left-hand-side as a transducer rather than as an `<input> -> <output>` mapping.

```
(<upper>):(<lower>) -> / <lcontext> _ <rcontext>
```

Using the transducer style, the consonant-devoicing rule can also be written as

```
b:p | d:t | g:k -> / _ #
```

which is arguably more readable.

Transducer-style rules can also be used to effect arbitrary numbers of epenthetic insertions in the output, doing what Xfst mark-up rules do, and much more. See the user manual for more explanations and examples of the range of rule types supported in Kleene.[29]

16.3.3 Right-Linear Phrase Structure Grammars

While regular expressions are mathematically capable of describing any regular language or regular relation, some linguistic phenomena—especially productive morphological compounding and derivation—can be awkward to describe this way. Kleene therefore provides right-linear phrase-structure grammars that are similar in semantics and purpose, though not in syntax, to the Lexc language (Beesley and Karttunen, 2003, pp. 203–78).

A Kleene phrase-structure grammar is defined as a set of productions, each bound to a production variable with the `$>` sigil. Productions may include right-linear references to themselves or to other pro-

[29] The user manual is downloadable from `http://www.kleene-lang.org`.

ductions, which might not yet be defined. The productions can also use normal definitions and function calls. The productions are parsed immediately but are not evaluated until the entire grammar is built into an FSM via a call to the built-in function `$^start()`, which takes one production name as its argument and treats it as the starting production of the whole grammar. The fact that productions are not evaluated immediately allows a top-down approach to grammar writing. The following example models a fragment of Esperanto noun morphotactics, including noun-root compounding, using right-linear productions.

```
$>Root = (kat | hund | elefant | dom)
               ( $>Root | $>AugDim ) ;
//         cat   dog   elephant  house
$>AugDim = ( eg | et )? $>Noun ;
//            aug  dim
$>Noun = o $>Plur ;  // obligatory o suffix for nouns
$>Plur = j? $>Case ;
//       optional plural suffix
$>Case = n? ;
//       optional accusative case suffix

$nouns = $^start($>Root) ;
```

The syntax on the right-hand side of productions is identical to the regular-expression syntax, but allowing right-linear references to productions of the form `$>`*Name*.

16.4 Kleene FSMs

16.4.1 FST Object Design

Each Kleene finite-state machine consists of an OpenFst FSM, under the default Tropical Semiring, wrapped in a Java object that stores the private alphabet of each machine.[30]

In Kleene, it is not necessary or possible to declare the whole alphabet of symbols being used; symbols appearing overtly in regular expressions, alternation rules, and right-linear phrase-structure grammars are added automatically to the alphabet and are stored automatically as OpenFst integer arc labels using their Unicode code point value, and this includes Unicode supplementary characters. Programmer-defined symbols with multi-character names, represented in the syntax with surrounding single quotes, e.g., `'+Noun'` and `'+Verb'`, or, using another

[30]More precisely, each Java object of the class Fst contains a long integer field that stores a pointer to the OpenFst machine, which actually resides in OpenFst's C++ memory space.

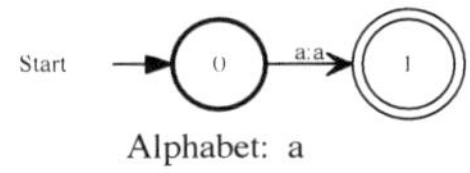

FIGURE 1 The FSM created for regular expression a.

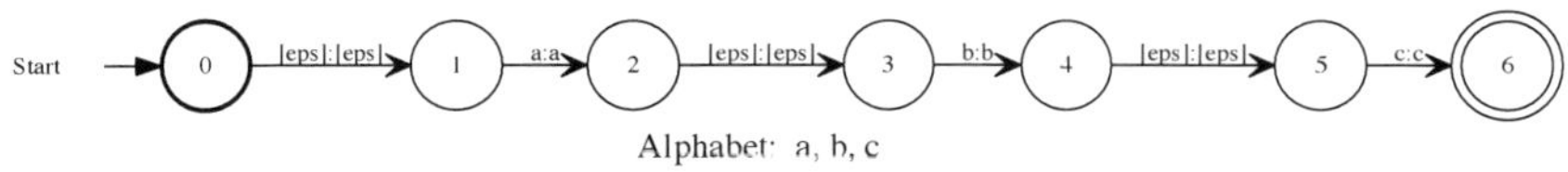

FIGURE 2 The FSM created for abc, before epsilon removal.

common convention, '[Noun]' and '[Verb]', also need no declaration and are automatically stored using code point values from a Unicode Private Use Area.

The dot (.) denotes *any* symbol, and it translates non-trivially into reserved arc labels that denote and match OTHER (i.e., unknown) symbols.[31]

16.4.2 FST Construction and Optimization

The FSM for the simple regular expression a is shown in figure 1. Note that the FSM consists of one start state, explicitly labeled and displayed as a heavy circle, one final state, marked with a double circle, and one arc labeled a:a, where the first a indicates *a* on the input projection, and the second a indicates *a* on the output projection. In OpenFst, and therefore in Kleene, each label always has both an input and an output label. If for each arc in an FSM the input label is equal to the output label, the FSM can be viewed and used as either an acceptor or an identity transducer.[32]

```
$a = a ;
draw $a ;

// or just
// draw a ;
```

Each single symbol like a, b, and c is initially interpreted to create a two-state FSM as shown in figure 1. So the regular expression a b c

[31]The treatment of FSM-specific alphabets and the handling of OTHER symbols is modeled on the Xerox/PARC implementation (Beesley and Karttunen, 2003, pp. 56–60).

[32]In the OpenFst visualization of FSMs, there is always an "input" projection and an "output" projection. In the traditional Xerox visualization, which emphasizes the bidirectionality of FSMs, it is traditional to think in terms of "upper" and "lower" projections, so a:a is <upper>:<lower>.

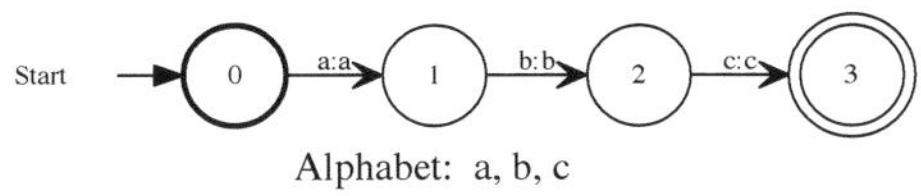

FIGURE 3 The FSM created for `abc`, after epsilon removal, which is applied by default.

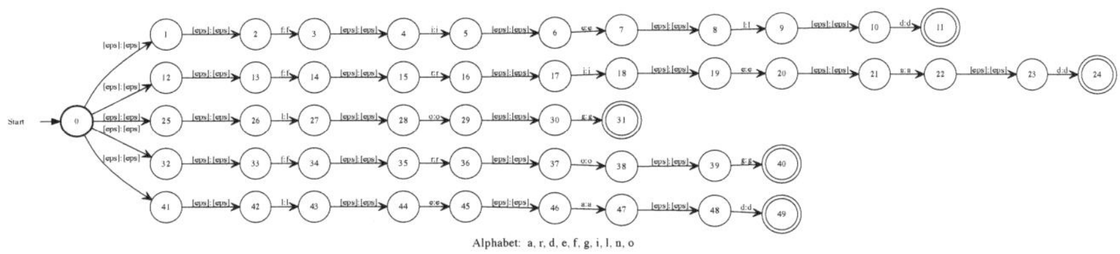

FIGURE 4 The FSM created for `field | friend | log | frog | lead`, before optimization.

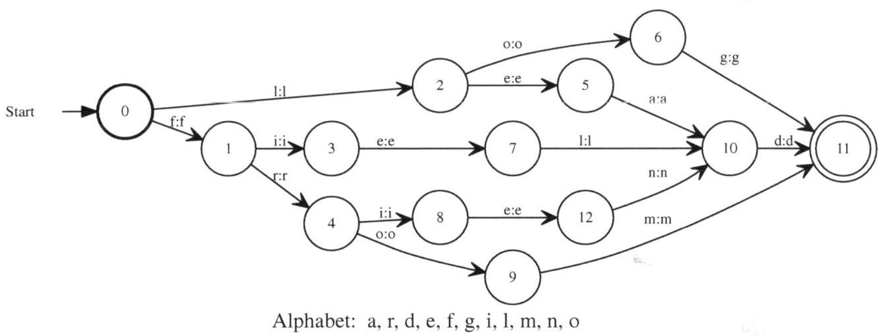

FIGURE 5 The FSM created for `field | friend | log | frog | lead`, after optimization.

initially results in three such FSMs that are subsequently concatenated together as shown in figure 2 by creating epsilon (empty-string) arcs from the final state of `a` to the start state of `b`, making the final state of `a` non-final, and making the start state of `b` a normal (non-start) state, and the same for the transition from `b` to `c`. Figure 2 shows the result before epsilon removal, which is normally turned on to produce the FSM shown in figure 3.

Optimization, which is normally performed by default, includes determination, minimization and epsilon removal. If optimization is turned off, the regular expression `field | friend | log | frog | lead` is interpreted to create the FSM shown in figure 4; after normal optimization, the result is as shown in figure 5.

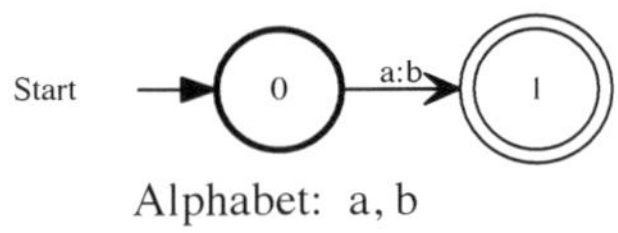

FIGURE 6 The FSM created for `a:b`.

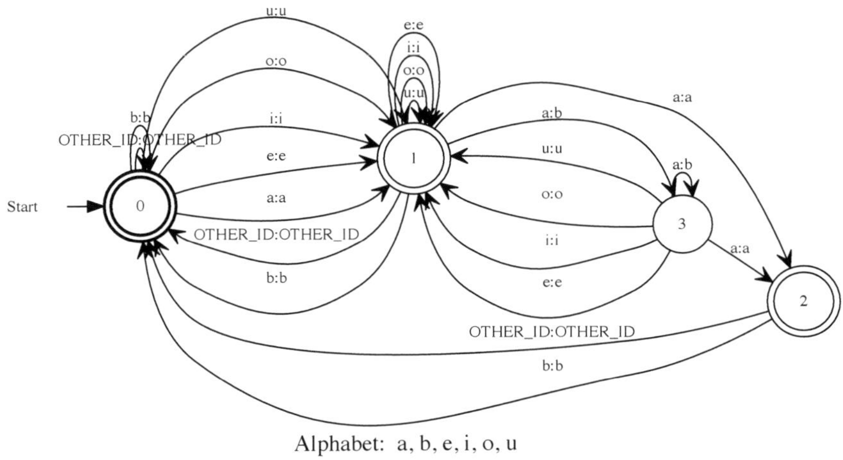

FIGURE 7 The FSM created for the alternation rule `a -> b / [aeiou] _ [aeiou]`.

The simplest non-identity transducers can be specified in regular expressions using the cross-product operator `:` as in `a:b`, which is interpreted to create the FSM shown in figure 6. Alternation rules also compile into transducers, as in the FSM for `a -> b / [aeiou] _ [aeiou]`, shown in figure 7.

Finally, the treatment of weights, under the Tropical Semiring, is of some interest. The regular expression `<0.1>`, which consists of just a weight expression, is interpreted to create the FSM shown in figure 8; the one arc is an epsilon arc, matching the empty string and carrying the specified weight. If weights are inserted into a larger regular expression, such as `a <0.1> b <0.2> c`, the result before optimization is shown in figure 9. After optimization, the equivalent FSM is shown in figure 10, which illustrates that during epsilon-removal the weights are pushed from the weighted epsilon arcs onto an adjacent arc and are combined using the extension operation of the Tropical Semiring, which is simple addition.[33]

[33]The weight of a path, in the Tropical Semiring, is the sum of all the weights on

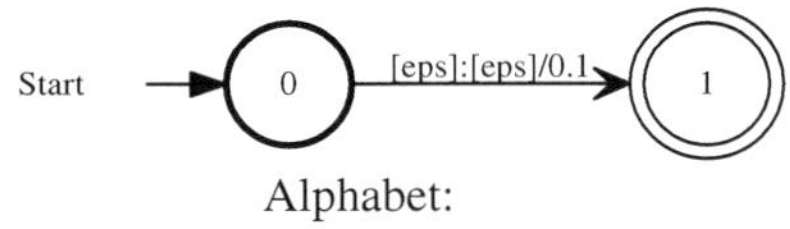

FIGURE 8 The FSM created for the regular expression `<0.1>`.

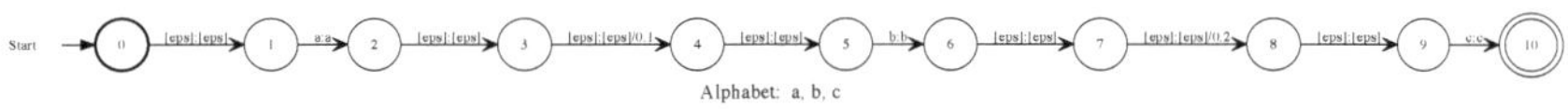

FIGURE 9 The FSM created for the weighted regular expression `a <0.1> b <0.2> c`, before optimization.

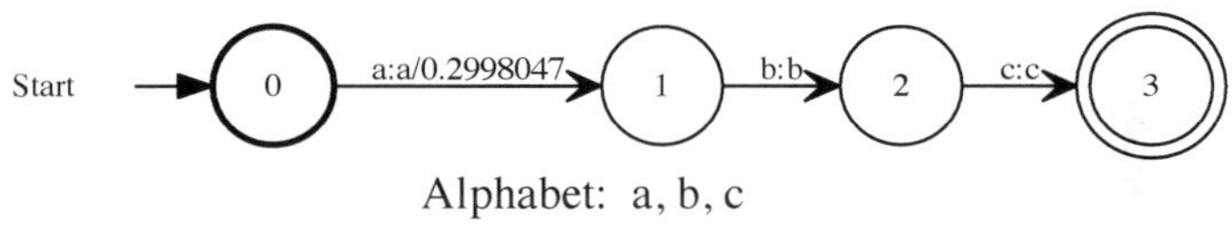

FIGURE 10 The FSM created for the weighted regular expression `a <0.1> b <0.2> c`, after optimization.

16.5 Status

At the time of writing, Kleene version 0.9.5.0 is an advanced beta project. It is used by Mans Hulden in his classes at the University of Colorado, and it has been used to model edit distance, Dutch noun pluralization, and Spanish verb morphology.

For integration of Kleene FSMs into larger NLP applications, the still experimental **fst2java** code translates a Kleene FSM into executable Java code in the form of a class that provides methods to take an input Java String object as an argument and return a String or Strings, in various user-controllable formats, as the output.

16.6 Future Work

The work remaining to be done includes:

- Writing of **fst2cpp** code to translate Kleene FSMs into executable C++ code.
- Writing of runtime applications and APIs to apply in-memory FSMs to input and return output.
- Expansion to handle semirings other than the default Tropical Semiring of OpenFst.

---

all the arcs in the path. Thus the "extension" operation of the Tropical Semiring is simple addition; in the OpenFst terminology, the extension operation is called the "Times()" operation.

- Testing in non-trivial applications to determine memory usage and performance.

References

Allauzen, Cyril, Michael Riley, Johan Schalkwyk, Wojciech Skut, and Mehryar Mohri. 2007. OpenFst: A general and efficient weighted finite-state transducer library. In *Proceedings of the Ninth International Conference on Implementation and Application of Automata (CIAA 2007)*, vol. 4783 of *Lecture Notes in Computer Science*, pages 11–23. Springer.

Antworth, Evan L. 1990. *PC-KIMMO: a two-level processor for morphological analysis*. No. 16 in Occasional publications in academic computing. Dallas: Summer Institute of Linguistics.

Beesley, Kenneth R. 1991. Computer analysis of Arabic morphology: A two-level approach with detours. In B. Comrie and M. Eid, eds., *Perspectives on Arabic Linguistics III: Papers from the Third Annual Symposium on Arabic Linguistics*, pages 155–172. Amsterdam: John Benjamins. Read originally at the Third Annual Symposium on Arabic Linguistics, University of Utah, Salt Lake City, Utah, 3-4 March 1989.

Beesley, Kenneth R., Tim Buckwalter, and Stuart N. Newton. 1989. Two-level finite-state analysis of Arabic morphology. In *Proceedings of the Seminar on Bilingual Computing in Arabic and English*. Cambridge, England. No pagination.

Beesley, Kenneth R. and Lauri Karttunen. 2003. *Finite State Morphology*. Palo Alto, CA: CSLI Publications.

Copeland, Tom. 2007. *Generating Parsers with JavaCC*. Alexandria, VA: Centennial Books.

Friedl, Jeffrey E.F. 2006. *Mastering Regular Expressions*. Cambridge: O'Reilly, 3rd edn.

Hulden, Mans. 2009a. *Finite-State Machine Construction Methods and Algorithms for Phonology and Morphology*. Ph.D. thesis, The University of Arizona, Tucson, AZ.

Hulden, Mans. 2009b. Foma: a finite-state compiler and library. In *Proceedings of the EACL 2009 Demonstrations Session*, pages 29–32. Athens, Greece.

Kaplan, Ronald M. and Martin Kay. 1981. Phonological rules and finite-state transducers. In *Linguistic Society of America Meeting Handbook, Fifty-Sixth Annual Meeting*. New York. Abstract.

Kaplan, Ronald M. and Martin Kay. 1994. Regular models of phonological rule systems. *Computational Linguistics* 20(3):331–378.

Karttunen, Lauri and Kenneth R. Beesley. 1992. Two-level rule compiler. Tech. Rep. ISTL-92-2, Xerox Palo Alto Research Center, Palo Alto, CA.

Karttunen, Lauri and Kenneth R. Beesley. 2005. Twenty-five years of finite-state morphology. In A. Arppe, L. Carlson, K. Lindén, J. Piitulainen,

M. Suominen, M. Vainio, H. Westerlund, and A. Yli-Jyrä, eds., *Inquiries into Words, Constraints and Contexts: Festschrift in the Honour of Kimmo Koskenniemi on his 60th Birthday*, pages 71–83. Saarijärvi, Finland: Gummerus Printing. Preprint, to be published in CSLI Studies in Computational Linguistics ONLINE.

Karttunen, Lauri, Kimmo Koskenniemi, and Ronald M. Kaplan. 1987. A compiler for two-level phonological rules. In M. Dalrymple, R. Kaplan, L. Karttunen, K. Koskenniemi, S. Shaio, and M. Wescoat, eds., *Tools for Morphological Analysis*, vol. 87-108 of *CSLI Reports*, pages 1–61. Palo Alto, CA: Center for the Study of Language and Information, Stanford University.

Kempe, André, Christof Baeijs, Tamás Gaál, Franck Guingne, and Florent Nicart. 2003. WFSC – A new weighted finite state compiler. In O. Ibarra and Z. Dang, eds., *Proc. 8th Int. Conf. on Implementation and Application of Automata (CIAA'03)*, vol. 2759 of *Lecture Notes in Computer Science*, pages 108–119. Santa Barbara, CA, USA: Springer Verlag.

Koskenniemi, Kimmo. 1983. Two-level morphology: A general computational model for word-form recognition and production. Publication 11, University of Helsinki, Department of General Linguistics, Helsinki.

Koskenniemi, Kimmo. 1984. A general computational model for word-form recognition and production. In *COLING'84*, pages 178–181.

Roark, Brian and Richard Sproat. 2007. *Computational Approaches to Morphology and Syntax*. Oxford Surveys in Syntax & Morphology. Oxford: Oxford University Press.

Schmid, Helmut. 2005. A programming language for finite state transducers. In *FSMNLP'05*. Helsinki.

17

Simplified Two-level Morphophonology

KIMMO KOSKENNIEMI

17.1 Introduction

Writing two-level grammar rules and entire two-level grammars is sometimes consider difficult as in (Beesley and Karttunen, 2003, pp. 12–13):

> TWOLC rules conceptually apply simultaneously; this avoids the ordering problems but means that sets of twolc rules must be carefully written to avoid nasty and often mysterious conflicts among rules. Correct, non-conflicting TWOLC rule sets are notoriously difficult to write when some of the rules perform deletion or, especially, epenthesis.

This paper elaborates a simplified version of the two-level model which appears to avoid most of the sources of the complexity that some users of the standard model have experienced.[1] In the simplified model, separate morphophonemes are used more freely for alternations which have different causes or patterns. Generally, there is less need for creative or artistic solutions when using the new model. A technical difference is that in the present model, all rules are strictly conjunctive as they were in Koskenniemi (1983). Rules are also usually written for each morphophoneme separately.

In the simplified model, some tasks can be done automatically for the linguist. It is claimed here that building morphophonological grammars

[1] An earlier version of the simplified two-level morphology was presented in Koskenniemi (2013b). That version contained some of the features presented in this paper.

Tokens of Meaning: Papers in Honor of Lauri Karttunen.
Cleo Condoravdi and Tracy Holloway King (eds.).

is easier when using the simplified model. Even if one needs more rules, each rule is simpler.

The simplified model is expected to be best suited for languages which have morphophonemic alternations and use a phonemic or near-phonemic alphabet. Therefore, the terms 'letter' and 'phoneme' are sometimes used interchangeably in this paper.

The proposed method consists of a number of steps:

1. A linguist collects a relevant set of examples of inflected word forms from a grammar or a dictionary and lays them out as a table together with some grammatical information. The word forms that are collected are plain surface forms, see Section 17.2.
2. The linguist inserts boundary symbols manually between the morphs in the word forms, see Section 17.2.
3. An algorithm aligns the morphs belonging to each morpheme by inserting some zero symbols (Ø) as necessary. The letters in corresponding positions of the aligned allomorphs form the raw morphophonemes, see Section 17.3.
4. The linguist labels the raw morphophonemes implied by the alignment. Many raw morphophonemes are usable as morphophonemes as such. Some raw morphophonemes may be so similar that they can be unified by giving them the same label. In other cases, somewhat similar raw morphophonemes are better kept apart because the triggering conditions or alternation patterns are quite different, see Section 17.4.
5. The lexical representations of morphemes are mechanically established according to the alignment and the labeling of the morphophonemes,[2] see Section 17.4.
6. A set of positive examples is produced mechanically by combining the lexical representations and the aligned examples, see Section 17.4.
7. A tentative raw two-level rule is computed for each morphophoneme by using the set of examples and a set of negative examples produced for that morphophoneme. Such raw rules always work correctly with the given examples, but they may not be general enough to handle all other words and forms correctly, see Section 17.5.

[2] In (Beesley and Karttunen, 2003, p. 21) the importance of first setting up examples and only thereafter writing the rules is pointed out. It is not easy to establish the lexical representations in advance. The method presented here provides a method and guidelines for finding useful lexical representations in an objective manner.

8. Raw rules are refined into final rules by performing the following steps separately for each morphophoneme as defined above, see Section 17.6:
   (a) Tune the raw rule for this morphophoneme by generalizing its contexts as appropriate to simplify the rule.
   (b) Compile the rule into a finite-state transducer using a rule compiler and let a program check whether this rule accepts all positive examples.
   (c) Let a program produce the set of negative examples for this morphophoneme and check whether this rule rejects all these negative examples.
   (d) Proceed to the next rule if checks were successful. Improve the rule if some checks failed. Repeat with a revised version of the rule.

17.2 Examples and Morph Boundaries

Grammars and dictionaries often describe the inflection of words (i.e. declension and conjugation) by defining a number of classes of lexemes so that within each class the words are inflected in a similar way. The classes are presented using a selection of characteristic inflectional forms (so called principal parts) which determine the rest of the forms. In this way, all different forms of the stems and the affixes (i.e. their allomorphs) are explicitly included in the examples. Examples in this article are partly from the Reverse Dictionary of Modern Standard Finnish Tuomi (1980).

The information given in such sources is usually compact and useful. Such lists and tables are available for many languages which have a grammar or a dictionary, and they provide good starting point for building a morphophonological analyzer. Of course, one has to be prepared to augment the set of examples in order to cover all relevant morphophonemic alternations.

The linguist has to add some information into the plain example word forms in order to make the material suitable for the present method. Firstly, one must indicate what lexemes and what grammatical forms each example consists of. One could produce a two-column list where the left column has the inflected word form and the right column lists some names identifying the morphemes. Secondly, one must mark the boundaries between the morphs, e.g. as in Table 1.[3] Note

[3]Methods for automatically finding the places for the boundaries has been discussed at least in Theron and Cloete (1997). It is an interesting topic and would deserve more attention. The assumption that the boundaries are already placed makes the process much simpler.

katu	KATU
kadu+lla	KATU+ADE
kadu+i+lla	KATU+PL+ADE
katu+j+en	KATU+PL+GEN

TABLE 1 Segmented word forms with morpheme identifiers.

that only the morphemes that are actually present in the examples are segmented and listed by their name. In the examples, there is no overt morpheme for singular, thus neither a boundary nor an identifier for singular number is needed.

The dictionaries often give the inflectional information as a table so that each row represents a lexeme and each column represents a form. So, each cell in the table has one stem morph for that row and inflectional morphs for that column. Table 2 presents a small table of that type with appropriate column and row labels.

ID	STEM	STEM+ADE	STEM+PL+ADE	STEM+PL+GEN
KATU	katu	kadu+lla	kadu+i+lla	katu+j+en
HIIRI	hiiri	hiire+llä	hiir+i+llä	hiir+i+en
NIEMI	niemi	nieme+llä	niem+i+llä	niem+i+en
KALA	kala	kala+lla	kalo+i+lla	kalo+j+en
RIITA	riita	riida+lla	riido+i+lla	riito+j+en

TABLE 2 Example words as a table

One must include relevant examples of the phenomena to be described. Otherwise, it is unlikely that the rules will perform correctly when applied to further data. For Finnish, one ought to include example words not only for each inflectional class but also take care that there are examples of different types of consonant gradation and examples of stems and endings with front and back harmony. Typically, a few hundred examples are needed.

17.3 Phoneme by Phoneme Alignment of Allomorphs

From the segmented examples, one can automatically collect the different allomorphs (morphs representing the same morpheme). E.g. *katu*, *kadu* are the two stem allomorphs of the lexeme *KATU* and *lla* and *llä* are the allomorphs of *ADE*. In this step, the morphs for each morpheme will be aligned by adding zero symbols *Ø* where that is necessary or desirable to make the phonemes in corresponding positions match properly. It is assumed that consonant may not be aligned with vowels or vice versa, except that semivowels may correspond to some consonants or vowels. Otherwise, identical phonemes match perfectly, and similar ones better than those differing in several features.

One may align the allomorphs of each stem and each affix using a finite-state algorithm which weights the similarity of different phonemes and the inserted zeros, and finds the optimal places where to insert the zeros, see e.g. Koskenniemi (2017) for the method and an experiment with aligning Estonian noun stems. As a result, we have the morphs aligned letter by letter so that the correspondences of letters in the same position is optimal in some sense. From Table 2 we would get the morphs for each morpheme as in Table 3

`KATU:`	`katu, kadu`
`HIIRI:`	`hiiri, hiire, hiirØ`
`NIEMI:`	`niemi, nieme, niemØ`
`KALA:`	`kala, kalo`
`RIITA:`	`riita, riida, riido`
`ADE:`	`lla, llä`
`PL:`	`i, j`
`GEN:`	`en`

TABLE 3 Aligned morphs of the morphemes.

The linguist might check the result of the alignment in order to find mistakes in the examples or in the positioning of the boundaries. Boundaries in wrong positions would show up as excessive zeros in the alignment.

17.4 Morphophonemic Representations

The alignment was made so that the phonemes in each position correspond to each other as closely as possible, e.g. for `KATU`:

```
k a t u
k a d u
```

The first, second and fourth phonemes are identical in the two morphs. The third position contains `t` and `d` and gives rise for a morphophoneme. The only task here is to give a name for the morphophoneme, and here we call it `{td}`. Similarly, the illative morpheme `ILL` consists of aligned morphs where the third letter is either `a` or `ä` which is a morphophoneme which we decide to denote with `{aä}`. After such decisions, we have morphophonemic representations for all morphemes:

```
KATU:   k a {td} u
HIIRI:  h i i r {ieØ}
NIEMI:  n i e m {ieØ}
KALA:   k a l {ao}
RIITA:  r i i {td} {ao}
ADE:    l l {aä}
PL:     {ij}
GEN:    e n
```

After the alignment and the adding of some zero symbols, our examples consist of equal length morphemes. Thus, we can combine the aligned examples with the morphophonemic representations and get examples which consist of pairs, where each of them consists of either identical phonemes or a morphophoneme and a phoneme as in Table 4. Note that pairs of identical symbols are abbreviated, e.g. *k* stands for *k:k*.

```
k a {td}:t u
k a {td}:d u l l {aä}:a
k a {td}:d u {ij}:i l l {aä}:a
k a {td}:t u {ij}:j e n
h i i r {ieØ}:i
h i i r {ieØ}:e l l {aä}:ä
h i i r {ieØ}:Ø {ij}:i l l {aä}:ä
h i i r {ieØ}:Ø {ij}:i e n
n i e m {ieØ}:i
n i e m {ieØ}:e l l {aä}:ä
n i e m {ieØ}:Ø {ij}:i l l {aä}:ä
n i e m {ieØ}:Ø {ij}:i e n
k a l {ao}:a
k a l {ao}:a l l {aä}:a
k a l {ao}:o {ij}:i l l {aä}:a
k a l {ao}:o {ij}:j e n
r i i {td}:t {ao}:a
r i i {td}:d {ao}:a l l {aä}:a
r i i {td}:d {ao}:o {ij}:i l l {aä}:a
r i i {td}:t {ao}:o {ij}:j e n
```

TABLE 4 Examples as sequences of pairs.

17.5 Raw Rules

The method presented here resembles somewhat that of Theron and Cloete (1997). In that article, there is a brief survey of other relevant approaches, and see also (Koskenniemi, 2013a, pp. 159–161) for a short survey of discovering morphophonological rules.

The examples which have been augmented with morphophonemes are positive examples which all rules must accepted. For each morphophoneme-symbol pair, one can start with a set of rules where each example (where that pair occurs) forms a context. A program then checks step by step whether the contexts can be truncated by one or more symbols without any loss of accuracy within the set of examples.

Rules with truncated context still accept the positive examples, but they might fail to reject some cases which they are expected to reject. A good approximation for the negative examples for a morphophoneme can be produced from the original examples by substituting each occurrence of the morphophoneme by all possible pairs of the morphophoneme and subtracting the original examples from these corrupted examples. Suppose we are working on a morphophoneme {*ao*} which can correspond to *a* or *o*, and there are (positive) examples as in Table 5.

```
k a l {ao}:a
k a l {ao}:a l l {aä}:a
k a l {ao}:o {ij}:i l l {aä}:a
k a l {ao}:o {ij}:j e n
r i i {td}:t {ao}:a
r i i {td}:d {ao}:a l l {aä}:a
r i i {td}:d {ao}:o {ij}:i l l {aä}:a
r i i {td}:t {ao}:o {ij}:j e n
```

TABLE 5 Positive examples for {*ao*}.

The program starts with rules as in Table 6.

```
{ao}:a =>
        .#. k a l _ .#. ;
        .#. k a l _ l l {aä}:a .#. ;
        .#. r i i {td}:t _ .#. ;
        .#. r i i {td}:d _ l l {aä}:a .#. ;
{ao}:o =>
        .#. k a l _ {ij}:i l l {aä}:a .#. ;
        .#. k a l _ {ij}:j e n
        .#. r i i {td}:d _ {ij}:i l l {aä}:a .#. ;
        .#. r i i {td}:t _ {ij}:j e n
```

TABLE 6 Initial raw rules.

These rules clearly accept all positive examples but they would not accept any other words with the same inflection classes. Thus, the program tries to truncate the context parts in order to make the rules more general. In order to constrain the truncation, the program builds a set of negative examples for this morphophoneme. First, it creates all variations of the correspondences of the current morphophoneme as in Table 7.[4]

When the original correct examples are subtracted, the incorrect examples remain as in Table 8.

The program tries to truncate the left context parts which initially have a maximum length of four. By shortening them to three, two, one and zero lengths does not change the fact that even the truncated rules reject all of the negative examples of $\{ao\}$. Thus, we get a somewhat simpler raw rule as in Table 9.

We can eliminate identical copies of contexts and simplify the rule further as in Table 10.

When trying to truncate the right hand contexts, we notice that reducing the length to three, two and finally one, all negative examples are still rejected. There the program[5] stops and produces the following

[4]One might consider corrupting the correspondences for all morphophonemes, not only those of the current morphophoneme. A problem in that approach is that the raw rules for this morphophoneme would not discard all bad examples even if some other raw rule would. In that setup, the raw rules could not be processed separately.

[5]Producing the raw rules is simple, if we have the examples available in their morphophonemic form. No finite-state technology is necessary. One may represent both the positive and negative contexts as pairs of strings. Accepting negative examples is manifested as non-empty intersections of sets of truncated positive and negative contexts.

```
k a l {ao}:a
k a l {ao}:o
k a l {ao}:a l l {aä}:a
k a l {ao}:o l l {aä}:a
k a l {ao}:o {ij}:i l l {aä}:a
k a l {ao}:a {ij}:i l l {aä}:a
k a l {ao}:o {ij}:j e n
k a l {ao}:a {ij}:j e n
r i i {td}:t {ao}:a
r i i {td}:t {ao}:o
r i i {td}:d {ao}:a l l {aä}:a
r i i {td}:d {ao}:o l l {aä}:a
r i i {td}:d {ao}:o {ij}:i l l {aä}:a
r i i {td}:d {ao}:a {ij}:i l l {aä}:a
r i i {td}:t {ao}:o {ij}:j e n
r i i {td}:t {ao}:a {ij}:j e n
```

TABLE 7 Example with corrupted $\{ao\}$.

```
k a l {ao}:o
k a l {ao}:o l l {aä}:a
k a l {ao}:a {ij}:i l l {aä}:a
k a l {ao}:a {ij}:j e n
r i i {td}:t {ao}:o
r i i {td}:d {ao}:o l l {aä}:a
r i i {td}:d {ao}:a {ij}:i l l {aä}:a
r i i {td}:t {ao}:a {ij}:j e n
```

TABLE 8 True negative examples for $\{ao\}$.

```
{ao}:a =>
        _ .#. ;
        _ l l {aä}:a .#. ;
        _ .#. ;
        _ l l {aä}:a .#. ;
{ao}:o =>
        _ {ij}:i l l {aä}:a .#. ;
        _ {ij}:j e n
        _ {ij}:i l l {aä}:a .#. ;
        _ {ij}:j e n
```

TABLE 9 Left truncated raw rules for $\{ao\}$.

```
{ao}:a =>
        _ .#. ;
        _ l l {aä}:a .#. ;
{ao}:o =>
        _ {ij}:i l l {aä}:a .#. ;
        _ {ij}:j e n
```

TABLE 10 Left truncated raw rules for {*ao*} without duplicate contexts.

raw rules as in Table 11.

```
{ao}:a =>
        _ .#. ;
        _ l ;
{ao}:o =>
        _ {ij}:i ;
        _ {ij}:j ;
```

TABLE 11 Final raw rules {*ao*}.

One can readily see that the raw rules we get depend on the examples we have selected. If we would have had more case endings, we would have had more context parts in the first raw rule. The raw rules are not perfect but they serve as a useful starting points for refining them into a general and correct final rules.

The procedure succeeded well in the above example. Some other morphophonemes end up having plenty of long contexts. E.g. the raw rule for vowel harmony lists almost the full left context of each word where the morphophoneme occurs. Some linguistic knowledge is needed for refining such rules.

If the morphophoneme has free variation, one ought to prepare the collection of examples so that it contains examples of both variants. Otherwise the program cannot find useful raw rules. In general, free variation or optional alternations cause no problems when producing the raw rules. Raw rules are all right-arrow rules and in such cases, their contexts just happen overlap.

No raw left-arrow rules are proposed. Instead, right-arrow rules are proposed for all realizations of each morphophoneme. Often one of those right-arrow rules has an apparently complex contexts which often turns out to be a complement of the other context (or the union of other contexts). Note that in traditional two-level grammars, one uses mostly double-arrow rules.

17.6 Refining Raw Rules into Two-level Rules

The strategy in refining the raw rules is to generalize some contexts to accept also other similar examples. Each raw context consists of the left context and the right context and initially both of these parts consist of sequences of symbol pairs. The first step is to generalize the context by replacing some symbol pairs with expressions which stand for several distinct pairs of symbols as long as the rule rejects all negative examples. A common expression can represent a set of symbol pairs e.g. by using brackets parenthesis and vertical bars, e.g. [l|n|s|{Øt}:t]. Typically, vowels are combined with vowels and consonants with consonants. Generalizing one context may make it include some other contexts. Such other context are obviously redundant and they can be discarded.

The alphabets or lexical and surface characters and their feasible pairs are not explicitly declared in the present approach. The examples define them implicitly. Let *Pair* denote the expression which allows any of those feasible symbol pairs (but just one). In two-level rule expressions a colon *:* (separated by space from neighboring symbols) denotes *Pair*.

Quite often, one can generalize a symbol pair, e.g. {*ao*}*:a* into an expression that corresponds to all pairs which have the second symbol i.e. *a* as their second part. Let *:a* denote the set of such pairs and the set is defined as the composition *Pair .o. a*. Similarly, {*aä*}*:* denotes the set of all pairs which have e.g. {*aä*} as their first part and the set is defined as {*aä*} *.o. Pair*.

With a slightly larger set of examples one could get the following two raw rules:

```
{ao}:a =>
        _ {Øt}:Ø ;
        _ .#. ;
        _ {Øh}:Ø ;
        _ {Øt}:t ;
        _ {i}:i ;
{ao}:o =>
        _ {ij}:i ;
        _ {ij}:j ;
```

One could generalize the second rule into the following by substituting {*ij*}*:i* and {*ij*}*:j* both with {*ij*}*:* and removing the second context as an identical copy of the first:

```
{ao}:o => _ {ij}: ;
```

Because this context is not overlapping with the contexts in the first raw rule and there are just these two pairs, one can generalize the contexts of the first rule so that *{ao}:a* can occur anywhere except before *{ij}::*

```
{ao}:a /<= _ {ij}: ;
```

Together these two refined sub-rules results in a final double-arrow rule:

```
{ao}:o <=> _ {ij}: ;
```

Let us study a slightly more complicated raw rule which accounts for the form of the plural ending:

```
{ij}:j =>
    e _ e ;
    e _ {Øt}:Ø ;
    {iieØ}:e _ {Øt}:Ø ;
    {iiØeØ}:e _ {Øt}:Ø ;
    {ØieØ}:e _ {Øt}:Ø ;
    {ao}:o _ {Øt}:Ø ;
    o _ e ;
    {ao}:o _ e ;
    o _ {Øt}:Ø ;
    {aoØ}:o _ {Øt}:Ø ;
    u _ e ;
    u _ {Øt}:Ø ;
```

One could substitute the pairs with a vowel with surface vowels and remove duplicate contexts:

```
{ij}:j =>
    :e _ :e ;
    :e _ {Øt}:Ø ;
    :o _ :e ;
    :o _ {Øt}:Ø ;
    :u _ :e ;
    :u _ {Øt}:Ø ;
```

From the symbols of our original examples we have a vowels $Vowel = [a \mid e \mid i \mid \ldots]$, consonants $Consonant = [b \mid c \mid d \mid f \mid \ldots]$ and semivowels, e.g. $Glide = [j \mid \ldots]$. Two-level rules operate in the domain of symbol pairs. Therefore all relevant sets must be expressed using symbol pairs and as regular expressions which construct sets out of elementary pairs or other sets. As opposed to the traditional two-level formalism, the simplified model uses no definitions for the alphabet nor any character sets.

The the content of following sets are implicitly defined by the collection of examples:

1. The set *SurfV* consisting of symbol pairs that are called *surface vowels* is defined by the composition: *[[:] .o. Vowel]* (where *.o.* stands for composition operator as in the XFST regular expressions). Note that Ø was not a vowel and therefore pairs such as *{ieØ}:Ø* do not belong to *SurfV*.
2. The set *SurfC* consisting of symbol pairs that are called *surface consonants* is the composition: *[[:] .o. Consonant]*.
3. The set *Cons* consisting of symbol pairs which are called *morphophonemic or underlying consonants* is defined as *[SurfC.u .o. [:]]* (where *.u* is the unary operator for the input, upper or left side of the relation or transducer).

Using such sets one can still generalize the above rule without losing any accuracy:

```
{ij}:j =>
        SurfV _ SurfV ;
        SurfV _ {Øt}:Ø ;
```

This is how far one can go blindly without looking the examples and using some linguistic knowledge. One notes that *{tØ}:Ø* always precedes a vowel. So the final form for the rule could be:

```
{ij}:j => SurfV _ (:Ø) SurfV ;
```

17.7 Rule Compilation

Simplified two-level grammars can be compiled using the Xerox TWOLC or HFST-TWOLC rule compiler. The larger number of morphophonemes causes some more work when maintaining various sets and keeping them consistent with the increasing set of examples. Writing yet another two-level rule compiler is not difficult any more, especially because the finite-state calculus can now be used also from higher level languages like Python. In order to integrate the rule compiler with the processing of positive and negative examples the author wrote an entirely new two-level rule compiler using the formulas presented in Yli-Jyrä and Koskenniemi (2006). The linguist can compile and test single rules (or bunches of rules) against the examples and get immediate feedback after the compilation of each rule. The compiler reports any rejected positive examples or accepted negative ones.

The compiler is simpler than the Xerox TWOLC or HFST-TWOLC by omitting definitions of the alphabet and character sets. Only definitions are used. Four types of rules (=>, <=, <=> and / <=) are supported but neither *where* clauses nor conflict resolution is included. They are not needed when following the principles of simplified two-level grammars where one proceeds morphophoneme by morphophoneme and each morphophoneme gets its own rule(s).

One could expect that with such tools, even less experienced linguists could have a fairly smooth start and a reasonable learning curve when writing comprehensive morphological analyzers.

17.8 Testing Rules

Not only the writing of two-level rules is claimed to be difficult. Also the testing of them has been considered difficult: (Beesley and Karttunen, 2003, p. 13):

> A system of replace rules is relatively easy to check and modify because each rule can be applied individually. The output from one rule can be typed as input to the next rule and the effect of a whole cascade of replace rules can be checked step by step. When we move to TWOLC rules, however, the semantics of the rules demand that we conceive of them always as simultaneously applied constraints on the relation between the lexical language and the surface language. Because twolc rules are designed to apply in parallel, it is difficult to test them individually.

In the simplified model, the compilation of a rule and its testing are integrated so that after the compilation of a rule, the program tests the rule against all positive examples as a FST, then builds a FST which corresponds to the negative examples for this rule, and finally tests those against the compiled rule.

One can see that corrupting one morphophoneme at a time when producing negative examples might not be sufficient. Let us, thus, assume that the set of examples contains all possible surface correspondences that can be correctly generated out of the lexical representations of the examples. Under this assumption, all multiply corrupted negative examples will be rejected by some rule, i.e. if not a rule for every morphophoneme, anyway at least by some. Building such a multiply corrupted set of negative examples with finite-state calculus is easy, and the test can be made by intersecting that FST with all rules. Admittedly, this final check can be made only after we have all rules available.

There is also another way of making this total test. One can extract the lexical side of the examples and compose-intersect it with the combination of all rules. The surface side of that operation ought to be equivalent with the surface side of the original examples.

One can reduce the need for such testing of all rules simultaneously by choosing context expressions which refer to the lexical symbols alone, or sets which can be expressed as unions of such, e.g. use *Cons* rather than *SurfC*.

Epenthesis does not exist in a technical sense within simplified two-level grammars. The lexical representations never contain plain zeros. Where a linguist sees epenthesis, the method sees an alternation between zero and e.g. *e*. This ends up as a morphophoneme {*Øe*} which must be present in the lexicon entry of that morpheme.

One may speculate that the most crucial part of building a two-level rule grammar will be the selection and preparation of relevant examples. While a set of examples is established, the later steps such as the alignment and building raw and refined rules probably are fast and easy but they are likely to trigger revisions in the set of examples and in the positioning of the morph boundaries.

Moving any boundaries slightly left or right might cause significant changes in the morphophonemes and the results. Similarly important are the initial decisions about grammatical morphemes, e.g. whether one postulates one affix for a grammatical form or perhaps several if the morphs are substantially different. Comprehensive testing is probably needed in order to find guidelines for such decisions.

17.9 Future

One could establish a measure of the goodness of a collection of morphophonemes as they are produced by the insertion of the morph boundaries. This measure would evaluate the success of those steps. One could test different choices for the boundary positions and choose the best of them. Ultimately, this might lead to the automation of that step.

One could establish a measure of the complexity of individual rules on the basis of the number of contexts, the lengths of the context and naturalness of the sets present in the contexts. A measure could be used for guiding the refinement of raw rules more or less automatically. The total sum of such measures could be used as a further measure of the success of the whole grammar. It could also be used for deciding between the earlier alternative steps of the procedure including the naming or merging of morphophonemes.

A permissive full scale morphological analyzer for Early Modern Standard Finnish ought to be built. Such an analyzer could be applied to classical literature and 19th century newspapers etc. In addition and more importantly, it could be used as a component in comparing modern language and historical texts, and also when comparing Finnish with other Uralic languages, cf. Koskenniemi (2013a).

The simplified two-level model could be applied to build a morphological analyzer for Inari Saami, a language with particularly complex morphophonemics including vowel and consonant quantity alternations.

References

Beesley, Kenneth R. and Lauri Karttunen. 2003. *Two-Level Rule Compiler*. Xerox PARC. https://web.stanford.edu/~laurik/.book2software/.

Koskenniemi, Kimmo. 1983. *Two-level Morphology: A General Computational Model for Word-Form Recognition and Production*. No. 11 in Publications. University of Helsinki, Department of General Linguistics.

Koskenniemi, Kimmo. 2013a. Finite-state relations between two historically closely related languages. In *Proceedings of the workshop on computational historical linguistics at NODALIDA 2013; May 22-24; 2013; Oslo; Norway*, no. 87 in NEALT Proceedings Series 18, pages 53–53. Linköping University Electronic Press; Linköpings universitet.

Koskenniemi, Kimmo. 2013b. An informal discovery procedure for two-level rules. *Journal of Language Modelling* 1(1):155–188.

Koskenniemi, Kimmo. 2017. Aligning phonemes using finite-state methods. In *Proceedings of the 21st Nordic Conference on Computational Linguistics*, pages 56–64. Gothenburg, Sweden: Association for Computational Linguistics.

Theron, Pieter and Ian Cloete. 1997. Automatic acquisition of two-level morphological rules. In *Proceedings of the Fifth Conference on Applied Natural Language Processing*, ANLC '97, pages 103–110. Stroudsburg, PA, USA: Association for Computational Linguistics.

Tuomi, Tuomo. 1980. *Suomen kielen käänteissanakirja / Reverse Dictionary of Modern Standard Finnish*. No. 274 in Toimituksia. Suomalaisen Kirjallisuuden Seura, 2nd edn.

Yli-Jyrä, Anssi and Kimmo Koskenniemi. 2006. Compiling generalized two-level rules and grammars. In T. Salakoski, F. Ginter, S. Pyysalo, and T. Pahikkala, eds., *Advances in Natural Language Processing, Proceedings of the 5th International Conference on NLP, FinTAL 2006, Turku, Finland, August 2006*, vol. 4139 of *Lecture Notes in Computer Science*, pages 174–185. Springer.

18

Tokenization and Morphological Analysis for Malagasy*

MARY DALRYMPLE, MARIA LIAKATA, AND LISA MACKIE

18.1 Introduction

We present a tokenizer and finite-state morphological analyzer (Beesley and Karttunen, 2003) for Malagasy, based primarily on the discussion of Malagasy morphology in Keenan and Polinsky (2001) and Randriamasimanana (1986). Words in Malagasy are built from roots by means of a variety of morphological operations such as compounding, affixation, and reduplication. We analyze productive patterns of nominal and verbal morphology, describing genitive compounding and suffixation for nouns, and various derivational processes involving compounding and affixation for verbs. Our work offers a computational analysis of Malagasy morphology, and forms the basis of our computational grammar and lexicon of Malagasy within the framework of the PARGRAM project.

*Lauri Karttunen's seminal and influential work on finite-state morphology is the basis upon which our proposals are built. We are grateful to Lauri and to the late Charles Randriamasimanana for help in the development of the system. The Verb-Initial Grammars subproject of PARGRAM initiative was supported by a grant from the Economic and Social Research Council, UK (Project RES-000-23-0505).

This paper is a revised and updated version of Dalrymple et al. (2006). We thank the editors of the *International Journal of Computational Linguistics and Chinese Language Processing* for permission to publish this paper, and we are very grateful to Ron Kaplan and an anonymous reviewer for helpful comments on this version.

Tokens of Meaning: Papers in Honor of Lauri Karttunen.
Cleo Condoravdi and Tracy Holloway King (eds.).

18.2 Malagasy in the PARGRAM Project

Malagasy is an Austronesian language spoken by about seventeen million people on the island of Madagascar (Lewis et al., 2015). It was one of the target languages in the Verb-Initial Grammars subproject[1], a collaborative project within the PARGRAM initiative to develop computational lexicons and grammars of the verb-initial languages Malagasy and Welsh within the shared linguistic framework of Lexical Functional Grammar (Butt et al., 2002). As with the other grammar development projects within the PARGRAM initiative, our grammar is implemented within the XLE grammar development environment[2] (Crouch et al., 2008), which implements LFG theory. The project was a partnership between the University of Oxford and the University of Essex, and ran from 2004 to 2007.

The objective of the PARGRAM initiative is to develop parallel grammars for a range of different languages[3] using a shared linguistic framework and shared grammar writing techniques and technology. All members of the PARGRAM initiative strive for accurate, linguistically well-motivated grammatical analyses according to a common set of linguistic principles and assumptions: the grammars are "parallel" in the sense that differences among grammars reflect empirically demonstrable differences between languages, not theoretical disagreements or arbitrary decisions on the part of individual grammar writers. Within the space of these common goals, the projects within the PARGRAM umbrella have a range of practical motivations. For example, the English, German, and Japanese grammars aim for very broad and robust coverage for industrial applications. In contrast, although all of the PARGRAM grammars have the capacity to feed into large practical applications, the primary focus of attention in the Urdu and Hungarian projects is on theoretical linguistic issues: whether a coherent large-scale grammar and lexicon of these languages can be written in conformance with the linguistic assumptions common to all the PARGRAM grammars. The Welsh and Malagasy grammars fall at this end of the PARGRAM spectrum; the focus of the project was to produce coherent, internally consistent, linguistically well-motivated large-scale grammars and lexicons of these languages, following the common PARGRAM assumptions and using the common tools. As our grammar development work for Welsh and Malagasy progressed, we found that our analyses of these languages as exemplars of the verb-initial type share a good deal of

[1] `http://users.ox.ac.uk/~cpgl0015/pargram/`

[2] `http://www2.parc.com/isl/groups/nltt/xle/`

[3] For details see the main PARGRAM webpages, `http://pargram.b.uib.no/`.

commonality at the phrase structure level of analysis, creating theoretical synergy within the Verb-Initial Grammars subproject. However, the languages also differ in interesting ways: most importantly, Welsh is a VSO language, whereas Malagasy is VOS. Exploring differences between these languages has enhanced our understanding of the range of variation possible within the verb-initial type. A web-based interface to a number of PARGRAM grammars, including the Malagasy grammar, is available from the Norwegian INESS project webpages.[4]

Like all grammars within the PARGRAM project, our Malagasy grammar relies heavily on a computational component for morphological analysis. The need for automatic morphological analysis for Malagasy is acute, since entering into the lexicon each of the many hundreds of surface forms associated with a single verb, noun, or adjective root would miss important linguistic generalizations and impede progress in grammar development. For most of the other PARGRAM grammar development efforts, the task of building a morphological analyzer does not arise, since large-scale morphological analyzers already exist for many of the PARGRAM languages. For those grammars, the task is instead to incorporate these already existing morphological analyzers, which had often been originally created for shallow grammatical analysis or information retrieval applications, and which therefore tend not to contain detailed grammatical information and, indeed, to contain unnoticed mistakes, gaps, and inconsistencies. As discussed by Kaplan and Newman (1997), the challenge for PARGRAM projects incorporating a pre-existing morphological analyser is to overcome the problems arising from the lack of detailed grammatical information that these analyzers make available; Kaplan and Newman discuss ways of alleviating these problems by combining pre-existing analyzers with additional transducers to correct and augment their results.

The Malagasy grammar shares with a few of the other Pargram grammars (Arabic, Turkish, Urdu, Welsh) the opportunities and difficulties that arise when a morphological analyzer is developed in tandem with a syntactic grammar and lexicon. The advantages are that the morphological analyzer can be tuned to provide exactly the syntactic information that the grammar writer expects, and the division of labor between the morphology and syntax can be made in a well-motivated manner, rather than being imposed on the grammar writer by a pre-existing morphology component. The disadvantages are that the grammar development effort tends to be delayed if any problems arise in developing the morphological analyzer, and any changes to the

[4]`http://clarino.uib.no/iness/xle-web`

architecture of the morphological analyzer can necessitate overhauling the syntactic lexicon and grammar to restore compatibility between the two. In related work, Çetinoğlu and Oflazer (2006) explore some issues in developing a morphological analyzer for Turkish, an agglutinative, morphologically complex language, in the context of the PARGRAM project.

For our Malagasy morphological analyzer, we use the Xerox finite-state tools LEXC and XFST (Beesley and Karttunen, 2003), which are employed by many of the PARGRAM grammars. As with any finite-state morphological transducer, our Malagasy morphological analyzer is bidirectional: it can be used in grammatical analysis to produce morphologically analyzed input to a parser, or in generation to produce a surface form from a specification of lexical properties (Beesley and Karttunen, 2003). In the following, we often describe the tokenizer and morphological component in terms of analysis as opposed to generation of a surface string, but this is only for expository purposes.

18.3 Malagasy Morphology: An Overview

As Keenan and Polinsky (2001) note, there is very little inflectional morphology in Malagasy: there is no verb agreement or nominal inflection for agreement features, for example. Keenan and Polinsky (2001) analyze certain alternations in deictic forms and demonstratives as inflection, but since the forms involved belong to a small closed class, we treat them by listing them in the lexicon. The morphological analyzer described here handles many of the productive cases of nominal and verbal derivational morphology, consisting primarily of affixal verbal morphology and genitive compounding.

Besides verbal affixation and genitive compounding, Malagasy also exhibits root reduplication (Keenan and Razafimamonjy, 1998, Keenan and Polinsky, 2001), usually giving a diminished, attenuated, or pejorative meaning. In reduplication, the stressed syllable of the root and the material to its right are copied, and there is often adjustment to the final syllable of the full root and/or the initial syllable of the reduplicant along the lines described for genitive compounding on page 423, including dropping of the weak endings *ka/tra/na*. Keenan and Polinsky (2001) provide the following examples:

(1)

Root	Reduplicated root
bé 'big, numerous'	bèbé 'fairly big, numerous'
fótsy 'white'	fòtsifótsy 'whitish'
hadíno 'forget'	hadìnodíno 'forget a bit'
éntana 'baggage'	èntanéntana
fántatra 'known'	fàntapántatra
résaka 'conversation'	rèsadrésaka

Reduplicated roots participate in the same morphological processes as unreduplicated roots except for prefixation with the passive prefix *tafa-*, which is possible only with non-reduplicated roots.

It is well known that reduplication requires special treatment in a finite-state morphological model, and the COMPILE-REPLACE algorithm described by Beesley and Karttunen (2000, 2003) provides a means of treating these cases. We have implemented a preliminary treatment of Malagasy reduplication using the COMPILE-REPLACE algorithm, but in the following we leave aside discussion of reduplication, concentrating instead on our treatment of nominal and verbal morphology using the standard LEXC and XFST tools.

18.4 Lexical Information

Malagasy roots consist of one or more syllables. Roots with more or fewer than three syllables are regular or 'strong', and have penultimate stress if they are multisyllabic. Three-syllable roots take penultimate stress unless they end in one of the 'weak syllables' *na/ny, ka, tra*, in which case they usually receive antepenultimate stress and are called 'weak roots' (Keenan and Polinsky, 2001). Weak and strong roots behave differently in the processes we treat, and are listed separately in our morphological lexicon.

Our lexicon contains 2,446 roots, including 2,033 roots which form nouns, adjectives or verbs, 288 roots which form adjectives or verbs, and 125 roots which form only verbs. Indeclinable forms, including proper names, adverbs, some prepositions, and free pronouns, are not listed in the morphological lexicon, and so are passed through the morphological analyzer unchanged and treated by the syntax as unanalyzed tokens. We also allow for guessed roots, defined in terms of permissible root patterns; these roots are marked with the tag `+Guess`, and are permitted, though dispreferred, in syntactic analysis. In our treatment of guessed forms, we define Syllable (`Syll`) as in (2); this allows the definition of weak guessed roots as consisting of two syllables followed by one of the weak endings *na, ka, tra*. Strong guessed roots are then defined as consisting of one to four syllables, and subtracting the weak root patterns.

(2) Guessed roots:

```
Syll = [((Nasal) ([t|d]) Consonant) (Vowel) Vowel];
WeakKTRoot = [Syll^2 [[[T|t] [R|r]|[K|k]] [A|a]]];
WeakNRoot = [Syll^2 [[N|n] [A|a]]];
StrongRoot = [Syll^{1,4} - [WeakKTRoot|WeakNRoot]];
```

The definitions in (2) follow standard XFST notation, as defined by Beesley and Karttunen (2003): square brackets '[' ']' indicate grouping, parentheses '(' ')' indicate optionality, '|' indicates union or disjunction, '−' indicates subtraction of the second set of strings from the first set of strings, and '^' followed by a number or range of numbers indicates the number of times the immediately preceding string is repeated. Guessed roots participate in the same morphological processes as known roots, and interact with other components of the morphological analyzer in the same way: the LEXC and XFST components do not distinguish between known and guessed roots.

18.5 Genitive Compounding

Our analysis of verbal and nominal morphology closely follows the exposition of Keenan and Polinsky (2001). Nominal morphology consists mainly in the formation of genitive compounds, and the rules governing genitive compounding are quite regular and consistent. Genitive compounds are of the form Head+NP_{gen}, where the Head can be any of the following: noun (in which case NP_{gen} expresses the possessor), passive verb (NP_{gen} is the agent), preposition (NP_{gen} is the prepositional object) or adjective (NP_{gen} is an agent or indirect cause). In such expressions, the Head and NP_{gen} are concatenated, and the concatenation is regulated by rules referring to properties of the final syllable in the Head and the first syllable in NP_{gen}.

18.5.1 Target Phenomena

The following informal rules follow the treatment of Keenan and Polinsky (2001), and represent alternations in the final and first syllables of Head and NP_{gen} respectively. The hyphen, which sometimes alternates with apostrophe, is part of Malagasy orthography. The expressions 'C', 'C′' stand for consonants and 'V' and 'V′' stand for vowels, while 'S' denotes a stop consonant. The lowercase characters denote the corresponding letters. The expression to the left of the '+' sign stands for the final portion of the head word, consisting of some strong consonant 'C' and some vowel 'V' in the case of (1a) and (2) and some vowel 'V' followed by one of the weak endings *ka*, *tra*, *na* in (1b). The expression to the right of the '+' sign stands for the initial character of the NP_{gen}.

1. Head is weak, that is, ends in one of *ka*, *tra*, *na*
   (a) NP_{gen} begins with a vowel V:
   CV + V → C-V (remove final vowel in Head and concatenate)
   (b) NP_{gen} begins with a consonant C with corresponding stop consonant S:
      i. Head ends in *na*:
      Vna + C → Vn-S (S not bilabial), or
      Vna + C → Vm-S (S bilabial)
      ii. Head ends in *ka* or *tra*:
      V[ka|tra] + C → V-S
2. Head is not weak:
   (a) NP_{gen} begins with a vowel V′:
   CV + V′ → CVn-V′ (prefix *n-* and concatenate)
   (b) NP_{gen} begins with a consonant C′ with stop consonant S:
   CV + C′ → CVn-S (S not bilabial), or
   CV + C′ → CVm-S (S bilabial)

Keenan and Polinsky (2001) provide the following examples of genitive compounding with full nominal genitives:

(3)

Head	NP_{gen}	Compound	rule
tóngotra	akóho	tòngotr'akóho	(1a)
'foot'	'chicken'	'chicken's foot'	
órona	sáka	òron-tsáka	(1b.i)
'nose'	'cat'	'a cat's nose'	
táolana	bíby	tàolam-bíby	(1b.i)
'bones'	'animal'	'bones of animals'	
sóroka	záza	sòro-jáza	(1b.ii)
'shoulder'	'child'	'a child's shoulder'	
tóngotra	fàrafára	tòngo-pàrafára	(1b.ii)
'foot'	'bed'	'foot of a bed'	
tráno	andríana	trànon'andríana	(2a)
'house'	'noble'	'a noble's house'	
tráno	soavály	trànon-tsoavály	(2b)
'house'	'horse'	'house for horses'	
tráno	bíby	trànom-bíby	(2b)
'house'	'animal'	'house for animals'	

Similar to noun genitive expressions are pronominal suffixed genitives. If the Head ends in a non-weak syllable or *na*, then the GEN1 suffixes are attached to the Head. Otherwise, the GEN2 suffixes are attached.

(4)

	GEN1 suffix	GEN2 suffix
1SG	ko	o
2SG	nao	ao
3SG or PL	ny	ny
1PL.INCL	ntsika	tsika
1PL.EXCL	nay	ay
2PL	nareo	areo

Keenan and Polinsky (2001) provide the following examples of pronominal genitive compounding:[5]

(5)

	GEN1 tráno 'house'	GEN2 sóroka 'shoulder'	GEN2 tóngotra 'foot'
1SG	tránoko	sóroko	tóngotro
2SG	tranonáo	sorokáo	tongotráo
3SG or PL	tránony	sórony	tóngony
1PL.INCL	tranontsíka	sorotsíka	tongotsíka
1PL.EXCL	tranonáy	sorokáy	tongotráy
2PL		sorokaréo	tongotraréo

18.5.2 Implementation

The XLE grammar development environment requires a tokenizer and morphological analyzer for the language being analyzed, and allows the specification of a sequence of alternative morphological analyzers to be used when analysis with the first alternative fails. Our implementation relies on the Xerox finite-state calculus, with a tokenizer written in XFST, a lexicon written in LEXC, and more general orthographic and phonological rules written in XFST (Beesley and Karttunen, 2003). The output of the morphological analyzer is a lemma (generally the root form) and a set of morphological tags, which is the input to syntactic analysis; this obviates the need for listing each surface form separately in the syntactic lexicon. Instead, the syntactic component contains information about the syntactic content and behavior of each lemma and morphological tag, as analyzed by the morphological component. We discuss the interface between XLE and the morphological component and display some example parses in Section 18.7.

Tokenization

XLE expects a string as input, which is first tokenized according to the rules of the tokenizer for the language being analyzed. Each token

[5]Keenan and Polinsky (2001) do not list the second-person plural possessor form for *tráno* 'house'.

is then individually passed to the morphological analyzer for finite-state morphological analysis. Most grammars within the PARGRAM initiative employ at least two morphological analyzers: an analyzer for known forms, and a guesser for forms that fail to be analyzed by the known-form analyzer. Following this paradigm, our known-form transducer and guesser are extracted separately, and applied to the output of the tokenizer in sequence; only forms that fail to obtain an analysis with the known-form analyzer are passed to the guesser.

In most cases, tokenization in Malagasy is straightforward, with tokens usually delimited by whitespace. For the sentence *Hanketo izy.* 'he will come here', the tokenizer produces the following result, where TB indicates a token boundary:

(6) hanketo TB izy TB .

The tokenizer (optionally) decapitalizes the first word of the sentence, inserts token boundaries at spaces, and separates punctuation by a token boundary. Each token is then passed separately to the morphological analyzer for analysis.

In the case of non-pronominal genitive compounding, the situation is more complex. The compound form *akanjon-olona* 'a person's clothes' consists of two noun roots *akanjo* 'clothes' and *olona* 'person', and has the following structure:

(7) akanjon-olona
akanjo (epenthetic 'n'; cf. 2a above) (compound boundary) olona

In our original treatment of non-pronominal genitive compounding, this form was treated as a single token, and was handled by the morphological analyzer (Dalrymple et al., 2005). However, this approach interacted badly with the standard configuration of XLE grammars, where the known-form analyzer and guesser are separate transducers, applied in sequence. If both roots are known, both can be analyzed by the known-form transducer; however, if one root is unknown, the entire compound fails to be recognized by the known-form analyzer. This means that the entire compound must be handled by the guesser, even if one of the roots is known. This undesirable result has led us to revise the treatment of non-pronominal genitive compounds, moving most of the work to the tokenizer.

In our current treatment, the tokenizer 'undoes' the effects of the compounding rules given above, proposing one or more underlying forms for analysis by the morphological component. For example, the compound form *akanjon-olona* is tokenized as follows:

(8) `akanjo TB +GEN+ TB olona`

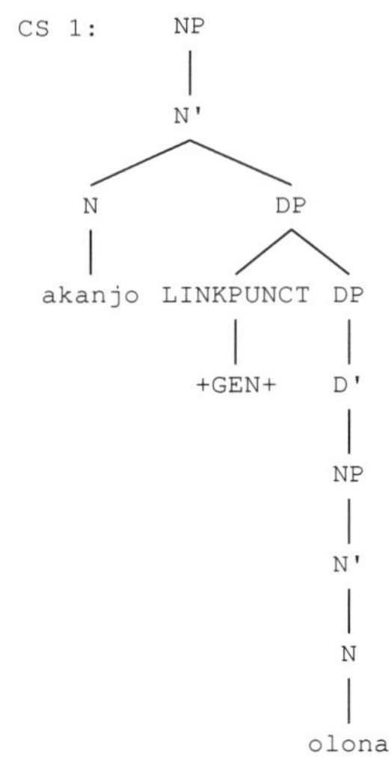

FIGURE 1 Phrase structure tree for *akanjon-olona*.

The root *akanjo* is a three-syllable root; the hypothetical root *akanjona* would have four syllables, which is impossible for a weak root. For this reason, rule 1 above, which requires that Head is a weak root, does not apply. Rule 2a covers the case in which the second member of the compound begins with a vowel; "undoing" rule 2a entails removing the epenthetic *n* inserted after the Head, producing *akanjo.* The compound boundary is treated as a separate token, represented by the special symbol `+GEN+`, to signal to the syntactic analysis component that genitive compounding has taken place. The phrase structure tree that is produced for *akanjon-olona* is shown in Figure 1, in which the leaves of the tree correspond to the tokens produced by the tokenizer.

Some forms can be tokenized in more than one way. For example, the compound *volon-dRabe* 'Rabe's month'/'Rabe's money' is ambiguous (Keenan and Polinsky, 2001):

1. Head is weak, reconstructed by the tokenizer as *volana* 'month', with Rule 1a requiring removal of the final vowel; or
2. Head is strong, reconstructed by the tokenizer as *vola* 'money', with Rule 2a requiring insertion of *-n*

After tokenization, the morphological analyzer is presented with all possible forms resulting from 'undoing' the compounding rules. Analysis proceeds as for the simple cases, with forms recognized by the known-form analyzer given preference in syntactic analysis over hypothetical forms analyzed by the guesser.

Our current treatment of genitive compounding relies on the presence of the hyphen or apostrophe to signal the compound boundary. In a small minority of cases, however, genitive compounding involves only concatenation of roots, and is not signaled by special punctuation. We have left the treatment of these forms for future work, since we are unsure how the treatment of such forms will interact with the guesser: almost any simple form can be given a spurious analysis as a compound composed of two hypothetical, guessed roots.

Pronominal Genitives

Pronominal genitive compounds, on the other hand, are best treated by the morphological analysis component, which we now describe. The LEXC lexicon is a finite-state transducer which specifies a relation between an Upper 'lexical' string and a Lower 'surface' string for a form (Beesley and Karttunen, 2003). Roots and affixes are organized into sublexicons according to their phonological and prosodic properties, e.g. whether the root is weak or strong. The lexicon also specifies possibilities for transitions when a particular form is encountered.

For example, the noun root *akanjo* 'clothes' is listed in the Noun sublexicon with continuation class `Nstrong`, meaning that it takes the strong root suffixes listed in the `Nstrong` sublexicon. The `Nstrong` sublexicon adds the `+Noun` tag to the lexical side of the transducer, and permits the form to terminate with no suffixation, or alternatively allows genitive suffixation. Thus, the transducer relates the surface string, the unsuffixed noun *akanjo*, to the morphologically analyzed lexical string which forms the input to syntactic analysis:

(9) LEXC transducer:
Lexical: `akanjo +Noun`
Surface: `akanjo`
'clothes'

The related form *akanjoko* 'my clothes' involves pronominal genitive suffixation; the `NStrong` sublexicon relates the first person singular genitive suffix *ko* on the surface side to the tag `+1SgGen` on the lexical side:

(10) LEXC transducer:
Lexical: `akanjo +Noun +1SgGen`
Surface: `akanjoko`
'my clothes'

Here, the LEXC lexicon on its own is sufficient for analysis of the combination of the root *akanjo* and the pronominal genitive suffix *-ko*.

18.6 Verbal Morphology

In many cases, we also need a set of XFST rules to cater for phonological and orthographic alternations induced by morphological operations. The XFST rules define an XFST transducer, which is composed with the LEXC transducer in full morphological analysis (Karttunen et al., 1992). The XFST transducer is controlled by diacritics introduced by LEXC, orthographically distinguished by use of a carat '^'. These diacritics appear neither in the surface string nor in the lemma and morphological tags that are provided to the syntactic component, but are crucial in the definition of the XFST rules, as we now describe.

18.6.1 Target Phenomena

Malagasy exhibits rich and complex verbal morphology (Randriamasimanana, 1986, Keenan and Polinsky, 2001). Verbs are classified according to the case of their arguments: nominative, accusative and genitive. Verbs which take a genitive complement are non-active verbs, a category which includes passive verbs and circumstantial verbs. Passive verbs are formed in three different ways, each corresponding to different semantics. The following discussion follows Keenan and Polinsky (2001), though simplifying somewhat.

The schematic relation for verbal patterns encoded by the LEXC transducer is given in Figure 2. The first line in each category represents the lexical side of the LEXC transducer, and the second line represents the surface side, which is input to the XFST transducer. Ellipses (...) represent surface strings of varying form: for example, ROOT is realized as any root form, and GEN is realized as any of the pronominal genitive suffixes in (4). ROOTTYPE is a diacritic encoding the type of the root, one of `^StrongRoot`, `^WeakKTRoot` or `^WeakNRoot`; this information is needed by the XFST rules to control certain morphological alternations. The LEXC transducer is composed with the XFST transducer, which performs necessary adjustments as the morphemes are concatenated.

The first category defined in Figure 2 is root passives: that is, roots which are passive verbs. These refer more to the result than the process. The pattern for passive roots is very similar to patterns for noun roots with optional pronominal genitive suffixation:

(11)

Root passive	With genitive suffix
araka 'be followed'	arany 'be followed by him/them'

The largest category of passive verbs are suffix passives. These are formed by the suffixation of *ina* or *ana* to a root, which is usually

Passive roots

```
ROOT  +Verb     (GEN)
...   ROOTTYPE  ...
```

Suffix passives

```
TENSE (Caus) ROOT +Verb     (C)VnaPass (GEN|IMP)
...     amp   ... ROOTTYPE (C)ina/ana  ...
```

Prefix passives

```
VTPass    ROOT +Verb     (GEN|IMP)
voa/tafa  ...  ROOTTYPE  ...
```

Active Verbs

```
(TENSE|NOM) [(Recip)(Caus)][ACTIVE PassROOT|NullPrefROOT]
 ...           if     amp    i/an   ...

+Verb    (IMP)
ROOTTYPE ...
```

Circumstantial form

```
TENSE (Caus)(ACTIVE) ROOT +Verb     (C)VnaPass
...     amp   i/an    ... ROOTTYPE (C)ina/ana
```

FIGURE 2 Verbal patterns in the LEXC transducer.

preceded by a root-dependent consonant C epenthesis. They can appear with a past or future tense prefix, represented as TENSE, optionally followed by a causal prefix *amp*. This form can also undergo genitive compounding or imperative suffixation. Keenan and Polinsky (2001) provide the following examples of suffix passives; these examples do not contain a TENSE prefix or any additional suffixation:

(12)

Root	Suffix passive	
áraka 'follow'	aráhina 'be followed'	$k \to h$, *-ina*
rákotra 'cover'	rakófana 'be covered'	$tr \to f$, *-ana*
tóhy 'continue'	tohízina 'be continued'	$\emptyset \to z$, *-ina*

A third type of passive is prefix passives. These are formed by prefixing a root with any of *a*, *voa*, *tafa*. Passives in *a* refer to the process rather than the result, and usually their subject functions as an instrument. The imperative is formed by prefixing with *a* and adding the corresponding passive imperative suffix. Passives in *voa/tafa* refer to the end result rather than the process and have a perfective meaning. *Voa/tafa* passives may not be prefixed by a tense prefix, while *a* passives do take a tense prefix. Keenan and Polinsky (2001) provide the following examples of prefix passives:

(13) Prefix passive:

Root	Prefix passive	
tolotra 'offer'	atolotra 'be offered'	*a*
arina 'put upright'	tafarina 'get up'	*tafa*
araka 'follow'	voaraka 'be followed'	*voa*

There are a few active verb roots, but the majority of active verbs are derived from roots by means of the active prefixes *i, an*. Active verbs can be marked for tense via a tense prefix TENSE (distinguishing past, present, and future). Genitive suffixing is not allowed, but the formation of imperatives is possible: present tense (*m-*) actives take suffix *a*, where consonant mutation and epenthesis (-*(C)a*) apply. If no epenthetic consonant intervenes, they fuse the -*a* imperative with root final -*a*. They can also receive a prefix for causality and reciprocation. The active verb roots may also appear with causative *ank-/amp-*.

In the circumstantial form of a verb, an oblique argument or adjunct of an active verb is made the subject. The circumstantial is built from roots prefixed by primary active affixes *i, an* and, possibly, secondary causative affixes *ank-, amp-* by means of the suffixation -*Cana*, where *C* is the root-specific epenthetic consonant mentioned above in the context of suffix passives. Tense is marked in the same way as for suffix passives. Keenan and Polinsky (2001) provide the following examples of present active forms and circumstantials:

(14)

Root	Present active	Circumstantial
omé	manomé 'gives'	anomézana
sóratra	manóratra 'writes'	anorátana
íla	míla 'needs'	ilána
ánatra	miánatra 'studies'	ianárana
tóhy	mitóhy 'continues'	itohízanax

18.6.2 Implementation

As discussed above, the LEXC lexicons contain information about subclasses of individual roots as well as more general structural information regarding verb forms. For example, verbs are formed on the basis of a tense prefix sublexicon which contains separate past, present and future prefixes, including a `^TNS^` tag to control morphological alternations with overt tense prefixes. In the following, 0 represents the empty string.

```
LEXICON Tense
PresentTense+:0          Secondary;
PastTense+:no^TNS^       Secondary;
FutureTense+:ho^TNS^     Secondary;
```

```
PresentTense+:0          Vroot;
PastTense+:no^TNS^       Vroot;
FutureTense+:ho^TNS^     Vroot;
```

The lexicon VPassRoot represents the passive verbs: inherently passive roots, or guessed passive verbs ending in either a strong or weak syllable. In the compilation step, the transducer for guessed roots is extracted separately from the transducer for known roots, since XLE requires application of the known root transducer and the guessed root transducer in sequence. However, since known and guessed roots exhibit the same morphological patterns, they are defined together in the LEXC lexicons.

```
LEXICON VPassRoot
PassiveRoot ;
<StrongRoot %+Guess:0>  StrongSuff ; ! guessed Strong root
<WeakKTRoot %+Guess:0>  KTWeak ; ! guessed Weak KT root
<WeakNRoot %+Guess:0>   NWeak ; ! guessed Weak N root
```

Roots are listed in the lexicon with information about the continuation classes of their suffixes:

```
LEXICON PassiveRoot
araka          WeakSuff; ! be followed
fantatra       TR2RWeak; ! be known
```

In this example *araka* is a passive root; its continuation class indicates that it is a member of the class of morphologically weak roots. *Fantatra* is a weak passive root with final syllable *tra*, where the TR2RWeak continuation class indicates that the *tra* suffix for this root is replaced with *r* during passive suffixation or the formation of imperatives. Thus, the passive form corresponding to *fantatra* is *fantarina*.

As above, the XFST rules deal with surface phenomena such as syllable deletion and consonant and vowel epenthesis, which take place during affixation. In the previous example, the continuation class TR2RWeak is used with roots where the weak final root syllable *tra* is converted to *r* during passive suffixation or the formation of imperatives. Other weak roots convert *tra* to one of a number of other consonants which must be lexically specified for each root. One way of handling these alternations would be to have a continuation class for each of the possible combinations of suffixes and final syllables of roots. Thus, even though there are only two passive suffixes *ina/ana*, we would need separate continuation classes for the formation of passives for weak roots ending in *tra* where *tra* is transformed to *r*, *f*, *t*, or other consonants.

However, this would result in an over-sized, untidy lexicon. Instead, we keep a small number of continuation classes corresponding to possible suffixes, and signal the final syllable root transformations by means of tags referenced by rules of the XFST transducer. These tags provide the context for the application of XFST rules for the various cases of epenthesis, deletion and transformation. For instance, the `TR2RWeak` continuation class is defined in the following way:

```
LEXICON TR2RWeak
+Verb:^WeakKTRoot         WeakKTEnding ;
+Verb:^WeakKTRoot^Ftr2r   Suffixes ;
```

The feature `^Ftr2r` is referenced by the XFST rule in (15), which transforms *tra* to *r* if the *tra* syllable is followed by the feature `^Ftr2r`.

(15) `[t r a]` $\rightarrow$ `r` | _ `^Ftr2r`

This XFST rule applies to the underlying grammatical form, the output of LEXC. Formally, it resembles a standard context-sensitive phrase structure rule: the expression to the left of the arrow is replaced by the expression to the right of the arrow in a certain context. The context of application is separated from the rule by double bars, '|'. Here, the sequence *'tra'* is replaced by *'r'* in the context immediately preceding the tag `^Ftr2r`. This rule applies after removal of the tag `^WeakKTRoot`, which separates the root from the `^Ftr2r` tag in the surface string of the LEXC transducer. Directly after the application of this rule, the rule to remove the tag `^Ftr2r` applies, preventing its appearance in the surface string and its interference with the application of other rules. Similar rules cater for alternations with prefixation, passive and imperative formation.

Features are an efficient way of modeling local morphological dependencies and alternations. However, in the morphology of Malagasy verbs there are long distance dependencies which cannot be modeled by standard FST techniques. For instance, there are roots which can form the passive in either *ana* or *ina* but not both. Thus, we want *fantarina* and not *fantarana* to be recognized as the correct passive form of *fantatra*. This is a problem both in recognition and generation as we do not want our rules to accept or generate incorrect forms. A tag could be added to the root *fantatra* to exclude the passive formation in *ana*, but the tag may be separated from the position of *ina/ana* by other morphemes and tags during passive formation.

For example, if we decided to implement the requirement for passive suffixation in *-ina* rather than *-ana* as a feature, the lexical entry for *fantatra* in the lexicon would be accompanied by a feature `^Fpassi` on the surface level as below. In the following hypothetical lexicon, the root and its associated tags are grouped together by angled brackets '<' and '>' as is standard in LEXC:

```
LEXICON OtherRoot
<{fantatra} 0:^Fpassi> TR2RWeak;
```

However, this means that when the features `^WeakKTRoot^Ftr2r` are added by the continuation class `TR2RWeak`, they are not immediately next to the root, but rather ^Fpassi stands in the way. As a result the rule (15) above for the transformation of the weak syllable *-tra* to *-r*, which precedes passive suffixation, cannot apply.

Fortunately, XFST allows for the treatment of such dependencies by the use of flag diacritics, non-FST handles which can store information that is not compiled into the FST. This information is used at runtime, when a certain phrase is being analyzed or generated. We use two sorts of flag diacritics: U-type (where 'U' stands for "unification"), and R-type (where 'R' stands for "requires"). Importantly, the use of flag diacritics does not change the formal power of the system (Karttunen, 2006). In our Malagasy morphological analyzer, we use flag diacritics to store root-specific information: therefore, they are entered together with the lexical entry for the root. Because they do not take effect until the interpretation phase, they do not interfere with the XFST rules. Thus, the lexical entry for *fantatra* in the previous section becomes:

```
LEXICON OtherRoot
<{fantatra} @U.PASS.I@> TR2RWeak;
```

This information uses a U-type flag diacritic, here represented as `@U.PASS.I@`, to associate the feature PASS with the value I for this root. This feature ensures that the root *fantatra* takes a passive in *ina* and not in *ana*. This is coupled with matching flag diacritics for the passive suffixes:

```
LEXICON PassaSuff
<+Passa:a 0:n 0:a @U.PASS.A@>   #;

LEXICON PassiSuff
<+Passi:i 0:n 0:a @U.PASS.I@>  #;
```

The passive suffix *ina* is associated with the flag diacritic `@U.PASS.I@`, which is defined as above as specifying the value I for the feature PASS, while the suffix *ana* is associated with the flag diacritic `@U.PASS.A@` specifying the value A for the same feature. Whenever flag diacritics meet, they must match; therefore the form *fantarana* is not accepted, as the flag diacritics of *ana* do not match the flag diacritics of *fantatra*.

We also make use of R-type flag diacritics to model long distance dependencies between prefixes and suffixes. R-type flag diacritics are similar in structure to U-type diacritics, and are specified in the same way; crucially, however, R-type diacritics check that a certain value of a feature has been previously set by another flag diacritic specification. For example, Malagasy verbs may be formed from roots which are lexically nouns or adjectives. Since this is a very general fact about Malagasy, we do not list every root form in both the noun lexicon and the verb lexicon. Nevertheless, we must ensure that the prefixes that appear with a root are compatible with its suffixes, since if a root appears with verbal prefixes, it allows verbal and not nominal suffixes.

We handle this by setting the flag `POS` (part of speech) to `VERB` or `NOUN` at the beginning of the word, depending on what prefixes have been encountered. We then check that the suffixes that appear with a root are compatible with its prefixes. For example, the strong noun root *halatra* 'theft' is specified with the continuation class `NStrong`, which allows either the `+Noun` tag and noun suffixes with the continuation class `NStrongEnding`, or the `+Verb` tag and verbal suffixes with the continuation class `VStrongEnding`. `NStrongEnding` uses an R-type flag diacritic to check that the flag diacritic `POS` has been set to `NOUN`, preventing noun suffixes from appearing with verb prefixes; similarly, the `VStrongEnding` lexicon checks that the flag `POS` is set to `VERB`.

The continuation classes, together with the rules and flag diacritics, give a general model for the construction of different verb forms. In our analysis of Malagasy verbal morphology, there are many exceptions to be taken into account which render the task of modeling verb morphology non-trivial. For instance, a root may not accept a certain affix; this can be handled by more sophisticated flag diacritics which govern the permissible affixes that each root can accept. Our analyzer uses flags encoding 9 features with various values for the different affixes, which can be negatively specified by particular roots to disallow particular affixes or affix combinations.

As noted by Beesley and Karttunen (2003), more general cases can be ruled out by means of filters, which are sets of rules that apply on the lexical level – that is, on the lexical side of the LEXC transducer. Such filters are used to prevent groups of continuation classes from combining with a certain affix, or to merge together morphological information. For instance, the lexical tag `+Passa` indicates that we have a passive form in *ana*, which can signal either a suffix passive or a circumstantial form. However, if it is preceded by the tag `ActiveAN+`, it is unambiguously a circumstantial form. Our treatment incorporates 5 filters disallowing certain affix combinations for all roots. Encoding such interactions in the morphological analyzer provides important constraints for syntactic analysis.

18.7 Grammatical Outputs

In syntactic analysis, the XLE grammar development environment makes crucial use of both the lexical and surface sides of the morphological analyzer. The surface form is treated as a single leaf node of the tree in the display of the phrasal analysis. XLE also requires the specification of a set of sublexical grammar rules for analysis of the lemma and tags, each of which is associated with a functional description specifying its grammatical contribution. Example (10), repeated here, shows the lexical and surface side of the transducer for the form *akanjo* 'my clothes', composed of the noun root *akanjo* with a pronominal genitive suffix.

(16) Lexical: **akanjo +Noun +1SgGen**
Surface: **akanjoko**
'my clothes'

The standard LFG phrase structure tree for *akanjoko* is shown on the left side of Figure 3: the leaf node in this tree is the surface form *akanjoko*. The lexical side of the transducer also plays a crucial analytic role, since the lemma and morphological tags are analyzed by sublexical phrase structure rules, and information associated with them is assembled to form the syntactic and semantic constraints contributed by *akanjoko*. XLE provides a special mode for display of this sublexical structure: the right side of Figure 3 shows the sublexical structure and sublexical rules for *akanjoko*, with the lemma and tags as leaves of the sublexical tree.

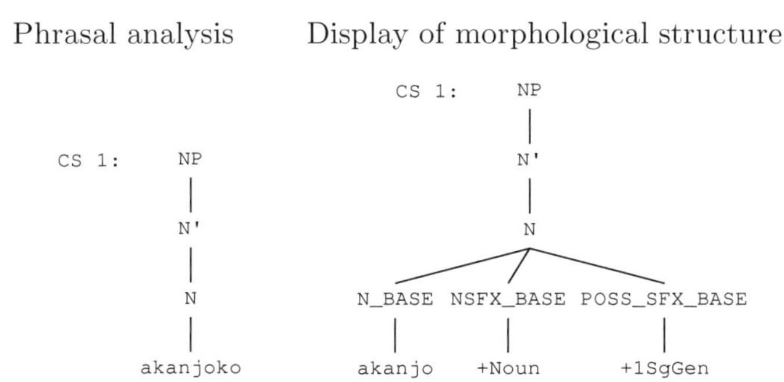

FIGURE 3 Analysis of *akanjoko*.

The phrase structure analysis of the full sentence in (17) is shown in

Figure 4, and Figure 5 displays the morphological structure (lemmas and tags) for the verb *nindrana* 'borrowed' and *vola* 'money'.

(17)

nindrana	vola	i	Paoly
n-indrana	vola	i	Paoly
PAST-borrow	money	DET	Paul

'Paul borrowed (some) money.'

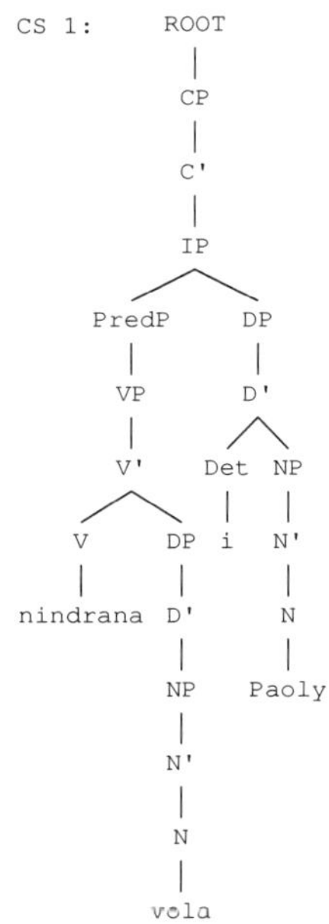

FIGURE 4 Analysis of *nindrana vola i Paoly* 'Paul borrowed some money'.

18.8 Conclusion

We have described a computational implementation of the productive nominal and verbal morphology of Malagasy, concentrating on our treatment of genitive compounding and affixal verb morphology. Our approach closely follows the analysis of Keenan and Polinsky (2001) and realizes the aforementioned morphological processes in terms of LEXC continuation classes, associated with groups of productive roots and general structural information, and general orthographic and phonetic rules implemented as XFST rules.

Our morphological analyzer provides a solid basis for our syntactic lexicon and grammar of Malagasy. The syntactic lexicon has been

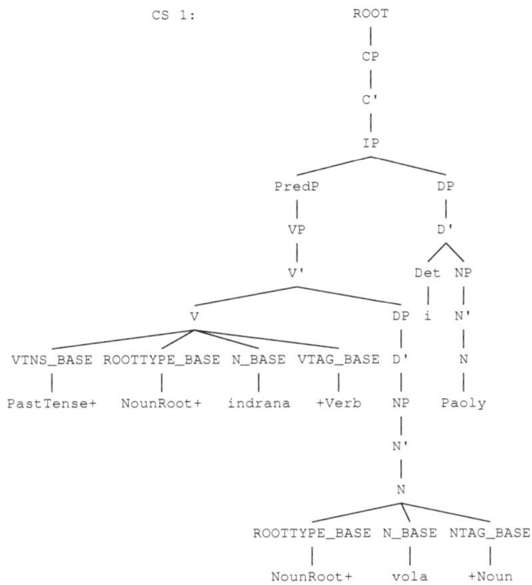

FIGURE 5 Analysis of *nindrana vola i Paoly* showing morphological analysis of *nindrana* and *vola*.

populated with the lemmas and tags generated by the morphological analyzer, and accepts these forms as input to syntactic analysis. We have encoded the syntactic contributions of each affix as well as default syntactic contributions for large classes of verb, noun, and adjective roots, together with refining the lexicon to account for subclasses of roots with exceptional, non-default behavior. Our Malagasy grammar comprises 22 preterminal categories appearing on the left-hand side of phrase-structure rules with regular-expression right-hand sides covering a number of possible expansions.

References

Beesley, Kenneth R. and Lauri Karttunen. 2000. Finite-state non-concatenative morphotactics. In *Proceedings of the Fifth Workshop of the ACL Special Interest Group in Computational Phonology (SIGPHON-2000)*, pages 1–12. Association for Computational Linguistics.

Beesley, Kenneth R. and Lauri Karttunen. 2003. *Finite-State Morphology*. Stanford: CSLI Publications.

Butt, Miriam, Helge Dyvik, Tracy Holloway King, Hiroshi Masuichi, and Christian Rohrer. 2002. The Parallel Grammar Project. In *Proceedings of the International Conference on Computational Linguistics*

(COLING2002) Workshop on Grammar Engineering and Evaluation, pages 1–7. International Committee on Computational Linguistics, Taipei.

Çetinoğlu, Özlem and Kemal Oflazer. 2006. Morphology-syntax interface for Turkish LFG. In *Proceedings of the 21st International Conference on Computational Linguistics and 44th Annual Meeting of the ACL*. Association for Computational Linguistics, Sydney.

Crouch, Dick, Mary Dalrymple, Ronald M. Kaplan, Tracy Holloway King, John T. Maxwell, III, and Paula S. Newman. 2008. *XLE Documentation*. Palo Alto Research Center, Palo Alto, CA.

Dalrymple, Mary, Maria Liakata, and Lisa Mackie. 2005. A two-level morphology of Malagasy. In *19th Pacific Asia Conference on Language, Information and Computation*. PACLIC Steering Committee, Taipei.

Dalrymple, Mary, Maria Liakata, and Lisa Mackie. 2006. Tokenization and morphological analysis for Malagasy. *International Journal of Computational Linguistics and Chinese Language Processing* 11(4):315–332.

Kaplan, Ronald M. and Paula Newman. 1997. Lexical resource reconciliation in the Xerox Linguistic Environment. In D. Estival, A. Lavelli, K. Netter, and F. Pianesi, eds., *Computational Environments For Grammar Development and Linguistic Engineering*, pages 54–61. Proceedings of a workshop sponsored by the Association for Computational Linguistics, Madrid, Spain, July 1997.

Karttunen, Lauri. 2006. Numbers and Finnish numerals. *SKY Journal of Linguistics* 19:407–421.

Karttunen, Lauri, Ronald M. Kaplan, and Annie Zaenen. 1992. Two-level morphology with composition. In *Proceedings of the International Conference on Computational Linguistics (COLING92)*. International Committee on Computational Linguistics, Nantes.

Keenan, Edward L. and Maria Polinsky. 2001. Malagasy. In A. Spencer and A. M. Zwicky, eds., *The Handbook of Morphology*, pages 563–623. Oxford: Blackwell.

Keenan, Edward L. and Jean Paulin Razafimamonjy. 1998. Reduplication in Malagasy. In *The Structure of Malagasy III*, UCLA Working Papers in Syntax and Semantics. Department of Linguistics, UCLA, Los Angeles.

Lewis, M. Paul, Gary F. Simons, and Charles D. Fennig. 2015. *Ethnologue: Languages of the World*. SIL International. 18th Edition.

Randriamasimanana, Charles. 1986. *The Causatives of Malagasy*. Honolulu: University of Hawai'i Press.

19

Urdu Morphology and Beyond: Why Grammars Should not Live without Finite-State Methods

TINA BÖGEL, MIRIAM BUTT, AND TRACY HOLLOWAY KING

19.1 Introduction

The first thing I ever said to Lauri Karttunen was: "Nice to meet you. I fell in love with your FSM book". He blushed. And smiled.

This paper examines the role that Finite State Transducers (FST) play in the Urdu ParGram grammar.[1] Like most of the ParGram grammars, the Urdu grammar uses FSTs for **tokenization** and for **morphological analysis**. In addition to these basic components, the Urdu grammar is special among the ParGram grammars in that it also integrates a **transliteration** FST. This transliteration component allows the Urdu grammar to function as the core engine for the parsing and generation of both Urdu and Hindi. Urdu and Hindi are structurally similar enough that they are often treated as versions of one language. However, Urdu is written in a version of the Arabic script and Hindi is written in Devanagari. The transliteration component takes input from both scripts and converts it into an underlying Latin transliteration that can be used for both languages.

[1]We would like to thank Tafseer Ahmed, Ghulam Raza, and an anonymous reviewer for their help. Parts of this research was funded by the Urdu ParGram project funded by the Deutsche Forschungsgemeinschaft. Research for this paper by the third author was done prior to her joining Amazon.

Tokens of Meaning: Papers in Honor of Lauri Karttunen.
Cleo Condoravdi and Tracy Holloway King (eds.).

Urdu/Hindi has relatively complex morphology. Our implementation of the Urdu/Hindi morphological component uses all the capabilities of finite-state morphology (FSM) introduced by Beesley and Karttunen (2003), including **phonological rules** and **reduplication**. These interact in a complex manner with the FST transliteration component. We also use the morphological component for the dynamic formation of **morphological complex predicates**, i.e., to model the Urdu/Hindi morphological causative. Complex predication in the Urdu grammar (Butt et al., 2003, 2009) is implemented in the syntax via the restriction operator (Kaplan and Wedekind, 1993) and phrase structure rules and in the morphological component via sublexical rules. The implementation uses standard capabilities provided by FSM and its interface to the syntax in the grammar development platform XLE (Crouch et al., 2016, Kaplan et al., 2004). However, it raises questions with respect to the interaction of lexical rules with the restriction operator. In particular, it raises issues of how morphology and syntax interface with respect to argument structure operations such as passivization and causativization.

We address these topics as part of the paper. The system architecture is presented in section 19.2, the core tokenization in section 19.3, the script transliterator in section 19.4 and the morphological component in section 19.5. Section 19.6 describes how these are specified in the XLE implementation. The interaction between morphology and syntax with respect to complex predicate formation is the topic of section 19.7. Section 19.8 concludes that an integration of FSTs into a computational grammar taps into a powerful yet intuitive and user-friendly technology that is compatible with theoretical proposals concerning the role of morphology in a modular architecture of grammar (Karttunen, 2003, Dalrymple, 2015). It is thus a technology that no computational grammar should have to do without.

The major conclusion of our paper is that we, as a field, are indebted to Lauri Karttunen for playing a crucial role in developing this theory-driven technology. Without his combination of theoretical and implementational genius, this technology would not have been taken as far and would not have become as available to the community in its intuitive and accessible manner.[2]

[2]We are personally immeasurably indebted to Lauri Karttunen for his long-term involvement in the ParGram project, his avid interest in different applications for FSTs, and his boundless encouragement for our work.

19.2 System Architecture

The Urdu grammar (Butt and King, 2002) is part of the Parallel Grammar (ParGram) project (Butt et al., 1999, 2002). The ParGram project originally focused on three closely related European languages: English, French, and German. Once grammars for these languages were established, more languages were added, including Urdu. Grammars have been developed for Arabic, Georgian, Hungarian, Indonesian, Irish, Japanese, Malagasy, Norwegian, Polish, Tigrinya, Turkish, Welsh and Wolof. The ParGram project uses the XLE parser and grammar development platform (John T. Maxwell and Kaplan, 1993, Crouch et al., 2016). The grammars use the Lexical-Functional Grammar (LFG) formalism which produces c(onstituent)-structures (trees) and f(unctional)-structures (attribute-value matrices or AVMs) as syntactic analyses. A parallel treebank across several of the ParGram languages has been developed (Sulger et al., 2013) and is accessible via the INESS treebanking technology (Rosén et al., 2009, 2012b,a).

LFG assumes a version of Chomsky's Universal Grammar hypothesis that all languages are governed by similar underlying structures. Within LFG, f-structures encode a language universal level of analysis, reflecting cross-linguistic parallelism. The ParGram project aims to test the LFG formalism for its universality and coverage limitations, determining how far parallelism can be maintained across languages. Where possible, the analyses produced for similar constructions in each language are parallel. The standardization of the analyses has the computational advantage that the grammars can be used in similar applications and this standardization can simplify cross-language applications (Frank, 1999).

Most of the ParGram grammars use finite-state tokenizers and morphologies (Beesley and Karttunen, 2003). None of them uses a full-form lexicon. Having access to a morphological analyzer is crucial for large-scale, robust coverage for morphologically complex languages.

In this paper, we focus on the roles FSTs play in the Urdu ParGram grammar. There are three types of FSTs in the Urdu grammar: an Urdu↔Latin transliterator, a tokenizer, and a morphology. Within the ParGram context, the transliteration step is unique: it was introduced to allow the grammar to parse both Urdu, written in Arabic script, and Hindi, written in Devanagari,[3] using Latin alphabet forms as a lingua franca.

The following sections discuss the components in Figure 1 from the

[3]We do not discuss Devanagari here, focusing on the Urdu transliteration which is a significantly more complex task.

Tokenizer + Transliterator (FST)

$\downarrow$

Morphology (FST)

$\downarrow$

LFG ParGram Grammar

FIGURE 1 Configuation of the FSTs in the Urdu Grammar (Parsing)

perspective of parsing. LFG grammars are reversible and hence are also used for generation. That is, an f-structure can be given as input to a grammar and the appropriate strings generated. We focus mainly on parsing within this paper. See Maxwell (2006), Kaplan and Wedekind (2000), Wedekind and Kaplan (2012), Zarrieß et al. (2011) and Crouch et al. (2016) on LFG and generation.

19.3 Tokenizer

The first step in the natural language processing (NLP) of text is that of tokenization, i.e., of breaking a text into words or tokens. Languages differ in the punctuation systems they use as well as in the conventions used to indicate word boundaries. Therefore, many of the ParGram grammars have developed specialized tokenizers. The Urdu grammar integrates a cascade of FSTs, including a transliterator, a morphological analyzer and a component for the identification of multi-word expressions (MWE). The special needs of Urdu are taken care of by the combination of these components and the default XLE tokenizer that is included as part of the XLE grammar development platform (Crouch et al., 2016). This default tokenizer is based on the tokenizer described in chapter 9 of the FSM book (Beesley and Karttunen, 2003) and has been elegantly augmented by Ron Kaplan (Kaplan, 2005, Forst and Kaplan, 2006).

As a standard FST, the tokenizer is bidirectional. In the Urdu grammar, the tokenizer is used for parsing and generation. In order to parse and generate Urdu script, it is combined with the transliterator described in the next section.

19.4 Transliterator

One of the characteristics of the Urdu ParGram grammar is its aim to cover both Urdu and Hindi. The architectural design involves a core grammar written in Latin script flanked by two FSTs, one for Urdu script and one for Devanagari, which makes it possible to switch from one language to the other while using a single underlying grammar.

This section describes the Urdu FS transliterator[4] and how it deals with Urdu-specific orthographic issues by integrating restrictional components to minimize the generation of words not found in Urdu. The transliterator is based on a non-probabilistic FST compiled with the **lexc** language (Lexicon Compiler), which is designed to build finite state networks and analyzers implemented with the Xerox finite state technology (XFST) (Beesley and Karttunen, 2003). The resulting network is compatible with one written with, e.g., regular expressions, but is human readable. The underlying transliteration scheme was developed by Malik et al. (2010), following Glassman (1986).

19.4.1 Urdu Script Issues

Urdu is written in a version of the Persian alphabet (itself derived from the Arabic alphabet). The direction of the script is from right to left and the shapes of most characters are context sensitive, i.e., depending on its position within the word a character assumes a certain form.

There is no one-to-one transliteration from Urdu to Latin script and vice versa. The main reason for this are the diacritics and semivowels. Table 19.4.1 represents the four most frequent diacritics (of a total of 15; Malik (2006, 13)) in combination with the letter ب 'b' and the sounds represented by the semi-vowels ي 'yeh' and و 'wao', respectively.

ب + diacritic	Name	Latin transliteration
بَ	Zabar	ba
بِ	Zer	bi
بُ	Pesh	bu
بّ	Tashdid	bb
Semivowels		
و	Wao	v, O, U, o
ي	Yeh	y, E, I, e

TABLE 1 The four most frequently used Urdu diacritics and the two semivowels

[4]This section is based extensively on Bögel (2012), written by the first author.

The vowels signified by the diacritics are always short. Long vowels are indicated by capital letters (e.g., 'E'); short vowels are in lower case (e.g., 'e'). The Tashdid indicates gemination.

A difficulty for Urdu NLP is that the diacritics are generally not used in Urdu text. Coupled with the range of interpretative possibilities for the semivowels, this results in the (over-)generation of words which are not part of the Urdu language. Consider Figure 2, where the word کتا kuttA 'dog' is to be transliterated. The word contains two vowels and a geminated consonant. Without diacritics, the written word consists of just three letters: k, t and A. If the transliteration system hypothesizes all possible short vowels and geminated consonants, there are six possibilities.

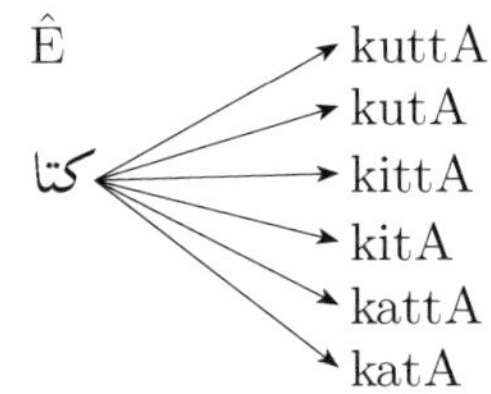

FIGURE 2 Overgeneration for the sequence کتا kuttA 'dog'

Phonotactic constraints usually reduce the number of forms. For example, Urdu does not generally allow consonant clusters, with a schwa added to loan words like *school* or *station* to make them conform to Urdu phonotactics (*səkul* or *əsteʃon*). Strings such as `ktA` therefore do not form part of the search space that needs to be considered for words as in Figure 2. Furthermore, final short vowels should not be hypothesized as they are always indicated in the script (*`ktAi`). These and other phonotactic constraints were implemented in transliterator to reduce the number of possible outcomes.

However, even with phonotactic constraints, there is still usually more than one logically possible option for transliteration, often several, as in Figure 2. One way to reduce the number of possibilities are lists of Urdu words that the system can match against. However, static word lists do not allow for alternate spellings and exclude 'mixed' words in which some of the diacritics are written, but not all of them. Furthermore, a word list is never complete, as languages constantly coin or import new words. English has been a major source of new lexical items in Urdu, due to intensive language contact over several centuries. Urdu texts thus often include English words in Latin script.

As a result of these considerations, the Urdu-Latin transliterator was designed to include: (a) a word list against which known words are matched; (b) a default transliteration component that allows the transliteration of unknown words in the Urdu script. Furthermore, the system includes a default Latin 'transliterator' to allow for words in the Latin script to be parsed as well. The next section describes these components in detail.

19.4.2 Basic Components

The Urdu transliterator integrates three layers of restrictions that constrain the transliteration possibilities for a word in Urdu script.

First, a word list is incorporated. The FS transliterator works with a Latin script list of Urdu words derived from two resources: (a) a word list that was compiled in the process of creating a dictionary and was shared with us by our colleagues from CRULP;[5] (b) a word list compiled from the Urdu finite state morphology (Bögel et al., 2007, 2009) (section 19.5). The second word list increases automatically whenever an item is added to the Urdu finite state morphology.

Second, based on the phonotactics of the language, regular expression filters reduce the possibilities proposed by the transliterator. Consider the filter in (1).

(1) [~[y A [a |i |u]]]

In Urdu a combination of [*y A short vowel*] is not allowed, as indicated by the negation (complement) symbol ~. A filter like (1) disallows all generations that match the sequence.

Third, the FST must be able to deal with unknown items. In the UrduGram FST architecture, items that do not match the word list are first passed through the phonotactic constraints filter before being fed into the default transliterator, thus allowing a maximum number of transliterations while preventing extensive overgeneration.

These three components are implemented with the finite state techniques proposed in Beesley and Karttunen (2003). To compose these within a single network, while maintainging efficiency, several layers of the transliterator are re-used during the transliteration process.

[5]The Center for Research in Urdu Langauge Processing (CRULP) was located at the National University of Computer and Emerging Sciences in Lahore, Pakistan. It has been superseded by the Center for Language Engineering (CLE) at the University of Engineering and Technology in Lahore, Pakistan (http://www.cle.org.pk/).

19.4.3 The Overall Transliterator Architecture

Figure 3 illustrates typical instances of transliteration with respect to two sequences: کتاب *kitAb* 'book' and کت. The latter transliterates to an unknown word *kt*, potentially corresponding to the surface forms *kut, kat* or *kit.* Recall that neither consonant clusters nor final short vowels should be hypothesized by the system (cf. section 19.4.2).

Step 1	**Transliterator** (Urdu to Latin)	**Default Urdu/Latin** (identity relation)
	↓ ... *kitAib* *kut* *kitAub* *kit* *kattAb* *kat* *kuttAab* ...	↓ `Uscript+`کت `Uscript+`کتاب
	↓	
Step 2	**Latin word list:** Tagging matching Latin words with `+match`	
	Filter: Keep only tokens with tags [`Uscript+` |`+match`]	
	↓ *kitAb* `+match` `Uscript+`کتاب	↓ `Uscript+`کت
	↓	
Step 3	**Urdu word list:** Delete matching Urdu words	
	Filter: Delete all tags	
	↓ *kitAb* ↓	↓ کت ↓
Step 4	**Default Urdu/Latin** (identity relation)	**Transliterator** (Urdu to Latin)
	↓ *kitAb*	↓ *kat* *kit* *kut*
Step 5	**Further processing/Tokenization**	

FIGURE 3 Transliteration of کت and کتاب

Step 1: Transliteration part 1 Step 1 of the FST contains a character mapping from Urdu to Latin (left column) and an identity mapping component for both Urdu and Latin (right column). Even though phonotactic filters are applied during the Urdu-Latin mapping, the output of the basic transliterator shows (part of) the overgeneration caused by the underspecified nature of the script, e.g., for the word کتاب, a total of 24 transliterations are possible.

The network also contains a default Urdu and a default Latin component (right column) where the respective characters are matched against themselves (e.g. k:k, r:r). That is, an Urdu script word will not only be transliterated into the corresponding Latin script, but will also be 'transliterated' into itself plus an identificational tag. The Urdu script default one-to-one mappings are marked with a special identification tag (`[+Uscript]`) for further processing.

Step 2: Word list matching and tag deletion In step 2, the output is matched against the Latin word list (s.a.). When there is a match (as it is the case for *kitAb*), the respective word is tagged `[+match]`. Following the matching, a filter is applied which erases all output forms that contain no tags, neither `[+match]` nor `[Uscript+]`. Consequently, there are two choices left for کتاب *ktAb* (one transliterated 'matched' form and one default Urdu form) while کتب *ktb* is left with only the default Urdu form.

Step 3: Distinguishing unknown from overgenerated entities The Urdu word list applied in step 3 is a transliteration of the original Latin word list, which was transliterated via the present FS transliterator system. That is, the Urdu word list is a mirror image of the Latin word list. During step 3, the Urdu script words are matched against the Urdu word list, *deleting* all the words that *find* a match. By definition, all of the words that found a match in the Latin word list in step 2 will also find a match in the Urdu word list in step 3, while all unknown entities will fail to match. As a result, any Urdu script version of an already correctly transliterated word is deleted, while the Urdu script of an unknown entity is kept for further processing. Finally, the tags of the remaining entities are deleted, which leaves the correct transliteration of the known word *kitAb* and the unknown Urdu script word كتب.

Step 4: Transliteration part 2 The remaining words are again sent into the FST of step 1. The Latin transliteration *kitAb* passes through the default Latin transliterator, effectively matching *kitAb* against *kitAb*. The unknown Urdu script word is transliterated into all three possible forms *kit, kut, kat.*

Step 5: Final adjustments So far, the transliterator only applies to single words. To allow the transliterator to process entire texts, the FST network is composed with a standard tokenizer (section 19.3). Effectively, the tokenizer first breaks the text into words and then the transliterator applies to each word. The resulting composed FST is used within the Urdu ParGram MCONFIG, which specifies the tokenizers and morphologies used for parsing and generation (see Section 19.6).

19.4.4 Transliteration Summary

The Finite State Transducer for Urdu $\leftrightarrow$ Latin transliteration described above is a constrained, yet flexible, efficient, and robust system. The price of ensuring dynamic flexibility in the transliteration from Urdu to Latin is that the system generates non-existent words due to the underspecified nature of the Urdu script. This overgeneration is reduced by applying layers of restrictions based on Urdu phonotactics and the incorporation of word lists. The transliterator thus distinguishes between items unknown to the word list (*kat, kut, kit*) and non-existent items like *kittAub*, thus restricting the possible combinations while always producing at least one transliteration.

The nature of an FST is that parsing input equals generation output. For the transliterator this means that if diacritics are optionally parsed, then they will be optionally generated. To avoid this, two transliterators were created for generation: one which obligatorily generates Urdu script with diacritics and one which generates text without any diacritics; mixed cases are not allowed. Both generators use the architecture described above and only require minimal adjustments. The transliterator can also be used to convert text without diacritics to text that contains diacritics by parsing a text without diacritics and then generating one with diacritics. Texts with partial diacritics can be transliterated and then generated either as fully without or fully with diacritics.

19.5 Morphological Analysis

Urdu ParGram grammar provides a basis for processing both Urdu and Devanagari scripts by means of transliterators to Latin script. Thus, the input to the Urdu morphological analyzer must be in Latin script.

The morphological analyzer is similar to those used in other ParGram grammars and was custom-built for use in the Urdu grammar following the guidelines in Beesley and Karttunen (2003).[6] Although the morphology was built for the Urdu grammar, it was designed to function as a stand-alone module. For example, it can be used as a lemmatizer, to provide potential parts of speech, and as a morphological analyzer for other grammars.

The Urdu morphological analyzer associates surface forms of words with a canonical form (a lemma) and a series of morphological tags that provide grammatical information about that form. An example for English is shown in (2) and for Urdu in (3).

(2) pushes: push +Verb +Pres +3sg
push +Noun +Pl

(3) bOlA: bOl +Verb +Perf +Masc +Sg

(2) states the English *pushes* can either be the third singular form of the verb *push* or the plural of the noun *push.* (3) states that the Urdu *bOlA* is the perfect masculine singular form of the verb *bOl* 'speak'.

In developing the Urdu morphological analyzer, we found that the finite-state tools and solutions to problems like the application of phonological rules or reduplication outlined in Beesley and Karttunen (2003) met the challenges posed by the Urdu morphological system.[7]

19.5.1 Morphological Coverage

The morphology covers all the inflected forms for nouns, verbs, adjectives, and adverbs, as well as closed-class words such as postpositions and conjunctions. Table 2 shows how many lemmata of the major verb classes are covered by the morphology. The focus in building the morphological analyzer was to cover all of the types of verbal paradigms. This work is complete and now new lemmata can be added very simply into the existing word classes.

Beesley and Karttunen's (2003) definition of finite-state morphology allows for non-concatenative morphology, the integration of phonological rules, long-distance dependencies and a treatment of reduplication. The Urdu morphological analyzer depends on all of these, particularly phonological rules and reduplication (Bögel et al., 2007). It also makes heavy use of flags for long-distance dependencies.

The number of simple verbs in Urdu is between 500–800 (Humay-

[6]Not all ParGram grammars use custom-built morphologies: some ParGram grammars (e.g. English, German) incorporate existing morphological analyzers (Butt et al., 1999).

[7]This includes derivational morphology and compounding.

Part of Speech	Number of lemmata
Nouns	210
Verbs	100
Adjectives	124
Adverbs	71

TABLE 2 Lemma coverage of the Urdu/Hindi morphology

oun, 2006). The majority of verbal predication is achieved via complex predicates, which can be composed of nouns, verbs, adjectives or adpositions in combination with a light verb (Butt, 1995, Mohanan, 1994). A significant part of the Urdu grammar development effort concerned the treatment of complex predicates (Hautli et al., 2012, Ahmed et al., 2012, Butt et al., 2012, Hautli-Janisz, 2014, Sulger and Vaidya, 2014, Hautli-Janisz et al., 2015). Morphological issues around predicate formation arose with respect to morphological causative complex predicates (section 19.7).

In addition to the lemmata specified in the morphology, the morphology contains a guesser. In many of the ParGram grammars, this guesser is a separate FST which processes words which receive no analysis from the core finite state morphology. In the Urdu grammar, there is a single finite-state morphology which contains both the known words and a guesser to handle forms unknown by the morphology. The guesser was designed primarily for unknown names, but is also able to guess verbs and adjectives. The guesser was designed according to the specifications in chapter 9 of Beesley and Karttunen (2003).

The Urdu morphological analyzer represents a realizational morphology (Karttunen, 2003), which is formally equivalent to Paradigm Function Morphology, an inferential realizational theory of inflectional morphology (Stewart and Stump, 2006). As such, several pieces of morphology may correspond to one feature, or one piece of abstract morphological information may be "realized" by several different overt markers. Our design decisions are consonant with this approach.

Several issues arose around the design of the morphological tag set. Recall from (2) and (3) that the morphological analyzer associates a surface form with a lemma and a set of tags. These tags are a combination of part-of-speech information such as +Verb, +Noun or +Country[8] and tags representing information such as +Fem, +Sg and +3P for feminine, singular and third person. Most of the tags follow straight-

[8]The latter are particularly useful for named entity recognition applications, hence we included them as part of the morphological analysis.

forwardly from the lingusitically motivated morphological analysis of Urdu. However, we faced several design decisions.

First, it is possible to combine different types of information into one tag, as in the +3sg tag in the English example in (2). However, we separated out all of pieces of morphological information since that led to an interface that is independent of the Urdu ParGram grammar.

Second, although we generally designed the morphological analyzer to be as explicit as possible, in some cases explicit analyses lead to unncessary ambiguity. Consider the future forms. The future is formed via the verb plus subjunctive morphology which also provides information about number and person. This is followed by the future marker *g*, which is inflected for number and gender morphology (*A/I/E*). An example is shown in (4). In Hindi the verb and the future marking are written together, while in Urdu they are written as separate words. As such, examples as in (4) present an issue for tokenization (section 19.3) and morphological analysis. We normalize the different writing practices in our transliterator and treat the verb plus its future marking as one lexical item.

(4) mArUNgI ⇔
mAr+Verb+Subjunct+1P+Sg+Fut+Fem

From the perspective of the syntax, marking the form as both subjunctive and future is redundant: every future form also carries subjunctive meaning. Experience gathered with respect to the German grammar (Butt et al., 1999) showed that it is better to eliminate tags of this kind from the morphology, since dealing with them complicates the morphology-syntax interface. For example, Urdu also uses the subjunctive morphology as a real subjunctive, see (5).

(5) mArUN ⇔
mAr+Verb+Subjunct+1P+Sg

Given that these subjunctive uses exist in parallel with the future use in (4), the interpretation of the +Subjunct tag by the morphology-syntax interface would need to differ depending on whether it is found in conjunction with future morphology or not, thus complicating the interface. We therefore eliminated the +Subjunct tag from the morphological analysis of future forms, allowing for a cleaner morphology-syntax-semantics interface.

This same problem is found with respect to infinitives as in *dEkHnA* 'to look/looking',[9] which are used as verbal nouns. The morphology could potentially provide both the analyses in (6).

[9] Capital H in the transliteration indicates aspiration of the preceding consonant.

(6) dEkHnA ⇔
    a. dEkH+Verb+Inf+Masc+Sg
    b. dEkH+Noun+Deverb+Masc+Sg

However, this would result in unnecessary ambiguity since all infinitives are also deverbal nouns. Instead, this option has been encoded as part of the morphology-syntax interface (next section). The entry in (7) shows how the grammar interprets the abstract tag +Inf. The tag is associated with a functional annotation that states that words with this tag can optionally (denoted by the round brackets) be used as a noun whose type is deverbal.

(7) +Inf   ((↑ NTYPE) = deverbal).

This solution pushes the ambiguity from the morphology into the syntax, where syntax can resolve the ambiguity via other information from the clausal context.

19.5.2 Morphology-Syntax Interface

In this section, we show how the output of the Urdu FST morphology is integrated into the Urdu LFG grammar. The morphology-syntax interface is as described in Kaplan et al. (2004). The intuition behind the interface is that the lemma and tags can be treated on a par with lexical items. For example, in the lexicon, a tag +Past can be associated with the information that the value of tense is past, as in (8).

(8) +Past (↑ TNS-ASP TENSE)=past

The "lexical items" coming out of the morphology, namely the lemma and the tags, are assembled via sublexical rules into a word. LFG grammars assume the notion of Lexical Integrity, which means that the terminal leaves are syntactically independent items (fully formed words or clitics). With the integration of a finite-state morphology, these terminal nodes of fully formed lexical items are replaced by the output of the morphology. The grammar uses the output of the morphology as the leaves of the c(onstituent)-structure tree. For example, the noun *haftA* 'week' forms a c-structure tree as in (9).

(9)

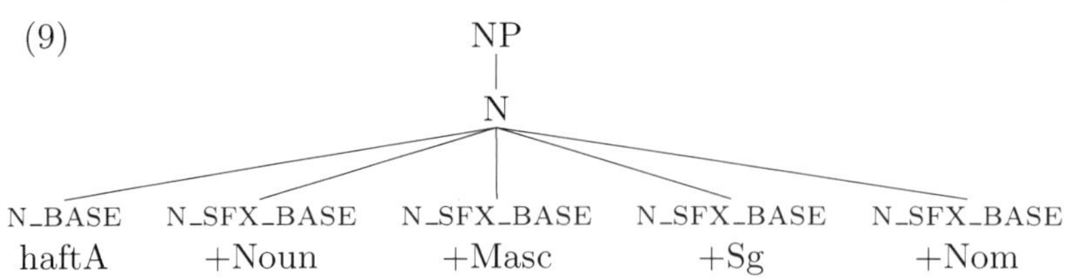

The standard XLE LFG context-free rule formalism is used to assemble the lemmata and tags into a sublexical tree as in (9). A sample context free c-structure rewrite rule that produces the tree in (9) is shown in (10). The rule states that an N is composed of an N_BASE and at least one N_SFX_BASE as indicated by the Kleene +.[10]

(10) N $\longrightarrow$ N_BASE
N_SFX_BASE+

Each of the leaf nodes in (9) has a lexical entry which provides the c-structure information used to produce the tree and the f(unctional)-structure information used to produce the syntactic LFG analyses. Like standard c-structure rules, sublexical rules and lexical entries can be annotated with information about f-structural information.

For common nouns like *haftA* 'week', no lexical entry is necessary. The Urdu grammar only stipulates lexical entries for nouns which specify an unpredictable subcategorization frame (e.g., nouns used with complex predication). In the case of *haftA* 'week', no such information needs to be stated. The lemma *haftA* is contained in the morphological analyzer and the grammar makes use of this by accessing it via XLE's -*unknown* facility. This facility provides a default lexical entry -*unknown* which can match any lexical item from the morphology. Through it, the morphology itself provides the lexical items, while the -*unknown* lexical entry provides the information used to build the c- and f-structures. A simplified version of -*unknown* for Urdu is shown in (11).

(11)	-unknown	N	XLE	($\uparrow$ PRED)='%stem'
				($\uparrow$ NTYPE)=common
		NAME	XLE	($\uparrow$ PRED)='%stem'
				($\uparrow$ NTYPE)=proper
		A	XLE	($\uparrow$ PRED)='%stem'
				($\uparrow$ ATYPE)

The %stem matches the form output by the morphology, in this case *haftA* and is passed to the f-structure syntactic represention to create ($\uparrow$ PRED)='haftA' as well as contributing ($\uparrow$ NTYPE)=common.

Besides the mapping between surface form and abstract tags and lemmata, the morphology-syntax interface allows for a many-to-many

[10] The only way that these rules differ from standard c-structure rules is the presence of _BASE which indicates to XLE that these are *sublexical* rules. XLE uses this sublexical indication for a default collapsed display of the c-structure so that only the N node is shown with the inflected form under it, as shown in (i).

(i) NP
|
N
|
haftA

mapping between lemmata/tags and functional/syntactic information. Lemmata and tags may be associated with simple or complex functional annotations or not be annotated at all and thus be "suppressed" for the purposes of syntactic analysis.

The major advantage of integrating a finite-state morphology into a grammar, however, is that the lexicons for the grammar can be relatively small. This is because lexicons are not needed for words whose syntactic lexical entry can be determined based on their morphological analysis and for which nothing special need be said (i.e. as described for the *-unknown* entry in (11)). This is particularly true for nouns, adverbs and adjectives. Items whose lexical entry cannot be predicted based on the morphological tags need explicit lexical entries. This is the case for items whose subcategorization frames are not predictable, primarily for verbs. For each verb lemma, a lexical entry is created with the required subcategorization information. Due to the FST morphology, only a single entry is needed, corresponding to that of the lemma; no entry is needed for the inflected forms, thus avoiding the need for multiple entries for forms in morphologically complex languages and simplifying grammar maintenance.

19.6 Specifying Configurations — MCONFIG

The FSTs used for tokenization, transliteration and morphological analysis can in principle be invoked in different combinations. In the XLE platform the arrangement of the FSTs is specified in the "MCONFIG" file (short for "morphological configuration") (Crouch et al., 2016). In this section, we show how the Urdu grammar makes use of the power and flexibility afforded by combination of FSTs.

The function of the MCONFIG file is to interface an XLE grammar with external components. Within ParGram, these have generally been FST tokenizers and morphological analyzers. The MCONFIG file is also the place where further transducers can be introduced. For example, the transducer which recognizes Multi-Word Expressions (MWE) and tokenizes these as one token, e.g., for *New York* or *Saudi Arabia*. The Urdu grammar also makes use of a MWE FST (Hautli and Sulger, 2011), as seen in the Urdu MCONFIG file in Figure 4.

The first line in the MCONFIG in Figure 4 is an identificatory line. The TOKENIZE section invokes the files relevant for tokenization. It allows for the specification for two different files: one for parsing (indicated by P!) and one for generation (indicated by G!). Since parsing and generation have different goals, they often involve different tokenizers.[11]

[11]For example, the parser needs to parse errors such as two commas in a row,

STANDARD URDU MORPHOLOGY (1.0)

TOKENIZE:
P!TranslitParse.fst G!TranslitGenNoDia.fst

ANALYZE USEFIRST:
morph.override
urdu.fst

PARAMETERS:
*NOCAP

BuildMultiwordsFromMorphology:
Tag = +PreferMWToken

FIGURE 4 Urdu MCONFIG

The Urdu MCONFIG file calls an FST that consists of the tokenizer and the transliterator composed together (section 19.4). For generation, the version here does not generate diacritics in the Urdu script. However, an alternative version `TranslitGenWithDia.fst` can instead be used to always produce diacritics.

The Urdu grammar also allows for a further option. Rather than taking Urdu script input, it is possible to specify in the MCONFIG file that already-transliterated input be parsed and generated. This is useful for debugging as it separates issues of script from issues of morphological and syntactic analysis. In this case, rather than the custom-made transliterator plus tokenizer, the default tokenizers for parsing and generation available as part of the XLE package are called: `P!/usr/local/xle/bin/default-parse-tokenizer.fsmfile G!/usr/local/xle/bin/default-gen-tokenizer.fst`.

The Urdu morphology is invoked in the `ANALYZE` section with `urdu.fst`. There are two files: the Urdu morphology proper and an FST specificying multiword expressions. The `USEFIRST` option specifies that the first file applies before the Urdu morphology. This has the effect that the FST for multiwords, `morph.override`, is applied first. Furthermore, as the last two lines of the MCONFIG file show, multiword expressions are provided with a tag that allows the multiword version to be preferred (Frank et al., 1998).

Finally, the `PARAMETERS` option allows for the specification of further parameters. The parameter shown here pertains to capitalization. Since neither the Urdu script, nor Devanagari nor the common Latin

whereas the generator should not allow for this possibility to be output (see Jurafsky and Martin (2006) for detailed discussions).

transliteration scheme need to be normalized for capitalization, this option is set to `NOCAP`.

This section concludes the description of how finite-state morphologies are used in the Urdu grammar. The design decisions laid out in Beesley and Karttunen (2003) for morphological analyzers provide flexibility and formal power while also being well designed for developers. The finite-state morphologies can be integrated into grammar development platforms such as XLE and provide grammar writers with the tools necessary for an efficient and robust morphological analysis. Urdu is morphologically complex, but the formal power in Beesley and Karttunen's finite-state technology allows for a straightforward treatment of the morphology and provides a way to separate the morphological issues from the complexities of Urdu-Latin transliteration.

19.7 Causatives and the Morphology-Syntax Interface

This section describes an issue that arose with respect to the ParGram treatment of complex predication in conjunction with sublexical rules (section 19.5.2). The issues were observed in both the Turkish (Çetinoğlu, 2009, Çetinoğlu and Oflazer, 2009) and Urdu grammars. Here we illustrate the underlying problem with respect to Urdu.[12]

19.7.1 Complex Predicates via Restriction

The Urdu grammar uses the *restriction operator* (Kaplan and Wedekind, 1993) to model complex predication. The restriction operator allows for features of f-structures to be "restricted out", i.e., to cause the grammar to function as if these features did not exist. This operation is applied to complex predication in order to build complex predicate-argument structures dynamically (Butt et al., 2003, 2009).

Consider (12). (12) is a noun-verb complex predicate in which *kahAnI* 'story' is an argument that is contributed by the noun *yAd* 'memory', but that functions as the direct object of the clause. The finite verb *kI* 'did' has two arguments: Nadya and *yAd* 'memory'. The noun *yAd* 'memory' thus plays a double role: it is an argument of the finite verb and it contributes to the overall predication of the clause (Mohanan, 1994).

The details of theoretical and computational analyses of complex predication have been discussed in depth elsewhere (e.g., Butt 1995, Mohanan 1994, Butt et al. 2009). The f-structure analysis is as in (13) (simplified to show only the predicate-argument relations).

[12]We would like to acknowledge Özlem Çentinoğlu, who was the first to track down the root of the problem in the Turkish grammar.

(12) nAdiyah=nE kahAnI yAd k-I
Nadya.F.Sg=Erg story.F.Sg.Nom memory.F.Sg.Nom do-Perf.F.Sg
'Nadya remembered a/the story.'

(13)
$$\begin{bmatrix} \text{PRED} & \text{'do<SUBJ,'memory<OBJ>'>'} \\ \text{SUBJ} & \begin{bmatrix} \text{PRED} & \text{'Nadya'} \end{bmatrix} \\ \text{OBJ} & \begin{bmatrix} \text{PRED} & \text{'story'} \end{bmatrix} \end{bmatrix}$$

This f-structure is achieved by a dynamic composition of the subcategorization frames contributed by *kar* 'do' and *yAd* 'memory'. The restriction operator is invoked in f-structure annotations on the c-structure rules. While the individual annotations differ according to the type of complex predicate that is involved, (14) illustrates the general schema.

(14)
$$\begin{array}{lcc} \text{Vcp} \rightarrow & \text{X} & \text{Vlight} \\ & \downarrow\backslash\text{OLDGF}\backslash\text{PRED}=\uparrow\backslash\text{OLDGF}\backslash\text{PRED} & \uparrow=\downarrow \\ & (\downarrow\text{OLDGF}) = (\uparrow\text{NEWGF}) & \\ & (\uparrow \text{ PRED ARG2})=(\downarrow \text{ PRED}) & \end{array}$$

To allow the predicate composition, the light verb is associated with a subcategorization frame that is incomplete. In the case of *kar* 'do', the subcategorization frame is as in (15). The %Pred stands for a variable that needs to be filled in, following the XLE notation for variables.

(15) (↑ PRED) = 'kar< SUBJ %Pred >'

The *kar* 'do' contributes a subject to the predication and also encodes the fact that it needs a predicate to fill its variable slot. This further predicate is provided by the X in (14). The X could be a noun, an adjective, a verb or an adposition. In our example, it is the noun *yAd* 'memory'. The annotation (↑ PRED ARG2)=(↓ PRED) substitutes the PRED value of *yAd* into the second argument of the light verb. The subcategorization frame of *yAd* is lexically specified as in (16) and contributes an object to the overall predication.

(16) (↑ PRED) = 'yAd<OBJ>'

The restriction operator restricts out those pieces of information which are "changed" as part of complex predication.[13] For one, the overall PRED value changes, since a value has been substituted for the

[13] As LFG is formally monotonic, the f-structures are not in fact changed. Rather, new information is added onto already existing information. Pretty printing then gives the effect of an f-structure "changing" into another one.

variable. For another, the complex predication may require grammatical functions to be renamed. This does not occur in our example, but does occur with causatives, discussed below. The OLDGF stands for a grammatical function, be it a SUBJ, OBJ, OBL OR OBJ_θ that is being reassigned to a NEWGF. To accomplish this, it is restricted out and the new correspondence is established via the (↓OLDGF) = (↑NEWGF) equation.

The restriction operator is able to model different types of complex predicates in the Urdu grammar and can model cases of stacked complex predicates (Butt et al., 2009).

19.7.2 Causatives and Passives

Problems with the restriction operator arise in the interaction of passives with causatives. Causatives in Urdu are formed morphologically, as in (17), where the causative morpheme *-A* effectively adds an argument, the causer. (17a) is an example of a simple transitive verb. In the causativized version in (17b),[14] the subject of the transitive is realized as the causee and is marked with the dative/accusative *kO*. This is an example of a "change" in grammatical function that can be effected via the restriction operator.

(17) a. yassIn=nE kHAnA kHa-yA
Yassin=Erg food.M.Sg.Nom eat-Perf.M.Sg
'Yassin ate food.'

b. nAdyA=nE yassIn=kO kHAnA kHil-A-yA
Nadya=Erg Yassin=Dat food.M.Sg.Nom eat-Caus-Perf.M.Sg
'Nadya had Yassin eat (fed Yassin).'

Causatives are also complex predicates since the overall argument structure is co-determined by more than one predicational element. Crosslinguistically, causatives can be either morphological or syntactic but the constraints on the formation of complex predicate-argument structures are the same (Alsina, 1993). Following this insight from theoretical linguistics, the Urdu grammar treats syntactically formed complex predicates like the N-V complex predicates discussed above and morphologically formed causatives on a par. The predicate-argument structure is calculated dynamically based on the information contributed by each of the predicational parts and the final, joint subcategorization frame is effected by the restriction operator. With morphological causatives, this occurs at the level of sublexical rules.

The morphological analyzer provides the analysis in (18) for the verb

[14]The stem also changes in this case. The verb *kHA* 'eat' is one of a handful of verbs in Urdu which shows an irregular stem formation in the causative.

kHilAyA 'made to eat'. As the tags are terminal nodes of sublexical rules, the `+Caus` tag provides a phrase-structure locus for the restriction operator so that it can be analyzed similarly to syntactically formed complex predicates. The sublexical rule for the causative in (17b) is as in (19).

(18) kHilAyA ⇔ kHA +Verb +Caus +Perf +Masc +Sg

(19) V → V-S_BASE CAUS_BASE

$$\begin{array}{ll} \downarrow\backslash\text{PRED}\backslash\text{SUBJ}=\uparrow\backslash\text{PRED}\backslash\text{SUBJ} & \uparrow=\downarrow \\ (\downarrow\text{SUBJ})=(\uparrow\text{OBJ-GO}) & \\ (\uparrow\text{PRED ARG2})=(\downarrow\text{PRED}) & \end{array}$$

The causative tag is lexically associated with a subcategorization frame that is parallel to that of the light verb *kar* 'do':

(20) (↑ PRED) = 'cause< SUBJ %Pred >'

The variable is filled by the PRED value of the main verb, the transitive verb *kHA* 'eat'. The basic f-structure for the non-causative version in (17a) is shown in (21). When causativized, the SUBJ is realized as an OBJ-GO. This is the result of the equations in (19) and the resulting complex subcategorization frame is shown in (22).

(21)
$$\begin{bmatrix} \text{PRED} & \text{'eat<SUBJ,OBJ>'} \\ \text{SUBJ} & [\text{PRED 'Yassin'}] \\ \text{OBJ} & [\text{PRED 'food'}] \end{bmatrix}$$

(22)
$$\begin{bmatrix} \text{PRED} & \text{'cause<SUBJ,'eat<OBJ-GO,OBJ>'>'} \\ \text{SUBJ} & [\text{PRED 'Nadya'}] \\ \text{OBJ-GO} & [\text{PRED 'Yassin'}] \\ \text{OBJ} & [\text{PRED 'food'}] \end{bmatrix}$$

Now consider the interaction with passivization. Passives in Urdu are formed by combining the verb *jA* 'go' with the perfect form of the main verb. The subject/agent of the base verb is realized as an adjunct and is marked with *se* 'with/from', as shown in (23).

(23) a. yassIn=nE kHAnA kHa-yA
Yassin=Erg food.M.Sg.Nom eat-Perf.M.Sg
'Yassin ate food.'

b. kHAnA yassIn=sE kHa-yA ga-yA
food.M.Sg.Nom Yassin=Inst eat-Perf.M.Sg go-Perf.M.Sg
'The food was eaten by Yassin.'

Passivization of the causative in (17b), repeated here in (24a), is as in (24b), where the subject/agent of the causative is realized as an adjunct marked by *se* 'with/from'.

(24) a. nAdyA=**nE** yassIn=kO kHAnA kHil-**A**-yA
Nadya=Erg Yassin=Dat food.M.Sg.Nom eat-**Caus**-Perf.M.Sg
'Nadya had Yassin eat (fed Yassin).'

b. yassIn=kO nAdyA=**sE** kHAnA kHil-**A**-yA
Yassin=Dat Nadya=Inst food.M.Sg.Nom eat-**Caus**-Perf.M.Sg
ga-yA
go-Perf.M.Sg
'The food was fed to Yassin by/through Nadya.'

As originally implemented, the Urdu grammar did not parse examples as in (24b) as grammatical. Moreover, it judged examples as in (25) as grammatical. In this case the former indirect object (OBJ-GO) *Yassin* has been analyzed as a former subject that is now realized as an agentive adjunct.

(25) *nAdyA=**nE** yassIn=sE kHAnA kHil-**A**-yA
Nadya=Erg Yassin=Inst food.M.Sg.Nom eat-**Caus**-Perf.M.Sg
ga-yA
go-Perf.M.Sg
'Nadya made the food be eaten by/through Yassin.'

The underlying problem is architectural. Passivization has traditionally been handled by lexical rules in LFG (Bresnan, 1982). These lexical rules apply in the lexicon directly to the specification of subcategorization frames. For example, the transitive verb *kHA* 'eat' has the subcategorization specification in (26) as part of its lexical entry. (26) states that there is a predicate 'P' (*kHA* in our example) which has a subject and an object and which can optionally undergo passivization. The '@' sign signals a template call (Dalrymple et al., 2004) to the template PASS, which effects the passivization via a lexical rule.

(26) TRANS(P) = @(PASS (↑ PRED)='P<(↑ SUBJ) (↑ OBJ)>').

Since this is specified in the lexical entry of *kHA* 'eat', passivization **always** applies before causativization. That is, the lexical rule is applied to the V-S_Base in (19). This is followed by the application of the causativization restriction operator. However, passivization should operate on the entire complex predicate, so that passivization follows causativization. Once this problem was identified, passivization was moved to be part of the sublexical rules via the restriction operator, rather than the lexical rules.

19.7.3 Summary and Discussion

While the current solution to the passive-causative interaction works, it is not satisfactory. The interaction between causativization and passivization revealed an architectural problem in how argument alternations are treated in the implementation. Within theoretical linguistics, argument alternations are stated at a level of a(rgument)-structure and are independent of particular morphological or syntactic realizations. In the ParGram grammars, passivization continued to be treated via lexical rules, as per classic LFG (but see Wedekind and Ørsnes 2003). One reason for this is that a-structure is not implemented in XLE: predicate arguments are modeled solely via subcategorization frames pertaining to grammatical functions. The interaction between causativization and passives at the morphology-syntax interface highlights that traditional lexical rules do not allow for the right order of application when causativization is morphological but passivization is part of the syntax. This realization was only made possible by the integration of the computational morphological component represented by a finite-state morphology á la Beesley and Karttunen (2003).

19.8 Conclusion and Discussion

We conclude that an integration of finite-state morphology, as well as tokenizing and in the case of Urdu transliterating finite-state transducers, into a computational grammar taps into a powerful yet intuitive technology that enhances grammar engineering substantially. It is thus a technology that no computational grammar should do without. In the case of the finite-state technology provided by Beesley and Karttunen (2003), the morphologial analysis and the morphology-syntax interface is in line with theoretical ideas on the place of morphology in a modular architecture of grammar (Karttunen, 2003, Dalrymple, 2015).

References

Ahmed, Tafseer, Miriam Butt, Annette Hautli, and Sebastian Sulger. 2012. A Reference Dependency Bank for Analyzing Complex Predicates. In *Proceedings of the Eight International Conference on Language Resources and Evaluation (LREC'12)*, pages 3145–3151. Istanbul, Turkey: European Language Resources Association (ELRA). ISBN 978-2-9517408-7-7.

Alsina, Alex. 1993. *Predicate Composition: A Theory of Syntactic Function Alternations*. Ph.D. thesis, Stanford University.

Beesley, Kenneth and Lauri Karttunen. 2003. *Finite-State Morphology*. CSLI Publications.

Bögel, Tina. 2012. Urdu-Roman transliteration via finite state transducers. In *Proceedings of the 10th International Workshop on Finite State Methods and Natural Language Processing (FSMNLP)*.

Bögel, Tina, Miriam Butt, Annette Hautli, and Sebastian Sulger. 2007. Developing a finite-state morphological analyzer for Urdu and Hindi. In T. Hanneforth and K. M. Würzner, eds., *Proceedings of the Sixth International Workshop on Finite-State Methods and Natural Language Processing*, pages 86–96. Potsdam: Potsdam University Press.

Bögel, Tina, Miriam Butt, Annette Hautli, and Sebastian Sulger. 2009. Urdu and the modular architecture of ParGram. In *Proceedings of the Conference on Language and Technology 2009 (CLT09)*. CRULP, Lahore.

Bresnan, Joan, ed. 1982. *The Mental Representation of Grammatical Relations*. Cambridge, MA: MIT Press.

Butt, Miriam. 1995. *The Structure of Complex Predicates in Urdu*. Stanford: CSLI Publications.

Butt, Miriam, Tina Bögel, Annette Hautli, Sebastian Sulger, and Tafseer Ahmed. 2012. Identifying urdu complex predication via bigram extraction. In *In Proceedings of COLING 2012, Technical Papers*, pages 409 – 424. Mumbai, India.

Butt, Miriam, Helge Dyvik, Tracy Holloway King, Hiroshi Masuichi, and Christian Rohrer. 2002. The Parallel Grammar project. In *Proceedings of COLING 2002: Workshop on Grammar Engineering and Evaluation*.

Butt, Miriam and Tracy Holloway King. 2002. Urdu and the Parallel Grammar project. In *Proceedings of COLING2002, Workshop on Asian Language Resources and International Standardization*, pages 39–45.

Butt, Miriam, Tracy Holloway King, and John T. Maxwell, III. 2003. Complex predicates via restriction. In M. Butt and T. H. King, eds., *The Proceedings of the LFG '03 Conference*, pages 92–104. Stanford, CA: CSLI Publications. University at Albany, State University of New York.

Butt, Miriam, Tracy Holloway King, María-Eugenia Niño, and Frédérique Segond. 1999. *A Grammar Writer's Cookbook*. CSLI Publications.

Butt, Miriam, Tracy Hollowy King, and Gillian Ramchand. 2009. Complex predication: Who made the child pinch the elephant? In L. Uyechi and L. H. Wee, eds., *Reality Exploration and Discovery: Pattern Interaction in Language and Life*, pages 231–256. Stanford: CSLI Publications.

Çetinoğlu, Özlem. 2009. *A Large Scale LFG Grammar for Turkish*. Ph.D. thesis, Sabanci University.

Çetinoğlu, Özlem and Kemal Oflazer. 2009. Integrating derivational morphology into syntax. In N. N. et al., ed., *Recent Advances in Natural Language Processing V*. Amsterdam: John Benjamins.

Crouch, Dick, Mary Dalrymple, Ron Kaplan, Tracy King, John T. Maxwell, III, and Paula Newman. 2016. Xle documentation. Tech. rep., Palo Alto Research Center, http://ling.uni-konstanz.de/pages/xle/doc/xle_toc.html.

Dalrymple, Mary. 2015. Morphology in the LFG architecture. In M. Butt and T. H. King, eds., *Proceedings of LFG15*, pages 64–83. Stanford: CSLI Publications.

Dalrymple, Mary, Ron Kaplan, and Tracy Holloway King. 2004. Linguistic generalizations over descriptions. In *Proceedings of LFG04*. CSLI On-line Publications.

Forst, Martin and Ron Kaplan. 2006. The importance of precise tokenizing for deep grammars. In *Fifth Language Resource and Evaluation Conference (LREC2006)*.

Frank, Anette. 1999. From parallel grammar development towards machine translation. In *Proceedings of MT Summit VII*, pages 134–142.

Frank, Anette, Tracy Holloway King, Jonas Kuhn, and John T. Maxwell, III. 1998. Optimality Theory style constraint ranking in large-scale LFG grammars. In M. Butt and T. H. King, eds., *Proceedings of the LFG98 Conference*. CSLI On-line Publications.

Glassman, Eugene H. 1986. *Spoken Urdu*. Lahore: Nirali Kitaben Publishing House, 6th edn.

Hautli, Annette and Sebastian Sulger. 2011. Extracting and Classifying Urdu Multiword Expressions. In *Proceedings of the 49th Annual Meeting of the Association for Computational Linguistics: Human Langauge Technologies (ACL-HLT '11): Student Session*, pages 24–29.

Hautli, Annette, Sebastian Sulger, and Miriam Butt. 2012. Adding an Annotation Layer to the Hindi/Urdu Treebank. *Linguistic Issues in Language Technology* 7(3):1–18s.

Hautli-Janisz, Annette. 2014. *Urdu/Hindi Motion Verbs and Their Implementation in a Lexical Resource*. Ph.D. thesis, University of Konstanz.

Hautli-Janisz, Annette, Tracy Holloway King, and Gillian Ramchand. 2015. Encoding event structure in urdu/hindi verbnet. In *Proceedings of the 3rd Workshop on EVENTS: Definition, Detection, Coreference, and Representation (NAACL 2015)*, pages 25–33.

Humayoun, Muhammad. 2006. *Urdu Morphology, Orthography and Lexicon Extraction*. Master's thesis, Department of Computing Science, Chalmers University of Technology.

John T. Maxwell, III and Ron Kaplan. 1993. The interface between phrasal and functional constraints. *Computational Lingusitics* 19:571–589.

Jurafsky, Daniel and James H. Martin. 2006. *Speech and language processing : an introduction to natural language processing, computational linguistics, and speech recognition*. Upper Saddle River, NJ: Pearson Prentice Hall.

Kaplan, Ron and Jürgen Wedekind. 2000. LFG generation produces context-free languages. In *Proceedings of the 18th International Conference on Computational Linguistics*, pages 425—431.

Kaplan, Ronald M. 2005. A method for tokenizing text. In *Festschrift in Honor of Kimmo Koskenniemi's 60th anniversary*. Stanford, CA: CSLI Publications.

Kaplan, Ronald M., John T. Maxwell, III, Tracy Holloway King, and Richard Crouch. 2004. Integrating finite-state technology with deep LFG grammars. In *Proceedings of the European Summer School on Logic, Language and Information (ESSLLI) Workshop on Combining Shallow and Deep Processing for NLP*.

Kaplan, Ronald M. and Jürgen Wedekind. 1993. Restriction and correspondence-based translation. In *Proceedings of the 6th Conference of the Association for Computational Linguistics European Chapter (EACL)*, pages 193–202. Utrecht University.

Karttunen, Lauri. 2003. Computing with realizational morphology. In A. Gelbukh, ed., *Computational Linguistics and Intelligent Text Processing*, pages 205–216. Springer Verlag.

Malik, Abbas. 2006. *Hindi Urdu Machine Transliteration System*. Master's thesis, University of Paris.

Malik, Muhammad Kamran, Tafseer Ahmed, Sebastian Sulger, Tina Bögel, Atif Gulzar, Ghulam Raza, Sarmad Hussain, and Miriam Butt. 2010. Transliterating Urdu for a Broad-Coverage Urdu/Hindi LFG Grammar. In *Proceedings of the Seventh Conference on International Language Resources and Evaluation (LREC 2010)*. European Language Resources Association (ELRA).

Maxwell, John T., III. 2006. Efficient generation from packed input. In M. Butt, M. Dalrymple, and T. H. King, eds., *Intelligent Linguistics Architectures: Variations on Themes by Ronald M. Kaplan*, pages 19–34. Stanford: CSLI Publications.

Mohanan, Tara. 1994. *Argument Structure in Hindi*. CSLI Publications.

Rosén, Victoria, Koenraad De Smedt, Paul Meurer, and Helge Dyvik. 2012a. An Open Infrastructure for Advanced Treebanking. In *META-RESEARCH Workshop on Advanced Treebanking at LREC2012*, pages 22–29. Istanbul, Turkey.

Rosén, Victoria, Paul Meurer, and Koenraad de Smedt. 2009. LFG Parsebanker: A Toolkit for Building and Searching a Treebank as a Parsed Corpus. In *Proceedings of the 7th International Workshop on Treebanks and Linguistic Theories (TLT7)*, pages 127–133. Utrecht: LOT.

Rosén, Victoria, Paul Meurer, Gyri Smørdal Losnegaard, Gunn Inger Lyse, Koenraad De Smedt, Martha Thunes, and Helge Dyvik. 2012b. An integrated web-based treebank annotation system. In I. Hendrickx, S. Kübler, and K. Simov, eds., *Proceedings of the Eleventh International Workshop on Treebanks and Linguistic Theories (TLT11)*, pages 157–167. Lisbon, Portugal: Edições Colibri.

Stewart, Thomas and Gregory Stump. 2006. Paradigm function morphology and the morphology-syntax interface. In G. Ramchand and C. Reiss, eds., *The Oxford Handbook of Linguistic Interfaces*, pages 383–421. Oxford: Oxford University Press.

Sulger, Sebastian, Miriam Butt, Tracy Holloway King, Paul Meurer, Tibor Laczkó, György Rákosi, Cheikh Bamba Dione, Helge Dyvik, Victoria Rosén, Koenraad De Smedt, Agnieszka Patejuk, Ozlem Cetinoglu, I Wayan Arka, and Meladel Mistica. 2013. Pargrambank: The pargram parallel treebank. In *Proceedings of the 51st Annual Meeting of the Association for Computational Linguistics (Volume 1: Long Papers)*, pages 550–560. Sofia, Bulgaria: Association for Computational Linguistics.

Sulger, Sebastian and Ashwini Vaidya. 2014. Towards identifying hindi/urdu noun templates in support of a large-scale lfg grammar. In *Proceedings of the Fifth Workshop on South and Southeast Asian Natural Language Processing*, pages 1–10. Dublin, Ireland: Association for Computational Linguistics and Dublin City University.

Wedekind, Jürgen and Ron Kaplan. 2012. LFG generation by grammar specialization. *Computational Linguistics* 38(4):867–915.

Wedekind, Jürgen and Bjarne Ørsnes. 2003. Restriction and verbal complexes in LFG: A case study for Danish. In M. Butt and T. H. King, eds., *Proceedings of LFG03*. CSLI On-line Publications.

Zarrieß, Sina, Aoife Cahill, and Jonas Kuhn. 2011. Underspecifying and predicting voice for surface realisation ranking. In *Proceedings of the 49th Annual Meeting of the Association for Computational Linguistics: Human Language Technologies*, pages 1007–1017.

20

Optimal Kornai-Karttunen Codes for Restricted Autosegmental Representations*

Anssi Yli-Jyrä

20.1 Introduction

Any finite-state implementation for autosegmental grammars requires, among other things, a way to encode its phonological representations during the transductions. In this article, I argue that Kornai and Karttunen's triple alphabet in Kornai (1995) can be modified and used to define a regular set of code words in such a way that the encoding function is compositional and invertible. This would contradict the negative result of Wiebe (1992) unless floating was treated outside the encoding as latent variation. This out-of-the-box manoeuvre suggests that the linear encoding (Kornai, 1995, Yli-Jyrä, 2013) and the model-theoretic approach (Bird and Klein, 1990, Jardine, 2013) can and perhaps should be combined to tackle the implementation challenge.

Proving the constructive regularity of practical Autosegmental Phonology (AP) (Goldsmith, 1976) grammars has turned out to be a long-term effort, much harder than showing the regularity of typical seg-

*The author has received funding as Research Fellow from the Academy of Finland (dec. No 270354 – A Usable Finite-State Model for Adequate Syntactic Complexity) and as Clare Hall Fellow from the University of Helsinki (dec. RP 137/2013). As the response to the reviews, the article was heavily revised during the author's 2017 visit to the USA under the mobility funding of the Faculty of Arts of the University of Helsinki (Dean's dec. N1/2017). The title of the original version was *Some Transition Systems and Codes for Bistrings.*

Tokens of Meaning: Papers in Honor of Lauri Karttunen.
Cleo Condoravdi and Tracy Holloway King (eds.).

mental grammars (Johnson, 1972). This situation is particularly interesting because AP has been presented (Ristad, 1990) as being easier than vanilla Generative Phonology.

The unfinished challenge of AP is not generally realized in the modern phonological theory-making — although perhaps it should. It is particularly notable that the fundamental questions concerning the description, encoding and derivation of the aligned parallel strings used in autosegmental phonology are reincarnated outside the AP framework (Kempe, 2010, Yli-Jyrä, 2016, Hulden, 2017). Moreover, these questions have started to receive renewed code-theoretic and model-theoretic concern (Jardine 2013, Jardine and Heinz 2015, Jardine 2017, Yli-Jyrä and Niemi 2006, Yli-Jyrä 2013, 2015, Yli-Jyrä 2016). In the long run, the potential extended impact of the fundamental questions may range from historical linguistics to paradigmatic morphology and alignments in machine translation.

This article revisits the linear encoding scheme presented in Kornai (1995) for autosegmental structures and evaluated further in Wiebe (1992). The prior evaluation left us with the conclusion that an **optimal linear encoding** is impossible. Yet there are many newer attempts to encode autosegmental graphs as linear strings (Eisner, 1997, Yli-Jyrä and Niemi, 2006, Jardine and Heinz, 2015, Yli-Jyrä, 2015). I have personally used a linear encoding (Yli-Jyrä, 2013) for a restricted set of autosegmental structures to combine a complete fragment of an AP grammar with a transducer that has morphemic tone. It is therefore necessary to check whether the assumptions of Kornai and Wiebe actually missed the opportunity for these practical results as they led to a conclusion that it is impossible to construct a coding scheme that satisfies all the requirements of an optimal linear encoding.

The current exposition avoids the conflict with Wiebe's and Kornai's negative results with an out-of-the-box solution:

- I first observe that the set of code words in a code does not have to be finite although the code alphabet is. This lets us construct an unambiguously factorizable domain over which an optimal linear encoding can be defined.
- Secondly, I acknowledge that the coding is only one part of the solution as the AP description may be underspecified about the linear order between the floating elements. To make the described structures linearly encodable, we assume a latent linear order that completes the underspecified description.

Thus, the unambiguous linear encoding and the model-theoretic description of floating via the latent linear order seem to have complementary functions and they may both be needed in a successful and full implementation of AP.

20.1.1 The Challenge of AP

While Autosegmental Phonology (Goldsmith, 1976) is antique from the perspective of modern theories, it is a valuable tool (Hyman, 2011) in descriptive linguistics, and its proper formalisation is still an intriguing problem for many good reasons:

1. AP views morphemes as combinations of multiple tiers
2. AP aligns the tiers by means of associations
3. AP describes and rewrites the resulting **aligned multistrings**
4. AP assumes that aligned multistrings are linearly pronounceable.

Each of these four aspects is non-trivial, and requires complicated linguistic underpinnings and solutions to computational challenges. Our focus will be on aligned multistrings — the objects that may be processed by autosegmental rewriting rules or described by autosegmental constraints.

Autosegmental rewriting rules cannot be easier to implement than segmental rewriting rules. The proper treatment of the latter have relied on the availability of a rich set of regular operations that include concatenation, star, union, intersection, difference, composition and projection. For regular languages and relations, the **closure properties** under these operations have been discovered before the 1970s. Meanwhile, the corresponding theory for graphs — including the graphs used in AP — has been growing during the last two decades (Engelfriet and Vereijken, 1996, Courcelle and Engelfriet, 2012, Jardine, 2017). The theory has provided us with a declarative formalism that can be used to define graph rewriting rules elegantly at a high level without constant bothering about the closure properties, decidability and implementation matters.

Although we now have a much richer theory of graphs (Courcelle and Engelfriet, 2012), we have to remember that the graphs in AP are particularly restricted and they resemble linearised graphs and string languages. For example, phonological representations in AP are typically non-crossing (Sagey, 1988). If the unassociated nodes are also ordered as in Yli-Jyrä (2015), they can be seen as non-crossing ordered graphs and they thus have a well-behaving, context-free code (Yli-Jyrä and Gómez-Rodríguez, 2017). But even this code has more power than what is necessary for AP graphs.

Another reason to look for a more refined declarative theory and the best possible linear encoding for multistrings is that lexical transducers

(Karttunen, 1994) may contain a huge or even an infinite number of lexical entries. Its synthesis with declaratively specified AP rules requires more than just brute force enumeration and the decidability of the individual rules. We should be able to compose the whole lexicon with the whole phonology and produce just the regular two-level relation between the underlying morphemes and the processed surface. Once we have reached the two-level relation, we realize that the choice of the phonological theory, the specific declarative formalism and even the alternations used to build internal representations are of secondary importance, as long as we are satisfied with the descriptive adequacy of the lexical transducer.

We are now convinced that, in order to address the formalization challenge of AP, any implementation of autosegmental rules over multistrings must have an encoding that is easy to get rid of once the regular lexicon-surface relation has been defined. This concern requires us to postpone the design aspects of a declarative formalism. We realize that some linear encoding — even with limitations — is going to be necessary for any ultimate solution to the AP challenge.

20.1.2 Bistrings

In order to study the linear encoding of autosegmental structures, we now restrict ourselves to bistrings that are a two-tiered special case of multistrings.

A **non-crossing (aligned) bistring** is a triple $S = (\sigma_n, \tau_m, E)$ where

- σ_n and τ_m are, respectively, partially $\varnothing$-padded strings $s_1 s_2 \ldots s_n$ and $t_1 t_2 \ldots t_m$ over alphabet $\Sigma \cup \{\varnothing\}$, and
- E is a subset of $[1..n] \times [1..m]$ called the **association relation**.
- E does not contain any pairs (i, k), (j, l) such that $i < j$ but $k > l$.
- E does not contain any pair (i, j) such that $s_i = \varnothing$ and $t_j = \varnothing$.

The operation of **(disjoint) concatenation** of bistrings (σ_n, τ_m, E) and (α, β, F), denoted by $(\sigma_n, \tau_m, E) \cdot (\alpha, \beta, F)$, is defined as the bistring $(\sigma_n \alpha, \tau_m \beta, E \cup \{(i+n, j+m) : (i, j) \in F\})$. Notice that no associations are added to connect the component bistrings to each other.

An association $(i, j) \in E$ is **nonzero** if $s_i \neq \varnothing$ and $t_j \neq \varnothing$, and **zero** otherwise. In a **non-zero associated bistring** (20.3), all elements have non-zero associations. For example, the bistring (color, colour, E) with associations $E = \{(1,1), (2,2), (3,3), (4,4), (5,4), (6,5)\}$ is non-zero associated:

(20.3)

The bistring (ondjaba,HLH,{(5,1),(7,2)}) in (20.4) has one floating tone (H) and one segment (o) that could bear a tone association but does not. This Kwanyama word means ‘elephant (predicative)’ (Halme, 2004) and it is derived from the underlying form *o H(L) - ndjaba HH.*

```
        H   L H
        |   |
o n d j a b a
```
(20.4)

The structure in (20.4) is a perfect example of a bistring that occurs in the AP literature. If we add some assumptions of the relative order of its unassociated elements with respect to adjacent words in the phonological string, we obtain a more specific kind of bistring (20.5) that contains zero associations. This kind of specificity makes a huge difference in the existence of an optimal linear encoding, as we will see later.

```
∅ ∅ ∅ ∅ H ∅ L H
| | | | | | | |
o n d j a b a ∅
```
(20.5)

Space limitations do not allow us to discuss the generalisations of non-crossing bistrings. These would have included multistrings (Clements, 1985, Kornai, 1995, Yli-Jyrä, 2016), bistrings with crossing associations (Bagemihl, 1989, Yli-Jyrä, 2016) and bistrings outside AP, for example in machine translation.

There is already a notable body of literature about the computational treatment of bistrings. The known approaches can be classified into four perspectives:

- *declarative description* (Bird and Klein, 1990, Bird and Ellison, 1994, Jardine, 2017) of bistrings
- *linear models* of bistrings that could satisfy these descriptions (Eisner, 1997, Yli-Jyrä and Niemi, 2006, Yli-Jyrä, 2013, 2015).
- *generative processes* that generate aligned multistrings (Kay, 1987, Wiebe, 1992, Kornai, 1995, Jardine and Heinz, 2015).
- *alignment models* that try to discover the associations when the component strings are given (studied mainly outside AP).

These perspectives are interrelated and most contributions seem to have more than one perspective in them. For example, Bird and Ellison (1994) presented a synthesis of a logical formalism for constraint-based description of the structures, model-theoretic semantics of the formalism and a generative process for the models. Therefore, this classification does not do full justice to individual works.

20.1.3 An Optimal Coding Function

In order to process bistrings as strings, we need to have a way to encode the source messages – bistrings – and then to decode the encoded bistrings from code strings. In our case, the bistrings consist of fragments Y and the code strings consist of factors X.

Let X^* and Y^* be two sets of structures that are closed under the concatenation operation with respective neutral elements, both denoted by ϵ. A partial function $f : Y^* \to X^*$ can be used to encode any message $y \in Y^*$ if

- f is **total** and thus computable
- f is invertible, having an **inverse function** $f^{-1} : X^* \to Y^*$ such that $f^{-1}(X^*) = Y^*$.

Thus, in order to be able to encode and decode, we need a bijective total function f from the concatenation-closed family Y^* of bistings to the concatenation-closed set X^*.

Because it is better that the coding function f not be cryptic but that the fragments X in the message and the factors Y in the encoded message correspond to each other one-to-one, Kornai (1995) defines two additional important properties for a coding function:

- f is **iconic** if it retains the local structure of its source message in the encoded message.
- f is **compositional** (and a monoid morphism) if $f(\epsilon) = \epsilon$ and $f(u)f(v) = f(uv)$ for all $u, v \in Y^*$.

The importance of iconic coding is in the need to describe bistring structures and their alternations using predicates over the encoded structures. A cryptographic encoding would be difficult for model-theoretic semantics of the grammar and the binding of formulas.

Compositionality is desirable because we want to perform operations over encoded structures without the need to decode these structures first back to their source structures. Especially, if we concatenate regular languages containing an infinite number of encoded structures, we can compute the concatenation only if the concatenation of the encoded structures gives the same result as the encoding of the concatenation of the decoded structures.

If a coding function f has all four of these properties (total, invertible, iconic and composition), it is an **optimal** coding function (Kornai, 1995).

20.1.4 The Original Triple Code

The current paper focuses on finding a balance between the set of source bistrings and the corresponding code words. When this balance is found, we can have an optimal coding function.

The triple code of András Kornai and Lauri Karttunen are the earliest attempts to encode bistrings as strings that can be processed by simple computers. The first known record of the triple code is in Kornai's 1991 Stanford dissertation that was supervised by Paul Kiparsky. The original version of the code became known as Kornai's triple code (Wiebe, 1992, Bird and Ellison, 1994). Kornai encoded every association between a segment s and an autosegment t with a triple $(s1t)$. In addition, the code used the short codewords b and t to tell if the most recent element of one component string has an additional association. In addition, there were some ways to encode the lack of association between two synchronized elements of the component strings, but these were never completely satisfactory.

We will now use Karttunen's variant because its syntax is simpler. Karttunen's variant (Kornai 1995, p. 22) reduces Kornai's informative triples and mentions each (auto)segment only once. This is the idea that we call **Kornai-Karttunen code**. Since the code was later assessed critically by other authors (Wiebe, 1992, Bird and Ellison, 1994), the published work (Kornai, 1995) contains extensions that accommodate to the criticism and its implications.

The years around 1987-1991 when Kornai studied in Stanford were interesting times in finite-state phonology. In the early 1980's, Kaplan and Kay had developed rapidly spreading ideas for finite-state phonology in Palo Alto. These ideas influenced the birth of two-level morphology (Koskenniemi, 1983). Lauri Karttunen (1983) reimplemented Kimmo Koskenniemi's model (the KIMMO model) and later got involved with the development of the first two-level compiler (Karttunen et al., 1987) in the Xerox Palo Alto Research Center (PARC). Lauri's PARC colleague, Martin Kay (1987), wrote about the possibility of applying multi-tape automata in the 1986 Prosodic Morphology (McCarthy and Prince, 1996). In addition to proposing a modification to Kornai's original triple code, Lauri was working on other encoding schemes that included a binary encoding for finite state networks (Karttunen, 1990).

This fundamental research in finite-state phonology required some implicit or explicit knowledge in coding theory. For example, Koskenniemi (1983) encoded same-length regular relations using a pair alphabet. The coding theory for autosegmental phonology started to be developed in Kornai's dissertation. More generally, we know that any linear encoding (Berstel et al., 2010) splits the source messages into fragments or "source letters" that correspond to **code words**. Each code word then consists of **code letters** of the code alphabet.

Kornai and Karttunen's triples can be viewed either as the code words or as code letters, depending on the perspective: In the original treatment (Kornai, 1995), the code alphabet for Karttunen's variant consists of the tier letters and three symbols: 0, 1, and underscore (_). The triples constructed from these were regarded as code words. However, the triples can themselves be seen as a code alphabet that is used to form longer code words. This kind of amendment will be our final perspective as it gives us more flexibility in defining what bistrings are actually encodable and what structures can be concatenated with each other.

20.1.5 The Critical Assessment and Its Limitations

If we strip bistrings of all association links, we obtain string tuples $\Sigma^* \times \Sigma^*$. A set of such unassociated bistrings is regular if it is recognized by a finite two-tape automaton that has transition labels Λ. The existence of a two-tape automaton gives us a decoding function $f^{-1} : \Lambda^* \to \Sigma^* \times \Sigma^*$.

However, no encoding function $f : \Sigma^* \times \Sigma^* \to \Lambda^*$ is compositional in the sense that the equivalence $f(\alpha\beta) = f(\alpha)f(\beta)$ would hold for all unassociated bistrings $\alpha, \beta \in \Sigma^* \times \Sigma^*$. This limitation of encoding functions is a well known fact in automata theory (Sakarovitch, 2009).

Wiebe (1992) found that unassociated multistrings have a similar problem. Since bistrings that lack associations are special cases of autosegmental representations, Wiebe's theorem can be narrowed to them.

Theorem 1 *An invertible linear encoding (using transition labels) for string pairs $\Sigma^* \times \Sigma^*$ cannot be compositional.*

While the theorem is true, it involves two assumptions that have been questioned only partially:

1. Wiebe ignored the possibility that the encoded bistrings could have **latent timing** between their unassociated elements, in a similar way to that illustrated in Bird and Ellison (1994).
2. Wiebe ignored the possibility that the factors of bistrings could be restricted to a (lexical) supply of **larger fragments** whose concatenation can be compositional, depending on the careful choice of the available fragments (Jardine and Heinz, 2015, Yli-Jyrä, 2015).

20.1.6 The Amending Avenues

In this article, I am arguing for a better version of the Kornai-Karttunen code by introducing unassociated elements with latent timing and code words for larger fragments.

Latent timing for unassociated elements refines the description of a bistring without postulating the usual associations. For example, Bird and Ellison (1994) showed how to describe a multistring and compute a linear encoding for all alternative models of the described object. They merely describe bistrings with a semi-declarative formalism that compiles to automata. The models generated by the compiled automata satisfy the declarative description despite having a more detailed timing between the elements. However, even Bird and Ellison (1994) fail to define a linear encoding that would respect concatenation, although the existence of a compositional, multilinear concatenation is pointed out in this context (Wiebe, 1992, Bird and Ellison, 1994).

Larger fragments could allow unspecified timing between the elements without affecting the compositionality. This idea has been explored recently in two contributions. Jardine and Heinz (2015) considered a finite, language-specific lexicon of bistring fragments. Yli-Jyrä (2015) considered an infinite set of fragments and showed that this set corresponds to a regular set of code words. Outside of AP, we have prior examples of transregular codes that are based on Dyck primes (Berstel et al., 2010) or a subset of these (Yli-Jyrä and Gómez-Rodríguez, 2017).

When the input of the coding function has a total order and the codewords as well as the corresponding fragments of bistrings have richer structure, we have a realistic hope of proceeding towards an optimal coding function in the sense of Kornai (1995). This idea of an amended triple code will be explained in the following main sections of this article.

20.1.7 The Impact

The current contribution is a part of a larger agenda to develop finite-state transducers for aligned multistrings. The amended triple code is an instructive example of a coding scheme, but it is not the only solution. In fact, there are bijections between different encoding schemes (Yli-Jyrä, 2015), which suggests that the differences between them may be an artefact having only secondary importance in the larger picture.

The choice between the encoding schemes can be made in the context of a model-theoretic implementation of AP. A model-theoretic implementation will have a descriptive formalism that describes either the local **replace relations** (in a derivative AP) or a GEN relation (in a constraint-based AP). Because these relations potentially generate multiple output candidates in a similar way as an undirected string replacement (Karttunen, 1995), these also need a **worsener aka preference relation** (Gerdemann, 2009, Yli-Jyrä, 2008, Yli-Jyrä, 2013) that disambiguates the output. If the bistring encoding is linear, the descriptions based on AP can be compiled, as in Yli-Jyrä (2013), into finite-state string transducers that have good closure properties. The resulting FST can then be combined with a one-way lexical transducer (Karttunen, 1994).

The replace relations and the ranking relations can be expressed with the finite-state transducer calculus, as was done successfully in Yli-Jyrä (2013). Alternatively, MSO definable transductions (Engelfriet and Hoogeboom, 2001, Courcelle and Engelfriet, 2012, Jardine, 2017) can be compiled from an elegant logical formalism which is, however, much more verbose than the classical AP rule formalism (Goldsmith, 1976).

Mature finite-state technology for aligned multistrings potentially has a wide impact in NLP. Compilation of the existing autosegmental grammars can help to improve the morphological disambiguation in speech recognition of morphologically rich tonal languages, such as Kwanyama (Halme, 2004) and Ikoma as the labelled training data is still too small for statistical modelling. The constructed transducers can also help to validate descriptive grammars that are based on autosegmental or OT phonology (Karttunen, 2006) or to produce training examples for a statistical model of phonology. Besides these obvious applications in generative phonology, aligned bistrings and multistrings are crucial in morphological induction, syntax and parallel texts (Yli-Jyrä, 2016). A new finite-state technology for bistrings might also provide a principled search space for many tasks and help to relate explainable structures to neural networks (Rastogi et al., 2016).

20.2 A Two-Tape Transition System

The possibility of applying multi-tape automata to autosegmental structures goes back to Kay (1987). In this model, each component string sits on a separate tape and the automaton coordinates the time steps needed to read the contents of each tape and to implicitly generate the associations between the elements of these strings.

In the present work, two-tape automata are viewed as transition systems that operate on tape-like memory structures. This view is chosen because transition systems represent a standard perspective in today's language technology and parsing (Nivre, 2008) and the conditions of the transitions can be expressed neatly. Working out the correspondence between the two-tape transition system and a two-tape finite automaton is left as an exercise to the advanced reader.

Valid Computations

A **transition system** is a quadruple $S = (C, \Lambda, \delta, c_0, F)$ where

- C is a set of *configurations* defined below
- Λ is a set of *transition labels*,
- $\delta : (C \times \Lambda) \to C$ is a partial *transition function*
- $c_0 \in C$ is an *initial configuration.*
- $F \subseteq C$ is a set of *final configurations.*

Transitions $\delta(c_i, \lambda) = c_j$ may be written as $c_i \xrightarrow{\lambda} c_j$ or $\lambda : c_i \to c_j$ and a **computation** of the transition system may be written as

$$c_i \xrightarrow{\lambda_i} c_{i+1} \xrightarrow{\lambda_{i+1}} c_{i+2} \cdots \xrightarrow{\lambda_{n-1}} c_n.$$

Such a computation is **valid** if $c_i = c_0$ and $c_n \in F$.

Two-Tape Configurations

By defining the set of configurations of the transition system, we specialize the type of the transition systems to a particular automaton structure. A **configuration** of a *two-tape transition system* is a 6-tuple $(q, \alpha, \beta, \sigma_n, \tau_m, E)$, where

- $q \in Q$ is a *state*,
- $\alpha, \beta \in \mathbb{N}^*$ are stacks of string positions
- $\sigma_n = s_1 s_2 ... s_n$, $\tau_m = t_1 t_2 ... t_m$ are strings over the alphabet $\Sigma \cup \{\varnothing\}$,
- $E \subset \mathbb{N} \times \mathbb{N}$ is the set of associations gathered so far.

For now, there are two states in Q. The state 0 means that the bistring is complete, while the state 1 indicates the situation where one more association must be added to the the last position of σ_n or τ_m, respectively, before the bistring is complete.

We fix the initial configuration $c_0 = (0, [\,], [\,], \epsilon, \epsilon, \{\})$ and restrict the final configurations F to those whose state is 0. A valid transition sequence of the form

$$(0, [\,], [\,], \epsilon, \epsilon, \{\}) \xrightarrow{\lambda_0} \xrightarrow{\lambda_1} \cdots \xrightarrow{\lambda_p} (q, \alpha, \beta, \sigma_n, \tau_m, E)$$

is said to generate the bistring (σ_n, τ_m, E). Since $(0, [\,], [\,], \epsilon, \epsilon, \{\})$ is also a final configuration; the empty bistring $(\epsilon, \epsilon, \{\})$ is generated without any transitions.

Transitions

In order to complete the definition of the transition system, we need to define the set of transition labels Λ and the partial transition function δ. Karttunen's triples in Kornai (1995) are defined for elements $s, t \in \Sigma$ as $(s0t)$, $(s0\_)$, $(\_0t)$, $(s1t)$, $(\_1t)$, $(s1\_)$. For purposes of the current discussion, we add also the triples $(s01)$, $(10t)$, $(s00)$, $(00t)$ whose use is more restricted than that of $(s0\_)$ and $(\_0t)$. These triples can be visualized as in (20.6) to make them easier to read:.

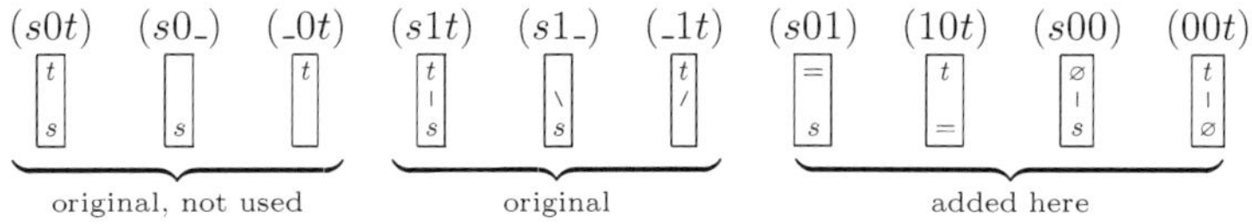

(20.6)

The transitions $(s0\_)$, $(\_0t)$, and $(s0t)$ add the letter s or/and t to the respective component string and leave the most recent letter (if any) in each component string available for further associations:

 $: (0, \alpha, \beta, \sigma_n, \tau_m, E) \mapsto (0, [n{+}1], [m{+}1], \sigma_n s, \tau_m t, E)$

 $: (0, \alpha, \beta, \sigma_n, \tau_m, E) \mapsto (0, [n{+}1], \beta, \sigma_n s, \tau_m, E).$

 $: (0, \alpha, \beta, \sigma_n, \tau_m, E) \mapsto (0, \alpha, [m{+}1], \sigma_n, \tau_m t, E).$

Using these transitions would lead to ambiguous coding. Therefore, we will not use then at all. Instead, we add new triples that encode zero associations and unassociated elements in specific safe contexts.

The triples $(s1\_)$, $(\_1t)$, and $(s1t)$ add the letter s or/and t to the respective component string, and then create an association between the last positions of the component strings. Finally, they leave the last positions available for further associations. The transitions $(s1\_)$ and $(\_1t)$ require that the matching position i is available in one of the strings that remains constant:

 $: (q, \alpha, [i], \sigma_n, \tau_m, E) \mapsto (0, [n{+}1], [i], \sigma_n s, \tau_m, E \cup \{(n{+}1, i)\})$

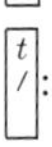 $: (q, [i], \beta, \sigma_n, \tau_m, E) \mapsto (0, [i], [m{+}1], \sigma_n, \tau_m t, E \cup \{(i, m{+}1)\})$

 $: (0, \alpha, \beta, \sigma_n, \tau_m, E) \mapsto (0, [n{+}1], [m{+}1], \sigma_n s, \tau_m t, E \cup \{(n{+}1, m{+}1)\})$

The triples $(\varnothing 1t)$ and $(s1\varnothing)$ behave like $(s1t)$ but they add a zero association and do not leave any last positions open for new associations:

$$\boxed{\begin{smallmatrix}\varnothing\\ |\\ s\end{smallmatrix}}: (0,\alpha,\beta,\sigma_n,\tau_m,E) \longrightarrow (0,[\,],[\,],\sigma_n s,\tau_m\varnothing,E\cup\{(n{+}1,m{+}1)\})$$

$$\boxed{\begin{smallmatrix}t\\ |\\ \varnothing\end{smallmatrix}}: (0,\alpha,\beta,\sigma_n,\tau_m,E) \longrightarrow (0,[\,],[\,],\sigma_n\varnothing,\tau_m t,E\cup\{(n{+}1,m{+}1)\})$$

The transitions ($s01$) and ($10t$) add the letter s or t to the respective component string, without associating it. They require, however, that the last element is available in the component that remains constant. This element must later be associated before the bistring can be recognized:

$$\boxed{\begin{smallmatrix}=\\ \\ s\end{smallmatrix}}: (q,\alpha,[i],\sigma_n,\tau_m,E) \mapsto (1,[],[i],\sigma_n s,\tau_m,E).$$

$$\boxed{\begin{smallmatrix}t\\ \\ =\end{smallmatrix}}: (q,[i],\alpha,\sigma_n,\tau_m,E) \mapsto (1,[i],[],\sigma_n,\tau_m t,E).$$

For example, the transition sequence (20.7)

$$\begin{array}{|c|c|c|c|c|c|c|}\hline \mathrm{j} & \mathrm{o} & \mathrm{y} & \mathrm{e} & \mathrm{u} & \mathrm{x} & \varnothing\\ | & | & | & | & | & | & |\\ \mathrm{j} & \mathrm{o} & \mathrm{y} & \mathrm{e} & \mathrm{u} & \mathrm{s} & \mathrm{e}\\ \hline\end{array} \tag{20.7}$$

gives rise to a valid sequence (20.8) of transitions that compute the bistring (joyeuse, joyeux∅, $\{(1,1),...,(5,5),(6,6),(7,7)\}$).

$$\begin{array}{l}
(0,[\,],[\,],\epsilon,\epsilon,\{\}) \xrightarrow{\boxed{\begin{smallmatrix}\mathrm{j}\\ |\\ \mathrm{j}\end{smallmatrix}}}\\
(0,[1],[1],\mathrm{j},\mathrm{j},\{(1,1)\}) \xrightarrow{\boxed{\begin{smallmatrix}\mathrm{o}\\ |\\ \mathrm{o}\end{smallmatrix}}}\\
(0,[2],[2],\mathrm{jo},\mathrm{jo},\{(1,1),(2,2)\}) \xrightarrow{\boxed{\begin{smallmatrix}\mathrm{y}\\ |\\ \mathrm{y}\end{smallmatrix}}} \cdots\\
(0,[5],[5],\mathrm{joyeu},\mathrm{joyeu},\{(1,1),...,(5,5)\}) \xrightarrow{\boxed{\begin{smallmatrix}\mathrm{x}\\ |\\ \mathrm{s}\end{smallmatrix}}}\\
(0,[6],[6],\mathrm{joyeus},\mathrm{joyeux},\{(1,1),...,(5,5),(6,6)\}) \xrightarrow{\boxed{\begin{smallmatrix}\varnothing\\ |\\ \mathrm{e}\end{smallmatrix}}}\\
(0,[\,],[\,],\underbrace{\mathrm{joyeuse},\mathrm{joyeux}\varnothing,\{(1,1),...,(5,5),(6,6),(7,7)\}}_{\text{the computed bistring}}).
\end{array} \tag{20.8}$$

20.3 The Amended Triple Code

In this section, we will show that transition systems can be used to define linear codes and coding functions that are compositional, invertible, iconic and computable for the corresponding families of bistrings.

The best way to ensure compositionality of encoded structures is to ensure that both the source fragment and the code strings have corresponding, unambiguous factorisations. A **code** is a set of code words X over a **code alphabet** A such that the strings in X^* have an unambiguous factorisation into a concatenation of the code words X. Ideally, the source bistring consists of corresponding unambiguous factors Y.

Although the size of the factors have no restrictions, they are still called source letters as they should be in a one-to-one correspondence with the code words.

Peculiarly enough, a code can be infinite. For example, the set of code words known as Dyck primes can be used to encode sequences of trees. One Dyck prime (code word) corresponds to an arbitrarily large tree. Every ordered non-crossing graph can also be encoded as a concatenation of code words that constitute a context-free language (Yli-Jyrä and Gómez-Rodríguez, 2017). Under this concatenation, the adjacent components share an articulation node. There are also infinite codes that are regular languages.

There are different kinds of codes (Berstel et al., 2010). A code $X \subseteq A^*$ is a **suffix code** if no proper suffix of a code word is itself a code word. Yli-Jyrä (2015) gives three codes all of which encode the same family of bistrings.

Source Factorisation

In order to use the code, we first have to make sure that the source message is factorised unambiguously. This is not possible if the relative order of elements is not fixed at the factor boundaries.

Associated elements of a bistring form bipartite caterpillar trees that have an almost unambiguous natural linear order when the strings are ordered. But the unassociated elements t_3, s_4 and $t_5, ..., t_7, s_6, ..., s_8$ in (20.9) lack a similar linear order:

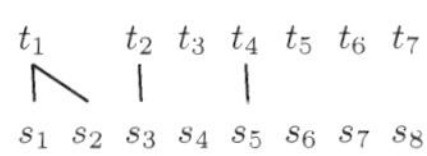

(20.9)

The unassociated elements can lead to alternative factorisations of the bistring:

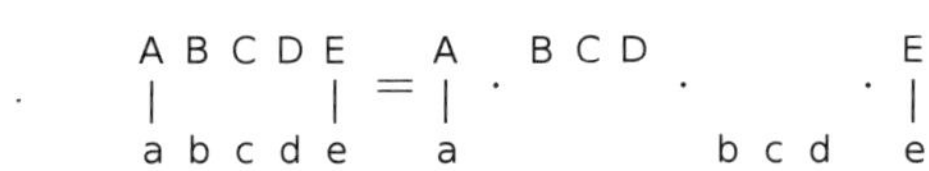

(20.10)

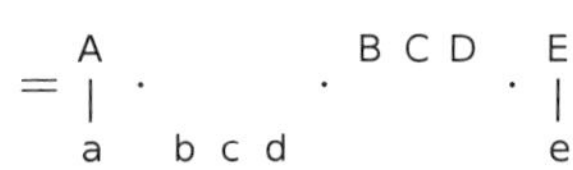

(20.11)

This inherent factorisation ambiguity of unassociated bistrings means that the two component strings can be delayed (arbitrarily) far under concatenation without changing the identity of the concatenated bistring:

$$\begin{array}{c}\mathsf{B\ C\ D\ B\ C\ D}\\ \\ \end{array} \cdot \begin{array}{c} \\ \mathsf{b\ c\ d\ b\ c\ d}\end{array} = \begin{array}{c} \\ \mathsf{b\ c\ d\ b\ c\ d}\end{array} \cdot \begin{array}{c}\mathsf{B\ C\ D\ B\ C\ D}\\ \\ \end{array} \qquad (20.12)$$

In an AP grammar that processes potentially an infinite set of phonological strings, the unbounded delay between the component strings is a big problem. For example, the equivalence of two regular sets of unassociated bistrings – two regular relations – is undecidable when the delay is unbounded.

The synchronisation delay is also a problem in coding. If the bistrings can be factorised in two different ways, both factorisations should map to the same code string, i.e. the coding function is compositional. For our examples (20.10 and 20.11) of alternative factorisations, a compositional function means concretely that the following equations hold:

$$f\begin{pmatrix}\mathsf{B\ C\ D}\\ \\ \end{pmatrix} f\begin{pmatrix} \\ \mathsf{b\ c\ d}\end{pmatrix} = f\begin{pmatrix}\mathsf{B\ C\ D}\\ \mathsf{b\ c\ d}\end{pmatrix} \qquad (20.13)$$

$$f\begin{pmatrix} \\ \mathsf{b\ c\ d}\end{pmatrix} f\begin{pmatrix}\mathsf{B\ C\ D}\\ \\ \end{pmatrix} = f\begin{pmatrix}\mathsf{B\ C\ D}\\ \mathsf{b\ c\ d}\end{pmatrix} \qquad (20.14)$$

Since Wiebe (1992) has already shown that the required kind of encoding function does not exist for all bistrings, we must avoid trying to encode all bistrings. Instead, we will restrict the domain of source bistrings and their factorisations in such a way that the factorisation ambiguity is never encountered. This idea is expressed by the following theorem:

Theorem 2 *Let Y be a recursive set of bistrings such that all elements of Y^* are unambiguously factorisable into a concatenation of elements of Y, then there is a code X and a compositional bijection $f : Y^* \to X^*$ that respects concatenation.*

Proof. In order to have a compositional bijection $f : Y^* \to X^*$, where Y^* is unambiguously generated by Y, it suffices to show that X is a code of the same cardinality and that restriction $f|_Y$ is a bijection between Y and X. Since every recursive set is a recursively enumerable, the set Y is a countable and there is a (countable) bijection g from Y to a subset of natural numbers. Each natural number $\{0, 1, 2, ...\}$ is itself encoded via a bijective function h that maps the numbers to strings of nested parentheses $\{(), (()), ((())), ...\}$. After setting $X = h(g(Y))$, we observe that X is a code and that the restriction $f_{|Y}(\cdot) = h(g(\cdot))$ is a bijection. There is an unambiguous factorisation $y = y_1 y_2 ... y_n$ such that $y_1, y_2, ..., y_n \in Y$ and this factorisation lifts $f_{|Y}$ to set Y^* by the definition $f(y) = f_{|Y}(y_1)f_{|Y}(y_2)...f_{|Y}(y_n)$. It is easy to see that f then respects concatenation because Y^* factorises unambiguously. □

I have found two main strategies that help to find the set of bistring factors Ysuch that Y^* is then unambiguously factorisable:

1. **We can introduce latent linear order.** Zero associations can be used for padding strings so that they have equivalent lengths, as in example 20.15.

   j o y e u x ∅
   | | | | | | |
   j o y e u s e (20.15)

   Padding can also be partial and it does not have to make the component strings have equivalent lenths. Zero associations help to introduce linear order in noncrossing bistrings. The linear order of elements in concatenation is fully determined when the elements in the operands have zero associations:

   A B C D ∅ ∅ ∅ E   A B C D ∅ ∅ ∅ E
   | | | | · | | | | = | | | | | | | |
   a ∅ ∅ ∅ b c d e   a ∅ ∅ ∅ b c d e (20.16)

   Historically, zero associations have been crucial to the KIMMO model (Koskenniemi, 1983, Karttunen, 1983, Yli-Jyrä and Koskenniemi, 2006), allowing Boolean operations over regular sets of one-to-one associated bistrings.

2. **We can use larger source fragments.** For example, we can allow unassociated elements that occur inside the elements of Y. An unassociated element i in s is an **interruption** if there are two elements j and k in the same component string and an element l such that $j < i < k$ and $(j, l), (k, l) \in E$ or $(j, l), (k, l) \in E^{-1}$.

If all non-interrupting elements in the bistring have a (zero or non-zero) association, the unassociated elements of bistring are totally ordered. For example, bistring (20.17) contains some interruptions and the other elements are associated either with a zero or a non-zero element.

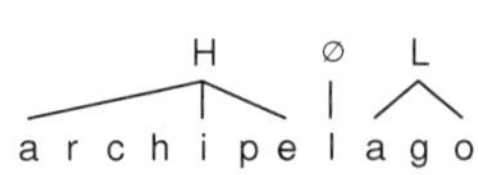

(20.17)

There are further ways to introduce more fragments that contain unassociated elements. For example, we could allow unassociated tones before an associated element and unassociated segments after an associated element. However, enforcing linear order on unassociated elements by such restricted positions does not add anything to what is already achieved when we replace unassociated elements with elements that have zero associations and thus an unambiguous position with respect to the surrounding elements.

Optimal Codes

In this section, we build codes that let us enumerate some useful families of bistrings. Each code X is such that its closure X^* corresponds to a family of unambiguously factorizable bistrings Y^*. The factors Y and the code X are bijectively related, and it is then easy to see that the coding function has all the properties of an optimal coding function (Kornai, 1995).

1. A bistring (s, t, E) is **one-to-one** if every symbol in s and t has exactly one (zero or non-zero) association. The family of **one-to-one non-crossing bistrings** is encoded with the transition system $S_{\text{1-1}}$ that has transitions $\boxed{\begin{smallmatrix}t\\ \mid\\ s\end{smallmatrix}}$, $\boxed{\begin{smallmatrix}\varnothing\\ \mid\\ s\end{smallmatrix}}$, and $\boxed{\begin{smallmatrix}t\\ \mid\\ \varnothing\end{smallmatrix}}$ for $s, t \in \Sigma$. In this case, the set of code words (20.18) are the same as the code alphabet.

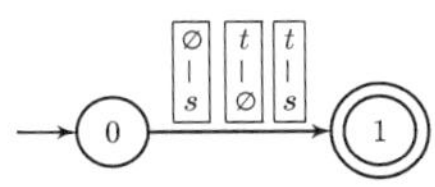

(20.18)

2. The family of **non-zero-associated non-crossing bistrings** is encoded with the transition system $S_{\text{non-zero}}$ that has transitions $\boxed{\begin{smallmatrix}t\\ \mid\\ s\end{smallmatrix}}$, $\boxed{\begin{smallmatrix}\ \\ \backslash\\ s\end{smallmatrix}}$, and $\boxed{\begin{smallmatrix}t\\ /\\ \ \end{smallmatrix}}$ for $s, t \in \Sigma$. In this case, the set of code words (20.19) is an infinite suffix code.

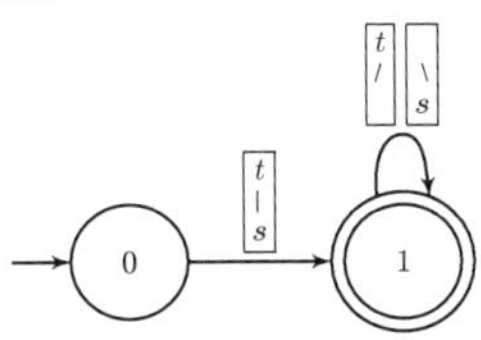

(20.19)

3. A non-crossing bistring is **inertial** (Yli-Jyrä, 2015) if every actual symbol in s and t is either non-zero/zero associated or an interruption. A bistring is **proper** (Kornai, 1995) if no element is an interruption. Note that properness excludes interruptions, while inertial bistrings exclude the opposite kind of unassociated elements.
The family of **proper inertial bistrings** is encoded with the transition system S_{propiner} that has transitions $\boxed{\begin{smallmatrix}t\\ \mid\\ s\end{smallmatrix}}$, $\boxed{\begin{smallmatrix}\varnothing\\ \mid\\ s\end{smallmatrix}}$, $\boxed{\begin{smallmatrix}t\\ \mid\\ \varnothing\end{smallmatrix}}$, $\boxed{\begin{smallmatrix}\ \\ \backslash\\ s\end{smallmatrix}}$, and

$\boxed{\substack{t \\ / \\ }}$ for $s, t \in \Sigma$. In this case, the set of code words (20.20) is an infinite suffix code.

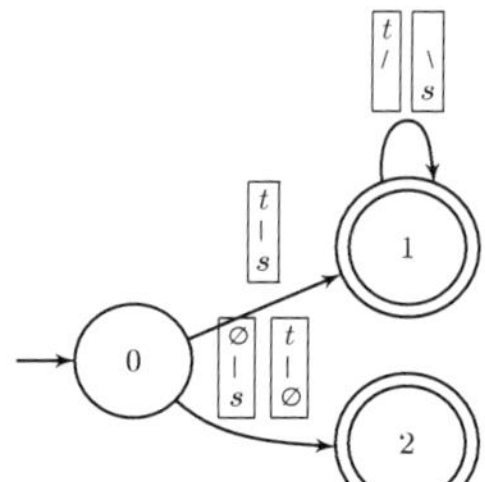

(20.20)

4. The family of **inertial bistrings** is encoded with the transition system S_{inertial} that has transitions $\boxed{\substack{t \\ | \\ s}}$, $\boxed{\substack{\varnothing \\ | \\ s}}$, $\boxed{\substack{t \\ | \\ \varnothing}}$, $\boxed{\substack{= \\ \\ \varnothing}}$, $\boxed{\substack{t \\ \\ =}}$, $\boxed{\substack{ \\ \backslash \\ s}}$, and $\boxed{\substack{t \\ / \\ }}$ for $s, t \in \Sigma$. In the transition system, the states and stack contents of the configurations implement constraints that make the transitions of intervening elements and zero associations behave in a certain way. The transitions such as $\boxed{\substack{= \\ \\ s}}$ and $\boxed{\substack{t \\ \\ =}}$ can be used only to form non-proper structures, while $\boxed{\substack{\varnothing \\ | \\ s}}$ and $\boxed{\substack{t \\ | \\ \varnothing}}$ are used only for zero associations:

$$\begin{array}{|c|c|c|c|} \mathsf{A} & \mathsf{B} & = & \\ | & / & & \backslash \\ \mathsf{a} & & \mathsf{b} & \mathsf{C} \end{array} \quad \begin{array}{|c|c|c|} \mathsf{A} & \mathsf{B} & \varnothing \\ | & / & | \\ \mathsf{a} & & \mathsf{c} \end{array}. \tag{20.21}$$

   - These transitions cannot (*) replace one another:

$$* \begin{array}{|c|c|c|c|} \mathsf{A} & \mathsf{B} & \varnothing & \\ | & / & | & \backslash \\ \mathsf{a} & & \mathsf{b} & \mathsf{C} \end{array} \quad * \begin{array}{|c|c|c|} \mathsf{A} & \mathsf{B} & = \\ | & / & \\ \mathsf{a} & & \mathsf{c} \end{array} \tag{20.22}$$

   - Moreover, the interruption transition cannot move earlier:

$$* \begin{array}{|c|c|c|c|} \mathsf{A} & = & \mathsf{B} & \\ | & & / & \backslash \\ \mathsf{a} & \mathsf{b} & & \mathsf{C} \end{array} \quad * \begin{array}{|c|c|c|} \mathsf{A} & = & \mathsf{B} \\ | & & / \\ \mathsf{a} & \mathsf{c} & \end{array} \tag{20.23}$$

Under these constraints, the set of code words (20.24) is an infinite suffix code over the code alphabet.

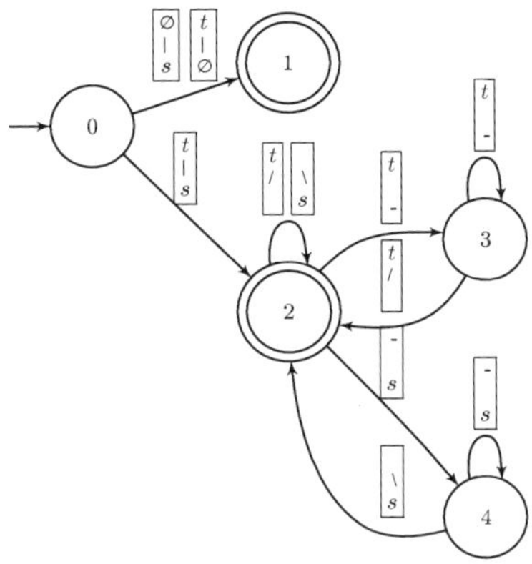

(20.24)

Lemma 3 *All four families of bistrings mentioned in this section have a code that is a regular language.* □

Lemma 4 *All four families of bistrings mentioned in this section have a computable encoding function.*

Proof. Availability of the transitions depends only on the three first elements of each configuration: state q, and stacks α and β. Since the stack never contains more than one symbol, the history of the transitions of Section 20.2 has a finite number of states. Thus, the valid transition sequences are finite-state and thus computable. □

Lemma 5 *All four families of bistrings mentioned in this section have a invertible encoding function.*

Proof. All these transition systems are deterministic and thus map each sequence of transition labels into a unique bistring. Thus the encoding is invertible. □

Lemma 6 *All four families of bistrings mentioned in this section are iconic.*

Proof. The fully associated noncrossing bistring in Figures 20.3 and 20.17 are very similar to their respective transition sequences (20.25).

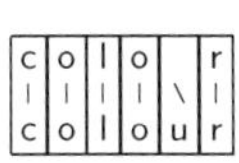

and
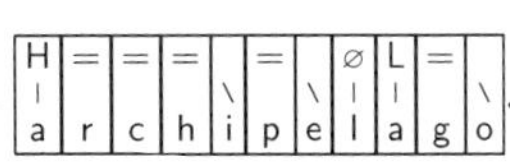

. (20.25)

From these examples, it is intuitively obvious that the code is iconic and it is easy to locate individual elements of the strings and the associations in the code strings. □

Lemma 7 *All four families of bistrings mentioned in this section have a compositional encoding function.*

Proof. It suffices to show that the code for inertial bistrings corresponds to a unique factorisation of bistrings. The first symbol of its code words is one of the "semaphores" (Berstel et al., 2010) $\boxed{\substack{\varnothing \\ \mid \\ s}}$, $\boxed{\substack{t \\ \mid \\ \varnothing}}$, or $\boxed{\substack{t \\ \mid \\ s}}$ that indicate the boundary of the code word. Now we need to show that every inertial bistrings is uniquely factorized into fragments that are generated by the code.

By definition, every element in component strings is either an interruption or has a nonzero or a zero association. Every string element that has a zero association constitutes a bistring fragment that splits the bistring into left and right parts that are recursively factorized. Further splits in the bistrings occur between two adjacent associations that do not share an incident element in the component strings. The interruptions remain inside the bistring fragments and do not introduce new splits. For example, (20.17) has three unambiguous fragments (20.26).

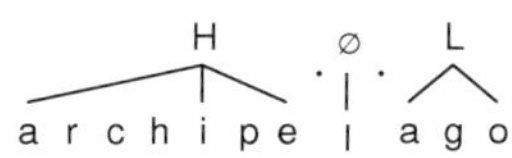

(20.26)

All inertial bistrings are obtained by concatenating these fragments. To encode them, we encode each part separately (20.27) and get the code string for the whole as the concatenation of the encoded parts.

(20.27)

We see now that the coding function is compositional by definition. □

Theorem 8 *All four families of bistrings mentioned in this section have an optimal coding function.* □

The following theorem can be proven with the techniques of Yli-Jyrä (2015), and is therefore left to the reader:

Theorem 9 *The currently amended Kornai-Karttunen triple code for inertial bistrings is bijectively related to three other regular codes (see Yli-Jyrä 2015) for inertial bistrings.*

References

Bagemihl, Bruce. 1989. The crossing constraint and 'backwards languages'. *Natural Language & Linguistic Theory* 7(4):481–549.

Berstel, Jean, Dominique Perrin, and Christophe Reutenauer. 2010. *Codes and Automata*, vol. 129 of *Encyclopedia of Mathematics and Its Applications*. Cambridge University Press.

Bird, Steven and T. Mark Ellison. 1994. One-level phonology: autosegmental representations and rules as finite automata. *Computational Linguistics* 20(1):55–90.

Bird, Steven and Ewan Klein. 1990. Phonological events. *Journal of Linguistics* 26(1):33–56.

Clements, George. N. 1985. The geometry of phonological features. *Phonology Yearbook* 2:225–252.

Courcelle, Bruno and Joost Engelfriet. 2012. *Graph Structure and Monadic Second-Order Logic: A Language-Theoretic Approach*. New York, NY, USA: Cambridge University Press.

Eisner, Jason. 1997. Efficient generation in primitive optimality theory. In *Proceedings of the 35th Annual ACL and 8th European ACL*, pages 313–320. Madrid.

Engelfriet, Joost and Hendrik Jan Hoogeboom. 2001. Mso definable string transductions and two-way finite-state transducers. *ACM Trans. Comput. Logic* 2(2):216–254.

Engelfriet, Joost and JanJoris Vereijken. 1996. Concatenation of graphs. In J. Cuny, H. Ehrig, G. Engels, and G. Rozenberg, eds., *Graph Grammars and Their Application to Computer Science*, vol. 1073 of *Lecture Notes in Computer Science*, pages 368–382. Springer Berlin Heidelberg.

Gerdemann, Dale. 2009. Mix and match replacement rules. In *Proceedings of the Workshop on Adaptation of Language Resources and Technology to New Domains*, AdaptLRTtoND '09, pages 39–47. Stroudsburg, PA, USA: Association for Computational Linguistics.

Goldsmith, John. 1976. *Autosegmental Phonology*. Ph.D. thesis, MIT.

Halme, Riikka. 2004. *A tonal grammar of Kwanyama*. Köln: Rüdiger Köppe Verlag.

Hulden, Mans. 2017. Rewrite rule grammars with multitape automata. *Journal of Language Modelling* 5(1):107–130.

Hyman, Larry. 2011. Tone: Is it different? In J. A. Goldsmith, J. Riggle, and A. C. L. Yu, eds., *The Blackwell Handbook of Phonological Theory*, pages 197–238. Wiley-Blackwell.

Jardine, Adam. 2013. Logic and the generative power of autosegmental phonology. In *Proceedings of Phonology 2013*.

Jardine, Adam. 2017. The expressivity of autosegmental grammars. Manuscript.

Jardine, Adam and Jeffrey Heinz. 2015. A concatenation operation to derive autosegmental graphs. In *Proceedings of the 14th Meeting on the Mathematics of Language (MoL 2015)*, pages 139–151. Chicago, USA: Association for Computational Linguistics.

Johnson, C. Douglas. 1972. *Formal Aspects of Phonological Description*. The Hague: Mouton.

Karttunen, Lauri. 1983. KIMMO: A general morphological processor. *Texas Linguistic Forum* 22:163–186.

Karttunen, Lauri. 1990. Binary encoding format for finite-state networks. Tech. Rep. SSL-90-17 [P90-00019], Xerox, System Sciences Laboratory, Palo Alto Research Center, Palo-Alto, California.

Karttunen, Lauri. 1994. Constructing lexical transducers. In *15th International Conference on Computational Linguistics, COLING 1994, Kyoto, Japan, August 5-9, 1994*, pages 406–411.

Karttunen, Lauri. 1995. The replace operator. In *Proceedings of the 33rd Annual Meeting on Association for Computational Linguistics*, ACL '95, pages 16–23. Stroudsburg, PA, USA: Association for Computational Linguistics.

Karttunen, Lauri. 2006. The insufficiency of paper-and-pencil linguistics: the case of Finnish prosody. In *Intelligent Linguistic Architectures: Variations on Themes by Roland M. Kaplan*, CSLI Publications, pages 287–300. Stanford, CA: Center for the study of language and information.

Karttunen, Lauri, Kimmo Koskenniemi, and Ronald Kaplan. 1987. *A compiler for two-level phonological rules*, vol. CSLI Report CSLI-87-108. Palo Alto, CA: Center for the Study of Language and Information, Stanford University.

Kay, Martin. 1987. Nonconcatenative finite-state morphology. In B. Maegaard, ed., *EACL 1989, 3rd Conference of the European Chapter of the Association for Computational Linguistics, April 1-3, 1987, University of Copenhagen, Copenhagen, Denmark*, pages 2–10. The Association for Computer Linguistics.

Kempe, André. 2010. Selected operations and applications of n-tape weighted finite-state machines. In A. Yli-Jyrä, A. Kornai, J. Sakarovitch, and B. Watson, eds., *Finite-State Methods and Natural Language Processing: 8th International Workshop, FSMNLP 2009, Pretoria, South Africa, July 21-24, 2009, Revised Selected Papers*, pages 31–46. Berlin, Heidelberg: Springer Berlin Heidelberg.

Kornai, András. 1995. *Formal Phonology*. New York: Garland Publishing.

Koskenniemi, Kimmo. 1983. *Two-Level Morphology: A General Computational Model for Word-Form Recognition and Production*. Ph.D. thesis, University of Helsinki.

McCarthy, John J. and Alan Prince. 1996. *Prosodic Morphology 1986*. No. 13 in Linguistics Department Faculty Publication Series. University of Massachusetts - Amherst, MA.

Nivre, Joakim. 2008. Algorithms for deterministic incremental dependency parsing. *Computational Linguistics* 34(4):513–553.

Rastogi, Pushpendre, Ryan Cotterell, and Jason Eisner. 2016. Weighting finite-state transductions with neural context. In K. Knight, A. Nenkova, and O. Rambow, eds., *NAACL HLT 2016, The 2016 Conference of the North American Chapter of the Association for Computational Linguistics: Human Language Technologies, San Diego California, USA, June 12-17, 2016*, pages 623–633. The Association for Computational Linguistics.

Ristad, Eric Sven. 1990. Computational structure of generative phonology and its relation to language comprehension. In *Proceedings of the 28th Annual Meeting on Association for Computational Linguistics*, ACL '90, pages 235–242. Pittsburgh, Pennsylvania.

Sagey, Elizabeth. 1988. On the ill-formedness of crossing association lines. *Linguistic Inquiry* 19:109–118.

Sakarovitch, Jacques. 2009. *Elements of Automata Theory*. Cambridge University Press.

Wiebe, Bruce. 1992. *Modelling autosegmental phonology with multitape finite state transducers*. Master's thesis, Simon Fraser University.

Yli-Jyrä, Anssi. 2008. Transducers from parallel replacement rules and modes with generalized lenient composition. In T. Hanneforth and K.-M. Würzner, eds., *Finite-State Methods and Natural Language Processing, 6th International Workshop, FSMNL-2007, Potsdam, Germany, September 14–16, Revised Papers*, pages 197–212. Potsdam: Potsdam University Press.

Yli-Jyrä, Anssi. 2013. On finite-state tonology with autosegmental representations. In M. Nederhof, ed., *Proceedings of the 11th International Conference on Finite State Methods and Natural Language Processing, FSMNLP 2013, St. Andrews, Scotland, UK, July 15-17, 2013*, pages 90–98. The Association for Computer Linguistics.

Yli-Jyrä, Anssi. 2015. Three equivalent codes for autosegmental representations. In T. Hanneforth and C. Wurm, eds., *Proceedings of the 12th International Conference on Finite-State Methods and Natural Language Processing, FSMNLP 2015, Düsseldorf, Germany, June 22-24, 2015*. The Association for Computer Linguistics.

Yli-Jyrä, Anssi. 2016. Aligned multistring languages. In *TTATT 2016, Proceedings of the Workshop, Workshop on Trends in Tree Automata and Tree Transducers*. Seoul, South Korea.

Yli-Jyrä, Anssi and Carlos Gómez-Rodríguez. 2017. Generic axiomatization of families of noncrossing graphs in dependency parsing. In *Proceedings of the 55th Annual Meeting of the Association for Computational Linguistics*, pages 1745–1755. Vancouver, Canada.

Yli-Jyrä, Anssi and Kimmo Koskenniemi. 2006. Compiling generalized two-level rules and grammars. In T. Salakoski, F. Ginter, S. Pyysalo, and T. Pahikkala, eds., *Advances in Natural Language Processing*, vol. 4139 of *Lecture Notes in Computer Science*, pages 174–185. Springer Berlin Heidelberg. ISBN 978-3-540-37334-6.

Yli-Jyrä, Anssi and Jyrki Niemi. 2006. Pivotal synchronization languages: A framework for alignments. In A. Yli-Jyrä, L. Karttunen, and J. Karhumäki, eds., *Finite-State Methods and Natural Language Processing*, vol. 4002 of *Lecture Notes in Computer Science*, pages 271–282. Springer Berlin Heidelberg.

21

Formal Verification in Optimality Theory*

MANS HULDEN

21.1 Introduction

Formal verification methods—tools and mindsets routinely found in the computational sciences—aim to establish watertight, mathematically rigorous proofs regarding the correct behavior of complex systems such as algorithms and digital circuits. In disciplines with engineering applications, such practice is indispensable in safety-critical processes when human life is at stake. Who would trust the software behind a radiation therapy device to deliver the correct dose if the engineer's response to the question "Is the software bug-free"? is simply "I should think so—I haven't found any bugs yet"?

In the context of linguistics, stakes are not quite as high, and failures to foresee subtle errors in a new generalization usually amount to nothing more than ill-spent time or, perhaps, a few sleepless nights worrying about blunders in a freshly proposed analysis. Nevertheless, as I will argue below, such waste of mental effort is in many cases completely avoidable. In fact, formal verification techniques can be put to use as a guide when *developing* a linguistic generalization, and also for *verifying* and *proving* correctness post hoc.

*I want to thank Ken Beesley and an anonymous reviewer for valuable comments on earlier versions of this paper. Thanks also to Dale Gerdemann for providing very fruitful discussions regarding finite-state OT, including the problem of implementing Finnish prosody exactly. Lastly, I am indebted to Lauri Karttunen for prompting this research, and for his helpful support over the years.

Tokens of Meaning: Papers in Honor of Lauri Karttunen.
Cleo Condoravdi and Tracy Holloway King (eds.).

It is perhaps not a coincidence that one of the principal components in the field of formal verification (Baier and Katoen, 2008), finite state technology, is also the foremost technology for the implementation of phonological and morphological analyzers and generators (Beesley and Karttunen, 2003). As we shall see, the fact that superficially divergent theories—of phonology in particular—can be formulated in terms of the language of finite state machines, offers far-reaching opportunities for correctness proofs.

A classic scenario which avails itself of formal verification techniques is the following: we have two different generalizations X and Y that both purport to characterize some linguistic phenomenon Z. We may assume that the generalizations in question are also being formulated in two different theoretical frameworks, each with its own language and notational peculiarities. The burning question that inevitably arises is: is X equivalent to Y? Might there not exist some counterexample that I haven't thought of that would prove that X behaves differently from Y on occasion?

A case for the need for computational help when analyzing the complex interaction of constraints that arises in Optimality Theory (OT) (Prince and Smolensky, 1993) was brilliantly put forth in Karttunen (2006a,b). In those articles, two different OT analyses of Finnish prosodic patterns (those of Elenbaas (1999), Elenbaas and Kager (1999) and Kiparsky (2003)) were put under the loupe through a method of compiling OT grammars into finite state transducers (Karttunen, 1998). This allowed for the rapid testing of the outputs that the OT grammars produce when input a corpus of words, revealing very subtle errors in the OT analyses.[1]

This paper shows how to extend this methodology to a more general level, taking Karttunen's analysis of Finnish Prosody as the starting point. I will show that by combining already developed methods by Karttunen (1998), Gerdemann and van Noord (2000), Gerdemann and Hulden (2012), and by introducing some formal verification techniques, the traps and pitfalls in OT analyses, including those found in Finnish prosody, can be investigated in a completely automatic fashion, potentially freeing the linguist from even having to possess any knowledge of the language in question. In other words, we will see how to move beyond the need to explicitly find counterexamples in a corpus when investigating an analysis.[2]

---

[1] Neque semper arcum tendit Apollo.

[2] Indeed, Karttunen's counterexample words to the two previous OT analyses are quite rare and, I would argue, difficult to come up with. A quick Google search reveals that one of them, **järjestelmällisyydelläni** ('with my systematicity'), re-

First, I will discuss a traditional rule-based transducer analysis of Finnish prosody, as implemented by Lauri Karttunen. Following this, I will show how to modify Karttunen's implementation of two OT analyses that attempt to model the same prosodic patterns produced by the rule-based one. This modification will produce a finite transducer that models the two OT grammars precisely for any input word of any length. Having done so, we will be in a position to formally compare the various grammars—or their transducer representations—for discrepancies, letting the finite automata algorithms do the work for us, telling us which input the grammars disagree on and produce different outputs. As will be seen, there are an infinite number of such patterns. Lastly, equipped with the formal verification tools necessary, we can easily correct the existing OT analyses and encounter one that can be *proven* to be equivalent to traditional analyses of Finnish prosody.

In this exposition, I will use the Xerox regular expression formalism for modeling finite automata and transducers, as documented in Beesley and Karttunen (2003), an overview of which is found in table 1. The code that implements the description and verification discussed below can be compiled with both the **xfst** or **foma** toolkits (Hulden, 2009b).[3]

21.2 Finnish Prosody

For the purposes of what follows, we can express the fundamental rules of primary and secondary stress assignment in Finnish as follows:

(a) The main stress always falls on the first syllable, regardless of its weight.

(b) Secondary stress falls on subsequent odd-numbered syllables, except in cases where an odd light syllable is followed by a heavy syllable. In such cases the stress shifts to the heavy syllable, and counting is reset.

Some simple cases are illustrated below:

(1)	(pé.rus).(tèl.la)	'to justify' (Inf)
(2)	(pé.rus).(tè.li).sin	'to justify' (1p Sg Pres Cond)
(3)	(ká.me).le.(ònt.ti)	'chameleon' (Nom Sg)
(4)	(kóm.mu).ni.(kòin.nis).sa	'communication' (Ine Sg)

ceives only 47 hits, almost all of them being somehow related to Karttunen's paper. In other words, a corpus as large as Google's may not contain the crucial examples one would like to find, motivating the need for automating this part somehow, without the need for corpora at all. One cannot, after all, count on all linguists having this kind of knack for coming up with the apposite counterexample.

[3]The code to reproduce everything in this paper is available at `https://github.com/mhulden/otverification`.

<table>
<tr><td>AB</td><td>Concatenation</td></tr>
<tr><td>A|B</td><td>Union</td></tr>
<tr><td>A*</td><td>Kleene star (zero or more)</td></tr>
<tr><td>A+</td><td>Kleene plus (one or more)</td></tr>
<tr><td>~A</td><td>Complement of language</td></tr>
<tr><td>?</td><td>Any symbol in alphabet</td></tr>
<tr><td>0</td><td>The empty string</td></tr>
<tr><td>\A</td><td>Any single symbol except those in A</td></tr>
<tr><td>$A</td><td>Contains a string from A, $A = ?* A ?*</td></tr>
<tr><td>X/A</td><td>X, ignoring intervening instances of A</td></tr>
<tr><td>%</td><td>Escape symbol for reserved characters</td></tr>
<tr><td>[and]</td><td>Grouping brackets</td></tr>
<tr><td>A:B</td><td>Cross product</td></tr>
<tr><td>T1 .o. T2</td><td>Composition of T1 and T2</td></tr>
<tr><td>T.u, T.l</td><td>Input, output projection of transducer T</td></tr>
<tr><td>T.i</td><td>Inverse of T</td></tr>
<tr><td>A -> B</td><td>Rewrite strings in a A with strings from B</td></tr>
<tr><td>A -> B ... C</td><td>Insert B and C around instances of A</td></tr>
<tr><td>[..] -> B</td><td>Insert (epenthesize) exactly one instance of B</td></tr>
<tr><td>|| C _ D</td><td>Context specifier</td></tr>
<tr><td>.#.</td><td>End or beginning of string</td></tr>
<tr><td>def F(X1,...,Xn) [regex]</td><td>Definition of macro</td></tr>
<tr><td>def X [regex]</td><td>Definition of language constant</td></tr>
</table>

TABLE 1 Regular expression notation used in this article.

In (1) and (2), we see the standard trochaic pattern. In (3) and (4) we see the result of encountering an odd light syllable, leading to the stress shifting over to the following heavy syllable.[4]

A number of corner cases exist which will not be of concern here and are ignored. For example, a final heavy syllable can be optionally stressed, as in **(ós.tin).pas/(ós.tin).pàs** 'I bought'. Likewise, some derivational morphemes, such as **-Oi-** (where **O** harmonizes as either **o** or **ö**), seem to attract stress even in cases where they would normally be relegated to the unstressed position in a foot, e.g. **(ár.gu).men.(tòi.da)** 'to debate (Inf.)'(Hakulinen et al., 2004).[5] The complex interaction of prosody and allomorph selection in Finnish (touched upon in Kiparsky (2003)) will also be avoided here, for rea-

[4] Because the OT analyses assume all feet to be binary, I am describing the phenomenon in terms of binary feet. In more traditional approaches, one would talk about the alternation of binary and ternary feet, and (3) would be described as (ká.me.le).(ònt.ti). This is largely irrelevant since the ultimate goal is to examine the correctness of stress assignment rather than the foot assignment.

[5] It may be tempting to regularize such shifts by attributing them to stress shifting from a lighter CVC-syllable to the following, presumably heavier CVV (Karvonen, 2005). But a vast number of counterexamples exist to such an analysis: **(ká.lus).(tèt.tui).na** 'furnished (Ess Pl)', **(ái.neel).(lìs.tuu).ko** 'materialize (3p +QP)', etc., prompting me to leave this complicated question aside.

FIGURE 1 Illustration of a traditional analysis implemented as a sequence of replacement rules.

sons of space.

21.3 A Rule-based Description

Lauri Karttunen has implemented the traditional analysis above[6] as a composition of finite-state transducers expressed as replacement rules (Kaplan and Kay, 1994, Karttunen, 1995). This implementation works as follows: the input is syllabified by a syllabification transducer, and subsequently composed with transducers that lay down ternary feet and binary feet where appropriate, then assigning stresses to the head of each foot. These transducers are built in a transparent way, and the end result, a monolithic transducer that assigns primary and secondary stresses to any input sequence of Finnish letters, can be assumed to fairly represent the traditional analysis. In what follows, I will reference this resulting transducer as the *gold standard* or the *traditional analysis*, and its transducer representation as `Karttunen`.

The rule-based description can be seen as a direct translation of the principles outlined above. First, a syllabifying transducer, `Syllabify` is constructed, it is composed with a transducer `TernaryFeet` which handles the ternary foot case, which in turn is composed with a transducer `BinaryFeet` which groups the remaining material into feet. This is followed by composition with transducers that mark primary stress on the first syllable in the first foot, and then secondary stresses on the first syllables or the remaining feet. Part of this chain is illustrated in figure 1.

This analysis and the resulting transducer will serve as the starting point for the formal verification of the subsequent OT analyses. The goal is to convert the OT grammars into transducers which can be manipulated and compared against the *gold standard*.[7]

21.4 OT Implementations as Finite Transducers

Finite-state devices are well known in theory to lack the capacity to model arbitrary OT grammars, even if identification of where constraints are violated can be expressed as a finite automaton (Frank and

[6] `http://web.stanford.edu/~laurik/fsmbook/examples/FinnishProsody.html`

[7] Karttunen's traditional grammar allows for ambiguous stress patterns in that final heavy syllable can be optionally stressed. I have removed this part for the sake of comparability with the OT grammars that do not model this.

Satta, 1998), and violation 'markup' could henceforth be performed by a finite state transducer. This circumstance is intuitively clear since finite-state devices have no memory and therefore cannot be harnessed to keep track of a unbounded number of constraint violations; i.e. producing a transducer that is capable of distinguishing between k and $k+1$ violations for arbitrary k is not possible. This is also of practical consequence since there exist very simple grammars that only include the most fundamental constraints assumed by OT practitioners yet are not implementable as finite transducers. One such grammar is given in Gerdemann and Hulden (2012).

21.4.1 A Counting Approximation

Karttunen (1998) showed that one could implement an approximation to an OT grammar with finite transducers by defining an abstract operation similar to regular composition of transducers, called *lenient composition*, denoted `.O.`. The method in essence is as follows: one can define violation markup transducers `R` that decorate candidates with a symbol, say `*`, whenever a violation of an OT constraint occurs. At the same time, a transducer `C` removes strings that contain some fixed number of violations, say k or more. Now, if R is composed with C in regular fashion, it might be the case that all candidates corresponding to some underlying form get purged, an unwanted circumstance. To prevent this from occurring, an alternative definition of composition is used, one that in essence composes `R` with `C` for those inputs that still map to *some* output in `R .o. C`. For those that do not, only `R` applies. The `.u`-operation which extracts the input projection of a relation is used in conjunction with negation `~` to achieve this type of filtering effect:

(5) `R .O. C = [R .o. C] | [~[R .o. C].u .o. R]`

This, in essence, allows one to model the effect of an OT grammar as the lenient composition of a sequence of transducers. The GEN mechanism can be cast into a transducer representation, as can the constraints. The constraint transducers themselves do nothing except mark violations with `*`-symbols. These are then further 'leniently' composed with a transducer that removes all candidates that incur more than k violations, followed by a transducer that removes those with more than $k-1$ violations, etc. etc. The end result can be described as follows:

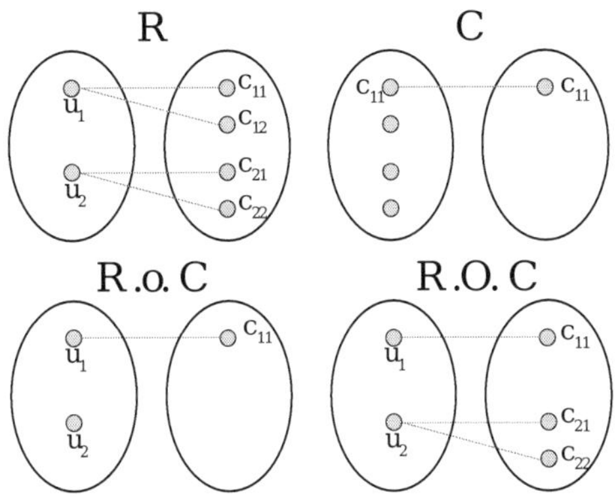

FIGURE 2 Illustration of regular composition (`R .o. C`) and lenient composition (`R .O. C`).

```
(6)  Gen .o.  MarkC1 .O. Violk .O. ...  .O. Viol1 .o. P
              MarkC2 .O. Violk .O. ...  .O. Viol1 .o. P
              ...
              MarkCn .O. Violk .O. ...  .O. Viol1 .o. P
```

In this sequence, `P` is a transducer that simply removes the violation decorations. Much of this bookkeeping can be automated and wrapped into macros as illustrated in Karttunen (2006a), resulting in a practical method for quickly testing the effect of OT grammars against a corpus of words, so long as one can define the transducers that identify violations, and so long as an upper bound k of the number of violations that can be distinguished in candidates is appropriate.

21.4.2 A Matching Approximation

Another approach to implementing OT through transducer composition, inspired by the earlier effort of Karttunen (1998) is given in Gerdemann and van Noord (2000), and is further elaborated upon in Gerdemann and Hulden (2012). This is based on the idea that, instead of counting violations at the crucial moment of filtering out strings that contain *-markup, one uses the set of existing candidates to define the worse ones, i.e. those that need to be filtered out.

Consider some of the forms after marking up the violations of an OT constraint STRESS-TO-WEIGHT on the input **kalastelemme**. The constraint militates against stressing nonheavy syllables, and the set of outputs might be the following:

(7) ☞ (ká*.las).te.(lèm.me)
(8) (ká*.las).(tè*.lem).me

Now, we can define the worse candidates in terms of the better candidates by adding at least one violation marker to each candidate. For example, from (7) we could, by adding at least one violation marker in an arbitrary location, produce something that is very close to (8), ignoring for the moment the placement of feet and stress marks. Since the output side of such a 'worsening' transducer is itself a regular set, we can use that regular set to subtract suboptimal candidates from the original set of candidates. In the finite state calculus, this can be expressed in three steps. First we undo and redo the effects of Gen, so that the footings and stress marks are arbitrarily permuted so that e.g. (7) can match (8) with respect to footing and stress. Assuming `Gen` is a transducer that syllabifies words and inserts footing markup arbitrarily, this can be expressed as composing the inverse of a `Gen`-transducer with `Gen` itself, ignoring the presence of violation markup: `[Gen.i .o. Gen]/{*}`.[8] Secondly, we add at least one violation to this new set, the effect of which can be achieved by the transducer `[?* 0:{*} ?*]+`. Finally, we compose the original set `X` with the complement of the output language of the new set which contains 'worse' candidates, and remove violation markers: `X .o. ~[[X .o. Worsen].l] .o. {*} -> 0`. This incantation can be wrapped into a macro called `Eval`, which takes as an argument a transducer that performs markup of violations for some constraint.

```
def AddViol    [?* 0:{*} ?*]+;
def Worsen     [Gen.i .o. Gen]/{*} .o. AddViol;
def Eval(X)    X .o. ~[[X .o. Worsen].l] .o. {*} -> 0;
```

As long as we have markup transducers for constraints, we are now in a position to compile OT grammars in a principled way, e.g. for a three-constraint system, we can say:

(9) `Eval(Eval(Eval(Gen .o. Con1) .o. Con2) .o. Con3)`

The above strategy allows one—under some circumstances—to compile exact transducers that model an OT grammar with no bound on the number of constraints that are distinguished. If the best candidate incurs k violations, for any k, and if all worse candidates have violation

[8] In an actual implementation, it is more efficient to simply remove and reinsert arbitrarily any markup symbols that `Gen` makes use of, but the formalization with the inversion of `Gen` is more principled and generic.

marks that coincide with those of the winner and some more besides, the method will produce a transducer that is not limited in its ability to distinguish between violations.

One case, however, where the approach may fail is if the constraint violations do not align perfectly. Consider a number of outputs after marking up STRESSTOWEIGHT for **ostamisestakohan**:

(10) ☞ (ós.ta).mi.(sès.ta).(kò*.han)
(11) (ós.ta).(mì*.ses).(tà*.ko).han

In this case, the better candidate (10) cannot be manipulated to coincide in shape with the worse candidate (11) by simply moving feet around and adding violation markers, since the markers do not align; (10) has a violation on **ko**, while (11) does not, and the method fails to distinguish between the two. To handle such cases, one can, after adding violations, permute the markers in the candidates some finite distance by declaring a transducer that moves a marker arbitrarily until the next or the previous marker position. This allows the definition of a strictly stronger `Eval`-function, one that can distinguish between more unaligned markup than `Eval` can.

```
def Perm   [?* ["*":0 \"*"* 0:"*"|0:"*" \"*"* "*":0]*
                                                    ?*]*;
def EvalP1(X)  X .o. ~[[X .o. Worsen .o. Perm].l] .o.
                                                {*} -> 0;
```

Naturally, one can compose with `Perm` multiple times and so cover more and more unaligned violations. Although this need for permutation of violation markers arises very rarely in modeling OT grammars, it does occasionally happen. One strong point of the method is that it is possible to formally ascertain when permutation is needed, and how many times. After the evaluation of a constraint, instead of removing the markers, we can compose the result with a transducer that removes everything except the violation marks. For the above input **ostamisestakohan**, before permutation, the system would produce two outputs: * and **. This would be an error and would reflect the fact that the system treats having one violation on an equal basis to having two. Formally speaking: the transducer in question does not represent a function (since it maps some input to more than one output). Now, whether an arbitrary transducer represents a function is a decidable question (Blattner and Head, 1977, Culik II, 1978), and an efficient algorithm exists for testing whether this is the case (Hulden, 2009a).[9]

[9]Implemented through the command `test functional` in *foma*.

The upshot is that (a) we can detect when permutation is needed to produce an 'exact' representation of OT grammars and (b) be safe in the knowledge that the method has produced an exact representation which distinguishes correctly between an unbounded number of violations.

It is possible, though, to find pathological OT grammars for which no amount of permutation will suffice (Gerdemann and Hulden, 2012), but this formal blemish of OT is, in my experience, not a practical concern for real-world grammars.

In short, the method has the disadvantage that one may not always end up with a transducer that accurately models the OT grammar in question, for any input. The success is entirely grammar-dependent. However, it is possible to detect when convergence has happened and an exact transducer is produced.

The fundamental advantage of the method with respect to formal verification is that once an OT grammar is implemented this way, we can ask universal questions about the resulting transducer, and can bring formal analyses to bear on the grammar, such as automated comparisons between transducers representing some other grammar, alleviating the need to test against a corpus and manually search for counterexamples.

21.5 Implementing the Constraint Systems

Below, I will make use of Karttunen's existing code for marking up the different constraint violations and build upon those transducers to develop an exact monolithic transducer that encodes the OT grammar in question for words of arbitrary length, as does the rule-based implementation. This circumstance then allows the two to be formally compared using standard Boolean operations on automata.

21.5.1 The Constraints

The constraints used in the proposed two grammars are as follows.

(a) MainStress: Primary stress on first syllable.

```
[B MSS ~$MSS]
```

(b) Clash: Adjacent syllables can't be stressed.

```
SS -> ... {*} || SS B _
```

(c) Left-Headedness: A stressed syllable must be foot-initial.

```
SV -> ... {*} || .#. ~[?* "(" C*] _
```

(d) FootBin: Feet have minimally two morae and maximally two syllables.

```
["(" Light ")" | "(" S ["." S]^>1] -> ... {*}
```

(e) LAPSE: every unstressed syllable must be adjacent to a stressed syllable or the word edge.

```
US -> ... {*} || [B US B] _ [B US B]
```

(f) NON-FINAL: The final syllable must not be stressed.

```
SS -> ... {*} || _ ~$S .#.
```

(g) STRESS-TO-WEIGHT: Stressed syllables need to be heavy.

```
[SS & Light] -> ... {*} || _ ")" | E
```

(g') *(L̀H): No feet of the form (L̀H)

```
def LHfoot "(" [Light & SS] "." Heavy ")"
[..] -> ... {*} || LHfoot _
```

(h) LICENSE-σ: Syllables have to be parsed into feet.

```
S -> ... {*} || E _ E
```

(i) ALL-FEET-LEFT: Every foot coincides with left edge of prosodic word.

[Not implementable as markup transducer]

The first constraint, MAINSTRESS, is a categorical one which is used simply to filter out any candidate that violates it, without any inter-candidate comparison. Beginning with CLASH, we apply the filtering mechanism described above to successively remove suboptimal candidates. Using the techniques for detecting when permutation of violation markers is required, we note that the STRESS-TO-WEIGHT-constraint requires one round of permutation for the grammar to achieve exactness. The two constraints (g) and (g') are where the grammars of Kiparsky (2003) and Elenbaas (1999) differ. We will look at both variants, but for the time being compile the grammar using (g): STRESS-TO-WEIGHT.

Excluding the final constraint, ALL-FEET-LEFT, we can model everything up to that point by the expression:

```
def Kiparsky  Eval(EvalP1(Eval(Eval(Eval(Eval(Eval(
              Gen .o. MainStress .o. Clash) .o.
              LeftHeadedness) .o. FootBin) .o. Lapse) .o.
              NonFinal) .o. StressToWeight) .o. Parse);
```

Pausing here for a moment before dealing with the last remaining constraint allows for some illustration of the power of formal verification techniques. If we were in the process of developing this OT generalization, a natural question to ask at any point when adding a new constraint would be this: are these constraints enough to allow for an unambiguous output for every possible input string? The question is not trivial. First, as mentioned above, we can check if the resulting transducer is a function, in which case we wouldn't need any more constraints since we would be safe in the knowledge that every input maps uniquely to a single output. However, testing for this shows that it is not a function; i.e. there exists some input which yields more than one output. Furthermore, we can formally calculate, for example, the shortest such input string, which is a good debugging strategy. Apart from simply testing whether a transducer is a function, finite state calculus techniques allow one to take an existing transducer and split it into two parts: one part representing those input strings that induce more than one path through the transducer, and another part that doesn't (Hulden, 2009a). Those paths that are ambiguous usually reflect differing outputs as well.[10] The *foma*-toolkit contains a `_ambpart()` operation to that effect, which allows us to perform this diagnostic:

```
def KiparskyAmbiguous _ambpart(Kiparsky);
```

Examining this new transducer that only contains the ambiguous paths, we can ask the question: what is the shortest string in the input side of this relation? The answer is:

```
foma[1]: print shortest-string
Upper: uebuea
Lower: (ú.e).bu.(è.a)
```

Since the transducer has no awareness of a lexicon, the shortest string is of course nonsense. But, we can glean the information that five light syllables in a row is the shortest input which yields an ambiguous output. A real-world example would be **kotonaniko** 'home 1P Poss + QP', which indeed receives the below two footings and stresses.

(12) (kó.to).na.(nì.ko)
(13) (kó.to).(nà.ni).ko

At this point we can be sure that the last constraint is needed and can move on to investigating that, which poses a special complication.

Generalized Alignment Constraints

The only remaining constraint is ALL-FEET-LEFT. This is a so-called gradient, or alignment constraint, which dictates a violation for each distance of a syllable that a foot is displaced from the left edge of the word. For example, a foot assignment such as the one below would receive the sum total of violations caused by each foot $(0+3+5=8)$:

[10] A minor technical point: we may encounter grammars that have multiple paths for some input but where the output is identical. In general, it is undecidable by algorithm whether this is the case, but the above technique is a good heuristic.

(14) (má.te).ma.(tìi.kas)***.(sà.ni)*****

Now, clearly, there is no finite transducer that can perform the markup required here for an input word of arbitrary length. At this point, to maintain the design goal of having an exact transducer that represents the entire grammar appears infeasible because of the gradient constraint. There is an out, however. We can reformulate the constraint as an approximation, and hope (for the moment!) that the approximation is sufficient. The idea is again based on the notion of trying to capture all the candidates that are worse than the winning one by putting the candidates in internal competition. To model this competition, we can rig a transducer to produce at least *some* of the worse candidates in a pool by taking the set of current candidates and (a) moving a foot an arbitrary amount to the right, or (b) adding a foot anywhere, except in the beginning, or (c) both. For example, in the system at hand, after the last constraint discussed so far, STRESSTOWEIGHT, we have the remaining candidates for the input *järjestelmällistämätöntä*:

(15) ☞	(jǟr.jes).(tèl.mäl).(lìs.tä).mä.(tȍn.tä)	0+2+4+7 = 13
(16)	(jǟr.jes).(tèl.mäl).lis.(tȁ.mä).(tȍn.tä)	0+2+5+7 = 14
(17)	(jǟr.jes).tel.(mȁl.lis).(tȁ.mä).(tȍn.tä)	0+3+5+7 = 15

In this example, the candidate (15), which is to be preferred under ALL-FEET-LEFT can be modified to match the worse candidates (16) and (17) with this idea. Since the right parentheses are irrelevant to the constraint (violations depend on where the foot begins), we can focus on the position of the left parentheses only. If we (a) removed all the right parentheses in (15), and (b) moved one of the left parentheses rightward and (c) reinserted arbitrary right parentheses, we can from (15) produce something that exactly matches (16) and (17). This allows us to filter out the 'worse' candidates, exactly as for the categorical constraints. To this end, we may define a function like the following:

```
def  EvalAllFeetLeft(X)  X .o. ~[X .o. WorsenFeet].l ;
```

Here, `WorsenFeet` is a transducer which moves left parentheses rightward and/or inserts additional left parentheses, while at the same time arbitrarily removing and re-inserting right parentheses.

It should be noted that such a strategy will only be able to target *some* of the worse candidates. The danger here is that there may exist worse candidates corresponding to some input that will slip between the cracks. An example case is illustrated by the following two hypothetical candidates, assuming they are the only two candidates left in the pool:

(18)	☞	$\sigma.\sigma.\sigma.\sigma.(\sigma)$	4
(19)		$\sigma.\sigma.(\sigma).(\sigma).\sigma$	$2 + 3 = 5$

Indeed, the maneuver described above does not allow for (18) to be transformed into (19) by simply moving parentheses to the right or adding them. It is possible to make the `WorsenFeet` relation more complex and to ultimately catch such cases as the above, but again, everything imaginable cannot be caught, and we rely on the approximation to be *good enough for the grammar at hand* to yield an exact representation of the system.[11]

But how do we know if this model of the gradient constraint is *good enough*? This time we cannot rely on the functionality test in conjunction with the markers to ascertain that we succeeded in producing an exact model for the simple reason that there are no marker symbols around. However, there is one possibility of making sure the model was correct for this particular grammar: the constraint in question is the very last one in a long chain of constraints, and presumably, if the grammar is valid, it should yield a functional transducer—one where every input maps to exactly one output. If that should happen, then we know, by virtue of this uniqueness, that the constraint model for the very last constraint was valid and did not miss knocking out an inferior candidate.

The compilation of the entire grammar can be expressed as:

```
def Kiparsky  EvalAllFeetLeft(Eval(EvalP1(Eval(Eval(Eval(
              Eval(Eval(Gen .o. MainStress .o. Clash) .o.
              LeftHeadedness) .o. FootBin) .o. Lapse) .o.
              NonFinal) .o. StressToWeight) .o. Parse));
```

We are in luck! The resulting transducer is *functional.* It has 168 states and $3,129$ arcs and represents the OT grammar in question exactly—assigning a syllabified, footed, and stress-marked output for any combination of Finnish characters, no matter how long the input word and no matter how many violations it incurs for some constraint.

[11] Jason Eisner has forcefully argued against both alignment constraints and violation counting and has suggested they be replaced by directional violation evaluation, which would guarantee regularity (Eisner, 2000, 2002). In essence, my reformulation of All-Feet-Left given here is similar in flavor to Eisner's directionality constraints.

21.6 Analyzing and Debugging

We now have two transducers `Karttunen` and `Kiparsky` which both lay down feet and assign stress—one representing the traditional analysis, and the other representing a specific OT analysis. These can easily be tested for equivalence. Note that transducer equivalence is an undecidable problem in the general case (Griffiths, 1968).[12] However, in the special case when at least *one of the two transducers* represents a function, equivalence is easy to test. In our case, both transducers represent functions, and this avenue is open to us. Composing a regular relation with the inverse of the other will yield a relation that represents an identity relation if and only if the original relations are equivalent—an identity relation being one where every input word maps to itself. While testing if a transducer represents an identity relation is non-trivial, an efficient algorithm exists for that purpose (Hulden, 2009a). In this case, we immediately see that

```
[Kiparsky.i .o. Karttunen]
```

yields a non-identity transducer, by which we know that the two differ in some way.

One way in which the two differ is a foregone conclusion—they represent different footings. The traditional analysis includes ternary feet, and the OT approach relies on only binary feet, allowing for unfooted material now and then. In order to do a fair comparison, the foot-markers should be removed by composition with a transducer that does so before the above is done. Even so, the transducers differ.

In a similar way as we constructed `Kiparsky`, we can construct the alternative analysis `Elenbaas`, which substitutes the STRESS-TO-WEIGHT constraint (g) with *(L̀H) (g'). Again, after removing the foot-markers, we can calculate:

```
[Elenbaas.i .o. Karttunen]
```

and reach the conclusion that this analysis also differs from the traditional analysis.

21.6.1 Pattern Analysis

We know that Karttunen's approximation of the system revealed two words in a corpus with outputs that differ from the traditional analysis: **kalasteleminen** and **järjestelmällisyydelläni**. By virtue of having two transducers that are not bounded by the length of input they can

[12]Two transducers may appear structurally quite different yet represent the same relation.

correctly assign outputs to, we are now in a position to perform an exhaustive analysis of all the differing patterns in the OT and traditional analyses, without reference to specific lexical items—indeed, we need not possess any knowledge of Finnish whatsoever to perform a comprehensive error analysis of the OT grammar.

The first step is to transform the three transducers `Karttunen`, `Kiparsky`, and `Elenbaas` into a more generic representation, one that reveals all the patterns of stressing sequences of light and heavy syllables. We do so by composing the stress-marking transducers by a transducer that converts the syllables into sequences over symbols `H,H́,L,Ĺ`.[13]

```
def Collapse  [Heavy & $SV]  -> H́ || E _ E ,,
              [Heavy & ~$SV] -> H || E _ E ,,
              [Light & $SV]  -> Ĺ || E _ E ,,
              [Light & ~$SV] -> L || E _ E ;
```

This simply maps all syllables to a one letter description when found between edge markers `E`, syllable or word boundaries. The resulting transducers (composing `Kiparsky` and `Elenbaas` with `Collapse`), now map word inputs into `HL`-sequences, e.g.:

(20) `matematiikassani` → `ĹLLH́HĹL`

The output side of these transducers represent regular languages over only four symbols which we can extract and examine. We will call these `KarttunenC`, `KiparskyC`, and `ElenbaasC`. In particular, the set of sequences over those four symbols implicitly encode how the grammar assigns stress, since if an `ĹLLH́HĹL` appears in the language, we know that this is how the grammar stresses any `LLLHHLL` patterned input.

Since regular languages (as opposed to regular relations) are closed under all the Boolean operations, we can easily analyze the three grammars for discrepancies across the board. For example, to see the totality of patterns stressed differently by the STRESSTOWEIGHT OT grammar and the traditional analysis, we simply calculate the *symmetric difference* of the two:[14]

---

[13]All three grammars could of course have been developed to operate only on `L` and `H` symbols in the first place. Still, a working linguist would likely want to test and debug actual words during development instead of using abstract `L`'s and `H`'s, and the workflow here is meant to model such a preference.

[14]If two sets A and B are identical, their symmetric difference yields the empty set, otherwise the result contains all the elements that are in one but not the other.

```
def DiffKK [KiparskyC - KarttunenC] |
           [KarttunenC - KiparskyC]
```

This yields an automaton that encodes all the differences between the two grammars, and we can proceed to ask questions. A simple question is: what is the shortest string where the two grammars differ? The answer is that there are 32 strings of length 6 where they differ, one of them being `ĹHLĹLL`, corresponding to the counterexample ***(ká.las).te.(lè.mi).nen**, discovered in Karttunen (2006b). Furthermore, there are an infinite number of inputs where this OT analysis differs from the traditional one.

To better make sense of the differences, we can further manipulate the resulting 'difference' automaton to remove the stress marks as we are primarily interested in what types of heavy-light sequences are in disagreement. We can therefore compose the `DiffKK` with a transducer that collapses the distinction between `Ĺ` and `L` as well as `H́` and `H`:

```
def CollapseAccents(X) [X .o. H́ -> H , Ĺ -> L].l
```

The results of calculating the difference between Kiparsky's and Elenbaas' analyses and the traditional one, and then collapsing accent marks, are shown in figures 3 and 4. Both are cyclic automata, and both hence have an unbounded number of discrepancies. The shortest counterexample to both is six syllables long, and discrepancies only occur with certain weight patterns, illustrating the difficulty of coming up with counterexamples. The STRESS-TO-WEIGHT analysis has by far more differing patterns than the *(ĹH)-analysis. The *(ĹH)-analysis only differs in some circumstances when the word ends in a heavy syllable (which is a clue to how to go about fixing the grammar).

In both cases, however, we can draw the conclusion that the differences are pervasive; starting with six-syllable words, patterns of every length are included in both automata. Making one more generalization—collapsing those patterns where there is no difference between an `L` and an `H` in terms of prediction, and replacing those with `X` symbols allows for an exhaustive, holistic analysis of all the differences. A selection of these are given in table 2.

21.7 A Provably Correct Solution to Ternary Stress

To conclude, I will present an OT constraint system for Finnish prosody that is provably correct (i.e., provably equivalent to the traditional analysis).[15] Once the computational tools are in place, finding any number

[15]Lauri Karttunen's website lists this as an exercise: "Can you suggest other changes, new constraints, some reranking or reformulation of existing constraints

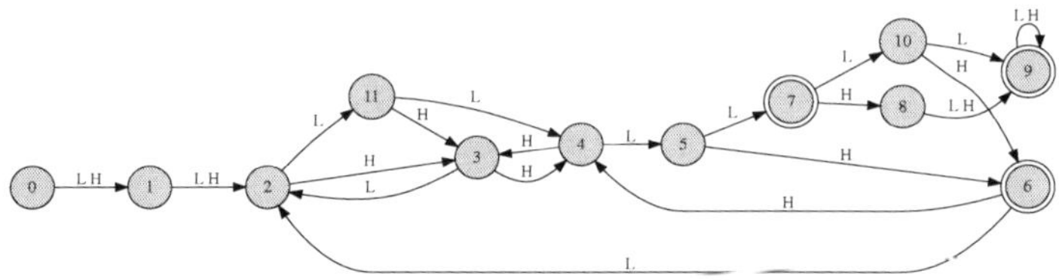

FIGURE 3 An automaton that represents the set of patterns in which the STRESS-TO-WEIGHT OT analysis differs from the traditional analysis of Finnish stress.

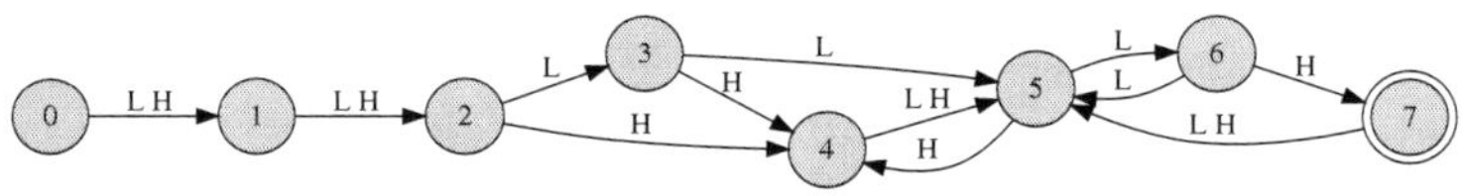

FIGURE 4 An automaton that represents the set of patterns in which the *(L̀H) OT analysis differs from the traditional analysis of Finnish stress.

	6	7	8	9
(a)	XXHXLH	XXLHXLH	XXHXHXLH	XXHXLHXLH
	XXLLLH		XXHXLLLH	XXLHXHXLH
			XXLLHXLH	XXLHXLLLH
			XXLLLLLH	XXLLLHXLH
	6	7	8	9
(b)	XXHHLX	XXLHHLX	XXHHHHLX	XXHHLHHLX
	XXLLLX		XXHHLLXX	XXHHLLHXX
			XXHLLLLX	XXHHLLLLX
			XXHLHHLX	XXHLLHHLX
			XXLLHHLX	XXLHHHHLX
			XXLLLLXX	XXLHHLLXX
				XXLHLHHLX
				XXLHLLLLX
				XXLLLHHLX
				XXLLLLHXX
				XXLLLLLLX

TABLE 2 All patterns of length 6 – 9 syllables where the (a) *(L̀H) analysis and the (b) STRESS-TO-WEIGHT analysis differ from the traditional analysis.

of solutions is not very difficult. I will not argue for my solution on typological grounds, but considering the problem at hand, it has the advantage of being very close to already proposed ones—in fact, the code for a solution compatible with the traditional analysis differs in exactly *one character* from the above code for producing `Elenbaas`.

As is convincingly shown by Karttunen, the reason the OT analyses presented above run aground is the insufficiency of either the *(L̀H)-constraint or the STRESS-TO-WEIGHT-constraint to produce an effect of skipping a light syllable if such a maneuver would be rewarded by allowing stress on a heavy one. The problem with a constraint such as STRESS-TO-WEIGHT is that an unstressed syllable will be skipped *even if there is no reward*, as in

(21) (ká*.las).(tè*.le).(mì*.nen)
(22) (ká*.las).te.(lè*.mi).nen

Obviously, (21) is the preferred configuration, but the STRESS-TO-WEIGHT-constraint penalizes it implicitly for having one more foot than the candidate that should be the suboptimal configuration (22). But the suboptimal candidate never gains a heavy stressed syllable by skipping a syllable in the footing.

The *(ĹH)-constraint also fails because the constraint in essence penalizes an LH-foot at the end of a word, again, *even if there is no reward*:

(23) (kés.kus).te.(lè.mi).nen
(24) (kés.kus).(tè.le).(mì.nen*)

That is, the **(mi.nen)**-foot is dispreferred, even in final position when there is no new initial-heavy binary foot to be formed by skipping **mi**, yielding an incorrect winner, (23).

What is common to both constraints and their failure is that they exhibit no lookahead beyond the foot to capture the intuitive idea that a constraint must favor moving a foot to the right if and only if doing so gains us a (H̀.X) foot. With this in mind, it seems that a simple fix is to modify the constraints by giving them the minimal lookahead they need to distinguish whether skipping a light syllable is a gain. Indeed, we can start with the Elenbaas analysis, and change the *(L̀H)-constraint to

that would give the desired output in the two cases above, of course, without getting something else wrong?"
(`http://web.stanford.edu/~laurik/fsmbook/exercises/FinnishOTProsody.html`)

something like *(L̀H)..., the three dots signifying that something must follow the foot for the constraint to apply:

(g”) *(LH)...: avoid non-final LH-feet.

```
def LH2 [..] -> {*} || LHfoot ? _ ;
```

Is this solution correct? We already have the entire framework set up for testing and analyzing an OT description equivalence with the traditional analysis, and can do so again, modifying only the constraint in question and maintaining the ranking MainStress >> Clash >> Left-Headedness >> FootBin >> Lapse >> NonFinal >> *(LH)... >> Parse >> All-Feet-Left. Doing so, and compiling the result into `OTnew`, we can calculate the symmetric difference of the two sets of outputs:

```
[Karttunen - OTnew] | [OTnew - Karttunen]
```

Doing so yields the empty set as a result—i.e. there is no input string for which the predictions of the two differ. There is no need to test a single word to establish this. ■

21.7.1 A Small Ablation Study

Having modified one of the constraints, albeit minimally, may of course have brought significant changes to the overall system. We have established that the solution is equivalent to the traditional analysis, but a subsequent question of interest is whether all the constraints are really needed to achieve this equality with the traditional analysis. This can easily be ascertained by removing a constraint from the system, recompiling, and checking for equivalence with the full grammar. In this case, the result is that *all the constraints are needed*; removing a single one yields a grammar that is different from the full grammar. Doing so also produces a non-functional transducer as the end product, meaning that some input words correspond to multiple winning candidates.

We can also pose a more subtle question: can some of the constraints be loosened? It turns out that they can: the *(L̀H)...-constraint need not care about the L-syllable being stressed. It can be reformulated as simply *(LH)...: avoid non-final *LH*-feet, with identical results. This is also true of the original Elenbaas grammar, the *(L̀H)-constraint could be renamed *(*LH*) with no effect on the grammar.

21.8 Conclusion

Wikipedia lists the longest non-compound word in Finnish to be *epäjärjestelmällistyttämättömyydelläänsäkäänköhän*,[16] ‘I wonder if—

[16] https://en.wikipedia.org/wiki/Longest_words

even with his/her quality of not having been made unsystematized'. Feeding it to the OT GEN transducer yields 636,873,197,339,181 different combinations of footings and stress placements; that is, 636 trillion(!). Out of these candidates, the OT cascades above select one as the winner. What's more, the number of initial candidates would be far larger if we had decided to syllabify Finnish through OT constraints as well. As it stands, the syllabification part was performed by a ready-made transducer for that purpose, allowing us to focus on the stress and footing constraints. With such astronomical numbers, human error has plenty of opportunity to sneak in and computational help is indispensable.

Looking at the specific problem of ternary stress from a computational and mathematical standpoint—or indeed any phonological generalization that claims equivalence to a more traditional analysis—it seems obvious that the first order of affairs is to prove that a particular solution has the desired properties. Only after that detail is dispensed with should a discussion about the merits of the constraints, their elegance, their naturalness, and their typological justifiability commence. Karttunen's message, that "paper-and-pencil methods are insufficient to test a theory," should be taken seriously lest the phonologist risk being drawn into a protracted back-and-forth, exchanging examples and counterexamples. Those who take heed will have gained a new approach to phonological argumentation, and, possibly, a better night's sleep.

References

Baier, Christel and Joost-Pieter Katoen. 2008. *Principles of Model Checking*. MIT press.

Beesley, Kenneth R. and Lauri Karttunen. 2003. *Finite State Morphology*. Stanford, CA: CSLI Publications.

Blattner, Meera and Tom Head. 1977. Single-valued a-transducers. *Journal of Computer and System Sciences* 15(3):328–353.

Culik II, Karel. 1978. Some decidability results about regular and push down translations. Research Report CS-78-09, University of Waterloo, Waterloo, Ontario, Canada.

Eisner, Jason. 2000. Directional constraint evaluation in optimality theory. In *Proceedings of the 18th conference on Computational linguistics*, pages 257–263. Association for Computational Linguistics.

Eisner, Jason. 2002. Comprehension and compilation in optimality theory. In *Proceedings of the 40th Annual Meeting on Association for Computational Linguistics*, pages 56–63. Association for Computational Linguistics.

Elenbaas, Nine. 1999. *A unified account of binary and ternary stress: considerations from Sentani and Finnish*. Ph.D. thesis, Utrecht University.

Elenbaas, Nine and René Kager. 1999. Ternary rhythm and the lapse constraint. *Phonology* pages 273–329.

Frank, Robert and Giorgio Satta. 1998. Optimality theory and the generative complexity of constraint violability. *Computational Linguistics* 24(2):307–315.

Gerdemann, Dale and Mans Hulden. 2012. Practical finite state optimality theory. In *Proceedings of the 10th International Workshop on Finite State Methods and Natural Language Processing*, pages 10–19. Donostia–San Sebastián: Association for Computational Linguistics.

Gerdemann, Dale and Gertjan van Noord. 2000. Approximation and exactness in finite state optimality theory. In *Proceedings of the Fifth Workshop of the ACL Special Interest Group in Computational Phonology*.

Griffiths, Timothy V. 1968. The unsolvability of the equivalence problem for λ-free nondeterministic generalized machines. *Journal of the ACM (JACM)* 15(3):409–413.

Hakulinen, Auli, Riitta Korhonen, Maria Vilkuna, and Vesa Koivisto. 2004. *Iso Suomen Kielioppi [Comprehensive Finnish Grammar]*. Suomalaisen kirjallisuuden seura.

Hulden, Mans. 2009a. *Finite-state Machine Construction Methods and Algorithms for Phonology and Morphology*. Ph.D. thesis, University of Arizona.

Hulden, Mans. 2009b. Foma: a finite-state compiler and library. In *EACL 2009 Proceedings*, pages 29–32.

Kaplan, Ronald M. and Martin Kay. 1994. Regular models of phonological rule systems. *Computational Linguistics* 20(3):331–378.

Karttunen, Lauri. 1995. The replace operator. In *Proceedings of the 33rd annual meeting on Association for Computational Linguistics*, pages 16–23. Association for Computational Linguistics.

Karttunen, Lauri. 1998. The proper treatment of optimality theory in computational phonology. In *Proceedings of the International Workshop on Finite State Methods in Natural Language Processing (FSMNLP)*.

Karttunen, Lauri. 2006a. A finite-state approximation of optimality theory: the case of Finnish prosody. In *Advances in Natural Language Processing*, pages 4–15. Springer.

Karttunen, Lauri. 2006b. The insufficiency of paper-and-pencil linguistics: the case of Finnish prosody. *Rutgers Optimality Archive* .

Karvonen, Daniel H. 2005. *Word Prosody in Finnish*. Ph.D. thesis, University of California, Santa Cruz.

Kiparsky, Paul. 2003. Finnish noun inflection. In *Generative approaches to Finnic linguistics.*. Stanford, CA: CSLI.

Prince, Alan and Paul Smolensky. 1993. Optimality theory: Constraint interaction in generative grammar. *Ms. Rutgers University Cognitive Science Center* .

22

Truth or *dare**

ANDRÁS KORNAI

22.1 Background

Thirty years ago, September 1986 to be precise, when I arrived at Stanford, Dwight Bolinger threw a barbeque for the incoming linguistics class. I was absolutely shocked. Bolinger was a demigod[1] of linguistics, someone I knew only through his work and stories, both transmitted to me by Ferenc Kiefer, and now I get to talk to him in person, eat his pulled pork, and drink his beer? I was delighted to see that, retired or not, he was just as sharp in real life as his work. There were plenty of CSLI people and other folks loosely affiliated with the linguistics department around – this was the first time I met Lauri. When my student Gábor Recski came back from *Sem 2015, he told me a very similar story: in a sea of younger faces there was this older guy, asking very sharp questions about all aspects of the work, and he was stunned to find out this was Lauri Karttunen himself! Somehow, some of the interests and esthetics of the older generation will rub off on the students, and (largely unbeknownst to me) a great deal of what Lauri thought was interesting I also ended up being interested in.

Following on many years of research in this direction, recently Kart-

*Thanks to Tibor Beke (UMass Lowell), Tim Fernando (Trinity College Dublin), Ferenc Kiefer (HAS Research Institute of Linguistics), Márton Makrai (HAS RIL), Chris Piñón (Université Lille 3), Gábor Recski (HAS RIL) and Károly Varasdi (Henrich Heine University, Düsseldorf) for cogent criticism of the draft version.

[1] http://zvon.org/comp/r/ref-Jargon_file.html#Terms~demigod

Tokens of Meaning: Papers in Honor of Lauri Karttunen.
Cleo Condoravdi and Tracy Holloway King (eds.).

tunen (2014) offered a force dynamics[2]-like analysis of what he calls *two-way implicatives* following Karttunen (1971), verbs like English *manage* and Finnish *hennoa*, the implication of which Karttunen illustrates with *Hennoitko tappaa kissan?* 'Did you overcome your pity to kill the cat?', akin to 'overcome your fear' for *dare*. Here we will look at a finite-state account of these verbs, finally bringing together two of the main threads of Lauri's research so far held together only by the esthetics. While hard to put in words exactly, clearly this esthetics has something to do with *mechanization*, going back at the very least to the the Calculus Ratiocinator of Leibniz, himself a tinkerer, building his Stepped Reckoner[3] from cogwheels the same way as Lauri builds his morphophonology from FSTs. For Leibniz, the elementary pieces were Monads, for Karttunen they are finite mechanisms which must be, in a sense we will make more precise in Section 22,4, *memoryless*. The luxury of a Turing Machine *tape* is not given to us, everything we remember we must remember at great cost, building it into the state space of the machinery as we go along. Crucially, there are no variables, and there is no variable binding, so who does what to whom will need to be specified by a different mechanism. We will use *cases* for this purpose.

Frege (1892) already notes that the failure of the implicatures that such verbs carry will not render false the sentence that uses the verb, and most subsequent authorities, including Karttunen, share this view. What needs to be made explicit in this regard is that sentences whose meaning cannot be tied to truth conditions (other than truth conditions pertaining to the mind-state of the speaker and the hearer) actually demonstrate that truth-conditional semantics is a blunt instrument, incapable of assigning meaning to sentences. Indeed, our main thesis here will be that either we are interested in truth, or we are interested in what verbs like *dare* mean.

Our goal in this paper is to formalize a lexically driven analysis in terms of a mechanical, finite state calculus. Since such an analysis, practically the only one that makes sense from the perspective of the grammar, is compatible only with a weak form of commonsense reasoning, as opposed to a muscular Tarski-style theory of truth, we obtain the result claimed in the title.

[2] `https://en.wikipedia.org/wiki/Force_dynamics`

[3] `https://en.wikipedia.org/wiki/Stepped_Reckoner`

22.2 The Elementary Pieces

The good thing is that we already know what *dare* means: 'to be brave enough to do something difficult or dangerous' (Cambridge Dictionary of English); 'to be brave enough to do something that is risky or that you are afraid to do' (Longman); 'to have enough courage or confidence to do something, to not be too afraid to do something' (Merriam-Webster). This is a special case of the general analysis that Karttunen offers for the whole class of verbs: 'overcoming an obstacle' with the obstacle being *fear* for *dare*, *indifference* for *bother*, *empathy* for *hennoa* and so on.

Here and in what follows we will rely heavily on the 'algebraic' style of lexical semantics first described in Kornai (2010a) and Kornai (2012) and now spelled out in far greater detail in Kornai (in press) and in a series of more computationally oriented papers such as Kornai et al. (2015). Remarkably, no part of the apparatus employed in this paper was developed with implicative verbs in mind.

We will use hypergraph-style notation with two kinds of concepts, unaries, which we will write in `typewriter font` and binaries, written in SMALL CAPS. There are only three types of edges: 0 used both for attribution *John is brave* and for IS_A indiscriminately. In larger graphs, we will write dashed arrows, $- \to$ instead of $\xrightarrow{0}$. The two other arrow types are the familiar '1' (ordinary $\to$ in larger graphs) for subject, and '2' (dotted arrow) for object. For ease of presentation, we introduce a special symbol @ that will be placed in the middle of arrows that should *in their entirety* be the terminal point of some other arrow, so that we can display the object of seeing in *video patrem venire* as

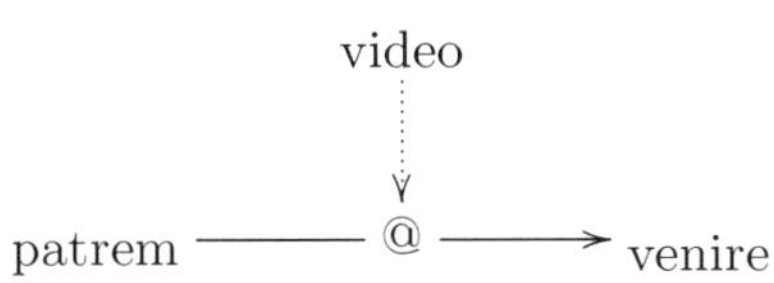

Figure 1. *Video patrem venire*

John dares VP is taken to mean *John does VP* in conjunction with *VP is risky*, and for the moment we leave open the issue whether it's risky for John, or really risky for everybody. What we did here was to incorporate a hidden element, 'object being risky' for *dare*, 'object being boring' or 'subject being indifferent' for *bother*, and 'subject being humane' for *hennoa*. As it happens, the calculus we use is detached from part of speech, and we make no distinction between the adjective *risky*, the V' *is risky*, and the noun *risk*, but this lack of morphosyntactic typing will not be relied on heavily in what follows, except for making it easier to draw the graphs and talk about their nodes.

A significant advantage of relying on such hidden elements is that they all fit in the category of `difficulty`. As a result, they will participate in a larger frame involving `virtue` $\stackrel{1}{\leftarrow}$ OVERCOME $\stackrel{2}{\rightarrow}$ `difficulty`. The virtue, be it `bravery` as in the Cambridge and Longman dictionaries, or courage/confidence, as in Merriam-Webster, comes for free here, in that `bravery` $\stackrel{0}{\rightarrow}$ `virtue`, `diligence` $\stackrel{0}{\rightarrow}$ `virtue`, `decency` $\stackrel{0}{\rightarrow}$ `virtue`, etc. come from the lexical definition of these concepts, and no doubt `winter-hardiness`, required in the analysis of *tarjeta*, is a virtue, perhaps a monomorphemic one in Finnish, if Sapir-Whorf has any bite.[4]

Now it is plausible that `fear` $\stackrel{0}{\rightarrow}$ difficulty (or `obstacle`, as Karttunen (2014) has it) is somehow a piece of lexical knowledge, but this does not work for the other cases: it is rather unlikely that `indifference` or `empathy` are lexically specified for genus `difficulty/obstacle`. Such a conclusion, if not available lexically, must somehow be derived by a process of typecasting. The essence of the force-dynamic analysis is that *dare* and *hennoa* both IS_A OVERCOME. There is every reason to suppose that OVERCOME subcategorizes for a `power` subject and an `obstacle` object, and to make some action an instance of OVERCOME, its subject must be typecast to `power` and its object to `obstacle`. That virtue IS_A `power` is hard to deny, and by transitivity of IS_A we can treat all implicative subjects under this heading. With the implicative objects, this is less trivial: `empathy` gets to be an obstacle only because *hennoa* IS_A OVERCOME, and outside this frame we cannot draw the usual conclusions, e.g. that obstacles are bad things and therefore being humane is a bad thing.

Before turning to the details of the finite state analysis, let us consider how an ordinary sentence, such as *John dared to criticize the mayor* will be analyzed. The matrix verb is *dare* and it is John who does the daring, so we have `John` $\stackrel{1}{\leftarrow}$ DARE, and it is also John who does the criticizing, so we have `John` $\stackrel{1}{\leftarrow}$ CRITICIZE. How the subject equi is effected during the parsing process is something we leave to the phenogrammar, the point here is that few grammarians (including LFGers who would use an XCOMP here) would seriously doubt that the subject of both verbs is the same `John`. The object of the criticism is no doubt the `mayor`, and the object of daring is the entire *criticizing*

[4] Inquiries to Finnish-speaking friends produced *pakkasenkestävä*, but with a cautionary note that this is probably more appropriate for plants than for animals or humans, and *kylmänkestävä* with perhaps a bit less strict subcategorization.

the mayor.

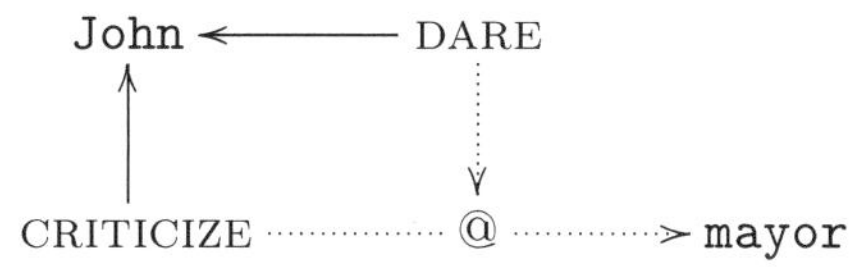

Figure 2. *John dared to criticize the mayor*

As we said, *dare* IS_A *overcome*, and whoever *dares* actually HAS `power`, or at least he thinks he does, to overcome `risk`. In fact, we can rely on a dictionary definition of *bravery, courage* as 'power to overcome risk' or 'power to overcome fright caused by risk', or even 'power to overcome one's own fright caused by risk'. Neither the final cause nor the precise application site of the power ends up being very relevant for the task at hand, which is to explain certain implications, whose non-fulfillment makes sentences using *dare* infelicitous, but not outright false. With *criticizing the mayor* it is rather clear that mayors are powerful people, and criticizing the powerful is dangerous. But when we say

(1) *#John dared to chew gum*

we need to abductively infer some theory that makes chewing gum dangerous. Perhaps John had throat surgery, and the wounds have not quite healed. Perhaps he is in the presence of some superior who considers this disrespectful. Perhaps he was told the gum could be laced with poison. There are many theories that would make the use of *dare* felicitous, and we need not choose among them. But we do need to draw the implication from *dare* to `risk` or `danger`. As with `obstacle` versus difficulty above, we need not be very precise which of these terms is operative here. What matters is the semantic concept, not the (English) printname we assign to it.

We will posit DARE $\xrightarrow{2}$`danger` as part of the lexical entry of *dare*, i.e. the selectional restriction that its object is dangerous. Similarly, the object of *deign* is low status (or perhaps the subject is high status), that of *remember* is hard to memorize, and so on. *Manage* has an object that is simply difficult, manner unspecified. Since it is the relationship of the subject to the object that is getting characterized by the implicative verb, we often have a choice between alternative framings: e.g. with *deign* we may be describing (i) the subject as high status; (ii) the object as low status; or (iii) the subject as higher status than the object. These alternatives are logically equivalent, since by default things are neither high nor low status. Yet it is quite conceivable that different speakers have different lexical entries for *deign*, and different lexicalization options may play differently with negation. Translational near-equivalents in different languages may also differ only in the choice between (i)-(iii).

22.3 The Mechanism

Again we begin with the easy pieces. The theory we rely on takes unaries simply to be bundles of essential properties, so for example the *fox* is `four-legged, animal, hairy, red, clever`. Since we make no distinction between attribution (*the fox is hairy*) and IS_A (*the fox is an animal*), we need not worry about the type signature of selectional restriction: by demanding DARE $\xrightarrow{2}$`danger` we have accomplished DARE $\xrightarrow{2} X, X \xrightarrow{0}$`danger` without lifting a finger. In general (not just for the sake of making this particular case come out right) IS_A is a derived notion, simply there to achieve economy in the system by means of lazy default inheritance. If x IS_A y, then the small set of essential properties associated to x is a superset of those associated to y, and elementary pieces of link-tracing logic, such as x IS_A $y \wedge y$ IS_A $z \Rightarrow x$ IS_A z, or x IS_A $y \wedge y$ HAS $z \Rightarrow x$ HAS z follow without any stipulation.

We make purposely very little distinction between an individual fox, the species *Vulpes vulpes,* the set of foxes in the world, or the class of potential foxes in all possible worlds. Even though such differences can be sufficient for distinguishing different senses of the same word, (compare *Jack is blond* 'has blond hair' to *Jack is a blond* 'fulfills the criteria for the stereotype), this is a peculiarity of English syntax, and as such it has no place in the semantics.

What implicative verbs bring to the table (working memory) are little lexically prespecified hypergraphs that demand abductive inferencing over and above the normal inferencing process, which we take to be (hyper)graph unification. We assume, as is standard, that verbs can subcategorize for their arguments: for example *elapse* demands a time interval subject. If we read that *A sekki elapsed* we know that this must refer to some time period even if we do not know the details of the sekki[5] system. This is part and parcel of knowing what *elapse* means: people who cannot make this inference are not in full possession of the lexical entry. In the representation of *elapse* there is thus a direct prespecification time_period $\xleftarrow{1}$ *elapse*, which contrasts with the prespecification inherited from a nominative linker NOM that subjects are agentive (active, causing, volitional).

There is little reason to suppose that time intervals are inherently

[5]`http://eco.mtk.nao.ac.jp/koyomi/faq/24sekki.html.en`

active, that they causally contribute to their own elapsing. To the contrary, time_interval IS_A `abstract_object` and would therefore inherit features of the latter such as LACK $\xrightarrow{2}$ `volition` that would directly contradict agentivity. But once *sekki* appears in the subject slot of *elapse*, it IS_A `time_interval` and the inheritance of non-volitionality from `abstract_object` is blocked, since the specific, lexically prespecified case will block the general inheritance mechanism as a matter of course. Similarly, in the representation of *dare*, the object of daring IS_A `risk`, and this will block the general assessment that e.g. chewing gum is not normally considered a risk.

Another aspect of the analysis that is relatively easy in the framework presented here is adding *overcoming* to the small set of preexisting force dynamic primitives *letting, hindering,* and *helping.* Since this would take us far afield from the issue at hand, we only sketch the basic mechanism: verbs can, and often do refer to the state *before* and *after* the action they depict: for example *go* simply means the conjunction `before` AT `source`, `after` AT goal; while telic verbs carry the specification `after done`. With these pieces at hand, we can dispense with the force-dynamic diagrams entirely in favor of analytic statements such as *overcome* 'the agent, initially weaker than the object, is subsequently stronger'. Since before and `after` are independently justified by other verbal phenomena, as is the generic comparative binary relation ER (abstracted from *greater, bigger, more*), we can say `before` (`force` $\xleftarrow{2}$ OVERCOME ER `force` $\xleftarrow{1}$ OVERCOME), `after` (force $\xleftarrow{1}$ OVERCOME ER `force` $\xleftarrow{2}$ OVERCOME). As usual, it matters but little whether we call the basis of the comparison *force, power, might, heft, momentum,* or something else, there is a single concept here, and we chose to call it `force` mainly to make clear our indebtedness to Talmy (1988) and Jackendoff (1990).

In a standard system of logic such as first order predicate calculus (FOPC) we would need at least two variables x and y, a one-place predicate *force* and seven two-place predicates *SubjectOf, ObjectOf, Before, After, IsA, Has,* and $>$, to express approximately the same meaning in a conjunctive formula:

(2) *Before((x IsA force & SubjectOf(x,overcome) & y IsA force & ObjectOf(y,overcome) & y > x),overcome) & After((x IsA force & SubjectOf(x,overcome) & y IsA force & ObjectOf(y,overcome) & x > y),overcome)*

even with the dubious expedient of reusing x and y in the *Before* and *After* subformulas. To simplify matters, notice that the variable x is just a paraphrase 'the force of the subject of overcome' and similarly y is 'the force of the object of overcome' so what we need to handle first are binary relations that have a first and a second argument.

As readers of Kornai (2010a) will know, we will use *machines* in the sense of Eilenberg (1974) toindexEilenberg machines do this work. A binary machine will have three *partitions*. The 0th or common partition will store all properties that hold for the entirety of the machine, e.g. that its printname is OVERCOME, or that various things may hold BEFORE or AFTER the overcoming. As with unaries, we do not make strict distinctions between a machine, its printname, or a pointer to the machine. The distinguished 1st partition will store properties true of the subject (1st argument), and the undistinguished 2nd partition to store properties that hold of the object (2nd argument).

This skeletal apparatus is already sufficient for providing the meaning representation of the bound morpheme *-er*: this will be a machine that has printname ER, and the only property it enjoys is that the relation $>$ holds between whatever is stored on its distinguished (1st) and undistinguished (2nd) partition. Largely similar is the machine for the possessive relation: we give it printname HAS (but it could be called OWN or POSS just as well) and this has implications for the subject, seen as the controller, and the active maintainer of the possession relation; and also for the object, seen as the controlled element, the one that cannot end the relation by itself.

We have already discussed unaries, seen as Eilenberg machinesindex-Eilenberg machines with two partitions, the 0th holding the printname, and the 1st (distinguished) partition holding (pointers to) the characteristic properties of the word being modeled (recall `fox` above). Note that IS_A is not a machine: we say `x` IS_A `y` iff the properties associated to `x` are a superset of those associated to `y`. Here `x` and `y` are variables in the metalanguage, not in the object language. There are no ternary or higher arity predicates – this is discussed in Kornai (2012).

We use *cases* such as NOM and ACC to effect the linking of subjects to the first, and objects to the 2nd partition at least in nominative-accusative languages: for ergative-absolutive this would be different. At this level, the mechanism is very similar to the linking theories of Kiparsky (1987) and Bierwisch (1988), see Chapter 5.5.1 of Butt (2006). The main technical innovation is the elimination of variable binding by means of machine substitution, taking advantage of the extra modeling capability offered by the relational monoid X that is at the base of Eilenberg machines. Members of X are relations (subsets of X^2), and if X has only two elements u, v we can use right multiplication with the one-member relation (v, v) to model binding at u, and right multiplication with (u, u) to model binding at v. This way we can guarantee, without recourse to variables, that the formula (or hypergraph) associated to *Brutus killed Caesar* differs exactly in the expected way from the one associated to *Caesar killed Brutus*.

Putting this all together, we start from highly skeletal lexical entries such as *dare* = `brave, do`, and obtain, by finite state means, implications such as *John chewed gum* and *chewing gum was risky (for John)*. Again, it should be noted that the lexical entry for *dare* was not created post festa, just to support this analysis, but existed in the 4lang conceptual dictionary for some years now, see github.[6] We owe a recent bugfix, shifting the verbal base from *try* to *do*, to the heightened scrutiny the entry received during the writing of this paper, but this does not affect the main point, which is to get from the subject's bravery (as posited in the actual entry) to the object's riskiness (the notion we relied on above).

This inferencing is accomplished by the same process, substitution *salva veritate* of the definition of *brave* in the subject position, so that we obtain 'subject HAS `courage`'. Now what about *courage*? Again substituting the definition '`will` ER `fear`' we obtain 'subject has greater willpower than fear' and it is by yet another substitution, that `fear` is not just any old mental state, but one that `danger` CAUSE that we finally derive the conclusion that the object of *dare* is indeed dangerous. As in many parts of the lexicon, there can be serious disagreement over how much of this is precomputed and already stored in the lexicon, see e.g. Pinker and Prince (1988), and defending one analysis over the other would take as far afield from the central theme of this paper, which is the finite state mechanism, the weak (proto)logic calculus one can use in deriving the meaning of the whole from the meanings of the parts.

22.4 Memory

Starting perhaps with Yngve (1961), linguists have long wrestled with assessing the impact on sentence processing of the limitations of short-term or working memory (Miller, 1956). The bulk of this work concerns syntax and takes it for granted that the central issue is dealing with the linear succession of words. Island parsing techniques, based on the idea that a full parse may be built from well-understood subgrammars, came two decades later (Carroll, 1983), and it was only under the impact of Ken Church's famous declaration, *parsers don't work*, that interest in partial parses, such as offered by light parsing (Abney, 1991), was

[6] `https://github.com/kornai/4lang`

beginning to be seen as legitimate.

If our focus is with semantics, the defining data structure of sequential processing, the tapes common to FSA, FSTs, and Turing machines, appear neither relevant nor particularly useful. Clearly, humans have huge long-term memory, but there is no reason whatsoever to suppose that this memory is sequentially organized outside of procedural/episodic memory. In particular, the bulk of linguistic information is stored in the lexicon, a device that is best thought of as random access. The classic model of computation best suited to random access of this sort is the Kolmogorov Б-complex (**КБС**), originating with Kolmogorov (1953) – for a more accessible introduction see Ch. 1 of Uspensky and Semenov (1993). There are more modern concepts, in particular the Storage Modification Machine of Schönhage (1980), the Pointer Machine of Shvachko (1991), and the Random Access Computer of Angluin and Valiant (1979) – for a good discussion, see Gurevich (1988).

We are in no position to make a compelling case for one over the other, but the key issue, as emphasized by Gurevich, is that all these models are "more appropriate for lower time complexities like real time or linear time" than the standard Turing Machine. There is in fact an important line of research, starting with Quillian (1967) and today best exemplified by the Abstract Meaning Representation (AMR) theory Banarescu et al. (2013), that shares much of the tools, concepts, and formal underpinnings of the theory described above. All these theories, called 'algebraic conceptual representation' (ACR) in Kornai and Kracht (2015), take the lexical entries, and the knowledge representations, to be (hyper)graphs, just as the **КБС** family of models. While AMR operates with hypergraph rewriting, and the theory presented here uses Eilenberg machinesindexEilenberg machines to build larger graphs from the elementary (lexical) pieces, **КБС** directly transduces one graph to the next one.

Whichever model we choose (and there is quite a rich variety to choose from, for example Kornai (1987) uses equational systems as defined in Curry and Feys (1958)), the key, most compelling notion these theories have since Quillian is *spreading activation.* This is island parsing writ large, beginning with nouns, named entities, and NPs, detection of case marking, assembly of clausal structure, and verbal slot filling. At every stage, morphemes, words, or larger lexical entries are active, and by spreading activation so are their links. A structure is detected whenever two such spreading waves of activation meet. Pragmatics, in the sense relevant to our understanding of *dare* and other implicatives, is simply an effort to find paths where none initially exist. There is clearly no link, at least initially, from *chewing gum* to `danger`.

But the post-verbal position really compels a reading whereby *chewing gum* is the object of *dare*, so we make the link, and now *chewing gum* is risky. Speakers are of course very aware that such sense-making activity is under way. They use it to eliminate redundancy, and abuse it to set up semantic traps like *when did you stop beating your wife.*

22.5 Conclusions

The lower predicate calculus (FOPC) is a wonder to behold: it is highly expressive, has good model theory, excellent proof theory, and a completeness theorem cementing the link between these two. It enjoys the compactness and Löwenheim-Skolem properties – in fact, according to Lindström's Theorem, it is the strongest among those systems of logic that have these two properties. Though Montague (1973) had good reasons to reach for higher order calculi, there have been continued efforts to bring natural language semantics down to first order, see in particular Blackburn and Bos (2005). But these efforts do not go far enough to curb the logic's hunger for resources: the simple task of checking that each quantifier bounds some variable is conjectured (Marsh and Partee, 1984) to be properly context sensitive, outside the power of indexed grammars, let alone the mildly context sensitive class.

Given that the mainstream theory of linguistic quantification still leaves a lot to be desired (Kornai, 2010b), a less ambitious form of logic that reduces quantification to genericity (use of defaults), and sacrifices scope effects may actually be a better fit with the semantics of natural language, and this is what we propose here. The system presented here is not even fully Boolean: conjunctions are everywhere, but disjunction is hard, and negation practically nonexistent, except for overt marking of failure of defaults, for example in taking `blind` to mean LACK $\stackrel{2}{\to}$ `sight`, or even a unuary analysis with `sight` $\stackrel{0}{\to}$ `lack`. This actually goes a long way towards explaining classic pragmatic puzzles, why *#blind stone* is infelicitous, and how can a *cup* be felicitously defined as a 'small round container for liquids, with or without a handle', given that everything is with or without a handle. At the same time it suggests caution with regards to relying on negation as *the* touchstone for implicature, especially as there is a whole lot of inferencing going on in positive contexts already, and the kind of logical semantics that takes Booleans for granted has no traction whatsoever over the central body of primary linguistic data.

Broadly speaking, all 'algebraic' approaches (among which we count not just classic AI models and AMR, but also Pāṇini) are like Generative Semantics[7] in that they proceed from meaning representation to surface form directly, without any reliance on LF, and view interpretation as the inverse task, analysis by synthesis. Such systems have no room for quantifier scoping,[8] and have been roundly rejected by AI greats like McCarthy (2005): "people who put knowledge into computers need mathematical logic, including quantifiers, as much as engineers need calculus". However, putting knowledge into computers is a goal very different from the goals of linguistics, in that people can acquire a great deal of knowledge for which there is no language-level support, starting with elementary arithmetic. To sustain this kind of scientific knowledge needs a logic that is considerably stronger than the protologic we rely on here.

The problem with these stronger logics is not so much that they are undecidable (they are), or hard to compute with (all systems in common use carry SAT[9] and other NP-complete problems), for clever limitations placed on the mechanism can avoid these pitfalls. The problem is that they are *unlearnable* in a strong sense. What we need is not just a model, but a path from primary data to this particular model within a reasonable hypothesis space. The general problem of learning FSA is already incredibly hard (Angluin, 1987), but somehow we all learn what *dare* means, so this must be a rather simple information object, selected from a very narrow hypothesis space. Our candidate information object is a graph with a few links to nodes already in the system. Here we laid out a plausible path toward a learnable theory, but there is a clear esthetics-driven choice here: one must decide whether to search for *truth*, in the narrow sense of catering to the needs of knowledge engineers, or try to build explanatory models that can learn *dare*.

References

Abney, Steven. 1991. Parsing by chunks. In R. Berwick, S. Abney, and C. Tenny, eds., *Principle-based parsing*, pages 257–278. Kluwer Academic Publishers.

Angluin, Dana. 1987. Learning regular sets from queries and counterexamples 75:87–106.

Angluin, Dana and Leslie Valiant. 1979. Fast probabilistic algorithms for Hamiltonian circuits and matchings 18:155–193.

Banarescu, Laura, Claire Bonial, Shu Cai, Madalina Georgescu, Kira Griffitt, Ulf Hermjakob, Kevin Knight, Philipp Koehn, Martha Palmer, and

[7] https://en.wikipedia.org/wiki/Generative_semantics

[8] A clever escape route may be left open by micro-timing the spreading, but this is a rabbit hole we do not want to go down.

[9] https://en.wikipedia.org/wiki/Boolean_satisfiability_problem

Nathan Schneider. 2013. Abstract meaning representation for sembanking. In *Proceedings of the 7th Linguistic Annotation Workshop and Interoperability with Discourse*, pages 178–186. Association for Computational Linguistics.

Bierwisch, Manfred. 1988. *Thematic grids as the interface between syntax and semantics*. Lectures.

Blackburn, Patrick and Johan Bos. 2005. *Representation and Inference for Natural Language. A First Course in Computational Semantics*. CSLI.

Butt, Miriam. 2006. *Theories of Case*. Cambridge University Press.

Carroll, John A. 1983. *An island parsing interpreter for the full augmented transition network formalism*. ACL Proceedings, First European Conference.

Curry, Haskell B. and Robert Feys. 1958. *Combinatory Logic I*. North-Holland.

Eilenberg, Samuel. 1974. *Automata, Languages, and Machines*, vol. A. Academic Press.

Frege, Gottlob. 1892. On sense and reference. In A. Martinich, ed., *The Philosophy of Language*, pages 36–56. Oxford University Press (4th ed, 2000).

Gurevich, Yuri. 1988. On Kolmogorov Machines and related issues 35:71–82.

Jackendoff, Ray S. 1990. *Semantic Structures*. MIT Press.

Karttunen, Lauri. 1971. Implicative verbs 47(2):340–358.

Karttunen, Lauri. 2014. Three ways of not being lucky.

Kiparsky, Paul. 1987. *Morphosyntax*. ms.

Kolmogorov, Andrei N. 1953. O ponyatii algoritma 8(4):175–176.

Kornai, András. 1987. Finite state semantics. In U. Klenk, P. Scherber, and M. Thaller, eds., *Computerlinguistik und philologische Datenverarbeitung*, pages 59–70. Georg Olms.

Kornai, András. 2010a. The algebra of lexical semantics. In C. Ebert, G. Jäger, and J. Michaelis, eds., *Proceedings of the 11th Mathematics of Language Workshop*, LNAI 6149, pages 174–199. Springer.

Kornai, András. 2010b. The treatment of ordinary quantification in English proper 54(4):150–162.

Kornai, András. 2012. Eliminating ditransitives. In P. de Groote and M.-J. Nederhof, eds., *Revised and Selected Papers from the 15th and 16th Formal Grammar Conferences*, LNCS 7395, pages 243–261. Springer.

Kornai, András. in press. *Semantics*. Springer Verlag.

Kornai, András, Judit Ács, Márton Makrai, Dávid Márk Nemeskey, Katalin Pajkossy, and Gábor Recski. 2015. Competence in lexical semantics. In *Proceedings of the Fourth Joint Conference on Lexical and Computational Semantics (*SEM 2015)*, pages 165–175. Association for Computational Linguistics.

Kornai, András and Marcus Kracht. 2015. Lexical semantics and model theory: Together at last? In *Proceedings of the 14th Meeting on the Mathematics of Language (MoL 14)*, pages 51–61. Association for Computational Linguistics.

Marsh, William and Barbara Partee. 1984. How non-context-free is variable binding? In M. Cobler, S. MacKaye, and M. Wescoat, eds., *Proceedings of the West Coast Conference on Formal Linguistics III*, pages 179–190.

McCarthy, John J. 2005. Human-level ai is harder than it seemed in 1955.

Miller, George A. 1956. The magical number seven, plus or minus two: some limits on our capacity for processing information 63:81–97.

Montague, Richard. 1973. The proper treatment of quantification in ordinary English. In R. Thomason, ed., *Formal Philosophy*, pages 247–270. Yale University Press.

Pinker, Steven and Alan S. Prince. 1988. On language and connectionism: Analysis of a parallel distributed processing model of language acquisition 28:73–194.

Quillian, M. Ross. 1967. Semantic memory. In Minsky, ed., *Semantic information processing*, pages 227–270. MIT Press.

Schönhage, A. 1980. Storage modification machine 9(3):490–508.

Shvachko, Konstantin V. 1991. Different modifications of pointer machines and their computational power. In *Proc. 16th Mathematical Foundations of Computer Science*, pages 426–441. Springer.

Talmy, L. 1988. Force dynamics in language and cognition 12(1):49–100.

Uspensky, Vladimir and Alexei Semenov. 1993. *Algorithms: Main Ideas and Applications*. Springer.

Yngve, Victor H. 1961. The depth hypothesis. In R. Jakobson, ed., *Structure of Language and its Mathematical Aspects*, pages 130–138. American Mathematical Society.

23

Finite-state Methods Featuring Semantics*

TIM FERNANDO

23.1 Introduction

"It may turn out to be very useful for semantic representations too." So concludes the abstract of Lauri Karttunen's COLING 84 paper, Features and values (F&V), referring to "the new Texas version of the 'DG (directed graph)' package" which was "primarily intended for representing morphological and syntactic information" (page 28). That the directed graph was essentially a finite automaton may have been too obvious an observation for F&V to state — or, assuming it had already been stated, restate. Be that as it may, this observation is used in Fernando 2016 to extract typed features structures from Robin Cooper's record type approach to frames (Fillmore 1982, Cooper 2012). I restate the observation here to develop its uses for semantic representations further, egged on by the aforementioned statement from F&V, and (as with Kornai 2017) the prospects of bringing together "two lines of research that lie at the opposite ends on the field" (Karttunen 2007). Just *how* to view feature structures as finite automata is detailed in the next section (section 2); *why* this view might pay off is explored in section 3.

As bottom-dwellers in the Chomsky hierarchy, finite automata have well-known limitations to test the maxim *keep it simple*. Finite-state

*My thanks to Cleo Condoravdi for inviting me to contribute to this Festschrift, András Kornai for feedback on this paper, and, not to forget, Lauri Karttunen for setting standards towards which to aspire.

Tokens of Meaning: Papers in Honor of Lauri Karttunen.
Cleo Condoravdi and Tracy Holloway King (eds.).

methods are structured below around semantic notions $\models$ of satisfaction between models and sentences, kept simple through Leibniz's Law, Identity of Indiscernibles. A logical formalism well-known from Hennessy & Milner 1985 (among other papers) is applied to feature structures in section 2 broadly along the lines of Blackburn 1993, but with particular attention to certain sets of strings to which directed graphs can be reduced, called trace sets. A set Σ of attributes is paired with a trace set $T \subseteq \Sigma^*$ for a *signature* (Σ, T), picking out the set $Mod(\Sigma, T)$ of trace sets L sandwiched between T and Σ^*

$$T \subseteq L \subseteq \Sigma^*.$$

A trace set $L \in Mod(\Sigma, T)$ is a (Σ, T)-*model*, as the notation $Mod(\Sigma, T)$ suggests, against which to evaluate a Σ-sentence. A (Σ, T)-model L can be construed as a record of record type (Σ, T) with an s-component L_s, for every string $s \in T$, that is a trace set satisfying a Σ-sentence φ precisely if L satisfies the Σ-sentence $\langle s \rangle \varphi$

$$L \models \langle s \rangle \varphi \iff L_s \models \varphi.$$

To analyze satisfaction $\models$, it suffices to keep the set Σ in a signature (Σ, T) finite, and integrate different signatures within a category (following the so-called Grothendieck construction). Behind the somewhat technical details below is the intuition that signatures are bounded granularities that simplify calculations of satisfaction $\models$. That simplification, called the *Translation Axiom* in Barwise 1974 (page 235) and the *Satisfaction Condition* in Goguen & Burstall 1992 (page 102), applies to unification in F&V with negative and disjunctive constraints that refine the sets $Mod(\Sigma, T)$.

Supposing a typed feature structure can be viewed as a finite automaton (which section 2 takes pains to show), *so what*? To make the view compelling, we turn in section 3 to runs of finite automata with the eventual goal of understanding these runs as uses of linguistic resources encoded by typed feature structures. An approach to temporality in which time arises from running automata is presented paralleling section 2, with Monadic Second Order logic in place of Hennessy-Milner logic, and superposition in place of unification (for building models bottom-up, subject to constraints). Careful attention is paid to shifts in bounded granularity and to the assorted forces that take shape as granularity is refined. This is in contrast to the practice of fixing some space of possible worlds once and for all, without any provisions for varying granularity.

23.2 From Features to Strings and Types

Some notions taken up in F&V are collected in the first column of Table 1, which we analyze in this section according to the second column.

path $\langle a_1 \cdots a_n \rangle$ of attributes	string $a_1 \cdots a_n$
(rooted) directed graph G	set $L(G)$ of strings
generalize(G, G')	$L(G) \cap L(G')$
constraints C	set Φ_C of sentences with $\neg, \vee$
unify$_C(G, G')$	$L(G) \cup L(G')$ if it satisfies Φ_C

Table 1

We take for granted in Table 1 a set Σ of *attributes* $(a, a_i, \ldots)$, and define a Σ-*deterministic system* to be a partial function $\delta : Q \times \Sigma \rightharpoonup Q$ to some set Q of nodes from the set $Q \times \Sigma$ of node-attribute pairs. We picture a triple $(q, a, \delta(q, a))$ in δ as a deterministic transition $q \xrightarrow{a} \delta(q, a)$, and formulate a (rooted) directed graph G as a pair (δ, q) of a Σ-deterministic system δ and a node $q \in Q$. To define the language $L(G) \subseteq \Sigma^*$, let $\delta_q : \Sigma^* \rightharpoonup Q$ be the $\subseteq$-smallest subset F of $\Sigma^* \times Q$ such that

(i) $(\epsilon, q) \in F$, and
(ii) $(sa, q'') \in F$ whenever $(s, q') \in F$ and $(q', a, q'') \in \delta$.

Now, if the directed graph G is the pair (δ, q), then its language $L(G)$ is the set $dom(\delta_q)$ of strings s for which $\delta_q(s)$ is defined. The language $dom(\delta_q)$ is called the *trace set of* (δ, q), and strings in $dom(\delta_q)$ are called *traces of* (δ, q).

Next, with Σ fixed, we express constraints through the set $sen(\Sigma)$ of sentences φ generated from attributes $a \in \Sigma$ by the grammar

$$\varphi \quad ::= \quad \top \mid \langle a \rangle \varphi \mid \neg \varphi \mid \varphi \vee \varphi'$$

interpreted against a Σ-deterministic system $\delta : Q \times \Sigma \rightharpoonup Q$ by a binary relation $\models^\delta \subseteq Q \times sen(\Sigma)$ that treats $\top$ as a tautology

$$q \models^\delta \top \quad \text{for every } q \in Q,$$

$\langle a \rangle$ as the Diamond modal operator with accessibility relation $\delta(\cdot, a)$

$$q \models^\delta \langle a \rangle \varphi \iff (q, a) \in dom(\delta) \text{ and } \delta(q, a) \models^\delta \varphi,$$

$\neg$ as Boolean negation

$$q \models^\delta \neg \varphi \iff \text{not } q \models^\delta \varphi$$

and $\vee$ as Boolean disjunction

$$q \models^\delta \varphi \vee \varphi' \iff q \models^\delta \varphi \text{ or } q \models^\delta \varphi'$$

(Hennessy & Milner 1985, Blackburn 1993). Collecting the sentences in $sen(\Sigma)$ that $q \models^\delta$-satisfies in

$$sen_\Sigma(\delta, q) \; := \; \{\varphi \in sen(\Sigma) \mid q \models^\delta \varphi\},$$

it turns out that directed graphs satisfy the same subset of $sen(\Sigma)$ precisely if they have the same trace set

$$sen_\Sigma(\delta, q) = sen_\Sigma(\delta', q') \iff dom(\delta_q) = dom(\delta'_{q'}) \qquad (23.28)$$

(Hennessy & Milner 1985).[1] Under Leibniz's Identity of Indiscernibles, with discernibility based on $sen(\Sigma)$, (23.1) reduces a directed graph (δ, q) to its trace set $dom(\delta_q)$. The trace set captures a fragment of $sen(\Sigma)$

$$dom(\delta_q) \; = \; \{s \in \Sigma^* \mid \langle s \rangle \top \in sen_\Sigma(\delta, q)\}$$

consisting of sentences of the form $\langle s \rangle \top$, where for every $\varphi \in sen(\Sigma)$, the sentence $\langle s \rangle \varphi$ in $sen(\Sigma)$ is defined by induction on $s \in \Sigma^*$, starting with the null string ϵ,

$$\langle \epsilon \rangle \varphi \; := \; \varphi$$

and using modal operators $\langle a \rangle$ elsewhere

$$\langle as \rangle \varphi \; := \; \langle a \rangle \langle s \rangle \varphi$$

so that $\langle a_1 \cdots a_n \rangle \varphi$ is $\langle a_1 \rangle \cdots \langle a_n \rangle \varphi$ and

$$q \models^\delta \langle s \rangle \varphi \iff s \in dom(\delta_q) \text{ and } \delta_q(s) \models^\delta \varphi. \qquad (23.29)$$

In the remainder of this section, we replace q and δ in (23.2) by a prefix-closed language over Σ with derivatives (in §2.1), and expand Σ to flesh out Table 1 (in §2.2), systematized category-theoretically (in §2.3) to link up with section 3.

23.2.1 Languages and Transitions to Derivatives

Given a set $L \subseteq \Sigma^*$ of strings over Σ and a string s over Σ, the *s-derivative of* L is the set

$$L_s \; := \; \{s' \mid ss' \in L\}$$

of strings that put after s belong to L (Brzozowski 1964). For any Σ-deterministic system $\delta : Q \times \Sigma \rightharpoonup Q$ and node q, one can check that $dom(\delta_q)$ is the set of strings s such that the null string ϵ is in the s-derivative of $dom(\delta_q)$

$$s \in dom(\delta_q) \iff \epsilon \in (dom(\delta_q))_s$$

[1] Readers familiar with, for example, Barwise & Moss 1996 will note that determinism simplifies matters considerably, reducing bisimulation equivalence between (δ, q) and (δ', q') to trace equivalence $dom(\delta_q) = dom(\delta'_{q'})$, and allowing us to talk of sets of strings instead of non-well-founded sets.

and that for every $s \in dom(\delta_q)$, the s-derivative of $dom(\delta_q)$ is the trace set of $(\delta, \delta_q(s))$

$$(dom(\delta_q))_s = dom(\delta_{q'}) \text{ where } q' = \delta_q(s).$$

Indeed, the chain of equivalences

$$\begin{aligned} a_1 a_2 \cdots a_n \in L &\iff a_2 \cdots a_n \in L_{a_1} \\ &\iff \cdots \iff \epsilon \in L_{a_1 \cdots a_n} \end{aligned}$$

from $a_1 \cdots a_n$ to the null string ϵ means that L is accepted by the deterministic automaton with

- s-derivatives L_s as states
- initial state $L = L_\epsilon$
- a-transitions from L_s to L_{sa} (for every symbol $a \in \Sigma$)
- final (accepting) states L_s such that $\epsilon \in L_s$.

The s-derivative of L equals the s'-derivative of L precisely if s and s' concatenate with the same strings to produce strings in L

$$L_s = L_{s'} \iff (\forall w \in \Sigma^*)\ (sw \in L \iff s'w \in L)$$

so that the Myhill-Nerode Theorem says that for finite Σ,

$$L \text{ is regular} \iff \{L_s \mid s \in \Sigma^*\} \text{ is finite}$$

(e.g. Hopcroft & Ullman 1979). Note that L_s is non-empty precisely if s is the prefix of some string in L. Moreover, if L_s is empty then so is L_{sa} for every $a \in \Sigma$. That is, $\emptyset$ is a sink state that we may safely exclude from the states of the automaton above, at the cost of making the transition function partial.

Let us call a language L *prefix-closed* if for all $sa \in L$, $s \in L$. Note that trace sets are prefix-closed and non-empty. Let $Mod(\Sigma)$ denote the set

$$Mod(\Sigma) := \{L \subseteq \Sigma^* \mid L \neq \emptyset \text{ and } L \text{ is prefix-closed}\}$$

of non-empty prefix-closed subsets of Σ^*, and let us refer to an element of $Mod(\Sigma)$ as a Σ-*state*. Not only are trace sets Σ-states, but conversely, if $\hat{\delta}$ is the Σ-deterministic system

$$\{(L, a, L_a) \mid L \in Mod(\Sigma) \text{ and } a \in \Sigma \cap L\}$$

then every Σ-state L is the trace set of $(\hat{\delta}, L)$. Keeping $\hat{\delta}$ implicit, a Σ-state L makes an s-transition to its s-derivative L_s precisely if $s \in L$, specializing the biconditional (2) from the previous page to

$$L \models \langle s \rangle \varphi \iff s \in L \text{ and } L_s \models \varphi.$$

23.2.2 Adding Attributes, Types and Constraints

Identity as indiscernibility relative to $sen(\Sigma)$ presupposes that all differences which matter are captured by the set Σ. An obvious problem is that the single trace set $\{\epsilon\}$ cannot differentiate between atomic values. But it is easy enough to introduce for every atomic value v, a fresh attribute a_v to Σ for say, the trace set $\{a_v, \epsilon\}$. At least two objections can be made to this move. The first is that a trace set of $\{\epsilon\}$ is arguably what it means for a value v to be atomic; any larger trace set would make v non-atomic. If "atomic" is understood this way, identity as indiscernibility leaves us no choice but to differentiate between values by making all but perhaps one of them non-atomic. A more serious objection is that if the alphabet Σ is to be finite, then we cannot introduce fresh attributes to Σ indefinitely. Or can we? Given any set $\mathcal{A}$, no matter how large, we can form its set $Fin(\mathcal{A})$ of finite subsets

$$Fin(\mathcal{A}) \ := \ \{\Sigma \subseteq \mathcal{A} \mid \Sigma \text{ is finite}\}$$

and let Σ vary over members of $Fin(\mathcal{A})$; each attribute $a \in \mathcal{A} - \Sigma$ added to Σ leads to the different member $\Sigma \cup \{a\}$ of $Fin(\mathcal{A})$. The challenge then becomes to implement the variations in Σ systematically. This is where signatures and institutions enter.

But first, it will prove convenient to expand $sen(\Sigma)$ with a modal operator $\Diamond$ for a sentence $\Diamond\varphi$ equivalent to the disjunction over all $s \in \Sigma^*$ of the sentences $\langle s \rangle\varphi$. More precisely,

$$q \models^{\delta} \Diamond\varphi \iff (\exists s \in \Sigma^*) \ q \models^{\delta} \langle s \rangle\varphi \tag{23.30}$$

for any Σ-deterministic system $\delta : Q \times \Sigma \rightharpoonup Q$ and node $q \in Q$. Incorporating $\Diamond$ into $sen(\Sigma)$ and $sen_\Sigma(\delta, q)$ for $sen^{\Diamond}(\Sigma)$ and $sen^{\Diamond}_{\Sigma}(\delta, q)$ respectively, it is not dfficult to verify that trace equivalence remains indiscernibility up to $sen^{\Diamond}(\Sigma)$

$$sen^{\Diamond}_{\Sigma}(\delta, q) = sen^{\Diamond}_{\Sigma}(\delta', q') \iff dom(\delta_q) = dom(\delta'_{q'}).$$

Thus, we can again reduce (δ, q) to its trace set $dom(\delta_q)$ and $\models^{\delta}$ to a binary relation $\models_\Sigma \subseteq Mod(\Sigma) \times sen^{\Diamond}(\Sigma)$ between a Σ-state L and a sentence $\varphi \in sen^{\Diamond}(\Sigma)$, simplifying (23.3) to

$$\begin{aligned} L \models_\Sigma \Diamond\varphi &\iff (\exists s \in \Sigma^*) \ L \models_\Sigma \langle s \rangle\varphi \\ &\iff (\exists s \in L) \ L_s \models_\Sigma \varphi \end{aligned}$$

(adding the subscript Σ to prepare for the aforementioned variations). As usual, we let $\Box\varphi$ abbreviate $\neg\Diamond\neg\varphi$ for

$$L \models_\Sigma \Box\varphi \iff (\forall s \in L) \ L_s \models_\Sigma \varphi$$

alongside the Boolean conventions $\varphi \supset \psi$ for $\psi \vee \neg\varphi$, and $\varphi \wedge \psi$ for $\neg(\neg\varphi \vee \neg\psi)$. Given a subset Φ of $sen^{\Diamond}(\Sigma)$, we say a Σ-state L is a

Σ-*model of* Φ, and write $L \models_\Sigma \Phi$, if it satisfies every sentence in Φ

$$L \models_\Sigma \Phi \iff (\forall \varphi \in \Phi)\ L \models_\Sigma \varphi.$$

Now, to pick out a particular Σ-state through a sentence φ, let $Uniq_\Sigma(\varphi)$ be the set

$$Uniq_\Sigma(\varphi) := \{\Diamond(\varphi \wedge \psi) \supset \Box(\varphi \supset \psi) \mid \psi \in sen(\Sigma)\}$$

of implications $\Diamond(\varphi \wedge \psi) \supset \Box(\varphi \supset \psi)$ ensuring that if ψ should ever occur with φ, it always occurs with φ. Since trace equivalence is indiscernibility with respect to $sen(\Sigma)$, it follows that the sentences ψ appearing in $Uniq_\Sigma(\varphi)$ can be restricted to those of the form $\langle s\rangle\top$ for $s \in \Sigma^*$ without changing the Σ-models of $Uniq_\Sigma(\varphi)$, and that

(†) for any Σ-model L of $Uniq_\Sigma(\varphi)$, and $s, s' \in L$,

$$\text{if } L_s \models_\Sigma \varphi \text{ and } L_{s'} \models_\Sigma \varphi \text{ then } L_s = L_{s'}.$$

If we are to introduce an attribute a_v to name a particular value v through the sentence $\langle a_v\rangle\top$, then we must restrict our $(\Sigma\cup\{a_v\})$-states to $(\Sigma \cup \{a_v\})$-models of $Uniq_{\Sigma\cup\{a_v\}}(\langle a_v\rangle\top)$. An attribute a might also be introduced to name a type that applies to more than one $(\Sigma \cup \{a\})$-state, implicating a $(\Sigma\cup\{a\})$-state that fails to satisfy some sentence in $Uniq_{\Sigma\cup\{a\}}(\langle a\rangle\top)$. There is a curious twist here on treatments of "identity and mere likeness" (F&V, page 29) and re-entrancy (connected with a feature path s that appears in the present set-up as a subscript in L_s and inside a modal operator in $\langle s\rangle\varphi$). Σ-states L and L' can be distinct only if some sentence in $sen(\Sigma)$ differentiates them (shifting, as it were, the burden of proof from identification to differentiation, and suggesting refinements of identity through expansions of Σ).

Additional attributes may serve purposes other then refining discernibility. For example, they may provide representations of sentences in $sen^\Diamond(\Sigma)$ as follows. Given a subset Φ of $sen^\Diamond(\Sigma)$, a sentence $\varphi \in sen^\Diamond(\Sigma)$, and a string $s \in \Sigma^*$, let us agree that s (Σ, Φ)-*represents* φ if every Σ-model of Φ satisfies

$$\Box(\varphi \equiv \langle s\rangle\top)$$

where $\varphi \equiv \psi$ is $(\varphi \supset \psi) \wedge (\psi \supset \varphi)$, and consequently, for any Σ-state L,

$$L \models_\Sigma \Box(\varphi \equiv \psi) \iff (\forall s \in L)(L_s \models_\Sigma \varphi \iff L_s \models_\Sigma \psi).$$

Because we can build φ with the connectives $\neg$ and $\vee$, we cannot expect there to be a string that $(\Sigma, \emptyset)$-represents φ. But we can always introduce an attribute $a_\varphi \notin \Sigma$ and set Φ to $\{\Box(\varphi \equiv \langle a_\varphi\rangle\top)\}$ so that a_φ $(\Sigma \cup \{a_\varphi\}, \Phi)$-represents φ. And we can put together attributes a_φ and a_ψ that (Σ, Φ)-represent φ and ψ respectively, as Σ-models of Φ

satisfy

$$\Box\,((\varphi \wedge \psi) \;\equiv\; (\langle a_\varphi\rangle\top \wedge \langle a_\psi\rangle\top)).$$

We can then avoid the addition of $a_{\varphi\wedge\psi}$, provided we generalize our notion of representation to a language $\hat{L} \subseteq \Sigma^*$ as follows. We say $\hat{L}$ (Σ,Φ)-*represents* φ if for every Σ-model L of Φ and $s \in L$,

$$\begin{aligned} L_s \models_\Sigma \varphi \;&\Longleftrightarrow\; (\forall s' \in \hat{L})\; L_s \models \langle s'\rangle\top \\ &\Longleftrightarrow\; \hat{L} \subseteq L_s \end{aligned} \tag{23.31}$$

Clearly, a string s (Σ,Φ)-represents φ iff the singleton language $\{s\}$ (Σ,Φ)-represents φ. But why should we care about representing sentences by languages?

Table 1 at the beginning of the present section mentions not only directed graphs G and G' but also constraints C. Directed graphs are formulated here as Σ-states (models), and constraints as subsets of $sen^\diamond(\Sigma)$. A Σ-state can be viewed as a token, and a sentence φ in $sen^\diamond(\Sigma)$ as the type

$$Mod_\Sigma(\varphi) \;:=\; \{L \in Mod(\Sigma) \mid L \models_\Sigma \varphi\}$$

of Σ-states satisfying φ. A set $\Phi \subseteq sen^\diamond(\Sigma)$ of sentences amounts to the conjunction $\bigwedge \Phi$ specifying the type

$$Mod_\Sigma(\Phi) \;:=\; \bigcap_{\varphi\in\Phi} Mod_\Sigma(\varphi)$$

of Σ-states satisfying every sentence in Φ. Inclusion $\subseteq$ between sets of strings over Σ in (23.4) is easily confused with that between sets $Mod_\Sigma(\varphi)$ and $Mod_\Sigma(\psi)$ of such sets

$$Mod_\Sigma(\varphi) \subseteq Mod_\Sigma(\psi) \;\Longleftrightarrow\; (\forall L \in Mod(\Sigma))\; L \models_\Sigma \varphi \supset \psi$$

signifying an entailment from φ to ψ (and reversing the direction in (23.4) from the less informative $\hat{L}$ to the more informative L_s). Converting a sentence φ to a Σ-state that (Σ,Φ)-represents it requires a set Φ of constraints that we can find in, if necessary, an expansion of Σ. Resorting to Φ as $\{\Box(\varphi \equiv \langle a_\varphi\rangle\top)\}$ with a_φ thrown into Σ is perhaps too easy, shoving all the work over to Φ. But there is surely a role for Φ, since L can only $(\Sigma,\emptyset)$-represent a sentence with the same Σ-models as $\{\langle s\rangle\top \mid s \in L\}$, leaving out many sentences formed with negation $\neg$ and disjunction $\vee$. The models of a sentence φ that a language $(\Sigma,\emptyset)$-represents are closed under inclusion $\subseteq$

$$(\forall L \in Mod_\Sigma(\varphi))(\forall L' \in Mod(\Sigma))\; L \subseteq L' \text{ implies } L' \models_\Sigma \varphi$$

and intersection $\cap$

$$(\forall L \in Mod_\Sigma(\varphi))(\forall L' \in Mod_\Sigma(\varphi))\; L \cap L' \models_\Sigma \varphi.$$

But closure under intersection fails for the negation $\neg\langle a\rangle\top$, and closure under intersection fails for the disjunction $\langle a\rangle\top \vee \langle a'\rangle\top$ (with two different $\subseteq$-minimal models, for $a \neq a'$).

As a binary operation on directed graphs, unification in F&V is defined on Σ-states, and, pace Blackburn 1993, *not* on sentences (in terms of the connective $\wedge$). The constraints determining when two directed graphs are unifiable does, however, bring in $sen^{\diamond}(\Sigma)$, as does talk of negative and disjunctive features inasmuch as these involve the $sen^{\diamond}(\Sigma)$-connectives $\neg$ and $\vee$. Evidently, a mix of Σ-states and Σ-sentences is required. Accordingly, let us pair Σ with a language $T \subseteq \Sigma^*$, revising $Mod(\Sigma)$ to

$$Mod(\Sigma, T) \ := \ \{L \in Mod(\Sigma) \mid T \subseteq L\}$$

and $Mod_{\Sigma}(\Phi)$, for $\Phi \subseteq sen^{\diamond}(\Sigma)$, to

$$Mod_{\Sigma,T}(\Phi) \ := \ \{L \in Mod_{\Sigma}(\Phi) \mid T \subseteq L\}.$$

Then relative to constraints Φ, we can analyze the unification of Σ-states L and L' in terms of $Mod_{\Sigma,L\cup L'}(\Phi)$, which may be empty even if neither $Mod_{\Sigma,L}(\Phi)$ nor $Mod_{\Sigma,L'}(\Phi)$ is, accounting for the partiality of unification

$$L \text{ and } L' \text{ are unifiable relative to } \Phi \quad \iff \quad Mod_{\Sigma,L\cup L'}(\Phi) \neq \emptyset.$$

Negation and disjunction in features may (or may not) require expanding Σ with $a_{\neg\varphi}$ and $a_{\varphi\vee\psi}$, and Φ with constraints

$$\Box(\varphi' \equiv \langle a_{\varphi'}\rangle\top) \qquad \text{for } \varphi' \in \{\neg\varphi, \varphi\vee\psi\}.$$

Fixing some large set $\mathcal{A}$ to which all the required attributes belong, we let Σ vary over the set $Fin(\mathcal{A})$ of finite subsets of $\mathcal{A}$, and note

Fact 1 *Let $\Sigma' \in Fin(\mathcal{A})$, $\Sigma \subseteq \Sigma'$, $\varphi \in sen(\Sigma)$, and $L' \in Mod(\Sigma')$. Then $L' \cap \Sigma^* \in Mod(\Sigma)$ and*

$$L' \models_{\Sigma'} \varphi \quad \iff \quad L' \cap \Sigma^* \models_{\Sigma} \varphi$$

and moreover, for every $s \in L' \cap \Sigma^*$, $(L' \cap \Sigma^*)_s \in Mod(\Sigma)$ and

$$L' \models_{\Sigma'} \langle s\rangle\varphi \quad \iff \quad (L' \cap \Sigma^*)_s \models_{\Sigma} \varphi.$$

The first part of Fact 1 says that the attributes that matter in satisfying φ are only those that appear in φ,[2] while the second part interprets

[2]Fact 1 leaves $\diamond$ out of φ precisely because $\diamond$ does not identify the attributes relevant to the satisfaction of sentences built with $\diamond$. To bring $\diamond$ into φ in Fact 1, we can add subscripts X ranging over subsets of Σ to make the pertinent attributes in $\diamond_X$ explicit, with

$$q \models^{\delta} \diamond_X \psi \iff (\exists s \in X^*)\ q \models^{\delta} \langle s\rangle\psi$$

(Fernando 2016).

the modal operator $\langle s\rangle$ against Σ'-states L' under the presupposition that s belongs to L'.

23.2.3 The Grothendieck Construction and an Institution

Some category-theoretic structure lurking in Fact 1 will resurface in section 3 under a different guise and is worth spelling out. We fix a large set $\mathcal{A}$ of attributes, and for each finite subset $\Sigma \in Fin(\mathcal{A})$ of $\mathcal{A}$, turn the set $Mod(\Sigma)$ of Σ-states into a category $\mathcal{Q}(\Sigma)$ as follows. A $\mathcal{Q}(\Sigma)$-morphism from Σ-state L to Σ-state L' is a pair (L, s) with $s \in L$ and $L_s = L'$. $\mathcal{Q}(\Sigma)$-morphisms compose by concatenating strings

$$(L, s); (L_s, s') \ := \ (L, ss')$$

and (L, ϵ) is the identity morphism for L. Whenever $\Sigma \subseteq \Sigma' \in Fin(\mathcal{A})$, we define the functor $\mathcal{Q}(\Sigma', \Sigma) : \mathcal{Q}(\Sigma') \to \mathcal{Q}(\Sigma)$ from $\mathcal{Q}(\Sigma')$ to $\mathcal{Q}(\Sigma)$ mapping

- a Σ'-state L' to the Σ-state $L' \cap \Sigma^*$, and
- a $\mathcal{Q}(\Sigma')$-morphism (L', s) to the $\mathcal{Q}(\Sigma)$-morphism $(L' \cap \Sigma^*, \pi_\Sigma(s))$

where $\pi_\Sigma(s)$ is the longest prefix of s in Σ^*

$$\pi_\Sigma(\epsilon) \ := \ \epsilon$$

$$\pi_\Sigma(as) \ := \ \begin{cases} a\,\pi_\Sigma(s) & \text{if } a \in \Sigma \\ \epsilon & \text{otherwise.} \end{cases}$$

Construing $Fin(\mathcal{A})$ as a category with morphisms given by inclusion $\subseteq$, the foregoing defines a contravariant functor $\mathcal{Q} : Fin(\mathcal{A})^{op} \to \mathbf{Cat}$ into the category **Cat** of small categories. The *Grothendieck construction* (e.g., Tarlecki, Burstall & Goguen 1991) applied to $\mathcal{Q}$ yields the category $\int \mathcal{Q}$ where

- an object is a pair $(\Sigma, L) \in Fin(\mathcal{A}) \times Mod(\Sigma)$, and
- a morphism from (Σ', L') to (Σ, L) is a pair

  $$((\Sigma', \Sigma), (L'', s))$$

  of a $Fin(\mathcal{A})^{op}$-morphism (Σ', Σ) and a $\mathcal{Q}(\Sigma)$-morphism (L'', s) such that

  $$L'' = L' \cap \Sigma^* \text{ and } L = L''_s.$$

Reversing the morphisms in $\int \mathcal{Q}$ for the category **Sign** of *signatures* (Σ, L), we define two functors from **Sign**, one covariant and the other contravariant

(i) sen : **Sign** $\to$ **Set** with $sen(\Sigma, L) := sen(\Sigma)$ and

$$sen((\Sigma, \Sigma'), (L'', s)) : \ \varphi \mapsto \langle s\rangle\varphi$$

(ii) Mod : $\mathbf{Sign}^{op} \rightarrow \mathbf{Cat}$ where the set $Mod(\Sigma, L)$ of Σ-states that $\subseteq$-contain L is turned into a full subcategory of $\mathcal{Q}(\Sigma)$, and

$$Mod((\Sigma', \Sigma), (L'', s)) : \hat{L} \mapsto (\hat{L} \cap \Sigma^*)_s.$$

To build an *institution* (Goguen & Burstall 1992) from **Sign**, *sen*, and *Mod*, it remains to form, for every signature (Σ, L), a relation $\models_{\Sigma,L}$ by intersecting $\models_{\Sigma}$ with $Mod(\Sigma, L) \times sen(\Sigma)$. Fact 1 is essentially the *Satisfaction Condition* characterizing institutions

for every signature (Σ', L'), subset Σ of Σ', string $s \in L' \cap \Sigma^*$, sentence $\varphi \in sen(\Sigma)$, and $\hat{L} \in Mod(\Sigma', L')$,

$$\hat{L} \models_{\Sigma', L'} \langle s \rangle \varphi \iff (\hat{L} \cap \Sigma^*)_s \models_{\Sigma, L} \varphi$$

where the subscript L above is short for $(L' \cap \Sigma^*)_s$.

Introduced by Goguen and Burstall to cope with the proliferation of logical systems in computer science, the notion of an institution has attracted considerable attention and found numerous applications (e.g. Diaconescu 2012, Kutz et al 2010). Under Fact 1, features and values can be seen as part of that body of work.

23.3 Time for and from Running Automata

It is one thing to encode a linguistic resource as a feature structure equivalent to a finite automaton. It is quite another matter to understand the use of such a resource as the use of a finite automaton. To use a finite automaton is (arguably first and foremost) to run it, accepting strings that end in a final/accepting state. But such runs take place in isolation, whereas it is only in combination with other resources that the encoding or use of a linguistic resource is interesting. The whole point of the category-theoretic approach from the previous section is to relate different feature structures. Similarly, the present section considers runs of an automaton *not* so much in isolation as in combination with other automata, constructing a notion of time from such runs. A simple way to superpose runs of two finite automata is defined in §3.1, and related to the approximation of Priorean temporal models in §3.2 by strings constructed from temporal propositions. We adopt the custom from Artificial Intelligence of referring to temporal propositions as *fluents*. We fix some large set Θ of fluents much as we fixed a large set $\mathcal{A}$ of attributes in the previous section. The plan roughly is to fill out Table 2, embracing Leibniz's Identity of Indiscernibles (as in section 2), with granularity given by a finite subset A of Θ (analogous to $\Sigma \in Fin(\mathcal{A})$ in section 2) to form strings over the alphabet 2^A of subsets of A. The $\subseteq$-larger the subset A, the more refined the A-models and the more expressive the A-sentences can be.

	section 2	section 3
information merge	unify graphs	superpose strings
large set	$\mathcal{A}$ of attributes	Θ of fluents
grain/signature	$\Sigma \in \mathit{Fin}(\mathcal{A})$	$A \in \mathit{Fin}(\Theta)$
model	language over Σ	string over 2^A
sentence	Hennessy-Milner	Monadic Second-Order

Table 2

Helpful examples for orientation are provided by representations of a calendar year at various granularities. The set $A = \{\text{Jan, Feb, ..., Dec}\}$ of months suggests the string

$$s_A := \boxed{\text{Jan}}\boxed{\text{Feb}} \cdots \boxed{\text{Dec}}$$

of length 12. Enlarging A with days d1,d2,...,d31

$$A' := A \cup \{\text{d1,d2...,d31}\}$$

refines s_A to the string

$$s_{A'} := \boxed{\text{Jan,d1}}\boxed{\text{Jan,d2}} \cdots \boxed{\text{Jan,d31}}\boxed{\text{Feb,d1}} \cdots \boxed{\text{Dec,d31}}$$

of length 366 for a leap year. We draw boxes (instead of the usual curly braces { and }) around sets *qua* symbols to suggest a film strip. A change in A can cause a box to split (much like hairs in Shan 2015), as $\boxed{\text{Jan}}$ in s_A does (30 times) on adding days

$$\boxed{\text{Jan}} \rightsquigarrow \boxed{\text{Jan,d1}}\boxed{\text{Jan,d2}} \cdots \boxed{\text{Jan,d31}}$$

in $s_{A'}$. Similarly, a common Reichenbachian account of the progressive puts a *reference time* R inside the event time E, splitting $\boxed{\text{E}}$ into 3 boxes

$$\boxed{\text{E}} \rightsquigarrow \boxed{\text{E}}\boxed{\text{E,R}}\boxed{\text{E}}$$

(one before, one simultaneous, and one after R). This and many other examples in tense and aspect are taken up at length in Fernando 2015. The aim of the present section is to link that work with the previous section through the notion of an institution. The hope is that this might contribute to understanding the use of linguistic resources encoded as feature structures in terms of runs of finite automata — runs that give rise to time at bounded granularities.

23.3.1 From Superposition to Reducts and MSO

Given two equally long strings $s = \alpha_1 \cdots \alpha_n$ and $s' = \alpha'_1 \cdots \alpha'_n$ of sets α_i and α'_i, let use define the *superposition s&s′ of s and s′* to be the string obtained by their componentwise unions $\alpha_i \cup \alpha'_i$

$$\alpha_1 \cdots \alpha_n \,\&\, \alpha'_1 \cdots \alpha'_n := (\alpha_1 \cup \alpha'_1) \cdots (\alpha_n \cup \alpha'_n).$$

For example,

$$\boxed{\text{E}|\text{E}|\text{E}} \;\&\; \boxed{\;|\text{R}|\;} \;=\; \boxed{\text{E}|\text{E,R}|\text{E}}.$$

Extending the operation to sets L and L' of strings of sets, the *superposition $L\&L'$ of L and L'* is the set of superpositions of strings of the same length from L and L'

$$L \;\&\; L' \;:=\; \{s\&s' \mid (s,s') \in L \times L' \text{ and length}(s) = \text{length}(s')\}$$

allowing us to conflate a string s with its singleton language $\{s\}$ (making $s\&s' = \emptyset$ in case s and s' differ in length). Given finite automata accepting L and L', the usual product construction on finite automata for their intersection $L \cap L'$ (e.g. Hopcroft & Ullman 1979) can be adjusted to combine transitions $\rightarrow_L$ for L and $\rightarrow_{L'}$ for L' to form non-deterministic transitions

$$(q,q') \overset{\alpha\cup\alpha'}{\rightarrow} (r,r') \quad \iff \quad q \overset{\alpha}{\rightarrow}_L r \text{ and } q' \overset{\alpha'}{\rightarrow}_{L'} r'$$

for $L\&L'$ in lockstep but with labels that may differ. We will loosen the lockstep requirement in §3.2, but first consider constraints that we might impose on superposition (analogous to C on unify$_C(G,G')$ in section 2).

For example, we may wish to require that a fluent a is never followed by a fluent b, as expressed by the predicate logic formula

$$(\forall x)(\forall y)(P_a(x) \wedge S(x,y) \supset \neg P_b(y))$$

where x and y range over string positions, and

$$S(x,y) \text{ says: next after position } x \text{ is } y$$

while for every fluent $a \in \Theta$,

$$P_a(x) \text{ says: } a \text{ occurs at position } x.$$

More precisely, given a string $s = \alpha_1 \cdots \alpha_n$ of n sets α_i of fluents, we can interpret S as the binary relation

$$S_n \;:=\; \{(1,2),(2,3),\ldots,(n-1,n)\}$$

on the set

$$[n] \;:=\; \{1,2,\ldots,n\}$$

of integers from 1 to n, and P_a as the subset

$$P_a^s \;:=\; \{i \in [n] \mid a \in \alpha_i\} \qquad (\text{where } s = \alpha_1 \cdots \alpha_n)$$

of $[n]$, for each fluent a. That is, a string $s \in (2^\Theta)^n$ specifies a structure

$$M_s \;:=\; \langle [n], S_n, \{P_a^s\}_{a\in\Theta}\rangle$$

against which to interpret predicate logic formulas built from S and the P_a's such as the *formulas φ of Monadic Second-Order Logic* (MSO;

e.g. Libkin 2010) generated by the seven clauses

$$\varphi \quad ::= \quad S(x,y) \mid P_a(x) \mid X(x) \mid \varphi \vee \varphi' \mid \neg\varphi \mid \exists x\varphi \mid \exists X\varphi$$

from three disjoint infinite sets Var_1, Var_2 and Θ of first-order variables $x, y \in Var_1$, second-order variables $X \in Var_2$, and fluents $a \in \Theta$, respectively. For any such MSO-formula φ, only finitely many fluents may occur in φ, which we collect in φ's *vocabulary*, $voc(\varphi) \in Fin(\Theta)$

$$\begin{aligned} voc(S(x,y)) &= voc(X(x)) \;=\; \emptyset \\ voc(P_a(x)) &= \{a\} \\ voc(\varphi \vee \varphi') &= voc(\varphi) \cup voc(\varphi') \\ voc(\neg\varphi) &= voc(\exists x\varphi) \;=\; voc(\exists X\varphi) \;=\; voc(\varphi). \end{aligned}$$

An MSO-*sentence* is understood to be an MSO-formula in which all variable occurrences are bound. For every $A \in Fin(\Theta)$, we put every MSO sentence with vocabulary contained in A into the set $MSO(A)$

$$MSO(A) := \{\varphi \mid \varphi \text{ is an MSO-sentence and } voc(\varphi) \subseteq A\}$$

and define a binary relation

$$\models_A \;\subseteq\; (2^A)^* \times MSO(A)$$

between $(2^A)^*$ and $MSO(A)$ in the usual Tarskian manner, associating a string $s \in (2^A)^*$ with M_s. (Apologies for reusing the symbol $\models$.) For any string s of sets of fluents, let the *A-reduct* $\rho_A(s)$ *of* s be the componentwise intersection of s with A

$$\rho_A(\alpha_1 \cdots \alpha_n) \;:=\; (\alpha_1 \cap A) \cdots (\alpha_n \cap A)$$

(so-called because $\rho_A(s)$ is precisely the part of s needed to extract from M_s its A-reduct $\langle [n], S_n, \{P_a^s\}_{a \in A}\rangle$).

Fact 2 *For all* $A \in Fin(\Theta)$, $\varphi \in MSO(A)$ *and* $s \in (2^A)^*$,

$$s \models_A \varphi \quad \Longleftrightarrow \quad \rho_{voc(\varphi)}(s) \models_{voc(\varphi)} \varphi\ .$$

With Fact 2, the relations $\{\models_A\}_{A \in Fin(\Theta)}$ become an institution with signature category $Fin(\Theta)$ provided we

(i) extend the map $A \mapsto MSO(A)$ to pairs (A, A') such that $A \subseteq A' \in Fin(\Theta)$, setting $MSO(A, A')$ to the inclusion $MSO(A) \hookrightarrow MSO(A')$ mapping $\varphi \in MSO(A) \subseteq MSO(A')$ to itself, and

(ii) turn the map $A \mapsto (2^A)^*$ into a contravariant functor $\mathbf{M}$ from $Fin(\Theta)$ so that whenever $A \subseteq A' \in Fin(\Theta)$, $\mathbf{M}(A', A) : (2^{A'})^* \to (2^A)^*$ is the restriction of ρ_A to $(2^{A'})^*$

$$\mathbf{M}(A', A)(s) \;=\; \rho_A(s) \qquad \text{for all } s \in (2^{A'})^*.$$

Büchi's theorem equating sentences in $MSO(A)$ with regular languages over A (e.g. Libkin 2010, page 124) holds also in the present set-up for languages over 2^A (the advantage of 2^A over A being the availability of reducts for Fact 2).

23.3.2 Compression, Branching and Superposition Modified

A string $s \in (2^A)^*$ is understood above to have granularity A. Variations in A are described in Fact 2 that preserve string length using A-reducts. It is natural, however, to expect the length of a string to grow with A, as hinted by the discussion above of

$$s_A \ := \ \boxed{\text{Jan}}\boxed{\text{Feb}}\cdots\boxed{\text{Dec}}$$

and

$$s_{A'} \ := \ \boxed{\text{Jan,d1}}\boxed{\text{Jan,d2}}\cdots\boxed{\text{Jan,d31}}\boxed{\text{Feb,d1}}\cdots\boxed{\text{Dec,d31}}.$$

Put the other way around, the A-reduct of $s_{A'}$

$$\rho_A(s_{A'}) \ = \ \boxed{\text{Jan}}^{31}\boxed{\text{Feb}}^{29}\cdots\boxed{\text{Dec}}^{d31}$$

has substrings such as $\boxed{\text{Jan}}^{31}$ which we might compress to $\boxed{\text{Jan}}$ for

$$\mathit{bc}(\rho_A(s_{A'})) \ = \ \boxed{\text{Jan}}\boxed{\text{Feb}}\cdots\boxed{\text{Dec}} \ = \ s_A$$

where for any string s, $\mathit{bc}(s)$ compresses blocks α^n of $n > 1$ consecutive occurrences in s of the same symbol α to a single α, leaving s otherwise unchanged

$$\mathit{bc}(s) \ := \ \begin{cases} \mathit{bc}(\alpha s') & \text{if } s = \alpha\alpha s' \\ \alpha\ \mathit{bc}(\alpha' s') & \text{if } s = \alpha\alpha' s' \text{ with } \alpha \neq \alpha' \\ s & \text{otherwise.} \end{cases}$$

To require that time progress only with change (discernible at some bounded granularity A), let us work with strings $\alpha_1\alpha_2\cdots\alpha_n$ that are *stutter-free* in that $\alpha_i \neq \alpha_{i+1}$ for i from 1 to $n-1$. That is,

$$\text{a string } s \text{ is stutter-free} \quad \Longleftrightarrow \quad s = \mathit{bc}(s).$$

The restriction of bc to any finite alphabet is computable by a finite-state transducer, as are, for all $A' \in \mathit{Fin}(\Theta)$ and $A \subseteq A'$, the composition $\rho_A; \mathit{bc}$ for bc_A

$$\mathit{bc}_A(s) \ := \ \mathit{bc}(\rho_A(s)) \qquad \text{for } s \in (2^{A'})^*.$$

Without the compression bc in bc_A, we are left with the map ρ_A that leaves the ontology intact (insofar as the domain of an MSO-model is given by the string length), whilst restricting the vocabulary (for A-reducts). The institution described by Fact 2 can be adjusted to another institution in which

- the models are stutter-free strings[3]
- the reducts ρ_A are replaced by bc_A, and
- the satisfaction relations $\models'_A$ are given by explicitly referring to the sentence's vocabulary

$$s \models'_A \varphi \iff \mathit{bc}_{voc(\varphi)}(s) \models_{voc(\varphi)} \varphi.$$

Compressing strings via bc_A allows us to lengthen the strings by inversion. The *inverse limit* $\mathrm{IL}(\Theta, \mathit{bc})$ *of* Θ, bc consists of functions $\mathbf{a} : \mathit{Fin}(\Theta) \to \mathit{Fin}(\Theta)^*$ that respect the projections bc_A

$$\mathbf{a}(A) = \mathit{bc}_A(\mathbf{a}(A')) \quad \text{whenever} \quad A \subseteq A' \in \mathit{Fin}(\Theta).$$

The prefix relation on strings

$$s \text{ prefix } s' \iff s' = s\hat{s} \text{ for some } \hat{s}$$

lifts to maps $\mathbf{a}$ and $\mathbf{a}'$ in $\mathrm{IL}(\Theta, \mathit{bc})$ by universal quantification for an irreflexive relation

$$\mathbf{a} \prec \mathbf{a}' \iff \mathbf{a} \neq \mathbf{a}' \text{ and } (\forall A \in \mathit{Fin}(\Theta))\ \mathbf{a}(A) \text{ prefix } \mathbf{a}'(A)$$

that is *tree-like* on $\mathrm{IL}(\Theta, \mathit{bc})$ — i.e., transitive and left linear: for every $\mathbf{a} \in \mathrm{IL}(\Theta, \mathit{bc})$, and all $\mathbf{a}_1 \prec \mathbf{a}$ and $\mathbf{a}_2 \prec \mathbf{a}$,

$$\mathbf{a}_1 \prec \mathbf{a}_2 \quad \text{or} \quad \mathbf{a}_2 \prec \mathbf{a}_1 \quad \text{or} \quad \mathbf{a}_2 = \mathbf{a}_1.$$

In other words, time branches at the inverse limit $\mathrm{IL}(\Theta, \mathit{bc})$.

Even if the strings we are interested in are stutter-free, strings that are not stutter-free can be useful. For instance, to relax the requirement of $L\&L'$ that L and L' run in lockstep, let us collect the strings bc-equivalent to a string in L in

$$L^{\mathit{bc}} := \{s \in (2^{\Theta})^* \mid (\exists s' \in L)\ \mathit{bc}(s) = \mathit{bc}(s')\}$$

and define the *bc-superposition* $L\&_{\mathit{bc}}L'$ *of* L *and* L' to be the image under bc of the superposition of L^{bc} and L'^{bc}

$$L \&_{\mathit{bc}} L' := \{\mathit{bc}(s) \mid s \in L^{\mathit{bc}} \& L'^{\mathit{bc}}\}$$

(a regular language, if L and L' are). Then for any two fluents $a, a' \in \Theta$, the bc-superposition $\boxed{}\boxed{a}\boxed{} \&_{\mathit{bc}} \boxed{}\boxed{a'}\boxed{}$ is the set

$$\{\mathit{bc}(s) \mid s \in (2^{\{a,a'\}})^* \text{ and } \mathit{bc}_{\{a\}}(s) = \boxed{}\boxed{a}\boxed{} \text{ and } \mathit{bc}_{\{a'\}}(s) = \boxed{}\boxed{a'}\boxed{}\}$$

consisting of 13 strings, one for each interval relation in Allen 1983. More generally, for any finite set $A = \{a_1, \ldots, a_n\} \in \mathit{Fin}(\Theta)$ of fluents,

[3] Apart from applying bc, a string can also be made stutter-free by superposition with $(\boxed{}\boxed{\text{tic}})^*(\boxed{} + \epsilon)$ for some fresh fluent tic. The crucial point is that stutter-freeness ensures the vocabulary is large enough to express the distinctions of interest (lengthening a string if necessary).

the $\&$-superposition

$$\boxed{}\boxed{a_1}\boxed{} \;\&_{bc} \cdots \&_{bc} \boxed{}\boxed{a_n}\boxed{}$$

represents the event structures over A in the sense of Russell-Wiener (Kamp & Reyle 1993, Fernando 2015).

23.3.3 Taking Stock

What are we to make of the difference between the institutions in sections 2 and 3? At its simplest, the difference is between, on the one hand, a program or automaton (as piece of code) and, on the other hand, an execution or run of it — a modern incarnation of the Aristotelian dichotomy between potentiality and actuality. Focusing on applications to natural language semantics, Table 3 lists contrasts based not only on the widespread encoding of linguistic resources as feature structures (including frames), but also on the notion defended in Carlson 1995 that the truth of a generic statement rests not on "the episodic instances but rather the causal forces behind those instances" (page 225), as well as the distinction between *individual-level* and *stage-level* predicates (Carlson 1977).

section 2	section 3
automata	run
resource	use
generic	episodic
causal	temporal
force	event
universal	particular/instance
individual-level	stage-level

Table 3

Much work remains to flesh out Table 3, and win over the skeptical reader. At stake in Table 3 is justification for viewing the directed graphs in F&V as finite automata.

References

Allen, James F. 1983. Maintaining knowledge about temporal intervals. In *Communications of the ACM*, vol. 26, pages 832–843.

Barwise, Jon. 1974. Axioms for abstract model theory. *Annals of Mathematical Logic* 7:221–265.

Barwise, Jon and Larry Moss. 1996. *Vicious Circles: On the Mathematics of Non-Wellfounded Phenomena.*. CSLI.

Blackburn, Patrick. 1993. Modal logic and attribute value structures. In M. de Rijke, ed., *Diamonds and Defaults*, pages 19–65. Kluwer.

Brzozowski, Janusz A. 1964. Derivatives of regular expressions. *Journal of the ACM* pages 481–494.

Carlson, Greg N. 1977. A unified analysis of the English bare plural. *Linguistics & Philosophy* 1:413–458.

Carlson, Greg N. 1995. Truth conditions of generic sentences: Two contrasting views. In *The Generic Book*, pages 224–237. University of Chicago Press.

Cooper, Robin. 2012. Type theory and semantics in flux. In R. Kempson, T. Fernando, and N. Asher, eds., *Philosophy of Linguistics*, pages 271–323. North-Holland.

Diaconescu, Răzvan. 2012. Three decades of institution theory. In J.-Y. Beziau, ed., *Universal Logic: An Anthology*, pages 309–322. Springer.

Fernando, Tim. 2015. The semantics of tense and aspect: A finite-state perspective. In S. Lappin and C. Fox, eds., *The Handbook of Contemporary Semantic Theory, Second Edition*, pages 203–236. Wiley.

Fernando, Tim. 2016. Types from frames as finite automata. In A. Foret, G. Morrill, R. Muskens, and R. Osswald, eds., *Formal Grammar 2015/2016*, pages 19–40. Springer.

Fillmore, Charles J. 1982. Frame semantics. In *Linguistics in the Morning Calm*, pages 111–137. Hanshin Publishing Co.

Goguen, Joseph and Rod Burstall. 1992. Institutions: Abstract model theory for specification and programming. *Journal of the ACM* 39:95–146.

Hennessy, Matthew and Robin Milner. 1985. Algebraic laws for nondeterminism and concurrency. *Journal of the ACM* 32:137–161.

Hopcroft, John and Jeffrey Ullman. 1979. *Inroduction to Automata Theory, Languages, and Computation.* Addison-Wesley.

Kamp, Hans and Uwe Reyle. 1993. *From Discourse to Logic.* Kluwer.

Karttunen, Lauri. 1984. Features and values (F&V). In *COLING '84*, pages 28–33.

Karttunen, Lauri. 2007. Word play. *Computational Linguistics* 33:443–467.

Kornai, András. 2017. Truth or *dare*. This volume.

Kutz, Oliver, Till Mossakowski, and Dominik Lücke. 2010. Carnap, goguen, and the hyperontologies: Logical pluralism and heterogeneous structuring in ontology design. *Logica Universalis* 4:255–333.

Libkin, Leonid. 2010. *Elements of Finite Model Theory*. Springer.

Shan, Chung-chieh. 2015. Splitting hairs. In *Proceedings of the 20th Amsterdam Colloquium*, pages 363–367.

Tarlecki, Andrzej, Rod Burstall, and Joseph Goguen. 1991. Some fundamental algebraic tools for the semantics of computation: Part 3 indexed categories. *Theoretical Computer Science* pages 239–264.

24

What are Grammars Good for? Reflections on Twenty Years of Grammatical Framework*

Aarne Ranta

Lauri Karttuselle.

24.1 Introduction

The methods of computational linguistics are often divided into **symbolic** and **statistical**. Church (2007) uses the more philosophical terms **rationalist** and **empiricist**, noting that the popularity of these methods follows a pendulum movement, where each swing takes about 20 years. Thus Church was expecting a new swing from empiricism to rationalism. However, nine years have passed, and the main stream of computational linguistics is still empiricist. It seems that much of the community has lost faith in symbolic methods. They are considered inefficient, brittle, and expensive. As a result, the motivation for teaching and learning them has been lost. A young scientist who wants to make a career in natural language processing may think that grammars and other symbolic methods are of no use.[1]

A part of the pendulum movement can be explained by the intended

*I am grateful to Bengt Nordström and to an anonymous referee for valuable comments and suggestions.

[1]A new factor that has stopped the pendulum from swinging back is the expectation that neural networks will eliminate the need of linguistic abstractions in natural language processing (Manning, 2015).

Tokens of Meaning: Papers in Honor of Lauri Karttunen.
Cleo Condoravdi and Tracy Holloway King (eds.).

applications. Thus grammars played a strong role in sublanguage applications (Burton and Brown, 1977), such as special-purpose query systems (Woods, 1973) and teaching software (Karttunen, 1989). As a continuation of this tradition, grammars still excel in the field of **controlled languages** (Kuhn, 2014). But sublanguage applications are no longer main stream: many natural language processing practitioners regard them as "toys". They are often considered toys by theoretical linguists as well, since they do not scale up to the whole language.

In this paper, we will look at some uses of computational grammars beyond sublanguages, possibly in combination with statistical methods. Much of the reported work belongs to a context that Lauri Karttunen has been one of the creators of. In his early work, he stressed the role of semantics and pragmatics as the foundation of all linguistic work: we are not just processing language by arbitrary rules, but by rules that refer to its *meaning* (e.g. (Karttunen, 1977)). In his work on D-PATR (Karttunen, 1986), he stressed the design of grammar formalisms that are pure and simple mathematical systems, free from linguistic hypotheses and thereby giving grammarians a freedom of expression. The Xerox Finite State Tool (XFST) (Beesley and Karttunen, 2003) also follows this design. It is an uncontestable example of a grammatical approach that is scalable and productive.

It was in this context that we started GF (Grammatical Framework) (Ranta, 2004, 2011) at Xerox Research Centre Europe (XRCE) in Grenoble in 1997–1999. Most examples in this paper are about making GF grammars scalable, robust, and cost-efficient. This should not be taken to imply that other grammar formalisms (LFG, HPSG, TAG, CCG) cannot achieve similar, or even better, results, possibly by design choices different from those in GF. But in the development of GF as a software system, XFST has had a greater influence than the major syntactic formalisms. On the theoretical side, the main ideas of GF come from constructive type theory (Martin-Löf, 1984), Montague grammar (Montague, 1974), and the programming language idea of multilingual grammars with a shared abstract syntax (Landin, 1966).

24.2 Classifiers vs. Transducers

In formal language theory, a language L is a set of strings. A grammar G is a set of rules that defines L. A string s belongs to L if and only if s is generated by G.

The ideas of formal language theory were immediately adopted in natural language, by their very inventor (Chomsky, 1956). Thus a **generative grammar** was to be a set of rules that defines all and only the grammatical sentences of a natural language. A grammar should be a **binary classifier** of strings into grammatical sentences and ungrammatical garbage.

The demand of binary classification has been challenged by probabilistic approaches. For instance, the introduction of the standard textbook (Manning and Schütze, 1999) argues that grammaticality judgements are not binary but **gradient**. One argument is language change: at any given moment in a living natural language, there are utterances that some speakers accept, some others rejects, and some are uncertain about. This gradience is given as a reason to switch from grammatical to probabilistic models of language. In later research, similar arguments can be found e.g. in (Clark et al., 2013).

It is easy to find examples of gradience. Finnish, for instance, has a long history of the usage of the so-called first vs. third infinitive when forming the complement of the verb *alkaa* ("to start"). Thus *it started raining* can be expressed by both of

alkoi sataa (first infinitive)

alkoi satamaan (third infinitive illative)

The grammaticality judgements of Finns are often affected by official standards imposed by schools. Thus most people from earlier generations "know" that the third infinitive is incorrect, even though they use it in spontaneous speech. Those with less influence from school education might be unsure, perhaps about both of the alternatives. In 2014, the third infinitive was in fact declared to be correct in this context as a variant of the first infinitive. But old-school Finns may still feel uncomfortable in judging the third infinitive to be grammatical. They might end up with a gradient grammaticality judgement, where the third infinitive is not completely wrong but less good than the first infinitive.

But does the gradience of grammaticality judgements imply that grammars are useless? Certainly not. A Finnish grammar can obviously describe the formation of sentences and verb forms of both kinds. Such a grammar need not decide which forms are correct: it should be able to analyse both kinds of forms. The resulting analyses can be used for instance to give frequency counts and trace the distribution of the constructions over time. Similarly, if the grammar is used in machine translation, it should not judge whether an utterance is correct or not. It should just analyse it the best it can and return the best possible translation.

In other words, we should not see a grammar as a classifier but as a **transducer** (or a component of a transducer), which accepts its input and returns some output. A transducer should never just reject its input. On top the grammar, we can of course add layers that say if a construction is rare or against certain norms. Such layers are needed for instance when the grammar is used for normative grammar checking. But the grammar itself should just analyse, not accept or reject.

Empiricists are not the only ones who reject grammars as binary classifiers. Also linguists working in theoretical syntax have done this. One argument is exactly gradience: the uncertainty on when to "put stars" on sentences. A well-known example is wh movement, which has more and more refined exceptions and exceptions of exceptions (for instance, exceptions called "island constraints"). A grammar that tries to capture them all becomes more and more complicated, covers less and less ground, and must rely on less and less certain evidence (Hofmeister and Sag, 2010). A better alternative is to tolerate overgeneration, keep the grammar simple, and explain the gradient judgements by other factors. An "overgenerating" grammar that translates a sentence that violates an island constraint into a similar violation in the target language is usually better than a grammar that rejects the source sentence because of a "syntax error".

24.3 Concepts vs. Methods

Like any theory, a grammar must define a set of concepts, **grammatical concepts**. These concepts can be useful independently of whether and how the grammar is used in processing, Thus, when describing the uses of the Finnish verb *alkaa*, we used terms such as first infinitive, complement verb phrase, third infinitive illative. Without these concepts, we could only refer to generic concepts such as strings. Then we might specify a list of forms of *alkaa*, together with a list of third infinitive illatives. Alternatively, we could propose generalizations such as "strings with the prefix *alk* followed by strings ending with *maan*". Such a description would easily miss some forms of *alkaa*, e.g. *aloin*, ("I started"), or give false positives such as *alkoholi*. It could mix up noun forms (*satamaan* "to the harbour") with true third infinitive inessives. Even if it managed to analyse the words properly, it could still get the syntax wrong. Thus *aloin juuri nukkumaan* ("I just started to sleep") could be missed because there is an intervening word, or, if intervening words can be skipped over, *aloin mennä nukkumaan* ("I started to go to sleep") could create a false positive.

We thus need grammatical concepts in order to **describe** utterances properly. Without such concepts, we would be like botanists going to the field with only layman concepts such as colours, shapes, and sizes of plants. We might be able to compute the relative frequencies of red and blue flowers, but we would not come close to what we would achieve if we knew the concepts of Linnaeus' taxonomy.[2]

Grammar is to language what Linnaeus' taxonomy is to plants. It gives us concepts for further investigations. In these further investigations, we can use different methods: **statistical** and **rule-based**. This division of methods should not be conflated with the statistical vs. symbolic division of *concepts*. The division of methods is orthogonal to the division of concepts. Thus we can apply both statistical and rule-based methods to both "raw strings" and to grammatically analysed objects. The following table gives examples of all four combinations:

	statistical	**rule-based**
strings	unsupervised stemming	Porter stemmer
grammar	probabilistic parsing	finite-state morphology

In this paper, we focus on methods that operate on grammatical concepts, be it by statistical or by rule-based methods.[3]

As shown by finite-state morphology, rule-based grammatical method can scale up to entire languages (Koskenniemi, 1983, Beesley and Karttunen, 2003). Part-of-speech tagging is another good example (Chanod and Tapanainen, 1995). These methods even extend to machine translation: Apertium (Forcada et al., 2011) is a transducer-based system, where morphological analysis is piped to lexical transfer, which in turn is piped to morphological surface form generation. Apertium reaches state of the art results when translating between closely related languages (e.g. Spanish to Catalan), even though its lack of syntactic analysis to capture long-distance dependencies makes it less suitable for many other language pairs.

There is a simple principle to guide the selection of concepts and methods: *don't guess if you know* (from the title of Tapanainen and Voutilainen (1994)). It is both uninformed and wasteful not to use the knowledge that there is: we should rely on the vast body of linguistic knowledge accumulated since the Ancient Greeks and Panini. At the same time, we must acknowledge that we do not always know. This is often the case when we go to higher levels of linguistic analysis than

[2]This comparison fits nicely with Bresnan (2016), "The Garden and the Bush". For examples, a move from the "garden" of grammar to the "bush" of quantitative concepts was needed to make it possible to predict the dative constructions in English. In this task, grammar-based attempts miserably failed to decide grammaticality. But the *concept* that was in focus is nonetheless a grammatical concept: the dative construction. Thus the concepts learnt in the garden can still be valid in the bush, even though their application is less easy to predict.

[3]The Porter stemmer is described in (Porter, 1980).

morphology or part of speech tagging. Semantics, translation, sentiment analysis: these are fields where we sometimes have to guess. The problem is very often **disambiguation**: a grammar gives us many alternative analyses, but we do not know which one should be chosen in the given context, since the utterance taken in isolation does not contain all the information that is needed for disambiguation. Whether this is because of the nature of things, or just because of our currently incomplete knowledge, can be left open.

When applying statistical methods to grammatical concepts, the role of grammars is to define the data on which we make statistics. Grammatically analysed objects then play the same role as strings do in "purely statistical" approaches. From the probabilistic point of view, grammars define the **sample space**. Thus we do not calculate the probabilities for words or n-grams, but for morphological descriptions, syntax trees, semantic objects, and other objects that are *more abstract* than strings.

24.4 Overcoming Sparse Data

sparse data—)

Raising the level of abstraction is a key to coping with **sparse data**. Finnish is a good source of examples. Every Finnish noun and verb produces thousands of strings by morphological inflections and suffixes. In addition, there is an infinite number of possible compounds. It is easy to see that this is a problem for methods such as traditional string-based statistical machine translation (Brown et al., 1990).

Examples of failures are easy to find by for instance generating a set of Finnish word forms and dumping them to Google translate. The word *olut* ("beer") shows a typical outcome: of the 26 number-case forms, 7 are left without translation[4]. One of them is *oluelta* ("from beer", singular ablative), which is surprising, since this form is very common. It is used in the idiom *tulla oluelta* ("to come back from having a beer") and as a complement of the verb *maistua* ("to taste like something").

The singular ablative is not the problem, since it is recognized by Google translate for many other words. Also the lemma (dictionary form) *olut* is recognized. One could hence profit from the use of **factored translation**, where lemmas and their morphological descriptions are treated separately (Koehn, 2010). To put it simply, we no longer need data for the translation

```
oluelta  -  from beer
```

[4]https://translate.google.comhttps://translate.google.com 8 December 2016

but it is be enough to have

```
olut   -  beer
+Abl   -  from
```

This solves the data sparseness problem, but of course requires the use of grammatical objects as data, as well as preprocessing the input with a morphological analyser.

Analogous problems can be found in syntax. Here is another example from Google translate:

Pidän tästä oluesta.	*I like this beer.*
Enkö pitäisi tästä oluesta?	*Did not I be this beer?*

The first translation is good. The second one should be *Wouldn't I like this beer?* It is a regular and predictable variant of the first sentence: a negative conditional question with the same propositional content (and even the same verb, subject, and object) as the first sentence.

In analogy with morphologically factored translation, one would profit from using **syntactically factored translation** to solve the data sparsity problem. Instead of storing pairs of complete sentences

```
enkö pitäisi tästä oluesta - wouldn't I like this beer
```

one could store pairs of "sentence lemmas" and tag sequences, such as

```
pidän tästä oluesta  - I like this beer
+Neg +Cond +Quest    - wouldn't
```

The "sentence lemma" is here shown as the positive indicative declarative. The "inflection forms" are constructed from polarity, tense, mood, speech act type, etc. These forms need only be stored once, not repeated for each sentence lemma. It is an easy task for a grammar to put together the lemma and the form description in parsing and generation.

24.5 Abstract Syntax

Now, what is a "syntactic lemma"? A lemma for a word is an abstract identifier that uniquely determines a part of speech and a set inflection forms. This could be refined to a **word sense**, which also determines a meaning. Lemmas with meanings are the natural choice in meaning-preserving translation. But what about longer phrases and sentences?

One possible answer is **logical propositions**. Thus a declarative and a question can have the same proposition just "inflected" in different ways. However, logical propositions may be *too* abstract, since they omit too much syntactic information. For instance, first order logic replaces *in situ* quantification with variables, which corresponds to several different structures in syntax. In applications like translation, one may want to preserve more of the syntactic structure.

The rationale of lemmas is to abstract away from morphological details. Similarty, when analysing a phrase, we want to abstract away from some details. We want to identify the meaningful parts of the phrase are and how they are put together. But we do not need to know what word strings are used and in what precise order.

A representation that preserves meaning and syntactic structure but ignores the ultimate words and their order is the **abstract syntax tree**. This concept was introduced by McCarthy (1962), as the way in which LISP expressions should be understood. It has become a central concept in compiler construction (Landin, 1966, Appel, 1998). In compilers, the source and machine languages may look totally different at surface, yet have the same abstract syntax. The textbook example is arithmetic expressions, where the infix order of source languages is converted to the postfix order of stack machines via a shared abstract syntax. For example, the expression `2+1` in Java compiles to `iconst_2 iconst_1 iadd` in Java Virtual Machine.

In linguistics, the programming language concept of abstract syntax is surprisingly little known. The **tectogrammatical structure** of (Curry, 1961) comes closest. Under a proper interpretation (Dowty, 1982), also Montague's **analysis trees** (Montague, 1974) can be seen as abstract syntax trees. This idea was also used in the Rosetta machine translation system (Landsbergen, 1982, Rosetta, 1994). But when GF was born, we knew of no other grammar formalism available as software and enabling a systematic use of abstract syntax. But the idea gained popularity soon later, e.g. in ACG (Abstract Categorial Grammar) (de Groote, 2001).[5]

Abstract syntax trees are built from applications of **constructor functions**. The simplest example is a tree consisting of just one constant, i.e. function with no arguments. Lemmas of words, possibly refined to word senses, are examples of this. Thus the noun *beer* is declared as a function (in GF notation)

```
fun beer_CN : CN
```

stating that `beer_CN` is a (zero-place) function of type `CN`. The declaration

[5] The f-structures of LFG (Bresnan, 1982) and the ID/LP distinction of GPSG (Gazdar et al., 1985) share some characteristics with abstract syntax, in particular the unspecified word order. But they are not fully abstract, since the representations contain words and morphological features of concrete languages.

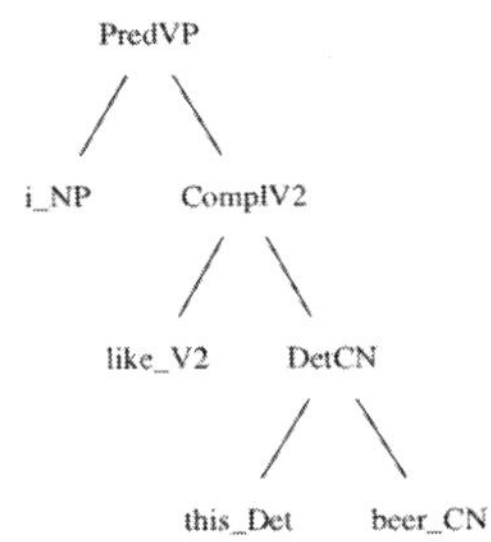


```
(PredVP i_NP (ComplV2 like_V2 (DetCN this_Det beer_CN)))
```

FIGURE 1 An abstract syntax tree for *I like this beer*: the nodes and leaves are abstract syntax functions, shown graphically and as a LISP-like functional term.

```
fun PredVP : NP -> VP -> Cl
```

states that `PredVP` is a two-place function with argument types `NP` and `VP`, and value type `Cl`. If we add the functions for complementation and determination

```
fun ComplV2 : V2 -> NP -> VP
fun DetCN   : Det -> CN -> NP
```

and the lexical functions

```
fun i_NP : NP
fun this_Det : Det
fun like_V2 : V2
```

we can build the abstract syntax tree in Figure 1.

Abstract syntax is related to actual strings by **linearization functions**, which are compositional, reversible mappings from trees to surface structures. The surface structure need not be just a string. It can be an **inflection table** containing all forms of a lemma. The layout of the table—the **linearization type**—depends on the part of speech and language. Thus nouns in English have a tables with two forms,

```
lin beer_CN = table {Sg => "beer" ; Pl => "beers"}
```

In Finnish, they have 26 forms depending on number and case: *olut, oluen, olutta*, etc. In French, nouns have a gender in addition to a table. The table and the gender are collected into a **record**:

```
lin beer_CN = {
  s = table {Sg => "bière" ; Pl => "bières"} ;
  g = Fem
```

```
  }
```

Inflection tables can also be assigned to complex phrases. Thus the table for the noun phrase *this beer*,

```
DetCN this_Det beer_CN
```

in Finnish has 14 case forms: *tämä olut, tämän oluen*, etc. These forms are generated by the concrete syntax rule for DetCN, which passes the number of the determiner to the noun and the case of the whole construction to both the determiner and the noun:

```
lin DetCN det cn = {
  s = table {c => det.s ! c ++ cn ! det.n ! c} ;
  n = det.n
  }
```

The choice of the case is determined by the syntactic structure in which the noun phrase is used. A typical example is Finnish verbs determining the case of the complement. Thus the abstract syntax word like_V2 used in our example has beed linearized to a two-place verb whose complement case is the elative. As the case is language-specific, it is not shown in the abstract syntax tree.

Finally, the inflection tables for clauses have forms for modal, temporal, and aspectual variations, as well as polarities. The exact set of forms is again language-dependent: English clauses have future forms, which Finnish does not have, whereas Finnish has potential forms (*pitänen tästä oluesta*, "I probably like this beer"). The form is determined by a wider syntactic context, where the clause is used in an utterance or as an embedded sentence. On this level, *I like this beer* has the abstract syntax tree

```
Decl Pos Indic
 (PredVP i_NP (ComplV2 like_V2 (DetCN this_Det beer_CN)))
```

which has no other inflection forms, whereas *wouldn't I like this beer* has the tree

```
Quest Neg Cond
 (PredVP i_NP (ComplV2 like_V2 (DetCN this_Det beer_CN)))
```

built from the same clause but with different mood, polarity, and tense.

In Finnish, the clause inflection table may moreover allow for variations of word order decided on a higher level, such as topicalization and the insertion of discourse clitics (Karttunen and Kay, 1985). The general form permitting this is a record with several strings and tables. treating the clause as a **discontinuous constituent**. Most of its parts are inherited from the verb phrase, which is itself discontinuous:

```
lin PredVP np vp = {
  subj  = np ! vp.subjcase ;
  verb  = vp.verb ;
  compl = vp.compl ;
  adv   = vp.adv
  }
```

From a record of this form, linearization can also produce *tästä oluesta minä pidän*, *pidänhän minäkin tästä oluesta*, etc, compositionally by applying discourse functions to one and the same clause "lemma" (Ranta, 2012).

24.6 Grammar Composition

GF was designed to support **multilingual grammars** where many languages have a shared abstract syntax. We first believed that this notion would only scale up to sublanguages, where the abstract syntax encodes the semantic structures of some special domain. The purpose of GF was to provide a declarative grammar formalism to make it easier to implement sublanguage systems. In this respect, GF followed the model of **Logical Frameworks** (LF) (Harper et al., 1993), which are frameworks for defining new logics for theorem proving, programming language semantics, and software verification. The abstract syntax format of GF is in fact precisely a kind of LF, using constructive type theory (Martin-Löf, 1984) to define types and trees.[6]

Abstract syntax can vary greatly from one application domain to the other, because the semantically relevant structures are different. Thus mathematical texts need a different abstract syntax from tourist phrasebooks, However, the concrete syntax involves similar details of morphology and "surface syntax" in both cases. To avoid repeating the implementation of these details, the idea emerged for a general purpose library that defines these "low-level" linguistic details once and for all. The result was a **resource grammar library** (RGL) (Khegai, 2006, Ranta, 2009), a grammar that can be used like a software library to implement domain grammars. The RGL has an abstract syntax based on syntactic structures, such as NP-VP predication in the previous section. Such structures are typically too concrete and fine-grained for semantic domain grammars, which work on more abstract concepts such as logical predicates. To give an example, the expression

the product of x and y

[6]The very name "Grammatical Framework", GF, was meant to indicate that GF is a Logical Framework with a surface grammar added.

should in a mathematical grammar have an abstract syntax tree just stating that it is a product of x and y,

```
product x y
```

The linguistic RGL tree says that it is a definite article determination of a noun modified by a noun phrase conjunction:

```
DetCN the_Det (ModCN product_N (ConjNP and_Conj x y))
```

The idea of RGL as a library is that we define the linearization of the former tree in terms of the latter tree:

```
lin product x y =
  DetCN the_Det (ModCN product_N (ConjNP and_Conj x y))
```

The grammarian who writes the latter might be a mathematician who does not know about linguistics. The complexities of the concrete syntax are thus delegated to the linguist who wrote the RGL.

The way RGL is used can be seen as **grammar composition**: we have the grammar MathRGL that converts math trees to RGL trees, and compose it with the grammar RGLEng that converts RGL trees to English strings. We can borrow XFST notation to express this:

```
MathEng = MathRGL .o. RGLEng
```

Now, since since the RGL trees are shared by many different languages, we also obtain

```
MathFin = MathRGL .o. RGLFin
```

which linearizes `product x y` to

x:n ja y:n tulo

24.7 Increasing the Coverage

By the end of 2016, the RGL has grown to cover 32 languages from many different families. Its shared abstract syntax can be expected to cover 80% of the structures of each language. The RGL also has modules for language-specific extensions of the common structures (e.g. the discourse clitics of Finnish). However, even if the GF-RGL covers 80% of syntactic structures of a language, this is not yet sufficient for wide-coverage parsing and translation. More things are needed:

- a **lexicon**, containing enough words (preferably, refined to word senses) in all involved languages
- a method for **disambiguation**, to select among the grammatically possible analyses
- a **runtime system** powerful enough to perform the processing with large grammars, lexica, and input

- a method for **smoothing**, to deal with input that the grammar does not cover

As for the lexicon, GF currently uses a set of 70,000 abstract syntax lemmas. There are 16 languages that have linearizations of at least 20,000 of these lemmas. The lexicon is based on the Princeton WordNet (Miller, 1995) and some of its sense distinctions. Linked Wordnets such as FinWordNet (Carlson and Lindén, 2010) have been available for creating concrete syntax in some languages. For other languages, other free resources such as Wiktionary[7] have been used. The resulting GF lexicon is sufficient for finding translations in most cases, but has not yet stabilized to anything near the conclusiveness of the RGL syntax. The lexicon is perhaps the main object of research and engineering in wide-coverage GF applications currently.[8]

As for disambiguation, GF uses probabilistic pruning based on a GF version of the Penn treebank (Marcus et al., 1993), in a way inspired by Clark et al. (2002). The probabilities are context-free in the sense that we look at the relative frequency of every abstract syntax function in its category, but without looking at the context in the tree. Since the abstract syntax functions are shared, we can use the same probabilities for parsing all languages. This has turned out to work surprisingly well for syntactic combination functions. However, when word senses or context-dependent probabilities are needed in disambiguation, the current model is far from sufficient. Disambiguation is therefore another object of continuous research and engineering.

We will discuss the runtime system in Section 24.10. But let us first take a closer look at smoothing.

24.8 Smoothing

Smoothing is needed for **robustness**: to deal with all input in a sensible way. When we encounter an utterance, we want to say something rather than nothing, even if we cannot say everything. To give an example,

I likes this beer

cannot be parsed as a sentence in GF-RGL, because it has an agreement error. However, if we look at its parsing bottom up, we notice that we can find a noun phrase (*I*) and a verb phrase (*likes this beer*). If we translate these two separately to Finnish, we get

minä pitää tästä oluesta

[7]http://www.wiktionary.orghttp://www.wiktionary.org

[8]Here one can find inspiration in work from older interlingua approaches, for example (Dorr, 1997).

which is a reasonable translation, just with a similar agreement error as the source sentence.

Similar things can happen with grammatical sentences that are just not covered by the RGL, or words not in the lexicon. We can still analyse parts of such sentences and treat them separately. These parts can be called **chunks**, following (Abney, 1991), who suggests that chunk-sized structures (such as noun phrases) have a stricter grammar than complete sentences. Thus the RGL might not have rules for all possible combinations of phrases to complete sentences, but it can still recognize all parts as chunks.[9]

The formation of chunks relies on ordinary RGL rules for noun phrases, verb phrases, etc. We just need to add rules for treating them as chunks, as well a rule that accepts a list of chunks as a tree in the start category:

```
fun ChunkNP  : NP -> Chunk
fun ChunkVP  : VP -> Chunk
fun ChunkS   : S  -> Chunk
fun ChunkN   : N  -> Chunk
...
fun Chunks   : ListChunk -> Start
```

The size of chunks thus ranges from individual words (`N`) to complete sentences (`S`). The weights in the probabilistic parser are set in such a way that long chunks are favoured over short ones. This idea is similar to the linear interpolation of n-grams, where for instance missing 3-grams are smoothed by 2-grams in the first place and 1-grams on the second place. When applied to abstract syntax trees, "missing 3-gram" means that a chunk with 3 leaf nodes is not recognized by the grammar.

Grammars aimed for wide coverage often favour shallow structures over deeply nested ones—for instance, NP-V2-NP instead of NP-VP. For chunk-based smoothing, however, nested structures are better than shallow ones. For instance, the example above relies on the grammar having verb phrases. With a flat NP-V2-NP structure, the translation of *beer* would not be connected with the verb *pitää* ("like"), and the elative case of the complement would not be correctly generated.

24.9 Abstract Syntax and Universal Dependencies

Language-neutral structures have not been popular in natural language processing, except in semantics. However, the recent **Universal Dependencies** initiative (UD) (McDonald et al., 2013) has changed the

[9]This solution turned out to be very similar to the technique of *fragments* used for LFG parsing in Riezler et al. (2002).

picture. UD tries to maximize the sharing of part of speech tags and dependency labels in different languages. The expected benefits are partly the same as in GF's RGL: to transfer analyses and applications between languages.

In UD, parsers are built from treebanks by machine learning. The bottleneck is the construction of the treebanks, which is done by manual annotation. As a result, the data is sparse in many languages. Now, since GF can map its abstract trees to many languages, could it be used for bootstrapping UD treebanks?

The first question to answer is formal: how do the abstract syntax trees of GF relate to dependency trees? Aren't they more like phrase structure trees? It has turned out that abstract trees actually combine the information in both kinds of trees. The nonterminals of phrase structure trees can be obtained from the value types of functions in abstract trees. The labels of dependency trees can be obtained from the argument places of the functions, if we attach a label to each argument place. All this information can be derived from function type signatures annotated with **dependency configuration**:

```
PredVP  : NP -> VP -> S    -- nsubj head
ComplV2 : V2 -> NP -> VP   -- head  dobj
DetCN   : Det -> CN -> NP  -- det   head
```

Thus the first argument (NP) of Pred gets the label nsubj, its second argument (VP) is the head, and so on.

Phrase structure trees and dependency trees are obtained as different **projections** of the abstract syntax trees (Kolachina and Ranta, 2016). The derivation starts by linking the words of a surface string to its smallest spanning subtree in the abstract tree, following the linearization rules. The next step is to erase the constructor functions from each node but remember some of the information: to derive a phrase structure tree, we remember the value types of each function; to derive a dependency tree, we remember the dependency labels of each subtree. Figure 2 shows an abstract syntax tree and its conversions.

The actual UD annotation manuals include labels that are specific to languages, such as for copulas and tense auxiliaries. Such dependencies could be argued not to be universal. These dependencies can still be obtained from GF by generalizing the abstract dependency configurations to ones that inspect the context in the tree or the generated surface words (Kolachina and Ranta, 2016). However, the great majority of labels in the 30 GF-RGL languages tested (more than 70% in every language) can be obtained by simple configurations only marking the immediate arguments of functions. This makes GF grammars usable in

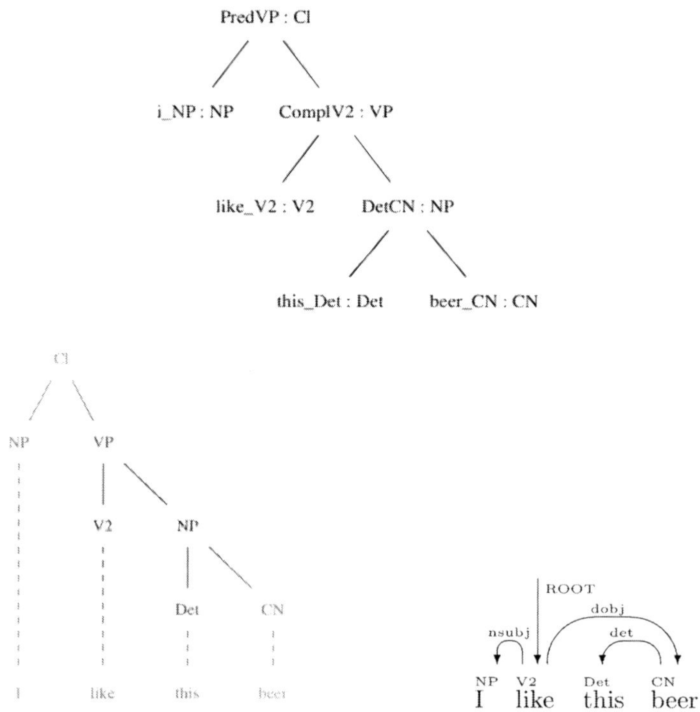

FIGURE 2 An abstract syntax tree decorated with value types with the phrase structure and dependency trees projected from it.

a new way to overcome data sparsity: treebanks can be automatically ported to new languages, without the need of labour-intensive manual annotations of trees. If a full coverage of UD labels is wanted, some language-speficic rules may have to be added.

In the opposite direction, UD parsers trained with large treebanks can be used to improve GF parsing and disambiguation. This is one of the current lines of development in wide-coverage parsing and translation in GF.

24.10 The Grammar Formalism

Grammars are programs, and grammar formalisms should therefore be seen as programming languages. Since grammars are large and demanding programs, grammar formalisms should have powerful **compilers**.

One of the most useful things a compiler can do is the separation of source code and machine code. Source code should be high level, abstract, rich, and programmer-friendly. Machine code should be low level, simple, austere, and machine-friendly. The compiler can bridge this gap in a way invisible to both the programmer and the machine.

Formal language theory provides a variety of languages for both purposes, together with algorithms for building the compiler. A prime example is **regular expressions**, which is usable as a source language and compiles to **finite state automata**. Thus grammarians do not need to construct automata by hand, let alone optimize them to deterministic and minimal ones. This is an important factor that has made finite-state techniques productive and scalable.

However, a source language consisting of the minimal set of five or six regular expression forms would still be too austere. Grammars written directly by using only the minimal operators would be very verbose and hard to understand. Moreover, the **linguistic generalizations** that grammarians have in their minds could not be expressed in the code, but get lost in the complex combinations of the minimal operators. A key success factor in XFST has thus been the abundance of special operators capturing higher-level idioms such as the replace operator (Karttunen, 1995). Since these operators can still be compiled into finite state automata (including transducers), the power of the run-time technology is retained.

But even the special operators defined by system providers may lag behind the generalizations the programmers might want to have. In XFST, the additional power is provided by **macros**, which enable programmers to express their own generalizations. On the level of source code, macros enable a style of **functional programming**, even though the target code does not support functions. The XFST language thus looks quite expressive, even though the macros compile down to the simple form of finite state transducers in the end.

Another advantage of separating source and run-time formats is that the formats can be used independently of each other. For instance, an automaton compiled from XFST regular expressions can be delivered as binary code and run in an interpreter. This interpreter is much simpler than the compiler that generates automata from source code. Conversely, regular expression code written for XFST twenty years ago can today be compiled by other tools to generate automata in other formats. Both of these properties make grammars **portable**, which is essential for the accumulation and sharing of knowledge that grammar-based NLP needs to make real progress.

Many of the architectural features of GF are similar to XFST. Thus the division between source and run-time language is there, although the run-time model of GF is more expressive so that it can express abstract syntax and linearization rules. The model is PMCFG (Parallel Multiple Context-Free Grammars, (Seki et al., 1991)), which guarantees run-time termination and gives parsing complexity bounds. Ordinary context-free (CFG) rules correspond to GF rules that generate strings, wheras PMCFG rules generate tuples of strings, which are needed to encode tables and records. The equivalence of PMCFG with GF was theoretically proved a few years after GF started, in (Ljunglöf, 2004). This theoretical result led to rapid development, which led to scaling up GF parsing. The resulting binary format PGF (Portable Grammar Format, (Angelov et al., 2009, Angelov, 2011)), is simple enough to be run e.g. on mobile phones independently of the GF compiler (Angelov et al., 2014) and supports efficient statistical parsing (Angelov and Ljunglöf, 2014).

On the other hand, GF source language has made PMCFG more usable for grammar writing, since raw PMCFG grammars are too low-level to be written manually. The heart of the GF source language is functional programming, with algebraic datatypes, pattern matching, tables, and records hiding the low-level assembly of string tuples. GF also supports functions, and grammar composition (Section 24.6) is seen as an instance of function composition. The main difference from XFST macros is that GF functions are **typed**, which we believe helps keep the code consistent and communicate programmers' intentions in collaborative projects. Unlike full-scale functional programming, the GF compiler eliminates most functions when generating PGF, just like macros are eliminated in XFST.[10] The reason is ultimately the same: in order for the grammar formalism to be reversible and have predictable complexity, it cannot have the full power of Turing-complete languages.[11]

24.11 Conclusion

We have identified a number of things that grammars are good for:

- They define concepts for talking about language with more precision than strings.
- They define mathematical structures for modelling language more abstractly than by strings.
- They can relieve the problem of sparse data in statistical processing.
- They can support abstract structures shared between languages.

We have also suggested some features that help grammars to reach their full potential:

- Grammars should be seen as transducers rather than as binary classifiers.
- Grammars of different levels should be composable into pipelines.
- Grammars should be kept simple and achieve full coverage by smoothing.
- Grammar formalisms should be based on simple mathematical models whose run-time behaviour is well understood.
- A grammar formalism should also have a high-level source language that supports linguistic generalizations but ultimately compiles to the simple run-time model.

XFST is a prime example of a useful grammar formalism, particularly in morphology and shallow parsing. GF is an attempt to extend the usability of grammars to syntax, cross-linguistic structures, and translation. Its notion of abstract syntax is a generalization of the notion of a lemma from the word level to the syntax level.

References

Abney, Steven. 1991. Parsing by chunks. In *Principle-Based Parsing*, pages 257–278. Kluwer Academic Publishers.

[10]The lexical rules of GF reduce to finite-state automata in the same way as in Huet's Zen toolkit (Huet, 2005), and can be exported as XFST and LEXC code.

[11]Instead of XFST, GF might have followed the existing tools for syntax, such as XLE (Maxwell and Kaplan, 1993) and LKB (Copestake, 2002)? However, these tools focused on parsing rather than transduction and were based on the computational model of unification, which is stronger and thereby less tractable than GF's PMCFG model.

Angelov, Krasimir. 2011. *The Mechanics of the Grammatical Framework*. Ph.D. thesis, Chalmers University of Technology.

Angelov, Krasimir, Björn Bringert, and Aarne Ranta. 2009. PGF: A Portable Run-Time Format for Type-Theoretical Grammars. *Journal of Logic, Language and Information* 19:201–228.

Angelov, Krasimir, Björn Bringert, and Aarne Ranta. 2014. Speech-enabled hybrid multilingual translation for mobile devices. In *Proceedings of the Demonstrations at the 14th Conference of the European Chapter of the Association for Computational Linguistics*, pages 41–44. Gothenburg, Sweden.

Angelov, Krasimir and Peter Ljunglöf. 2014. Fast statistical parsing with parallel multiple context-free grammars. In *Proceedings of the 14th Conference of the European Chapter of the Association for Computational Linguistics*, pages 368–376. Gothenburg, Sweden: Association for Computational Linguistics.

Appel, Andrew. 1998. *Modern Compiler Implementation in ML*. Cambridge University Press.

Beesley, Kenneth and Lauri Karttunen. 2003. *Finite State Morphology*. CSLI Publications.

Bresnan, Joan, ed. 1982. *The Mental Representation of Grammatical Relations*. MIT Press.

Bresnan, Joan, 2016. *Linguistics: The Garden and the Bush*. ACL Lifetime Achievement Award speech.

Brown, Peter F., John Cocke, Stephen A. Della Pietra, Vincent J. Della Pietra, Fredrick Jelinek, John D. Lafferty, Robert L. Mercer, and Paul S. Roossin. 1990. A statistical approach to machine translation. *Computational Linguistics* 16(2):76–85.

Burton, Richard R. and John Seely Brown. 1977. *Semantic Grammar: A Technique for Constructing Natural Language Interfaces to Instructional Systems*. BBN report. ERIC Clearinghouse.

Carlson, Lauri and Krister Lindén. 2010. FinnWordNet – WordNet på finska via översättning. *LexicoNordica – Nordic Journal of Lexicography* 17:119–140.

Chanod, Jean-Pierre and Pasi Tapanainen. 1995. Tagging French: Comparing a statistical and a constraint-based method. In *Proceedings of the Seventh Conference on European Chapter of the Association for Computational Linguistics*, EACL '95, pages 149–156.

Chomsky, Noam. 1956. Three models for the description of language. *IRE Transactions on Information Theory* 2:113–124.

Church, Kenneth. 2007. A pendulum swung too far. *Linguistic Issues in Language Technology* 2.

Clark, Alexander, Gianluca Giorgolo, and Shalom Lappin. 2013. Towards a statistical model of grammaticality. *Proceedings of the 35th Annual Conference of the Cognitive Science Society* pages 2064–2069.

Clark, Stephen, Julia Hockenmaier, and Mark Steedman. 2002. Building deep dependency structures with a wide-coverage ccg parser. In *ACL 2002*, pages 327–334.

Copestake, Ann. 2002. *Implementing typed feature structure grammars*. CSLI publications Stanford.

Curry, Haskell B. 1961. Some logical aspects of grammatical structure. In R. Jakobson, ed., *Structure of Language and its Mathematical Aspects: Proceedings of the Twelfth Symposium in Applied Mathematics*, pages 56–68. American Mathematical Society.

de Groote, Philippe. 2001. Towards Abstract Categorial Grammars. In *Association for Computational Linguistics, 39th Annual Meeting and 10th Conference of the European Chapter, Toulouse, France*, pages 148–155.

Dorr, Bonnie J. 1997. Large-scale dictionary construction for foreign language tutoring and interlingual machine translation. *Machine Translation* 12:271 – 322.

Dowty, David. 1982. Grammatical relations and Montague grammar. In P. Jakobson and G. Pullum, eds., *The Nature of Syntactic Representation*, pages 79–130. Dordrecht: D. Reidel.

Forcada, Mikel, Mireia Ginesti-Rosell, Jacob Nordfalk, Jim O'Regan, Sergio Ortiz-Rojas, Juan Perez-Ortiz, Felipe Sanchez-Martinez, Gema Ramirez-Sanchez, and Francis Tyers. 2011. Apertium: a free/open-source platform for rule-based machine translation. *Machine Translation* 24:1–18.

Gazdar, Gerald, Ewan Klein, Geoffrey Pullum, and Ivan Sag. 1985. *Generalized Phrase Structure Grammar*. Oxford: Basil Blackwell.

Harper, Robert, Furio Honsell, and Gordon Plotkin. 1993. A Framework for Defining Logics. *JACM* 40(1):143–184.

Hofmeister, Philip and Ivan A Sag. 2010. Cognitive constraints and island effects. *Language* 86(2):366.

Huet, Gerard. 2005. A Functional Toolkit for Morphological and Phonological Processing, Application to a Sanskrit Tagger. *The Journal of Functional Programming* 15(4):573–614.

Karttunen, Lauri. 1977. Syntax and semantics of questions. *Linguistics and Philosophy* 1(1):3–44.

Karttunen, Lauri. 1986. D-patr: A development environment for unification-based grammars. In *Proceedings of the 11th Coference on Computational Linguistics*, COLING '86, pages 74–80. Association for Computational Linguistics.

Karttunen, Lauri. 1989. Translating from English to Logic in Tarski's World. *Journal of Information Science and Engineering* 5(4):323–348.

Karttunen, Lauri. 1995. The replace operator. In *Proceedings of the 33rd Annual Meeting on Association for Computational Linguistics*, ACL '95, pages 16–23.

Karttunen, Lauri and Martin Kay. 1985. Parsing in a free word order language. In D. Dowty, L. Karttunen, and A. Zwicky, eds., *Natural Language Parsing, Psychological, Computational, and Theoretical Perspectives*, pages 279–306. Cambridge University Press.

Khegai, Janna. 2006. GF Parallel Resource Grammars and Russian. In *Coling/ACL 2006*, pages 475–482.

Koehn, Philipp. 2010. *Statistical Machine Translation*. Cambridge University Press.

Kolachina, Prasanth and Aarne Ranta. 2016. From Abstract Syntax to Universal Dependencies *Linguistic Issues in Language Technology* 13(3):1–57.

Koskenniemi, Kimmo. 1983. *Two-Level Morphology: A General Computational Model for Word-Form Recognition and Production*. Ph.D. thesis, University of Helsinki.

Kuhn, Tobias. 2014. A Survey and Classification of Controlled Natural Languages. *Computational Linguistics* 40(1):121–170.

Landin, Peter. 1966. The next 700 programming languages. *Communications of the ACM* 9:157–166.

Landsbergen, Jan. 1982. Machine translation based on logically isomorphic Montague grammars. In *COLING-1982*.

Ljunglöf, Peter. 2004. *The Expressivity and Complexity of Grammatical Framework*. Ph.D. thesis, Dept. of Computing Science, Chalmers University of Technology and University of Gothenburg.

Manning, Christopher D. 2015. Computational linguistics and deep learning. *Computational Linguistics* 41(4):701–707.

Manning, Christopher D. and Hinrich Schütze. 1999. *Foundations of Statistical Natural Language Processing*. Cambridge, MA, USA: MIT Press. ISBN 0-262-13360-1.

Marcus, Mitchell P., Beatrice Santorini, and Mary Ann Marcinkiewicz. 1993. Building a Large Annotated Corpus of English: The Penn Treebank. *Computational Linguistics* 19(2):313–330.

Martin-Löf, Per. 1984. *Intuitionistic Type Theory*. Napoli: Bibliopolis.

Maxwell, John T and Ronald M Kaplan. 1993. The interface between phrasal and functional constraints. *Computational Linguistics* 19(4):571–590.

McCarthy, John. 1962. Towards a mathematical science of computation. In *Proceedings of the Information Processing Cong. 62*, pages 21–28. Munich, West Germany: North-Holland.

McDonald, Ryan, Joakim Nivre, Yvonne Quirmbach-Brundage, Yoav Goldberg, Dipanjan Das, Kuzman Ganchev, Keith Hall, Slav Petrov, Hao Zhang, Oscar Täckström, Claudia Bedini, Núria Bertomeu Castelló, and Jungmee Lee. 2013. Universal Dependency Annotation for Multilingual Parsing. In *Proceedings of the 51st Annual Meeting of the Association for Computational Linguistics (Volume 2: Short Papers)*, pages 92–97. Sofia, Bulgaria: Association for Computational Linguistics.

Miller, George A. 1995. WordNet: A Lexical Database for English. *Commun. ACM* 38(11).

Montague, Richard. 1974. *Formal Philosophy*. New Haven: Yale University Press. Collected papers edited by Richmond Thomason.

Porter, M.F. 1980. An algorithm for suffix stripping. *Program* 14(3):130–137.

Ranta, Aarne. 2004. Grammatical Framework: A Type-Theoretical Grammar Formalism. *The Journal of Functional Programming* 14(2):145–189.

Ranta, Aarne. 2009. The GF Resource Grammar Library. *Linguistic Issues in Language Technology* 2(2):1–63.

Ranta, Aarne. 2011. *Grammatical Framework: Programming with Multilingual Grammars*. Stanford: CSLI Publications.

Ranta, Aarne. 2012. On the syntax and translation of Finnish discourse clitics. In *Shall We Play the Festschrift Game?*, pages 227–241. Springer Berlin Heidelberg.

Riezler, Stefan, Tracy H King, Ronald M Kaplan, Richard Crouch, John T. Maxwell III, and Mark Johnson. 2002. Parsing the Wall Street Journal using a lexical-functional grammar and discriminative estimation techniques. In *Proceedings of the 40th Annual Meeting on Association for Computational Linguistics*, pages 271–278. Association for Computational Linguistics.

Rosetta, M. T. 1994. *Compositional Translation*. Dordrecht: Kluwer.

Seki, H., T. Matsumura, M. Fujii, and T. Kasami. 1991. On multiple context-free grammars. *Theoretical Computer Science* 88:191–229.

Tapanainen, Pasi and Atro Voutilainen. 1994. Tagging accurately - don't guess if you know. In *In Proceedings of ANLP '94*, pages 47–52.

Woods, William A. 1973. Progress in natural language understanding: An application to lunar geology. In *Proceedings of the June 4-8, 1973, National Computer Conference and Exposition*, AFIPS '73, pages 441–450. ACM.

25

Types as Learnable Cognitive Resources in PyTTR

Robin Cooper

25.1 Introduction

I first got to know Lauri well in 1975 when I was teaching for a year at UT Austin. (I think we first met at the 1974 Linguistic Institute in Amherst.) This was the time when he was working on his seminal paper on the semantics of questions. The next time when Lauri and I spent a significant amount of time together was in 1981 when we were both in Stanford. Things had changed a lot in the intervening time. Lauri had become a computational linguist and an expert lisp programmer. At the time I was a computer illiterate and was very suspicious of computers as any kind of useful tool. Lauri gently suggested that perhaps I should learn some lisp as programming was, he assured me, of theoretical interest. He patiently and painstakingly introduced me to both basic concepts (like *file*) and took me through exercises in Daniel Friedman's *The Little Lisper*. He also arranged for me to get an account on the DEC20 machine in Austin that I could access via the ARPANET on a terminal (a big improvement over the lineprinter with a keyboard which was the computer equipment originally available at the Centre for Advanced Study in the Behavioral Sciences back then). Lauri's patience and generosity in all this caused a major change in my intellectual life which eventually led to my holding a chair in computational linguistics at Gothenburg 1995-2012. For this and for much other kindness and inspiration over the years I will always be grateful.

Tokens of Meaning: Papers in Honor of Lauri Karttunen.
Cleo Condoravdi and Tracy Holloway King (eds.).

In this paper,[1] I will present some aspects of the beginning of a Python implementation[2] of TTR (Type Theory with Records, Cooper, 2012, Cooper and Ginzburg, 2015, Cooper, in prep). There was a previous implementation of TTR in Oz/Mozart[3] in which I got further than the core of TTR which is currently implemented in PyTTR. However, the Python implementation is a good deal more readable and structured that the previous implementation and so I am hopeful for adding the functionality of the previous implementation to the new implementation. The hope is that a Python implementation will make the work more accessible and useful to people working in computational linguistics.

By the "core of TTR" I mean the type theory (with no linguistic applications) including the features in (1).

(1) Basic types
Ptypes (types constructed with predicates and their arguments)
Meet (intersection) types
Join (union) types
Function types
List types
Record types
String types
Judging (assigning objects to types)
Querying (asking whether an object is of a type)
Adding witness conditions to types
Creating objects of types
Subtyping
Type merging (including asymmetric type merging)
Possibilities (types may have different witnesses in different possibilities)

After some general remarks about TTR and how it relates to other type theories, I will give a brief account of the majority of these features and their implementation.

[1]This paper was supported by the project Networks and Types, Swedish Research Council project VR 2013-4873.

[2]Available on `https://github.com/GU-CLASP/pyttr`.

[3]Available on `https://github.com/GU-CLASP/ttr-tool`.

25.2 Rich Type Theory and Cognition

The type theory that Montague (1973) employed is a version of *simple type theory*. It provides a regimentation of the objects in a semantic universe in a way that will avoid set theoretic paradoxes and provide a backbone for compositional semantic interpretation. It provides types for basic ontological classes, which for Montague were entities, truth values, time points, possible worlds and total functions between these objects. I contrast this kind of type theory with what I call *rich type theories* stemming from the original work of Martin-Löf (1984). (Luo, 2010, 2011 and elsewhere has used the term *modern type theory* to refer to this kind of type theory.) Rich type theories provide a more general collection of types. For example, in our type theory there can be a type *Tree*, the type of all trees, or a type of situations *Hugging of a dog by a boy*, the type of all situations in which a boy hugs a dog. While TTR uses many of the insights and techniques of Martin-Löf type theory it is distinguished from it in a number of ways. For example, it is not intuitionistic or constructive in the way that Martin-Löf type theory is and it is not engaged in the project of developing type theory as an alternative to set theory (though it seems to me quite possible that the set theory that is used in TTR might well be ultimately recast in terms of type theory, but this is not a task I feel qualified to undertake).

Central to type theory is the notion of *judgement* as indicated in (2).

(2) a. (An agent judges that) object a is of type T.
b. $a : T$

In standard versions of rich type theory, the notion of judgement is central, although there is not consideration of the agent making the judgement. This is reflected in the notation in (2b) meaning that the object a is of type T. In the work on TTR we take more seriously the idea that judgements are acts carried out by an agent and this will be reflected in the way the implementation is set up. This is part of a general attempt to put a cognitive spin on type theory. If an agent, A, perceives a tree then she judges that object to be of type *Tree*. Similarly, if she sees a boy hugging a dog she judges that situation to be of type *Hugging of a dog by a boy*. Both of these types can be thought of as modelling what Gibson (1986) would call an *invariance*, at least in the sense that it was adopted in the early work on situation semantics (Barwise and Perry, 1983). In order to make these perceptions, the agent, A, must have access to cognitive resources corresponding to these types. Different agents will have access to different types as resources.

For example, a bee may land on a tree or collect nectar from its flowers but we suspect that it does not classify the tree as belonging to the type *Tree* as A does and possibly doesn't even have a perception of the complete tree as an object at all. It seems even less likely that a bee could classify a situation as a boy-hugging-dog situation even if lands on the dog's nose. It is not only members of different species which apparently have access to different types. Agents can acquire types and modify them based on their experience. For example, having read this far in this paper you have a type *Rich type theory* that you possibly did not have before and perhaps the type *Type theory* which you had previously has now changed at least in the sense that you count more things as belonging to the type that you did before. What I am calling here *having access to a type as a resource* corresponds to the notion of *attunement* which the situation semanticists took from Gibson. One could talk of A being attuned to the types *Tree* and *Hugging of a dog by a boy*.

If A is a human agent attuned to these types then there must be some pattern of brain activity corresponding to these types. Otherwise A would not be able to distinguish these objects and situations from objects and situations belonging to other types to which she is attuned. In this paper, we will not attempt to address how these types could be represented by patterns of activation on a neural network although that is something that is taken up in Cooper (2017) which describes the PyTTR module `nu`[4]. The current implementation is an attempt to build a computational language that will enable us to reason about types in the sense of resources available to an agent which can be modified by experience. One potential application of this is in the programming of artificial robotic agents that can learn from experience.

25.3 Judgements

The notion of *judgement* in type theory allows us to model the processing of a cognitive agent as it dynamically discovers new objects in the world and assigns types to them.

The Python class `Type` of types in TTR has a method `judge()`. `BType` is a class which inherits from `Type`. It is the class of basic types, that is, those which do not have components. Consider (3).

[4]See `https://github.com/GU-CLASP/pyttr/blob/master/nu.ipynb`

(3)
```
Ind = BType()

Ind.judge('j')
Ind.judge('k')
Ind.judge('l')
Ind.judge('m')

print(Ind.witness_cache) ==> ['j', 'k', 'l', 'm']
```

The first line creates a new basic type and sets it to be the value of the variable `Ind`. (The intuitive idea is that this should be the type of individuals.) The next four lines judge some objects to be of this type, that is, they are judged to be *witnesses* of this type. Here the individuals are implemented as Python strings such as `'j'`. As a result of this, the objects will be stored in an attribute of the type called `witness_cache` as shown in the last line of (3).

There are two ways the `judge`-method can be used in a program. One way is to initialize objects witnesses of types at the beginning of a program creating a static environment in which computations can be made, but no new witnesses can be added to a type after the initialization. This would be similar to the kind of static system we are familiar with from classical model theoretic semantics where the denotations of basic expressions such as predicates are defined at the outset by the model. The other way to use the `judge`-method is to allow it to be called anywhere in a computation. A cognitive agent wandering around in an environment does not start out with a complete inventory of all the individuals it may encounter as might be suggested by a traditional model-theoretic approach to semantics. Rather it has the ability to judge things to be individuals (or to be witnesses of any other type) at the point at which it encounters them. In addition to the `judge`-method, there is also a `query`-method which will just ask whether something is a witness for a type, rather than assert that it is a witness. Thus if all we have run is the code in (3) then the query in (4) will return `False` since we have not seen that `'h'` is of type `Ind`.

(4)
```
print(Ind.query('h')) ==> False
```

How then could an agent go about recognizing something that it has never seen before as being of a particular type other than by making an arbitrary judgement as in (3)? Types also have an attribute `witness_conditions`. This is a collection of functions which return a boolean value. If one of these functions returns `True` for the putative witness then it may be judged to be of the type. These functions can make arbitrary Python calls. They can be used as an interface between TTR and other computational modules. For example, they might make reference to sensor input. One way to do this is to have the witness condition call a classifier trained by traditional machine learning methods. In this way we could model how a cognitive agent could over time dynamically refine its view of what counts as a witness for a given type by retraining the classifier associated with the type by the witness condition on the basis of experience. Types also have a method `learn_witness_condition()` which will add such a function to the `witness_conditions` attribute. Thus not only do we have the possibility of modifying a classifier associated with a type, but we also have a possibility provided by TTR of associating a new witness condition with the type either as a replacement for witness conditions already there or as an addition. If a type is associated with several witness conditions, the satisfaction of any one of them will allow us to judge an object to be a witness of the type. This could be used, for example, to model the fact that we can recognize, say, an apple, by its visual appearance or its taste or the way it feels in your hand and so on. As we learn more about apples, we may develop new ways of recognizing them. Two cognitive agents which have access to different sensory modalities, for example, one with and one without vision, may nevertheless be aligned on other witness conditions associated with apples such as taste or touch.

Like `judge()`, the method `learn_witness_condition()` can be used in one of two ways. We can use it to initialize our types before running any computation to achieve a classical static system. Or we can allow new witness conditions to be learned at any point during a computation. This corresponds to a cognitive agent learning in real time, for example, as it moves through its environment.

Not all types allow the learning of witness conditions. We call these *logical* types. (We will see some examples below.) Thus whereas on traditional approaches logical constants are those which have the same interpretation in each model, we characterize the notion of logicality from a cognitive viewpoint in terms of learning theory. Thus you may learn about new kinds of trees and add appopriate witness conditions to the type *Tree* but you cannot learn new witness conditions for "and".

Witness conditions that do not make calls external to the type theory module have a similar role to meaning postulates in a traditional model theoretic semantics for natural language. Those which make external calls, for example, to sensor readings, give us an opportunity to ground our types in the external world in a way that goes beyond the aims of traditional model theoretic approaches. Witness conditions used as a hook to external machine learning modules such as classifiers that are trained on the basis of experience provide the possibility of placing a type theoretic layer for reasoning on top of a machine learning architecture. This means that there are two levels of learning that we may consider: one concerning modifications to the witness conditions associated with a type and another where the witness conditions remain constant but call a machine learning module such as a classifier whose output can be modified as a result of learning.

Letting witness conditions for types call classifiers could introduce probabilistic aspects into the judgements made by a cognitive agent. This raises the question of whether this kind of probability could be associated with the type theory itself as in the probabilistic type theory discussed by Cooper et al. (2015). This seems feasible though it has not been implemented yet. The plan is to add a module to PyTTR in which witness caches do not correspond simply to sets of witnesses for the types but sets of witness-probability pairs.

Types also have a method `create()` which allows you to create an object of the type which did not exist before. This is illustrated in (5).

(5)
```
print(Ind.create()) ==> _a0
```

This method is particularly useful for types of events. This is illustrated in (6).

(6)
```
run = Pred('run',[Ind])
p = PType(run,['j'])
p.create()
print(p.witness_cache) ==> ['_e0']
```

Here we create a predicate `run` which has the arity `[Ind]`, that is, it takes one argument of type `Ind`. Then we create a ptype, `p`, which has two components: the predicate `run` and a list of arguments, `['j']`, which matches its arity. Ptypes can be thought of as types of situations.[5] Creating an object of type `p` results in an event being added to `p`'s witness cache. Clearly, in a robot application one might want something more exciting to happen, for example, assuming `'j'` is the robot, then one would expect that the robot carries out the action of running, thereby actually creating an event of the type.

[5]They correspond to *infons* or *soas* in the old situation theory. An alternative within TTR is to take a neo-Davidsonian approach to predication using record types as discussed below. We do not discuss this option further here.

25.4 Some Logical Types

We said above that logical types are those for which it is not possible to learn new witness conditions. We now discuss some examples of what we are considering to be logical types. Consider (7).

(7)
```
T1 = Type()
T2 = Type()
T1.judge('a')
T2.judge('a')
T1.judge('b')
T = MeetType(T1,T2)
print(T.query('a')) ==> True
print(T.query('b')) ==> False
```

Here we introduce two types `T1` and `T2`. In TTR we allow objects to be of more than one type. Here we judge `'a'` to be a witness for both `T1` and `T2`. However, we only judge `'b'` to be of type `T1`. Now we let `T` be the meet type whose components are `T1` and `T2`. What are called meet types in TTR are often called intersection types in other type theoretic literature. They correspond to classical conjunction. An object will be a witness for `T` just in case it is a witness for both `T1` and `T2`. Thus we get the results represented in the last two lines of (7). While we could learn new witness conditions for `T1` and `T2`, the system will not allow us to learn new witness conditions for `T`.

In addition to meet types, TTR also has join types (often called union types elsewhere). (8) continues (7).

(8)
```
T3 = JoinType(T1,T2)
print(T3.query('a'))  ==> True
print(T3.query('b'))  ==> True
print(T3.create())    ==> _a1
print(T3.witness_cache) ==> ['a', 'b', '_a1']
print(T1.witness_cache) ==> ['a', 'b']
print(T2.witness_cache) ==> ['a']
```

Here we introduce `T3` as a join type whose components are the types `T1` and `T2` from (7). An object will be of this type just in case it is either of type `T1` or of type `T2`. Thus both `'a'` and `'b'` are of type `T3`. As with all other types, it is possible to create a new object of the type `T3` which will then show up in `T3`'s witness cache, as shown. It is perhaps a little unsettling to note that the created object `'_a1'` appears in `T3`'s witness cache without appearing in the witness caches of either `T1` or `T2`. This is because the witness caches represent aspects of an agent's cognitive state rather than the state of the world. Certainly it is possible to have the information that an object is, say, either a tree or a bush without having information about which of the two it is.

25.5 Subtyping and Record Types

Types in PyTTR are provided with a method `subtype_of()` which returns `True` if the type is a subtype of the argument supplied to the method. Thus, continuing the example from above, we have (9).

(9)
```
print(T1.subtype_of(T1)) ==> True
print(T.subtype_of(T1))  ==> True
print(T1.subtype_of(T3)) ==> True
print(T3.subtype_of(T1)) ==> False
print(T.subtype_of(T3))  ==> True
```

Types are subtypes of themselves. A meet type is a subtype of either of its components. A type is a subtype of a join type of which it is a component but a join type is not in general a subtype of one of its components. A meet type is a subtype of a join type with the same components. These examples are not treated as separate cases in the implementation. There is a general strategy for computing whether a type, `T1`, is a subtype of a type, `T2`. This is to create a *hypothetical object* of type `T1` and then check whether this object is of type `T2`. Types come with a method, `create_hypobj()`, for creating hypothetical objects. Hypothetical objects are like other objects except that (i) they only exist locally to a particular subtyping computation (and never appear in witness caches) and (ii) they have an attribute `types` which represent which types they are hypothesized to be witnesses of. This attribute is checked by the `query`-method when it is presented with a hypothetical object as opposed to a real object.

Record types have been introduced into type theory as a way of having a limited and controlled kind of subtyping. There are a number of variants of record types within the type theory literature. My original inspiration was Tasistro (1997), Betarte (1998), Betarte and Tasistro (1998) with important subsequent insights from Coquand et al. (2004), though I would not hold any of these people responsible for what I have done with the ideas. An illustration of how record types work in PyTTR is given in (10).

(10)
```
T1 = RecType({'x':Ind})
T2 = RecType({'x':Ind,
              'y':Ind})
r1 = Rec({'x':'j',
          'y':'k',
          'z':'e1'})
r2 = Rec({'x':'j'})
print(show(T2))  ==> {x : Ind, y : Ind}
print(show(r1))  ==> {x = j, y = k, z = e1}
print(T1.query(r1)) ==> True
print(T2.query(r2)) ==> False
print(T2.subtype_of(T1)) ==> True
```

We first introduce a record type, `T1`, which has one field consisting of the label `'x'` and the type `Ind`, for individuals as introduced earlier. We then introduce `T2`, a record type with two fields, with labels `'x'` and `'y'` both of which are associated with the type `Ind`. `r1` is a record (i.e. the kind of object that can be a witness for a record type). It has three fields, labelled `'x'`, `'y'` and `'z'`, which contain respectively the objects `'j'`, `'k'` and `'e1'`. It is important for this example to recall that `'j'` and `'k'` were judged in our previous examples to be witnesses for `Ind`. That information is carried over here. `r2` is another record which only has one field. We have a way of displaying both record types and records in a more standard and readable notation with ':' separating the label and type in a field in a record type and '=' separating the label and object in a field in a record. This is illustrated here for `T2` and `r1`.[6] It is important to notice that `r1`, with its three fields, is a witness for `T1`, with its single field. This is because in checking whether a record is of a record type, we only check that fields with the same labels as in the record type are present in the record and that the objects in the fields in the record are witnesses for the type in the corresponding field in the record type. Fields in the record with labels not mentioned in the type are not checked. However, `r2`, with its single field, is not a witness for `T2` since it does not contain a field labelled `'y'` with an object of type `Ind` as required by `T2`. This fact about the way witnesses of record types are checked is what leads to a subtyping structure on record types. Any record that is of type `T2` will also be of type `T1`, that is, `T2` is a subtype of `T1` as shown in the last line of (10).

In order to facilitate our general strategy of checking subtyping using hypothetical objects we make the hypothetical objects of types of

[6]Perhaps in a future version of PyTTR it will be possible to enter records and record types in this format as well.

structured objects (like record types) themselves structured. This is illustrated in (11).

(11)
```
h = T2.create_hypobj()
print(show(h))           ==> {x = h8, y = h9}
T1.query(h)              ==> True
```

The hypothetical object `h` is not an atom but a record with two fields containing hypothetical objects which can then be straightforwardly checked as to whether it is a witness for `T1`. This strategy of creating structured hypothetical objects becomes important as we look at more complex kinds of record types, such as dependent record types.

25.6 Dependent Record Types

Dependent record types are record types where the type that you check against in a particular record field can depend on the object of another field in the record. (12) is an example using the abbreviatory notation normally employed in the TTR literature (and other literature on record types).

(12) a. $\begin{bmatrix} \text{x} & : & \textit{Ind} \\ \text{e} & : & \text{man(x)} \end{bmatrix}$

b. $\begin{bmatrix} \text{x} & = & a \\ \text{e} & = & s_1 \end{bmatrix}$

c. $\begin{bmatrix} \text{x} & = & b \\ \text{e} & = & s_2 \end{bmatrix}$

(12a) can be thought of intuitively as the type of situation where there is a man. (12b) will be of this type just in case a is of type *Ind* and s_1 (a situation) of type man(a). (12c) will be of the type (12a) just in case b is of type *Ind* and s_2 is of type man(b). Thus which type is to be checked for the 'e'-field depends on what object is chosen in the 'x'-field in the record being checked. There are a couple of reasons why (12a) is only a convenient and readable abbreviation. Firstly, 'man(x)' is not a ptype. It is something that becomes a ptype when the label 'x' is replaced with an individual. Secondly, when we have a more complex record type with record types embedded in record types and where the label 'x' may occur at different levels in unrelated fields, we need something to make clear which of the occurrences of 'x' is being referred to. For these reasons the "official", though less readable, notation for (12a) is (13).

(13) $\begin{bmatrix} \text{x} & : & \textit{Ind} \\ \text{e} & : & \langle \lambda v{:}\textit{Ind}\ .\ \text{man}(v),\ \langle \text{x} \rangle \rangle \end{bmatrix}$

Here, instead of a ptype with a label inside it we have a pair consisting of firstly a function which, when applied to an appropriate argument, will return a type and secondly a sequence of paths to fields in the record where the arguments are to be found (a singleton sequence in this case because the function only takes one argument). A function which returns a type is known as a *dependent type*. Thus a dependent field like the 'e'-field in (13) contains a pair consisting of a dependent type and a list of paths pointing to objects which will resolve the dependencies of the type. While this explicit version is harder to read it is more convenient to compute with.

Consider (14).

(14)
```
R1 = RecType({'x':Ind,
         'y':(Fun('v',Ind,SingletonType(Ind,'v')),['x']),
         'e': (Fun('v',Ind,PType(man,['v'])),['y'])})
R2 = RecType({'x':Ind,
         'y':Ind,
         'e': (Fun('v',Ind,PType(man,['v'])),['y'])})
print(show(R2)) ==>
  {x : Ind, e : (lambda v:Ind . man(v), [y]),
   y : Ind}
print(show(R1)) ==>
  {x : Ind, e : (lambda v:Ind . man(v), [y]),
   y : (lambda v:Ind . Ind_v, [x])}
print(R1.subtype_of(R2)) ==> True
```

In the standard abbreviatory notation R1 and R2 are represented as in (15).

(15) $\texttt{R1} = \begin{bmatrix} \text{x} & : & \textit{Ind} \\ \text{y=x} & : & \textit{Ind} \\ \text{e} & : & \text{man(y)} \end{bmatrix}$

$\texttt{R2} = \begin{bmatrix} \text{x} & : & \textit{Ind} \\ \text{y} & : & \textit{Ind} \\ \text{e} & : & \text{man(y)} \end{bmatrix}$

The field $[\text{y=x}{:}\textit{Ind}]$ in R1 is known as a *manifest field*. It corresponds to restricting the type *Ind* to a singleton type, that is, a type which has exactly one witness, in this case, whatever it is in the 'x'-field of the record being checked. The standard notation for a type T restricted to a singleton type whose only witness is a is T_a. This is reflected in the 'y'-field of the output produced by `print(show(R1))`. The two types are then similar except that in `R1` the object in the 'y'-field is required to be identical to that in the 'x'-field. Thus `R1` is a subtype of `R2` but not the other way around. With our strategy for checking subtyping using hypothetical objects we cover such cases automatically based on the structure of the hypothetical objects without having to implement special cases in the `subtype_of`-method. (16) shows a hypothetical object for `R1`.

(16)
```
h = R1.create_hypobj()
print(show(h))     ==>  {x = h14, e = h15, y = h14}
print(show(h.e.types)) ==> [man(h14)]
```

We can see that the 'x' and 'y'-fields of the hypothetical object contain the same hypothetical object. Furthermore when we inspect the type associated with the hypothetical object in the 'e'-field we see that it is the type of situation in which that object is a man.

Although the implementation of subtyping is useful and powerful, once we introduce dependent record types there is no guarantee that it is complete in the sense illustrated in (17).

(17) a. $T_1 \sqsubseteq T_2$ iff for any assignment M of witnesses to basic types and ptypes $a :_M T_1$ implies $a :_M T_2$.

b. `T1.subset_of(T2) ==> True` implies $T_1 \sqsubseteq T_2$ ("sound")

c. $T_1 \sqsubseteq T_2$ does not imply `T1.subset_of(T2) ==> True` ("but not complete")

The characterization of subtype in TTR (given in (17a)) is modal in the sense that T_1 is a subtype of T_2 just in case everything that is of type T_1 is also of type T_2 no matter what gets assigned to basic types and ptypes. I would like to claim that the implementation of subtype is *sound* in the sense of (17b), but perhaps not complete in the sense of (17c).

25.7 Merging of Record Types

Dependent record types can, among other things, be used to model feature structures from linguistic theory (Cooper, 2008). The question then arises, what would correspond to unification in type theory. We shall introduce a notion of *merge* which will unify two dependent record types into a single record type.

Record types have a special relationship with meet types. Consider (18).

(18)
```
T1 = RecType({'x':Ind})
T2 = RecType({'y':Ind})
T3 = MeetType(T1,T2)
T4 = RecType({'x':Ind,'y':Ind})
T3.subtype_of(T4) ==> True
T4.subtype_of(T3) ==> True
print(show(T1.merge(T2)))  ==>  {y : Ind, x : Ind}
print(show(T4.merge(T1)))  ==> {y : Ind, x : Ind}
```

Given any two record types there will always be a single record type which is equivalent to the meet of the two record types, in the sense that they will be subtypes of each other. (Note that this does not require that the two types are identical in TTR.) We introduce a method `merge()` which for any two types, `T1` and `T2`, will return the record type equivalent to the meet type if both `T1` and `T2` are record types and otherwise will return the meet of `T1` and `T2`.

Type merging is closely related to graph unification in feature based systems. Like unification, merge is symmetric as illustrated in (19) where `T1` and `T2` are as in (18).

(19)
```
print(show(T1.merge(T2)))  ==>  {y : Ind, x : Ind}
print(show(T2.merge(T1)))  ==>  {y : Ind, x : Ind}
```

Also like unification, merge is recursive as illustrated in (20).

(20)
```
T3 = RecType({'z' : T1})
T4 = RecType({'z' : T2})
print(show(T3.merge(T4)))  ==>
        {z : {y : Ind, x : Ind}}
```

Unlike unification, however, merge will not fail if it is presented with two distinct non-record types or a record type and a non-record type. This is because it returns the meet of such types. This is illustrated in (21).

(21)
```
T1 = RecType({'a' : PType(man, ['j'])})
T2 = RecType({'a' : PType(man, ['m'])})
print(show(T1.merge(T2)))  ==>
                    {a : (man(j)&man(m))}
```

It may be the case that merge returns a type that is contradictory, that is, a type that has no witnesses whatever you might assign to basic types and ptypes. Returning a contradictory type is potentially more useful than simply failing since much information can be read off the type. I would like to think that this has an application in robust parsing where contradictory types could be entered on a chart and used when all else fails using ideas similar to those in Vogel and Cooper (1994). This remains for future work, however.

It is interesting that type merging works together with dependent record types, although working out the details is not entirely trivial. (22) presents some reasonably simple examples of some of the subtlety involved. (We show only the more readable printout versions of the types.)

(22)
```
print(show(T1)) ==>
   {e : (lambda v:Ind . man(v), [x]),
    x : Ind}
print(show(T2)) ==> {e : man(j)}
print(show(T1.merge(T2)))  ==>
   {e : (lambda v0:Ind . (man(v0)&man(j)), [x]),
    x : Ind}
print(show(T3)) ==>
   {e : (lambda v:Ind . man(v), [x]),
    x : Ind_j}
print(show(T1.merge(T3)))  ==>
   {e : (lambda v2:Ind . man(v2), [x]),
    x : Ind_j}
```

Merging `T1` and `T2` involves merging a dependent type and a non-dependent type. Since the non-dependent type `man(j)` in `T2` is not connected to a field labelled by `'x'` it should not be associated with the 'x'-field in the result. The resulting merge requires both that 'x' is a man and `j` is a man. In `T3`, however, there is a field labelled by 'x' and the object in the 'x'-field is required to be `j` (because of the singleton type) and also a man (because of the 'e'-field). Thus in the resulting merged type no meet type is introduced in the dependent type but the restriction that the 'x'-field contain `j` is present.

In addition to the method `merge()`, PyTTR also provides a method `amerge()` for *asymmetric merge* which is similar to priority unification. It is like the `merge`-method except that when confronted with two types which are not both record types it will return the second one rather than the meet of the two. This is illustrated in (23) with a simple example inspired from the work on dialogue processing which requires non-monotonic update rules. This example involves the planning and execution of non-linguistic action.

(23)
```
print(show(T1)) ==>
{agenda : (lambda v:Ind . [Ty]_[{e : run(v)}], [x]),
 latest_move : [Re]_[],
 x : Ind}

print(show(T2)) ==>
{agenda : [Ty]_[],
 latest_move : (lambda v:Ind . {e : run(v)}, [x]),
 x : Ind}

print(show(T1.amerge(T2))) ==>
{agenda : [Ty]_[],
 latest_move : (lambda v:Ind . {e : run(v)}, [x]),
 x : Ind}
```

`T1` and `T2` both have three fields: an 'x'-field for an individual, intuitively the agent who plans and carries out the action. The 'agenda'-field is required to be a list of types (that is, objects of type `Ty`, the type of types). `T1` requires there to be an agenda which is a singleton list of types containing the type of events where 'x' runs. The 'latest_move'-field requires a list of records (i.e. objects of type `Re`) and in `T1` that is required to be the empty list. `T2` on the other hand requires the agenda to be the empty list and the latest move to be a single object of the type which in `T1` occurs on the agenda. This could be the result of an update rule (not represented here) which says if you create something of the first type on the agenda list, record the latest move as being of that type and remove the type from the agenda. Such updates in the way they are formulated in Cooper (in prep) involve an asymmetric merge of the type of the current information state with the type of the new information state. Such asymmetric merges have the effect of maintaining everything in the previous information state not explicitly addressed by the update rule.

25.8 Conclusion

We have given a brief account of some of the features of the PyTTR implementation which covers the core of TTR with a view to future applications of linguistic and non-linguistic agents perceiving and interacting with their environment. One hope for this work is that it will give us a way of interfacing logical approaches to information and action with low-level perceptual and motor apparatus as well as allowing for connections with low-level learning (e.g. in terms of modifying classifiers by experience) and high-level learning involved in acquiring new witness conditions for types. There is still much work to be done, but the direction of the work is beginning to become clear. A significant change between this TTR implementation and the earlier one is that the dynamic aspects of the system allowing for learning are central to the implementation of the type system.

References

Barwise, Jon and John Perry. 1983. *Situations and Attitudes*. Bradford Books. Cambridge, Mass.: MIT Press.

Betarte, Gustavo. 1998. *Dependent Record Types and Algebraic Structures in Type Theory*. Ph.D. thesis, Department of Computing Science, University of Gothenburg and Chalmers University of Technology.

Betarte, Gustavo and Alvaro Tasistro. 1998. Extension of Martin-Löf's type theory with record types and subtyping. In G. Sambin and J. Smith, eds., *Twenty-Five Years of Constructive Type Theory*, no. 36 in Oxford Logic Guides. Oxford: Oxford University Press.

Cooper, Robin. 2008. Type theory with records and unification-based grammar. In F. Hamm and S. Kepser, eds., *Logics for Linguistic Structures*, pages 9–34. Mouton de Gruyter.

Cooper, Robin. 2012. Type theory and semantics in flux. In R. Kempson, N. Asher, and T. Fernando, eds., *Handbook of the Philosophy of Science*, vol. 14: Philosophy of Linguistics, pages 271–323. Elsevier BV. General editors: Dov M. Gabbay, Paul Thagard and John Woods.

Cooper, Robin. 2017. Neural TTR and possibilities for learning. In S. Dobnik and S. Lappin, eds., *CLASP Papers in Computational Linguistics: Proceedings of the Conference on Logic and Machine Learning in Natural Language (LaML 2017), Gothenburg, 12–13 June*, vol. 1 of *CLASP Papers in Computational Linguistics*. Department of Philosophy, Linguistics and Theory of Science (FLOV), University of Gothenburg, Gothenburg, Sweden: CLASP, Centre for Language and Studies in Probability.

Cooper, Robin. in prep. Type theory and language: from perception to linguistic communication. Draft of book chapters available from `https://sites.google.com/site/typetheorywithrecords/drafts`.

Cooper, Robin, Simon Dobnik, Shalom Lappin, and Staffan Larsson. 2015. Probabilistic Type Theory and Natural Language Semantics. *Linguistic Issues in Language Technology* 10(4):1–45.

Cooper, Robin and Jonathan Ginzburg. 2015. Type theory with records for natural language semantics. In S. Lappin and C. Fox, eds., *The Handbook of Contemporary Semantic Theory*, pages 375–407. Wiley-Blackwell, 2nd edn.

Coquand, Thierry, Randy Pollack, and Makoto Takeyama. 2004. A logical framework with dependently typed records. *Fundamenta Informaticae* XX:1–22.

Gibson, James J. 1986. *The Ecological Approach to Visual Perception*. Lawrence Erlbaum Associates.

Luo, Zhaohui. 2010. Type-theoretical semantics with coercive subtyping. In *Proceedings of SALT 20*, pages 38–56.

Luo, Zhaohui. 2011. Contextual Analysis of Word Meanings in Type-Theoretical Semantics. In S. Pogodalla and J.-P. Prost, eds., *Logical Aspects of Computational Linguistics: 6th International Conference, LACL 2011*, no. 6736 in Lecture Notes in Artificial Intelligence, pages 159–174. Springer.

Martin-Löf, Per. 1984. *Intuitionistic Type Theory*. Naples: Bibliopolis.

Montague, Richard. 1973. The Proper Treatment of Quantification in Ordinary English. In J. Hintikka, J. Moravcsik, and P. Suppes, eds., *Approaches to Natural Language: Proceedings of the 1970 Stanford Workshop on Grammar and Semantics*, pages 247–270. Dordrecht: D. Reidel Publishing Company.

Tasistro, Alvaro. 1997. *Substitution, record types and subtyping in type theory, with applications to the theory of programming*. Ph.D. thesis, Department of Computing Science, University of Gothenburg and Chalmers University of Technology.

Vogel, Carl and Robin Cooper. 1994. Robust chart parsing with mildly inconsistent feature structures. In *AAAI Technical Report FS-94-04*, pages 127–136.

Index